1966

PERSPECTIVES ON REALITY

Readings in Metaphysics from
Classical Philosophy to Existentialism

The Harbrace Series in Philosophy

UNDER THE GENERAL EDITORSHIP OF
Jesse A. Mann and Gerald F. Kreyche

REFLECTIONS ON MAN
Readings in Philosophical Psychology from
Classical Philosophy to Existentialism

PERSPECTIVES ON REALITY
Readings in Metaphysics from
Classical Philosophy to Existentialism

APPROACHES TO MORALITY
Readings in Ethics from
Classical Philosophy to Existentialism

PERSPECTIVES ON REALITY

Readings in Metaphysics from
Classical Philosophy to Existentialism

UNDER THE GENERAL EDITORSHIP OF

Jesse A. Mann, *Georgetown University*
Gerald F. Kreyche, *DePaul University*

CONTRIBUTING EDITORS:

George F. McLean, O.M.I., *The Catholic University of America*
Thomas N. Munson, S.J., *Loyola University, Chicago*
Robert J. Roth, S.J., *Fordham University*
Jerzy A. Wojciechowski, *University of Ottawa*
Helen James John, S.N.D., *Trinity College, Washington, D.C.*

Harcourt, Brace & World, Inc.
New York / Chicago / Burlingame

Library of Congress Catalog Card Number: 66-16063

Printed in the United States of America

The experience of past ages, the progress of the sciences, and the treasures hidden in the various forms of human culture, by all of which the nature of man himself is more clearly revealed and new roads to truth are opened, these profit the Church, too. For, from the beginning of her history she has learned to express the message of Christ with the help of the ideas and terminology of various philosophers, and has tried to clarify it with their wisdom, too.

From the text of the Second Vatican Council's Pastoral Constitution on the Church in the Modern World, promulgated December 7, 1965.

The philosophical disciplines are to be taught in such a way that the students are first of all led to acquire a solid and coherent knowledge of man, the world, and of God, relying on a philosophical patrimony which is perennially valid and taking into account the philosophical investigations of later ages. This is especially true of those investigations which exercise a greater influence in their own nations. Account should also be taken of the more recent progress of the sciences. The net result should be that the students, correctly understanding the characteristics of the contemporary mind, will be duly prepared for dialogue with men of their time.

From the text of the Second Vatican Council's Declaration on Priestly Training, promulgated October 28, 1965.

Foreword

Most Christians sooner or later decide that philosophy solves no ultimately important problems by itself.

I hasten to add that only the dullest anti-intellectual, dull to the point of perverse, would be tempted on that account to hold philosophy in anything less than solid esteem. I also add that the Catholic Christian acknowledges that, in principle at least, philosophy could come up with rational solutions to many (theoretically, perhaps, most) of the natural problems which embarrass or intrigue human reason.

The First Vatican Council confirmed what the Apostle Paul had suggested concerning the power of reason (the philosopher's proper and characteristic tool) to solve with considerable certainty even the "problem of God," at least as far as God's existence and some of His essential attributes are concerned. But in the concrete human condition the Christian may well conclude that pure philosophy (to the extent that philosophy can be isolated from the total experience of man made in God's image, fallen from original justice, supernaturally redeemed) raises more questions than it can possibly solve and that, unaided, it solves practically none.

The unbeliever arrives at a like conclusion more often than not, and, if the conclusion be bleak, the unbeliever sometimes expresses it with wistful beauty. Edward Fitzgerald echoes Omar Khayyám:

> *Myself when young did eagerly frequent*
> *Doctor and Saint, and heard great Argument*
> *About it and about: but evermore*
> *Came out by the same Door as in I went.*

But the Christian's conclusion need not be so bleak. His love for philosophy may—indeed, should—be as passionate as that of the unbeliever, but his dependence on it is never more than partial. Not only for salvation hereafter but for sanity here, he has the light of faith to illumine the testimonies of reason and the resources of theology to supply for the inadequacies of philosophy.

For example, he may see no possibility of a satisfactory philosophy of history, as I, for one, see none. However, the Incarnation (which utterly eludes the domain of reason) gives history such meaning as a Christian can bring to his meditations upon it; but the Incarnation is the object of faith and reflection upon it provides the stuff of a theology of history. Philosophy brings cold comfort to the problem of evil; only the Cross (which is, for the philosophers, still the foolishness that Paul confessed it to be) lifts from this mystery the dreadful burden it places on the human heart.

The very "problem of God," mentioned above, illustrates how pathetically inadequate, however certain, are the answers of philosophy to the demands of the devout heart, let alone of the unbelieving mind. The "God of the philosophers," the neat and convenient God who emerges patly as the logical conclusion from lines of cold reasoning much as a mathematical formula emerges, inevitably and inexorably, from a mass of data— this sterile God of the debating halls is by no means to be denied by reason or rejected out of hand by the believer. But He, like reason itself, is only a part of total reality and a meager answer to our total need; He is a poor thing, however logically necessary, beside the God of Abraham, the God of Job, and above all the God of Jesus Christ and His saints.

The Christian perceives a mutual need between philosophy and theology, between reason and revelation, that is satisfied only in the integral wisdom that comes from the interplay of faith asking reason and reason asking faith for their respective witnesses. Hence his special regret when confronted by the excessive mutual exclusions between reason and faith set up by those in whom the method of Descartes speedily resulted in a mood which has permeated our culture to the hurt, the Christian considers, of both philosophy and theology. Hence, too, the special temptation of the devout sometimes to fuse with excessive simplicity the concerns and functions of philosophy and theology. The unity of philosophical experience is an attainable goal for the sophisticated traveler equipped with reliable maps; otherwise, it can be a mirage, a pot of fool's gold at the end of a rainbow that has many broad bands but, in fact, no end. *Myself when young. . . .*

But whatever the abstract power of philosophy in the face of the questions which excite or torment the human spirit, it is not, I submit, the business of philosophy to solve problems. Even in their best efforts to answer the riddles of life, the philosophers make their chief contribution when they succeed, as they have done, in pounding out more clear and pointed statements of the questions. It is probably not the vocation of the philosopher to give *answers,* least of all *final answers;* it is, one suspects, his essential task and his most valuable contribution to uncover, to phrase, and to press the *questions.*

In the present crisis of our culture, this may be of all vocations the most difficult, and one of the most urgent. When Gertrude Stein was dying, she wearily asked the friends clustered about her bed: *What is the answer?* No one replied; no theologian was present. *In that case,* she insisted, *what is the question?* The silence remained unbroken; philosophy, too, was without a representative. It has become the imperative role of philosophers to help us at least to state the question in an age of the dusty answers that "gets the soul when hot for certainties in this, our life."

Herein lies both the justification and great merit for Christian students of the present comprehensive collection of readings from widely differing philosophers. These volumes bring together historic attempts to answer perennial problems which engage human speculation. But the chief value of the publication lies (as it should) not in the enduring worth of any answers suggested, but in the contribution that each tentative answer inevitably makes to the posing of the so elusive questions, to the clarification of the elements of problems—a full answer to which may never be afforded by philosophy but the analysis of which is a built-in demand of the human intellect and an incomparable delight of the human spirit.

No small achievement this, the clarification of the terms of the problems. One suspects that most of the ultimate answers will turn out to be somehow *simple,* with the simplicity that traditional Christian philosophical speculations about God attribute to the Divine Nature. It is the statement of the questions that is tough—that plus, perhaps, the acceptance of the consequences, moral and intellectual, of some of the answers.

And so, if the Church is grateful to the philosophers for stating so many of the questions before which men, in bewilderment, turn to her, it is no less true that the sensitive philosopher is grateful to the Church for the manner in which she, even when lacking specific answers, somehow herself serves as the answer to the master-knots of human fate. She does so by her teaching concerning the Incarnation and the consequent premises for salvation history. She does so by her preaching of Christ, the Alpha and Omega of human experience, and especially of Christ Crucified. She does so supremely in the recollection of the mystery of the Resurrection.

But in all this there is that reciprocity between faith and reason required by the mutual dependencies to which we refer above. The Church, therefore, looks to the philosophers, in varying degrees and with varying profit but to them all without exception, not only for help in stating the questions but for guidance in the phrasing of the articulated responses of the Spirit. This is the clear sense of the Second Vatican Council's Constitution on the Church in the Modern World when it says:

> Just as it is in the world's interest to acknowledge the Church as an historical reality, and to recognize her good influence, so the Church herself knows how richly she has profited by the history and development of humanity.
>
> The experience of past ages, the progress of the sciences, and the treasures hidden in the various forms of human culture, by all of which the nature of man himself is more clearly revealed and new roads to truth are opened, these profit the Church, too. For from the beginning of her history she has learned to express the

message of Christ with the help of ideas and terminology of various philosophers, and has tried to clarify it with their wisdom, too. . . . [And] thus the ability to express Christ's message in its own way is developed in each nation, and at the same time there is fostered a living exchange between the Church and the diverse cultures of people. To promote such exchange, especially in our days, the Church requires the special help of those who live in the world, are versed in different institutions and specialties, and grasp their innermost significance in the eyes of both believers and unbelievers. With the help of the Holy Spirit, it is the task of the entire People of God, especially pastors and theologians, to hear, distinguish and interpret the many voices of our age, and to judge them in the light of the divine word, so that revealed truth can always be more deeply penetrated, better understood and set forth to greater advantage.

The editors of these volumes have acted in response to the implicit plea of the Council's pastoral declaration. That is not the least of the reasons why their work is so welcome.

✠ JOHN WRIGHT
BISHOP OF PITTSBURGH

Epiphany, 1966

Preface

The three text-anthologies in the Harbrace Series in Philosophy—*Perspectives on Reality, Reflections on Man,* and *Approaches to Morality*—offer a genuinely pluralistic approach to the basic issues in Metaphysics, Philosophy of Man, and Ethics. Their publication comes at a time when this approach is being encouraged within the entire Christian world. As His Excellency, Bishop John Wright, has pointed out in the Foreword, the Church "looks to the philosophers, in varying degrees and with varying profit but to them all without exception, not only for help in stating the questions but for guidance in the phrasing of the articulated responses of the Spirit."

An openness to truth wherever it may be found is revealed in various documents promulgated at the Second Vatican Council. In the Declaration on Priestly Training, for example, no one system is singled out for exclusive treatment; rather, seminarians are urged to study the "philosophical patrimony which is perennially valid" and to become acquainted with those investigations that have influenced their own country.

The pluralistic attitude affirmed by the Council has, in recent years, been the dominant approach in many Catholic colleges and universities in the United States. The significance of the *aggiornamento* in philosophy is that the philosophical pluralism initiated by some is now enjoined upon all. Such a positive attitude is in keeping with the demands of the society in which we live. Students of philosophy must know the dynamic currents of thought which are expressed in a free society. It is obvious that valuable insights are to be gained from considering more than one philosophical approach, especially when the pluralism exists within the framework of Christian philosophy itself. The fact that by design Aquinas is systematic and Marcel is unsystematic does not deprive the student from gaining wisdom from both. It is just as true that one can benefit philosophically from a study of philosophies beyond the Christian tradition or even hostile to it. Aquinas did not feel he had to baptize Aristotle before he could study him with profit.

Clearly there is no substitute for reading the philosophers themselves. The great thinkers have a right to be heard on their own; they present their own cases most effectively and are their own best interpreters. The objection is sometimes raised that primary sources are too difficult for the beginning student. This is not the case, however, when the readings have been carefully chosen by specialists in their respective fields and are accompanied by detailed commentary. Such a judicious selection of texts enables the introductory student to read the works of the great philosophers and to study their conception and development in a historical context.

The text-anthologies in this series give the beginning student a substantial introduction to different philosophical perspectives that are relevant to the contemporary American scene. Accordingly, each volume in the series presents materials from Classical and Scholastic Thought, Dialectical Thought, American Naturalist and Pragmatic Thought, Analytic and Positivist Thought, and Existentialist and Phenomenological Thought. A number of other traditions (Cartesian Rationalism and Utilitarianism, for example) have great historical value, but are not directly and dynamically relevant to the contemporary American scene. Although such traditions are not represented in the readings, they are covered in the General Introduction and are discussed in the section introductions where pertinent.

The series has been planned so that one volume does not presuppose the others. There is no fixed order in which the books have to be studied, although in most colleges the courses in Philosophy of Man and Metaphysics are taught to freshmen and sophmores while Ethics is usually a junior- or senior-level course. The five sections of each book have been edited by expert philosophers and teachers, each of whom has worked and written in the subject matter of his field. The Contributing Editors have chosen readings for their respective sections that are both representative of key issues and are within the competence of the beginner. Each selection is an ample, self-contained unit that provides a full argument and an adequate sampling of the philosopher's style. Some of the readings (Brunner's and Husserl's selections in *Reflections on Man* and the sections of the *Vienna Manifesto* in *Perspectives on Reality*) appear in English for the first time, thus making available important works that would be otherwise inaccessible to the vast majority of undergraduate students.

The editors introduce their sections with long essays that discuss the basic issues and place the readings in their historical and philosophical framework. As a further aid to the student's understanding of the subject, the editors provide a glossary of important philosophical terms for each section. No attempt has been made to include all terms or to give exhaustive definitions. The definitions are brief and descriptive, and are intended to serve as a convenient reference for the student as he reads the primary sources. Other editorial aids include headnotes that provide biographical data on each philosopher; footnotes (identified by the initials of the philosopher, editor, translator, or section editor) that clarify references, foreign phrases, or difficult terms; and annotated bibliographies of primary sources and commentaries, selected with the beginning student in mind.

Within each section are questions that test the student's comprehension of the selections he has read. In addition, there are two sets of questions at the end of each section: the first set is for the section as a whole; the second relates the section to other parts of the book. These questions may be used as topics for term papers or as guidelines for those classes conducted in the dialogue or Socratic method; they also are an excellent means of review.

The volumes can be used in the classroom in a variety of ways. Some instructors may want to cover the entire book in the course semester, while others may choose to concentrate on certain sections and assign remaining ones for home study. Because of the extensive editorial aids included, such assignments are feasible. Moreover, the sections do not have to be taken up in the order in which they appear in the books. Most instructors will want to begin with the General Introduction, which explains the nature and historical development of philosophy and analyzes the basic problems, topics, and issues of the particular subject of the volume. Once the student has had this orientation, the teacher may take up any philosophical tradition he chooses. In fact, the pluralistic approach of the volumes makes it possible for teachers with different areas of specialization to collaborate in teaching the course. They can also take advantage of the many excellent films now available that are related to the teaching of philosophy.[1]

The General Editors assume overall responsibility for the three books in the Harbrace Series in Philosophy; their specific responsibility was in writing the General Introduction and Preface for each volume and in coordinating the program of study aids. The Contributing Editors wrote the introductory essays and selected the readings for their respective sections. The series represents a genuinely collaborative effort on the part of seventeen editors to present philosophy as a meaningful enterprise for students. The attitude of pluralistic openness makes it possible for students to enter into the act of philosophizing with initiative, spontaneity, and enthusiasm; it also prevents philosophy from being a subject easily contained in a parcel of memorized formulas. Great philosophers have not been interested in the tidy definition but in a disciplined reflection on the world of truth and value. Students who resist memorized formulas will respond to philosophical materials that have obvious relevance to the world in which they find their problems and project their own solutions. It is precisely such materials that the editors have sought to include in these volumes.

J.A.M.
G.F.K.

January, 1966

---

[1] A very helpful list of films, and their distributors, has been compiled by Caroline E. Schuetzinger of Mercy College, Detroit. This list appeared in *The New Scholasticism*, XXXIX, 2 (April, 1965), 224–29.

Contents

PART II
DIALECTICAL THOUGHT:
Kant, Hegel, Engels, Marx

EDITED BY Thomas N. Munson, S.J., *Loyola University, Chicago*

PART III
AMERICAN PRAGMATIC-NATURALIST THOUGHT:
James, Peirce, Dewey

EDITED BY Robert J. Roth, S.J., *Fordham University*

PART IV
ANALYTIC-POSITIVIST THOUGHT:
Hume, Russell, Carnap, Tarski, Ayer

EDITED BY Jerzy A. Wojciechowski, *University of Ottawa*

PART V
EXISTENTIALIST AND PHENOMENOLOGICAL THOUGHT:
Heidegger, Sartre, Tillich, Marcel, Berdyaev, Buber

EDITED BY Helen James John, S.N.D., *Trinity College, Washington, D.C.*

General Introduction

BY *Jesse A. Mann* AND *Gerald F. Kreyche*

It has been said that every man is a philosopher, and in a very real sense this statement is true. As Aristotle remarked many centuries ago, it was because men began to wonder that philosophy first came about. One might even say that the history of the human race could be written as an exercise in wonder—but this must be qualified. As we probe more deeply into the things men have wondered about, we find that the topics fall into two main divisions: those of a transitory nature and those dealing with ultimates.

The searches men conducted in one age, together with the problems that interested them, have often been abandoned in the next. For several centuries during the Middle Ages, the alchemists' quest for the "philosopher's stone," which would transmute base metals into gold, and the philosophical problem of whether there was one intellect shared by all men were of pressing concern. These no longer occupy our attention.

There is another class of things, however, that has been a continual source of wonder to men of all ages. Although we might have only a latent interest in them, certain events can direct our conscious attention to them again. We might take for example the atomic catastrophe at Hiroshima or the orbiting of the earth for the first time. Such events provoked men to rethink certain basic philosophical problems and to ask questions that have been of perennial concern to all human beings. What is the meaning of life? What is the world coming to? What are the implications for man and his continued earthly existence? Is man's need for God greater than before? Can man really prove God's existence? If there is a God, how could he tolerate the obvious and almost overwhelming presence of evil? What is my relationship to such a being? In this changing world, is it true that the more things change, the more they remain the same?

The list could go on and on. But the important thing to note is that these are questions with which men have been preoccupied, are preoccupied now, and will be preoccupied in the future. Because such questions deal with ultimates and seek definitive answers, they are properly called metaphysical questions, that is, philosophical problems of the highest order. It is to such questions that this book addresses itself.

To qualify our original statement that every man is a philosopher: to the extent that man wonders, he engages in the philosophical enterprise. Nonetheless, few men persevere in this endeavor in a technical and professional way. Those who do are, in the more proper sense of the term, philosophers. (This is similar to the truth that all men employ psychology at various times, but few can lay claim to being professional psychologists.) To pursue the perennial questions about life, reality, goodness, evil, truth, and God, we should use certain guides, for these are difficult matters to investigate. Yet the philosophers represented in this volume should be seen *only* as guides, for no man can have another do his thinking for him. One cannot hope to answer philosophical questions by indoctrination; each must arrive at his own conclusions. This volume is written specifically to encourage philosophical thinking.

What Is Philosophy?

The word "philosophy" means a love of wisdom. Although knowledge and wisdom are related in meaning, they are still somewhat apart. It is not enough for a person to have knowledge in order to be characterized as a wise man, but neither could he be called wise if he lacked knowledge. Wisdom implies knowledge, but it also demands the deepest kind of knowledge, the kind that involves the search for ultimates. At this level, one can only ask the questions, not provide all the answers. Yet as a lover of wisdom one pursues those questions that deal with ultimates and that transcend the passing interest of his age.

One may now ask: Why raise questions that cannot always be answered? This objection presupposes two basic fallacies. First, it assumes one can ask an intelligent question on a subject he knows nothing about. Such is clearly impossible, for the ability to phrase and to ask an intelligent question presupposes considerable knowledge of the subject and also of the direction one must take in order to find the answer. What intelligent question could be asked of subatomic physics by one who knows virtually nothing about the topic? What question could the musically illiterate pose about the fugues of Bach?

The second fallacy assumes that in attempting to answer a question, one must either answer it completely or not at all. Philosophy, however, is not just a quantitative or factual study. Although its answers may be true and legitimate, they can always be improved upon. Philosophical progress normally involves progress in depth: there is always another insight that can be added to the mystery of good and evil or to the meaning of reality —insight that deepens our previous grasp and understanding. To some extent, that is why philosophers have always been interested in the history of philosophy. What the laboratory is to the scientist, the history of philosophy is to the philosopher. That is also why philosophy is alive, organic, perennial, and, to some extent, at one with its tradition. It feeds on its past in order to grow with the future.

The Division of Philosophy

We have described in a general way what might be called the spirit of philosophy; we must now turn to a more specific discussion of the exact character of philosophy. "Philosophy" is a broad term that extends collectively to a group of specialized enquiries or sciences, which though separate are still related. Let us consider each of these studies briefly.

LOGIC.   Although it is generally grouped together with the philosophical disciplines, logic is technically not a division of philosophy proper, since it pertains to all scientific enquiry. Stated very simply, logic is the science and art of correct reasoning. It is concerned with the methodology of drawing valid inferences and of avoiding basic fallacies.

PHILOSOPHY OF NATURE.   This branch of philosophy is ordinarily restricted to an investigation of the material world to uncover its basic constitutive principles. It is especially interested in the character of motion, not in measuring it but in asking what motion is and what its implications are. This study is sometimes referred to as "cosmology" or "philosophical physics."

PHILOSOPHY OF MAN.   Basically, this is a study of the nature of man, his activities, and his destiny. It attempts to ascertain the nature of the ultimate principle within man on which all of his operations depend. Of special concern to the philosophy of man are the problems of man's knowledge, freedom, unity, and immortality. This study is occasionally referred to as "rational" or "philosophical psychology."

METAPHYSICS.   Normally regarded as the highest of the philosophical disciplines, metaphysics covers the entire breadth of reality and is concerned with that which makes a thing to be ultimately real. Metaphysics also investigates the reality of the true, of good and evil, and probes the existence, nature, and operations of God. (This study of God is often regarded as a separate enquiry called "natural theology.")

EPISTEMOLOGY.   Formerly regarded as a branch of metaphysics, but now often accepted as a separate enquiry, epistemology is principally interested in discovering the limitations of man's knowledge. This discipline provides a general critique of the theory of knowledge and investigates the reasonableness of its claims to attain the real.

ETHICS.   The science of human conduct, ethics attempts to discover the criteria for human actions properly to be judged as morally good or bad. When this science directs its attention to those actions of men that have bearing upon communal institutions rather than to the acts of individuals, it is termed "social ethics."

ESTHETICS.   To understand and appreciate the nature of the beautiful is the concern of esthetics. It also attempts to analyze the poetic experience of man in relation to the beautiful.

In reviewing the above, we see that philosophy is sometimes *practical,* sometimes *speculative.* Its knowledge is said to be practical when such knowledge is ordained to the order of action, that is, when it seeks truth in order to do something with it. Its knowledge is said to be speculative when such knowledge is desired for its own sake and because man is perfected by it, regardless of whether such knowledge is useful. In short, the purpose of speculative knowledge is the mere possession and consideration of the truth, while the purpose of practical knowledge is to possess the truth so as to be able to apply it to some useful end.

Engineering, for example, involves practical knowledge, for it is concerned, among other things, with the building of bridges. Pure mathematics and metaphysics are speculative, for their knowledge is sought for its own sake and not for the sake of solving some day-to-day problem.

Not all philosophers would find themselves in agreement with the above divisions and explanations. Some would even rule out the possibility of philosophy. But paradoxically their position in such a matter itself constitutes a philosophical position. (This is particularly true of the analytic-positivist school of philosophy, which will be discussed in detail later.)

Philosophy is, therefore, a group of closely knit disciplines that seek to discover and to probe the ultimate principles and causes of reality, insofar as reality is accessible to human reason and experience. Most philosophers would at least find basic agreement on this description, although they would differ widely as to the extent to which this goal is possible.

We can best see the validity of this description, as well as the differing viewpoints on how far the human mind can probe into philosophical matter, by surveying briefly the history of philosophy from pre-Christian Greece to the present day. The reader should bear in mind at all times the continuity of philosophical experiences, although radically diverse solutions were often offered for the same problem. He should look for the development of the various branches of philosophy, for philosophy did not simply burst upon the scene all at once. It appeared at first only inconspicuously with cosmological enquiry, and later rose to a consideration of psychological, ethical, and metaphysical problems.

The History of Philosophy

The Greek Period

Philosophy in the Western world traces its beginnings to Miletus, the capital of the Greek colony of Ionia, now located in Turkey. It was here in the sixth century B.C. that Thales (*c.* 624–546 B.C.) began a systematic investigation into the material universe in which we live. He observed that the world manifests itself in many different forms and yet possesses an underlying principle of unity. He searched for that principle of unity that could somehow take on the different appearances of the changing world, and concluded that it is water. He chose water because it readily manifests the ability to take on a liquid, solid, or gaseous state. Since all known reality exhibited one or another of these forms, his solution at that time was plausible.

Although his answer was soon seen to be inadequate, we must credit Thales for raising the important problem of the "one and the many," which runs throughout the history of philosophy and touches upon nearly every aspect of it. The problem can be grasped by posing a number of questions from the various branches of philosophy. How can the world manifest so *many* variations of things and still be a *uni*-verse (*one*)? How can all men (the *many*) have the same (*one*) common nature as human beings? How can *many* things be designated by *one* idea? For example, my idea of chair refers equally well to a hardback chair, a stuffed chair, or a folding chair. How can things always be changing, manifesting *many* different aspects, and still retaining essentially their own unity (*one*)? Man grows from a zygote to an embryo to a child to an adolescent to an adult and to an old man, and still he is the same person. How can all things (the *many*) in the world somehow be attributed to *one* God, that is, *many* creatures but *one* Creator? How can the *many* different moral acts of man be governed by a single (*one*) objective norm of morality, enabling us to judge the action as good or bad?

We do not mean to imply that the early philosophers were so sophisticated as to formulate these questions, much less to answer them. However, they began the search for the principle of unity. Because Thales was the first to attempt a rational investigation of the causes of things, he is regarded as the "father of Western philosophy." Several other philosophers, also from Ionia, offered different answers to the problem of the make-up of the world. Anaximander (*c.* 610–546 B.C.) held that the principle common to all things must necessarily be "indeterminate" or unformed, since it was to take on different characteristics. Anaximenes (*c.* 588–524 B.C.) made air the principle of all things. His reasoning was based in part on the observation of rarefaction and condensation, whereby air, becoming warm, produced fire, and becoming condensed, produced water in different basic forms.

The Ionian tradition in philosophy, as developed by Thales, Anaximander, and Anaximenes, was eclipsed by the military conquest of Miletus in 494 B.C. What should be noted about the thinkers of this tradition is that they sought an ultimate rather than a proximate explanation of reality. They were *monists,* for they held to a single principle as the explanation of all things. They were *hylozoists,* for they made no distinction between organic and inorganic things, apparently accepting everything as alive in some way. Lastly, they were *materialists,* at least in the sense that their thought never went beyond the level of matter as the explanation of the world.[1]

Around the middle of the sixth century B.C., a group of thinkers interested in mathematics, religion, and science, combined their studies into a broad philosophy termed Pythagoreanism, named after their leader, Pythagoras (580–500 B.C.). Because everything was construed as a combination of points, lines, and surfaces, they explained reality as ultimately based on numerical and mathematical forms. They also accepted a theory of transmigration of human souls. What is of particular import is that because they explained things in terms of numbers, they advanced beyond a merely material explanation of the world to the consideration of *structure* as well as content.

In the fifth and fourth centuries B.C., a considerable advance in philosophy was made by the philosophers of the Eleatic school, named after the city of Elea from which its principal exponent, Parmenides, hailed. Parmenides (530–444 B.C.) is sometimes called the "father of metaphysics," for he was the first to raise the problem of "being."

Reality, the senses tell us, is continually changing. Yet if this is so, nothing we can say about it is true. For example, the moment we point to an arrow in flight and say, "There it is!" we are mistaken, for it is no longer there, but has traveled to another place. Change, according to Parmenides, is an illusion—an untrue vision relayed to us by deceiving senses. Only the intellect should be followed, and it tells us that change or "becoming" is impossible. Reality or "being" then is one and is unchanging. According to this school of thought, being cannot change *from* something and *into* something because, something is already being. Parmenides reasoned that a thing does not become what it already is. Hence, if it already is being, it cannot become being. The same is true with respect to changing *into* something. The only other alternative is for being to change from nothing into nothing, or "non-being." Yet this is clearly impossible, for from nothing, nothing comes. Being, or reality, then, has the same meaning (univocal) when applied to what we see about us. Things cannot change or be different, or be many, for being is one and immutable. Qualified pantheism—the position maintaining that all reality is part of one reality, God—prevails.

The Eleatics advanced philosophy by raising the question of the validity of knowledge at the twofold levels of sensory and intellectual cognition. They chose the latter as the only true kind of knowledge. Since in such a system thought and being become roughly identical, the Eleatics can be credited with giving the first philosophical exposition of idealism. They

---

[1] This label of "materialism" should not be confused with the same label applied to those such as the Atomists, Karl Marx, or Ludwig Feuerbach, who denied God. At this early stage of philosophy, the problem of God was not yet fully considered. Hence, materialism as applied by the Ionians simply means they limited their perspectives to this order.

made the first effort to grasp the fundamental problem of metaphysics, the meaning of reality, or the meaning of "being as being."

At that time, however, such a view was sharply challenged by Heraclitus (*c.* 540–475 B.C.), who held that "becoming" or change is more real than being. If we considered the matter rightly, argued Heraclitus, we would see that change is what is real about reality. For a man to stop changing or becoming is for that man to be dead. He *is,* only so long as he is changing. Reality should be seen as a river, always flowing, always in flux. No part of it is ever the same. To illustrate this notion, Heraclitus chose fire as the symbol for the ultimate constituent of reality. Fire's being consists in its becoming. Its generation consists in the continual corruption of something else. Yet Heraclitus' thought is somewhat vague when he also refers to a divine or rational principle of mind of the One (*Logos*), of which all reality partakes. Hence his thought too is pantheistically inclined.

Reverting back to materialism, another philosopher, Empedocles (*c.* 490–430 B.C.), attempted to synthesize previous thought by holding that objects as wholes change, but their parts (the four elements—earth, air, fire, and water) remain constant. The basic elements remain the same, although they can be brought together in new combinations, owing to the operations of mechanistic laws. An analogy can be drawn with respect to the three primary colors, or red, blue, and yellow, which are able to produce various shades and "new" color combinations.

Anaxagoras (*c.* 500–428 B.C.) held that everything consists of a number of particles of everything else. Those particles that are dominant determine what the object appears to be. For example, if we mix different colors but put in more red than any other, our result will be red, even though all the other colors are included in the mixture. He also raised the hypothesis of Mind (*Nous*) as entering into reality, a principle that was needed to explain the obvious order in the world. Unfortunately, he did not pursue this latter idea to any great extent.

During this same period, Leucippus (fl. 460 B.C.) and Democritus (*c.* 460–370 B.C.) bequeathed to philosophy the atomist tradition. Thoroughgoing materialists, they sought to free the Greeks from religious superstition, such as belief in an afterlife. They selected three principles as the source of all philosophical explanation: *matter, motion,* and the *void.*

Matter is ultimately nothing more than the smallest particles termed atoms, having various shapes and configurations but not differing essentially from one another. These atoms are in continual motion in a void (space) and through collision can account for generation and corruption. Generation is explained by the collision of atoms that happened to stick together; corruption, by the atoms that hit these combinations and broke them apart. Everything is accounted for by matter and chance; there is no need to appeal to Mind or any other cause. The Atomists applied these principles to all of the known branches of philosophy. In cosmology, the world is seen as entirely material; in psychology, man is viewed as a combination of quantitatively but not qualitatively different matter particles accidentally united; in ethics, since man's death was his dissolution, there is no concern for immortality. The Atomists were probably the most consistent materialistic philosophers of the period.

Toward the end of the fifth century B.C., a group of traveling teachers, the Sophists, brought their influence to bear upon the philosophical scene. For them, all knowledge and morality is relative to man. To an extent their views were brought about by previous disagreements among philosophers. In some respects, they were the pragmatists of ancient Greece, for they accepted the useful as the criterion of truth.

It was Socrates (470–399 B.C.) who fought the Sophists and their destructive influence on an already decaying Athens. Socrates upheld the absolute value of virtue and of man's intellectual ability to know truth. He tried to express this by his search for definitions, especially to the question, "What is virtue?" Ethical matters were his principal concern.

With Plato (c. 427–347 B.C.), the student of Socrates, philosophy began to reach its full heights.[2] If the Atomists' account of reality can be labeled purely physical or empirical, Plato's can be characterized as almost purely intellectual or ideal.

In his dialogue *Timaeus,* Plato asked the question, "What is always becoming but never is; what always is but is never becoming?" In answering the question he drew from several of his predecessors. With Heraclitus, Plato agreed that the sensible, material world is in flux or change and that accordingly it can contain no truth or give us scientific knowledge. With Parmenides, he agreed that reality in its highest form is unchanging and eternal and grasped only by intelligence. Reconciling the thought of these two men, Plato accepted two levels of reality: the sensory world in which we presently live, and the intelligible world of unchanging reality, termed the world of forms or ideas, which we aspire to know and attain and which is the "really" real world. Accordingly the sense world is "always becoming, but never is," and the intelligible world "always is but is never becoming."

The sense world can but generate *opinion* in man, for it is always becoming. The intelligible world of ideas, however, is not the world of becoming but of being, and only it can give us *knowledge.* The two worlds are related in that the ideal world is like a blueprint, and according to its archetypes or forms the sensory world is fashioned. The sensory world is a shadow, and the intelligible world is the tree that casts the shadow. Whatever reality the shadow has, it has by virtue of the tree that casts it. Yet the converse is not true. While the shadow (sensory world) is always changing and depicts reality in various forms (the shadow at noon is very small,

---

[2] Alfred North Whitehead, the famous British mathematician and philosopher, declared that "all Western philosophy is but a footnote to Plato."

while at dusk it is elongated), the tree (intelligible world) remains fundamentally the same. Yet both the shadow (sense world) and the tree (intelligible world) require the sun for the shadow to be seen and for the tree to continue to exist; both of the Platonic worlds require a higher principle called the One or the Good, in which both participate for unity. Christians were later to identify this One or Good with God, although there is some dispute as to Plato's meaning on this point.

If we ask of Plato what is it to be real, Plato's response is that it is to be after the manner of the intelligible world; it is to be essence or self-identity, unchanging and eternal. The philosopher aspires to a knowledge of these "eternal verities," and his life is taken up by the attempt to reach them through what Plato calls "dialectic." Dialectic implies a speculative and a moral ascent to the highest good, which is at one with the most intelligible. There are then religious and mystical elements in his thought which others later developed to greater fullness.

Although in his early years Aristotle (384–322 B.C.) was influenced by Plato, he eventually developed doctrines that were quite different from those of his teacher. Instead of retaining Plato's two worlds, Aristotle attempted to combine the sensory world of Heraclitus and the intelligible world of Parmenides. He did this by pointing out that all knowledge, even intellectual knowledge, comes through the senses. Yet intellectual knowledge is superior to sensory knowledge because it understands in the sensible object more than what is perceived by the senses. It does this by a peculiar ability to abstract or grasp the essence or nature of the object.

The senses attain the object through its accidental, changing, and nonessential features; for example, a man is seen as tall or heavy set. The intellect grasps the object at a deeper level where it understands its substantial nature and unchanging essence; for example, man is seen as rational animal. This is termed the *form* of the object. Aristotle then agreed with Plato that the purpose of intellectual knowledge is to grasp the essence or form, but he corrected Plato by asserting that the form is in the material world before us, and not "in another world." In establishing his position, Aristotle recognized the validity of matter *and* of form. In combining them he saw himself as unifying what is true in both empiricism and idealism.

Applying such principles to the problem of motion and change, Aristotle concluded that change requires a principle that remains (matter) to account for stability and sameness, and a principle that is gained (form) to account for the new. Contrary to Parmenides, change is real, but, it does not proceed from being or non-being. Rather, it proceeds from potentiality, that is, the fact that a thing changes argues to its having had a capacity or potentiality for such change. From this capacity or potentiality, as actualized or "moved" by an agent, change comes about. Parmenides' basic error lay in not granting a dual meaning to "being," whereby it could be understood as "being-in-act" *or* "being in potency."

Matter and form are, in fact, causes of change. The matter (material cause) is that out of which the thing is made or changed; the form (formal cause) is that determining principle that makes a thing to be or to become what it is. Besides these two intrinsic causes, Aristotle elaborated two extrinsic causes, the efficient and the final. The former is simply the agent cause or the motor cause that intitiates the activity; the latter is the end or purpose for which such change has occurred.

Aristotle applied all of these causes to the various branches of philosophical enquiry. He was the first man to introduce such orderly, causal enquiry into philosophy, and his influence upon future philosophers will equal if not exceed that of Plato.

In addition, Aristotle was the first to give us a fully developed science of metaphysics, or first philosophy and divine science, as he called it.[3] He pointed out that there are some indisputable and self-evident truths that cannot be denied and òn which all proof is ultimately based. One of these is that reality itself is intelligible. Since it is intelligible, it should be investigated, not simply piecemeal, as is done by cosmology, psychology, or ethics, but precisely insofar as it is real. He carries the study of "being as being" into his metaphysics; it will be discussed at length further in this essay.

With the death of Aristotle, Greek philosophy went into a period of general decline. There were some stirrings with the school of Neoplatonism, headed by Plotinus (205–270), but as the name suggests this philosophy was only a new synthesis of Platonic thought, combined with certain Aristotelian viewpoints.

The Medieval Period

St. Augustine (354–430) is considered to be within the Platonic tradition, but he was more a theologian than a philosopher. It was not until the Middle Ages, with Arabian philosophers and especially with St. Thomas Aquinas (1225–74), that philosophy rose again and attempted to reach new heights.

Although open to the insights of Plato and others, St. Thomas must be placed primarily in the Aristotelian tradition. For him, Aristotle was always *the* philosopher; he accepted his basic positions and developed them to greater depths. In addition, St. Thomas' philosophy accented the fact of existence as of greater import than essence; on this point Aquinas made a great advance over Aristotle. Aristotle apparently accepted form or substance as the highest principle of reality, presupposing of course the fact of its existence. Aquinas draws our specific attention to the latter as the focal

---

[3] Aristotle did not know the word "metaphysics," for it was coined in the first century A.D. Andronicus of Rhodes used the expression to characterize the writings of Aristotle dealing with "first philosophy." Since Andronicus edited Aristotle's writings and placed Aristotle's treatise on "First Philosophy" after the latter's treatises on Physics, Andronicus designated this treatise as "Meta," that is, after "Physics."

point of metaphysics and reality. He describes God as the very act of existence, as *ipsum esse subsistens*—self-subsistent being.

Aquinas' greatest contribution lay in providing a Christian synthesis in which Greek philosophy (especially Aristotelian thought) and theology were seen as mutually complementary. His specific philosophical advancements were primarily with those topics of most concern to Christianity, such as the nature of person and natural law.

Many other medievals attempted such a synthesis (as is evidenced by the number of *summae* that were written), but Aquinas' efforts, known today as Thomism, have met with the greatest success.

The latter part of the medieval period saw another stage of philosophic decline. The disputes became more verbal than real and the doctrines were promulgated more by decree than by careful thought. At the end of this stage a new genius, René Descartes (1596–1650), ushered in the period of modern philosophy.

The Modern Period

Descartes studied the "scholastic" philosophy emanating from the decadent half of the Middle Ages, but was impressed only by the disagreements that he found there. Possessed of an orderly mathematical mind, Descartes sought to restore philosophy to a position of prominence. For that to happen, it would have to be based, like mathematics, on a bedrock foundation. Once all philosophers agreed on the foundation, they would hopefully come to the same conclusions. Descartes sought to supply this foundation by giving philosophy a new methodology—the method of doubt and of the clear and distinct idea.

Descartes wished to begin his philosophical enquiry with an indubitable principle with which all would have to agree. To arrive at such a principle, he doubted everything he could in order to see if anything was indubitable. Since he could clearly doubt the existence of the world, for his senses might be deceiving him, Descartes chose instead to start with the idea of himself. He gave us his famous *Cogito, ergo sum* (I think, therefore I am). Only an existing being can doubt his existence, so whether I doubt or affirm my existence, I must at least *be* in order to do so. Here then was a truth that could not be doubted—the fact of one's own existence. Once this idea was obtained, Descartes examined its characteristics, which, if attached to other ideas, would be signs or criteria of their own truth and indubitability. Those characteristics were clarity and distinctness, the tools Descartes needed to pursue philosophy to whatever conclusions it could give to the human mind.

Examining another idea within him, that of God, Descartes saw that it, too, is clear and distinct, and so is true. Descartes used both ideas to prove the validity of one's impression of a real world. I experience the fact that I think there is a real world outside of myself. In addition, God, whose attribute of goodness is clearly seen, would be deceiving me if I thought a real world existed when, in fact, such is not the case. Deception, as incompatible with God's goodness, could therefore be ruled out, and the world I seem to experience can now be taken for granted.

By starting out with the idea, rather than with the real object outside the knower, Descartes initiated the movement of rationalism which was carried on by Benedict Spinoza (1632–77), Gottfried Wilhelm Leibniz (1646–1716), Immanuel Kant (1724–1804), and G. W. F. Hegel (1770–1831). Basically, rationalism is an attempt to emphasize the ability of the intellect to know reality and its laws independently of sense experience. In a qualified way, it sees reality as following the patterns of the mind, instead of the converse. It is completely optimistic with respect to the ability of mind to know all.

As was to be expected, another philosophical camp reacted strongly and protested against this "highhanded" philosophical attitude toward experience. Known as "empiricism," this movement in modern philosophy found such exponents as Thomas Hobbes (1588–1679), John Locke (1632–1704), George Berkeley (1685–1753), and David Hume (1711–76). Generally, empiricism insists that sense experience is the only root experience available to man. If our ideas cannot be traced to it, they contain no philosophical validity. Moreover, empiricism usually denies man's ability to know the essence of things as a reality more basic to the object than the information attained by the senses. Abstraction is replaced by association of ideas; intellect assumes an organizational function, rather than an abstractive one that arrives at insights into nature.

Issuing a strong critique of rationalism, David Hume denied that causality was speculatively verifiable. Although he did grant the practical utility of this concept, he claimed that we cannot uncover in reality the necessary connection between cause and effect. Previously this was regarded as the very base on which the causal notion rests. Hume claimed that the association of ideas explains our connecting cause and effect, and such being the case science and all philosophy are rejected. Philosophically, Hume wound up in the camp of scepticism, maintaining the paradoxical position that "the truth is, there is no truth."

Immanuel Kant, who had been brought up in the philosophical environment of rationalism, could neither remain unaffected by the rigorous Humean critique nor desert the validity of science, especially the Newtonian physics and mathematics of the day. By applying Hume's critique to metaphysics Kant rejected metaphysics; but to retain science, he had to formulate an entirely new system of philosophy based upon a radically different theory of knowledge than had been previously developed.

Instead of *deriving* meaning from things, Kant declared that we *impose* meaning on them. The object of knowledge now revolves around the knower, rather than the knower around the object. This has aptly been termed Kant's Copernican Revolution in the field of knowledge. Accordingly, we do not know the way things are but only the way they appear, because we *make* them appear that way. By the term *noumenon,* or the thing in itself, Kant referred to the world of reality; by the term *phenomenon,* Kant referred to the thing as it appears. Certain necessary ways to see things (a priori categories) are built into man's knowing structure. He cannot escape this mode of knowing—causing objects to be seen as appearances—any more than he can escape being human. It is as if at the moment of birth a pair of rose-colored glasses were placed on a child in such a way that they could not be removed, and were considered part of his natural apparatus for seeing. Whatever the child would see would be rose colored; he could never know if things were different from the way in which they appeared to him. Similarly, given our knowing structure, Kant said we can never know if things really are or are not the way we see them.

Since science claims only to know phenomena (things as they appear), it is valid; metaphysics, however, which purports to deal with the reality (noumenon) behind the appearance, can never attain that reality, and is a frustrated search. The categories of substance and cause are meaningful only when applied to the phenomenal order of appearance. Hence, because of the structure of man's cognitive make-up, he can never attain the possibility of metaphysics as a science.

G. W. F. Hegel saw no necessity for the Kantian dualism of reality and mind. As an absolute idealist, he identified the forms of thought and reality, declared that the real is rational and the rational is real, and thereby eliminated the distinction between appearance and thing in itself. Reality now as appearance is all there is to know and our only aim should be to know it as completely as possible. This could be done only through consciousness of self—of individual mind, eventually seeing the union of all things in the Absolute Mind or Spirit. Reality, in the last analysis, is the dynamic manifestation of Mind or Spirit, evolving dialectically toward an ever more perfect state. According to a common interpretation of Hegel, God is not yet, but he is becoming.

Karl Marx (1818–83) applied Hegel's dynamic methodology to the evolution of matter rather than of mind; in so doing, he put "Hegel on his feet, instead of on his head." Just as the history of matter reveals progress through opposition of forces, so human history reveals progress and perfection through the opposing forces of class struggles. Examples are the opposition of the slave and the master, the serf and the feudal baron, and the worker and the employer. It is not God (who is nonexistent) but the classless society that is becoming but is not yet. Since the laws of progress are necessary and inevitable, man should recognize his destiny in order that the end be attained more quickly. This requires that man recognize his freedom as an "insight into necessity." It also requires collectivization of men in a social setting, for outside this setting, they may be men but they will not be human. Society makes man human.

Contemporary Philosophy

Philosophy after Hegel was brought more and more back to the level of the concrete. For the Marxists, this meant the concrete of the "collective," while for the existentialists it meant the concrete of the individual.

Søren Kierkegaard (1813–55), regarded by many as the "father of existentialism," made this clear in his protest against Hegelian inroads being made upon Protestant Christianity, especially in Denmark. Kierkegaard upheld the validity of the individual as the only important thing in Christianity. He protested against a militant Christianity being turned into the abstract "Christendom" of a Church triumphant on earth. Progress for the Christian lay not in moving *forward* in Hegelian fashion, but by going *backward* to Christ. This was the only way in which the human person living in time could go on to eternity, namely, by joining with Christ, who as man exists in time but who as God is eternal.

Friedrich Nietzsche (1844–1900) also decried the de-emphasis on the individual by proposing a theory of the superman—*Übermensch*—who by his strength justifies a new order. This order could come about only by declaring, as does Zarathustra, that *Gott ist tot!* God is dead. Man would have to rely upon himself and not look to another.

Jean-Paul Sartre (b. 1905) echoes a similar theme, declaring with Dostoevski that "if God does not exist, all things are possible." The world for Sartre is not big enough for man and God. He banishes God, in order that man be able to exercise freedom. Yet a world without God, a world in which man is "condemned to be free" and in which each of us is responsible for all mankind, is a stark reality to face. Sartre asks that we face it and accept the fact that we live in a desert of despair. We must avoid falling into *mauvaise foi,* or bad faith, which is a life sustained by the myth of a God's existence.

Gabriel Marcel (b. 1889), a Christian existentialist, admits that dread and anxiety are native to the human condition, but asks nonetheless that we play the "entire existential keyboard" with its additional notes of love, hope, and fidelity. Through interpersonal relationships meaning is seen and absurdity is dispelled. We must reveal "who we are" instead of merely "what we have." Marcel accuses our age of confusing "being" with "having"—that is, mistakenly identifying "who a man is" with "what he has." Accordingly, we regard a man as "somebody" only when he has something. Vigorously opposed to philosophical idealism (to which he originally had strong tendencies), Marcel insists at all times on realism and on the necessity of paying attention to the concrete. Since it is through the body that one has contact with the world of reality, an incarnational rather than a spiritual metaphysics needs to be developed.

Because of their distaste for the abstract, signified especially in definitions, the existentialists have almost unanimously employed the phenomenological method. This method attempts to describe rather than to define that which is attained by consciousness. By insisting on the unity between consciousness and that which it grasps, it opposes the dualism of Kantian thought. Yet phenomenology disassociates itself from a merely psychological presentation of cognitive activities. It is thoroughly philosophical and, in the words of its founder, Edmund Husserl (1859–1938), it seeks to get back to "the things themselves."

In addition, existentialism openly acknowledges the element of the irrational in the world. Its stress is on the concrete, the individual, and the primacy of sense experience encountered by humans, a position that also places the movement in sharp opposition to idealistic philosophies.

These allied views can also be found in the movements of pragmatism and naturalism. Philosophers in these movements hold several basic principles in common, which could be summed up generally as: the useful is the only workable criterion for truth; meaning is to be found not in static idealizations of objects but in the interaction of thought and reality; appeals to meaning should be kept within the natural order as verifiable by experience having a sensory base. Foremost among the philosophers in the pragmatic-naturalist movements are Charles Sanders Peirce (1839–1914), William James (1842–1910), John Dewey (1859–1952), and Sidney Hook (b. 1902).

Related to this school are the analytic and the positivist philosophers. Positivism holds that to arrive at truth we must imitate the method of the physical sciences. It declares as non-sense any sentence or proposition that one makes but cannot offer with it the method whereby it can be proven or disproven. One could declare, for example, "The moon is made of green cheese," and in so doing make a meaningful but false statement. One can at least see how the proposition could be verified, that is, by making a spectographic analysis and eventually sampling the material of the moon. But statements such as "God is" or "God is not" are non-sense statements, because they cannot have their validity investigated by possible proofs or disproofs acceptable to the methodology of positivism. Such sentences may express a wish and thus do have some degree of emotional significance.

It is to such philosophers as A. J. Ayer (b. 1910), Gilbert Ryle (b. 1900), and Ludwig Wittgenstein (1889–1951) that modern-day positivists owe this analytical approach. These men have stressed the investigation of sentence structure or syntax as a prerequisite to looking for solutions to philosophical problems. This method will generally "dissolve" the philosophical problem at hand by showing a statement to be tautological, contradictory, or incapable of verification. Before we can ask "Is it true that . . . ," we must be able to explain "what we mean by . . . ." To say "Before creation God existed" is implicitly to contradict ourselves. "Before" is agreed upon by all as a category, meaningful and applicable only to what exists in the temporal order. Even if God exists, we would be applying a "time category" to a nontemporal being—a procedure that is regarded as totally meaningless and contradictory by the analysts.

The methodology of positivism and analytic philosophy forces its proponents to dissolve philosophical problems or to maintain an agnostic attitude toward them. The indirect influence of Kant upon these philosophers is readily apparent, as is the fact that they are the modern continuators of the empiricist tradition of Locke and Hume.

The contemporary schools of thought are today becoming less restrictive than they were at the time of their origin. A. J. Ayer's thought, for example, has seen considerable modification and a greater spirit of openness. This is a characteristic of most philosophical traditions, especially of those that will be treated in the readings of this volume. Such progression from dogmatism to a greater willingness to hear new viewpoints and to a reevaluation of the old positions is a sign that the philosophy being held is both organic and developing. It also indicates that such philosophies have maintained a contact with the real, which, after all, is continually manifesting change amidst stability.

Metaphysics: Its Nature and Key Problems

Although there are different philosophies of man and different systems of ethics, there can be only one metaphysics. By its very nature metaphysics is a single science, and any variation in approach is either a further development of this basic metaphysics, a deviation from it, or a denial of it (antimetaphysics). In order to understand metaphysics, as well as its development, deviation, and denial, we must also discuss some of its basic problems. These problems vary with different philosophers: what is important in one tradition might be relatively unimportant in another.

Aristotle and Basic Metaphysics

The birth of metaphysics as a science is generally credited to Aristotle, although this does not mean that no metaphysical problems were raised prior to Aristotle. Certainly Parmenides, Heraclitus, and Plato raised metaphysical issues in their philosophies and attempted to give solutions to them. However, we must look to Aristotle for the original systematic and scientific treatment of metaphysics.

In attempting to distinguish this discipline from others, Aristotle observed that all other studies treated aspects of reality or "being," but none concerned itself with "being as such." [4] Consequently, the science of being as such would be the most basic, for in a sense all other "special sciences" presupposed it. If arranged hierarchically, the conclusions of one science would be seen as the principles of the next science. But there must be a science of first things or of the most real, and that science is metaphysics.

THE PROBLEM OF THE REAL. For Aristotle, being or reality is ap-

---

[4] It would be similar if in studying man only the various parts of man were studied in isolation, but never the whole man, precisely as man.

plied to various things not in the same way (univocally), nor in a completely different way (equivocally), but only in a similar manner (analogously). It is at once the broadest of terms and, in the language of later philosophers, a "transcendental," for it cannot be confined or limited to any single category of thought (to the exclusion of another category). Since we observe many different kinds of beings, we must ask ourselves in what way can we say of each that it is real, that it is a being? A tree, a cow, and a man are all real, but what is it that makes them to be real? If *to be real* were to be a tree as such, then all realities would be trees. The case is similar if applied to cows and men. On the other hand, if *to be real* meant *to be changing,* then whatever is unchanging could not be called real. Again, if *to be real* meant *to be material,* no nonmaterial thing could be real, that is, could exist.

The question then is: What does being signify chiefly and primarily? Aristotle replied that being (reality) means *substance.* By "substance" he meant a thing that exists in its own right, a subject that has predicates but itself is not predicated of anything else. For example, a cat is a substance but its predicates, or attributes, of being thin, black, and furry would not be substances. These latter characteristics are termed "accidents." The substance is simply "that which is" in its most basic character. Hence, metaphysics is first and foremost a study of substance—its causes and its principal attributes—and second a study of accidents. We should note that a substance is a unity; hence unity is a universal characteristic of being. But since being is applied analogously to different things, unity is likewise predicated analogously. The unity of man, dog, and tree is the same only in an analogous way.

THE PROBLEM OF THE CONTINGENT. If we examine the substances of our experience, we see that they manifest aspects of activity and passivity. They come to be and they pass away; they are capable of change; they acquire and lose perfections. Accordingly, within such substances there must be two complementary, united, but still diverse principles accounting for this perfection and capacity for further change and perfection. These principles are designated by the terms "act" and "potency." Act signifies that which is already in some way fulfilled and perfected; potency indicates the capacity for this perfection. For example, a child is potentially an adult; many years later, he actually is an adult. Being as we see it in our experience involves principles of potency (imperfection) and act (perfection). Gradations of perfection can be noted, for some things are more actual and less potential, or the converse. A young pupil has great potentiality for knowledge, but little actuality or perfection in this respect.

Because the things of our experience manifest change they manifest contingency, for they thereby show that they are imperfect and not wholly independent. They are, but they need not be. Since they come to be and cease to be, their explanation is rooted not in themselves but in another. They are contingent beings because they depend on another. Further, since

motion demands a mover, and since things that are composed of two principles (such as a substance that incorporates both act and potency) demand a cause for being united, there must be other substances beside those
we experience to account for these effects. Hence Aristotle concluded that
there are three kinds of substances: (1) the sensible and perishable substance of ordinary experience (a man, a tree, a cow); (2) the sensible and
nonperishable substance (stars and other celestial bodies, which, because
of his faulty astronomy, Aristotle included in this type); (3) the non-
sensible and nonperishable substance (the gods, or God).

THE PROBLEM OF GOD. Aristotle called the third substance "unmoved mover" or "uncaused cause." It is the source of all motion and accounts for motion without itself moving. It is not a composition of potency
and act but is exclusively act or perfection. Such a perfect being, a unity
par excellence, characterized by Aristotle as "self-thinking thought," can
be called God.[5] Since Aristotle considered goodness another name for perfection, this God is supremely good. Other things, having but a limited
measure of perfection or actuality, have only a measure of goodness. This
being is the most necessary, and in that respect the highest of all beings.
For this reason, it could not not be. Aristotle's proofs for the existence of
God all proceed from an observation and a consideration of effects to their
demand for a first cause.

St. Thomas Aquinas: Further Development of Basic Metaphysics

Aquinas accepted the Aristotelian metaphysics, but emphasized certain
problems that Aristotle left untreated or undeveloped, and drew out many
implications from Aristotle's metaphysical views. St. Thomas was especially interested in correcting what he considered to be the distortion of
Aristotle by preceding and contemporary Arabian philosophers. He covered in depth those problems of specific interest to the Christian, foremost
of which was the distinction between creatures and God and the relationship of the latter to the former.

THE PROBLEM OF ESSENCE AND EXISTENCE. While Aquinas emphasized with Aristotle the primacy of substance in metaphysics, he high-
lighted another principle of reality, one that was presupposed but virtually
disregarded by Aristotle. That principle is *esse,* the act of existence. Besides the composition of things in terms of substance and its modifications
(accidents) and the composition of matter and form found in sensible substances, Aquinas stressed in creatures the composition of essence and the
act of existence, the latter being that whereby they simply are or exist. If
substance or essence accounts for *what* a thing is, *esse* or the act of existence accounts for *whether* it is. This is the basic earmark of creatures and
indicates their dependency (contingency) upon an-other. Since their ex-

---

[5] We should not be led to believe that Aristotle saw this God in the manner of the
Judeo-Christian concept. But later thinkers in this tradition did view the supreme
being of Aristotle's thought in line with Christian views.

istence is not of themselves but from another, the roots of their being lead inexorably to one who does not simply *have* existence, but whose nature *is* existence. That being is God; he corresponds to the "I am Who am" of Exodus in the Old Testament. (Here is one example of how Aquinas christianized Aristotelian thought.)

Developing and adding to Aristotle's proof for God, Aquinas pointed to God as the source and cause of all that exists. Although in creatures the principles of essence and existence are united, they are not identical; in God, they are one and the same. God's essence is his existence; this manifests his supreme perfection and all other perfections result logically from this one. Existence is the most basic actuality or perfection, and while creatures enjoy it by virtue of God, God enjoys it by virtue of his own nature. Hence God is an absolutely necessary and simple being, while creatures are always contingent and composite.

Aquinas developed in greater detail than did Aristotle the specific proofs for God, from facts such as the order in the universe demanding an intelligent orderer and the multiplicity of things demanding a first, ultimate, external principle of unity. Like Aristotle, Aquinas did not accept any philosophical proof for God other than that which proceeds from experience, following always a movement from effect to cause. St. Thomas explicitly rejected any innate idea of God as having been given to man.

We find in St. Thomas an attempt to combine certain Platonic and Aristotelian views. Plato's world of ideas according to which all things are fashioned is put in the mind of God. Aquinas' God is the producer and creator of all things, an un-Aristotelian notion. For Aristotle the matter of the world is an irreducible principle; it does not have its explanation in God, who is the active irreducible principle. For Aquinas, God, as Creator, is the cause of matter; *all* things are explained ultimately in terms of only one irreducible principle, God. Accordingly, Aquinas' God is personal, providential, and closer to the world than the God of Aristotle.

THE PROBLEM OF EVIL. Although dealt with only indirectly by Aristotle and Plato, the problem of evil is given full treatment by Aquinas. St. Augustine also wrestled with this problem, and Aquinas owes much to him. Basically the problem is how to explain evil if there is only one God and he is all good. It would seem that if we are to account for good things in terms of a supremely good cause, we would have to account for evil things by positing a supremely evil cause.

St. Thomas dealt with this problem by introducing a distinction between that which is something and that which is nothing. With Aristotle, he pointed out that whatever is, insofar as it is, is an act—a perfection—and so a good. Obviously, nothing in this respect can be called evil. On the other hand, sheer nothingness is neither good nor evil. Evil is not something positive or negative, but it is privation, the lack of perfection that should normally accrue to a thing in virtue of being the kind of thing it is. When anything has that lack (privation), it has something evil about it.

We can take, for example, a dental cavity and ask: Is it something? No. Is it nothing? Not exactly. It is the lack of a perfection in a tooth where there should be a perfection. Thus, to an extent, evil is relative to a particular nature. For a mole, being unable to see is not evil; it is only a negation since vision is not proper to the nature of the mole. But for a man to be blind is an evil, for sight is of his nature. Similarly, evil (a corruption) requires the presence of the good, that is, that which it corrupts. If there were no tooth, there would be no cavity. In short, nothing could be completely evil, for then it would not be.

Viewed as a whole, the order of nature explains the presence of physical evil.[6] Nothing in nature is ordained to evil, for only the good attracts and nature is directed to the good. God, the cause of nature, both with respect to its parts and to its character as a whole, is the direct cause of goodness. Since accidentally this involves privation (evil) being present to some things, God is at the same time indirectly the cause of physical evil, but this is only in his role as cause of the good of the whole of nature.

A Variation of Basic Metaphysics: The Rationalists

The rationalist tradition in modern philosophy began with Descartes and continued through Spinoza, Leibniz, and Christian Wolff (1679–1754) on up to Kant and Hegel. We have seen that Descartes' philosophy began with an examination of two ideas that he considered to be innate, namely, the idea of self and the idea of God, by means of which Descartes verified the reality of the world and our knowledge of it. Since the existence of God is essential to Descartes' philosophy, it will be profitable to see how he established the latter's existence. The way this is done portrays well the rationalistic approach to philosophy.

DESCARTES: THE PROBLEM OF GOD, OF KNOWING THE REAL, AND OF SUBSTANCE. Descartes gave us two types of proof for God's existence. The first proceeds from effect to cause and can be termed an a posteriori approach to God, one that begins with a later experience and proceeds to the source of that experience. Basically that proof can be described as follows: I have in my mind an idea of an infinite and perfect being, but how can I explain the presence of such an idea? I cannot account for the idea of a *perfect* being by positing myself as the cause of it, for I am aware of my finitude and imperfection as evidenced by my ability to doubt. Hence to say that I could cause such an idea is to say that the imperfect could cause the perfect. For the same reason, the world cannot account for this idea, for it, too, is imperfect. There remains only one explanation for the idea within me of a perfect being: it must be produced by a being proportionate to the idea, that is, by an infinite and perfect being. Such a being then must exist and we call him God. (It should be noted that Descartes claimed to have a *positive* idea of an infinite being, and also that

---

[6] The problem of moral evil is solved in a similar fashion. But this is principally the concern of psychology and ethics.

he assumed, without examining it, the principle that the effect demands a cause and that the effect cannot be greater than the cause. Both notions were thoroughly rejected by Hume.)

The second proof Descartes gave for God is an a priori type of argument, which, by considering the nature of God as manifested in my innate idea of him, argues to the attribute of his necessary existence. Descartes argued that when one considers a triangle, one must also consider certain necessary characteristics that follow upon it—for example, the necessity of its having angles equal to 180 degrees. So, too, in understanding my idea of God, I grasp the fact that existence is his necessary attribute; I conclude that his existence is real because conceptually I see that his nature demands that he cannot not be.

Descartes also considered the problem of knowing the real and the problem of substance. In regard to the former, he reasoned that since God is perfect, he is good; since he is good, he cannot deceive. If my ideas and impressions of the outside world are illusory, God would be acting contrary to his nature as a nondeceiver. Thus, I can be assured that the world is as I know it.[7]

Descartes defined substance as "a thing which exists in such a way as to stand in need of nothing beyond itself in order to its existence." This definition, if taken strictly, could pertain only to God. However Descartes applied it loosely to two kinds of substance, mind and matter. The essence of mind is thought and the essence of matter is extension. Everything will henceforth be explained by one or the other; Descartes' metaphysics resolved in a dualism.

SPINOZA: THE PROBLEM OF GOD, SUBSTANCE, AND REALITY AS ONE. Spinoza accepted the Cartesian definition of substance more rigorously than Descartes himself cared to and logically concluded that God was the only existing substance. Everything else would be an aspect of God, which one must view in light of the eternal. We see Spinoza's philosophy as a pantheism in which only necessity prevails, and freedom is an illusion. Even God *must* act the way he does, for he must follow his nature. For Spinoza, any discussion about the free will of God is meaningless; the problem of what is reality is solved by answering that it is substance and that substance is God and everything else is an aspect of him.

LEIBNIZ: THE PROBLEM OF THE REAL AND THE PROBLEM OF GOD. Leibniz, like Descartes and Spinoza, was mathematically inclined and accepted the presence of innate ideas. Reality as we apprehend it through our senses is merely an illusion and is of the phenomenal order. Things are not extended nor are they in external motion as we see them. The real world is composed of an infinite number of simple, living, and inde-

---

[7] One should note that philosophers who accept some of the principles of Descartes, but who reject his argument for God, have no means of "getting to the world." With them a phenomenalism arises, that is, a view in which we know only appearances and cannot be sure they portray things as they really are.

pendent points of force, called "monads." They differ in their ability to know, that is, in their power to mirror or represent the world. Yet each thing is capable of cognition. Only those monads exist that have the greatest possibility for existence, either singly or in combination with other monads. This possibility for existence is determined by their degree of perfection: the more perfect the nature of the monad, the greater claim it has to existence. Hence, the world we know is the best possible world.[8]

One of Leibniz' proofs for God's existence follows this line of a priori reasoning: *God is thinkable; therefore he is possible; therefore he exists.* In explaining this, Leibniz said that (1) we can conceive of God. Since we cannot conceive of the impossible (for example, we are unable to conceive a square circle), whatever we conceive must at least be possible. Hence, if God is thinkable, (2) he is at least possible. Further, if God did not exist, he would not be possible, for nothing could bring him into existence. That is, if by definition God is the first being, then if he didn't exist, it would be impossible for him to come from nothing or to bring himself into existence. We must conclude then that if he is possible, he must be more than possible, (3) he must exist!

This is only an initiation into the rationalistic approach to metaphysics as characterized by its handling of the problem of the real and the problem of God. It should be clear that rationalism became less and less concerned with actuality and more and more concerned with the essence of things in their possibility. In fact, Christian Wolff, whose teachings influenced Kant, defined metaphysics as the science of pure possibles. Rationalism marked a sharp departure from Aristotelian metaphysics, although the former granted the validity of metaphysics as a science. Because rationalism had become wholly deductive, conceptual, and a priori, one could expect a strong reaction, which came in the form of an outright denial of the possibility of any metaphysics at all.

The Denial of Metaphysics

Those philosophers upholding or allied with the empirical and positivist traditions were generally inclined to write off metaphysics as illegitimate philosophy. With Auguste Comte (1798–1857), they viewed it as the kind of spurious thought which sustained man during a particular phase in his search for progress. However, this progress has now been assured and it is the positive sciences, not philosophy, that have made it possible. They were generally disinclined to look beyond "that which appears," affirming that what appears is all there is, or at least all that can be known by man. Immanuel Kant is the classic exponent of this latter position, but to some extent his thought is the culmination of those who preceded him. Accordingly, we will look briefly at several ideas of the pre-Kantians bearing on metaphysics.

---

[8] In the eighteenth century Voltaire remarked cynically against this "best possible world"; he stated that it was shattered by the great Lisbon earthquake!

THE DISMISSAL OF THE IDEA OF SUBSTANCE. The meaning and reality of substance are always prime objects of metaphysical investigation. Descartes' idea of substance, particularly as interpreted by Spinoza, varied considerably with Aristotle's and that of the scholastic tradition. Yet it is Descartes' idea that the empiricists investigated and found wanting. John Locke, who denied innate ideas in man, attempted to trace the notion of substance to experience, so that he could thereby justify it. Although Locke could not discover a valid basis for the idea of substance, he accepted it as "I know not what." He conceived of it as the support of the appearances or "accidents" of things that we perceive. The principal role of substance for him is that of serving as a base or substratum for the characteristics of things. But it is only the characteristics of things we perceive, not the substance itself.[9]

BERKELEY: THE PROBLEM OF THE REAL AND OF SUBSTANCE. George Berkeley, in explaining what we know, claimed that we only know our own impressions. These impressions are further identified with reality in such a way that "to be is to be perceived." To say that we perceive things is to say that we perceive our impressions. There is no legitimate reason for affirming a material world as other than the impressions of the knower. This is made clear by experiment: when we place one hand on something hot, the other on something cold, and then immerse both hands in a bucket of lukewarm water, the water will seem hot to the hand that touched something cold and cold to the other. Obviously, what we know is our impression, for the object (water) cannot simultaneously be hot and cold. Being or reality then consists in "being perceived."

Berkeley completely undermined Locke's position that the chief argument for substance was that it is a support for accidents or appearances. For Berkeley, it is the knower and not the material substance that supports the appearances, impressions, or accidents. He held that the concept of a material substance is wholly superfluous and should be dismissed; he denied the reality of the material world.

However, Berkeley did maintain the reality of spiritual substance, for the knower clearly supports his impressions. In addition to the spiritual substance of the finite knower, there is the spiritual substance of God. Yet it is patent that if the reality and meaning of substance is a chief enquiry of metaphysics, Berkeley's position cuts out a good deal of ground from under that discipline.

HUME AND KANT: THE REJECTION OF METAPHYSICS. David Hume

---

[9] We should note that serving as a base or substratum was not the principal role of substance for metaphysicians in the Aristotelian tradition. For them, the principal attribute of substance was to be "that which exists in its own right as a subject, not needing another to exist in." Accordingly, substance could and was predicated pre-eminently of God. The Lockean notion of substance could not be strictly applied to God, for God is simple and has no characteristics residing in a substratum of his nature, as accidents would reside in a substance. His "characteristics" and his nature are absolutely one.

went one step further and said that since in knowing myself, I only know my impressions, there is no basis for affirming material *or* spiritual substance. Accordingly, the notion of substance is completely excised from philosophical consideration. In addition, Hume's attack on causality persuaded many to follow his advice to regard as worthless any treatises on metaphysical problems.

Kant struck the deathblow to the variation of metaphysics as he knew it in the rationalist tradition. His theory of knowledge prohibited one's grasping the real order in any but a phenomenal way. Since metaphysics aspires to concerning itself primarily with reality in its deepest meaning— the level of things not as they appear but as they are—it was doomed by the Kantian critique to frustration in all of its efforts.

The only role left for it to play was that of investigating the limits of mind. Such notions as substance and causality have no validity except when applied to the order of appearances—an order that, according to Kant, a genuine metaphysics would prefer to ignore.

Thus Kant rejected any attempts at proofs for the existence of God, the freedom of man, and the immortality of the soul. He argued that previous efforts directed toward such proofs all involved specious and circular reasoning. Yet Kant apparently did accept the existence of God as a postulate for the practical order of morality. God's existence became more a matter for the will to decide, than for the intellect to understand. It was incapable of proof or disproof, for such a being, together with the other objects of metaphysics, lies beyond man's ken.

Kant's critique of "rationalist" metaphysics was so effective that, with the exception of Hegel, metaphysics as a discipline passed into relative obscurity.[10] But the denial of metaphysics itself constitutes a metaphysical position and, like a phoenix, metaphysics rises out of its own ashes.

The contemporary traditions of pragmatism and naturalism, as well as the positivist and analytic philosophies, have maintained strong criticism of metaphysics. While in some instances their rejection is arbitrary, generally they have grappled with the problems, at least to the extent that they have attempted to explain them away.

Representative Contemporary Traditions

Five traditions in philosophy have exerted and are still exerting a strong influence upon the contemporary scene. All have enriched the discussion of

---

[10] It was a "rationalist metaphysics" that Kant sent to the graveyard, rather than the basic metaphysics of the Aristotelian tradition. Hence, although rationalist metaphysics is no longer alive, Aristotelian metaphysics still shows many signs of current vitality. However, it is only fair to state that Kant thought he dispatched metaphysics as such.

metaphysical problems, and it is from these traditions that the readings in this volume have been selected.

The reader is invited to compare the key ideas in the selections in order to determine the compatibility, incompatibility, logical consistency, and implications that can be derived from them. Yet he should be cautioned not to expect these various traditions to employ the same language or concentrate on the same problems.

The Thomistic-Aristotelian Tradition

We are already familiar with this tradition, having discussed its essential features earlier. It helped to shape the mainstream of Western thought up to our own age, and it poses the basic problems with which men have always been primarily concerned, either to solve them or to dissolve and deny them. Readings typifying the viewpoints of this tradition have been chosen in order to state its answers to the basic problems.

One problem treated is the real, and man's knowledge of it. This tradition asserts and explains man's native ability to attain the real order and to know it as it is. It sees reality as in part material, in part spiritual. The necessity for upholding the superiority of intellectual knowledge to sensory knowledge, even though the former be based on the latter, is made clear. Covered also in the readings are the various meanings ascribed to being or reality, the characteristics of every being as one, true, and good. Specific attention is given to the proofs for the existence of God, and subsequent discussion indicates the relation of the world to him.

The Hegelian-Marxist Tradition

Hegelianism and Marxism are concerned with a world view, a systematic explanation of the full picture of reality. Accordingly, both constitute a metaphysical vision of reality, even though the name "metaphysics" sounds strange when used in conjunction with Marxism.

This tradition represents the divergent tendencies of idealism and materialism, although both follow a similar methodology, which recognizes and emphasizes the dynamic and dialectical character of the real. The real, in progressing toward perfection, makes its way through opposing forces to new and more perfect forms or syntheses. The Hegelians see this unfolding of reality as the manifestation of Mind; the Marxists view it as the development of matter. Both groups then are strict monists, accepting only a single principle as the explanation of the real.

The readings from Hegel explain his basic approach to philosophy and to a study of being, and also reveal his understanding of being as Mind. The life of Mind is discussed and the tendency of all things toward union in this rational principle is illustrated. Hegel's notion of substance is treated as is his understanding of causality and how the latter functions in history. The reader will see the overall thesis of Hegel that thought and reality are one. Hence, metaphysics and a dynamic logic came to the same thing: What is real is rational and what is rational is real.

The selections taken from Marx's works indicate his view that reality is fundamentally matter, but a matter that is always evolving and acquiring new forms, even to the point of human consciousness. Yet the reduction of all reality to matter is made clear. Marx's strong opposition to speculative (as opposed to revolutionary) philosophy is indicated and his critique of idealism is given. Of particular interest is Marx's theory of man's alienation and a discussion of the historical and philosophical causes that have encouraged it. Ideas such as God and religion play a role here, and the need for emancipation from both is indicated.

The readings from Friedrich Engels (1820–95) carry on the Marxist position and explain the laws according to which matter develops. Truth is seen to be evolving and temporal rather than static and eternal. The relation of thought to being, as seen by the Marxist, is also included in the selections and reveals a viewpoint opposite to the one expounded by Hegel.

The Pragmatic-Naturalist Tradition

This tradition, native to the American temperament, stresses the empirical method of investigation in philosophy. Suspicious of abstraction, it seeks to make evaluations always in terms of cold, objective, scientific facts. Concepts such as substance and spirit are rejected because they contain no empirical content. Equally suspicious of supernaturalism in philosophy, it restricts its explanations of things to principles understood by and in the natural order.

The stress on the real—"being" as process and knowing as an interaction between experience and nature—marks this school of thought. The movement makes a strong claim for humanism, and although Dewey rules out God, Peirce and James are open to his existence.

The selections from Dewey reveal his strong faith in the employment of scientific method in philosophy as the only means of assuring progress. His violent opposition to speculative philosophy as not only useless but as positively harmful to human progress is noted. The continuity of nature and experience is a constant theme in Dewey's readings. His humanism and naturalism are most apparent in his explaining the need to eliminate the supernatural element from religion. Dewey's rejection of God as a real being is given, together with his discussion of the idea of God as a human ideal toward which we can strive.

The readings taken from James reveal his ideas with respect to the nature of philosophy. Since he believes philosophy makes a difference in one's life, he considers it as a necessarily practical rather than speculative endeavor. Included in his selections is a discussion on the need for God varying in different individuals. James explains the types of philosophies dealing with God as appealing either to the "tough-minded" or to the "tender-minded."

The Analytic-Positivist Tradition

In England and America this tradition is currently the dominant philosophy; it often joins hands with the pragmatic-naturalist tradition. It owes its roots to the great iconoclast, David Hume, who rebelled against the abstract and universal character of metaphysics because he could not grasp the meaning of the terms, which seemed to roll so easily from the tongues of philosophers. To get at such meaning, he asked that we analyze our concepts and trace our ideas back to the sensation from which they were supposedly derived. If we cannot do so, he declared our ideas to be devoid of philosophical significance. The readings from Hume indicate his predilection for positivism; they also include his treatment of causality as an association of ideas and his own sceptical inclinations with respect to philosophy.

Others in our day have refined Hume's ideas and have developed specific techniques for testing the meaning of ideas. Yet their conclusions are not so far removed from Hume's in that they too are inclined to reject most of speculative philosophy. More interested in meaning than in truth (although the two are often closely related), this tradition sees past philosophy as the "disease of what it should be the cure." The task of philosophy should be analysis, not synthesis; language clarification, not verbal confusion. Scholastic philosophy with its many distinctions came particularly under fire. The classic problems of traditional metaphysics were scrutinized by the analysts and found to be based on vocabulary and syntactical problems. Linguistic clarification could dissolve such problems and show that they never should have arisen in the first place.

Positivists seized this method as bolstering their own position and helped formulate the famed principle of verifiability, which affirms as meaningless any statement not reducible to experiential terms. Since we have no such verifiable experiences of God, since we cannot know reality or our ideas of it, these problems are meaningless and should be expurgated from philosophy. The function of the new philosophy will henceforth be concerned with clarification of scientific and/or ordinary language. Only science will give progress in knowledge.

All the readings in this section are taken from philosophers who are positivists employing the methods of analysts. No readings are offered from the men who consider themselves analysts, but decry the label of positivists. The reason for this is because they regard themselves as "methodological purists" and want no traffic with positions strictly philosophical. Their sensitivity on this point cannot be overstressed, even though the distinction between contemporary positivism and analysis is commonly blurred.

The readings from Alfred Tarski (b. 1902) shows how semantics handles the concept of truth and also provide an excellent example of logical analysis. Carrying on in this tradition, Ayer reveals the nature of philosophical analysis and shows why, in his opinion, the only great philosophers of the past were the analysts such as Locke, Berkeley, and Hume, who exhibited this method, and not the metaphysicians. Accordingly, Ayer calls for a separation of metaphysics from philosophy.

The selections taken from Rudolf Carnap (b. 1891) illustrate his understanding of the principle of verifiability and apply it to a number of instances. The utility of the principle is shown not only for science and for philosophy, but for everyday use as well.

Bertrand Russell (b. 1872), who gave strong impetus to this movement, is represented in the readings as showing how bad metaphysics resulted from the faulty use of language. His own theory of logical atomism is explained; basically it posits that reality is made of discrete things or events that find their relatedness through the interference of mind. Yet mind and matter are not two different things so much as they are aspects of one reality.

The sharpest picture of what positivism is and the method of analysis which it employs is to be found in the selection drawn from the *Vienna Manifesto*. This is a document drawn up by Carnap, Otto Neurath (1882–1945), and Hans Hahn (1879–1934), members of the Vienna Circle of scientists and philosophers who gave birth to one extreme position of this now popular tradition. Founded in the 1920s and disbanded in the middle 1930s, the Vienna Circle attempted to settle the legitimate boundaries of philosophical enquiry. It was openly antimetaphysical and criticized the principal claims of traditional philosophy to cope with reality. The group exerted a strong influence on subsequent British and American philosophy, particularly in the area of philosophy of science.

The Existentialist-Phenomenological Tradition

This movement, which dominates current thinking on the European continent, emphasizes that the only view we can have of being or reality is through man's eyes. Accordingly it employs the phenomenological method, which examines things as they appear without considering their total reality in isolation from men. Current existentialism is antirationalistic and anti-idealistic. Suspicious of absolutes and "total objectivity," it dwells at great length on the subject's view of reality and truth, and it has adherents both in the theistic (Marcel) and the atheistic (Sartre) camps.

The existentialist-phenomenological tradition has few commitments to give it a common bond. The one unifying aspect found in all of its thinkers is its great concern with man as the focal point from which a view of being must be developed. Its stress on intuition or insights, instead of wholly discursive reasoning, must be noted.

The work of Edmund Husserl succeeded in giving a fresh start to philosophical method, namely, the phenomenological method. Only such a method could provide for a total philosophy.

Martin Heidegger's (b. 1889) selections portray the necessity for investigating man and being together instead of in separation. An insight into man's finitude as revealing an aspect of his nature gains for us a glimpse at how to provide a foundation for metaphysics. To raise the question of being, we must first raise the question of man who asks what being is.

Martin Buber's (1878–1965) selections highlight the differences between experience and relationship, as between that of an I-It and an I-Thou confrontation. I can *experience* things, but I can only *relate* to persons. The supreme relationship is between myself and God—the eternal I-Thou relation.

The readings from Sartre explain the basis for his atheistic humanism and tell why he feels it is the only authentic philosophy. His stress on human freedom finds a parallel in the writings of Nicolas Berdyaev (1874–1948), who discusses man's freedom in history.

Paul Tillich's (1886–1965) readings discuss the nature of philosophy and theology as a quest for being, although he indicates the differences between the two approaches. Together with Sartre he emphasizes the importance of recognizing the presence of non-being in the world today.

The readings from Marcel portray an exercise in the phenomenological method which he employs so fruitfully. Discussed here are such notions as presence, availability, modern man's loss of "a sense of being," philosophical realism, and the distinction between mystery and problem. Throughout, Marcel stresses man as already present in being. Consequently, his view of man is from one within being, rather than from one outside, the latter constituting the basic error of rationalistic thought.

Concluding Remarks

By way of summary, this essay has attempted (1) to introduce the reader to the nature of philosophical experience; (2) to accomplish this through a brief survey of the history of philosophy, thereby giving a sense of overall perspective to philosophy and its organic development; (3) to expose the key problems and solutions in that section of philosophy termed metaphysics.

By means of the above, the reader should now be prepared to read the expository essays and readings covering those major traditions most relevant to the contemporary scene. Yet covering this volume is but a preparatory step to its most important purpose: to encourage and guide the reader into philosophizing for himself. "The search for truth," said Aristotle, "is in one sense difficult, but in another it is easy."

> This is shown by the fact that while no one can obtain an adequate grasp of it, no one fails entirely. Every thinker has something true to say about the nature of the universe; and if individually they contribute little or nothing to the inquiry, taken together their conjectures amount to a good deal. In so far, then, as truth is like the proverbial door, which no one can miss, its study pre-

sents no difficulty; but the fact that we cannot, although having some grasp of the whole, grasp a particular part shows it on the other hand to be far from easy.

. . .

Justice requires our gratitude not only to those whose opinions we inherit, but also to those earlier thinkers whose superficial views gave the mind its necessary practice in thinking. If there had been no Timotheus we should lack much of our lyric poetry, but if there had been no Phrynis, there would have been no Timotheus. It is the same with those who have speculated about the nature of reality: we have derived certain views from the greatest among them, while these in turn have been indebted to others.

Moreover, philosophy is rightly called the knowledge of the truth. For the end of theoretical knowledge is truth, while that of practical knowledge is action; if the latter studies the truth, it is not eternal truth but that which is of the moment and relative to an object. Now we cannot know the truth without the cause; that which imparts to other things a certain character itself has that character in the highest degree, so that what makes other things true is itself most true. Hence the principles of eternal things must be true above all things; for they are not merely sometimes true, nor is there any cause of the existence of other things, so that as each thing is in respect of being, so it is in respect of truth. . . .[11]

To take the step toward his own philosophizing, the reader will be obliged to attempt to answer the basic questions and criticisms posed by the various traditions. In doing so, he will be required to weigh the evidence based upon his own insights and experiences as well as his reasoned thoughts about the matter. He will have to sort out those views that are inconsistent with each other. He will have to ask himself, frequently and honestly, what difference would it make if a conclusion other than the one given were reached? What are the implications of each conclusion with respect to a given problem?

To cite an example, let us take the problem of contingency. Do the things of our experience manifest their own *raison d'être?* Do they all point to themselves as the total explanation for themselves being, for being what they are, and for acting the way they do? Is there any respect in which they are "other directed," in which paradoxically they point to another as a fuller explanation of themselves? Should this be the case, in what precise manner is it so? Can we know anything about this "other" to which they are directed? Can such an "other-directedness" be explained by an infinite regress, or would such a procedure "beg the question"? Must one conclude eventually to a necessary termination of this series in a being to which all things point, but which itself is its own explanation?

---

[11] Taken from Aristotle, *Metaphysics,* Book I, as reprinted in *The Oxford Translation of Aristotle,* ed. by J. A. Smith and W. D. Ross (Oxford: Clarendon Press, 1928), vol. III.

On the other hand, what is the evidence against such contingency in the beings of our experience? If they reveal no "other-directedness," could any be related to each other? If such relationship seems to be present, how could it be explained or explained away? How would the answers to the other problems—the meaning of reality, the nature of truth, the existence of God—be seen in the light of the conclusions reached with respect to the first?

To ask such questions and to seek their answers is to engage in the task of metaphysics. At all times, in attempting to formulate his own metaphysics, the reader will be forced to ask what light others have shed on the problems. Yet he must also look to the answers given by others in their historical perspectives. He must determine to what extent such answers were conditioned by history and constitute a possible exaggerated reaction to what came before.

Such then is the task to be laid before the student. It is a weighty and difficult one. It must be approached without prior prejudices and assumptions. Its formulation must be subjected to rigorous and continual examination and reexamination. Despite the enormous difficulties such a task entails, the task should prove to be an enjoyable one. In wondering about the most ultimate questions of being, man is doing more than philosophizing; he is fulfilling his nature.

PART ONE

CLASSICAL
AND CHRISTIAN
THOUGHT:

Plato
Aristotle
Augustine
Aquinas

EDITED BY

George F. McLean, O.M.I.

THE CATHOLIC UNIVERSITY OF AMERICA

CLASSICAL AND CHRISTIAN THOUGHT:
Plato
Aristotle
Augustine
Aquinas

Introduction

Throughout history man has sought to extend his vision by searching for new facts and setting them in a broad and unifying perspective. This desire for an overall view is grounded in the realization that man can respond to the pressing needs of a particular moment only by seeing those needs in the light of the total situation. Modern technology, by giving contemporary man an ever greater responsibility in structuring his world, has intensified this need for a comprehensive view.

The importance of a world view can be illustrated by an example taken from Gestalt psychology, which emphasizes the perception of the whole rather than its parts. A sequence of still frames assumes full meaning when the frames are passed in rapid succession through a motion picture projector because this process manifests the unity of the sequence. Similarly, the proper concern of classical and Christian metaphysics has been to work out a unity of perspective in which all particular types and fields of knowledge achieve their full significance.

This unity of vision has undergone a continual historical development, each state of which provided new insights into the internal structure and external order of things. In this Introduction we shall explore the development of metaphysics from the earliest times through the work of St. Thomas Aquinas, and show the relation of metaphysics to other types of knowledge. We shall also treat in detail the particular types of problems to which classical and Christian metaphysicians directed their attention—the internal structure, the external principles or causes, and the general characteristics or properties of being.

Preludes to Classical-Christian Thought

Myth

Today, if the physicist discovers a number of infra-atomic particles, he is driven to the more important search for the unifying principle that will render the plurality intelligible. Even in the earliest days of human history a similar effort was made to discover the unity among things. Before there was anything that could rightfully be called science, successive civilizations had existed whose art and literature manifested an overall world view based upon the only mode of thought then available—the myth.

In myth intellectual insights were conceived in the form of personal symbols. Single parts of nature were personified as gods and the accounts of their quasi-human actions were statements of the relations between sectors of reality. When Hesiod joined the various myths together in his *Theogony* [1] to form a genealogy of the gods, he expressed the developing and unfolding unity of the universe.

There were important advantages to this mode of thinking. Paul Tillich (1886–1965) pointed out that to personify these forces allows one to place full value on the realm of spirit and on its influence in shaping a unified world,[2] even where the precise form of this unity has not been fully identified. For this reason the myth approach has never been completely relinquished by the human mind; it has continued to manifest itself wherever a romanticist element developed and has had a recent revival in the personalist orientations of much of contemporary thought. Nevertheless, to the degree that men began to pay more attention to the intellectual content of the myth as distinct from its anthropomorphic embellishments, it became possible for the human mind to be more precise in the development of its intellectual insights. The ways in which this took place manifest the various modes of human wisdom and their interrelation.

Hebrew Thought

The route that the Hebrews took in surpassing the stage of myth was intimately connected with their history as the chosen people. At first, in recognizing *their* God they seemed to feel that other people also had their independent gods. But the special providence which God exercised over the Hebrews gradually revealed that this was not so, and that *their* God had dominion over any other gods. By the time of the Babylonian exile, in the

---

[1] *Hesiod*, trans. by Hugh G. Evelyn-White (New York: Macmillan Co., 1914).
[2] Paul Tillich, *Systematic Theology* (Chicago: University of Chicago Press, 1956), p. 91; and Bernard Lonergan, *Insight* (New York: Philosophical Library, 1958), pp. 531–49.

sixth century B.C., it had become clear that there was no other God, and that all things were one in their dependence on the God of Israel.

This special providence also implied that all owed a return of love to the God who loved and protected them. Unity was seen in its personal dimension of love, in view of which unity was no longer expressed by anthropomorphic and symbolic terms, but by the concrete relation in which everything and every person depends upon God.

Although this advance from figurative to proper ideas was important, something more important remained to be done. In order to state in concrete terms the unifying dependence of all things on God, it was necessary for the Jews to repeat continually that God was the Lord of the sea, the Lord of the heavens. This repetition suggested the need for a new type of thinking and speaking that would state many things, not by enumerating them individually, but by referring precisely to that according to which they were one or alike. The development of this more precise and penetrating thought was to be the special accomplishment of the Greeks.

Early Greek Philosophy

The type of thought developed by the Greeks expressed things in abstract terms rather than in the figurative form of the myth or in the concrete Hebraic mode. By "abstract" is meant not simply the omission of part of the total reality referred to in concrete expression; its primary significance is in stating more precisely what the mind has actually obtained concerning the thing. The distinctive marks of the development of Greek thought were the attention to the evidence on which a thought sequence proceeds and the careful control of the intellectual content of the ideas derived therefrom. These characteristics marked the beginning of scientific procedures.

In this spirit the Greeks developed a series of sciences, each of which derived its unity from the distinctive subject or intelligible dimension of reality considered. The task of a science is to achieve an understanding of why its subject possesses its distinctive characteristics or properties by tracing them to their proper principles. Aristotle subsequently articulated this scientific pattern in his logic; it took the form of a syllogism that explains, in its major and minor propositions, why the predicate pertains to the subject in the conclusion.

The area immediately observable by the external senses was first considered to possess its unity from the fact that all derived from a single principle: water as the principle of unity for various states of vapor, liquid, and solid, or fire for its capacity of unifying that which darted up and died down. As it became evident that no one type of reality could adequately unify all others on the same level, Anaximander (c. 610–546 B.C.) expressed the actual intellectual content achieved concerning the unifying principle of this level by the term "boundless," that is, unlimited to any one type.

Pythagoras (580–500 B.C.) and his followers raised the search for unity to the mathematical level by using the evidence presented through the internal sense of imagination. Parmenides (530–444 B.C.) attained distinctively intellectual evidence concerning the level of being, that is, of things inasmuch as they are and act, rather than as pertaining to some physical type or mathematical set. This is the metaphysical level that is concerned not simply with one or another kind of reality but with reality as such, with what it means to be real, and hence with all reality. Some initial insight into the importance of this new development might be gained by contrasting it with the previously mentioned approaches to unity. It will be noted that for the first time the human mind could attend explicitly to that principle according to which *all* things are one—to that by which they are real and to the characteristics of the internal structures and external relations of all reality.

It is not surprising that Parmenides himself was not able to solve the problems he raised. Concluding that all reality must be one, he could not find room for any type of diversity, whether it be one of plurality or of change in things. It is important though that only the Parmenidean vision of everything as real makes possible the proper appreciation of all as one. This, in turn, enables the mind to attend to the question of the reality and meaning of difference itself—the question of the one and the many. Parmenides was the first to raise the key questions of metaphysics.

Evolution of Classical Metaphysics

Since truth is not an inert mass but a catalytic agent, the insight of Parmenides, when challenged by the Sophists, gave birth to the power and brilliance of the golden age of classical Greek thought. Parmenides' unification of all in being, in opposition to non-being, led him to deny the reality of the changing and developing world of common experience; the Sophists attempted to save the world of experience by rejecting the truth of his principle of non-contradiction (being is not non-being). Since they held the world to be composed of contradictories, unified only subjectively in the mind of the knower who could argue equally well on either side of any question, scepticism resulted, and the very name of the Sophists, the great teachers of the day, came to stand for captious or fallacious reasoners. Thus, at a time when the Greek city-states were evolving and it was imperative to find the real meaning and solid foundation for such moral absolutes as justice and piety, the individualistic and relativistic approaches of the Sophists asserted that any moral position was impossible.

Plato

Socrates (470–399 B.C.) initiated the search for moral values, such as justice, that transcend particular acts and are the criteria by which acts are judged. His pupil, Plato (*c.* 427–347 B.C.), was convinced of the need for this understanding because of the moral corruption that led to the death of Socrates. He saw the need for further development of the philosophy initiated by Socrates in order to discover the precise ontological status of those transcendent values and to clarify the reality of the multiple subordinate realities, their types and their interrelation. In this way, the sociopolitical situation provided an urgency to the conflict between the Parmenidean and Sophistic positions, which called forth some of the most profound insights of human thought.

The direction of Plato's thought is indicated in Book VI of the *Republic* (509–514). (See "Degrees of Knowledge" in the readings.) Plato spoke of a line divided into two unequal parts, each of which is again divided into unequal parts. The shorter part of the initial subdivision is the area of sensible reality, which corresponds to opinion. Of this part, the shorter subsection represents shadows grasped by conjecture, while the longer subsection corresponds to belief. The longer part of the initial division signifies the more important or intelligible sector of reality, which corresponds to knowledge. This section is subdivided between a shorter subsection, for images attained by a procedure based on hypotheses, and a longer subsection, which is the highest part of all and represents the ideas attained by intelligence or the dialectic.

In this simile of the line and also in that of the cave, there is a beguiling change of perspective. The immediately tangible things, of whose reality we are generally most aware, are spoken of as shadows in comparison with ideas, which we ordinarily consider most elusive. Similarly, sense images, with their multiple and vivid articulation of color, taste, and the like, are placed in a position subordinate to mathematical images. But there is more than a mere change of perspective, for Plato was speaking from considerable experience when he noted the degeneration of the Athenian social order, and he was quite precise in relating this to a loss of the significance of ideas such as truth, goodness, and justice. Until such notions were given absolute reality, all particular circumstances would remain at the arbitrary manipulation of forces, however unworthy their motives.

These important implications become still more manifest in the further development of Book VI of the *Republic*. In a passage parallel to the description of the divided line and immediately following upon it, Plato continued the development of his theme by describing the lower parts of the line as the state of prisoners in a cave. These he contrasted to men who are outside the cave and, in the highest part of the line, to those who are fully liberated. Hence, the shadows at the bottom of the line reflect not only the poor state of the reality found there, but the half life of persons who remain exclusively concerned with this type of reality. A truly worthy life for the Athenian consists rather in an ascension through the remaining phases of the line to the truly intelligible realm of ideas, the source of the intelligibility and meaning of all else. Education is precisely this process of ascent and it is the prerequisite for all who would be truly free.

The diagram below combines the discussion of the divided line with that of the simile of the cave.[3]

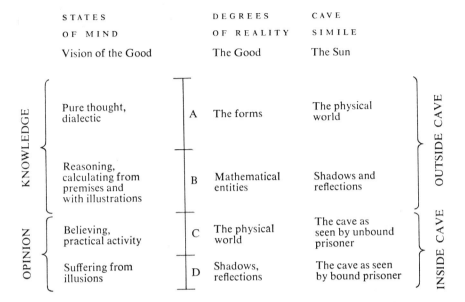

	STATES OF MIND		DEGREES OF REALITY	CAVE SIMILE	
	Vision of the Good		The Good	The Sun	
KNOWLEDGE	Pure thought, dialectic	A	The forms	The physical world	OUTSIDE CAVE
	Reasoning, calculating from premises and with illustrations	B	Mathematical entities	Shadows and reflections	
OPINION	Believing, practical activity	C	The physical world	The cave as seen by unbound prisoner	INSIDE CAVE
	Suffering from illusions	D	Shadows, reflections	The cave as seen by bound prisoner	

Plato here constructed an intelligible schema that went beyond Socrates' isolation of the ideas of truth and justice to identify their ontological reality. The general striving for this authentic intelligibility even enabled him to return to that study of the physical world that Socrates had abandoned in despair before the mass of conflicting and sophistical argumentation. In the third or mathematical section of the line the mind proceeds from hypotheses, such as order and even the basic types of figures, which necessitate the use of the imagination but are accepted by all men. These ideas more immediately correspond to the physical order, about which they allow the mind to reason to conclusions. This mathematical study of the physical world was to become so consuming for Plato's successors in the Academy that Aristotle observed that they considered mathematics to be all of philosophy.

Plato accomplished much, but not all. He retained the unity of vision with which the human mind had always been concerned and followed Parmenides to the level of reality at which it can be seen that this unity ultimately requires an absolute being to provide its full justification. He advanced beyond Parmenides and recognized the reality of many different re-

---

[3] Joseph Katz and Rudolph H. Weingartner, *Philosophy of the West* (New York: Harcourt, Brace & World, 1965), p. 69. Reprinted by permission of the publisher.

alities by subordinating them as participations, images, and shadows of the absolute ideas. The adequacy of such a statement for the reality of multiple beings remained a question. Similarly his explanation of the achievement of intellectual knowledge of the ideas by "recollection" also left room for considerable improvement. To the task of improving, not destroying, Aristotle (384–322 B.C.) dedicated his work.

Aristotle

The unity of vision, which had been the Greek heritage since the days of the myth and which had achieved its explicit intellectual articulation in Parmenides, had been reopened to the multiple and diverse world of experience by Plato's notion of participation in the ideas. However, the opening was only tentative while this world was described in terms of shadows. An articulation of this world of experience according to its own distinctive explanatory principles was needed. This conformed to the ideal for a science or philosophy of nature that would state not only what a thing was, but why it was that way and could not be otherwise. A similar type of knowledge would be sought for the mathematical realm.

Above all, metaphysics as a third and final body of speculative knowledge was needed to go beyond the changing things of sensible experience and beyond the mathematical. It would somehow include the most absolute of realities, and all else related thereto. This would be the highest type of knowledge, for it would attend to that by which all things from the most perfect to the most imperfect are one. By such knowledge the human intellect would reach its greatest fulfillment.

Aristotle showed the need and the dignity of this science in Book I, Chapters 1–2, of *Metaphysics,* and in Book IV he proceeded to a more particular identification of the subject with which this science would be concerned. (See "Science of Being as Being" in the readings.) His answer was different from Plato's, for he did not suggest that the mind intuit separate and transcendent ideas or attempt to recall such intuition. On the contrary, for Aristotle this science is concerned with being as being—with "what is" to whatever degree in which it is. Is such a science possible? Can any single body of knowledge be this extensive and exalted?

At first thought, it would seem that being as being could have only the minimal significance of opposition to nothingness as a least common denominator of all things. But this would hardly be adequate for a science whose aim is to know "to what end each thing must be done," to appreciate the difference between things, or to attend to the distinctive perfection of the divine. Being as being—the subject of metaphysics—must state what is the most meaningful in being.

In Book IV, Chapter 2, Aristotle identified this by tracing the various types of accidents to the substance they specify and manifest. Substance thus appears as the primary notion of being, while all else, whether accident, privation, or motion, is understood in relation to it. Throughout

Greek thought, the characteristics of substance—permanence and determined form—are the hallmarks of the real. For the Greeks, a living eternity is the proper characteristic of the divine. Hence, the science of metaphysics is concerned not merely with a minimal first step by which things escape nothingness, but with the full reality that the being possesses; it studies being to whatever degree of perfection it achieves. In this light the first principle of being (the principle of contradiction: being is not nonbeing) is the safeguard of the full range of being.

In Book VI, Chapter 1, Aristotle related this science to other levels of speculative thought. The physical sciences are also concerned with substances, but only insofar as they undergo change and imply matter. If there were only physical realities, these sciences would constitute the ultimate human intellectual perspective. However, because not everything is material, the science of being as being must be distinct from that of changing substances.

Does this imply that the subject of this science, being as being, is restricted not only to substance but to the nonmaterial, nonchanging, nonphysical—that is, to the separated or divine substance? Those who agree [4] insist that this is so in the sense of studying reality at the point at which all else obtains its significance. Still others [5] hold that the subject of metaphysics remains open to all substances, including the material, that are related to the separate substance by final causality.

Whatever may be decided on this point, some general factors concerning metaphysics in Greek philosophy should be kept in mind. While concerned with the unity of beings and with their identity, the Greek mind always presupposed that matter was eternal. [6] The direct question of existence as opposed to simple nonexistence was never radically posed. Attention was given rather to the form according to which beings achieved their specific identity and their general relation to other things within the overall gradation of being.

This concentration on form, which identifies the species rather than the individual, is also reflected in the restricted character of the attention given by the Greek mind to the person and his distinctive autonomy and responsibility in freedom and love. This area of insight could be enriched only by opening a perspective more penetrating than form and centering on that element in being, existence (*esse*), which is both unique and active. The development of this perspective remained the task of philosophers in the later, Christian period.

---

[4] See Joseph Owens, *A History of Ancient Western Philosophy* (New York: Appleton-Century-Crofts, 1959), pp. 332–34; and *The Doctrine of Being in the Aristotelian Metaphysics* (Toronto: Pontifical Institute of Medieval Studies, 1951).

[5] For one, Ralph McInerny, *A History of Western Philosophy* (Chicago: Henry Regnery Co., 1963), I, 285.

[6] W. Norris Clarke, "The Limitation of Act by Potency," *The New Scholasticism,* XXIX (1955), 181–83.

Christian Metaphysical Syntheses

Two points in the Christian perspective helped to bring into view the special significance of existence. One was the notion of creation which took the mind beyond the study of forms received by a preexisting matter to confrontation with the very question of existence. The other was the attention to the person as actively, freely, and responsibly disposing of himself.

The gateway to Christian philosophy is found in the impressive figure of St. Augustine (354–430). In time and thought he is close to Plotinus' (205–270) final attempt to systematize the thought of Plato with the help of some Aristotelian elements and to understand the world as the expression of the supreme ideas of the One, the True, and the Good. Removing the pantheistic overtones, Augustine used this schema to express the way in which all creation and especially the personal beings, men and angels, manifest the Trinity: Father (Unity or Power), Son (*Logos* or Truth), and Holy Spirit (Love or Goodness). It took centuries for medieval philosophy to develop the metaphysical implications of this improved understanding of person and creation. In time, however, it became clear that the question of being as being was not a question of form, nature, or substance, but one of being precisely inasmuch as it is or as related to existence. This provided a new perspective within which the rich contents of the Platonic and Aristotelian traditions could be more closely harmonized and their implications more profoundly drawn out.

St. Thomas Aquinas (1225–74) had the unique historical opportunity to stand at this juncture in the development of metaphysics, to live when the body of Aristotelian thought, long isolated from the continuing evolution of Platonism in Asia Minor, Africa, and Europe, was introduced to the medieval mind through the expansion of the Arabian culture and the Crusades. The patristic and medieval Christian insights into the notion of being made it possible for St. Thomas to synthesize the metaphysical Platonic tradition and the newly presented Aristotelian writings. He was able to relate the content of metaphysics to the physical world of experience and to derive therefrom, in a systematic manner, the manifestation of real being.

In his early work, *Commentary on the Trinity of Boethius* (see "Metaphysics and the Sciences"), St. Thomas distinguished two acts of intellect. The first was simple apprehension that concerns the nature of things and answers the question of *what* a thing is. This first act of the intellect gave rise to two distinct sciences—physics, and mathematics. It did this by a process called "abstraction," which consists simply in the selective apprehension of some aspects of what a thing is. What can be known of things as subject to physical changes and as manifest in the evidence achieved through the external senses was identified as physics, or the philosophy of nature. Material things as specified by the quantitative characteristics perceived through the internal senses constitute the subject of a separate science, mathematics.

After St. Thomas distinguished the two sciences on the basis of the abstractive work of the first act of the mind, he added a third science, metaphysics. He did this by means of the second act of the intellect in which the mind is concerned with things, not in regard to what they are, but rather in regard to their existence. This is what is meant by saying that being (what is) as being (inasmuch as it is) is the subject of metaphysics. The division of the sciences may be represented graphically in the following manner:

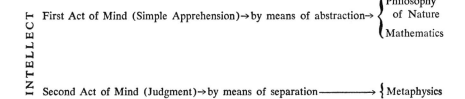

This division enabled St. Thomas to respond more adequately to the problem Aristotle foresaw for any science that would attend to all things: if being were constituted only by the form that states the distinctive way a thing exists, the mind could attend to this form universally only by choosing one form, the highest. In such a case the mind would but inadequately attend to the others, or would omit all the differences between forms, making the notion of being relatively meaningless. However, because St. Thomas recognized that what is most formal in being is existence, he attained being and all its differing realizations by focusing on that by which they are or exist. Therefore, being as that which is expresses the actuality of whatever is; it does not explicate its particular characteristics. Far from being the most meaningless of notions, it is on the contrary the richest in content, containing within itself the reality of any of the differences by which one being is distinguished from another. On this basis we are able to confront directly the perennial problems of the unity and difference of things.

From where and in what way does the mind achieve this rich notion of being? It is an Aristotelian realism that determined St. Thomas' approach to metaphysics. If the physical, sensible, and changing things about us are fully real and not mere images, and if our direct knowledge is the attainment of that reality rather than a recalling of ideas, then the content of metaphysics can be adequately explained only by identifying the way in which the mind, working from sensible and material reality, separates out its all-embracing insights concerning being as existing. The process will be essentially that of removing the initial limitation of the human mind to sensible or changing being as such. The mind frees itself from this limitation by its achievement of the knowledge that not all reality is material or changing.

It can achieve this knowledge in nonphilosophical ways by revelation and by a common-sense appreciation that there is something that transcends the body, and in philosophical ways by the conclusion that changing reality is insufficient to give an account of its motion (Aristotle, *Physics*), by the conclusion that the human soul is nonmaterial (Aristotle, *De Anima*), and by the appreciation of the nonmaterial character of man's ultimate goal (Aristotle, *Ethics*).

Thus all sectors of reality and all the speculative and practical sciences manifest that some realities are nonmaterial. This manifestation from all sectors of nonmetaphysical knowledge forces the mind to make the negative judgment that it is not necessary for something to be material in order to be; being as being is not material. In this way the material limitations of the mind's first notion of reality are removed, and the mind's perspective is expanded from material being to being as being.

For this reason the *Commentary on the Trinity of Boethius* (Question 6. Article 1) does not stop with the observation that divine science (metaphysics) "confers principles upon the other sciences, since intellectual consideration is the starting point of rational consideration, on which account it is called first philosophy." Nevertheless, first philosophy "is studied after physics [philosophy of nature] and other sciences, since intellectual speculation is the terminus of rational consideration, and consequently is called metaphysics or, as it were, *transphysica,* because it is attained by further process of analysis after (transcending) physics."

Key Problems in Classical-Christian Metaphysics

We have surveyed the progressive development of the body of thought called metaphysics in a basically historical sequence. We must now investigate the general problem areas considered by this metaphysics.

In classical-Christian philosophy Aristotle's pattern of science provides the basis for the distinction and organization of problem areas. Once the subject of a science has been identified, three areas must be investigated: internal structure, external principles or causes, and properties. For the study of metaphysics as the science of being as being these three areas will be: (1) the intrinsic principles of contingent being—existence and essence; (2) the Divine as the ultimate extrinsic cause of being; (3) the transcendental properties of being, here especially truth and beauty.

The Contingent

The unique accomplishment of the human mind by which it attains the notion of being raises a crucial problem. If the mind grasps being as one, can there be any multiplicity in reality? Is diversity an illusion of the senses? Parmenides responded by rejecting the very possibility of anything other than the one absolute being. St. Thomas' position, synthesizing the positions of Plato and Aristotle, is considerably different.

To begin with, since his route to the reality of being had been the Aristotelian path through direct sense encounter with multiple and changing things, he was committed to search for a solution to the Parmenidean negation of their reality. Furthermore, contrary to the Greek notion of a divine insouciance, he considered the God of the Christians as the protector of Israel and the Saviour of mankind. This led him to a deeper study of the human person and of all men in their unity as children of God. Both philosophy and theology called for a further philosophical development that would identify the real principles of this unity and diversity in things.

ESSENCE AND EXISTENCE. One finds this important philosophical development taking place within one of St. Thomas' earlier works, *Summa Contra Gentiles*. In Book II, Chapters 52–54, he asked how there can be anything other than the unique and absolute divine. (See "Act and Potency in Created Intellectual Substances" in the readings.) Upon reflecting he found that the answer does not lie in existence (*esse*). The reason for this is that the intelligible content of a form is unique, infinite, and indivisible. "Every form if abstractly considered has an infinity as regards its proper perfection. An example of this is whiteness," which of itself is neither limited to any particular realization of white nor multiplied among many. Existence, because it is most formal, distinctive, and specifying in being, if it were to be realized simply and by itself, would be unlimited and unique.

From this it follows that where beings are multiple, existence must be accompanied by an additional distinct and differentiating principle of *what is* namely, essence. St. Thomas proceeded to develop this thought on two levels and then to relate both of them. First, if existence itself is one, there can be many existents only if existence is joined to another principle that differentiates its various realizations. Second, since in its own right existence would be infinite, limited realities must also have the principle which determines that existence be limited and to what degree. Finally, the limited realizations of being must depend on a being that is simply existence and hence unlimited in perfection.

PARTICIPATION. In this principle lies the notion of participation which Plato had developed extensively in his dialogue *Parmenides*. Plato had stated it in terms of a composition of being with non-being. To constitute any single being it was necessary that what made it what it was needed to be complemented by that which made it not to be anything else. After Plato, the understanding of this non-being was advanced by medieval Christian and Arabian philosophers who understood it as determining "what" a being is. It was the merit of St. Thomas to clarify how essence (*essentia*) was really distinguished from existence (*esse*), while remaining related to it as a determined capacity or potency for existence.

For this notion he turned to Aristotle's act-potency composition of form and matter in changing things. Just as Plato's composition of being and non-being had been deepened to the level of existence and essence, so Aristotle's discovery of act and potency in the physical order was expanded and deepened by its application to being as existing. The result was neither Platonism nor Aristotelianism, but St. Thomas' synthesis of both within the deeper understanding of being, which was found to be composed of existence and essence related to each other as act is related to potency.

Thus, it was the evidence of multiplicity joined with the understanding of being as a relation to existence that allowed the mind to enter into the center of being and identify its internal structure as a composition of existence and essence related to each other as act and potency. The importance of this cannot be overemphasized. On the metaphysical level, it corresponds to the identification of the infra-atomic structure in the sciences of chemistry and physics. Just as that discovery allowed the mind to arrive at a new understanding of the relations among physical things, so this penetration into being made possible a scientific and objective appreciation of the hierarchical gradation and interaction of beings.

The Divine

For the Christian philosopher, it can be expected that the philosophy of God will be a matter of fundamental and personal commitment, but as St. Paul indicated in the Epistle to the Romans (1:19–20), the basis for knowledge of God is not restricted to revelation. In point of historical fact, an initial and gradually developing insight into the notion of the divine was manifested through the whole of classical thought without always arriving at a notion of the divine as that to which homage was due. This was apparent in some of the superior characteristics attributed to the gods in Greek mythology; it was also intimated in the pre-Socratic notion of the "boundless" [7] and was increasingly articulated by Plato and Aristotle.

EXISTENCE OF GOD. St. Augustine attempted to direct the mind to God by reflecting on its own interior consciousness and possession of truth. He saw this as only part of a long procedure in which the interior stages of reflection on the truth possessed are the natural consequence of extensive, direct, and abstractive knowledge of the exterior world. In his *Sermon* 241, 1–3, St. Augustine identified the many difficulties that can befall a person in proceeding to a philosophical knowledge of God. (See "To God Through Body and Spirit" in the readings.)

In response to these difficulties, Thomas, in *Summa Theologica,* I (Question 2. Articles 2–3), applied the ample classical and Christian metaphysical resources to the question of whether it can be demonstrated that God exists. He described the required conditions for such a demonstration and laid out his own plan which is to direct the attention of the

---

[7] Werner Jaeger, *The Theology of the Early Greek Philosophers* (Oxford: Clarendon Press, 1948), pp. 31–34.

mind to what in reality is distinctively an effect of God and to trace this effect to its cause. (See "The Five Ways.")

Since in the theological context of the *Summa Theologica* one already knows by revelation the existence of God and has some idea of his nature, this process may appear dependent upon a presupposed nominal definition of God. However, as is seen in the subsequent article about the famous five ways by which the mind is led to recognize the existence of God, these ways begin not from a definition, but from finite reality itself. This reality is divided according to five aspects: (1) dependence in being moved, (2) dependence on a cause in moving others, (3) the contingent character of mobile being, (4) the gradation of beings as more or less perfect, (5) the order among beings and their movement toward an end. Each of these aspects is applicable to every being in our experience. Each opens a basic route into the internal structure of finite being and the recognition that it is a composition of existence and essence, related as act and potency.

Upon this recognition follows a second step in each of the five ways, namely, the realization that beings thus structured cannot be self-explanatory. Essence as a capacity or a potency is not existence and does not explain existence. To hold that it does would be to identify something (existence) with nothing (the mere capacity or lack of existence) and to negate the principle of contradiction. (*Metaphysics,* IV, 3.) For this reason St. Thomas maintained that the mind must turn to existence and ultimately to that simple existence that is without potency and therefore unique, infinite, and absolute—the divine. (*Summa Contra Gentiles,* II, 52.)

It will be noted that the theological context is not essential to this argumentation. The problem is common to beings precisely as composed of essence and existence in their structure as being. Any road that leads the mind to an insight concerning the fact of this structure in finite beings must lead the mind still more deeply to the question of the cause of being as existing, that is, to the cause of being as being. This might be summarized in the more precise technical terms of the science of metaphysics: after distinguishing the subject of metaphysics (being as being, being as existing) and identifying the intrinsic principles that constitute multiple beings (essence and existence related as potency and act), one is forced to seek the extrinsic cause for the existence of such beings. The process toward this cause is precisely the way to God, the cause of the subject of metaphysics. Metaphysics does not set out to "search for God"; but, like any science, it must identify its own subject and the causes of this subject.[8] The cause of being as being can only be absolute being or God.

Though these five ways take the mind to the most profound depths of finite beings, these beings are within our immediate experience; though our mind is led to the most exalted being, this being is the cause of what we experience most profoundly. The ways to God are not arguments in favor

---

[8] Thomas C. O'Brien, *Metaphysics and the Existence of God* (Washington, D.C.: The Thomist Press, 1960), pp. 157–69.

of the imposition of an alien power but the recognition by man of his own limitations and of the living source by which he lives, knows, and loves. In their technical character the five ways are attempts to make this as precise, penetrating, and all-inclusive as possible.

NATURE AND THE ATTRIBUTES OF GOD. In the *Summa Contra Gentiles* St. Thomas considered the attributes of infinity and uniqueness (II, 52), and reflected upon the value of such names for God (I, 30). (See "Act and Potency in Created Intellectual Substances" and "The Names of God.") He applied a distinction taken from Aristotle, the one between the way in which something is signified in the mind (by the one who is thinking) and the thing itself that is signified. From this follows the recognition that the distinctive perfection of God is not only above the natures of sensible things, which are the proper object of the human intellect, but it is even above being as being, the subject of man's highest science, inasmuch as God's perfection is the cause of that subject. Consequently, since the knowledge of God in metaphysics must be according to the subject of that science, what can be known about God is what he is not rather than what he is, and how other things are related to him. This is not to deny knowledge concerning God; but it emphasizes that even knowledge concerning God must be relevant to man and constitutes a strong warning against any attempt by the human mind to manipulate God.

With this in mind St. Thomas proceeded to some considerations about God. The first concerned God as living and is of special interest because of the danger that, in proceeding on the metaphysical level to God as the cause of being as being, one might reduce him to a static or empty term.

Our notion of being as such was arrived at by a removal of restrictions and an opening of the mind to the full breadth and depth of reality. In this sense the attainment of being as being and the progression to its cause is a gradual opening of the mind to that unique plenitude of perfection in which all beings participate and that all manifest. This is perhaps best seen in considering God as living, inasmuch as life is the highest and hence most actual level of perfection. From this it can be seen that life is not incidentally or accidentally added to the divine being, as if without it he would still be God. On the contrary, it is his nature to be life in the fullest and most absolute way. The same is true of the intellectual level of this life, which, rather than being an incidental addition, is the very reality of absolute being.

St. Thomas next considered God as love. Because God is living and the fullness of life is love, the very life of God is love. The *Summa Theologica,* I(Question 20. Article 2), identifies this love in God as first of all love of his own goodness—an absolute adherence to the absolute good. (See "The Highest Degree of Life and Love—God.") There is no question of God willing evil in any sense. Furthermore, since all things other than God exist by the will of God, he must love them also and in proportion to their degree of perfection or being. Thus, God is absolute love; all else, to the degree that it is, participates in God and as such shares in divine love. This can be discovered in metaphysics because it is a statement not of an accidental situation, but of the very significance of being. In order for the finite being to be, he must be loved by God.

If, however, everything is by the love of God and all that happens takes place by this same love, can it be said that I really act, or that what I do really counts? In the *Disputed Questions on the Power of God* this question is discussed with particular reference to the Arabian philosophers, who hoped to reaffirm the power of God by reducing things other than God to fleeting moments continually recreated by God but incapable of acting and causing. St. Thomas, on the contrary, saw the power of God best manifest in the strength by which limited beings as effects of God affirm being in their own right, if not of themselves. (See "The Work of God in the Workings of Nature.") The power of God is nowhere seen more clearly than in the ability of his effects, by their own actuality, to cause others to be actual.[9]

At first sight this might seem to subtract from the causality of God by suggesting that God created only some original beings to which all subsequent beings are related instead of being direct creatures of God. The reason why this is not so is that any being causes or contributes actuality to another being only to the degree it itself is real, that is, according to its nature. Hence, there must be two causes: creatures (secondary causes) that, in causing according to their nature, cause the essence of their effects; and God (first cause) who, in causing according to his nature, causes the existence of these same beings.

Properties of Being

TRANSCENDENTAL PROPERTIES: UNITY, TRUTH, AND GOODNESS. A major contribution of metaphysics is to enable the mind to unify otherwise seemingly unrelated facets of reality. One may speak of things in three ways: their identity in themselves and in relation to others, their significance or meaning in our understanding, and their value or attractiveness to our will. Are these multiple facets of things related? Can our response to the attractiveness of things be more perfect by directing our understanding to their identity and their order among themselves? Is man creative and do things obtain their values because man desires them? Or do things possess a value by which they are able to contribute to the man who attains them? Or is there a relation between the two?

If these questions concerned restricted areas or types of things, they might be treated adequately in particular sciences. However, because they concern everything, they are the concern of metaphysics, which considers

---

[9] Etienne Gilson, *Elements of Christian Philosophy* (Garden City, N.Y.: Doubleday & Co., 1960), pp. 189–93.

the very reality of things in their identity or unity, their relation to the intellect or truth, and their relation to the will or goodness. These three—unity, truth, and goodness—are properties of being, but they are transcendental properties because they are as broad and as pervasive as being itself.

Since each of these is in reality being itself, each is distinguished from being only by the mind in what is called "distinction of reason." This is not to say that these transcendental properties are mere products of the imagination. On the contrary, it is because they include the same reality—being—that they can be distinguished from it only by reason. Nevertheless, this distinction is important because it explores the richness of the concept of being and allows for a clear understanding of the relation among its various aspects.

This relation among the transcendental properties may be expressed as follows: being is first expressed in identity or unity; being and unity are expressed in truth; and being, unity, and truth are expressed in goodness. Each property subsumes its predecessor: unity includes being; truth is the intelligibility of being as one; and goodness is the desirability of the being in its own intelligibility.

From this relationship follow two important considerations. One is the recognition that reality as such is intelligible. From this appreciation the mind derives the need, the obligation, and the courage to search for order and meaning wherever it finds being. As a result the mind of man is forever probing and ranging beyond the confines of past discoveries. Before the enigmas and problems of reality, the human mind has never long remained sceptical or despaired that things are absurd. Rather, it has taken them as a sign that more work needs to be done, that a new point of vision must be developed, that more intellectual effort is required.

Another implication is that it would be erroneous to consider the work of human intellection as a simply passive process of reflecting what exists in reality. Rather, intellection is a form of life, a perfective process drawing its reality from the active unity that constitutes being, and expressing this reality as the good or attractive, in such a way that it elicits an act of love. Man's relation to being as articulated by the transcendentals must be a dynamic and creative process.

This process is magnificently illustrated in the *Summa Contra Gentiles,* II, 45–51, for an understanding of which we now have the essential metaphysical perspectives. (See "The Personal in Creation—Immateriality and Freedom.") Having discovered the principles of limited beings, related them to the ultimate cause, and seen the truth or intelligibility of being, one can now recognize that the distinction or plurality of things is not "the result of chance, nor of a diversity of matter, nor of the intervention of certain causes or merits, but of the intention of God himself, who wills to give the creature such perfection as it is possible for it to have." (Chapter 45, 9.) The divine intellect sees the many ways in which the divine perfection can be manifested. But this work of truth also sees the way in which these many manifestations are ordered or related. Thus, in willing that a certain plurality of beings should exist, God wills their intelligible order. Indeed, to the degree that anything is, it is a participation in him and in his unity, truth, and goodness.

From this it becomes more clear that such a relation to the divine intellect and will does not subtract from the truth and goodness of lesser realities; instead, it is the relation to this divine perfection that makes possible the highest good in creatures. Thus, St. Thomas proceeds in Chapter 46 to show that the perfection of the universe positively requires intellectual creatures, and that such beings must have a will and be endowed with freedom. In a sense, the universe would be absurd without them in at least some phase of its development.

From this, one can note that creation, as seen in Christian metaphysics, is not simply a juxtaposition of unrelated items, but must, like God, have life by including both knowledge and love. As such, creation is itself creative. This is so not in the same sense as an absolute being is creative, but in the sense of a limited being possessing from God a responsible life that is open to the absolute in truth and goodness, from which it receives and in which it finds its ultimate inspiration and highest goal.

BEAUTY. The unity, truth, and goodness of being, particularly as realized in higher beings through knowledge and love, are in a continuing process of development. They develop, however, not in isolation, but as facets of a major synthesis called beauty. Wherever there is a plurality, there is a demand for a higher unity. If truth and goodness follow upon the one, there must be a unifying synthesis of the true and the good. This synthesis is the beautiful, described as that which pleases (goodness) when seen (truth).

Beauty, like truth and goodness, is realized diversely according to the level of the being's perfection. Further, beauty characterizes the relation between beings, and thus expresses the full order of being. Finally, beauty is realized most perfectly in God who, as absolute being, is absolute beauty and the source of the beauty of all else. The divine beauty is manifested in as many ways as there are things, and the total order of all beings has its own beauty within which the full significance of each part can be best appreciated.

St. Thomas provided the basis for a reunification of the insights both of those who would attend more directly to the truth of things and of those who would attend more specifically to the considerations related to the good, such as freedom, will, and love. He also warned against considering either of these aspects in isolation as absolutes or even as adequate in the solution of any concrete situation. This does not mean, for instance, that the truth of a thing is not relevant to its beauty; but it does mean that a thing must be true and good in unison in order to be beautiful. The elements of this unison are described in the commentary *On the De Nominibus Divinis.* (See "On Beauty.")

Finally, because God is absolute beauty, any striving for the beautiful must lead to the divine. If God is the end of all beings because he is their creative source, he is not an end to which man is simply physically moved. On the contrary, as truth God is to be known by man, as goodness he is to be loved by man, and as beauty he is the end to which man creatively directs himself and others. Man's freedom, guided by a metaphysics that offers a deep appreciation of beauty, unites all else and draws it into the supreme delight that is the active contemplative union with the beautiful.

Conclusion

Throughout this introduction to the development of classical-Christian thought, we have identified certain dominant themes. It is marked by a strong intellectual orientation, generally realistic and objective in character. For this reason, special attention is given to the development of abstraction or separation so that notions such as being, used in the science of metaphysics, would be open to the full breadth of human experience and rich in real content. Since there has also been a constant interest in discovering the internal structure of being, we have examined the intensive efforts to discover, clarify, and relate the principles of existence and essence. In turn, these have contributed notably to ordering the different levels of being and identifying the special dignity of the spiritual. Finally, we have seen that there was a constant concern to understand all things in the unity of their relation to the absolute.

This endeavor might be described as a mammoth project inspired by the soaring vision of Plato and technically elaborated according to the Aristotelian pattern of science. Deepening both and making their synthesis possible was the new dimension in the understanding of being offered by the work of Augustine and the early fathers and elaborated by Thomas Aquinas.

Much more has and will be done in philosophy to improve this body of thought. Linguistic philosophy will contribute to its logic, phenomenology to its materials, existentialism to its appreciation of the person, and transcendental philosophy to its critical self-awareness. A condition required of any authentic philosophy as "the study of all things" is openness to progressive and varied developments. It is the hallmark of its greatness that classical-Christian thought, by the breadth and balance of its principles and perspectives, remains a basis both for launching new philosophical investigations and for integrating their findings.

Glossary

ABSTRACTION:
The mental grasp of one form or note in a thing without attending to other of its aspects, thus opening the mind to any realizaion of that form.

ACCIDENT:
That which is or exists in another. For example, the *posture* of Socrates is an accident and requires Socrates the man as primary substance or subject in which to inhere.

ACT:
An intrinsic principle conferring a perfection on a being; an operation.

BEAUTY:
That which pleases when seen because of its integrity, due proportion, and splendor.

BEING:
That which is; that to which existence belongs.

CAUSE:
That which contributes to the being or change of something, either from within (intrinsic cause), or from without by its action (efficient cause) or by its attraction (final cause).

ESSENCE:
The internal principle of being by which is determined what (kind) the being is.

EXISTENCE:
The act by which a thing is or exists.

FORM:
The internal principle that specifies what a thing is. For example, the soul of Socrates is the substantial form of his body.

GOOD:
That which is perfect or perfective, and which therefore is desirable.

MATTER:
An intrinsic principle capable of receiving and being determined by form. For example, the marble of the statue can be changed by the sculptor.

METAPHYSICS:
The science of being as being, that is, the science of that which is and inasmuch as it is; also called wisdom, ontology, and first philosophy.

NATURE:
Essence (see above) as a principle of activity.

PARTICIPATION:

The limited realization of a perfection in relation to another being that is the unlimited realization of that perfection.

POTENCY:

Capacity for a perfection or act by which the capacity is determined. For example, Socrates is capable of being wise, and upon his achievement of wisdom he actually is wise.

PROPERTY:

A characteristic or attribute; a perfection that is not part of the essence. For example, the ability to laugh is a property of Socrates.

SUBSTANCE:

That which exists in itself, or to which such existence would be proper. For example, Socrates is a substance.

TRANSCENDENTAL PROPERTY:

Property that is had by any and all being, that is, unity, truth, goodness, and beauty.

TRUTH:

Correspondence of mind with thing (logical truth) or of thing with mind (ontological truth).

Plato

Degrees of Knowledge

BOOK VI

You have to imagine, then, that there are two ruling powers, and that one 509 of them is set over the intellectual world, the other over the visible. I do not say heaven, lest you should fancy that I am playing upon the name. May I suppose that you have this distinction of the visible and intelligible fixed in your mind?

I have.

Now take a line which has been cut into two unequal parts, and divide each of them again in the same proportion, and suppose the two main divisions to answer, one to the visible and the other to the intelligible, and then compare the subdivisions in respect of their clearness and want of clearness, and you will find that the first section in the sphere of the visible consists of images. And by images I mean, in the first place, shadows, 510 and in the second place, reflections in water and in solid, smooth and polished bodies and the like: Do you understand?

Yes, I understand.

Imagine, now, the other section, of which this is only the resemblance,

From pp. 771–80 of Plato, *Republic,* translated by B. Jowett, in *Dialogues of Plato,* vol. I. Copyright 1937 by Random House, Inc.

to include the animals which we see, and everything that grows or is made.

Very good.

Would you not admit that both the sections of this division have different degrees of truth, and that the copy is to the original as the sphere of opinion is to the sphere of knowledge?

Most undoubtedly.

Next proceed to consider the manner in which the sphere of the intellectual is to be divided.

In what manner?

Thus:—There are two subdivisions, in the lower of which the soul uses the figures given by the former division as images; the enquiry can only be hypothetical, and instead of going upwards to a principle descends to the other end; in the higher of the two, the soul passes out of hypotheses, and goes up to a principle which is above hypotheses, making no use of images as in the former case, but proceeding only in and through the ideas themselves.

I do not quite understand your meaning, he said.

Then I will try again; you will understand me better when I have made some preliminary remarks. You are aware that students of geometry, arithmetic, and the kindred sciences assume the odd and the even and the figures and three kinds of angles and the like in their several branches of science; these are their hypotheses, which they and every body are supposed to know, and therefore they do not deign to give any account of them either to themselves or others; but they begin with them, and go on until they arrive at last, and in a consistent manner, at their conclusion?

Yes, he said, I know.

And do you not know also that although they make use of the visible forms and reason about them, they are thinking not of these, but of the ideals which they resemble; not of the figures which they draw, but of the absolute square and the absolute diameter, and so on—the forms which they draw or make, and which have shadows and reflections in water of their own, are converted by them into images, but they are really seeking to behold the things themselves, which can only be seen with the eye of the mind?

511   That is true.

And of this kind I spoke as the intelligible, although in the search after it the soul is compelled to use hypotheses; not ascending to a first principle, because she is unable to rise above the region of hypothesis, but employing the objects of which the shadows below are resemblances in their turn as images, they having in relation to the shadows and reflections of them a greater distinctness, and therefore a higher value.

I understand, he said, that you are speaking of the province of geometry and the sister arts.

And when I speak of the other division of the intelligible, you will understand me to speak of that other sort of knowledge which reason herself attains by the power of dialectic, using the hypotheses not as first principles, but only as hypotheses—that is to say, as steps and points of departure into a world which is above hypotheses, in order that she may soar beyond them to the first principle of the whole; and clinging to this and then to that which depends on this, by successive steps she descends again without the aid of any sensible object, from ideas, through ideas, and in ideas she ends.

I understand you, he replied; not perfectly, for you seem to me to be describing a task which is really tremendous; but, at any rate, I understand you to say that knowledge and being, which the science of dialectic contemplates, are clearer than the notions of the arts, as they are termed, which proceed from hypotheses only: these are also contemplated by the understanding, and not by the senses: yet, because they start from hypotheses and do not ascend to a principle, those who contemplate them appear to you not to exercise the higher reason upon them, although when a first principle is added to them they are cognizable by the higher reason. And the habit which is concerned with geometry and the cognate sciences I suppose that you would term understanding and not reason, as being intermediate between opinion and reason.

You have quite conceived my meaning, I said; and now, corresponding to these four divisions, let there be four faculties in the soul—reason answering to the highest, understanding to the second, faith (or conviction) to the third, and perception of shadows to the last—and let there be a scale of them, and let us suppose that the several faculties have clearness in the same degree that their objects have truth.

I understand, he replied, and give my assent, and accept your arrangement.

BOOK VII

And now, I said, let me show in a figure how far our nature is enlightened   514
or unenlightened:—Behold! human beings living in an underground den,
which has a mouth open towards the light and reaching all along the den;
here they have been from their childhood, and have their legs and necks
chained so that they cannot move, and can only see before them, being prevented by the chains from turning round their heads. Above and behind
them a fire is blazing at a distance, and between the fire and the prisoners
there is a raised way; and you will see, if you look, a low wall built along the
way, like the screen which marionette players have in front of them, over
which they show the puppets.

I see.

And do you see, I said, men passing along the wall carrying all sorts of   515
vessels, and statues and figures of animals made of wood and stone and
various materials, which appear over the wall? Some of them are talking,
others silent.

You have shown me a strange image, and they are strange prisoners.

Like ourselves, I replied; and they see only their own shadows, or the shadows of one another, which the fire throws on the opposite wall of the cave?

True, he said; how could they see anything but the shadows if they were never allowed to move their heads?

And of the objects which are being carried in like manner they would only see the shadows?

Yes, he said.

And if they were able to converse with one another, would they not suppose that they were naming what was actually before them?

Very true.

And suppose further that the prison had an echo which came from the other side, would they not be sure to fancy when one of the passers-by spoke that the voice which they heard came from the passing shadow?

No question, he replied.

To them, I said, the truth would be literally nothing but the shadows of the images.

That is certain.

And now look again, and see what will naturally follow if the prisoners are released and disabused of their error. At first, when any of them is liberated and compelled suddenly to stand up and turn his neck round and walk and look towards the light, he will suffer sharp pains; the glare will distress him, and he will be unable to see the realities of which in his former state he had seen the shadows; and then conceive some one saying to him, that what he saw before was an illusion, but that now, when he is approaching nearer to being and his eye is turned towards more real existence, he has a clearer vision,—what will be his reply? And you may further imagine that his instructor is pointing to the objects as they pass and requiring him to name them,—will he not be perplexed? Will he not fancy that the shadows which he formerly saw are truer than the objects which are now shown to him?

Far truer.

And if he is compelled to look straight at the light, will he not have a pain in his eyes which will make him turn away to take refuge in the objects of vision which he can see, and which he will conceive to be in reality clearer than the things which are now being shown to him?

True, he said.

And suppose once more, that he is reluctantly dragged up a steep and 516 rugged ascent, and held fast until he is forced into the presence of the sun himself, is he not likely to be pained and irritated? When he approaches the light his eyes will be dazzled, and he will not be able to see anything at all of what are now called realities.

Not all in a moment, he said.

He will require to grow accustomed to the sight of the upper world. And first he will see the shadows best, next the reflections of men and other objects in the water, and then the objects themselves; then he will gaze upon the light of the moon and the stars and the spangled heaven; and he will see the sky and the stars by night better than the sun or the light of the sun by day?

Certainly.

Last of all he will be able to see the sun, and not mere reflections of him in the water, but he will see him in his own proper place, and not in another; and he will contemplate him as he is.

Certainly.

He will then proceed to argue that this is he who gives the season and the years, and is the guardian of all that is in the visible world, and in a certain way the cause of all things which he and his fellows have been accustomed to behold?

Clearly, he said, he would first see the sun and then reason about him.

And when he remembered his old habitation, and the wisdom of the den and his fellow-prisoners, do you not suppose that he would felicitate himself on the change, and pity them?

Certainly, he would.

And if they were in the habit of conferring honours among themselves on those who were quickest to observe the passing shadows and to remark which of them went before, and which followed after, and which were together; and who were therefore best able to draw conclusions as to the future, do you think that he would care for such honours and glories, or envy the possessors of them? Would he not say with Homer,

> "Better to be the poor servant of a poor master,"

and to endure anything, rather than think as they do and live after their manner?

Yes, he said, I think that he would rather suffer anything than entertain these false notions and live in this miserable manner.

Imagine once more, I said, such an one coming suddenly out of the sun to be replaced in his old situation; would he not be certain to have his eyes full of darkness?

To be sure, he said.

And if there were a contest, and he had to compete in measuring the shadows with the prisoners who had never moved out of the den, while his sight was still weak, and before his eyes had become steady (and the time which would be needed to acquire this new habit of sight might be very considerable), would he not be ridiculous? Men would say of him that up he went and down he came without his eyes; and that it was better not even to think of ascending; and if any one tried to loose another and lead him up to the light, let them only catch the offender, and they would put him to death.

No question, he said.

This entire allegory, I said, you may now append, dear Glaucon, to the previous argument; the prison-house is the world of sight, the light of the fire is the sun, and you will not misapprehend me if you interpret the journey upwards to be the ascent of the soul into the intellectual world according to my poor belief, which, at your desire, I have expressed—whether rightly or wrongly God knows. But, whether true or false, my opinion is that in the world of knowledge the idea of good appears last of all, and is seen only with an effort; and, when seen, is also inferred to be the universal author of all things beautiful and right, parent of light and of the lord of light in this visible world, and the immediate source of reason and truth in the intellectual; and that this is the power upon which he who would act rationally either in public or private life must have his eye fixed.

I agree, he said, as far as I am able to understand you.

Moreover, I said, you must not wonder that those who attain to this beatific vision are unwilling to descend to human affairs; for their souls are ever hastening into the upper world where they desire to dwell; which desire of theirs is very natural, if our allegory may be trusted.

Yes, very natural.

And is there anything surprising in one who passes from divine contemplations to the evil state of man, misbehaving himself in a ridiculous manner; if, while his eyes are blinking and before he has become accustomed to the surrounding darkness, he is compelled to fight in courts of law, or in other places, about the images or the shadows of images of justice, and is endeavouring to meet the conceptions of those who have never yet seen absolute justice?

Anything but surprising, he replied.

518   Any one who has common sense will remember that the bewilderments of the eyes are of two kinds, and arise from two causes, either from coming out of the light or from going into the light, which is true of the mind's eye, quite as much as of the bodily eye; and he who remembers this when he sees any one whose vision is perplexed and weak, will not be too ready to laugh; he will first ask whether that soul of man has come out of the brighter life, and is unable to see because unaccustomed to the dark, or having turned from darkness to the day is dazzled by excess of light. And he will count the one happy in his condition and state of being, and he will pity the other; or, if he have a mind to laugh at the soul which comes from below into the light, there will be more reason in this than in the laugh which greets him who returns from above out of the light into the den.

That, he said, is a very just distinction.

But then, if I am right, certain professors of education must be wrong when they say that they can put a knowledge into the soul which was not there before, like sight into blind eyes.

They undoubtedly say this, he replied.

Whereas, our argument shows that the power and capacity of learning exists in the soul already; and that just as the eye was unable to turn from darkness to light without the whole body, so too the instrument of knowledge can only by the movement of the whole soul be turned from the world of becoming into that of being, and learn by degrees to endure the sight of being, and of the brightest and best of being, or in other words, of the good.

Very true.

And must there not be some art which will effect conversion in the easiest and quickest manner; not implanting the faculty of sight, for that exists already, but has been turned in the wrong direction, and is looking away from the truth?

Yes, he said, such an art may be presumed.

And whereas the other so-called virtues of the soul seem to be akin to bodily qualities, for even when they are not originally innate they can be implanted later by habit and exercise, the virtue of wisdom more than anything else contains a divine element which always remains, and by this conversion is rendered useful and profitable; or, on the other hand, hurtful and 519 useless. Did you never observe the narrow intelligence flashing from the keen eye of a clever rogue—how eager he is, how clearly his paltry soul sees the way to his end; he is the reverse of blind, but his keen eye-sight is forced into the service of evil, and he is mischievous in proportion to his cleverness?

Very true, he said.

But what if there had been a circumcision of such natures in the days of their youth; and they had been severed from those sensual pleasures, such as eating and drinking, which, like leaden weights, were attached to them at their birth, and which drag them down and turn the vision of their souls upon the things that are below—if, I say, they had been released from these impediments and turned in the opposite direction, the very same faculty in them would have seen the truth as keenly as they see what their eyes are turned to now.

Very likely.

Yes, I said; and there is another thing which is likely, or rather a necessary inference from what has preceded, that neither the uneducated and uninformed of the truth, nor yet those who never make an end of their education, will be able ministers of State; not the former, because they have no single aim of duty which is the rule of all their actions, private as well as public; nor the latter, because they will not act at all except upon compulsion, fancying that they are already dwelling apart in the islands of the blest.

Very true, he replied.

Then, I said, the business of us who are the founders of the State will be to compel the best minds to attain that knowledge which we have already shown to be the greatest of all—they must continue to ascend until they arrive at the good; but when they have ascended and seen enough we must not allow them to do as they do now.

What do you mean?

I mean that they remain in the upper world: but this must not be allowed; they must be made to descend again among the prisoners in the den, and partake of their labours and honours, whether they are worth having or not.

But is not this unjust? he said; ought we to give them a worse life, when they might have a better?

You have again forgotten, my friend, I said, the intention of the legislator, who did not aim at making any one class in the State happy above the rest; the happiness was to be in the whole State, and he held the citizens together by persuasion and necessity, making them benefactors of the State, and therefore benefactors of one another; to this end he created them, not to please themselves, but to be his instruments in binding up the State.

520

True, he said, I had forgotten.

Observe, Glaucon, that there will be no injustice in compelling our philosophers to have a care and providence of others; we shall explain to them that in other States, men of their class are not obliged to share in the toils of politics: and this is reasonable, for they grow up at their own sweet will, and the government would rather not have them. Being self-taught, they cannot be expected to show any gratitude for a culture which they have never received. But we have brought you into the world to be rulers of the hive, kings of yourselves and of the other citizens, and have educated you far better and more perfectly than they have been educated, and you are better able to share in the double duty. Wherefore each of you, when his turn comes, must go down to the general underground abode, and get the habit of seeing in the dark. When you have acquired the habit, you will see ten thousand times better than the inhabitants of the den, and you will know what the several images are, and what they represent, because you have seen the beautiful and just and good in their truth. And thus our State which is also yours will be a reality, and not a dream only, and will be administered in a spirit unlike that of other States, in which men fight with one another about shadows only and are distracted in the struggle for power, which in their eyes is a great good. Whereas the truth is that the State in which the rulers are most reluctant to govern is always the best and most quietly governed, and the State in which they are most eager, the worst.

Quite true, he replied.

And will our pupils, when they hear this, refuse to take their turn at the toils of State, when they are allowed to spend the greater part of their time with one another in the heavenly light?

Impossible, he answered; for they are just men, and the commands which we impose upon them are just; there can be no doubt that every one of them will take office as a stern necessity, and not after the fashion of our present rulers of State.

521

Yes, my friend, I said; and there lies the point. You must contrive for your future rulers another and a better life than that of a ruler, and then you may have a well-ordered State; for only in the State which offers this, will they rule who are truly rich, not in silver and gold, but in virtue and wisdom, which are the true blessings of life. Whereas if they go to the administration of public affairs, poor and hungering after their own private advantage, thinking that hence they are to snatch the chief good, order there can never be; for they will be fighting about office and the civil and domestic broils which thus arise will be the ruin of the rulers themselves and of the whole State.

Most true, he replied.

And the only life which looks down upon the life of political ambition is that of true philosophy. Do you know of any other?

Indeed, I do not, he said.

And those who govern ought not to be lovers of the task? For, if they are, there will be rival lovers, and they will fight.

No question.

Who then are those whom we shall compel to be guardians? Surely they will be the men who are wisest about affairs of State, and by whom the State is best administered, and who at the same time have other honours and another and a better life than that of politics?

They are the men, and I will choose them, he replied.

And now shall we consider in what way such guardians will be produced, and how they are to be brought from darkness to light,—as some are said to have ascended from the world below to the gods?

By all means, he replied.

The process, I said, is not the turning over of an oyster-shell,[1] but the turning round of a soul passing from a day which is little better than night to the true day of being, that is, the ascent from below, which we affirm to be true philosophy?

Quite so.

And should we not enquire what sort of knowledge has the power of effecting such a change?

Certainly.

What sort of knowledge is there which would draw the soul from becoming to being? And another consideration has just occurred to me: You will remember that our young men are to be warrior athletes?

Yes, that was said.

Then this new kind of knowledge must have an additional quality?

What quality?

Usefulness in war.

Yes, if possible.

There were two parts in our former scheme of education, were there not?

Just so.

---

[1] In allusion to a game in which two parties fled or pursued according as an oyster-shell which was thrown into the air fell with the dark or light side uppermost. [B.J.]

QUESTIONS FOR STUDY AND DISCUSSION

1. What reversal of the common position concerning the value of experimental knowledge is introduced by Plato's division between the top two sections and the bottom two sections of his divided line?
2. Compare the types of knowledge expressed by the four sections of the divided line to the knowledge had by various groups in the allegory of the cave.
3. What importance does this passage attribute to the idea of the good in relation to the reality of all else?
4. What insight does this passage suggest concerning the nature of philosophy and especially of metaphysics?
5. What contribution to the good of society does Plato envisage for metaphysics in this passage?

Aristotle

ARISTOTLE was born in Stagira in 384 B.C., and spent his early youth at the Macedonian court, where his father was a physician. When he was eighteen he went to Athens and studied at the Academy for several years, leaving after the death of Plato. In 342 Aristotle accepted the position of tutor to Alexander the Great, but in 335 he returned to Athens and founded his own school, the Lyceum. For the next twelve years he directed the course of studies at the Lyceum, and it is presumed that he wrote most of his extant works during that time. The death of Alexander in 323 resulted in an anti-Macedonian reaction in Athens. Fearing that his fate would be the same as Socrates'—and because he did not want "the Athenians to sin twice against philosophy" —he went into exile in Chalcis, where he died in 322. Although famous in his day for his literary style, almost all his known works today are technical treatises covering logic, natural philosophy, metaphysics, and practical philosophy.

Science of Being as Being

BOOK I

1   All men by nature desire to know. An indication of this is the delight we   980ᵃ
take in our senses; for even apart from their usefulness they are loved for
themselves; and above all others the sense of sight. For not only with a
view to action, but even when we are not going to do anything, we prefer
seeing (one might say) to everything else. The reason is that this, most of
all the senses, makes us know and brings to light many differences between
things.

By nature animals are born with the faculty of sensation, and from sensation memory is produced in some of them, though not in others. And
therefore the former are more intelligent and apt at learning than those   980ᵇ
which cannot remember; those which are incapable of hearing sounds
are intelligent though they cannot be taught, e.g. the bee, and any other
race of animals that may be like it; and those which besides memory have
this sense of hearing can be taught.

From Aristotle, *Metaphysics,* in *The Oxford Translation of Aristotle,* vol. VIII, edited by J. A. Smith and W. D. Ross. Copyright 1928 by Clarendon Press, Oxford. Reprinted by permission of Clarendon Press, Oxford.

The animals other than man live by appearances and memories, and have but little of connected experience; but the human race lives also by art and reasonings. Now from memory experience is produced in men; for the several memories of the same thing produce finally the capacity for a single 981ᵃ experience. And experience seems pretty much like science and art, but really science and art come to men *through* experience; for "experience made art," as Polus says, "but inexperience luck." Now art arises when from many notions gained by experience one universal judgment about a class of objects is produced. For to have a judgment that when Callias was ill of this disease this did him good, and similarly in the case of Socrates and in many individual cases, is a matter of experience; but to judge that it has done good to all persons of a certain constitution, marked off in one class, when they were ill of this disease, e.g. to phlegmatic or bilious people when burning with fever—this is a matter of art.

With a view to action experience seems in no respect inferior to art, and men of experience succeed even better than those who have theory without experience. (The reason is that experience is knowledge of individuals, art of universals, and actions and productions are all concerned with the individual; for the physician does not cure *man,* except in an incidental way, but Callias or Socrates or some other called by some such individual name, who happens to be a man. If, then, a man has the theory without the experience, and recognizes the universal but does not know the individual included in this, he will often fail to cure; for it is the individual that is to be cured.) But yet we think that *knowledge* and *understanding* belong to art rather than to experience, and we suppose artists to be wiser than men of experience (which implies that Wisdom depends in all cases rather on knowledge); and this because the former know the cause, but the latter do not. For men of experience know that the thing is so, but do not know why, while the others know the "why" and the cause. Hence we think also that the master-workers in each craft are more honourable and know in a truer 981ᵇ sense and are wiser than the manual workers, because they know the causes of the things that are done (we think the manual workers are like certain lifeless things which act indeed, but act without knowing what they do, as fire burns—but while the lifeless things perform each of their functions by a natural tendency, the labourers perform them through habit); thus we view them as being wiser not in virtue of being able to act, but of having the theory for themselves and knowing the causes. And in general it is a sign of the man who knows and of the man who does not know, that the former can teach, and therefore we think art more truly knowledge than experience is; for artists can teach, and men of mere experience cannot.

Again, we do not regard any of the senses as Wisdom; yet surely these give the most authoritative knowledge of particulars. But they do not tell us the "why" of anything—e.g. why fire is hot; they only say *that* it is hot.

At first he who invented any art whatever that went beyond the common perceptions of man was naturally admired by men, not only because there was something useful in the inventions, but because he was thought wise and superior to the rest. But as more arts were invented, and some were directed to the necessities of life, others to recreation, the inventors of the latter were naturally always regarded as wiser than the inventors of the former, because their branches of knowledge did not aim at utility. Hence when all such inventions were already established, the sciences which do not aim at giving pleasure or at the necessities of life were discovered, and first in the places where men first began to have leisure. This is why the mathematical arts were founded in Egypt; for there the priestly caste was allowed to be at leisure.

We have said in the *Ethics* what the difference is between art and science and the other kindred faculties; but the point of our present discussion is this, that all men suppose what is called Wisdom to deal with the first causes and the principles of things; so that, as has been said before, the man of experience is thought to be wiser than the possessors of any sense-perception whatever, the artist wiser than the men of experience, the master-worker than the mechanic, and the theoretical kinds of knowledge to be more of the nature of Wisdom than the productive. Clearly then Wisdom   982ᵃ
is knowledge about certain principles and causes.

2   Since we are seeking this knowledge, we must inquire of what kind are the causes and the principles, the knowledge of which is Wisdom. If one were to take the notions we have about the wise man, this might perhaps make the answer more evident. We suppose first, then, that the wise man knows all things, as far as possible, although he has not knowledge of each of them in detail; secondly, that he who can learn things that are difficult, and not easy for man to know, is wise (sense-perception is common to all, and therefore easy and no mark of Wisdom); again, that he who is more exact and more capable of teaching the causes is wiser, in every branch of knowledge; and that of the sciences, also, that which is desirable on its own account and for the sake of knowing it is more of the nature of Wisdom than that which is desirable on account of its results, and the superior science is more of the nature of Wisdom than the ancillary; for the wise man must not be ordered but must order, and he must not obey another, but the less wise must obey *him*.

Such and so many are the notions, then, which we have about Wisdom more of the nature of Wisdom than the ancillary; for the wise man must belong to him who has in the highest degree universal knowledge; for he knows in a sense all the instances that fall under the universal. And these things, the most universal, are on the whole the hardest for men to know; for they are farthest from the senses. And the most exact of the sciences are those which deal most with first principles; for those which involve fewer principles are more exact than those which involve additional principles, e.g. arithmetic than geometry. But the science which investigates causes is also *instructive,* in a higher degree, for the people who instruct us are those who tell the causes of each thing. And understanding and knowledge pursued for their own sake are found most in the knowledge of that which is most knowable (for he who chooses to know for the sake of knowing will choose most readily that which is most truly knowledge, and such is the knowledge of that which is most knowable); and the first principles and the causes are most knowable; for by reason of these, and from these, all other things come to be known, and not these by means of the things subordinate to them. And the science which knows to what end each thing must be done is the most authoritative of the sciences, and more authoritative than any ancillary science; and this end is the good of that thing, and in general the supreme good in the whole of nature. Judged by all the tests we have mentioned, then, the name in question falls to the same science; this must be a science that investigates the first principles and causes; for the good, i.e. the end, is one of the causes.

982ᵇ

That it is not a science of production is clear even from the history of the earliest philosophers. For it is owing to their wonder that men both now begin and at first began to philosophize; they wondered originally at the obvious difficulties, then advanced little by little and stated difficulties about the greater matters, e.g. about the phenomena of the moon and those of the sun and of the stars, and about the genesis of the universe. And a man who is puzzled and wonders thinks himself ignorant (whence even the lover of myth is in a sense a lover of Wisdom, for the myth is composed of wonders); therefore since they philosophized in order to escape from ignorance, evidently they were pursuing science in order to know, and not for any utilitarian end. And this is confirmed by the facts; for it was when almost all the necessities of life and the things that make for comfort and recreation had been secured, that such knowledge began to be sought. Evidently then we do not seek it for the sake of any other advantage; but as the man is free, we say, who exists for his own sake and not for another's, so we pursue this as the only free science, for it alone exists for its own sake.

Hence also the possession of it might be justly regarded as beyond human power; for in many ways human nature is in bondage, so that according to Simonides "God alone can have this privilege," and it is unfitting that man should not be content to seek the knowledge that is suited to him. If, then, there is something in what the poets say, and jealousy is natural to the divine power, it would probably occur in this case above all, and all who excelled in this knowledge would be unfortunate. But the divine power cannot be jealous (nay, according to the proverb, "bards tell many a lie"), nor should any other science be thought more honourable than one of this sort. For the most divine science is also most honourable; and this science alone must be, in two ways, most divine. For the science which it would be most meet for God to have is a divine science, and so is any science that

983ᵃ

deals with divine objects; and this science alone has both these qualities; for (1) God is thought to be among the causes of all things and to be a first principle, and (2) such a science either God alone can have, or God above all others. All the sciences, indeed, are more necessary than this, but none is better.

Yet the acquisition of it must in a sense end in something which is the opposite of our original inquiries. For all men begin, as we said, by wondering that things are as they are, as they do about self-moving marionettes, or about the solstices or the incommensurability of the diagonal of a square with the side; for it seems wonderful to all who have not yet seen the reason, that there is a thing which cannot be measured even by the smallest unit. But we must end in the contrary and, according to the proverb, the better state, as is the case in these instances too when men learn the cause; for there is nothing which would suprise a geometer so much as if the diagonal turned out to be commensurable.

We have stated, then, what is the nature of the science we are searching for, and what is the mark which our search and our whole investigation must reach.

3 Evidently we have to acquire knowledge of the original causes (for we say we know each thing only when we think we recognize its first cause), and causes are spoken of in four senses. In one of these we mean the substance, i.e. the essence (for the "why" is reducible finally to the definition, and the ultimate "why" is a cause and principle); in another the matter or substratum, in a third the source of the change, and in a fourth the cause opposed to this, the purpose and the good (for this is the end of all genera- 983ᵇ tion and change). We have studied these causes sufficiently in our work on nature, but yet let us call to our aid those who have attacked the investigation of being and philosophized about reality before us. For obviously they too speak of certain principles and causes; to go over their views, then, will be of profit to the present inquiry, for we shall either find another kind of cause, or be more convinced of the correctness of those which we now maintain.

· · ·

7 Our review of those who have spoken about first principles and reality 988ᵃ and of the way in which they have spoken, has been concise and summary; but yet we have learnt *this* much from them, that of those who speak about "principle" and "cause" no one has mentioned any principle except those which have been distinguished in our work on nature, but all evidently have some inkling of *them,* though only vaguely. For some speak of the first principle as matter, whether they suppose one or more first principles, and whether they suppose this to be a body or to be incorporeal; e.g. Plato spoke of the great and the small, the Italians of the infinite, Empedocles of fire, earth, water, and air, Anaxagoras of the infinity of things composed

of similar parts. These, then, have all had a notion of this kind of cause, and so have all who speak of air or fire or water, or something denser than fire and rarer than air; for some have said the prime element is of this kind.

These thinkers grasped this cause only; but certain others have mentioned the source of movement, e.g. those who make friendship and strife, or reason, or love, a principle.

The essence, i.e. the substantial reality, no one has expressed distinctly. It is hinted at chiefly by those who believe in the Forms; for they do not suppose either that the Forms are the matter of sensible things, and the One the matter of the Forms, or that they are the source of movement (for they say these are causes rather of immobility and of being at rest), but they furnish the Forms as the essence of every other thing, and the One as the essence of the Forms.

That for whose sake actions and changes and movements take place, they assert to be a cause in a way, but not in this way, i.e. not in the way in which it is its *nature* to be a cause. For those who speak of reason or friendship class these causes as goods; they do not speak, however, as if anything that exists either existed or came into being for the sake of these, but as if movements started from these. In the same way those who say the One or the existent is the good, say that it is the cause of substance, but not that substance either is or comes to be for the sake of this. Therefore it turns out that in a sense they both say and do not say the good is a cause; for they do not call it a cause *qua* good but only incidentally.

All these thinkers, then, as they cannot pitch on another cause, seem to testify that we have determined rightly both how many and of what sort the causes are. Besides this it is plain that when the causes are being looked for, either all four must be sought thus or they must be sought in one of these four ways. Let us next discuss the possible difficulties with regard to the way in which each of these thinkers has spoken, and with regard to his situation relatively to the first principles.

·   ·   ·

BOOK IV

1003ª   1   There is a science which investigates being as being and the attributes which belong to this in virtue of its own nature. Now this is not the same as any of the so-called special sciences; for none of these others treats universally of being as being. They cut off a part of being and investigate the attribute of this part; this is what the mathematical sciences for instance do. Now since we are seeking the first principles and the highest causes, clearly there must be something to which these belong in virtue of its own nature. If then those who sought the elements of existing things were seeking these same principles, it is necessary that the elements must be elements of being not by accident but just because it *is* being. Therefore it is of being as being that we also must grasp the first causes.

2   There are many senses in which a thing may be said to "be," but all that "is" is related to one central point, one definite kind of thing, and is not said to "be" by a mere ambiguity. Everything which is healthy is related to health, one thing in the sense that it preserves health, another in the sense that it produces it, another in the sense that it is a symptom of health, another because it is capable of it. And that which is medical is relative to the   1003ᵇ medical art, one thing being called medical because it possesses it, another because it is naturally adapted to it, another because it is a function of the medical art. And we shall find other words used similarly to these. So, too, there are many senses in which a thing is said to be, but all refer to one starting-point; some things are said to be because they are substances, others because they are affections of substance, others because they are a process towards substance, or destructions or privations or qualities of substance, or productive or generative of substance, or of things which are relative to substance, or negations of one of these things or of substance itself. It is for this reason that we say even of non-being that it *is* non-being. As, then, there is one science which deals with all healthy things, the same applies in the other cases also. For not only in the case of things which have one common notion does the investigation belong to one science, but also in the case of things which are related to one common nature; for even these in a sense have one common notion. It is clear then that it is the work of one science also to study the things that are, *qua* being.—But everywhere science deals chiefly with that which is primary, and on which the other things depend, and in virtue of which they get their names. If, then, this is substance, it will be of substances that the philosopher must grasp the principles and the causes.

Now for each one class of things, as there is one perception, so there is one science, as for instance grammar, being one science, investigates all articulate sounds. Hence to investigate all the species of being *qua* being is the work of a science which is generically one, and to investigate the several species is the work of the specific parts of the science.

If, now, being and unity are the same and are one thing in the sense that they are implied in one another as principle and cause are, not in the sense that they are explained by the same definition (though it makes no difference even if we suppose them to be like that—in fact this would even strengthen our case); for "one man" and "man" are the same thing, and so are "existent man" and "man" and the doubling of the words in "one man and one *existent* man" does not express anything different (it is clear that the two things are not separated either in coming to be or in ceasing to be); and similarly "*one* existent man" adds nothing to "existent man," so that it is obvious that the addition in these cases means the same thing, and unity is nothing apart from being; and if, further, the substance of each thing is one in no merely accidental way, and similarly is from its very nature something that *is*:—all this being so, there must be exactly as many species of being as of unity. And to investigate the essence of these is the work of a science which is generically one—I mean, for instance, the discussion of the same and the similar and the other concepts of this sort; and nearly all contraries may be referred to this origin; let us take them as having been investigated in the "Selection of Contraries."

1004ᵃ

And there are as many parts of philosophy as there are kinds of substance, so that there must necessarily be among them a first philosophy and one which follows this. For being falls immediately into genera; for which reason the sciences too will correspond to these genera. For the philosopher is like the mathematician, as that word is used; for mathematics also has parts, and there is a first and a second science and other successive ones within the sphere of mathematics.

Now since it is the work of one science to investigate opposites, and plurality is opposed to unity—and it belongs to one science to investigate the negation and the privation because in both cases we are really investigating the one thing of which the negation or the privation is a negation or privation (for we either say simply that that thing is not present, or that it is not present in some particular class; in the latter case difference is present over and above what is implied in negation; for negation means just the absence of the thing in question, while in privation there is also employed an underlying nature of which the privation is asserted):—in view of all these facts, the contraries of the concepts we named above, the other and the dissimilar and the unequal, and everything else which is derived either from these or from plurality and unity, must fall within the province of the science above named. And contrariety is one of these concepts; for contrariety is a kind of difference, and difference is a kind of otherness. Therefore, since there are many senses in which a thing is said to be one, these terms also will have many senses, but yet it belongs to one science to know them all; for a term belongs to different sciences not if it has different senses, but if it has not one meaning *and* its definitions cannot be referred to one central meaning. And since all things are referred to that which is primary, as for instance all things which are called one are referred to the primary one, we must say that this holds good also of the same and the other and of contraries in general; so that after distinguishing the various senses of each, we must then explain by reference to what is primary in the case of each of the predicates in question, saying how they are related to it; for so some will be called what they are called because they possess it, others because they produce it, and others in other such ways.

It is evident, then, that it belongs to one science to be able to give an account of these concepts as well as of substance (this was one of the questions in our book of problems), and that it is the function of the philosopher to be able to investigate all things. For if it is not the function of the philosopher, who is it who will inquire whether Socrates and Socrates seated are the same thing, or whether one thing has one contrary, or what contrariety is, or how many meanings it has? And similarly with all other such questions. Since, then, these are essential modifications of unity *qua*

1004ᵇ

unity and of being *qua* being, not *qua* numbers or lines or fire, it is clear that it belongs to this science to investigate both the essence of these concepts and their properties. And those who study these properties err not by leaving the sphere of philosophy,[1] but by forgetting that substance, of which they have no correct idea, is prior to these other things. For number *qua* number has peculiar attributes, such as oddness and evenness, commensurability and equality, excess and defect, and these belong to numbers either in themselves or in relation to one another. And similarly the solid and the motionless and that which is in motion and the weightless and that which has weight have other peculiar properties. So too there are certain properties peculiar to being as such, and it is about these that the philosopher has to investigate the truth.—An indication of this may be mentioned:—dialecticians and sophists assume the same guise as the philosopher, for sophistic is Wisdom which exists only in semblance, and dialecticians embrace all things in their dialectic, and being is common to all things; but evidently their dialectic embraces these subjects because these are proper to philosophy.—For sophistic and dialectic turn on the same class of things as philosophy, but this differs from dialectic in the nature of the faculty required and from sophistic in respect of the purpose of the philosophic life. Dialectic is merely critical where philosophy claims to know, and sophistic is what appears to be philosophy but is not.

Again, in the list of contraries one of the two columns is privative, and all contraries are reducible to being and non-being, and to unity and plurality, as for instance rest belongs to unity and movement to plurality. And nearly all thinkers agree that being and substance are composed of contraries; at least all name contraries as their first principles—some name odd and even,[2] some hot and cold,[3] some limit and the unlimited,[4] some love and strife.[5] And all the others as well are evidently reducible to unity and plurality (this reduction we must take for granted), and the principles stated by other thinkers fall entirely under these as their genera. It is obvious then from these considerations too that it belongs to one science to examine being *qua* being. For all things are either contraries or composed of contraries, and unity and plurality are the starting-points of all contraries. And these belong to one science, whether they have or have not one single meaning. Probably the truth is that they have not; yet even if "one" has several meanings, the other meanings will be related to the primary meaning (and similarly in the case of the contraries); even if being or unity is not a universal and the same in every instance or is not separable from the particular instances (as in fact it probably is not; the unity is in some cases that of common reference, in some cases that of serial succession). And for this

1005ᵃ

---

[1] *Sc.* which they do not do. [W.D.R.]
[2] The Pythagoreans. [W.D.R.]
[3] Parmenides in the "Way of Opinion." [W.D.R.]
[4] The Platonists. [W.D.R.]
[5] Empedocles. [W.D.R.]

reason it does not belong to the geometer to inquire what is contrariety or completeness or unity or being or the same or the other, but only to presuppose these concepts and reason from this starting-point.—Obviously then it is the work of one science to examine being *qua* being, and the attributes which belong to it *qua* being, and the same science will examine not only substances but also their attributes, both those above named and the concepts "prior" and "posterior," "genus" and "species," "whole" and "part," and the others of this sort.

3   We must state whether it belongs to one or to different sciences to inquire into the truths which are in mathematics called axioms, and into substance. Evidently, the inquiry into these also belongs to one science, and that the science of the philosopher; for these truths hold good for everything that is, and not for some special genus apart from others. And all men use them, because they are true of being *qua* being and each genus has being. But men use them just so far as to satisfy their purposes; that is, as far as the genus to which their demonstrations refer extends. Therefore since these truths clearly hold good for all things *qua* being (for this is what is common to them), to him who studies being *qua* being belongs the inquiry into these as well. And for this reason no one who is conducting a special inquiry tries to say anything about their truth or falsity—neither the geometer nor the arithmetician. Some natural philosophers indeed have done so, and their procedure was intelligible enough; for they thought that they alone were inquiring about the whole of nature and about being. But since there is one kind of thinker who is above even the natural philosopher (for nature is only one particular genus of being), the discussion of these truths also will belong to him whose inquiry is universal and deals with primary substance. Physics also is a kind of Wisdom, but it is not the first kind.—And the attempts of some of those who discuss the terms on which truth should be accepted, are due to a want of training in logic; for they should know these things already when they come to a special study, and not be inquiring into them while they are listening to lectures on it.

1005ᵇ   Evidently then it belongs to the philosopher, i.e. to him who is studying the nature of all substance, to inquire also into the principles of syllogism. But he who knows best about each genus must be able to state the most certain principles of his subject, so that he whose subject is existing things *qua* existing must be able to state the most certain principles of all things. This is the philosopher, and the most certain principle of all is that regarding which it is impossible to be mistaken; for such a principle must be both the best known (for all men may be mistaken about things which they do not know), and non-hypothetical. For a principle which every one must have who understands anything that is, is not a hypothesis; and that which every one must know who knows anything, he must already have when he comes to a special study. Evidently then such a principle is the most certain of all; which principle this is, let us proceed to say. It is, that the same attribute cannot at the same time belong and not belong to the same subject and in the same respect; we must presuppose, to guard against dialectical objections, any further qualifications which might be added. This, then, is the most certain of all principles, since it answers to the definition given above. For it is impossible for any one to believe the same thing to be and not to be, as some think Heraclitus says. For what a man says, he does not necessarily believe; and if it is impossible that contrary attributes should belong at the same time to the same subject (the usual qualifications must be presupposed in this premiss too), and if an opinion which contradicts another is contrary to it, obviously it is impossible for the same man at the same time to believe the same thing to be and not to be; for if a man were mistaken on this point he would have contrary opinions at the same time. It is for this reason that all who are carrying out a demonstration reduce it to this as an ultimate belief; for this is naturally the starting-point even for all the other axioms.

. . .

BOOK VI

1   We are seeking the principles and the causes of the things that are, and   1025^b obviously of them *qua* being. For, while there is a cause of health and of good condition, and the objects of mathematics have first principles and elements and causes, and in general every science which is ratiocinative or at all involves reasoning deals with causes and principles, more or less precise, all these sciences mark off some particular being—some genus, and inquire into this, but not into being simply nor *qua* being, nor do they offer any discussion of the essence of the things of which they treat; but starting from the essence—some making it plain to the senses, others assuming it as a hypothesis—they then demonstrate, more or less cogently, the essential attributes of the genus with which they deal. It is obvious, therefore, that such an induction yields no demonstration of substance or of the essence, but some other way of exhibiting it. And similarly the sciences omit the question whether the genus with which they deal exists or does not exist, because it belongs to the same kind of thinking to show what it is and that it is.

And since natural science, like other sciences, is in fact about one class of being, i.e. to that sort of substance which has the principle of its movement and rest present in itself, evidently it is neither practical nor productive. For in the case of things made the principle is in the maker—it is either reason or art or some faculty, while in the case of things done it is in the doer—viz. will, for that which is done and that which is willed are the same. Therefore, if all thought is either practical or productive or theoretical, physics must be a theoretical science, but it will theorize about such being as admits of being moved, and about substance-as-defined for the most part only as not separable from matter. Now, we must not fail to notice the mode of being of the essence and of its definition, for, without this, inquiry is but idle. Of things defined, i.e. of "whats," some are like "snub," and some like "concave." And these differ because "snub" is bound up with matter (for what is snub is a concave *nose*), while concavity is independent of perceptible matter. If then all natural things are analogous to the snub in their nature—e.g. nose, eye, face, flesh, bone, and, in general, animal; leaf, root, bark, and, in general, plant (for none of these can be defined without reference to movement—they always have matter), it is clear how we must seek and define the "what" in the case of natural objects, and also that it belongs to the student of nature to study even soul in a certain sense, i.e. so much of it as is not independent of matter.

1026ª

That physics, then, is a theoretical science, is plain from these considerations. Mathematics also, however, is theoretical; but whether its objects are immovable and separable from matter, is not at present clear; still, it is clear that *some* mathematical theorems *consider* them *qua* immovable and *qua* separable from matter. But if there is something which is eternal and immovable and separable, clearly the knowledge of it belongs to a theoretical science—not, however, to physics (for physics deals with certain movable things) nor to mathematics, but to a science prior to both. For physics deals with things which exist separately but are not immovable, and some parts of mathematics deal with things which are immovable but presumably do not exist separately, but as embodied in matter; while the first science deals with things which both exist separately and are immovable. Now all causes must be eternal, but especially these; for they are the causes that operate on so much of the divine as appears to us.[6] There must, then, be three theoretical philosophies, mathematics, physics, and what we may call theology, since it is obvious that if the divine is present anywhere, it is present in things of this sort. And the highest science must deal with the highest genus. Thus, while the theoretical sciences are more to be desired than the other sciences, this is more to be desired than the other theoretical sciences. For one might raise the question whether first philosophy is universal, or deals with one genus, i.e. some one kind of being; for not even the mathematical sciences are all alike in this respect—geometry and astronomy deal with a certain particular kind of thing, while universal mathematics applies alike to all. We answer that if there is no substance other than those which are formed by nature, natural science will be the first science; but if there is an immovable substance, the science of this must be prior and must be first philosophy, and universal in this way, because it is first. And it will belong to this to consider being *qua* being—both what it is and the attributes which belong to it *qua* being.

---

[6] I.e. produce the movements of the heavenly bodies. [W.D.R.]

QUESTIONS FOR STUDY AND DISCUSSION

1. What are the characteristics of the wise man, and what does this manifest concerning Aristotle's understanding of metaphysics?
2. What one point of attention does Aristotle identify in order to constitute wisdom as a single body of knowledge which is nevertheless open to all things?
3. What certainty does Aristotle attach to the principle of contradiction? How does the understanding of this principle in metaphysics contribute to the other sciences?
4. What is the meaning of Aristotle's distinction between "what it is" and "that it is"?
5. How does Aristotle relate metaphysics to both the study of all things and the study of the divine?

St. Augustine

ST. AUGUSTINE was born in 354 at Tagaste (now Algeria) of a pagan father and a Christian mother, St. Monica. His education was primarily literary and rhetorical. After completing his studies in Tagaste and Carthage he taught in both places before moving on to Rome and later Milan, where he held the municipal chair of Rhetoric. He was influenced by the writings of Cicero and by the teachings of the Manichees, but in 386 he was converted to Christianity by St. Ambrose, Bishop of Milan. After returning to teach in Tagaste, he was ordained to the priesthood, and in 395 he became Bishop of Hippo. The first great Christian philosopher, Augustine wrote many and varied works, including his *Confessions, The City of God,* and *On the Trinity.* He died in 430.

To God Through Body and Spirit

SERMON 241

(1) The belief in the resurrection of the dead is the distinctive belief of Christians. Christ, our Head, in His own person revealed this to us, that is, the resurrection of the dead, and He furnished us an example of this belief, so that His members might have hope for themselves in regard to that which had already happened to their Head. Yesterday I informed you that wise men of the pagans whom they call philosophers, and who were outstanding among their own people, had made a thorough investigation of nature and had come to know the Creator from His works. [Sermon 240] They did not hear the Prophets; they did not receive the Law of God; but God, though silent, spoke to them in a certain way through the works of this world, and the outward aspect of the world challenged them to seek its Maker; they could not be convinced that the heavens and the earth existed without a Creator. The blessed Apostle Paul speaks thus concerning these philosophers [Rom. 1. 18–21]: "The wrath of God is revealed from heaven against all ungodliness." What does "against all ungodliness" mean? That the wrath of God is revealed from heaven not only against the Jews who received the Law and offended the Giver of the Law, but also against

From pp. 254–56 of St. Augustine, *Sermons on the Liturgical Seasons,* translated by Sister Mary Sarah Muldowney, in *Fathers of the Church,* vol. XXXVIII. © 1959 by Catholic University Press. Reprinted by permission of the publisher.

all the ungodliness of the pagans. And, lest anyone should say: "Why is that, since they did not receive the Law?" he went on to add: "and wickedness of those men who in wickedness hold back the truth." Now you ask: "What truth? For they did not receive the Law; they did not hear the Prophet." Learn what truth [from the words of the Apostle]: "Seeing that what may be known about God is manifest to them." How was it manifested? Hear the answer: "For God has manifested it to them." If you persist in asking: "How did He manifest it to those to whom He did not give the Law?" hear the reply: "For since the creation of the world his invisible attributes are clearly seen . . . being understood through the things that are made." "For his invisible attributes," that is, the invisible attributes of God, "since the creation of the world," that is, since the world was made, "are clearly seen . . . being understood through the things that are made," that is, those attributes, being understood through the things of creation, are clearly seen. I am giving the words of the Apostle, interweaving my own commentary: "His everlasting power also and divinity," you supply "being understood, are clearly seen." "And so they are without excuse." Why "without excuse"? Because "although they knew God, they did not glorify him as God or give thanks." He did not say "although they did not know God" but "although they knew God."

(2) How did those philosophers know God? From the things which He had made. Question the beautiful earth; question the beautiful sea; question the beautiful air, diffused and spread abroad; question the beautiful heavens; question the arrangement of the constellations; question the sun brightening the day by its effulgence; question the moon, tempering by its splendor the darkness of the ensuing night; question the living creatures that move about in the water, those that remain on land, and those that flit through the air, their souls hidden but their bodies in view, visible things which are to be ruled and invisible spirits doing the ruling;—question all these things and all will answer: "Behold and see! We are beautiful." Their beauty is their acknowledgment. Who made these beautiful transitory things unless it be the unchanging Beauty?

Finally, these philosophers, in order to be able to understand God, the Creator of the whole world, in man himself, investigated the two parts of man: his soul and his body. They investigated what they themselves possessed; they saw the body, they did not see the soul; but they saw the body only by means of the soul. For they saw through the eyes; but what looked out through the windows [of the eyes] was within them. Besides, when the dweller departs, the house lies empty; when that which guided withdraws, that which was guided falls; and since it falls, it is called a fallen body or a corpse. Are not those eyes unimpaired? They are wide open, but they see nothing; the ears are there, but the hearer has departed; the organ of speech remains, but the music which stirred it has gone. Therefore, the philosophers investigated these two parts of man, the body which is seen and the soul which is not seen, and they came to the conclusion that what is not seen is better than what is seen, that the invisible soul is superior and the visible body inferior. They saw these things; they considered them; they discussed both parts and they found that both parts of man were subject to change, that the body changed through the various stages of life, through the breaking down and the building up of tissues, through refreshment and wasting away, through life and through death. They turned their attention to the soul which they had recognized as undoubtedly superior and at which they marvelled even though it was invisible. They found that it, too, was subject to change, that now it wished and again it did not wish; that now it knew and again it did not know; that now it remembered and again it forgot; that now it feared and again it dared; that now it advanced toward wisdom and again it dropped back into foolishness. They saw that it, too, was subject to change; they passed on from it, also; they sought something which would not be subject to change.

(3) Thus, therefore, the philosophers came to the knowledge of God through the things which He had made. "But they did not glorify him as God or give thanks," says the Apostle, "but became vain in their reasonings, and their senseless minds have been darkened. For while professing to be wise, they have become fools." By arrogating to themselves what they had received, they lost what they possessed. Professing to be, as it were, great men, they became as fools. And what did they come to? The Apostle goes on: "They have changed the glory of the incorruptible God for an image made like to corruptible man." He refers to idols. And it was not enough to make an image like to man and to abandon the Maker for the likeness of His work; that was not enough. What else did they make? Images like to "birds and four-footed beasts and creeping things." They, as it were, great wise men, made all those dumb beasts and irrational objects as gods for themselves. I censured you when you adored the image of a man. What shall I do when you adore the image of a dog, the image of a serpent, the image of a crocodile? They descended even to those depths. Falling just as low as they had been carried aloft in their investigations, they were sunk in the depths, for the greater the height from which an object falls, the more deeply is it submerged.

QUESTIONS FOR STUDY AND DISCUSSION

1. What openings do the philosophers find for initiating some knowledge of God?
2. Which elements need clarification in order to strengthen these approaches to God?

St. Thomas Aquinas

ST. THOMAS AQUINAS was born in 1225 at Roccasecca of a noble Italian family. His early schooling was at the monastery of Monte Cassino, and in 1239 he went to the University of Naples; while a student there he entered the Dominican order. In Paris he studied philosophy and theology under Albert the Great and from 1248 to 1952 he taught with him at the University of Cologne. He wrote most of his works while at the Studium Generale of his order at Rome and later as a professor at the University of Paris. His most notable writings are *Summa Contra Gentiles, Summa Theologica, Commentaries* on Aristotle and on the Scriptures, and *Disputed Questions.* Through these he developed a synthesis of the newly introduced Aristotelian thought with the Platonism of the Christian West. Aquinas died in 1274 and was canonized in 1323.

Metaphysics and the Sciences

QUESTION 5. Concerning the division of speculative science.

ARTICLE 3. Whether mathematics considers objects that are without motion and matter?

. . .

Response. For the clarification of this question, we must know in what manner the intellect by its own operation is able to abstract. Therefore, according to the Philosopher (III *De Anima*), we should know that the operation of the intellect is twofold. By one, which is called the intelligence of indivisibles, it knows of anything what it is. By another operation, however, it composes and divides, as by formulating affirmative or negative enunciations, and these same two operations correspond to two aspects in regard to things. The first operation, indeed, regards the nature itself of the thing, according as a certain object of the intellect acquires a certain grade in being, whether it is a complete thing, as some whole, or incomplete, as a part or an accident. The second operation looks to the existence of the

From pp. 148–86 of St. Thomas Aquinas, *Commentary on the Trinity of Boethius* (Question 5, Articles 3 and 4; Question 6, Articles 1 and 2), in *The Trinity and the Unicity of the Intellect,* translated by Sister M. Rose Emmanuella Brennan, S.N.J.M. Copyright 1946 by B. Herder Book Company. This selection was edited by George F. McLean, with permission of the translator, and is complete except for the objections and their answers.

thing, which, indeed, results from an aggregation of principles in composites, or is concomitant with the simple nature of the thing in the case of simple substances. And because the truth of the intellect resides in this, that it is conformed to a thing, it is evident that according to this second operation the intellect is not able truly to abstract what, on the part of the thing, is joined to it, because in abstracting is signified that there is a separation according to the very existence of the thing, just as if I should abstract man from whiteness by saying: "Man is not white," and should signify separation in the thing. Whence if, in reality, man and whiteness are not separate, the intellect will be false. By this operation, therefore, the intellect cannot truly abstract except from things that are on the part of the object separate, as when it is said: "Man is not an ass." But, according to the first operation of the intellect, it is possible to abstract things which on the part of the object are not separate, not indeed all, but some.

For since everything is intelligible inasmuch as it is in act, as is said in X *Metaph.,* it must necessarily be that a nature or quiddity of a thing is known either according as it is a certain act (as happens in the case of forms and simple substances); or according to that which is its act (as composite substances are intelligible through their forms); or according to what is in place of act (as prime matter is known through its relationship to form, and a vacuum through privation of any objects located with it); and this connection with act is that by which each nature determines its definition.

Therefore when that by which the intelligibility of a nature of a thing is constituted, by which the very nature is understood, has an order and a dependence in regard to something else, then it is certain that such a nature cannot be understood apart from that other, whether it is joined to it in the same way as the part is joined to the whole (as a foot cannot be understood without comprehension of an animal, because that by reason of which foot has the meaning of a foot depends on that by which an animal is an animal); or whether it is united in the same way as form is joined to matter, as a part to another part, or accident to subject (as it is not possible to understand pug nose without understanding nose); or whether it is a separate thing (as "father" cannot be understood without an understanding of "son," although these relations are found in diverse things).

But if one thing does not depend upon another according as it constitutes the meaning of the nature, then the one can be abstracted from the other by the intellect so that it is understood without it. This is true only if they are separate in reality, as man and stone, but also if in reality they are joined, whether in the manner of part and whole (as a letter can be understood without the syllable, and the animal without a foot, but not conversely): or whether, indeed, this conjunction is after the manner of that by which form is joined to matter and accident to subject (as white can be understood without reference to man, and conversely).

So, therefore, the intellect distinguishes one from another differently according to either of these operations; because, according to the operation by which it composes and divides, it distinguishes one from another by this fact, namely, that it understands that the one is not in the other. But in the operation by which it understands what a thing is, it distinguishes one from another, while it understands what the thing is, not understanding anything concerning the other, or what may be with it, or what may be separate from it. Whence this manner of distinction is not properly termed separation, but the first type only. This kind of distinction, however, is rightly called abstraction in so far as the things of which one is understood without the other are objectively one and the same thing.

For an animal is not said to be abstracted from a stone, if by the intellect an animal is understood apart from a stone. Hence, since abstraction cannot take place, properly speaking, unless there is conjunction of things objectively, according to two modes of conjunction referred to above, namely, according as part is joined to whole, or form to matter, abstraction is twofold: one sort by which form is abstracted from matter; the other, by which the whole is abstracted from its parts. Now a form can be abstracted from matter if the intelligibility of its essence does not depend on matter. But a form cannot be abstracted by the intellect from that matter upon which the intelligibility of its essence depends. Therefore, since all accidents are compared to substances as forms to matter, and the nature of any accident is to depend upon substance, it is impossible for such a form to be separated from substance. But accidents are associated with substance in a certain order, for quantity is primarily related to it, then qualities, then passion and motion.

Therefore quantity can be understood in matter before there is understanding of the sensible qualities on account of which it is termed sensible matter. And so, according to its essential nature, quantity does not depend on sensible matter, but on intelligible matter only. For accidents having been removed, substances are comprehensible only by the intellect, since sensible potencies do not attain to the comprehension of substances. And concerning such abstractions is mathematics, which considers quantity and those things that follow upon quantity, such as figure and the like.

The whole, indeed, cannot be abstracted from just any parts. For there are certain parts upon which the meaning of the whole depends, when it is a whole of a certain kind because composed of such and such parts, as a syllable is related to letters, and a mixture to elements. Such parts are said to be parts of the species or form since without them the whole cannot be understood, but they are in the very definition of it. There are certain parts which are accidental to the whole as such, as, for instance, the semicircle is related to the circle. For, in the case of a circle, it happens that it can be divided into two equal parts, or even more: but in the case of a triangle it does not happen by chance that three lines are designated in respect to it, because by this very fact a triangle is a triangle. Similarly it pertains to a man *per se* that in him is found a rational soul and a body composed of the four elements. Since without these parts man cannot be understood, they must be posited in the very definition of man. Hence they are parts of the species or form. But finger, foot, and hand, and other parts of this sort add to that contained in the idea of man; wherefore the meaning of man does not essentially depend upon these since he can be understood without them. It matters not whether he has feet or not: as long as there is supposed the union of a rational soul and a body composed of the four elements properly commingled, which such a form requires, he is a man.

We call these parts of matter, which are not contained in the definition of the whole, but conversely suppose it; and so all signate parts are related to man as *this* soul and *this* body, *this* mouth, and the like. These are material parts which are, indeed, parts of the essence of Socrates and of Plato, but not of man inasmuch as he is man: and therefore man can be abstracted by the intellect from these parts, and such an abstraction is that of the universal from the particular.

Thus there are two abstractive operations of the intellect. One corresponds to the union of form with matter or accident with subject, and this is abstraction of form from sensible matter. The other corresponds to the union of whole or parts, and to this corresponds the abstraction of the universal from the particular and this is abstraction of the whole, in which some nature is considered absolutely, according to its essential meaning separated from all those parts which are not specific, but accidental.

Moreover, there are not any other abstractions different from these, in which part is abstracted from the whole or matter from form, because the part cannot be abstracted from the whole by the intellect, if it is one of the parts of matter in the definition of which the whole is posited: or, because it can exist without the whole if the part is specific, such as, a line without the triangle, or a letter without the syllable, or an element without the mixture. But, in the case of things which can exist separately, the process is one of separation rather than of abstraction. In like manner also, when we say that form has been abstracted from matter, we do not understand this of the substantial form, because the substantial form and the matter corresponding to it are mutually dependent, and one cannot be understood without the other, because the proper act must be in its own proper matter. Rather, this is understood of accidental form, namely, quantity and figure, from which sensible matter cannot be abstracted by the intellect, since sensible qualities cannot be understood without a prior comprehension of quantity, as is clear in the matter of surface quality and color: nor can a thing even be understood as a subject of motion unless it is so understood as possessing quantity.

Substance, however, which is the intelligible matter of quantity, can exist without quantity. Hence, to consider a substance apart from quantity pertains more to the nature of separation than to that of abstraction.

Thus, therefore, in the operation of the intellect, a threefold distinction is found. 1. According to the operation of the intellect as it composes and divides, which is properly called separation; and this mode relates to divine science or metaphysics. 2. According to the operation which formulates the quiddities of things; and this is abstraction of form from sensible matter, which pertains to mathematics. 3. According to the same operation, the abstraction of the universal from the particular; and this concerns even physics and is common to all the sciences, because in every science there is a disregarding of the accidental and a retaining of that which is *per se.*

Certain persons, not understanding the difference of the last two from the first, fell into error, so that they held mathematics and the universals to exist as separated from sensible things, as did the Pythagoreans and the followers of Plato.

. . .

ARTICLE 4. Whether divine science treats of those things that are without matter and motion?

. . .

Response. In order to clarify this question, it is necessary to know which one of the sciences ought to be called "divine science." It is to be noted, therefore, that any science which considers a particular class of things as its subject it must consider the principles of that class since science is not perfected except through knowledge of principles, as is stated by the Philosopher in the beginning of the *Physics.* But there are two kinds of principles.

1. There are certain principles that are in themselves complete natures, yet principles of other things, just as the heavenly bodies are in a certain way principles of inferior bodies, and simple bodies of those that are mixed. Consequently these things are considered by the sciences which treat of them not only as principles, but as things in themselves. On this account not only is there study of them in sciences that consider that of which they are principles, but they have also a distinct science of their own. Thus there is a certain branch of natural science that deals with heavenly bodies, apart from that branch in which inferior bodies are considered, and about the elements there is some science besides that which treats of the mixed bodies.

2. But there are certain other principles that are not complete natures in themselves, but are only principles of natures, as unity of number, and a point of a line, and form and matter of a physical body. Consequently principles of this kind are not dealt with except in a science that treats of the things of which they are the principles.

Now, as there are certain principles belonging to any determined class (or genus) and extending to all the principles of that class, so also all beings, according as they communicate in being, have certain principles that are the principles of all beings. These principles can be called common for two reasons, as Avicenna says in his *Sufficientia.*

1. In one way, by predication, as when I say that "form" is common to all forms because it is predicated of any form whatever.

2. In another way, because of a relation of causality, as we say that the sun, numerically one, is the principle of all things subject to generation.

Of all beings there are, then, common principles, not only according to this first mode, which the Philosopher (II *Metaph.*) calls having the same principles "according to analogy," but also according to another mode, as there are certain things numerically the same, existing as principles of all things, for example, principles of accidents are reduced to substances, and principles of corruptible substances to substances that are incorruptible. Thus in a certain grade and order all beings are reduced to certain principles. And because what is the principle of being for all things ought to be in the strictest sense being, as is said in II *Metaph.*, principles of this kind should be most complete, and on this account they must be supremely in act and have nothing, or the very least of potentiality, because act is prior to and more powerful than potentiality, as is said in X *Metaph.* Therefore these principles must be without matter, which is in potency, and without motion, which is the act of that existing in potency. Of such an order are divine things; because, if the divine anywhere exists, it exists above all in an immaterial and immobile nature, as is said in VI *Metaph.*

Thus, therefore, can divine things be considered in a twofold manner, because they are the principles of all being, and yet they are natures complete in themselves; in one way, for as much as they are the principles common to all beings, and according to another mode, inasmuch as they are certain things in themselves.

But first principles of this kind, although they are in themselves most knowable, yet in relation to our intellect they are as the light of the sun to the eyes of owls, as is said in II *Metaph.* Hence by the light of natural reason we are not able to attain to them except as we are led to them through their effects; and thus the philosophers arrived at a knowledge of them, as is said in Rom. 1:20: "The invisible things of Him, from the creation of the world, are clearly seen, being understood by the things that are made."

Therefore divine things are not dealt with by philosophers except in so far as they are the principles of all things; and hence they are considered in that science in which things common to all beings are studied, which has being inasmuch as it is being as its subject; and this science is termed among the philosophers "divine science." However, there is another manner of knowing things of this sort, not as they are made manifest through their effects, but according as they manifest themselves. And this manner the Apostle alludes to in I Cor. 2:11 f.: "The things also that are of God no man knoweth, but the Spirit of God. Now we have received not the spirit of this world, but the Spirit that is of God, that we may understand"; and (2:10), "To us God hath revealed them, by His Spirit."

And in this way divine things are considered according as they subsist in themselves, and not only in so far as they are the principles of all things. Thus theology, or divine science, is twofold. According to one approach, divine things are studied, not so much as the subject of the science but as the principle of its subject matter, and of this kind is that theology which the philosophers sought to master, which, according to another name, is called metaphysics.

But of another sort is that theology which considers divine things on their own account as the very subject matter of its science, and this is the theology taught in Sacred Scripture. Both types of theology are concerned with the things that exist separate from matter and from motion, but in different ways, according as a thing can exist separate from matter and motion in either of two ways.

According to one mode, a thing is called separate if by reason of its very nature it can in no way exist in matter and motion: and in this manner God and the angels are said to be separate from matter and motion.

In another way that can be called separate which is not by its very nature associated with matter and motion but can exist apart from both matter and motion, though sometimes it is found in matter. Thus being and substance, potency and act, are separated from matter and motion because, according to their very existence, they do not depend upon matter and motion, as do the objects of mathematics which never can have existence apart from matter, although they can be understood without sensible matter.

Philosophical theology treats of things separated in the second way, as its subject and of things separated in the first way as the principles of its subject. But the theology of Sacred Scripture treats of separate things in the first mode, as its own proper subjects, although in this science some things that are in matter and in motion may be considered because the manifestation of divine things requires this.

.　　.　　.

QUESTION 6. Concerning the modes attributed to speculative science.

Next, inquiry is made concerning the modes which Boethius has attributed to speculative science. In regard to this matter, four things are to be considered:

1. Whether in regard to the things of nature one proceeds by way of reason (*rationabiliter*) and in regard to mathematics, by way of learning (*disciplinabiliter*), and in regard to divine things, by way of intellect (*intelligibiliter*).

2. Whether in considering divine things imagination must be altogether relinquished.

3. Whether our intellect can contemplate the divine form or essence itself.

4. Whether this can be attained by way of any of the speculative sciences.

ARTICLE 1. Whether we ought to proceed by reason in regard to the natural sciences, by learning in regard to mathematics, and by intellect in regard to divine science?

.　　.　　.

Response to the first part. I answer that, in regard to the first part, it must be said that the process by which one advances in the sciences is called "rational" in a threefold manner.

1. In the first place, on the part of the principles by which we proceed, as when we advance to prove something by making use of beings of reason, that is, genus and species, and opposition, and concepts of this sort which logicians consider. And so a method is called rational when in any science use is made of the propositions that logic provides; namely, according as we make use of logic so far as it has a teaching function in relation to the other sciences. But this method of procedure cannot properly be said to be that of any particular science, for in them error will arise unless we proceed from certain principles belonging properly to each. However, this method is rightly applied in metaphysics and logic since it is common to each science, and they have, in a certain manner, the same subject matter.

2. In another sense we say that procedure is rational on account of the end which terminates the process. The ultimate goal, toward which the investigation of reason should lead, is the understanding of principles, in which we resolve our judgments. But when this is the result, it is called, not a reasonable process or a natural proof, but a demonstration. When, however, rational investigation does not attain to the ultimate goal, but stops in the investigation, when, namely, two possible paths still lie open to the investigator (which happens when one makes use of probable arguments which are adapted to produce opinion and faith, but not science), then rational investigation is distinguished from demonstration. And by this method we can proceed rationally in any science at all, as from probabilities the road is prepared for necessary conclusions. And this is another mode of logic made use of in the demonstrative sciences, not indeed as teaching, but as an instrument. According to these two ways a method is called "rational" from rational science, for logic, which is a rational science, is used in these two ways in demonstrative sciences, as the Commentator says in I *Physic.*

3. In a third way a method may be called rational in relation to a rational power, inasmuch as in the method we follow the manner proper to the rational soul in knowing; and under this aspect the rational method is proper to science. For natural science in its methods of proceeding observes the method proper to the rational soul in two ways.

a) As the rational soul receives from sensible things, which are more knowable as far as we are concerned, its knowledge of intelligible things, which in their own nature are more knowable (as I *Physic.* declares), so natural science proceeds from those things that are more knowable to us, but less knowable in their own nature as is evident in I *Physics.* Furthermore, the demonstration by means of a sign or effect is that most used in natural science.

b) In the second place, it is proper to reason to advance from one thing to another, and this is observed in the natural sciences where from the knowledge of one thing it proceeds to knowledge of another as from knowledge of an effect to that of a cause. And this procedure is not from one thing to another according to reason (or definition) alone which would not be according to the thing itself, as if from "animal" we advanced to the concept of "man." In mathematical science, indeed, procedure is through those things only that are the essences of things, since these sciences demonstrate only through formal cause. So there is in them no demonstration of one thing by means of another thing, but through the proper definition of that thing. For, although there are certain demonstrations made concerning a circle by means of a triangle, or conversely, this is only in so far as in the circle there is the triangle potentially, or conversely. But in natural science in which demonstration is made through extrinsic causes, one thing is proved by means of another thing altogether extrinsic to it. So the method of reason is especially observed by natural science and hence, among all others, natural science is most in conformity with the intellect of man. A rational mode of procedure, therefore, is attributed to natural science, not because it applies to it alone, but because it belongs to it particularly.

.　　.　　.

Response to the second part. To the second part it must be said that to proceed "by way of learning" is attributed to mathematics, not because it alone proceeds "by way of learning," but because this mode applies to it particularly. Therefore, since "to learn" means nothing else than to receive knowledge from another, we say that we proceed "by way of learning" when our advance leads us to certain knowledge, which is called science; and this occurs most perfectly in the mathematical sciences. For, although mathematics holds the middle place between natural science and divine science, it is more certain than either of these others. It is more certain than natural science because its investigation is freed from matter and motion, whereas the considerations of natural science treat of matter and motion. From the fact that natural science is concerned with what is material, it is dependent upon many things such as the consideration of matter and form, and of the material dispositions and properties consequent upon form as found in matter. Wherever it is necessary to consider many things in order to come to a knowledge of a thing, cognition is thereby the more difficult. Hence it is said in I *Poster.* that a science which is attained by adding on is less certain, as geometry in comparison with arithmetic. Indeed since the considerations of natural science are concerned with things in motion, and with those things that have no uniform relationships, knowledge of it is the less certain, because its demonstrations are for the greater part based upon something which is sometimes different.

Therefore, in proportion as any science approaches to a consideration of singulars, as do the sciences of operation, such as medicine, alchemy, and ethics, it is the less capable of possessing certitude, both because of the multitude of things that must be considered and whose omission will lead to error, and also because of the variability of the facts themselves.

Moreover, the procedure of mathematics is a more certain one than that of divine science, because those things that are the objects of divine science are farther removed from sensible things, from which our knowledge has its origin. This is true both as regards separated substances (for what we know by way of our senses gives us only inadequate knowledge of these objects), and as regards those things that are common to all beings (and so are furthest removed from those particular things that belong to sense knowledge). But the objects of mathematics are such as come under the senses and they are the subjects of our imagination, such as lines, figures, number, and the like. Hence the human intellect, receiving its knowledge from phantasms, the more easily and more certainly achieves knowledge in regard to these things than things purely intelligible, or even of such things as the quiddity of a substance, potency, act, and the like. So it is evident that mathematical inquiry is both easier and more certain than that of natural science or theology, and much easier and more certain than any of the practical or operative sciences. Therefore it is said to proceed by way of learning. This is what Ptolemy says in the beginning of *Almagest:* "The other kinds of speculation one should call opinion rather than scientific knowledge: theology, on account of its hidden and incomprehensible character; and physics, on account of the instability and obscurity of its matter. Mathematics alone will grant to the inquirer firm and abiding certitude, as a demonstration through indubitable procedures."

.   .   .

Response to the third part. It is answered that, just as to proceed by way of reason is attributed to natural philosophy because in it the method of reason is especially observed, so to proceed by way of intellect is attributed to divine science since in it an intellectual method is especially employed. Moreover, reason differs from intellect as multitude from unity. Therefore Boethius says in VI *De consolatione* that reason is related to intellect as time is to eternity, and as a circle is to its center. For it is the nature of reason to be concerned about many things and from them to establish some one, simple knowledge. Whence it is that Dionysius says (*De div. nom.,* chap. 7) that because souls have the power of reason they approach the truth of existing things from various directions. In this respect they are inferior to the angels; but as they resolve many things into one concept, after a certain manner they become the equals of the angels.

Conversely, intellect considers first unified and simple truth, and in it achieves its knowledge of a whole multitude of truths, as God, by knowing His own essence, knows all things.

Therefore Dionysius says (*ibid.*) that the minds of the angels have intellectuality inasmuch as they understand in a unified way the intelligible essences of divine truths.

Thus it is evident that the consideration of reason terminates in intellection (or understanding) by way of analysis, in which from many facts the reason gathers one, simple truth. And again, the intellectual consideration is the beginning of rational thinking in its way of composition and of invention, since intellect grasps many things in one. Hence that consideration, which is the terminus, or goal, of all human ratiocination is supremely intellectual. Moreover, the entire consideration of reason in all the sciences following the way of analysis has for its end the knowledge of divine science.

For sometimes, as has been said, the reason proceeds from one thing to another in the order of reality, as when demonstration is made through external causes or effects. This it does by a method of composing when the process is from causes to effects, as it were, analyzing them when the process is from effects to causes, since causes are simpler than effects and more immovable and uniformly permanent. The ultimate goal of this method of reduction is attained, therefore, when one has arrived at the supreme and simplest causes, which are separated substances.

But sometimes the process is from one thing to another, according to reason, as when the advance is made according to intrinsic causes. This is by a method of composing when from most universal forms we proceed to consider those more particular. But it is a process of resolving when the direction is the opposite one (particular to universal), since the more universal is the simpler. Now, the most universal things are those common to all beings. Hence the final goal in this process of reduction is the consideration of being and of the things that are attributes of being inasmuch as it is being.

However, these are the things that divine science treats of, as was said above, that is, separated substances and those things common to all beings. Hence it is apparent that its consideration is supremely intellectual. And so it also follows that it confers principles upon the other sciences, since intellectual consideration is the starting point of rational consideration, on which account it is called first philosophy. Yet it is studied after physics and other sciences, since intellectual speculation is the terminus of rational consideration, and consequently is called metaphysics or, as it were, *transphysica,* because it is attained by further process of analysis after (transcending) physics.

. . .

ARTICLE 2. Whether in speculation on divine things imagination must be altogether relinquished?

. . .

Response. I reply that it must be said that in any kind of cognition two things are to be considered: a beginning and an end or goal. The beginning, indeed, pertains to apprehension, but the end pertains to judgment, for the cognition is there perfected. Now the beginning of any of our cognitions is in sensation, because from apprehension of sensation arises apprehension of the phantasm, which is moved by sense, as the Philosopher says. From this then arises intellectual apprehension in us, since phantasms are to the intellective soul as objects, as is said in III *De Anima.* But the terminus, or goal, of cognition is not uniformly the same; for it is sometimes in sensation, sometimes in imagination, and sometimes in the intellect alone. When the properties and accidents of a thing, which are had by the senses, adequately disclose the nature of the thing, the judgment regarding the truth of the thing, which the intellect makes, ought to conform to what the senses reveal concerning it. Of this order are all things of the natural world which are determined to sensible matter. Hence, in natural science, cognition should be terminated in the senses since we judge of natural things in accordance with what sense experience manifests about them, as III *De coelo et mundo* declares. He who disregards the data of the senses in regard to natural things falls into error. And those things are "natural" which are associated with sensible matter and motion both in their existence and in consideration of them.

But in the case of certain other things the judgment of them does not depend upon the data perceived by means of the senses, because, although according to their existence they are in sensible matter, according to their definite nature they are abstracted from sensible matter. The judgment about anything is made chiefly according to the definite nature of the thing: but because, according to this definite nature, certain things do not abstract from matter altogether, but only from sensible matter and from sensible conditions, there still remains something imaginable. Therefore, in regard to such objects, judgment should be made according to that which imagination demonstrates; and of this order are mathematical objects. In mathematics, indeed, cognition as regards judgment should terminate in the imagination, not in the senses, because mathematical judgment goes beyond the apprehension of the senses. Wherefore a judgment made concerning a mathematical line is not the same as that concerning a line that is sensible. For example, that a straight line touches a sphere at a point only, which applies to an abstract (separate) straight line, but not to a straight line in matter, as is said in I *De Anima.*

But there are certain other things surpassing what falls under the senses and what belongs to imagination, as do those altogether independent of matter, both as to their existence and as to their consideration. Hence cognition of them, as to judgment, ought to be terminated neither at imagination nor at sensation.

Nevertheless we arrive at cognition of these things from the things comprehended by the senses or by imagination, either by way of causality, as when from an effect we know a cause (though this cause is not commensurate to its effect, but excels it), or by way of transcendence or negation when we separate from such things all those things which senses or imagination apprehend. These modes of arriving at knowledge of divine things from those that are sensible, Dionysius set forth in his book *De divinis nominibus.*

Therefore, in regard to divine things, we can use both sense and imagination inasmuch as they are principles or starting points of our speculation, but not as ends or goals; judging to be divine the very things which sense and imagination gave us initial apprehension of. However, to be led to something means to be terminated [or limited] by it. Hence in divine science we should not go either to the sense or to the imagination; though in mathematics we go to the imagination, but not on sensation; whereas in regard to natural things we go to the senses. Thus they err who maintain that in the three divisions of speculation the procedure is uniform.

· · ·

QUESTIONS FOR STUDY AND DISCUSSION

1. How do differences in things themselves lay the foundation for distinguishing between the physical and mathematical sciences?
2. How do differences in the operations of the mind contribute to the distinction of metaphysics from the other sciences and allow metaphysics to attain the special reality, unity, and universality of its proper subject matter?
3. How does St. Thomas distinguish between two kinds of theology, one of which is metaphysics, when both treat of divine things? What task does this indicate for philosophy concerning things that can be known from revelation?
4. How do the processes of analysis and synthesis cooperate in the gradual elaboration of that unity of insight and universality of application that characterize metaphysics?
5. In what way are the different levels of science related to the different human faculties for knowledge?

The Names of God

BOOK I: GOD

CHAPTER 30. The names that can be predicated of God.

[1] From what we have said we can further consider what it is possible to say or not to say of God, what is said of Him alone, and also what is said of Him and other things together.

[2] Since it is possible to find in God every perfection of creatures, but in another and more eminent way, whatever names unqualifiedly designate a perfection without defect are predicated of God and of other things: for example, goodness, wisdom, being, and the like. But when any name expresses such perfections along with a mode that is proper to a creature, it

From pp. 139–41 of *On the Truth of the Catholic Faith*, Book I, by St. Thomas Aquinas, translated by Anton C. Pegis. Copyright © 1955 by Doubleday & Company, Inc. Reprinted by permission of the publisher.

can be said of God only according to likeness and metaphor. According to metaphor, what belongs to one thing is transferred to another, as when we say that a man is a *stone* because of the hardness of his intellect. Such names are used to designate the species of a created thing, for example, *man* and *stone;* for to each species belongs its own mode of perfection and being. The same is true of whatever names designate the properties of things, which are caused by the proper principles of their species. Hence, they can be said of God only metaphorically. But the names that express such perfections along with the mode of supereminence with which they belong to God are said of God alone. Such names are the *highest good, the first being,* and the like.

[3]   I have said that some of the aforementioned names signify a perfection without defect. This is true with reference to that which the name was imposed to signify; for as to the mode of signification, every name is defective. For by means of a name we express things in the way in which the intellect conceives them. For our intellect, taking the origin of its knowledge from the senses, does not transcend the mode which is found in sensible things, in which the form and the subject of the form are not identical owing to the composition of form and matter. Now, a simple form is indeed found among such things, but one that is imperfect because it is not subsisting; on the other hand, though a subsisting subject of a form is found among sensible things, it is not simple but rather concreted. Whatever our intellect signifies as subsisting, therefore, it signifies in concretion; but what it signifies as simple, it signifies, not as *that which is,* but as *that by which something is.* As a result, with reference to the mode of signification there is in every name that we use an imperfection, which does not befit God, even though the thing signified in some eminent way does befit God. This is clear in the name *goodness* and *good.* For *goodness* has signification as something not subsisting, while *good* has signification as something concreted. And so with reference to the mode of signification no name is fittingly applied to God; this is done only with reference to that which the name has been imposed to signify. Such names, therefore, as Dionysius teaches, can be both affirmed and denied of God. They can be affirmed because of the meaning of the name; they can be denied because of the mode of signification.

[4]   Now, the mode of supereminence in which the above-mentioned perfections are found in God can be signified by names used by us only through negation, as when we say that God is *eternal* or *infinite,* or also through a relation of God to other things, as when He is called the *first cause* or the *highest good.* For we cannot grasp what God is, but only what He is not and how other things are related to Him, as is clear from what we said above.

1. What creates the difficulty involved in speaking validly about God?
2. What basic distinction is introduced here in order to save what is valid and sort out what is not?
3. This passage speaks of knowledge through negation and relation. Is there any positive content to our knowledge of God?
4. What is the special importance of negation in this knowledge? Must it be used sometimes or always?

The Personal in Creation—
Immateriality and Freedom

BOOK II: CREATION

CHAPTER 45. The true first cause of the distinction of things.

[1]   From the foregoing it can be shown what is truly the first cause of the distinction of things.

[2]   Since every agent intends to introduce its likeness into its effect, in the measure that its effect can receive it, the agent does this the more perfectly as it is the more perfect itself; obviously, the hotter a thing is, the hotter its effect, and the better the craftsman, the more perfectly does he put into matter the form of his art. Now, God is the most perfect agent. It was His prerogative, therefore, to induce His likeness into created things most perfectly, to a degree consonant with the nature of created being. But created things cannot attain to a perfect likeness to God according to only one species of creature. For, since the cause transcends the effect, that which is in the cause, simply and unitedly, exists in the effect in composite and multiple fashion—unless the effect attain to the species of the cause; which cannot be said in this case, because no creature can be equal to God. The presence of multiplicity and variety among created things was therefore necessary that a perfect likeness to God be found in them according to their manner of being.

[3]   Moreover, just as things made from matter lie in the passive potentiality of matter, so things made by an agent must exist in the active power of the agent. The passive potentiality of matter, however, would not be

From pp. 136–52 of *On the Truth of the Catholic Faith,* Book II, by St. Thomas Aquinas, translated by James F. Anderson. Copyright © 1956 by Doubleday & Company, Inc. Reprinted by permission of the publisher.

completely actualized if only one of the things to which matter is in potentiality were made from it. Therefore, if an agent whose power extends to a number of effects were to produce only one of them, its power would not be as fully actualized as when it produces several. Now, by the fact that the active power is actualized the effect receives the likeness of the agent. Hence, there would not be a perfect likeness of God in the universe if all things were of one grade of being. For this reason, then, is there distinction among created things: that, by being many, they may receive God's likeness more perfectly than by being one.

[4] Then, too, a thing approaches to God's likeness the more perfectly as it resembles Him in more things. Now, goodness is in God, and the outpouring of goodness into other things. Hence, the creature approaches more perfectly to God's likeness if it is not only good, but can also act for the good of other things, than if it were good only in itself; that which both shines and casts light is more like the sun than that which only shines. But no creature could act for the benefit of another creature unless plurality and inequality existed in created things. For the agent is distinct from the patient and superior to it. In order that there might be in created things a perfect representation of God, the existence of diverse grades among them was therefore necessary.

[5] Furthermore, a plurality of goods is better than a single finite good, since they contain the latter and more besides. But all goodness possessed by creatures is finite, falling short of the infinite goodness of God. Hence, the universe of creatures is more perfect if there are many grades of things than if there were but one. Now, it befits the supreme good to make what is best. It was therefore fitting that God should make many grades of creatures.

[6] Again, the good of the species is greater than the good of the individual, just as the formal exceeds that which is material. Hence, a multiplicity of species adds more to the goodness of the universe than a multiplicity of individuals in one species. It therefore pertains to the perfection of the universe that there be not only many individuals, but that there be also diverse species of things, and, consequently, diverse grades in things.

[7] Whatever acts by intellect, moreover, represents in the thing made the species present in its intellect, for thus does an agent that causes things by art produce his like. Now, as we have already shown [*SCG* II, 23], God, acting as an intellectual agent and not by natural necessity, made the creature. Hence, the species present in God's intellect is represented in the creature made by Him. But an intellect which understands many things is not adequately represented in only one thing. Therefore, since the divine intellect knows many things, as was proved in Book I [*SCG* I, 49], it represents itself more perfectly if it produces many creatures of all grades than if it had produced only one.

[8]   But there is more. The highest degree of perfection should not be lacking in a work made by the supremely good workman. But the good of order among diverse things is better than any of the members of an order, taken by itself. For the good of order is formal in respect to each member of it, as the perfection of the whole in relation to the parts. It was not fitting, therefore, that God's work should lack the good of order. And yet, without the diversity and inequality of created things, this good could not exist.

[9]   To sum up: The diversity and inequality in created things are not the result of chance [*SCG* II, 39], nor of a diversity of matter [*SCG* II, 40], nor of the intervention of certain causes [*SCG,* II, 41–43] or merits [*SCG* II, 44], but of the intention of God Himself, who wills to give the creature such perfection as it is possible for it to have.

[10]   Accordingly, in the Book of Genesis (1:31) it is said: "God saw all the things that He had made, and they were very good," each one of them having been previously said to be *good.* For each thing in its nature is good, but all things together are very good, by reason of the order of the universe, which is the ultimate and noblest perfection in things.

CHAPTER 46. That the perfection of the universe required the existence of some intellectual creatures.

[1]   Having determined the actual cause of the diversity among things, it remains for us to tackle the third problem that we proposed [*SCG* II, 5], namely, to inquire into those things themselves, as far as this concerns the truth of faith. And first we shall show that, as a result of the order established by God's assigning to creatures the optimum perfection consonant with their manner of being, certain creatures were endowed with an intellectual nature, thus being given the highest rank in the universe.

[2]   An effect is most perfect when it returns to its source; thus, the circle is the most perfect of all figures, and circular motion the most perfect of all motions, because in their case a return is made to the starting point. It is therefore necessary that creatures return to their principle in order that the universe of creatures may attain its ultimate perfection. Now, each and every creature returns to its source so far as it bears a likeness to its source, according to its being and its nature, wherein it enjoys a certain perfection. Indeed, all effects are most perfect when they are most like their efficient causes—a house when it most closely resembles the art by which it was produced, and fire when its intensity most fully approximates that of its generator. Since God's intellect is the principle of the production of creatures, as we have shown above [*SCG* II, 23–24], the existence of some creatures endowed with intelligence was necessary in order that the universe of created things might be perfect.

[3]   A thing's second perfection, moreover, constitutes an addition to its first perfection. Now, just as the act of being and the nature of a thing are

considered as belonging to its first perfection, so operation is referred to its second perfection. Hence, the complete perfection of the universe required the existence of some creatures which return to God not only as regards likeness of nature, but also by their action. And such a return to God cannot be made except by the act of the intellect and will, because God Himself has no other operation in His own regard than these. The greatest perfection of the universe therefore demanded the existence of some intellectual creatures.

[4] Moreover, in order that creatures might perfectly represent the divine goodness, it was necessary, as we have shown [*SCG* II, 45], not only that good things should be made, but also that they should by their actions contribute to the goodness of other things. But a thing is perfectly likened to another in its operation when not only the action is of the same specific nature, but also the mode of acting is the same. Consequently, the highest perfection of things required the existence of some creatures that act in the same way as God. But it has already been shown [*SCG* II, 23–24] that God acts by intellect and will. It was therefore necessary for some creatures to have intellect and will.

[5] Again. It is according to the form of the effect pre-existing in the agent that the effect attains likeness to the agent, for an agent produces its like with respect to the form by which it acts. Now, in some cases the form of the agent is received in the effect according to the same mode of being that it has in the agent; the form of the fire generated has the same mode of being as the form of the generating fire. But in other cases the form of the agent is received in the effect according to another mode of being; the form of the house that exists in an intelligible manner in the builder's mind is received, in a material mode, in the house that exists outside the mind. And the former likeness clearly is more perfect than the latter. Now, the perfection of the universe of creatures consists in its likeness to God, just as the perfection of any effect whatever consists in its likeness to its efficient cause. Therefore, the highest perfection of the universe requires not only the second mode in which the creature is likened to God, but also the first, as far as possible. But the form through which God produces the creature is an intelligible form in Him, since, as we have shown above [*SCG* II, 23–24], God is an intellectual agent. Therefore, the highest perfection of the universe demands the existence of some creatures in which the form of the divine intellect is represented according to intelligible being; that is to say, it requires the existence of creatures of an intellectual nature.

[6] Likewise, the only thing that moves God to produce creatures is His own goodness, which He wished to communicate to other things by likening them to Himself, as was shown in Book I of this work [*SCG* I, 74–81]. Now, the likeness of one thing is found in another thing in two

ways: first, as regards natural being—the likeness of heat produced by fire is in the thing heated by fire; second, cognitively, as the likeness of fire is in sight or touch. Hence, that the likeness of God might exist in things perfectly, in the ways possible, it was necessary that the divine goodness be communicated to things by likeness not only in existing, but also in knowing. But only an intellect is capable of knowing the divine goodness. Accordingly, it was necessary that there should be intellectual creatures.

[7]   Again, in all things becomingly ordered, the relation to the last term of the things intermediate between it and the first imitates the relation of the first to all the others, both intermediate and last, though sometimes deficiently. Now, it has been shown in Book I that God embraces in Himself all creatures. [*SCG* I, 54]. And in corporeal creatures there is a representation of this, although in an other mode. For we find that the higher body always comprises and contains the lower, yet according to quantitative extension, whereas God contains all creatures in a simple mode, and not by extension of quantity. Hence, in order that the imitation of God, in this mode of containing, might not be lacking to creatures, intellectual creatures were made which contain corporeal creatures, not by quantitative extension, but in simple fashion, intelligibly; for what is intellectually known exists in the knowing subject, and is contained by his intellectual operation.

CHAPTER 47. That intellectual substances are endowed with will.

[1]   Now, these intellectual substances must be capable of willing.

[2]   There is in all things appetite for the good, since, as the philosophers teach,[1] *the good is what all desire.* In things devoid of knowledge this desire is called *natural appetite;* thus it is said that a stone desires to be below. In things having sense knowledge this desire is called *animal appetite,* which is divided into concupiscible and irascible. In things possessed of understanding it is called intellectual or rational appetite, and this is *will.* Created intellectual substances, therefore, are endowed with will.

[3]   Moreover, that which exists through another is referred to that which exists through itself, as being prior to the former. That is why, according to Aristotle,[2] things moved by another are referred to the first self-movers. Likewise, in syllogisms, the conclusions, which are known from other things, are referred to first principles, which are known through themselves. Now, there are some created substances that do not activate themselves, but are by force of nature moved to act; such is the case with inanimate things, plants, and brute animals; for to act or not to act does not lie in their power. It is therefore necessary to go back to some first things that move themselves to action. But, as we have just shown [*SCG* II, 46], intel-

---

[1] Cf. Aristotle, *Nicomachean Ethics,* I, 1 (1094a 3). [J.F.A.]
[2] Aristotle, *Physics,* VIII, 5 (257a 30); 6 (259a 7). [J.F.A.]

lectual substances hold the first rank in created things. These substances, then, are self-activating. Now, to move itself to act is the property of the will, and by the will a substance is master of its action, since within such a substance lies the power of acting or not acting. Hence, created intellectual substances are possessed of will.

[4] The principle of every operation, furthermore, is the form by which a thing is in act, since every agent acts so far as it is in act. So, the mode of operation consequent upon a form must be in accordance with the mode of that form. Hence, a form not proceeding from the agent that acts by it causes an operation of which that agent is not master. But, if there be a form which proceeds from the agent acting by it, then the consequent operation also will be in the power of that agent. Now, natural forms, from which natural motions and operations derive, do not proceed from the things whose forms they are, but wholly from extrinsic agents. For by a natural form each thing has being in its own nature, and nothing can be the cause of its own act of being. So it is that things which are moved naturally do not move themselves; a heavy body does not move itself downwards; its generator, which gave it its form, does so. Likewise, in brute animals the forms sensed or imagined, which move them, are not discovered by them, but are received by them from extrinsic sensible things, which act upon their senses and are judged of by their natural estimative faculty. Hence, though brutes are in a sense said to move themselves, inasmuch as one part of them moves and another is moved, yet they are not themselves the source of the actual moving, which, rather, derives partly from external things sensed and partly from nature. For, so far as their appetite moves their members, they are said to move themselves, and in this they surpass inanimate things and plants; but so far as appetition in them follows necessarily upon the reception of forms through their senses and from the judgment of their natural estimative power, they are not the cause of their own movement; and so they are not master of their own action. On the other hand, the form understood, through which the intellectual substance acts, proceeds from the intellect itself as a thing conceived, and in a way contrived by it; as we see in the case of the artistic form, which the artificer conceives and contrives, and through which he performs his works. Intellectual substances, then, move themselves to act, as having mastery of their own action. It therefore follows that they are endowed with will.

[5] The active, moreover, should be proportionate to the passive, and the moving to the movable. But in things having cognition the apprehending power is related to the appetitive power as mover to movable, for that which is apprehended by sense or imagination or intellect moves the intellectual or the animal appetite. Intellectual apprehension, however, is not limited to certain things, but reaches out to them all. And this is why Aristotle, in *De Anima* III, says of the possible intellect that it is "that by

which we become all things." [3] Hence, the appetite of an intellectual substance has relationship to all things; wherefore Aristotle remarks in *Ethics* III,[4] that appetite extends to *both possible and impossible things*. Intellectual substances, then, are possessed of will.

CHAPTER 48. That intellectual substances have freedom of choice in acting.

[1] It is therefore clear that the aforesaid substances are endowed with freedom of choice in acting.

[2] That they act by judgment is evident from the fact that through their intellectual cognition they judge of things to be done. And they must have freedom, if, as just shown [*SCG* II, 47], they have control over their own action. Therefore, these substances in acting have freedom of choice.

[3] Also, "the free is that which is its own cause." [5] Hence, that which is not the cause of its own acting is not free in acting. But things that do not move nor act unless they are moved by other things are not the cause of their own acting. So, only things that move themselves act freely. And these alone act by judgment. For the thing that moves itself is divided into mover and moved; and the mover is the appetite moved by intellect, imagination, or sense, to which faculties judgment belongs. Among these things, therefore, those alone judge freely which in judging move themselves. But no judging power moves itself to judge unless it reflects on its own action; for, if it moves itself to judge, it must know its own judgment; and this only an intellect can do. Thus, irrational animals have in a certain way freedom of movement or action, but not of judgment, whereas inanimate things, which are moved only by other things, have not even free action or movement. Intellectual beings, on the other hand, enjoy freedom not only of action, but also of judgment; and this is to have free choice.

[4] Then, too, the apprehended form is a moving principle according as it is apprehended under the aspect of the good or the fitting; for the outward action in things that move themselves proceeds from the judgment, made through that form, that something is good or fitting. Hence, if he who judges moves himself to judge, he must do so in the light of a higher form apprehended by him. And this form can be none other than the very intelligible essence of the good or the fitting, in the light of which judgment is made of any determinate good or fitting thing; so that only those beings move themselves to judge which apprehend the all-embracing essence of the good or the fitting. And these are intellectual beings alone. Hence, none but intellectual beings move themselves not only to act, but also to judge. They alone, therefore, are free in judging; and this is to have free choice.

---

[3] Aristotle, *De Anima*, III, 5 (430a 15). [J.F.A.]
[4] Aristotle, *Nicomachean Ethics*, III, 2 (1111b 23). [J.F.A.]
[5] Cf. Aristotle, *Metaphysics*, I, 2 (982b 26). [J.F.A.]

[5] Movement and action, moreover, issue from a universal conception only through the intermediation of a particular apprehension. For movement and action have to do with particular things, whereas it is the nature of the intellect to grasp universals. Hence, for movement and action of any kind to result from the intellect's grasp of something, the universal conception formed by it must be applied to particulars. But the universal contains many particulars potentially; so that the universal conception can be applied to many and diverse things. For this reason the judgment of the intellect concerning things to be done is not determined to one thing only. It follows, in short, that all intellectual beings have freedom of choice.

[6] Furthermore, certain things lack liberty of judgment, either because they have no judgment at all, as plants and stones, or because they have a judgment determined by nature to one thing, as do irrational animals; the sheep, by natural estimation, judges the wolf to be harmful to it, and in consequence of this judgment flees from the wolf; and so it is in other cases. Hence, so far as matters of action are concerned, whatever things possess judgment that is not determined to one thing by nature are of necessity endowed with freedom of choice. And such are all intellectual beings. For the intellect apprehends not only this or that good, but good itself, as common to all things. Now, the intellect, through the form apprehended, moves the will; and in all things mover and moved must be proportionate to one another. It follows that the will of an intellectual substance will not be determined by nature to anything except the good as common to all things. So it is possible for the will to be inclined toward anything whatever that is presented to it under the aspect of good, there being no natural determination to the contrary to prevent it. Therefore, all intellectual beings have a free will, resulting from the judgment of the intellect. And this means that they have freedom of choice, which is defined as *the free judgment of reason.*

CHAPTER 49. That the intellectual substance is not a body.

[1] From the foregoing we proceed to show that no intellectual substance is a body.

[2] For it is only by quantitative commensuration that a body contains anything at all; so, too, if a thing contains a whole thing in the whole of itself, it contains also a part in a part of itself, a greater part in a greater part, a lesser part in a lesser part. But an intellect does not, in terms of any quantitative commensuration, comprehend a thing understood, since by its wholeself it understands and encompasses both whole and part, things great in quantity and things small. Therefore, no intelligent substance is a body.

[3] Then, too, no body can receive the substantial form of another body, unless by corruption it lose its own form. But the intellect is not corrupted; rather, it is perfected by receiving the forms of all bodies; for it is

perfected by understanding, and it understands by having in itself the forms of the things understood. Hence, no intellectual substance is a body.

[4] Again, the principle of diversity among individuals of the same species is the division of matter according to quantity; the form of this fire does not differ from the form of that fire, except by the fact of its presence in different parts into which the matter is divided; nor is this brought about in any other way than by the division of quantity—without which substance is indivisible. Now, that which is received into a body is received into it according to the division of quantity. Therefore, it is only as individuated that a form is received into a body. If, then, the intellect were a body, the intelligible forms of things would not be received into it except as individuated. But the intellect understands things by those forms of theirs which it has in its possession. So, if it were a body, it would not be cognizant of universals but only of particulars. But this is patently false. Therefore, no intellect is a body.

[5] Likewise, nothing acts except in keeping with its species, because in each and every thing the form is the principle of action; so that, if the intellect is a body, its action will not go beyond the order of bodies. It would then have no knowledge of anything except bodies. But this is clearly false, because we know many things that are not bodies. Therefore, the intellect is not a body.

[6] Moreover, if an intelligent substance is a body, it is either finite or infinite. Now, it is impossible for a body to be actually infinite, as is proved in the *Physics*.[6] Therefore, if we suppose that such a substance is a body at all, it is a finite one. But this also is impossible, since, as was shown in Book I of this work [*SCG* I, 20], infinite power can exist in no finite body. And yet the cognitive power of the intellect is in a certain way infinite; for by adding number to number its knowledge of the species of numbers is infinitely extended; and the same applies to its knowledge of the species of figures and proportions. Moreover, the intellect grasps the universal, which is virtually infinite in its scope, because it contains individuals which are potentially infinite. Therefore, the intellect is not a body.

[7] It is impossible, furthermore, for two bodies to contain one another, since the container exceeds the contained. Yet, when one intellect has knowledge of another, the two intellects contain and encompass one another. Therefore, the intellect is not a body.

[8] Also, the action of no body is self-reflexive. For it is proved in the *Physics*[7] that no body is moved by itself except with respect to a part, so that one part of it is the mover and the other the moved. But in acting the

---

[6] Aristotle, *Physics*, III, 5 (206a 8). [J.F.A.]
[7] Aristotle, *Physics*, VIII, 5 (256a 2–33). [J.F.A.]

intellect reflects on itself, not only as to a part, but as to the whole of itself. Therefore, it is not a body.

[9] A body's action, moreover, is not terminated in action, nor movement in movement—a point proved in the *Physics*.[8] But the action of an intelligent substance is terminated in action; for just as the intellect knows a thing, so does it know that it knows; and so on indefinitely. An intelligent substance, therefore, is not a body.

[10] Hence it is that sacred Scripture calls intellectual substances *spirits;* and this term it customarily employs in reference to the incorporeal God; as St. John says: "God is a spirit" (John 4:24); and in the Book of Wisdom (7:22–23) we read: "for in her" namely, divine Wisdom, "is the spirit of understanding, containing all intelligible spirits."

[11] This, then, does away with the error of the early natural philosophers, who supposed that no substance exists except the corporeal, and who therefore said that the soul is a body, either fire or air or water, or something of the kind [9]—an opinion which some have endeavored to introduce into the Christian faith by saying that the soul is the effigy of the body, like a body externally represented.

CHAPTER 50. That intellectual substances are immaterial.

[1] It clearly follows that intellectual substances are immaterial.

[2] For everything composed of matter and form is a body, since matter cannot receive diverse forms except with respect to its various parts. And this diversity of parts can exist in matter only so far as one common matter is divided into several by dimensions existing in matter; for, without quantity, substance is indivisible. But it has just been shown [*SCG* II, 49], that no intelligent substance is a body. It remains, therefore, that such a substance is not composed of matter and form.

[3] Furthermore, just as *man* does not exist apart from *this man,* so *matter* does not exist apart from *this matter.* Any subsistent thing that is composed of matter and form is, then, composed of individual form and individual matter. But the intellect cannot be composed of individual matter and form, because the species of things understood are made actually intelligible by being abstracted from individual matter. And as a result of being actually intelligible they become one with the intellect. That is why the intellect also must be without individual matter. Therefore, a substance endowed with intelligence is not composed of matter and form.

[4] Then, too, the action of anything composed of matter and form belongs not to the form alone, nor to the matter alone, but to the compos-

---

[8] Aristotle, *Physics,* V, 2 (225b 12 ff.). [J.F.A.]
[9] Cf. Aristotle, *De Anima,* I, 2 (403b 32–404a 15). [J.F.A.]

ite; for to act belongs to that which exists, and existence belongs to the composite through its form, so that the composite also acts through its form. So, if the intelligent substance is composed of matter and form, its act of understanding will be the act of the composite. Now, action terminates in a thing like the agent that produces it; that is why the composite, in generating, produces not a form but a composite. Hence, if the act of understanding is an action of the composite, neither the form nor the matter would be known, but only the composite. But this is patently false. Therefore, the intelligent substance is not composed of matter and form.

[5] Again. The forms of sensible things have a more perfect mode of existence in the intellect than in sensible things, for in the intellect they are simpler and extend to more things; thus, through the one intelligible form of man, the intellect knows all men. Now, a form existing perfectly in matter makes a thing to be actually such—to be fire or to be colored, for example; and if the form does not have that effect, then the form is in that thing imperfectly, as the form of heat in the air carrying it, and the power of the first agent in its instrument. So, if the intellect were composed of matter and form, the forms of the things known would make the intellect to be actually of the same nature as that which is known. And the consequence of this is the error of Empedocles, who said that "the soul knows fire by fire, and earth by earth"; [10] and so with other things. But this is clearly incongruous. Therefore, the intelligent substance is not composed of matter and form.

[6] And since a thing's mode of presence in its recipient accords with the latter's mode of being, it would follow, were the intellect composed of matter and form, that the forms of things would exist in it materially, just as they exist outside the mind. Therefore, just as they are not actually intelligible outside the mind, so they would not be actually intelligible when present in the intellect.

[7] Moreover, the forms of contraries, as they exist in matter, are contrary; hence, they exclude one another. But as they exist in the intellect the forms of contraries are not contrary; rather, one contrary is the intelligible ground of another, since one is understood through the other. They have, then, no material being in the intellect. Therefore, the intellect is not composed of matter and form.

[8] And again, matter does not receive a fresh form except through motion or change. But the intellect is not moved through receiving forms; rather, it is perfected and at rest while understanding, whereas movement is a hindrance to understanding.[11] Hence, forms are not received in the intellect as in matter or a material thing. Clearly, then, intelligent substances are immaterial, even as they are incorporeal, too.

---

[10] Cf. Aristotle, *De Anima,* I, 2 (404b 15). [J.F.A.]
[11] Cf. Aristotle, *Physics,* VII, 3 (247b 8 ff.). [J.F.A.]

[9]   Hence, Dionysius says: "On account of the rays of God's goodness all intellectual substances, which are known to be incorporeal and immaterial, have remained immutably in existence." [12]

CHAPTER 51. That the intellectual substance is not a material form.

[1]   From the same principles we proceed to show that intellectual natures are subsistent forms, and are not in matter as though their being depends on matter.

[2]   Forms dependent in being upon matter do not themselves have being properly, but being properly belongs to the composites through their forms. Consequently, if intellectual substances were forms of this kind, it would follow that they have material being, just as they would if they were composed of matter and form.

[3]   Moreover, forms that do not subsist through themselves cannot act through themselves; rather, the composites act through them. Hence, if intellectual natures were forms of this sort, it would follow that they do not themselves understand, but that it is the things composed of them and matter which understand. And thus, an intelligent being would be composed of matter and form; which is impossible, as we have just shown.

[4]   Also, if the intellect were a form in matter and not self-subsistent, it would follow that what is received into the intellect would be received into matter, since forms whose being is bound to matter receive nothing that is not received into the matter. But the reception of forms into the intellect is not a reception of forms into matter. Therefore, the intellect cannot possibly be a material form.

[5]   Moreover, to say that the intellect is not a subsistent form, but a form embedded in matter, is the same in reality as to say that the intellect is composed of matter and form. The difference is purely nominal, for in the first way the intellect will be called the form itself of the composite; in the second way, the composite itself. So, if it is false that the intellect is composed of matter and form, it will be false that it is a form which does not subsist, but is material.

QUESTIONS FOR STUDY AND DISCUSSION

1. What is the special importance of intellectual creatures for the whole of creation? Could God have created without including intellectual creatures?
2. Why does anything with an intellect have a will? How does the will fulfill the implications of intellectuality?
3. How does freedom unite and express the importance of both intellect and will? What is the significance of rationality for freedom?
4. How does one differentiate between the spiritual and the material?

---

[12] Pseudo-Dionysius, *De divinis nominibus*, IV (PG 3, col. 694). [J.F.A.]

Act and Potency in Created Intellectual Substances

BOOK II: CREATION

CHAPTER 52. That in created intellectual substances, being and what is differ.

[1] Although intellectual substances are not corporeal, nor composed of matter and form, nor existing in matter as material forms, it is not to be supposed that they therefore equal the divine simplicity. For a certain composition is found in them by the fact that in them *being* is not the same as what is.

[2] For, if being is subsisting, nothing besides this act itself is added to it. Because, even in things whose being is not subsistent, that which is in the existing thing in addition to its being is indeed united to the thing, but is not one with the thing's being, except by accident, so far as the thing is one subject having being and that which is other than being. Thus it is clear that in Socrates, beside his substantial being, there is white, which, indeed, is other than his substantial being; for to be Socrates and to be white are not the same except by accident. If, then, being is not in a subject, there will remain no way in which that which is other than being can be united to it. Now, being, as being, cannot be diverse; but it can be diversified by something beside itself; thus, the being of a stone is other than that of a man. Hence, that which is subsisting being can be one only. Now, we have shown in Book I that God is His own subsisting being [*SCG* I, 22]. Hence, nothing beside Him can be its own being. Of necessity, therefore, in every substance beside Him the substance itself is other than its being.

[3] Moreover, a common nature, if considered in separation from things, can be only one, although there can be a plurality of things possessing that nature. For, if the nature of *animal* subsisted as separate through itself, it would not have those things that are proper to a man or an ox; if it did have them, it would not be *animal* alone, but man or ox. Now, if the differences constitutive of species be removed, there remains the undivided nature of the genus, because the same differences which constitute the species divide the genus. Consequently, if this itself which is being is common as a

From pp. 152–58 of *On the Truth of the Catholic Faith,* Book II, by St. Thomas Aquinas, translated by James F. Anderson. Copyright © 1956 by Doubleday & Company, Inc. Reprinted by permission of the publisher.

genus, separate, self-subsisting being can be one only. But, if being is not divided by differences, as a genus is, but, as it is in truth, by the fact that it is the being of this or that, then it is all the more manifest that being existing through itself can only be one. Since God is subsisting being, it therefore remains that nothing other than He is its own being.

[4] Again, absolutely infinite being cannot be twofold, for being that is absolutely infinite comprises every perfection of being; hence, if infinity were present in two such things, in no respect would they be found to differ. Now, subsisting being must be infinite, because it is not terminated in some recipient. Therefore, there cannot be a subsisting being besides the first.

[5] Then, too, if there is a self-subsisting being, nothing belongs to it except that which is proper to a being inasmuch as it is a being, since what is said of a thing, not as such, appertains to it only accidentally, by reason of the subject. Consequently, if the thing so spoken of is held to be separated from the subject, it in no way belongs to it. Now, to be caused by another does not appertain to a being inasmuch as it is being; otherwise, every being would be caused by another, so that we should have to proceed to infinity in causes—an impossibility, as was shown in Book I of this work [SCG I, 13]. Therefore, that being which is subsisting must be uncaused. Therefore, no caused being is its own being.

[6] The substance of each and every thing, furthermore, belongs to it through itself and not through another; thus, it does not pertain to the substance of air to be actually luminous, since this quality it acquires through something else. But every created thing has its being through another; otherwise, it would not be caused. Therefore, the being of no created substance is that substance.

[7] Also, since every agent acts so far as it is in act, it belongs to the first agent, which is most perfect, to be most perfectly in act. Now, a thing is the more perfectly in act the more its act is posterior in the way of generation, for act is posterior in time to potentiality in one and the same thing that passes from potentiality to act. Further, act itself is more perfectly in act than that which has act, since the latter is in act because of the former. These things being posited, then, it is clear from what has been shown in Book I of this work [SCG I, 13] that God alone is the first agent. Therefore, it belongs to Him alone to be in act in the most perfect way, that is, to be Himself the most perfect act. Now, this act is being, wherein generation and all movement terminate, since every form and act is in potentiality before it acquires being. Therefore, it belongs to God alone to be His own being, just as it pertains to Him only to be the first agent.

[8] Moreover, being itself belongs to the first agent according to His proper nature, for God's being is His substance, as was shown in Book I

[*SCG* I, 22]. Now, that which belongs to a thing according to its proper nature does not belong to other things except by way of participation, as heat is in other bodies from fire. Therefore, being itself belongs to all other things from the first agent by a certain participation. That which belongs to a thing by participation, however, is not that thing's substance. Therefore, it is impossible that the substance of a thing other than the first agent should be being itself.

[9]   Wherefore in Exodus (3:14) the proper name of God is stated to be *"He who is,"* because it is proper to Him alone that His substance is not other than His being.

CHAPTER 53. That in created intellectual substances there is act and potentiality.

[1]   Now, from the foregoing it is evident that in created intellectual substances there is composition of act and potentiality.

[2]   For in whatever thing we find two, one of which is the complement of the other, the proportion of one of them to the other is as the proportion of potentiality to act; for nothing is completed except by its proper act. Now, in the created intellectual substance two principles are found: the substance itself and its being, which, as we have just shown [*SCG* II, 52], is not the substance itself. Now, being itself is the complement of the existing substance, for each and every thing is in act through having being. It therefore remains that in each of the aforesaid substances there is composition of act and potentiality.

[3]   There is also the consideration that whatever is present in a thing from an agent must be act, for it belongs to an agent to make something in act. Now, it was shown above [*SCG* II, 15], that all other substances have being from the first agent; and the substances themselves are caused by the fact that they have being from another. Therefore, being is present in caused substances as a certain act of their own. But that in which act is present is a potentiality, since act, as such, is referred to potentiality. Therefore, in every created substance there is potentiality and act.

[4]   Likewise, whatever participates in a thing is compared to the thing participated in as act to potentiality, since by that which is participated the participator is actualized in such and such a way. But it was shown above [*SCG* II, 15] that God alone is essentially a being, whereas all other things participate in being. Therefore, every created substance is compared to its own being as potentiality to act.

[5]   Furthermore, it is by act that a thing is made like its efficient cause, for the agent produces its like so far as it is in act. Now, as shown above [*SCG* II, 6] it is through being itself that every created substance is likened to God. Therefore, being itself is compared to all created substances as their

act. Whence it follows that in every created substance there is composition of act and potentiality.

CHAPTER 54. That the composition of substance and being is not the same as the composition of matter and form.

[1]   Now, these compositions are not of the same nature, although both are compositions of potentiality and act.

[2]   First, this is so because matter is not the very substance of a thing; for, if that were true, it would follow that all forms are accidents, as the early natural philosophers supposed. But matter is not the substance; it is only part of the substance.

[3]   Secondly, because being itself is the proper act, not of the matter, but of the whole substance; for being is the act of that whereof we can say that it *is*. Now, this act is predicated not of the matter, but of the whole. Hence, matter cannot be called that which *is;* rather, the substance itself is that which is.

[4]   Thirdly, because neither is the form the being itself, but between them there is a relation of order, because form is compared to being itself as *light* to *illuminating,* or *whiteness* to *being white.*

[5]   Then, too, because being is compared even to the form itself as act. For in things composed of matter and form, the form is said to be the principle of being, for this reason: that it is the complement of the substance, whose act is being. Thus, transparency is in relation to the air the principle of illumination, in that it makes the air the proper subject of light.

[6]   Accordingly, in things composed of matter and form, neither the matter nor the form nor even being itself can be termed that which is. Yet the form can be called *that by which it is,* inasmuch as it is the principle of being; the whole substance itself, however, is *that which is.* And being itself is that by which the substance is called a *being.*

[7]   But, as we have shown [*SCG* II, 50–51], intellectual substances are not composed of matter and form; rather, in them the form itself is a subsisting substance; so that form here is *that which is* and being itself is act and *that by which* the substance *is.*

[8]   And on this account there is in such substances but one composition of act and potentiality, namely, the composition of substance and being, which by some is said to be of *that which is* and being, or of *that which is* and *that by which a thing is.*

[9]   On the other hand, in substances composed of matter and form there is a twofold composition of act and potentiality: the first, of the substance itself which is composed of matter and form; the second, of the substance

thus composed, and being; and this composition also can be said to be of *that which is* and being, or of *that which is* and *that by which a thing is.*

[10]   It is therefore clear that composition of act and potentiality has greater extension than that of form and matter. Thus, matter and form divide natural substance, while potentiality and act divide common being. Accordingly, whatever follows upon potentiality and act, as such, is common to both material and immaterial created substances, as *to receive* and *to be received, to perfect* and *to be perfected.* Yet all that is proper to matter and form, as such, as *to be generated* and *to be corrupted,* and the like, are proper to material substances, and in no way belong to immaterial created substances.

QUESTIONS FOR STUDY AND DISCUSSION

1. What is there about limited and multiple substances that manifests in them an essence or principle of "what is" distinct from their being or existence?
2. What is the significance of isolating essence and seeing its relation to existence for understanding and evaluating any interaction with other things?
3. How does the relation of potency and act aid in better understanding the relation between essence and existence?
4. If both are relations of potency and act, what is the difference between essence and existence on the one hand, and matter and form on the other?
5. How could one schematize the internal structure of a material being?

The Five Ways

QUESTION 2. THE EXISTENCE OF GOD

ARTICLE 2. Whether it can be demonstrated that God exists?

Objection 1. It seems that the existence of God cannot be demonstrated. For it is an article of faith that God exists. But what is of faith cannot be demonstrated, because a demonstration produces scientific knowledge; whereas faith is of the unseen (Heb. xi. 1). Therefore it cannot be demonstrated that God exists.

Obj. 2. Further, the essence is the middle term of demonstration. But we cannot know in what God's essence consists, but solely in what it does

From pp. 12–14 of St. Thomas Aquinas, *Summa Theologica,* Part I, translated by the English Dominican Fathers. Copyright 1947 by Benziger Brothers, Inc. Reprinted by permission of Benziger Brothers, Inc., and Burns and Oates Ltd., London.

not consist; as Damascene says (*De Fid. Orth.* i. 4). Therefore we cannot demonstrate that God exists.

Obj. 3. Further, if the existence of God were demonstrated, this could only be from His effects. But His effects are not proportionate to Him, since He is infinite and His effects are finite; and between the finite and infinite there is no proportion. Therefore, since a cause cannot be demonstrated by an effect not proportionate to it, it seems that the existence of God cannot be demonstrated.

On the contrary, The Apostle says: *The invisible things of Him are clearly seen, being understood by the things that are made* (Rom. i. 20). But this would not be unless the existence of God could be demonstrated through the things that are made; for the first thing we must know of anything is, whether it exists.

I answer that, Demonstration can be made in two ways: One is through the cause, and is called *a priori,* and this is to argue from what is prior absolutely. The other is through the effect, and is called a demonstration *a posteriori;* this is to argue from what is prior relatively only to us. When an effect is better known to us than its cause, from the effect we proceed to the knowledge of the cause. And from every effect the existence of its proper cause can be demonstrated, so long as its effects are better known to us; because since every effect depends upon its cause, if the effect exists, the cause must pre-exist. Hence the existence of God, in so far as it is not self-evident to us, can be demonstrated from those of His effects which are known to us.

Reply Obj. 1. The existence of God and other like truths about God, which can be known by natural reason, are not articles of faith, but are preambles to the articles; for faith presupposes natural knowledge, even as grace presupposes nature, and perfection supposes something that can be perfected. Nevertheless, there is nothing to prevent a man, who cannot grasp a proof, accepting, as a matter of faith, something which in itself is capable of being scientifically known and demonstrated.

Reply Obj. 2. When the existence of a cause is demonstrated from an effect, this effect takes the place of the definition of the cause in proof of the cause's existence. This is especially the case in regard to God, because, in order to prove the existence of anything, it is necessary to accept as a middle term the meaning of the word, and not its essence, for the question of its essence follows on the question of its existence. Now the names given to God are derived from His effects; consequently, in demonstrating the existence of God from His effects, we may take for the middle term the meaning of the word "God."

Reply Obj. 3. From effects not proportionate to the cause no perfect knowledge of that cause can be obtained. Yet from every effect the existence of the cause can be clearly demonstrated, and so we can demonstrate the existence of God from His effects; though from them we cannot perfectly know God as He is in His essence.

ARTICLE 3. Whether God exists?

Objection 1. It seems that God does not exist; because if one of two contraries be infinite, the other would be altogether destroyed. But the word "God" means that He is infinite goodness. If, therefore, God existed, there would be no evil discoverable; but there is evil in the world. Therefore God does not exist.

Obj. 2. Further, it is superfluous to suppose that what can be accounted for by a few principles has been produced by many. But it seems that everything we see in the world can be accounted for by other principles, supposing God did not exist. For all natural things can be reduced to one principle, which is nature; and all voluntary things can be reduced to one principle, which is human reason, or will. Therefore there is no need to suppose God's existence.

On the contrary, It is said in the person of God: *I am Who am* (Exod. iii. 14).

I answer that, The existence of God can be proved in five ways.

The first and more manifest way is the argument from motion. It is certain, and evident to our senses, that in the world some things are in motion. Now whatever is in motion is put in motion by another, for nothing can be in motion except it is in potentiality to that towards which it is in motion; whereas a thing moves inasmuch as it is in act. For motion is nothing else than the reduction of something from potentiality to actuality. But nothing can be reduced from potentiality to actuality, except by something in a state of actuality. Thus that which is actually hot, as fire, makes wood, which is potentially hot, to be actually hot, and thereby moves and changes it. Now it is not possible that the same thing should be at once in actuality and potentiality in the same respect, but only in different respects. For what is actually hot cannot simultaneously be potentially hot; but it is simultaneously potentially cold. It is therefore impossible that in the same respect and in the same way a thing should be both mover and moved, *i.e.*, that it should move itself. Therefore, whatever is in motion must be put in motion by another. If that by which it is put in motion be itself put in motion, then this also must needs be put in motion by another, and that by another again. But this cannot go on to infinity, because then there would be no first mover, and, consequently, no other mover; seeing that subsequent movers move only inasmuch as they are put in motion by the first mover; as the staff moves only because it is put in motion by the hand. Therefore it is necessary to arrive at a first mover, put in motion by no other; and this everyone understands to be God.

The second way is from the nature of the efficient cause. In the world of sense we find there is an order of efficient causes. There is no case known (neither is it, indeed, possible) in which a thing is found to be the efficient cause of itself; for so it would be prior to itself, which is impossible. Now in efficient causes it is not possible to go on to infinity, because in all efficient causes following in order, the first is the cause of the intermediate cause, and the intermediate is the cause of the ultimate cause, whether the intermediate cause be several, or one only. Now to take away the cause is to take away the effect. Therefore, if there be no first cause among efficient causes, there will be no ultimate, nor any intermediate cause. But if in efficient causes it is possible to go on to infinity, there will be no first efficient cause, neither will there be an ultimate effect, nor any intermediate efficient causes; all of which is plainly false. Therefore it is necessary to admit a first efficient cause, to which everyone gives the name of God.

The third way is taken from possibility and necessity, and runs thus. We find in nature things that are possible to be and not to be, since they are found to be generated, and to corrupt, and consequently, they are possible to be and not to be. But it is impossible for these always to exist, for that which is possible not to be at some time is not. Therefore, if everything is possible not to be, then at one time there could have been nothing in existence. Now if this were true, even now there would be nothing in existence, because that which does not exist only begins to exist by something already existing. Therefore, if at one time nothing was in existence, it would have been impossible for anything to have begun to exist; and thus even now nothing would be in existence—which is absurd. Therefore, not all beings are merely possible, but there must exist something the existence of which is necessary. But every necessary thing either has it necessity caused by another, or not. Now it is impossible to go on to infinity in necessary things which have their necessity caused by another, as has been already proved in regard to efficient causes. Therefore we cannot but postulate the existence of some being having of itself its own necessity, and not receiving it from another, but rather causing in others their necessity. This all men speak of as God.

The fourth way is taken from the gradation to be found in things. Among beings there are some more and some less good, true, noble, and the like. But "more" and "less" are predicated of different things, according as they resemble in their different ways something which is the maximum, as a thing is said to be hotter according as it more nearly resembles that which is hottest; so that there is something which is truest, something best, something noblest, and, consequently, something which is uttermost being; for those things that are greatest in truth are greatest in being, as it is written in *Metaph.* ii. Now the maximum in any genus is the cause of all in that genus; as fire, which is the maximum of heat, is the cause of all hot things. Therefore there must also be something which is to all beings the cause of their being, goodness, and every other perfection; and this we call God.

The fifth way is taken from the governance of the world. We see that things which lack intelligence, such as natural bodies, act for an end, and this is evident from their acting always, or nearly always, in the same way, so as to obtain the best result. Hence it is plain that not fortuitously, but designedly, do they achieve their end. Now whatever lacks intelligence cannot move towards an end, unless it be directed by some being endowed with knowledge and intelligence; as the arrow is shot to its mark by the archer. Therefore some intelligent being exists by whom all natural things are directed to their end; and this being we call God.

Reply Obj. 1. As Augustine says (*Enchir.* xi): *Since God is the highest good, He would not allow any evil to exist in His works, unless His omnipotence and goodness were such as to bring good even out of evil.* This is part of the infinite goodness of God, that He should allow evil to exist, and out of it produce good.

Reply Obj. 2. Since nature works for a determinate end under the direction of a higher agent, whatever is done by nature must needs be traced back to God, as to its first cause. So also whatever is done voluntarily must also be traced back to some higher cause other than human reason or will, since these can change and fail; for all things that are changeable and capable of defect must be traced back to an immovable and self-necessary first principle, as was shown in the body of the *Article.*

QUESTIONS FOR STUDY AND DISCUSSION

1. What basic procedure does St. Thomas suggest for arriving at some knowledge of God?
2. What is fundamentally in question here, God's existence or mine?
3. Is the division of five points of departure for approaches to the knowledge of God arbitrary; is it exhaustive?
4. Is there any special significance to the two-stage character of the third way by which one advances first to what is at least necessary by another and then to what is necessary of itself?
5. What knowledge of God do the five ways provide?

The Highest Degree of Life and Love — God

QUESTION 18. THE LIFE OF GOD

ARTICLE 3. Whether life is properly attributed to God?

Objection 1. It seems that life is not properly attributed to God. For things are said to live inasmuch as they move themselves, as previously

From pp. 113–16 of St. Thomas Aquinas, *Summa Theologica,* Part I, translated by the English Dominican Fathers. Copyright 1947 by Benziger Brothers, Inc. Reprinted by permission of Benziger Brothers, Inc., and Burns and Oates Ltd., London.

stated (A. 2). But movement does not belong to God. Neither therefore does life.

Obj. 2. Further, in all living things we must needs suppose some principle of life. Hence it is said by the Philosopher (*De Anima* ii. 4) that *the soul is the cause and principle of the living body.* But God has no principle. Therefore life cannot be attributed to Him.

Obj. 3. Further, the principle of life in the living things that exist among us is the vegetative soul. But this exists only in corporeal things. Therefore life cannot be attributed to incorporeal things.

On the contrary, It is said (Ps. lxxxiii. 3): *My heart and my flesh have rejoiced in the living God.*

I answer that, Life is in the highest degree properly in God. In proof of which it must be considered that since a thing is said to live in so far as it operates of itself and not as moved by another, the more perfectly this power is found in anything, the more perfect is the life of that thing. In things that move and are moved a threefold order is found. In the first place the end moves the agent: and the principal agent is that which acts through its form, and sometimes it does so through some instrument that acts by virtue not of its own form, but of the principal agent, and does no more than execute the action. Accordingly there are things that move themselves, not in respect of any form or end naturally inherent in them, but only in respect of the executing of the movement; the form by which they act, and the end of the action being alike determined for them by their nature. Of this kind are plants, which move themselves according to their inherent nature, with regard only to executing the movements of growth and decay.

Other things have self-movement in a higher degree, that is, not only with regard to executing the movement, but even as regards the form, the principle of movement, which form they acquire of themselves. Of this kind are animals, in which the principle of movement is not a naturally implanted form; but one received through sense. Hence the more perfect is their sense, the more perfect is their power of self-movement. Such as have only the sense of touch, as shellfish, move only with the motion of expansion and contraction; and thus their movement hardly exceeds that of plants. Whereas such as have the sensitive power in perfection, so as to recognize not only connection and touch, but also objects apart from themselves, can move themselves to a distance by progressive movement. Yet although animals of the latter kind receive through sense the form that is the principle of their movement, nevertheless they cannot of themselves propose to themselves the end of their operation, or movement; for this has been implanted in them by nature; and my natural instinct they are moved to any action through the form apprehended by sense. Hence such animals as move themselves in respect to an end they themselves propose are superior to these. This can only be done by reason and intellect; whose province it is to know that proportion between the end and the means to that end, and duly coordinate them. Hence a more perfect degree of life is that of intelligent beings; for their power of self-movement is more perfect. This is shown by the fact that in one and the same man the intellectual faculty moves the sensitive powers; and these by their command move the organs of movement. Thus in the arts we see that the art of using a ship, *i.e.,* the art of navigation, rules the art of ship-designing; and this in its turn rules the art that is only concerned with preparing the material for the ship.

But although our intellect moves itself to some things, yet others are supplied by nature, as are first principles, which it cannot doubt; and the last end, which it cannot but will. Hence, although with respect to some things it moves itself, yet with regard to other things it must be moved by another. Wherefore that being whose act of understanding is its very nature, and which, in what it naturally possesses, is not determined by another, must have life in the most perfect degree. Such is God; and hence in Him principally is life. From this the Philosopher concludes (*Metaph.* xii. 51), after showing God to be intelligent, that God has life most perfect and eternal, since His intellect is most perfect and always in act.

Reply Obj. 1. As stated in *Metaph.* ix. 16, action is two-fold. Actions of one kind pass out to external matter, as to heat or to cut; whilst actions of the other kind remain in the agent, as to understand, to sense, and to will. The difference between them is this, that the former action is the perfection not of the agent that moves, but of the thing moved; whereas the latter action is the perfection of the agent. Hence, because movement is an act of the thing in movement, the latter action, in so far as it is the act of the operator, is called its movement, by this similitude, that as movement is an act of the thing moved, so an act of this kind is the act of the agent, although movement is an act of the imperfect, that is, of what is in potentiality; while this kind of act is an act of the perfect, that is to say, of what is in act as stated in *De Anima* iii. 28. In the sense, therefore, in which understanding is movement, that which understands itself is said to move itself. It is in this sense that Plato also taught that God moves Himself; not in the sense in which movement is an act of the imperfect.

Reply Obj. 2. As God is His own very existence and understanding, so is He His own life; and therefore He so lives that He has no principle of life.

Reply Obj. 3. Life in this lower world is bestowed on a corruptible nature, that needs generation to preserve the species, and nourishment to preserve the individual. For this reason life is not found here below apart from a vegetative soul: but this does not hold good with incorruptible natures.

. . .

QUESTION 20. GOD'S LOVE

We next consider those things that pertain absolutely to the will of God. In the appetitive part of the soul there are found in ourselves both the passions of the soul, as joy, love, and the like; and the habits of the moral virtues, as justice, fortitude, and the like. Hence we shall first consider the love of God, and secondly his justice and mercy. About the first there are four points of inquiry: (1) Whether love exists in God? (2) Whether He loves all things? (3) Whether He loves one thing more than another? (4) Whether He loves more the better things?

ARTICLE 1. Whether love exists in God?

Objection 1. It seems that love does not exist in God. For in God there are no passions. Now love is a passion. Therefore love is not in God.

Obj. 2. Further, love, anger, sorrow, and the like, are mutually divided against one another. But sorrow and anger are not attributed to God, unless by metaphor. Therefore neither is love attributed to Him.

Obj. 3. Further, Dionysius says (*Div. Nom.* iv): *Love is a uniting and binding force.* But this cannot take place in God, since He is simple. Therefore love does not exist in God.

On the contrary, It is written: *God is love* (1 John iv. 16).

I answer that, We must needs assert that in God there is love: because love is the first movement of the will and of every appetitive faculty. For since the acts of the will and of every appetitive faculty tend towards good and evil, as to their proper objects: and since good is essentially and especially the object of the will and the appetite, whereas evil is only the object secondarily and indirectly, as opposed to good; it follows that the acts of the will and appetite that regard good must naturally be prior to those that regard evil; thus, for instance, joy is prior to sorrow, love to hate: because what exists of itself is always prior to that which exists through another. Again, the more universal is naturally prior to what is less so. Hence the intellect is first directed by universal truth; and in the second place to particular and special truths. Now there are certain acts of the will and appetite that regard good under some special condition, as joy and delight regard good present and possessed; whereas desire and hope regard good not as yet possessed. Love, however, regards good universally, whether possessed or not. Hence love is naturally the first act of the will and appetite; for which reason all the other appetite movements presuppose love, as their root and origin. For nobody desires anything nor rejoices in anything, except as a good that is loved: nor is anything an object of hate except as opposed to the object of love. Similarly, it is clear that sorrow, and other things like to it, must be referred to love as to their first principle. Hence, in whomsoever there is will and appetite, there must also be love: since if the first is wanting, all that follows is also wanting. Now it has been shown that will is in God (Q. 19, A. 1), and hence we must attribute love to Him.

Reply Obj. 1. The cognitive faculty does not move except through the medium of the appetitive: and just as in ourselves the universal reason moves through the medium of the particular reason, as stated in *De Anima*

iii. 58, 75, so in ourselves the intellectual appetite, or the will as it is called, moves through the medium of the sensitive appetite. Hence, in us the sensitive appetite is the proximate motive-force of our bodies. Some bodily change therefore always accompanies an act of the sensitive appetite, and this change affects especially the heart, which, as the Philosopher says (*De part. animal.* ii. 1; iii. 4), is the first principle of movement in animals. Therefore acts of the sensitive appetite, inasmuch as they have annexed to them some bodily change, are called passions; whereas acts of the will are not so called. Love, therefore, and joy and delight, in so far as they denote acts of the sensitive appetite, are passions, in so far as they denote acts of the intellective appetite, they are not passions. It is in this latter sense that they are in God. Hence the Philosopher says (*Ethic.* vii): *God rejoices by an operation that is one and simple,* and for the same reason He loves without passion.

Reply Obj. 2. In the passions of the sensitive appetite there may be distinguished a certain material element—namely, the bodily change—and a certain formal element, which is on the part of the appetite. Thus in anger, as the Philosopher says (*De Anima* iii. 15, 63, 64), the material element is the kindling of the blood about the heart; but the formal, the appetite for revenge. Again, as regards the formal element of certain passions a certain imperfection is implied, as in desire, which is of the good we have not, and in sorrow, which is about the evil we have. This applies also to anger, which supposes sorrow. Certain other passions, however, as love and joy, imply no imperfection. Since therefore none of these can be attributed to God on their material side, as has been said (*ad* 1); neither can those that even on their formal side imply imperfection be attributed to Him; except metaphorically, and from likeness of effects, as already shown (QQ. 3, A. 2, *ad* 2 and 19, A. 11). Whereas, those that do not imply inperfection, such as love and joy, can be properly predicated of God, though without attributing passion to Him, as said before (Q. 19, A. 11).

Reply Obj. 3. An act of love always tends towards two things; to the good that one wills, and to the person for whom one wills it: since to love a person is to wish that person good. Hence, inasmuch as we love ourselves, we wish ourselves good; and, so far as possible, union with that good. So love is called the unitive force, even in God, yet without implying composition; for the good that He wills for Himself, is no other than Himself, Who is good by His essence, as above shown (Q. 6, AA. 1, 3). And by the fact that anyone loves another, he wills good to that other. Thus he puts the other, as it were, in the place of himself; and regards the good done to him as done to himself. So far love is a binding force, since it aggregates another to ourselves, and refers his good to our own. And then again the divine love is a binding force, inasmuch as God wills good to others; yet it implies no composition in God.

ARTICLE 2. Whether God loves all things?

Objection 1. It seems that God does not love all things. For according to Dionysius (*Div. Nom.* iv. 1), love places the lover outside himself, and causes him to pass, as it were, into the object of his love. But it is not admissible to say that God is placed outside of Himself, and passes into other things. Therefore it is inadmissible to say that God loves things other than Himself.

Obj. 2. Further, the love of God is eternal. But things apart from God are not from eternity; except in God. Therefore God does not love anything, except as it exists in Himself. But as existing in Him, it is no other than Himself. Therefore God does not love things other than Himself.

Obj. 3. Further, love is twofold—the love, namely, of desire and the love of friendship. Now God does not love irrational creatures with the love of desire, since He needs no creature outside Himself. Nor with the love of friendship; since there can be no friendship with irrational creatures, as the Philosopher shows (*Ethic.* viii. 2). Therefore God does not love all things.

Obj. 4. Further, it is written (Ps. v. 7): *Thou hatest all the workers of iniquity.* Now nothing is at the same time hated and loved. Therefore God does not love all things.

On the contrary, It is said (Wis. xi. 25): *Thou lovest all things that are, and hatest none of the things which Thou hast made.*

I answer that, God loves all existing things. For all existing things, in so far as they exist, are good, since the existence of a thing is itself a good; and likewise, whatever perfection it possesses. Now it has been shown above (Q. 19, A. 4) that God's will is the cause of all things. It must needs be, therefore, that a thing has existence, or any kind of good, only inasmuch as it is willed by God. To every existing thing, then, God wills some good. Hence, since to love anything is nothing else than to will good to that thing, it is manifest that God loves everything that exists. Yet not as we love. Because since our will is not the cause of the goodness of things, but is moved by it as by its object, our love, whereby we will good to anything, is not the cause of its goodness; but conversely its goodness, whether real or imaginary, calls forth our love, by which we will that it should preserve the good it has, and receive besides the good it has not, and to this end we direct our actions: whereas the love of God infuses and creates goodness.

Reply Obj. 1. A lover is placed outside himself, and made to pass into the object of his love, inasmuch as he wills good to the beloved; and works for that good by his providence even as he works for his own. Hence Dionysius says (*l.c.*): *On behalf of the truth we must make bold to say even this, that He Himself, the cause of all things, by His abounding love and goodness, is placed outside Himself by His providence for all existing things.*

Reply Obj. 2. Although creatures have not existed from eternity, except in God, yet because they have been in Him from eternity, God has known them eternally in their proper natures; and for that reason has loved them, even as we, by the images of things within us, know things existing in themselves.

Reply Obj. 3. Friendship cannot exist except towards rational creatures, who are capable of returning love, and communicating one with another in the various works of life, and who may fare well or ill, according to the changes of fortune and happiness; even as to them is benevolence properly speaking exercised. But irrational creatures cannot attain to loving God, nor to any share in the intellectual and beatific life that He lives. Strictly speaking, therefore, God does not love irrational creatures with the love of friendship; but as it were with the love of desire, in so far as He orders them to rational creatures, and even to Himself. Yet this is not because He stands in need of them; but only on account of His goodness, and of the services they render to us. For we can desire a thing for others as well as for ourselves.

Reply Obj. 4. Nothing prevents one and the same thing being loved under one aspect, while it is hated under another. God loves sinners in so far as they are existing natures; for they have existence, and have it from Him. In so far as they are sinners, they have not existence at all, but fall short of it; and this in them is not from God. Hence under this aspect, they are hated by Him.

ARTICLE 3. Whether God loves all things equally?

Objection 1. It seems that God loves all things equally. For it is said: *He hath equally care of all* (Wis. vi. 8). But God's providence over things comes from the love wherewith He loves them. Therefore He loves all things equally.

Obj. 2. Further, the love of God is His essence. But God's essence does not admit of degree; neither therefore does His love. He does not therefore love some things more than others.

Obj. 3. Further, as God's love extends to created things, so do His knowledge and will extend. But God is not said to know some things more than others; nor will one thing more than another. Neither therefore does He love some things more than others.

On the contrary, Augustine says (*Tract. in Joan.* cx): *God loves all things that He has made, and amongst them rational creatures more, and of these especially those who are members of his only-begotten Son; and much more than all, His only-begotten Son Himself.*

I answer that, Since to love a thing is to will it good, in a twofold way anything may be loved more, or less. In one way on the part of the act of the will itself, which is more or less intense. In this way God does not love some things more than others, because He loves all things by an act of the will that is one, simple, and always the same. In another way on the part of the good itself that a person wills for the beloved. In this way we are said to love that one more than another, for whom we will a greater good, though our will is not more intense. In this way we must needs say that God loves some things more than others. For since God's love is the cause of goodness in things, as has been said (A. 2), no one thing would be better than another, if God did not will greater good for one than for another.

Reply Obj. 1. God is said to have equally care of all, not because by His care He deals out equal good to all, but because He administers all things with a like wisdom and goodness.

Reply Obj. 2. This argument is based on the intensity of love on the part of the act of the will, which is the divine essence. But the good that God wills for His creatures, is not the divine essence. Therefore there is no reason why it may not vary in degree.

Reply Obj. 3. To understand and to will denote the act alone, and do not include in their meaning objects from the diversity of which God may be said to know or will more or less, as has been said with respect to God's love.

QUESTIONS FOR STUDY AND DISCUSSION

1. Would it make sense to consider life a type of activity added to God's existence or is it that very existence itself?
2. What connection allows the mind to move from life to intellect, thence to will, and from will to love in articulating the meaning of life in God?
3. What is the philosophical meaning of the statement: God is love?
4. If God loves himself with an infinite love, can he then also love others? What relation does this have to the perennial metaphysical problem of the "one and the many"?
5. Some have said that prosperity is a manifestation of special divine preference. In what way is this true? Are the poor really blessed?

The Work of God in the Workings of Nature

QUESTION 3. OF CREATION

ARTICLE 7. Does God work in operations of nature?

The seventh point of inquiry is whether God works in the operations of nature: and apparently the answer should be in the negative.

1. Nature neither fails in necessary things nor abounds in the super-

From pp. 123–35 of St. Thomas Aquinas, *On the Power of God,* translated by the English Dominican Fathers, in *Questiones Disputatae de Potentia.* Copyright 1952 by The Newman Press. Reprinted by permission of the publisher.

fluous. Now the action of nature requires nothing more than an active force in the agent, and passivity in the recipient. Therefore there is no need for the divine power to operate in things.

2. It may be replied that the active force of nature depends in its operation on the operation of God.—On the contrary as the operation of created nature depends on the divine operation, so the operation of an elemental body depends on the operation of a heavenly body: because the heavenly body stands in relation to the elemental body, as a first to a second cause. Now no one maintains that the heavenly body operates in every action of an elemental body. Therefore we must not say that God operates in every operation of nature.

3. If God operates in every operation of nature God's operation and nature's are either one and the same operation or they are distinct. They are not one and the same: since unity of operation proves unity of nature: wherefore as in Christ there are two natures, so also are there two operations: and it is clear that God's nature and man's are not the same. Nor can they be two distinct operations: because distinct operations cannot seemingly terminate in one and the same product, since movements and operations are diversified by their terms. Therefore it is altogether impossible that God operate in nature.

4. It will be replied that two operations can have the same term, if one is subordinate to the other.—On the contrary, when several things are immediately related to some one thing, one is not subordinate to the other. Now both God and nature produce the natural effect immediately. Therefore of God's operation and nature's one is not subordinate to the other.

5. Whenever God fashions a nature, by that very fact he gives it all that belongs essentially to that nature: thus by the very fact that he makes a man he gives him a rational soul. Now strength is essentially a principle of action, since it is the perfection of power, and power is a principle of acting on another which is distinct (*Metaph.* v, 12). Therefore by implanting natural forces in things, he enabled them to perform their natural operations. Hence there is no need for him also to operate in nature.

6. It might be replied that natural forces like other beings cannot last unless they be upheld by the divine power.—On the contrary, to operate on a thing is not the same as to operate in it. Now the operation whereby God either produces or preserves the forces of nature, has its effect on those forces by producing or preserving them. Therefore this does not prove that God works in the operations of nature.

7. If God works in the operations of nature, it follows that by so doing He imparts something to the natural agent: since every agent by acting makes something to be actual. Either then this something suffices for nature to be able to operate by itself, or it does not suffice. If it suffices, then since God also gave nature its natural forces, for the same reason we may say that the natural forces were sufficient for nature to act: and there will be no further need for God to do anything towards nature's operation be-

sides giving nature the natural forces. If on the other hand it does not suffice, he will need to do something more, and if this is not sufficient, more still and so on indefinitely, which is impossible: because one effect cannot depend on an infinite number of actions, for, since it is not possible to pass through an infinite number of things, it would never materialise. Therefore we must accept the alternative, namely that the forces of nature suffice for the action of nature without God operating therein.

8. Further, given a cause that acts of natural necessity, its action follows unless it be hindered accidentally, because nature is confined to one effect. If, then, the heat of fire acts of natural necessity, given heat, the action of heating follows, and there is no need of a higher power to work in the heat.

9. Things that are altogether disparate can be separate from each other. Now God's action and nature's are altogether disparate, since God acts by his will and nature by necessity. Therefore God's action can be separated from the action of nature, and consequently he need not operate in the action of nature.

10. A creature, considered as such, is like God inasmuch as it actually exists and acts: and in this respect it participates of the divine goodness. But this would not be so if its own forces were not sufficient for it to act. Therefore a creature is sufficiently equipped for action without God's operation therein.

11. Two angels cannot be in the same place, according to some, lest confusion of action should result: because an angel is where he operates. Now God is more distant from nature than one angel from another. Therefore God cannot operate in the same action with nature.

12. Moreover, it is written (Ecclus. xv, 14) that *God made man and left him in the hand of his own counsel.* But he would not have so left him, if he always operated in man's will. Therefore he does not operate in the operation of the will.

13. The will is master of its own action. But this would not be the case, if it were unable to act without God operating in it, for our will is not master of the divine operation. Therefore God does not operate in the operation of the will.

14. To be free is to be the cause of one's own action (*Metaph.* i, 2). Consequently that which cannot act without receiving the action of another cause is not free to act: now man's will is free to act. Therefore it can act without any other cause operating in it: and the same conclusion follows.

15. A first cause enters more into the effect than does a second cause. If, then, God operates in will and nature as a first in a second cause, it follows that the defects that occur in voluntary and natural actions are to be ascribed to God rather than to nature or will: and this is absurd.

16. Given a cause whose action suffices, it is superfluous to require the action of another cause. Now it is clear that if God operates in nature and will, his action is sufficient, since *God's works are perfect* (Deut. xxii, 4). Therefore all action of nature and will would be superfluous. But nothing

in nature is superfluous, and consequently neither nature nor will would do anything, and God alone would act. This, however, is absurd: therefore it is also absurd to state that God operates in nature and will.

On the contrary it is written (Isa. xxvi, 12): *Lord, thou hast wrought all our works in us.*

Moreover, even as art presupposes nature, so does nature presuppose God. Now nature operates in the operations of art: since art does not work without the concurrence of nature: thus fire softens the iron so as to render it malleable under the stroke of the smith. Therefore God also operates in the operation of nature.

Again, according, to the Philosopher (*Phys.* ii, 2) man and the sun generate man. Now just as the generative act in man depends on the action of the sun, so and much more does the action of nature depend on the action of God. Therefore in every action of nature God operates also.

Further, nothing can act except what exists. Now nature cannot exist except through God's action, for it would fall into nothingness were it not preserved in being by the action of the divine power, as Augustine states (*Gen. ad lit.*). Therefore nature cannot act unless God act also.

Again, God's power is in every natural thing, since he is in all things by his essence, his presence and his power. Now it cannot be admitted that God's power forasmuch as it is in things is not operative: and consequently it operates as being in nature. And it cannot be said to operate something besides what nature operates, since evidently there is but one operation. Therefore God works in every operation of nature.

I answer that we must admit without any qualification that God operates in the operations of nature and will. Some, however, through failing to understand this aright fell into error, and ascribed to God every operation of nature in the sense that nature does nothing at all by its own power. They were led to hold this opinion by various arguments. Thus according to Rabbi Moses some of the sages in the Moorish books of law asserted that all these natural forms are accidents, and since an accident cannot pass from one subject to another, they deemed it impossible for a natural agent by its form to produce in any way a similar form in another subject, and consequently they said that fire does not heat but God creates heat in that which is made hot. And if it were objected to them, that a thing becomes hot whenever it is placed near the fire, unless some obstacle be in the way, which shows that fire is the *per se* cause of heat; they replied that God established the order to be observed according to which he would never cause heat except at the presence of fire: and that the fire itself would have no part in the action of heating. This opinion is manifestly opposed to the nature of sensation: for since the senses do not perceive unless they are acted upon by the sensible object—which is clearly true in regard to touch and the other senses except sight, since some maintain that this is effected by the visual organ projecting itself on to the object—it would follow that a man does not feel the fire's heat, if the action of the fire does not produce in the sensorial organ a likeness of the heat that is in the fire. In fact if this heat-species be produced in the organ by another agent, although the touch would sense the heat, it would not sense the heat of the fire, nor would it perceive that the fire is hot, and yet the sense judges this to be the case, and the senses do not err about their proper object.

It is also opposed to reason which convinces us that nothing in nature is void of purpose. Now unless natural things had an action of their own the forms and forces with which they are endowed would be to no purpose; thus if a knife does not cut, its sharpness is useless. It would also be useless to set fire to the coal, if God ignites the coal without fire.

It is also opposed to God's goodness which is self-communicative: the result being that things were made like God not only in being but also in acting.

The argument which they put forward is altogether frivolous. When we say that an accident does not pass from one subject to another, this refers to the same identical accident, and we do not deny that an accident subjected in a natural thing can produce an accident of like species in another subject: indeed this happens of necessity in every natural action. Moreover, they suppose that all forms are accidents, and this is not true: because then in natural things there would be no substantial being, the principle of which cannot be an accidental but only a substantial form. Moreover, this would make an end of generation and corruption: and many other absurdities would follow.

Avicebron (*Fonts Vitæ*) says that no corporeal substance acts, but that a spiritual energy penetrating all bodies acts in them, and that the measure of a body's activity is according to the measure of its purity and subtlety, whereby it is rendered amenable to the influence of a spiritual force. He supports his statement by three arguments. His first argument is that every agent after God requires subject-matter on which to act: and no corporeal agent has matter subject to it, wherefore seemingly it cannot act. His second argument is that quantity hinders action and movement: in proof of which he points out that a bulky body is slow of movement and heavy: wherefore a corporeal substance being inseparable from quantity cannot act. His third argument is that the corporeal substance is furthest removed from the first agent, which is purely active and nowise passive, while the intermediate substances are both active and passive: and therefore corporeal substances which come last, must needs be passive only and not active.

Now all this is manifestly fallacious in that he takes all corporeal substances as one single substance; and as though they differed from one another only in accidental and not in their substantial being. If the various corporeal substances be taken as substantially distinct, every one will not occupy the last place and the furthest removed from the first agent, so that one will be able to act on another.—Again in the foregoing arguments the corporeal substance is considered only in respect of its matter and not in respect of its form, whereas it is composed of both. It is true that the corporeal substance belongs to the lowest grade of beings, and has no subject beneath it, but this is by reason of its matter, not of its form: because in respect of its form a corporeal substance has an inferior subject in any other substance whose matter has potentially that form which the corporeal substance in question has actually. Hence it follows that there is mutual action in corporeal substances, since in the matter of one there is potentially the form of another, and vice versa. And if this form does not suffice to act, for the same reason neither does the energy of a spiritual substance, which the corporeal substance must needs receive according to its mode.—Nor does quantity hinder movement and action, since nothing is moved but that which has quantity (*Phys.* vi, 10). Nor is it true that quantity causes weight. This is disproved in *De Cælo* iv, 2. In fact, quantity increases the speed of natural movement, thus a weighty body, the greater it is, the greater the velocity of its downward movement, and in like manner that of a light body in its movement upwards. And although quantity in itself is not a principle of action, no reason can be given why it should hinder action, seeing that rather is it the instrument of an active quality; except in so far as active forms in quantitative matter receive a certain limited being that is confined to that particular matter, so that their action does not extend to an extraneous matter. But though they receive individual being in matter, they retain their specific nature, by reason whereof they can produce their like in species, and yet are unable themselves to be in another subject. Hence we are to understand that God works in every natural thing not as though the natural thing were altogether inert, but because God works in both nature and will when they work. How this may be we must now explain.

It must be observed that one thing may be the cause of another's action in several ways. First, by giving it the power to act: thus it is said that the generator moves heavy and light bodies, inasmuch as it gives them the power from which that movement results. In this way God causes all the actions of nature, because he gave natural things the forces whereby they are able to act, not only as the generator gives power to heavy and light bodies yet does not preserve it, but also as upholding its very being, forasmuch as he is the cause of the power bestowed, not only like the generator in its becoming, but also in its being; and thus God may be said to be the cause of an action by both causing and upholding the natural power in its being. For secondly, the preserver of a power is said to cause the action; thus a remedy that preserves the sight is said to make a man see. But since nothing moves or acts of itself unless it be an unmoved mover; thirdly, a thing is said to cause another's action by moving it to act: whereby we do not mean that it causes or preserves the active power, but that it applies the power to action, even as a man causes the knife's cutting by the very fact that he applies the sharpness of the knife to cutting by moving it to cut.

And since the lower nature in acting does not act except through being moved, because these lower bodies are both subject to and cause alteration: whereas the heavenly body causes alteration without being subject to it, and yet it does not cause movement unless it be itself moved, so that we must eventually trace its movement to God, it follows of necessity that God causes the action of every natural thing by moving and applying its power to action. Furthermore we find that the order of effects follows the order of causes, and this must needs be so on account of the likeness of the effect to its cause. Nor can the second cause by its own power have any influence on the effect of the first cause, although it is the instrument of the first cause in regard to that effect: because an instrument is in a manner the cause of the principal cause's effect, not by its own form or power, but in so far as it participates somewhat in the power of the principal cause through being moved thereby: thus the axe is the cause of the craftsman's handiwork not by its own form or power, but by the power of the craftsman who moves it so that it participates in his power. Hence, fourthly, one thing causes the action of another, as a principal agent causes the action of its instrument: and in this way again we must say that God causes every action of natural things. For the higher the cause the greater its scope and efficacity: and the more efficacious the cause, the more deeply does it penetrate into its effect, and the more remote the potentiality from which it brings that effect into act. Now in every natural thing we find that it is a being, a natural thing, and of this or that nature. The first is common to all beings, the second to all natural things, the third to all the members of a species, while a fourth, if we take accidents into account, is proper to this or that individual. Accordingly this or that individual thing cannot by its action produce another individual of the same species except as the instrument of that cause which includes in its scope the whole species and, besides, the whole being of the inferior creature. Wherefore no action in these lower bodies attains to the production of a species except through the power of the heavenly body, nor does anything produce being except by the power of God. For being is the most common first effect and more intimate than all other effects: wherefore it is an effect which it belongs to God alone to produce by his own power: and for this reason (*De Causis,* prop. ix) an intelligence does not give being, except the divine power be therein. Therefore God is the cause of every action, inasmuch as every agent is an instrument of the divine power operating.

If, then, we consider the subsistent agent, every particular agent is immediate to its effect: but if we consider the power whereby the action is done, then the power of the higher cause is more immediate to the effect than the power of the lower cause; since the power of the lower cause is not coupled with its effect save by the power of the higher cause: wherefore it is said in *De Causis* (prop. i) that the power of the first cause takes the first place in the production of the effect and enters more deeply therein. Accordingly the divine power must needs be present to every acting thing, even as the power of the heavenly body must needs be present to every acting elemental body. Yet there is a difference in that wherever the power of God is there is his essence: whereas the essence of the heavenly body is not wherever its power is: and again God is his own power, whereas the heavenly body is not its own power. Consequently we may say that God works in everything forasmuch as everything needs his power in order that it may act: whereas it cannot properly be said that the heaven always works in an elemental body, although the latter acts by its power. Therefore God is the cause of everything's action inasmuch as he gives everything the power to act, and preserves it in being and applies it to action, and inasmuch as by his power every other power acts. And if we add to this that God is his own power, and that he is in all things not as part of their essence but as upholding them in their being, we shall conclude that he acts in every agent immediately, without prejudice to the action of the will and of nature.

Reply to the First Objection. The active and passive powers of a natural thing suffice for action in their own order: yet the divine power is required for the reason given above.

Reply to the Second Objection. Although the action of the forces of nature may be said to depend on God in the same way as that of an elemental body depends on the heavenly body, the comparison does not apply in every respect.

Reply to the Third Objection. In that operation whereby God operates by moving nature, nature itself does not operate: and even the operation of nature is also the operation of the divine power, just as the operation of an instrument is effected by the power of the principal agent. Nor does this prevent nature and God from operating to the same effect, on account of the order between God and nature.

Reply to the Fourth Objection. Both God and nature operate immediately, although as already stated there is order between them of priority and posteriority.

Reply to the Fifth Objection. It belongs to the lower power to be a principle of operation in a certain way and in its own order, namely as instrument of a higher power: wherefore, apart from the latter it has no operation.

Reply to the Sixth Objection. God is the cause of nature's operation not only as upholding the forces of nature in their being, but in other ways also, as stated above.

Reply to the Seventh Objection. The natural forces implanted in natural things at their formation are in them by way of fixed and constant forms in nature. But that which God does in a natural thing to make it operate actually, is a mere intention,[1] incomplete in being, as colours in

---

[1] I.e. not a permanent quality but something flowing "like colours in the air, or the energy of a craftsman in his tools," as St. Thomas explains elsewhere. [E.D.F.]

the air and the power of the craftsman in his instrument. Hence even as art can give the axe its sharpness as a permanent form, but not the power of the art as a permanent form, unless it were endowed with intelligence, so it is possible for a natural thing to be given its own proper power as a permanent form within it, but not the power to act so as to cause being as the instrument of the first cause, unless it were given to be the universal principle of being. Nor could it be given to a natural power to cause its own movement, or to preserve its own being. Consequently just as it clearly cannot be given to the craftsman's instrument to work unless it be moved by him, so neither can it be given to a natural thing to operate without the divine operation.

Reply to the Eighth Objection. The natural necessity whereby heat acts is the result of the order of all the preceding causes: wherefore the power of the first cause is not excluded.

Reply to the Ninth Objection. Although nature and will are disparate in themselves, there is a certain order between them as regards their respective actions. For just as the action of nature precedes the act of our will, so that operations of art which proceed from the will presuppose the operation of nature: even so the will of God which is the origin of all natural movement precedes the operation of nature, so that its operation is presupposed in every operation of nature.

Reply to the Tenth Objection. The creature has a certain likeness to God by sharing in his goodness, in so far as it exists and acts, but not so that it can become equal to him through that likeness being perfected: wherefore as the imperfect needs the perfect, so the forces of nature in acting need the action of God.

Reply to the Eleventh Objection. One angel is less distant from another in the degree of nature than God from created nature; and yet in the order of cause and effect God and the creature come together, whereas two angels do not: wherefore God operates in nature, but one angel does not operate in another.

Reply to the Twelfth Objection. God is said to have left man in the hand of his counsel not as though he did not operate in the will: but because he gave man's will dominion over its act, so that it is not bound to this or that alternative: which dominion he did not bestow on nature since by its form it is confined to one determinate effect.

Reply to the Thirteenth Objection. The will is said to have dominion over its own act not to the exclusion of the first cause, but inasmuch as the first cause does not act in the will so as to determine it of necessity to one thing as it determines nature; wherefore the determination of the act remains in the power of the reason and will.

Reply to the Fourteenth Objection. Not every cause excludes liberty, but only that which compels: and it is not thus that God causes our operations.

Reply to the Fifteenth Objection. Forasmuch as the first cause has more influence in the effect than the second cause, whatever there is of perfection in the effect is to be referred chiefly to the first cause: while all defects must be referred to the second cause which does not act as efficaciously as the first cause.

Reply to the Sixteenth Objection. God acts perfectly as first cause: but the operation of nature as second cause is also necessary. Nevertheless God can produce the natural effect even without nature: but he wishes to act by means of nature in order to preserve order in things.

QUESTIONS FOR STUDY AND DISCUSSION

1. Is God manifested in causing the operations of nature or in causing beings that can cause the operations themselves?
2. What reasons are there for holding that created beings can cause?
3. Is the ability to cause an addition to the reality of creatures or a natural implication of that reality?
4. Can the effect of a finite being still be called a creature of God, or were only the first finite beings creatures?
5. How is the causality of finite beings related to that of God in producing one thing?

What Is Truth?

QUESTION 1. TRUTH

ARTICLE 1. The problem under discussion is truth, and in the first article we ask: What is truth?

Difficulties: It seems that the true is exactly the same as being, for

1. Augustine says: "The true is that which is." But that which is, is simply being. The true, therefore, means exactly the same as being.

2. It was said in reply that the true and being are the same materially but differ formally.—On the contrary the nature of a thing is signified by its definition; and the definition of the true, according to Augustine, is "that which is." He rejects all other definitions. Now, since the true and being are materially the same, it seems that they are also formally the same.

3. Things which differ conceptually are so related to each other that one of them can be understood without the other. For this reason, Boethius says that the existence of God can be understood if for a moment we men-

---

From pp. 3–20 of St. Thomas Aquinas, *Truth,* translated by Robert W. Mulligan. Copyright 1952 by Henry Regnery Company. Reprinted by permission of the publisher.

tally separate His goodness from His existence. Being, however, can in no way be understood apart from the true, for being is known only in so far as it is true. Therefore, the true and being do not differ conceptually.

4. If the true is not the same as being, it must be a state of being. But it cannot be a state of being. It is not a state that entirely corrupts—otherwise, this would follow: "It is true. Therefore, it is non-being"—as it follows when we say: "This man is dead. Therefore, this is not a man."

Similarly, the true is not a state that limits. If it were, one could not say: "It is true. Therefore it is." For one cannot say that a thing is white simply because it has white teeth. Finally, the true is not a state which contracts or specifies being, for it is convertible with being. It follows, therefore, that the true and being are entirely the same.

5. Things in the same state are the same. But the true and being are in the same state. Therefore, they are the same. For Aristotle writes: "The state of a thing in its act of existence is the same as its state in truth." Therefore, the true and being are entirely the same.

6. Things not the same differ in some respect. But the true and being differ in no respect. They do not differ essentially, for every being is true by its very essence. And they do not differ in any other ways, for they must belong to some common genus. Therefore, they are entirely the same.

7. If they were not entirely the same, the true would add something to being. But the true adds nothing to being, even though it has greater extension than being. This is borne out by the statement of the Philosopher that we define the true as: "That which affirms the existence of what is, and denies the existence of what is not." Consequently, the true includes both being and non-being; since it does not add anything to being, it seems to be entirely the same as being.

To the Contrary. 1'. Useless repetition of the same thing is meaningless; so, if the true were the same as being, it would be meaningless to say: "Being is true." This, however, is hardly correct. Therefore, they are not the same.

2'. Being and the good are convertible. The true and the good, however, are not interchangeable, for some things, such as fornication, are true but not good. The true, therefore, and being are not interchangeable. And so they are not the same.

3'. In all creatures, as Boethius has pointed out, "to be is other than that which is." Now, the true signifies the existence of things. Consequently, in creatures it is different from that which is. But that which is, is the same as being. Therefore, in creatures the true is different from being.

4'. Things related as before and after must differ. But the true and being are related in the aforesaid manner; for, as is said in *The Causes:* "The first of all created things is the act of existence." In a study of this work, a commentator writes as follows: "Everything else is predicated as a specification of being." Consequently, everything else comes after being. Therefore, the true and being are not the same.

5'. What are predicated of a cause and of the effects of the cause are more united in the cause than in its effects—and more so in God than in creatures. But in God four predicates—being, the one, the true, and the good—are appropriated as follows: being, to the essence; the one, to the Father; the true, to the Son; and the good, to the Holy Spirit.

Since the divine Persons are really and not merely conceptually distinct, these notions cannot be predicated of each other; if really distinct when verified of the divine Persons, the four notions in question are much more so when verified of creatures.

Reply. When investigating the nature of anything, one should make the same kind of analysis as he makes when he reduces a proposition to certain self-evident principles. Otherwise, both types of knowledge will become involved in an infinite regress, and science and our knowledge of things will perish.

Now, as Avicenna says, that which the intellect first conceives as, in a way, the most evident, and to which it reduces all its concepts, is being. Consequently, all the other conceptions of the intellect are had by additions to being. But nothing can be added to being as though it were something not included in being—in the way that a difference is added to a genus or an accident to a subject—for every reality is essentially a being. The Philosopher has shown this [1] by proving that being cannot be a genus. Yet, in this sense, some predicates may be said to add to being inasmuch as they express a mode of being not expressed by the term *being*. This happens in two ways.

First, the mode expressed is a certain special manner of being; for there are different grades of being according to which we speak when we speak of different levels of existence, and according to these grades different things are classified. Consequently, *substance* does not add a difference to being by signifying some reality added to it, but *substance* simply expresses a special manner of existing, namely, as a being in itself. The same is true of the other classes of existents.

Second, some are said to add to being because the mode they express is one that is common, and consequent upon every being. This mode can be taken in two ways: first, in so far as it follows upon every being considered absolutely; second, in so far as it follows upon every being considered in relation to another. In the first, the term is used in two ways, because it expresses something in the being either affirmatively or negatively. We can, however, find nothing that can be predicated of every being affirmatively and, at the same time, absolutely, with the exception of its essence by which the being is said to be. To express this, the term *thing* is used; for, according to Avicenna, thing differs from being because being gets its name from to-be, but thing expresses the quiddity or essence of the being. There is, however, a negation consequent upon every being considered abso-

---

[1] Aristotle, *Metaphysics* III, 3 (998b 23). [G.F.M.]

lutely: its undividedness, and this is expressed by *one*. For the *one* is simply undivided being.

If the mode of being is taken in the second way—according to the relation of one being to another—we find a twofold use. The first is based on the distinction of one being from another, and this distinctness is expressed by the word *something,* which implies, as it were, *some other thing.* For, just as a being is said to be *one* in so far as it is without division in itself, so it is said to be *something* in so far as it is divided from others. The second division is based on the correspondence one being has with another. This is possible only if there is something which is such that it agrees with every being. Such a being is the soul, which, as is said in *The Soul,* "in some way is all things." The soul, however, has both knowing and appetitive powers. *Good* expresses the correspondence of being to the appetitive power, for, and so we note in the *Ethics,* the good is "that which all desire." *True* expresses the correspondence of being to the knowing power, for all knowing is produced by an assimilation of the knower to the thing known, so that assimilation is said to be the cause of knowledge. Similarly, the sense of sight knows a color by being informed with a species of the color.

The first reference of being to the intellect, therefore, consists in its agreement with the intellect. This agreement is called "the conformity of thing and intellect." In this conformity is fulfilled the formal constituent of the true, and this is what *the true* adds to being, namely, the conformity or equation of thing and intellect. As we said, the knowledge of a thing is a consequence of this conformity; therefore, it is an effect of truth, even though the fact that the thing is a being is prior to its truth.

Consequently, truth or the true has been defined in three ways. First of all, it is defined according to that which precedes truth and is the basis of truth. This is why Augustine writes: "The true is that which is"; and Avicenna: "The truth of each thing is a property of the act of being which has been established for it." Still others say: "The true is the undividedness of the act of existence from that which is."

Truth is also defined in another way—according to that in which its intelligible determination is formally completed. Thus, Isaac writes: "Truth is the conformity of thing and intellect"; and Anselm: "Truth is a rectitude perceptible only by the mind." This rectitude, of course, is said to be based on some conformity. The Philosopher says that in defining truth we say that truth is had when one affirms that "to be which is, and that not to be which is not."

The third way of defining truth is according to the effect following upon it. Thus, Hilary says that the true is that which manifests and proclaims existence. And Augustine says: "Truth is that by which that which is, is shown"; and also: "Truth is that according to which we judge about inferior things."

Answers to Difficulties. 1. That definition of Augustine is given for the true as it has its foundation in reality and not as its formal nature is given complete expression by conformity of thing and intellect. An alternative answer would be that in the statement, "The true is that which is," the word *is* is not here understood as referring to the act of existing, but rather as the mark of the intellectual act of judging, signifying, that is, the affirmation of a proposition. The meaning would then be this: "The true is that which is—it is had when the existence of what is, is affirmed." If this is its meaning, then Augustine's definition agrees with that of the Philosopher mentioned above.

2. The answer is clear from what has been said.

3. "Something can be understood without another" can be taken in two ways. It can mean that something can be known while another remains unknown. Taken in this way, it is true that things which differ conceptually are such that one can be understood without the other. But there is another way that a thing can be understood without another: when it is known even though the other does not exist. Taken in this sense, being cannot be known without the true, for it cannot be known unless it agrees with or conforms to intellect. It is not necessary, however, that everyone who understands the formal notion of being should also understand the formal notion of the true—just as not everyone who understands being understands the agent intellect, even though nothing can be known without the agent intellect.

4. The true is a state of being even though it does not add any reality to being or express any special mode of existence. It is rather something that is generally found in every being, although it is not expressed by the word *being*. Consequently, it is not a state that corrupts, limits, or contracts.

5. In this objection, *condition* [state] should not be understood as belonging to the genus of quality. It implies, rather, a certain order; for those which are the cause of the existence of other things are themselves beings most completely, and those which are the cause of the truth of other things are themselves true most completely. It is for this reason that the Philosopher concludes[2] that the rank of a thing in its existence corresponds to its rank in truth, so that when one finds that which is most fully being, he finds there also that which is most fully true. But this does not mean that being and the true are the same in concept. It means simply that in the degree in which a thing has being, in that degree it is capable of being proportioned to intellect. Consequently, the true is dependent upon the formal character of being.

6. There is a conceptual difference between the true and being since there is something in the notion of the true that is not in the concept of the existing—not in such a way, however, that there is something in the concept of being which is not in the concept of the true. They do not

---

[2] Aristotle, *Metaphysics* II, 1 (993b 27–30). [G.F.M.]

differ essentially nor are they distinguished from one another by opposing differences.

7. The true does not have a wider extension than being. Being is, in some way, predicated of non-being in so far as non-being is apprehended by the intellect. For, as the Philosopher says, the negation or the privation of being may, in a sense, be called being. Avicenna supports this by pointing out that one can form propositions only of beings, for that about which a proposition is formed must be apprehended by the intellect. Consequently, it is clear that everything true is being in some way.

Answers to Contrary Difficulties. 1'. The reason why it is not tautological to call a being true is that something is expressed by the word *true* that is not expressed by the word *being,* and not that the two differ in reality.

2'. Although fornication is evil, it possesses some being and can conform to intellect. Accordingly, the formal character of the true is found here. So it is clear that *true* is coextensive with *being.*

3'. In the statement, "To be is other than that which is," the act of being is distinguished from that to which the act belongs. But the name of being is taken from the act of existence, not from that whose act it is. Hence, the argument does not follow.

4'. The true comes after being in this respect, that the notion of the true differs from that of being in the manner we have described.

5'. This argument has three flaws. First, although the Persons are really distinct, the things appropriated to each Person are only conceptually, and not really, distinct. Secondly, although the Persons are really distinct from each other, they are not really distinct from the essence; so, truth appropriated to the Person of the Son is not distinct from the act of existence He possesses through the divine essence. Thirdly, although being, the true, the one, and the good are more united in God than they are in created things, it does not follow from the fact that they are conceptually distinct in God that they are really distinct in created beings. This line of argument is valid only when it is applied to things which are not by their very nature one in reality, as wisdom and power, which, although one in God, are distinct in creatures. But being, the true, the one, and the good are such that by their very nature they are one in reality. Therefore, no matter where they are found, they are really one. Their unity in God, however, is more perfect than their unity in creatures.

ARTICLE 2. In the second article we ask: Is truth found principally in the intellect or in things?

Difficulties. It seems that it is found principally in things, for

1. It was pointed out that the true is convertible with being. But being is found more principally in things than in the soul. The true, therefore, is principally outside the soul.

2. Things are not in the soul through their essences but, as pointed out

by the Philosopher,[3] through species. If, therefore, truth is found principally in the soul, truth will not be the essence of a thing but merely its likeness or species; and the true will be the species of a being existing outside the soul. But the species of a thing existing in the soul is not predicated of a thing outside the soul and is not convertible with it; for, if this were so, the true could not be converted with being—which is false.

3. That which is in something is based upon that in which it is. If truth, then, is principally in the soul, judgments about truth will have as their criterion the soul's estimation. This would revive that error of the ancient philosophers who said that any opinion a person has in his intellect is true and that two contradictories can be true at the same time. This, of course, is absurd.

4. If truth is principally in the intellect, anything which pertains to the intellect should be included in the definition of truth. Augustine, however, sharply criticizes such definitions, as, for example, "The true is that which is as it is seen." For, according to this definition, something would not be true if it were not seen. This is clearly false of rocks hidden deep in the earth. Augustine similarly criticizes the following definition: "The true is that which is as it appears to the knower, provided he is willing and able to know." For, according to this definition, something would not be true unless the knower wished and were able to know. The same criticism can be leveled against other definitions that include any reference to intellect. Truth, therefore, is not principally in the intellect.

To the Contrary. 1'. The Philosopher says: "The true and the false are not in things but in the mind."

2'. Truth is "the conformity of thing and intellect." But since this conformity can be only in the intellect, truth is only in the intellect.

Reply. When a predicate is used primarily and secondarily of many things, it is not necessary that that which is the cause of the others receive the primary predication of the common term, but rather that in which the meaning of the common term is first fully verified. For example, *healthy* is primarily predicated of an animal, for it is in an animal that the nature of health is first found in its fullest sense. But inasmuch as medicine causes health, it is also said to be healthy. Therefore, since truth is predicated of many things in a primary and a secondary sense, it ought to be primarily predicated of that in which its full meaning is primarily found.

Now, the fulfillment of any motion is found in the term of the motion; and, since the term of the motion of a cognitive power is the soul, the known must be in the knower after the manner of the knower. But the motion of an appetitive power terminates in things. For this reason the Philosopher speaks of a sort of circle formed by the acts of the soul: for a thing outside the soul moves the intellect, and the thing known moves the appetite, which tends to reach the things from which the motion origi-

---

[3] Aristotle, *De Anima* III, 8 (431b 29), [G.F.M.]

nally started. Since good, as mentioned previously, expresses a relation to appetite, and true, a relation to the intellect, the Philosopher says that good and evil are in things, but true and false are in the mind. A thing is not called true, however, unless it conforms to an intellect. The true, therefore, is found secondarily in things and primarily in intellect.

Note, however, that a thing is referred differently to the practical intellect than it is to the speculative intellect. Since the practical intellect causes things, it is a measure of what it causes. But, since the speculative intellect is receptive in regard to things, it is, in a certain sense, moved by things and consequently measured by them. It is clear, therefore, that, as is said in the *Metaphysics*,[4] natural things from which our intellect gets its scientific knowledge measure our intellect. Yet these things are themselves measured by the divine intellect, in which are all created things—just as all works of art find their origin in the intellect of an artist. The divine intellect, therefore, measures and is not measured; a natural thing both measures and is measured; but our intellect is measured, and measures only artifacts, not natural things.

A natural thing, therefore, being placed between two intellects is called *true* in so far as it conforms to either. It is said to be true with respect to its conformity with the divine intellect in so far as it fulfills the end to which it was ordained by the divine intellect. This is clear from the writings of Anselm and Augustine, as well as from the definition of Avicenna, previously cited: "The truth of anything is a property of the act of being which has been established for it." With respect to its conformity with a human intellect, a thing is said to be true in so far as it is such as to cause a true estimate about itself; and a thing is said to be false if, as Aristotle says, "by nature it is such that it seems to be what it is not, or seems to possess qualities which it does not possess."

In a natural thing, truth is found especially in the first, rather than in the second, sense; for its reference to the divine intellect comes before its reference to a human intellect. Even if there were no human intellects, things could be said to be true because of their relation to the divine intellect. But if, by an impossible supposition, intellect did not exist and things did continue to exist, then the essentials of truth would in no way remain.

Answers to Difficulties. 1. As is clear from the discussion, *true* is predicated primarily of a true intellect and secondarily of a thing conformed with intellect. *True* taken in either sense, however, is interchangeable with being, but in different ways. Used of things, it can be interchanged with being through a judgment asserting merely material identity, for every being is conformed with the divine intellect and can be conformed with a human intellect. The converse of this is also true.

But if *true* is understood as used of the intellect, then it can be converted with being outside the soul—not as denominating the same subject,

---

[4] Aristotle, *Metaphysics* X, 1 (1053a 33); X, 6 (1057a 9–13). [G.F.M]

but as expressing conformity. For every true act of understanding is referred to a being, and every being corresponds to a true act of understanding.

2. The solution of the second argument is clear from the solution of the first.

3. What is in another does not depend on that other unless it is caused by the principles of that other. For example, even though light is in the air, it is caused by something extrinsic, the sun; and it is based on the motion of the sun rather than on air. In the same way, truth which is in the soul but caused by things does not depend on what one thinks but on the existence of things. For from the fact that a thing is or is not, a statement or an intellect is said to be true or false.

4. Augustine is speaking of a thing's being seen by the human intellect. Truth, of course, does not depend on this, for many things exist that are not known by our intellects. There is nothing, however, that the divine intellect does not actually know, and nothing that the human intellect does not know potentially, for the agent intellect is said to be that "by which we make all things knowable," and the possible intellect, as that "by which we become all things." For this reason, one can place in the definition of a true thing its actually being seen by the divine intellect, but not its being seen by a human intellect—except potentially, as is clear from our earlier discussion.

ARTICLE 3. In the third article we ask: Is truth only in the intellect joining and separating?

Difficulties. It seems not, for

1. The true is predicated from the relation of being to intellect. But the first operation by which an intellect is related to things is that in which the intellect forms the quiddities of things by conceiving their definitions. Truth, therefore, is principally and more properly found in that operation of the intellect.

2. The true is a "conformity of thing and intellect." Now, although the intellect, in joining and separating, can be conformed with things, it can also be conformed with things in understanding their quiddities. Truth, therefore, is not merely in the intellect joining and separating.

To the Contrary. 1'. In the *Metaphysics* we read: "The true and the false are not in things but in the mind. In regard to simple natures and quiddities, however, it is not in the mind."

2'. In *The Soul* the statement is made that the true and the false are not to be found in simple apprehension.

Reply. Just as the true is found primarily in the intellect rather than in things, so also is it found primarily in an act of the intellect joining and separating, rather than in an act by which it forms the quiddities of things. For the nature of the true consists in a conformity of thing and intellect. Nothing becomes conformed with itself, but conformity requires distinct terms. Consequently, the nature of truth is first found in the intellect when the intellect begins to possess something proper to itself, not possessed by the thing outside the soul, yet corresponding to it, so that between the two—intellect and thing—a conformity may be found. In forming the quiddities of things, the intellect merely has a likeness of a thing existing outside the soul, as a sense has a likeness when it receives the species of a sensible thing. But when the intellect begins to judge about the thing it has apprehended, then its judgment is something proper to itself—not something found outside in the thing. And the judgment is said to be true when it conforms to the external reality. Moreover, the intellect judges about the thing it has apprehended at the moment when it says that something is or is not. This is the role of "the intellect composing and dividing."

For these reasons, the Philosopher says that composition and division are in the intellect, and not in things. Moreover, this is why truth is found primarily in the joining and separating by the intellect, and only secondarily in its formation of the quiddities of things or definitions, for a definition is called true or false because of a true or false combination. For it may happen that a definition will be applied to something to which it does not belong, as when the definition of a circle is assigned to a triangle. Sometimes, too, the parts of a definition cannot be reconciled, as happens when one defines a thing as "an animal entirely without the power of sensing." The judgment implied in such a definition—"some animal is incapable of sensing"—is false. Consequently, a definition is said to be true or false only because of its relation to a judgment, as a thing is said to be true because of its relation to intellect.

From our discussion, then, it is clear that the true is predicated, first of all, of joining and separating by the intellect; second, of the definitions of things in so far as they imply a true or a false judgment. Third, the true may be predicated of things in so far as they are conformed with the divine intellect or in so far as, by their very nature, they can be conformed with human intellects. Fourth, true or false may be predicated of man in so far as he chooses to express truth, or in so far as he gives a true or false impression of himself or of others by his words and actions; for truth can be predicated of words in the same way as it can be predicated of the ideas which they convey.

Answers to Difficulties. 1. Although the formation of a quiddity is the first operation of the intellect, by it the intellect does not yet possess anything that, properly speaking, is its own and can be conformed to the thing. Truth, accordingly, is not found in it.

2. From this the solution of the second difficulty is clear.

ARTICLE 4. In the fourth article we ask: Is there only one truth by which all things are true?

Difficulties. It seems that this is so, for

1. Anselm says that the relation of truth to all true things is like that of

time to all temporal things. But there is only one time to which all temporal things are related. Therefore, there will be only one truth to which all true things are related.

2. But it was said that truth is used in two ways. In one, it means the entity of a thing, as when Augustine says: "The true is that which is." If truth be understood in this sense, then there should be as many truths as there are essences of things. In the second way in which truth is used, it signifies truth as it is expressed in the intellect. Consequently, Hilary writes: "The true affirms existence." But since nothing can manifest anything to the intellect except in virtue of the first divine truth, all truths are, in some sense, one, inasmuch as they all move the intellect—just as colors are one in moving the sense of sight, since they all move it because of one thing: light.

On the contrary, however, time, the measure of all temporal things, is numerically one; and if truth is related to true things as time is related to temporal things, the truth of all true things must also be numerically one. It will not be sufficient for all truths to be one in their action of moving the intellect or to be one in their exemplary cause.

3. Anselm argues as follows: If there are as many truths as there are true things, then truths should change as true things change. But truths do not change with the changes of true things, for, even when true and correct things are destroyed, the truth and correctness by which they are true or correct remain. There is, therefore, only one truth. He proves the minor from this: When a sign is destroyed, the correctness of the signification remains, for it remains correct that the sign should signify that which it did signify. For the same reason, rectitude or truth remains even when a true or correct thing has been destroyed.

4. With regard to created things, nothing is identical with that whose truth it is. The truth of a man is not the man; the truth of flesh is not the flesh. But every created thing is true. No created thing, therefore, is truth. Consequently, every truth is uncreated, and so there is only one truth.

5. As Augustine says, only God is greater than the human mind. But, as he proves elsewhere, truth is greater than the human mind, for truth certainly cannot be said to be less than the human mind. If this were so, it would be within the competence of the mind to pass judgment on truth. This, of course, is false, for the mind does not judge truth but judges according to the truth, like a magistrate who does not pass judgment upon the law but, as Augustine himself says, judges according to the law. Similarly, the mind of man cannot be said to be equal to truth, for it judges everything according to truth. It does not judge everything according to itself. Truth, therefore, must be God alone, and so there is only one truth.

6. Augustine has proved that truth is not perceived by any bodily sense. His proof is that nothing is perceived by sense unless it is changeable. But truth is unchangeable. Truth, therefore, is not perceived by sense.

One could similarly argue that everything created is changeable. But truth is not changeable. Therefore, it is not a creature but is something uncreated. Consequently, there is only one truth.

7. Augustine offers another proof in the same place: "There is no sensible thing that does not have some similarity to what is false, and as a result, the two cannot be distinguished. To mention only one example: all that we sense through the body. Even when these objects are not present to the senses, we experience their images as though they were present, as when we are asleep or become delirious." Truth, however, has no resemblance to what is false. Therefore, truth is not perceived by a sense.

One could similarly argue that every created thing has some similarity to what is false in so far as it has some defect. Nothing created, therefore, is truth, and so there is only one truth.

To the Contrary. 1'. Augustine writes: "As likeness is the form of like things, so truth is the form of true things." But for many like things there are many likenesses. Therefore, for many true things there are many truths.

2'. Just as every created truth is derived from the uncreated truth as its model, and has its truth from it, so all intelligible light is derived from the first uncreated light as from its exemplary cause, and from it possesses its power of making things known. But we say that there are many intelligible lights, as is clear from the writings of Dionysius. Therefore, following this analogy, it seems we must likewise simply concede that there are many truths.

3'. Although all colors are able to affect the sense of sight in virtue of light, nevertheless, in themselves colors are distinct and different, and cannot be said to be one, except from a particular point of view. Consequently, even though all created truths manifest themselves in the intellect by virtue of the first truth, we cannot for this reason say that there is one truth, unless considered under this one aspect.

4'. Just as a created truth can manifest itself to the intellect only by virtue of the uncreated truth, so no power in a creature can act except by virtue of the uncreated power. Yet we do not say that somehow or other there is one power for all powers; so, in the same manner, we should not say that in some way there is one truth for all truths.

5'. God as a cause is related to things in three ways: as an efficient, an exemplary, and as a final cause. Consequently, by a kind of appropriation, the entity of things is referred to God as efficient cause, their truth to Him as an exemplary cause, their goodness to Him as a final cause—even though, properly speaking, each single one could be referred to each single cause. But in no manner of speaking do we say that there is one goodness for all good things, or one entity for all beings. Therefore, we should not say that there is one truth for all true things.

6'. Although there is one uncreated truth from which all created truths take their model, these truths are not modeled on it in the same way. For while it is true that the uncreated truth has the same relation to all, all do not have the same relation to it—as pointed out in *The Causes*. Necessary and contingent truths are modeled on the uncreated truth in quite different ways. But different ways of imitating the divine model cause diversity among created things. Consequently, there are many created truths.

7'. Truth is "the conformity of thing and intellect." But since things differ specifically, there cannot be a single conformity to the intellect. So, since true things are specifically different, there cannot be one truth for all true things.

8'. Augustine writes as follows: "One must believe that the nature of the human mind is so connected with intelligible things that it gazes upon all it knows by means of a unique light." Now, the light by whose means the soul knows all things is truth. Truth, therefore, belongs to the same genus as the soul and must be a created thing. Consequently, in different creatures there are different truths.

Reply. From our previous discussion it is clear that truth is properly found in the human or divine intellect, as health is found in an animal. In things, however, truth is found because of some relation to intellect —just as health is said to be in things other than animals in so far as they bring about or preserve animal health. Truth, therefore, is properly and primarily in the divine intellect. In the human intellect, it exists properly but secondarily, for it exists there only because of a relation to either one of the two truths just mentioned.

In his gloss on these words of Psalm 11 (v. 2), "Truths are decayed from among the children of men," Augustine writes that the truth of the divine intellect is one, and from it are drawn the many truths that are in the human intellect—"just as from one man's face many likenesses are reflected in a mirror." Now, there are many truths in things, just as there are many entities of things. But truth predicated of things because of their relation to the human intellect is, as it were, accidental to those things; for, supposing that human intellect did not or could not exist, things would still remain essentially the same. But truth predicated of things because of their relation to the divine intellect is inseparably attendant on them, for they cannot exist except by reason of the divine intellect which keeps bringing them into being. Again, truth is primarily in a thing because of its relation to the divine intellect, not to the human intellect, because it is related to the divine intellect as to its cause, but to the human intellect as to its effect in the sense that the latter receives its knowledge from things. For this reason, a thing is said to be true principally because of its order to the truth of the divine intellect rather than because of its relation to the truth of a human intellect.

So, if truth in its proper sense be taken as that by which all things are primarily true, then all things are true by means of one truth, the truth of the divine intellect. This is the truth which Anselm writes about. But if truth in its proper sense be taken as that by which things are said to be true secondarily, then there are many truths about many true things, and even many truths in different minds about one true thing. Finally, if truth in its improper sense be taken as that by which all things are said to be true, then there are many truths for many true things, but only one truth for one true thing.

Things are called true from the truth in the divine or human intellect, just as food is called healthy, not because of any inherent form, but because of the health which is in an animal. If, however, a thing is called true because of the truth in the thing, which is simply its entity conformed with intellect, then it is so called because of something inhering in it after the manner of a form, as food is said to be healthy because of a quality of its own—which is the reason for its being said to be healthy.

Answers to Difficulties. 1. Time is related to temporal things as a measure is related to the measured. It is clear, therefore, that Anselm is referring to that truth which is only the measure of all true things. There is only one such truth numerically, just as there is only one time—as the second argument concludes. However, the truth in the human intellect or in things themselves is not related to things as an extrinsic or common measure is related to those it measures. It is related as a measured thing is related to a measure, for such is the relation of truth in a human intellect to things, and it must, as a consequence, vary as things vary. Or, it is related as an intrinsic measure to the thing itself, as is the case with the truth that is in things themselves. Intrinsic measures must be multiplied as the number of things measured is multiplied—just as dimensions must be multiplied with multiplicity of bodies.

2. We concede the second argument.

3. The truth which remains after things are destroyed is the truth of the divine intellect, and this is numerically one. However, the truth which is in things or in the soul is diversified according to the diversity of things.

4. The proposition "Nothing is its own truth" is understood of things having a complete act of existence in reality. It is likewise said that "Nothing is its own act of existence," yet the act of existence of a thing is, in a sense, something created. In the same way, the truth of a thing is something created.

5. The truth by which the soul passes judgment on all things is the first truth; for, just as from the truth of the divine intellect there flow into the angelic intellects those intelligible species by which angels know all things, so does the truth of the first principles by which we judge everything proceed from the truth of the divine intellect as from its exemplary cause. Since we can judge by means of the truth of these first principles only in so far as this truth is a likeness of the first truth, we are said to judge everything according to the first truth.

6. That immutable truth is the first truth, which is neither perceptible by sense nor something created.

7. Although every creature has some similarity to what is false, created truth itself does not have this similarity. For a creature has some similarity to what is false in so far as it is deficient. Truth, however, does not depend on a creature in so far as it is deficient, but in so far as it rises above its deficiency by being conformed to the first truth.

Answers to Contrary Difficulties. 1'. Properly speaking, when two things are similar, likeness is found in both. Truth, however, being a certain agreement of intellect and thing, is not, properly speaking, found in both, but only in intellect; and since all things are true and said to be true in so far as they are in conformity with one intellect, the divine intellect, everything must be true according to one truth, even though in many like things there are many different likenesses.

2'. Although intelligible light has the divine light for its exemplary cause, light is nevertheless predicated in the proper sense of created intelligible lights. Truth, however, is not predicated in the proper sense of things having the divine intellect as their exemplary cause. Consequently, we do not say that there is one light in the same way that we say that there is one truth.

3'. Our reply given immediately above will answer the argument taken from colors, for visible is properly predicated of colors, also, even though they are not seen except by means of light.

4'–5'. Our answer to the fourth argument (from the nature of power) and to the fifth (from the nature of being) is the same.

6'. Even though things are modeled in different ways upon the divine truth, this does not keep things from being true in the proper sense of the term by a single truth—not by many truths. For that which is received in different ways in the things modeled upon the exemplar is not properly called truth with the same propriety as truth is said to be in the exemplar itself.

7'. Although things differing specifically are not on their own part conformed with the divine intellect by one conformity, the divine intellect to which all things are conformed is one, and on its part there is one conformity with all things—even though all things are not conformed to it in the same way. The truth of all things, therefore, is one in the manner described.

8' Augustine is speaking of truth in our mind as it is modeled upon the divine mind as the likeness of a face is reflected in a mirror; and, as we said, there are many reflections of the first truth in our souls. Or one can say that the first truth belongs to the genus of the soul if *genus* be taken in a broad sense, namely, in so far as everything intelligible or incorporeal is said to belong to one genus. *Genus* is used in this way in the Acts of the Apostles (17:28) where we read: "For we are also his offspring [*genus*]."

QUESTIONS FOR STUDY AND DISCUSSION

1. If being expresses the reality of all, show how one can proceed to identify "properties" that express what it means to be.
2. What does the relation of the transcendentals to being manifest concerning the reality of the transcendentals?
3. What does the relation of truth to intellect manifest concerning the importance of spirit for reality?
4. In what sense is being always between two intellects, God's and ours?
5. Does the relation of being to more than one intellect imply that there can be more than one truth; if so, are these truths related?

On Beauty

LECTIO 5. On the beautiful and how it is attributed to God?

He [Dionysius] shows how they are attributed to creatures. He says that the beautiful and beauty are distinguished in existing things according to the participant and the participated. Thus, the beautiful is called that which participates in beauty; beauty is the participation of the first cause which makes all things beautiful. Indeed, the beauty of a creature is nothing but the likeness of divine beauty participated in things.

Next, when he says, "The supersubstantial beautiful is called beauty because what is beautiful in each thing has been handed down from It to all existing things," he shows how the aforesaid items are attributed to God. First, how the beautiful is attributed to Him, in the text: "Now the beautiful is at once the most beautiful and the superbeautiful." Therefore, he says first that God, Who is the supersubstantially beautiful, is called Beauty, "because of the fact that He gives beauty to all created beings in accord with the limitations of each."

For, there is one kind of beauty of the spirit and another of the body and another of this and that body. And he shows in what the meaning of beauty consists, when he adds that God so hands down beauty that He is "the cause of harmony and brilliance" in all. Thus, we call a man beautiful because of a fitting proportion of members in size and position, and because of the fact that he possesses a brilliant and bright color. Hence, it should be taken proportionally in the case of others that each thing is called beautiful because it has the brillance of its genus, either spiritual or corporeal, and because it is established in due proportion.

He shows how God is the Cause of brilliance, when he adds that

God with a flash sends down to all creatures a share of His luminous ray, and it is the source of all light. These glittering communications of the divine ray should be understood according to the participation of likeness. And these communications are "pulchrifying," that is, producing beauty in things.

There is a twofold harmony in things. The first is according to the relation of creatures to God. He touches on this when he says that God is the cause of harmony, "as calling all things to Himself," in that He turns all toward Himself as to an end, as was said above. For this reason beauty is named *kalos* in Greek, which is derived from the verb "to call." The second kind of harmony is present in things by virtue of their ordering among themselves. He touches this point when he adds that He gathers all things to the same in all. And this can be understood according to the Platonic view that the higher things are present to the lower by participation, while the lower things are in the higher by eminence, and thus all things are in all. Finally, from the fact that all things are found in all by some order it follows that all things are ordered to the same ultimate thing.

Next, when he says, "The beautiful is at once the most beautiful and the superbeautiful and the superexistent according to the same," he shows how the beautiful is predicated of God. First, he shows that it is predicated by way of excess; second, that it is predicated by way of cause, in this text: "It is from the beautiful in itself that individually beautiful things exist according to a character of their own." He makes two remarks on the first point. In the first place, he advances the notion of *excess;* next, he explains it, in this statement: "and the superexistent according to the same." Now, excess is twofold: one sort is within a genus and it is signified by the comparative or superlative; another kind is beyond the genus and it is signified by the addition of the preposition *super*. For example, if we wish to say that fire is in excess, by virtue of an excess within the genus, we say that it is most hot—but the sun exceeds by an excess that goes beyond the genus, so we do not say that it is most hot but superhot, for its heat is not in it in the same way but more eminently. Now, though these two meanings of excess do not combine into identity in the case of caused things, yet, in the case of God, we say that He is most beautiful and superbeautiful, not in the sense that He is in a genus but that all that belong to any genus whatever are attributed to Him.

Then, when he says, "and the superexistent," he explains what he had said. First, he explains why God is called most beautiful; second, why He is called superbeautiful, in this text: "and like the One Who already possesses the source-beauty of every beautiful thing within Himself." Indeed, just as something is called white though it is mixed with black, so also is a thing called more beautiful by virtue of a removal of a deficiency of beauty. Now, there are two deficiencies of beauty in creatures. One occurs because certain things possess a variable beauty, as is evident in corruptible things. He first excludes this kind of deficiency from God, saying that God

is always beautiful in the same sense and the same way. Thus, the alteration of beauty is excluded. Moreover, there is in Him neither generation
nor corruption of beauty, nor again increase or decrease of it, such as we
find in bodily things. The second defect of beauty is the fact that all creatures have some sort of particular beauty, as they also have a particular
nature. He excludes this deficiency from God on the basis of every kind
of particularity and he says that God is not beautiful in one part and ugly
in another, as sometimes happens in particular things. Nor is He so in
one time and not so in another, as happens in those things whose beauty
falls within time. Nor, again, is He beautiful in regard to one aspect and
not in another, as happens in all things directed to one definite use or end
(if they are employed for something else, their harmony will not be maintained, nor will their beauty). Nor even is He beautiful in one place and
not beautiful in another, which in fact happens in some things because
they seem beautiful to some people and not so to others. Instead, God is
beautiful in the view of all and without qualification.

He gives the reason for all the foregoing when he adds that He is beautiful "according to Himself." By this phrase, these exclusions are made: He
is not beautiful in one part only, nor in a certain time only, nor in a certain
place only. In fact, that which belongs to a subject, in himself and primarily, belongs to Him as a whole, and always, and everywhere. Again,
God is beautiful in Himself and not in relation to some limited terminus;
thus, it cannot be said that for one He is beautiful and to another not beautiful; nor is He beautiful to some people and not so to others. Again,
He is uniformly beautiful and by this is excluded the first deficiency of
beauty, namely, variability.

Next, when he adds, "and like the One Who already possesses the
source-beauty by way of excess within Himself," he shows for what reason
God may be called superbeautiful, inasmuch as He possesses eminently in
Himself, and before all others, the source of beauty in its entirety. In that
simple and supernatural nature of all beautiful things that are derived from
it, every beauty and every beautiful thing pre-exist, not, of course, in a divided way but uniformly, in the manner whereby multiple effects pre-exist
in their cause.

Then, when he says, "It is from this beautiful thing that individually beautiful things exist according to a character of their own," he shows
how beautiful is predicated of God causally. He first asserts the causality of
the beautiful, then he explains it in this phrase: "And He is the Beginning
[*principium*] of all beautiful things." Therefore, he says, first, that being
comes to all existents from this Beautiful. Now, brilliance pertains to the
consideration of beauty, as has been said. Every form, by which a thing has
being [*esse*], is a participation in the divine brilliance. This is why he adds
that "individual things" are "beautiful according to a character of their
own," that is, in accord with a proper form. Hence, it is clear that the being

[*esse*] of all things is derived from the divine Beauty. Likewise, it was also said that harmony belongs to the intelligibility of beauty; hence, all things that pertain in any manner to harmony proceed from the divine Beauty. This is why he adds that for the sake of the divine good all things that pertain to rational creatures are "concordant" in regard to understanding (for those beings are concordant who agree to the same judgment), "and friendships" in regard to the effect, "and communions" in regard to the act, or toward any extrinsic thing whatever; and universally all creatures have, from the power of the beautiful, however much unification they may possess.

Next, when he says, "and He is the Beginning of all beautiful things," he explains what he had said on the causality of the beautiful: first, in regard to the meaning of causation; second, in regard to the diversity of effects, in this text: "This one good and beautiful being is in a singular manner the cause of all the many beautiful and good things." He makes two remarks on the first. One, he indicates according to what rational principle the beautiful may be called a cause; two, he infers a sort of corollary from the statement, in this phrase: "Because of this the beautiful is the same as the good."

First of all, he says, then, that "the beautiful is indeed the Beginning of all things, as an efficient cause," giving being, and like a "moving" cause, and like a "containing" cause, that is, conserving all things. But an agent cause acts by virtue of a desire of the end, because it is an imperfect agent not yet possessing what it desires. However, it pertains to a perfect agent to act by virtue of love for what it possesses, and for this reason he adds that the beautiful that is God is the efficient, moving, and containing cause, "by a love of His own Beauty." Since He has His own Beauty, he wishes to multiply it as far as possible, that is to say, by the communication of His likeness.

In the second place, he states that the beautiful that is God is "the end of all, like a final cause" of all things. Indeed, all things are made in order to imitate divine beauty in some fashion. Thirdly, He is the exemplary cause, for all things are distinguished in accord with the divinely beautiful, and the mark of this is that no one cares to make an image or a representation, except for the sake of the beautiful.

Next, when he says, "For this reason the beautiful is the same as the good," he infers a sort of corollary from the statement, saying that since the beautiful is the cause of all in so many ways, as a consequence the good and the beautiful are the same, for all things desire the beautiful and the good, as cause, in all ways. And since there is nothing that does not participate in the beautiful and good, and each thing is beautiful and good according to its own form, we might daringly say even this: "that the nonexistent," that is, prime matter, "participates in the beautiful and the good." For the first nonexistent being has a likeness to the divine beautiful and good, because the beautiful and good in God are praised by the removal of all. However, removal is considered in prime matter as a defect, while in God it is by way of excess, in that He supersubstantially exists. Now, although the beautiful and the good are the same in the concrete subject, since both brilliance and harmony are contained under the meaning of the good, nevertheless they are different in their rational intelligibility, for the beautiful adds to the good a directed relation to the power that knows an object of this kind.

LECTIO 6. Concerning the diversity of causes of the beautiful.

"This one, good and beautiful, is in a unique manner the cause of all the many and good things." After Dionysius has explained by what characteristic the beautiful is a cause, he here shows of what things it is the cause. On this point he makes two observations. First, he offers a general statement; second, he continues by distinguishing them in detail, in this text: "From this are the substantial essences of all existents."

So, he says first of all that "the good and beautiful," though one in being, is nevertheless "the cause of all good and beautiful things"—and they are many.

Next, when he says, "From this are the substantial essences of all existents," he continues in detail concerning those things of which the beautiful is the cause: first, in regard to being itself; secondly, in regard to the one, in the text: "unions and distinctions"; thirdly, in regard to their order, in the text: "the providences of higher things"; and fourthly, in regard to rest and movement, in the text: "all resting places and movements." Therefore, he says that all the substantial essences of beings are caused out of the beautiful. For, every essence is either a simple form or gets its perfection through form. Now, form is a certain irradiation coming forth from the first brilliance. Of course, brilliance belongs to the rational character of beauty, as we have said.

Then, when he adds, "unions and distinctions," he states the items that belong to the meaning of the one. On this we should observe that "one" adds indivision to the meaning of being. For, one being is undivided; hence, distinction or discreteness is the opposite to unity. So, he first states that the "unions and distinctions" of things are caused by divine Beauty. Now, a unit in substance produces the same, while a distinction in substance produces diversity; hence, he adds: "othernesses and diversities."

From a unit in quality a like thing is caused, while from a discrete distinction an unlike product results. So, he speaks next of "dissimilitudes." Similarly, a unit in quantity causes equality, and a discrete distinction inequality; but he does not speak of these because they belong to the commensuration of things, which he will treat later.

This may be noticed in things: that even the unlike items in something are in agreement, as, for instance, the contraries in a genus and in matter, and they are unified on some basis, but they remain distinct as parts within the whole. So, he adds, "the communions of contraries," in regard to the first point, and the "nonmixtures of unified items," in regard to the second. Now, all these points are reduced to the causality of the beautiful, since they pertain to harmony, and it is one of the rational characteristics of beauty, as was said.

Next he speaks of "the providences of higher things," and he names the items pertaining to the ordering of things. First, in regard to action, insofar as higher beings exercise providence over the lower ones, and he touches on this when he says, "the opposed relations of mutually ordered things," that is, of equals; again, insofar as lower things are turned to receive perfection and regulation from the higher ones, and this is where he speaks of "conversions of the less well-endowed." Second, he touches on those items that pertain to the existence of things in themselves, and this is where he adds that from the beautiful are "the dwelling places that preserve the same things," that is, of any things in themselves. For, something is preserved by the fact that it remains within the limits of its nature, for if it flows entirely beyond itself, it perishes. Yet, he adds, "and the not unlike collocations," that is, the foundations. For, just as something is preserved because it remains within itself, so something is not capable of passing away because it has something solid within itself on which it is based. Third, he states those items that pertain to the dwelling of one thing in another.

Consequently, we should note that when something requires to be constituted out of others, it is first of all necessary for the parts to be in agreement. For example, as the many stones from which a house is constructed must fit each other, likewise all the parts of the universe must agree in the principle of their existence. And so he says that not only are the dwelling places of things in themselves derived from the beautiful, but also "the communions of all things in all things in accord with what is proper to each." For all things are not in all in merely one way; instead, the higher things are in the lower ones by participation, while the lower are in the higher by eminence. Yet, all have something in common with all.

Secondly, it is a requirement of parts that in their very diversification they can be mutually adapted to each other. For a house is not made from cement and stone unless they be made suitable to each other. Likewise, the parts of the whole things are mutually adapted, so that they can fall under one ordering—and this is where he speaks of "adaptations."

Thirdly, it is required that one part be helped by another, as the wall and the roof are supported by the foundation, and the roof covers the wall and foundation. Likewise, in the whole of things the higher ones give perfection to the lower ones, and the strength of the higher is manifested in the lower ones. This is where he says, "and the unconfused friendships," because mutual assistance is without prejudice to the distinction of things.

Fourthly, there is required a due proportion among the parts, for instance, that the foundation be such as to fit the other parts. This is where he says, "and the harmony of the thing in the whole," that is, of all parts of the universe. For harmony is caused in the members as a result of a due proportion of numbers. With the parts so arranged, their composition into a whole follows. In this way, one universe of things is constituted out of all the parts of the whole. This is where he adds, "in everything," that is, in the whole, are "concretions." This concretion of parts in the whole is observed in two ways. First, by way of local containment, as the higher things are in beings in some way in the place of lower things (and this may be so either of spiritual or corporeal being). This is where he speaks of "unbreakable containers of existents," in the sense that the higher things contain the lower in an unbreakable order. Second, it pertains to temporal succession (but in this case only in things subject to generation and corruption, in which things the later ones come after the earlier ones). Here, he speaks of "the unfailing successions of things that are made." Now, they are called the unfailing successions of things, not in the sense that there are everlasting genera but that without any gap some members follow after others as long as the course of this world lasts. Now, all these features are caused by the beautiful, he says, because they belong to the meaning of harmony which is essential to beauty.

Then, when he speaks of "all the resting places and the movements," he continues in regard to rest and motion. These, too, belong to the meaning of harmony and beauty, in that they imply a relationship of one item to another. On this he makes three points. First, he states the causality of the beautiful in relation to rest and motion; second, he explains certain motions that seemed to be unmoved, in the phrase: "and indeed divine minds are said to be moved"; third, he offers a conclusion in the text: "therefore, the beautiful and good is the cause, the container, and the end, of three motions in these sensible things in this whole, and much more primarily of the dwelling places and resting places and collocations of each and every thing."

So, he asserts first of all the divine causation of "all resting places," that is, states of rest, "and motions," whether "of minds" or "of bodies." This he says, because that greatest part which is above all rest and motion is the cause of all things both at rest and in motion, in the sense that it gathers into place each thing in its proper essential character, in which the thing has its resting place, and in the sense that it moves all things toward the divine motion. For the motions of all things are ordered to the motion whereby they may be moved in God, in the same way that the motions toward secondary ends are related to the motion toward the ultimate end. Now, the form, on which the proper essence of the thing depends, pertains to brilliance; while the ordering to the end pertains to harmony. Thus, motion and rest are brought back to the causality of the beautiful.

QUESTIONS FOR STUDY AND DISCUSSION

1. How is beauty related to the other transcendentals?
2. What is the nature of the beautiful?
3. In what sense can it be said that God is beautiful?
4. In particular, what does the fact that the creator is beautiful imply concerning the beauty of creation?

TOPICS FOR DISCUSSION AND TERM PAPERS

A.

1. Did the Greek and Christian philosophers seek to unify the existing knowledge of their day into some coherent and systematic framework? Is this search for synthesis and striving for a unified knowledge an essential need for metaphysics? If so, why? Granted that Aquinas provided a synthesis of the knowledge of his own day, do you think such a synthesis is possible today?
2. Plato sought certainty in philosophical knowledge. When he could not find such certainty in the world of sense experience he claimed that certain knowledge could only be found in a world of pure forms and ideal essences, a realm totally apart from any possible sense experience. How did Aristotle base his metaphysics on the changeable beings in this world and still find the kind of certainty that Plato was after?
3. "Abstraction" is often taken to mean "emptying of real content." Is there a sense in which it can mean "opening to a more extensive real content"?
4. Is it true that Aquinas was the first to see the act of existing or to be as the prime character of reality? Did this insight make the metaphysics of Aquinas basically different from that of the Greeks? If so, how?
5. If Aquinas thinks that existing or the act of to be is the very internal structure of being, what role does he give to essence? For Plato, essence, especially the forms, had been beings in their own right. For Aristotle, primary substance was a being in its own right. Why does Aquinas see both form and substance as in some way potential to the act of existing? Does the doctrine of creation force Aquinas to claim that all beings other than God are in some way necessarily passive recipients of their very act of being?
6. Is there any way in which all the existing beings in the universe, including God, can be considered as having the same reality? Does a positive answer here lead to pantheism? Explain.
7. Discuss efficient causality from the point of view of its relation to the act character of being, and of its significance for the unity between finite beings.
8. If God must be transcendent in order to be God, does this mean that he is absent from or irrelevant to man? What does metaphysics contribute to the solution of the dilemma?
9. How can God be the end, goal, or purpose of all things and still be said to love everything?
10. How are metaphysics and art related in the contemplation of being as beautiful?

B.

1. For Aquinas the primary fact about being is the act of existing. For Dewey the primary fact about being is the fact of process. Are these two assessments incompatible? Explain.
2. How would you compare the particular attention of Aristotle to the realm

of sense experience with the emphasis found in modern empiricism and naturalism?

3. In view of St. Thomas' attention to the unique importance of intellectual creatures for the meaning of the finite world, what precisely has been added by the more recent philosophies (such as those of Sartre and Marcel) which center on the person and on subjectivity?
4. Does Christian commitment compel one to accept process and novelty, which recent philosophers have emphasized, as essential facts about the world?
5. Must a metaphysics of human freedom be a theistic or an atheistic metaphysics?

RECOMMENDED READINGS

Primary Sources

Aristotle. *Basic Works of Aristotle.* Ed. by Richard McKeon. New York: Random House, 1941. Most of the works by Aristotle now known are scientific in character. This is a fine collection of their major parts. The complete works of Aristotle from which these selections are taken consists of twelve volumes. (Ed. by W. D. Ross. Oxford: Clarendon Press, 1908–52.)

Augustine. *The Basic Writings of St. Augustine.* Ed. by Whitney J. Oates. New York: Random House, 1948. A selection of outstanding sections of Augustine's works, taken from the complete collection, which is in sixteen volumes. (Ed. by Marcus Dowds. Edinburgh: Clark, 1871–76.)

————. *The Essential Augustine.* Ed. by Vernon J. Bourke. New York: The New American Library, 1964. A collection of brief passages on the various phases of the thought of Augustine.

Plato. *The Dialogues of Plato.* Trans. by B. Jowett. 2 vols. New York: Random House, 1937. Almost all of Plato's extant writings in dialogue form.

St. Thomas Aquinas. *Basic Writings of St. Thomas Aquinas.* Ed., annot., and with Introd. by Anton C. Pegis. 2 vols. New York: Random House, 1945. The collection of extensive sections from different parts of the writings of St. Thomas.

————. *On the Truth of the Catholic Faith* (*Summa Contra Gentiles*). Trans. by Anton C. Pegis, James F. Anderson, Vernon J. Bourke, C. J. O'Neil. 4 vols. Garden City, N.Y.: Doubleday & Co., 1955–57.

————. *The Pocket Aquinas: Selections from the Writings of St. Thomas.* Ed. and with some passages newly trans. by Vernon J. Bourke. New York: Washington Square Press, 1960. A handy collection of brief passages from all sections of his writings and ordered according to the many types of issues which St. Thomas discussed.

————. *Summa Theologica.* Trans. by the English Dominican Fathers. 3 vols. New York: Benziger Bros., 1947–48. This is a complete edition of the *Summa Theologica.* A more recent translation which contains extensive descriptive notes and discussions is now being published in several volumes. (Ed. by Thomas Gilby and P. K. Meagher. New York: McGraw-Hill, 1964– .)

Commentaries

Allan, D. J. *The Philosophy of Aristotle*. London: Oxford University Press, 1958. An important study on the philosophy of Aristotle.

Bourke, Vernon J. *Aquinas' Search for Wisdom*. Milwaukee: Bruce Publishing Co., 1965. An excellent introduction to the writings of St. Thomas and the context of his intellectual work.

————. *Augustine's Quest for Wisdom: Life and Philosophy of the Bishop of Hippo*. Milwaukee: Bruce Publishing Co., 1945. A particularly useful introduction to the development of the thought of Augustine.

Chenu, M.-D. *Toward Understanding Saint Thomas*. Chicago: Henry Regnery Co., 1964. An important introduction to the structure of St. Thomas' writings and thought.

D'Arcy, Martin. *St. Thomas Aquinas*. Westminster, Md.: The Newman Press, 1954. A simple introduction to the thought of St. Thomas with particular comparison to various trends in modern thought.

Friedlander, Paul. *Plato*. Trans. by Hans Meyerhoff. 2 vols. New York: Random House, 1958, 1964. An excellent discussion of the central themes in the philosophy of Plato.

Gilson, Etienne. *The Christian Philosophy of St. Augustine*. Trans. by L. E. M. Lynch. London: Gollancz, 1961. A study of the themes of knowledge and faith leading to love and freedom in the thought of Augustine. A particularly scholarly insight into his philosophy.

————. *The Christian Philosophy of St. Thomas Aquinas*. Trans. by L. K. Shook. New York: Random House, 1956. A scholarly study of the main directions of the philosophy of St. Thomas with special attention to its relation to theology.

Jaeger, Werner. *The Theology of the Early Greek Thinkers*. Oxford: Clarendon Press, 1948. This work is especially effective in describing the metaphysical implications of pre-philosophic thought and the continuity of its development through the first period of Greek philosophy as it leads up to the formal initiation of metaphysics in Parmenides.

Kirk, G. S., and J. E. Raven. *The Pre-Socratic Philosophers*. New York: Cambridge University Press, 1957. The philosophy of the earliest Greek thinkers. Chapter I is particularly useful on pre-philosophic thought, and Ch. 6 compared to Ch. 10 describes the issues between the more dynamic and static metaphysical views as typified by Heraclitus and Parmenides.

Maritain, Jacques. *St. Thomas Aquinas*. Trans. and rev. by J. W. Evans and P. O'Reilly. New York: Meridian Books, 1958. A simple presentation of the religious and philosophical character of St. Thomas and the importance of his thought for the development of the Christian vision and its relation to modern problems.

Marrou, Henri. *St. Augustine and His Influence Through the Ages*. Trans. by P. Hepburne-Scott. New York: Harper & Bros., 1957. A simple presentation of the thought of Augustine with selected texts.

Pieper, Joseph. *Guide to Thomas Aquinas*. Trans. by R. and C. Winston. New York: Random House, 1962. A survey of the thought of St. Thomas and insight into its relation to the problems of science and religion in modern times.

Portalie, Eugene. *A Guide to the Thought of St. Augustine*. Trans. by R. Bastian. Chicago: Henry Regnery Co., 1960. A scholarly survey of the life and writings of St. Augustine originally written for an encyclopedia.

Randall, John Herman, Jr. *Aristotle*. New York: Columbia University Press, 1960. A competent study of the thought of Aristotle with special attention to the significance in relation to trends or perspectives in American philosophy.

Ross, W. D. *Aristotle: A Complete Exposition of His Works and Thought.* New York: Meridian Books, 1959. A fundamental work for any study of Aristotle.

Taylor, A. E. *Plato: The Man and His Work*. New York: Meridian Books, 1956. An excellent running commentary on the dialogues of Plato.

PART TWO

DIALECTICAL
THOUGHT:

Kant
Hegel
Engels
Marx

EDITED BY

Thomas N. Munson, S.J.
LOYOLA UNIVERSITY, CHICAGO

DIALECTICAL THOUGHT:
Kant
Hegel
Engels
Marx

Introduction

The Historical Setting

Today we speak of philosophy as a dialogue, and the philosopher as a man who is caught up in a swirl of ideas and events. Like everyone else he has been educated in a tradition, that is, he has been taught to listen to the past and to commune with the present, and so to express himself in a language that reflects our experience and our interest. The philosopher's gift to us is his vision. By his reflection he hopes to heighten our sensitivity to, and sharpen our insight into, the immediate. In a word, he would make us responsive to the ranging significance of the fleeting present.

If we accept this description as accurate and bear in mind the affinity of "dialectical" to "dialogue," then the problems encountered in understanding Hegel and Marx can be brought more sharply into focus. Aside from the language barrier (no English translation is wholly satisfactory), we might single out three problems as particularly formidable.

1. Only a detailed knowledge of intellectual history from the birth of Georg Wilhelm Friedrich Hegel (1770) to the death of Karl Marx (1883) can open to us "the world" upon which these thinkers reflected. The American and French Revolutions as incarnations of the spirit of freedom, the age of Goethe and Romanticism, the publication of Kant's *Critique of Pure Reason* in 1781, the rise and fall of Napoleon, the development of Prussian hegemony, the political upheaval of 1848, the Paris Commune—these were the events that quickened their thoughts and brought Hegel and Marx into dialogue with Kant, Fichte, Schelling, Novalis, the Schlegels, F. H.

Jacobi, Feuerbach, Bruno Bauer, Max Stirner, and others. Since Hegel as a rule only alluded to "the other" of his dialogues, we can easily lose our way and fail to appreciate his debater's points.

In comparison with Marx, whose work exhibits the simplicity and directness characteristic of the proletarian polemicist, Hegel is exceedingly complex. Not that he is less topical than Marx; his brief experience as a newspaper editor undoubtedly contributed to his philosophical preoccupation with "actuality." But to a remarkable degree Hegel exploited his classical and seminary education for illustrations of his dialectic. His reflections on art, history, religion, and government were intended to serve a metaphysical purpose, namely, to show the evolution of intelligence or the concrete development of thought in time. If the scope of this philosophy and its wealth of detail are obstacles to our comprehension of it, we must recognize that these are the features that account for its almost universal impact. Hegel, as French existentialist Merleau-Ponty remarked, is responsible for all that is outstanding in contemporary thought: Marxism, phenomenology, German existentialism, psychoanalysis. His distinguished group of disciples includes personalities as diverse and influential as the German Friedrich Nietzsche (1844–1900), the Italian Benedetto Croce (1866–1952), the Englishman F. H. Bradley (1846–1924), and the American Josiah Royce (1855–1916).

2. The Hegel and Marx in whom we are interested today are not purely historical personages. Contemporary Communism owes much to Lenin, Stalin, and innumerable theoreticians, whether Chinese, Russian, Yugoslavian, or other nationality. Moreover, we look at Hegel through Jean-Paul Sartre (b. 1905) and French existentialism, through Martin Heidegger (b. 1889), Nietzsche, and Søren Kierkegaard (1813–55), through his contributions to phenomenology and psychoanalysis. We find in Hegel or Marx what responds to our concerns and interpret accordingly. The reader of this volume should be forewarned of the conflicting potentialities of their thought so that he will approach the problem of interpretation with requisite caution.

3. Both Hegel and Marx thought dialectically. There is no simple starting point in systematic thought because knowledge is a circular movement. Any one point implies the entire system. Concretely, the *comprehension* of cellular mitosis actually requires a grasp of the whole science of biology, which in turn rests upon an understanding of other sciences (we contrast the validity of the "biological answer" with the "anthropological or chemical answer"), which likewise supposes familiarity with how man knows, and so forth. In Hegelian terms, the whole (the complexus of all knowledge) is the (complete) truth. In practice, this concept brings to light a major obstacle for the beginner. Marx and Hegel, and all philosophers for that matter, write from the viewpoint of their entire world view. How, then, does the uninitiated dip in to get a start? Every line presupposes an entire text!

Philosophy: The Hegelian-Marxist Interpretation

The Phenomenology of Mind

Let us begin with a general consideration of what Hegel and Marx meant by philosophy. One is tempted at first to regard their activities as diametrically opposed. Hegel's fundamental interest was the process of knowing. He traced the history of thought (Spirit, Mind) as if he were asking the question "What is the American mentality?" or "How does one detect the American Spirit?" "In our plastic art," we might reply, "or in our music, our literature, our architecture, our painting, or in our notions of science, of law, etc." And so Hegel looked at the ancient world—Egypt, Persia, Greece, Rome—and at the development of Western culture until his own day in order to discern what understanding or wisdom meant for diverse peoples in different historical contexts. The purpose of this phenomenology or description of "Spirit" operating in humanity was to afford an insight into the meaning and evolution of intelligibility. The questions, for example, that we ask today, and the types of evidence we acknowledge as pertinent are not necessarily those of even twenty years ago, much less of a century or a millennium ago. Human knowledge is "on the go." The discoveries of our nuclear age have opened up new problems and cast doubts on time-honored solutions. In philosophical circles we have had to take a fresh look at natural law, war, human rights, personality, and countless other issues. This continuous reassessment of our stock in trade, which is the burden of being human, not exclusively of being a chemist, a theologian, or a philosopher, piqued Hegel's curiosity. He was fascinated by the appearance and disappearance of essences or themes of attention on the screen of everyday consciousness. His philosophy articulates his wonder. Even his turgid prose does not completely drown out the optimism and triumphant finality of his study of being in time, of meaning in history, of the unity of forms of thought in the concretions of actual existence.

Praxis Versus Ideology

With Hegel in mind, Marx spoke of philosophy as an ideology—a speculative or purely ideal justification of what ordinarily presents itself as a contradiction in the real world. Basically, Marx's complaint was that Hegel's insight into understanding did not change anything or improve the world situation. How can a philosopher pretend to be involved if he occupies himself in playing word games and battling windmills? If he truly loves wisdom and would effectively benefit us, let him get down to the business of doing. Only a pragmatic knowledge or *praxis* deserves serious attention. Thus, in contrast to the contemplative Hegelian thought, which gives the impression that the spoils of victory over nature, science, history, and religion belong to the systematizer, that is, to the one who has grasped that process by which these various thought-unifications are accomplished, the thrust of Marxist thought is relentlessly destructive. His tone is strident, whereas Hegel's is subdued. At heart Marx was a revolutionary, and his work is a polemical critique of the philosophical criticisms of his day.

And yet Hegel and Marx were united by a bond other than the dialectical method which they inherited from their common ancestor, Johann Gottlieb Fichte (1762–1814). Both were bitter antagonists of what we have since called "alienation," from which has sprung the anxiety of modern man. In contemporary thought the theme of alienation is commonplace. In his meditations on freedom, Sartre has described its sinister growth in a context of one's finding himself over against, and in opposition to, "the other," whose presence limits his freedom and whose look depersonalizes him, that is, reduces him to a mere object or thing. For Heidegger *Angst* (anxiety) is part of man's fundamental existential structure. It is symptomatic of his need to go out of himself into otherness in order to discover and complete himself. Both of these contemporary thinkers borrowed this notion from Kierkegaard, who has graphically described man's fearsome situation as one of sober choice: either-or.

Marx extended Hegel's philosophical use of *Entfremdung* (estrangement) or *Entäusserung* (objectification) into the areas of his immediate practical interest. He blamed the capitalist system of private property for the proletarians' economic alienation because it unjustly deprived workers of the fruits of their labor. A social alienation resulted: society was split into the haves and the have-nots. The political alienation of proletarians was only an extension of their economic condition, for the rich manipulated the power of the State to maintain their financial domination. Finally, religion has always been a useful rationalization of alienation. Because the Church has operated on the principle that in order to safeguard its influence it must cater to the wealthy and aid in preserving the status quo, its ministers have mesmerized the socially and economically deprived workers with promises of spiritual blessedness for their practice of humility, meekness, and poverty. However sugar-coated, the pill of religion remains an "opiate of the people." It has lulled mankind into a soporific, unquestioning acceptance of things as they are.

Kant: Hegel's Point of Departure

The alienation proper to Hegelian thought is a philosophical concept that is wrapped up in the notion of self-consciousness. In his ordinary life a man is not philosophical. He does not begin to realize (Hegel would emphasize etymology: *real-ize*) what he is doing until he has reflected upon the import of his activity. Historically, Hegel hammered out this notion of a "return-to-self" or "being-at-home" in an effort to resolve the basic dilemma of Immanuel Kant's (1724–1804) metaphysics. The first selection in the readings is a clear statement of the program of Kant's *Critique of Pure Reason*. The second selection shows us what he actually accomplished, namely, a radical dichotomy of speculative and practical reason. Perhaps this alienation of thought from life's activity—the focal point of post-Kantian reflection—can be better understood from the following summary.

1. The rationalist tradition of Cartesian philosophy had stressed the clarity and distinctness of the mind's ideas as the immediate criterion of truth and certitude. The eventual reaction to this mental fixation was David Hume's (1711–76) empiricism, which emphasized the mind's passivity in knowledge and threw the weight of evidence on directly apprehended empirical data. Kant hoped to be the instrument of Providence in synthesizing these opposing philosophical traditions.

2. In the course of unfolding the structures of the mind, Kant uncovered a crucial distinction between the categories and concepts (e.g., cause, substance) of the understanding (*Verstand*), the exclusive function of which was to unify empirical data (perceived *phenomena*), and the reason (*Vernunft*), which operated with nonempirical, umbrella-like concepts (God, soul, world). Although these concepts were not empirically verifiable, they were deemed necessary as unifying schemes in the overall process of understanding or comprehending.

3. The upshot of this analysis was a metaphysics of finitude, that is, an affirmation of the essential dependence of man's knowledge upon sense data, with the important consequence that the unifying concepts of reason had to be thought of as postulates: objects of faith, not knowledge.

4. As a committed Newtonian scientist, Kant accepted the dogma of the causal determination of the natural world. But as a moralist, he could not deny freedom. He pulled together these centrifugal forces in his postulate of God as the supreme legislator and creator of the world who ultimately sanctions man's conduct. The irony of this position was that on the stringent terms of his metaphysics of finitude Kant could not *know* or *prove* any of these requirements for the specifically human or moral life. His own premises compelled him to leave man in suspended alienation, with knowledge and speculation divorced from faith and action.

Hegel: From the *Verstand* to the *Vernunft*

Hegel's resolution of Kant's dichotomy was effected by collapsing the abstractive or categorizing Kantian understanding into the dynamic or dialectical reason. In Kant's own terms, this means that the transcendental logic is absorbed by the transcendental dialectic, or, more generally, that the abstract universals or eternal essences of formal logic become moments or legitimate yet partial characterizations of things in the on-going process of human thought. The scientifically oriented Kantian thought is inductive-deductive, and therefore intrinsically connected with the promulgation of abstract forms or essences. Hegel's dialectic—the point bears repeating—is not a denial of the validity of this formal or scientific procedure. It is rather an insistence on the interplay of abstract and concrete, of universal and particular (hence of form and content) in the knowing situation. It is not wrong, for instance, to call John Doe a man, a being, a cause, or a substance. But it is myopic to believe that Doe's intelligibility is exhausted by these general classifications of abstract metaphysics.

In the preface to *Phenomenology of Mind* (1807), Hegel attempted to sketch his dialectic, in fact, to put into the hands of his reader the fulcrum of his ponderous system. But he was incapable of being popular, and the matter itself proved intractable. However, the strain caused by a critical reading of this important selection might be relaxed by keeping the following points in mind.

The Universal as Process

Hegel refused to dignify with the name of science the wholesale accumulation of facts. Even etymologically science means knowledge, which has traditionally been associated with generalization or universalized thought. Hegel shifted the emphasis to the process of universalization, since one can construe "universal" as meaning one-in-opposition-to-others (*unum versus alia*). Hegelian science, therefore, is organic; it consists in apprehending items in their interrelatedness. It is not, for example, a bare classification of the tissues, nerves, and bones of the hand, since this kind of conceptual or categorial thought is patently abstract or divisive. Instead, the prominent feature of Hegelian thought is the insistence on the total point of view, namely, of the whole body as necessary for a true (adequate) understanding of the hand.

PRINCIPAL DIALECTICAL TERMS. To enable us to come closer to that totality or unity that is life, Hegel urged that we recognize that even abstraction involves the reciprocity of form (that which) and ground (from which). As a result, Hegel's concept (*Begriff*) is the actual process of comprehending (*Begreifen,* understood as com-prehending), of holding together these two moments, form and ground, in their dynamic relationship. Accordingly, his reader must be wary of such terms as "universal," "idea," "life," "distinction," "determination," "negation." The first three of these are full-blown organic or dialectical notions; the movement or moments of existence are synthesized in them. The latter three attest to Hegel's indebtedness to Benedict Spinoza (1632–77) and his legacy to contemporary existentialists. The fact that man knows by means of a process of determination (one negates chairs by separating and distinguishing them from tables, trees, etc.) is the sign par excellence of the finitude of human nature. Here is the explanation for our need to complement our abstract and partial mode of apprehending by a reference to other aspects or further moments.

The Moments of the Dialectic

It is noteworthy that Hegel did not characterize this dialectic as thesis, antithesis, and synthesis. Still, these expressions are serviceable as long as they recall the process of philosophical thought or reflection. Experience begins with our immersion in the world. "Tossed" here, we are compelled to live with and react to "things." This is the moment of immediacy or unreflected position, which Hegel called the "in itself." Objects of all kinds are present to us to be treated or handled without their being formally characterized as determinate things in themselves. This further determination is the second moment of the dialectic, that of negation or particularity. The negation consists in knowing the object "for itself"; it has been located or specified in an intelligible world. In the next moment, that of full reflection, we are aware of our relationships to objects. We recognize that as subjects we have been thinking about a world, that is, rendering objects intelligible by classifying them as substances of various kinds. Subject and object stand in mutual dependence, in a union of the "in and for itself." This comprehensive moment is both a unification of the thought process and a realization, for in it the traditional universal concept and the particular are brought together to constitute the individual or *concrete* (realized) universal, the so-called negation of the negation.

The Concept as Process

The concrete or undivided (in-dividual) Hegelian universal is literally a con-cept, that is, a *taking together* of different or "contradictory" moments of thought. Thus Hegel designated the thought process an *Aufhebung,* a word that suggests a *suppression* or negation of what is partial or fragmentary, a *preservation* of the negated moment in the conservation of what is essential, and a *sublation* or sublimation to a higher or more comprehensive level of truth or reality. Because this thought process is a dialectical union of form-matter—in contrast to Kantian formalism in which the power of form (thought) works a unification upon the matter or content of knowledge—Hegel defined philosophical science as the unfolding of this process of making intelligible, or, in technical language, the exhibition of the concept. In brief, the con-cept offers us a systematic presentation of reality (the intelligible world).

Counterpositions

A significant portion of the preface to the *Phenomenology* is polemical. Hegel was elaborating his idea of philosophy or speculative thought in opposition to traditional and popular notions. If we accept his understanding of the con-cept (Idea, Notion) as the movement of thought and not as an eternal essence or product of abstraction, then we will take for granted that philosophical thinking and truth are evolutionary. Concretely this means that:

1. We do not begin philosophy from the privileged position of an immediately intuited ego or *cogito* (Descartes). In our experience, a disengaged ego is no primordial given; initial experience is a composite from which we extract an ego.

2. Philosophy does not commence with some sort of mystical intuition (Jacobi and Romantics) or obscure emotional knowledge (Hegel punned with Schleiermacher's name: a veil-maker). Nor can it be confused with the possession of an empty, formal concept, casually identified as the Absolute Idea (Schelling) or Being. Hegel charged the philosophers who have talked this way with formalism or abstractionism. For the sake of clarity they blotted out the distinctions and flux of life. In a way, everything is much simpler when we have to deal only with empty husks and common denominators. But this is to prefer the darkness to the light, to dwell in the night in which "all cows are black."

3. Diverse philosophical systems should not be juxtaposed in a rigid either-or, true-false fashion. Rather, each system can be regarded as having its truth and expressing its form of intelligibility, which subsequently developed systems refine or supplement. Because, for example, we have moved beyond Plato (*c.* 427–347 B.C.) in thinking our contemporary world, are we to condemn his philosophy as false? Alfred North Whitehead (1861–1947) captured Hegel's outlook when he remarked that all philosophy is only a series of footnotes to Plato.

4. The evolution of thought in time does not culminate in an insight into or grasp of an Absolute (a total view of reality or intelligibility) such that no further scientific developments are possible. Hegel's thought in this area is not as clear as might be desired. If we limit ourselves to the *Phenomenology,* we can readily entertain the idea that the course of evolution has halted and that we are now basking in the light of Absolute Spirit because we have understood the principle of dialectics. But to suppose that the logic of thought has been exhausted is not the same as to maintain that time has ended. Hegel's thought is that we have achieved the Absolute in the first sense. We have witnessed the unfolding of different patterns of thought in succeeding ages and have intimately experienced through "recollection" the entire history of our race.

5. This Absolute is the presupposition of Hegel's dialectical progress. Every evolutionary or teleological system requires a point toward which all development tends and from which the entire chain of events is intelligible. At the outset this focal point is implicit, and the task of reflection or philosophy is to unfold the total scheme of rationality concentrated in it. In other words, philosophy consists in an Aristotelian movement from potency to act. Its ultimate logical paradox is the "circle of knowledge"; such an actuation is possible only on the supposition that in some way act already precedes potency.

Hegel: Religion

If Kant's answer to Hume's empirical criticism was a metaphysics of forms of thought, Hegel's reply to the *Critique of Pure Reason* was a metaphysics in which the forms of thought are the modes of reality. Kant's transcendental logic was transfigured into the dialectical science of the *logos*. The religious overtones of this metamorphosis were not a pious flourish. In the *Lectures on the Philosophy of Religion,* Hegel was quite candid about the religious intention of his work:

> The aim of philosophy is to know the truth, to know God, for He is the absolute truth, inasmuch as nothing else is worth troubling about save God and the unfolding of God's nature. . . . Philosophy, which is theology, is solely concerned with showing the rationality of religion.[1]

There are superficial explanations for this religious concern: Hegel was a product of the Tübingen seminary and philosophers traditionally, even from the time of René Descartes (1596–1650), have exercised themselves on the problem of God. But the chosen selection, a part of the Introduction to the *Lectures,* will not make sense unless one keeps in mind Hegel's deep-seated opposition to the alienations that are summed up in Kant's word, "faith."

The Reduction of God to Man

It is evident that Kant's acceptance of the Humean starting point and the resultant restriction of "knowledge" to empirical data can be interpreted as a philosophical expression of his pietistic religious background. But whatever may have been the status of Kant's personal belief (his remarks in the *Opus Postumum* about seeking God only within ourselves leave us in a quandary about the exact tenor of his understanding of God), it is easy to recognize the danger of emphasizing divine immanence to the point of eliminating transcendence. As Karl Barth has warned us, whoever is concerned with the spirit, the heart, the conscience, and the inwardness of man must be confronted with the question of whether he is really concerned with God and not with the apotheosis of man. Beginning with Gotthold Lessing's (1729–81) criticism of historical Christianity and Kant's thoroughgoing rationalistic treatise, *Religion Within the Bounds of Reason Alone* (1793), the trend of religious thought was in the direction of a secular humanism. Practically all the significant writers of the late eighteenth, early nineteenth centuries—Schiller, Goethe, Herder, Hölderlin, Richter—

---

[1] *Lectures on the Philosophy of Religion, Together with a Work on the Proofs of the Existence of God,* trans. from the 2nd German ed. by E. B. Speirs and J. Burdon Sanderson (New York: Humanities Press, 1962), III, 48.

espoused a "rationalized" Christianity: a religion in which dogmas are forced to deliver their "true meanings," in which supernatural accounts are systematically demythologized, and in which religious conformity or practice is respected because of its bearing on "practical" life. Fichte's *Essay Towards a Critique of All Revelation* (1792) is a classical portrayal of this mentality. Regrettably, even the theologians succumbed to it and thus provided grist for Feuerbach's mill: "Theology is anthropology, that is, in that object of religion which we call *Theos* in Greek and *Gott* in German, nothing but the essence of man is expressed."

Hegel's works evince a lifelong involvement in this debate. Understandably, Christians of other denominations have disagreed with formulations that reflect Hegel's Lutheran commitment. But this difficulty is marginal when one confronts the obscurities, not to say contradictions, of the Hegelian texts which have richly documented conflicting opinions. The basic issue that split the Hegelians of the Right (the conservative, theistic group of young Hegelians) from those of the Left (the revolutionary, atheistic group that Marx joined) was this: Was Hegel the great reconciler who restored all things in Christ or the uncompromising rationalist who reduced a transcendent infinite to a finite human mind?

Hegel's Attack on Kant

It is possible to plot the general course of Hegel's religious thought without running into the controversy that surrounds this critical question. In attacking Kant's theory of knowledge, specifically the alienation of the nonempirical from the realm of scientific understanding, Hegel was actually making a direct assault on a perennial romanticism or mysticism to which the Kantian philosophy had lent an air of respectability. Mankind, it would appear, has had to be on constant guard against the temptation to make God utterly inconceivable and ineffable. An exaltation of his divine transcendence appeals to the fervor of some enthusiastic believers, as well as respects the scrupulosity of certain conscientious theologians. But how meaningful is it to claim that a wholly transcendent object of worship is man's God? From being intellectually unapproachable, God swiftly degenerates into something "emotional," pseudoscientific, and for intelligent people disreputable. Hegel was aware that Kant's empiricism celebrates just this kind of "bad infinite." To destroy this position, he planned a two-pronged counterattack:

1. He would free human reason from the empiricist's bonds and insist that in all human knowledge man "finds himself," that is, disclose the "rational" in things. An unknown God is a contradiction in terms. No one could speak of God at all if the infinite were not in some way assimilated to the finite.

2. He would carry this argument into the religious field by pointing to the Incarnation as the supreme example of the infinite's assimilation of

the finite, and by underlining the obvious fact that all divine revelation supposes an openness of the finite to the infinite. This is the sense of a remark he once made about Hamann, a friend of Kant:

> Hamann would not put himself to the trouble which in a higher
> sense God undertook. The ancient philosophers have described God
> under the image of a round ball. But if that be his nature, God has
> unfolded it; and in the actual world he has opened the closed shell
> of truth into a system of nature, into a state-system, a system of
> law and morality, in the system of the world's history. The shut
> fist has become the open hand, the fingers of which reach out to
> lay hold of man's mind and draw it to himself. Nor is the human
> mind a self-involved intelligence, blindly moving within its own
> secret recesses. It is no mere feeling and groping about in a vacuum,
> but an intelligent system of rational organization. Of that system
> thought is the summit in point of form: and thought may be de-
> scribed as the capability of going beyond the mere surface of God's
> self-expansion—or rather as the capability, by means of reflection
> upon it, of entering into it, and then when the entrance has been
> secured, of retracing in thought God's expansion of himself. To
> take this trouble is the express duty and end of ends set before the
> thinking mind, ever since God laid aside his rolled-up form and
> revealed himself.[2]

Having located Hegel's religious thought in its proper context, we have
not yet resolved its basic dilemma: Was the Absolute Hegel described in
the *Phenomenology* God or Man? A recent critic of Hegel has stated cate-
gorically that the "biography is of the human not of the absolute mind." [3]
Personally, I tend to agree with this verdict, but we should view with suspicion any facile answer that would bind Hegel to options that betray his
profession of Christianity. If we answer "God," does it follow that he was a
pantheist? Or if we say "Man," does that necessarily mean that he was an
atheist?

The Reaction to Hegelian Thought

Hegel died of cholera in 1831. By 1845 his philosophical theology, a
reconciliation of Christianity and the State, appeared to be doomed because the bourgeois-Christian world upon which it had been grounded was
tottering. Christianity bore the brunt of the attack. In *The Essense of Christianity* (1841), Ludwig Feuerbach (1804–72) reduced its essence to man;
David Friedrich Strauss (1808–74), especially in his *Life of Jesus*
(1835), attributed its gospels to the myth-making consciousness of the
Christian community; in a series of works Bruno Bauer (1809–82) denied

---

[2] William Wallace, *Prolegomena to the Study of Hegel's Philosophy and especially
of His Logic,* 2nd. ed. rev. (Oxford, 1894), p. 18. Cited as from Hegel's *Vermischten
Schriften,* II, 87.
[3] Jacob Loewenberg, *Hegel's Phenomenology: Dialogues on the Life of Mind* (La
Salle, Ill.: Open Court Publishing Co., 1965), p. 361.

the historicity and divinity of its founder; Marx credited its success to its promise of "pie in the sky" in compensation for the miseries of this life; Kierkegaard surrendered its historical reality—the Christian State, theology, the Church—for a despairing, decisive "leap of faith." Essentially, all of these thinkers had picked up the theme of alienation from Hegel. But they preferred self-estrangement to reconciliation, the moment of negation to the dialectical self-appropriation which Hegel had fancied as the freedom of the children of God.

Marxism: Engels and Marx

Friedrich Engels

The extent to which Hegel's dialectic had been secularized is evident in the first selection from the *Dialectics of Nature* of Friedrich Engels (1820–95), long-time collaborator and friend of Marx and author of a well-known treatise against German philosopher Eugen Dühring (1833–1921). In contrast to Hegel, whose alleged idealism had inclined him to stress the gambols of Spirit or "mere thought," Engels turned his attention completely to the physical or material world. His evolutionary naturalism is more likely to strike us today as a reflection of the scientific optimism of the decades immediately following the publication of Darwin's *Origin of Species* (1859) than as a companion piece to Marx's dialectic. Hence the pupil of Hegel will find little to approve in his work, and the disciple of Marx will wonder how Engels escaped the criticism that Marx had leveled at Feuerbach for conceiving nature as independent of man.

It will be apparent from Engels's treatment of *Feuerbach and the End of Classical German Philosophy* that he regarded himself in debt to Hegel for an evolutionary concept of truth and for a philosophy that had overcome the dichotomies of subject and object, of ideal and real, of form and content. The guiding passion of Hegel's philosophy, as Engels clearly saw, was the drive for the unity of thought and being: the real is rational and the rational is real. Yet, paradoxically, Engels joined forces with Marx in attacking the Hegelian idealism as a preoccupation with "essence" and, more broadly, with the demands of his system at the expense of the real problems of existence. Perhaps we can better appreciate these objections that are the foundation of the communist revolutionary point of view if we understand the reasons for a widespread disillusion with Hegel's Promised Land.

From Theory to Practice

At the beginning of his monumental study *Von Kant bis Hegel* (1921–24), Richard Kroner described the epoch of German idealism (1781–1821) in apocalyptic tones. A philosophical *parousia* appeared imminent. Kant, the "Moses of our nation" as Friedrich Hölderlin called him, declared at the end of his *Critique of Pure Reason:*

> If the reader has had the courtesy and patience to accompany me along the path, he may now judge for himself whether, if he cares to lend his aid in making this path into a high-road, it may not be possible to achieve before the end of the present century what many centuries have not been able to accomplish; namely, to secure for human reason complete satisfaction in regard to that with which it has all along so eagerly occupied itself, though hitherto in vain.

The youthful Hegel was nurtured by this illusion. In 1795 he announced to Friedrich Wilhelm Joseph von Schelling (1775–1854) the advent of the "kingdom of God" and later, while still under the influence of the spirit of romantic optimism, composed the utopian *Phenomenology of Mind.* Two characteristics of this work are noteworthy. First, its polemic against the Kantian and visionary "beyond," in which the philosophical balance is weighted in favor of an unrealized ought to be, can be looked at as an attempt to suppress a conception that disparaged the expectation of an impending kingdom. Second, having pursued the temporal development of Spirit in a fashion that gave to history an unprecedented philosophical role, Hegel, as we have already noted, brought evolution and history to a climax in the revelation of Absolute Spirit. Thus the forward surge of the *Phenomenology* has receded in the *Encyclopaedia of the Philosophical Sciences* (1817) and the *Philosophy of Right* (1821). Accordingly, since neither of these later works can be linked with eschatology, we are led to believe that for some reason Hegel shifted his sights from what becomes to what actually is. In religious terms, this reversal represents the fading of an Old Testament mood of anticipation before a New Testament contemplation of past salvific events.

The attitude of Marx and Engels toward this change of perspective oscillated between consternation and undisguised hostility. They were shocked at what amounted to a betrayal of the revolutionary cause. Hegel's mature philosophy was purged of activism; it braked the momentum in the direction of a world about to come in order to safeguard a respectable, bourgeois-Prussian conservatism.

Karl Marx

Many factors contributed to Marx's writing about the growing "Opposition of the Materialistic and Idealistic Outlook." But if we are to penetrate to the core of his methodology, of which the Preface to *Critique of Political Economy* (1859) is acknowledged to be a first-rate statement, we must concentrate our attention on the political issues that burst the bubble of philosophical optimism. During his university years in Tübingen, Hegel shared the passion of his fellow students for freedom. He read Rousseau. He was deeply sympathetic to the political stirrings across the Rhine. He responded enthusiastically to the idealistic slogans *Liberté, Égalité, Fra-*

ternité. It was the evolution of the "spirit of the fall of the Bastille" that he depicted in the *Phenomenology.* The course of this dialectic of freedom or self-consciousness is conspicuous for its sense of urgency, which undoubtedly Hegel felt because the World-Spirit incarnate in Napoleon was crashing through the gates of Jena. Anyone, we might suppose, could have predicted an inevitable letdown. Conquering armies are not famous for bestowing benefits. Instead of the eagerly awaited freedom, one experienced daily frustration. As a newspaper editor in Bamberg, Hegel was soon bogged down in the petty censorship of the bureaucratic State. It is not surprising that a sober realism gradually replaced his former chiliasm.

It is insufficient, therefore, to explain the differences between Hegel and Marx by appealing to an obvious lack of interest in economic questions on the part of Hegel. In his Germany liberty, not economic reform, was regarded as the mainspring of the French Revolution; during the Napoleonic period the country was too divided and turbulent for the development of a mass proletarian movement. Hegel's world of political and academic ideas had not as yet been touched by the deleterious effects of the Industrial Revolution. Then an untimely death intervened, which precluded any further emendations of the *Philosophy of Right,* the work that Marx savagely attacked as a glorification of the Prussian state. Perhaps Hegel's political philosophy is more correctly evaluated as a program, notwithstanding its pretense of being a factual analysis. At the time that he wrote the book, Hegel had no reason to question the good faith of Friedrich Wilhelm III's projected political reforms. Even if his composition had been blessed with Marx's hindsight (especially of the turn of events after 1848), it could scarcely have concealed the anguish of watching revolutionary hopes being washed away by tidal waves of reactionary conservativism.

Speculation Versus Action

Yet in a general assessment of Hegel and Marx, these historical factors recede into the background as merely contributory. Actually, they only articulate radically divergent views of the function of philosophy. Hegel was above all a speculative philosopher. His dialectic as a process of reflecting on experience describes the free activity of thought in rendering the world intelligible. In brief, his entire metaphysics can be summed up as an attempt to answer two questions: What is this comprehension of the world which we call knowledge? What is the reality of knowledge as a temporal process, or what is history?

Marx, on the contrary, was essentially an activist. He latched on to the futurist thrust of the *Phenomenology* (still the manual of the intellectuals among the French Communists) in order to exploit its reforming capacities. He dismissed epistemological and metaphysical problems as purely ideological. The question he wanted solved was: How can the world be changed to effect the economic, political, and social equality of all men? His answer is condensed in the cryptic phrase: "Philosophy cannot realise itself without abolishing the proletariat; the proletariat cannot abolish itself without re-alising philosophy." In other words, Hegel, Marx affirmed, would canonize whatever circumstance prevails in our world, even though it bristles with economic injustice and threatens the continued existence of the impover-ished workingman. Because philosophical comprehension means showing how rational a situation is, it suggests a moral approval of that situation and a reluctance to ameliorate it. Therefore, the only practical solution that cuts at the heart of the problem is to form a communist or classless society, with no bourgeois values for a philosophy or speculative understanding to preserve. Philosophy would be replaced by a working science of law, ethics, or politics.

This difference in outlook between Hegel and Marx should not blind us to their similarities, in particular the common humanism that separates them from Kantian scientism. Kant always remained at heart a devoted Newtonian. In his philosophical scheme, Reason (the Transcendental Dia-lectic) set goals, but "reasoning," understood as the process of knowledge, meant categorizing, working transcendental deductions, explaining how knowledge is possible by pointing to its structures. In brief, his model was the inductive-deductive procedure of natural science, which can be sum-marized as follows:

> "Logistic" methods are employed to construct systems of proof on the model of the mathematical deductions of geometry by giving simple terms literal and univocal definitions, by establishing simple relations among them, and by proceeding in long chains of deductive reasoning to the construction of more and more complex wholes. It has been assumed in all ages that knowledge would be more pre-cise and the grounds for its truth would be more easily ascertained if conclusions were deduced logically from postulate sets, and that the problems of human action and association would be solved more easily if a science of man were constructed on the model of the science of mechanics.[4]

The dialectic of Hegel and Marx is the humanist's response to the natu-ral scientist. Scientific criteria of exactness are irrelevant to that biblical or prophetic view of world history that fascinated Hegel. How, for example, does one measure scientifically the destiny of a people? In science one may, of course, classify Greek and Roman contributions to culture: in painting, in sculpture, and in literature. But he will need to broaden his scope, to free himself from the precisions of science, if he is to discuss a destiny or to bring out the full teleological implications of the phrase, "contributions to culture." In dialectical history the divisions are not dates but epochs, either in the pattern of Toynbee's rise and fall of civilizations in response to vari-ous challenges, or in a more pretentious evolutionary sweep such as that of

---

[4] Richard McKeon, *Freedom and History: The Semantics of Philosophical Contro-versies and Ideological Conflicts* (New York: Farrar, Straus & Giroux, 1952), pp. 14–15.

Pierre Teilhard de Chardin (1881–1955). Needless to say, this type of thought is condemned by empiricists as "philosophy in the grand manner," a holistic approach that applies different criteria of evidence from natural science's observation and classification.

Although both Hegel and Marx were dialectical thinkers, their thought, as we have seen, moved in opposite directions. Hegel's dialectic closely parallels the Christian view of things: a forward movement, as in the Old Testament, until the advent of the Absolute, followed by a static period of vision (the Christian's earthly pilgrimage during which he lives by grace a life in imitation of his Lord) embracing here and now the moments of past and future (the recollection of the sacrificial life of Christ accompanied by the expectation of his Second Coming). Even though this Hegelian outlook has often been criticized as blatantly rationalistic, Marx rejected it as a compromising Christocentric theology. For him the dialectical movement was not "idealist" thought but "materialist" action—the play of opposing groups that represent inevitably conflicting economic interests. One learns dialectic in the Marxian school in order to control this movement of history. And to shape history means nothing less than to be a revolutionary, since all the superstructures—political, social, and religious—which have been erected on our present capitalist economy are only reenforcements and expressions of the economic system of exploitation that must be toppled.

Marxist Religion

The Marxist critique of religion, of which the selection from Engels is an authentic sampling, is to be considered as a prerequisite for all criticism. Marx stated this clearly in a formulation of his program:

> It is therefore the duty of history, the beyond of truth having vanished, to establish the truth of this world. Philosophy is in the service of history. Its primary duty, once the sacred image of human self-estrangement has been unmasked, is to unmask self-estrangement in all its unholy forms. Criticism of heaven is transformed thereby into criticism of earth, criticism of religion into criticism of right, criticism of theology into criticism of politics.[5]

But this subsequent criticism of earth, right, and politics was not exclusively socioeconomic, because the Prussian state, the bastion of conservatism that Marx violently attacked, was in reality committed to upholding a bourgeois-Christian concept of man. Thus Marx's rebellion against the existing order was deeply rooted in a Promethean defiance of the Christian

---

[5] Karl Marx, *Marx-Engels Gesamtausgabe,* cited by Karl Löwith in *From Hegel to Nietzsche: The Revolution in Nineteenth-Century Thought,* trans. from the 3rd German ed. by David E. Green (New York: Holt, Rinehart & Winston, 1964), p. 97.

scheme of things. For this reason Marx honored Prometheus as the greatest martyr of the philosophic calendar and credited Epicurus with being the first mortal to defy the immortal gods.

It would be absurd to deny the far-reaching influence of Marx's work, but equally silly to suppose that the ground had not been prepared for his ideas.[6] As a result of the philosophy of the Enlightenment, in which man became the focal point of philosophical reflection, popular thought—that of Feuerbach, Arnold Ruge (1802–80), and Marx—attempted to formulate a humanism without God. But, as Nietzsche was to reveal, the death of God entailed the death of the traditional idea of man as a creature, defined, that is, by his relationship to God. Since God is dead, Nietzsche argued, we must revaluate all our values; we cannot merely take over the old notions in the absence of their ultimate point of reference.

As yet, however, the Nietzschean program has not been realized. Its urgency has been underlined by contemporary existentialist writers, whose faith in man has been severely shaken by the experience of two world wars. They offer us anew the perennial challenge: God or Man. But they also respect our freedom of choice, for we can no longer phrase the option in purely Hegelian or Marxist terms.

Conclusion

In this introductory essay we have emphasized that both Hegel and Marx were children of German idealism. They meditated the problem of man's freedom, that is, the risk each one of us runs in finding or losing himself in "the other." In the wake of Spinoza, Hegel concentrated on the freedom of the finite in its dialectical involvement with the infinite. Marx's preference, which was molded by the Feuerbachian critique of religion, alighted on freedom from economic domination. Both of these thinkers presuppose in their dialectics that the suppression of alienation (the condition of man's freedom) spells the end of history. This, we should note, is tantamount to the paradoxical assertion that the aim of philosophy, both speculative and practical, is to put itself out of business.

---

[6] In order to place Marx's attack on Christianity in its proper perspective, the student might profitably read Mircea Eliade, *The Sacred and the Profane* (New York: Harper & Row, 1961) and Erich Heller, *The Disinherited Mind* (New York: Farrar, Straus & Giroux, 1957). Both of these works, one through an examination of various forms of religious experience, the other through a study of the gradual exaltation of the scientific mode of thought, describe the phenomenon to which Marx is a faithful witness, namely, the progressive despiritualization of Western man.

Glossary

ABSOLUTE:
The totality of reality or intelligibility that is explicated by philosophy or reflective thought.

A PRIORI:
In Kant's terminology, thought which is not grounded in actual experience: the result of "purely conceptual considerations."

CONCEPT:
For Hegel, the activity of *com-prehension*: the holding together of different aspects or moments (e.g., form and content) which constitutes thought.

DIALECTIC:
1. The thought process as Hegel described it in opposition to Kantian abstractive or categorial thought. Thus to prove something is to show *how* it is rational, that is, to unfold its dialectic.
2. For Marxists generally, the reconciliation of opposites.

IDEOLOGY:
A manner of thinking characteristic of a class which serves to justify the prejudices of the class. Marx regarded philosophy as such a rationalization.

MEDIATION:
The process of reflection. For Hegel the immediate is the implicit and therefore stands in need of negation in order to be realized.

MOMENT:
A stage in the dialectical process; for example, the immediate or "in itself," the determined or "for itself."

NEGATION:
Hegel and contemporary thinkers are indebted to Spinoza for the dictum: "Determination is negation." The distinctions of the reflective process are successive negations.

REASON (*Vernunft*):
For Kant, the mind insofar as it is occupied with non-empirical, regulative ideas: God, World, Soul.

SPIRIT (*Geist*):
A difficult notion conveniently understood as *intelligibility*. Hegel was not developing precisely a phenomenology of *mind;* but he uses the term ambiguously, as we do in English, for the "spirit" of the times, that is, the "breath" or "wind" (as in Greek and Hebrew) which is a moving force.

UNDERSTANDING (*Verstand*):
For Kant, the mind insofar is it unifies empirical data under categories and concepts, such as cause, necessity, and substance.

UNIVERSAL:

The process of universalizing, that is, holding together abstract and concrete in the unity of reflection. Therefore the Hegelian *concrete* universal is a *con-cept*.

VORSTELLUNG:

An ambiguous term perhaps best translated by the equally vague Notion, although this has been the customary translation of Hegel's *Begriff*. For Hegel the *Vorstellung* is a level of thought accompanied by images, or still attached to its sensuous origins. Hegel gave the impression that mythopoeic thought (the level of *Vorstellung*) was included in, yet inferior to, "pure thought" (philosophy).

Immanuel Kant

IMMANUEL KANT was born in Koenigsberg in 1724 and was educated at
the university there. Throughout his life he never traveled beyond his
native East Prussia. After many years as a tutor at the university, he
was appointed professor of Logic and Metaphysics in 1770, a post he
held until his retirement in 1796. He died in 1804. His philosophical
reputation was assured by the publication of the *Critique of Pure Reason*
(1781), a work that attempted to establish the grounds of metaphysics.
The *Critique* forms part of a trilogy with the *Critique of Practical
Reason* (1788), a work on morals, and the *Critique of Judgment*
(1790), a study of beauty and teleology in nature.

Critical Thought in Metaphysics and Morals

Introduction to
Prolegomena to Any Future Metaphysics

My object is to persuade all those who think metaphysics worth studying
that it is absolutely necessary to pause a moment and, regarding all that
has been done as though undone, to propose first the preliminary question,
"Whether such a thing as metaphysics be even possible at all?"

If it be science, how is it that it cannot, like other sciences, obtain universal and lasting recognition? If not, how can it maintain its pretensions
and keep the human mind in suspense with hopes never ceasing, yet never
fulfilled? Whether then we demonstrate our knowledge or our ignorance in
this field, we must come once for all to a definite conclusion respecting the
nature of this so-called science, which cannot possibly remain on its present footing. It seems almost ridiculous, while every other science is continually advancing, that in this, which pretends to be wisdom incarnate, for
whose oracle everyone inquires, we should constantly move round the same
spot, without gaining a single step. And so its votaries having melted away,
we do not find men confident of their ability to shine in other sciences venturing their reputation here, where everybody, however ignorant in other

From pp. 2–8 of Immanuel Kant, the Introduction to *Prolegomena to Any Future
Metaphysics,* translated and edited by Paul Carus. Copyright 1902 by The Open
Court Publishing Company.

matters, presumes to deliver a final verdict, because in this domain there is actually as yet no standard weight and measure to distinguish sound knowledge from shallow talk.

After all it is nothing extraordinary in the elaboration of a science that, when men begin to wonder how far it has advanced, the question should at last occur whether and how such a science is possible at all. Human reason so delights building that it has several times built up a tower and then razed it to see how the foundation was laid. It is never too late to become reasonable and wise; but if the knowledge comes late, there is always more difficulty in starting a reform.

The question whether a science be possible presupposes a doubt as to its actuality. But such a doubt offends the men whose whole fortune consists of this supposed jewel; hence he who raises the doubt must expect opposition from all sides. Some, in the proud consciousness of their possessions, which are ancient and therefore considered legitimate, will take their metaphysical compendia in their hands and look down on him with contempt; others, who never see anything except it be identical with what they have elsewhere seen before, will not understand him, and everything will remain for a time as if nothing had happened to excite the concern or the hope for an impending change.

Nevertheless, I venture to predict that the independent reader of these *Prolegomena* will not only doubt his previous science, but ultimately be fully persuaded that it cannot exist unless the demands here stated on which its possibility depends be satisfied; and, as this has never been done, that there is, as yet, no such thing as metaphysics. But as it can never cease to be in demand—since the interests of common sense are so intimately interwoven with it—he must confess that a radical reform, or rather a new birth of the science, after a new plan, is unavoidable, however men may struggle against it for a while.

Since the *Essays* of Locke and Leibniz, or rather since the origin of metaphysics so far as we know its history, nothing has ever happened which could have been more decisive to its fate than the attack made upon it by David Hume. He threw no light on this species of knowledge, but he certainly struck a spark by which light might have been kindled had it caught some inflammable substance and had its smouldering fire been carefully nursed and developed.

Hume started chiefly from a single but important concept in metaphysics, namely, that of the connection of cause and effect (including its derivatives force and action, and so on). He challenged reason, which pretends to have given birth to this concept of herself, to answer him by what right she thinks anything could be so constituted that if that thing be posited, something else also must necessarily be posited; for this is the meaning of the concept of cause. He demonstrated irrefutably that it was absolutely impossible for reason to think *a priori* and by means of concepts such a combination, for it implies necessity. We cannot at all see why, in consequence of the existence of one thing, another must necessarily exist or how the concept of such a combination can arise *a priori*. Hence he inferred that reason was altogether deluded with reference to this concept, which she erroneously considered as one of her own children, whereas in reality it was nothing but a bastard of imagination, impregnated by experience, which subsumed certain representations under the law of association and mistook a subjective necessity (habit) for an objective necessity arising from insight. Hence he inferred that reason had no power to think such combinations, even in general, because her concepts would then be purely fictitious and all her pretended *a priori* cognitions nothing but common experiences marked with a false stamp. In plain language, this means that there is not and cannot be any such thing as metaphysics at all.

However hasty and mistaken Hume's inference may appear, it was at least founded upon investigation, and this investigation deserved the concentrated attention of the brighter spirits of his day as well as determined efforts on their part to discover, if possible, a happier solution of the problem in the sense proposed by him, all of which would have speedily resulted in a complete reform of the science.

But Hume suffered the usual misfortune of metaphysicians, of not being understood. It is positively painful to see how utterly his opponents, Reid, Oswald, Beattie, and lastly Priestley, missed the point of the problem; for while they were ever taking for granted that which he doubted, and demonstrating with zeal and often with impudence that which he never thought of doubting, they so misconstrued his valuable suggestion that everything remained in its old condition, as if nothing had happened. The question was not whether the concept of cause was right, useful, and even indispensable for our knowledge of nature, for this Hume had never doubted; but whether that concept could be thought by reason *a priori,* and consequently whether it possessed an inner truth, independent of all experience, implying a perhaps more extended use not restricted merely to objects of experience. This was Hume's problem. It was solely a question concerning the *origin,* not concerning the *indispensable* need of using the concept. Were the former decided, the conditions of the use and the sphere of its valid application would have been determined as a matter of course.

But to satisfy the conditions of the problem, the opponents of the great thinker should have penetrated very deeply into the nature of reason, so far as it is concerned with pure thinking—a task which did not suit them. They found a more convenient method of being defiant without any insight, namely, the appeal to *common sense.* It is indeed a great gift of God to possess right or (as they now call it) plain common sense. But this common sense must be shown in action by well-considered and reasonable thoughts and words, not by appealing to it as an oracle when no rational justification for one's position can be advanced. To appeal to common sense when insight and science fail, and no sooner—this is one of the subtile discoveries of modern times, by means of which the most superficial ranter can safely enter the lists with the most thorough thinker and hold his own. But as long as a particle of insight remains, no one would think of having recourse to this subterfuge. Seen clearly, it is but an appeal to the opinion of the multitude, of whose applause the philosopher is ashamed, while the popular charlatan glories and boasts in it. I should think that Hume might fairly have laid as much claim to common sense as Beattie and, in addition, to a critical reason (such as the latter did not possess), which keeps common sense in check and prevents it from speculating, or, if speculations are under discussion, restrains the desire to decide because it cannot satisfy itself concerning its own premises. By this means alone can common sense remain sound. Chisels and hammers may suffice to work a piece of wood, but for etching we require an etcher's needle. Thus common sense and speculative understanding are each serviceable, but each in its own way: the former in judgments which apply immediately to experience; the latter when we judge universally from mere concepts, as in metaphysics, where that which calls itself, in spite of the inappropriateness of the name, sound common sense, has no right to judge at all.

I openly confess my recollection of David Hume was the very thing which many years ago first interrupted my dogmatic slumber and gave my investigations in the field of speculative philosophy a quite new direction. I was far from following him in the conclusions at which he arrived by regarding, not the whole of his problem, but a part, which by itself can give us no information. If we start from a well-founded, but undeveloped, thought which another has bequeathed to us, we may well hope by continued reflection to advance farther than the acute man to whom we owe the first spark of light.

I therefore first tried whether Hume's objection could not be put into a general form, and soon found that the concept of the connection of cause and effect was by no means the only concept by which the understanding thinks the connection of things *a priori,* but rather that metaphysics consists altogether of such concepts. I sought to ascertain their number; and when I had satisfactorily succeeded in this by starting from a single principle, I proceeded to the deduction of these concepts, which I was now certain were not derived from experience, as Hume had attempted to derive them, but sprang from the pure understanding. This deduction (which seemed impossible to my acute predecessor, which had never even occurred to anyone else, though no one had hesitated to use the concepts without investigating the basis of their objective validity) was the most difficult task which ever could have been undertaken in the service of metaphysics; and the worst was that metaphysics, such as it is, could not assist me in the least because this deduction alone can render metaphysics possible. But as soon as I had succeeded in solving Hume's problem, not merely in a particular case, but with respect to the whole faculty of pure reason, I could proceed safely, though slowly, to determine the whole sphere of pure reason completely and from universal principles, in its boundaries as well as in its contents. This was required for metaphysics in order to construct its system according to a reliable method.

DIALECTIC OF PURE PRACTICAL REASON

If human nature is called upon to strive for the highest good, the measure of its cognitive faculties and especially their relation to one another must be assumed to be suitable to this end. But the critique of pure speculative reason demonstrates the utter insufficiency of speculative reason to solve the most weighty problems which are presented to it in a way satisfactory to its end; but that critique did not ignore the natural and unmistakable hints of the same reason or the great steps that it can take in approaching this great goal which is set before it but which it can never of itself reach even with the aid of the greatest knowledge of nature. Thus nature here seems to have provided us only in a stepmotherly fashion with a faculty needed for our end.

Now assuming that it had here indulged our wish and had provided us with that power of insight or enlightenment which we would like to possess or which some erroneously believe they do possess, what would be the consequence so far as we can discern it? In so far as our whole nature was not changed at the same time, the inclinations (which under any condition have the first word) would first strive for their satisfaction and, conjoined with reasonable consideration, for the greatest possible and most lasting satisfaction under the name of happiness. The moral law would afterward speak in order to hold them within their proper limits and even to subject them all to a higher end which has no regard to inclination. But instead of the conflict which now the moral disposition has to wage with inclinations and in which, after some defeats, moral strength of mind may be gradually won, God and eternity in their awful majesty would stand unceasingly before our eyes (for that which we can completely prove is as certain as that which we can ascertain by sight). Transgression of the law would indeed be shunned, and the commanded would be performed. But because the disposition from which actions should be done cannot be instilled by any command, and because the spur to action would in this case be always present and external, reason would have no need to endeavor to gather its strength to resist the inclinations by a vivid idea of the dignity of the law. Thus most actions conforming to the law would be done from fear, few would be done from hope, none from duty. The moral worth of actions, on which alone the worth of the person and even of the world depends in the eyes of supreme wisdom, would not exist at all. The conduct of man, so

From pp. 151–53 of Immanuel Kant, *Critique of Practical Reason,* translated by Lewis White Beck. Copyright © 1956 by The Liberal Arts Press, reprinted by permission of the Liberal Arts Press Division of The Bobbs-Merrill Company, Inc.

long as his nature remained as it now is, would be changed into mere mechanism, where, as in a puppet show, everything would gesticulate well but no life would be found in the figures.

But it is quite otherwise with us. With all the exertion of our reason we have only a very obscure and ambiguous view into the future; the Governor of the world allows us only to conjecture His existence and majesty, not to behold or clearly prove them; the moral law in us, without promising or threatening us with anything certain, demands of us a disinterested respect; finally, only when this respect has become active and dominating, it allows us a view into the realm of the supersensuous, though only a glimpse. Thus only can there be a truly moral character dedicated directly to the law and the rational creature become worthy of participating in the highest good corresponding to the moral worth of his person and not merely to his action.

Thus what the study of nature and of man has sufficiently shown elsewhere may well be true here, viz., that the inscrutable wisdom through which we exist is not less worthy of veneration in respect to what it denies us than in what it has granted.

QUESTIONS FOR STUDY AND DISCUSSION

1. Why does Kant call into question the validity of metaphysics?
2. What is the problem of the "a priori" and the "necessary"?
3. How does Hume resolve this difficulty?
4. What is Kant's idea of metaphysics?
5. In the brief passage from *Critique of Practical Reason,* what does Kant suggest as the function of morals in his philosophy?

G. W. F. Hegel

The Dialectic of Thought

In the case of a philosophical work it seems not only superfluous, but, in view of the nature of philosophy, even inappropriate and misleading to begin, as writers usually do in a preface, by explaining the end the author had in mind, the circumstances which gave rise to the work, and the relation in which the writer takes it to stand to other treatises on the same subject, written by his predecessors or his contemporaries. For whatever it might be suitable to state about philosophy in a preface—say, an historical sketch of the main drift and point of view, the general content and results, a string of desultory assertions and assurances about the truth—this cannot be accepted as the form and manner in which to expound philosophical truth.

Moreover, because philosophy has its being essentially in the element of that universality which encloses the particular within it, the end or final result seems, in the case of philosophy more than in that of other sciences, to have absolutely expressed the complete fact itself in its very nature; contrasted with that the mere process of bringing it to light would seem, prop-

From pp. 67–130 of G. W. F. Hegel, the Preface to *Phenomenology of Mind*, translated by J. B. Baillie. Copyright 1931 by The Macmillan Company. Reprinted by permission of George Allen and Unwin Ltd., London and Humanities Press, Inc.

erly speaking, to have no essential significance. On the other hand, in the general idea of e.g. anatomy—the knowledge of the parts of the body regarded as lifeless—we are quite sure we do not possess the objective concrete fact, the actual content of the science, but must, over and above, be concerned with particulars. Further, in the case of such a collection of items of knowledge, which has no real right to the name of science, any talk about purpose and such-like generalities is not commonly very different from the descriptive and superficial way in which the contents of the science—these nerves and muscles, etc.—are themselves spoken of. In philosophy, on the other hand, it would at once be felt incongruous were such a method made use of and yet shown by philosophy itself to be incapable of grasping the truth.

In the same way too, by determining the relation which a philosophical work professes to have to other treatises on the same subject, an extraneous interest is introduced, and obscurity is thrown over the point at issue in the knowledge of the truth. The more the ordinary mind takes the opposition between true and false to be fixed, the more is it accustomed to expect either agreement or contradiction with a given philosophical system, and only to see reason for the one or the other in any explanatory statement concerning such a system. It does not conceive the diversity of philosophical systems as the progressive evolution of truth; rather, it sees only contradiction in that variety. The bud disappears when the blossom breaks through, and we might say that the former is refuted by the latter; in the same way when the fruit comes, the blossom may be explained to be a false form of the plant's existence, for the fruit appears as its true nature in place of the blossom. These stages are not merely differentiated; they supplant one another as being incompatible with one another. But the ceaseless activity of their own inherent nature makes them at the same time moments of an organic unity, where they not merely do not contradict one another, but where one is as necessary as the other; and this equal necessity of all moments constitutes alone and thereby the life of the whole. But contradiction as between philosophical systems is not wont to be conceived in this way; on the other hand, the mind perceiving the contradiction does not commonly know how to relieve it or keep it free from its onesidedness, and to recognize in what seems conflicting and inherently antagonistic the presence of mutually necessary moments.

The demand for such explanations, as also the attempts to satisfy this demand, very easily pass for the essential business philosophy has to undertake. Where could the inmost truth of a philosophical work be found better expressed than in its purposes and results? and in what way could these be more definitely known than through their distinction from what is produced during the same period by others working in the same field? If, however, such procedure is to pass for more than the beginning of knowledge, if it is to pass for actually knowing, then we must, in point of fact, look on it as a device for avoiding the real business at issue, an attempt to combine the appearance of being in earnest and taking trouble about the subject with an actual neglect of the subject altogether. For the real subject-matter is not exhausted in its purpose, but in working the matter out; nor is the mere result attained the concrete whole itself, but the result along with the process of arriving at it. The purpose by itself is a lifeless universal, just as the general drift is a mere activity in a certain direction, which is still without its concrete realization; and the naked result is the corpse of the system which has left its guiding tendency behind it. Similarly, the distinctive difference of anything is rather the boundary, the limit, of the subject; it is found at that point where the subject-matter stops, or it is what this subject-matter is *not*. To trouble oneself in this fashion with the purpose and results, and again with the differences, the positions taken up and judgments passed by one thinker and another, is therefore an easier task than perhaps it seems. For instead of laying hold of the matter in hand, a procedure of that kind is all the while away from the subject altogether. Instead of dwelling within it and becoming absorbed by it, knowledge of that sort is always grasping at something else; such knowledge, instead of keeping to the subject-matter and giving itself up to it, never gets away from itself. The easiest thing of all is to pass judgments on what has a solid substantial content; it is more difficult to grasp it, and most of all difficult to do both together and produce the systematic exposition of it.

The beginning of culture and of the struggle to pass out of the unbroken immediacy of naïve psychical life has always to be made by acquiring knowledge of universal principles and points of view, by striving, in the first instance, to work up simply to the *thought* of the subject-matter in general, not forgetting at the same time to give reasons for supporting it or refuting it, to apprehend the concrete riches and fullness contained in its various determinate qualities, and to know how to furnish a coherent, orderly account of it and a responsible judgment upon it. This beginning of mental cultivation will, however, very soon make way for the earnestness of actual life in all its fullness, which leads to a living experience of the subject-matter itself; and when, in addition, conceptual thought strenuously penetrates to the very depths of its meaning, such knowledge and style of judgment will keep their due place in everyday thought and conversation.

The systematic development of truth in scientific form can alone be the true shape in which truth exists. To help to bring philosophy nearer to the form of science—that goal where it can lay aside the name of *love* of knowledge and be actual *knowledge*—that is what I have set before me. The inner necessity that knowledge should be science lies in its very nature; and the adequate and sufficient explanation for this lies simply and solely in the systematic exposition of philosophy itself. The external necessity, however, so far as this is apprehended in a universal way, and apart from the accident of the personal element and the particular occasioning influences affecting the individual, is the same as the internal: it lies in the form and shape in which the process of time presents the existence of its moments. To show that the time process does raise philosophy to the level of scientific system would, therefore, be the only true justification of the attempts which aim at proving that philosophy must assume this character; because the temporal process would thus bring out and lay bare the necessity of it, nay, more, would at the same time be carrying out that very aim itself.

When we state the true form of truth to be its scientific character—or, what is the same thing, when it is maintained that truth finds the medium of its existence in notions or conceptions alone—I know that this seems to contradict an idea with all its consequences which makes great pretensions and has gained widespread acceptance and conviction at the present time. A word of explanation concerning this contradiction seems, therefore, not out of place, even though at this stage it can amount to no more than a dogmatic assurance exactly like the view we are opposing. If, that is to say, truth exists merely in what, or rather exists merely *as* what, is called at one time intuition, at another immediate knowledge of the Absolute, Religion, Being—not being in the centre of divine love, but the very Being of this centre, of the Absolute itself—from that point of view it is rather the opposite of the notional or conceptual form which would be required for systematic philosophical exposition. The Absolute on this view is not to be grasped in conceptual form, but felt, intuited; it is not its conception, but the feeling of it and intuition of it that are to have the say and find expression.[1]

If we consider the appearance of a claim like this in its more general setting, and look at the level which the self-conscious mind at present occupies, we shall find that self-consciousness has got beyond the substantial fullness of life, which it used to carry on in the element of thought—beyond the state of immediacy of belief, beyond the satisfaction and security arising from the assurance which consciousness possessed of being reconciled with ultimate reality and with its all-pervading presence, within as well as without. Self-conscious mind has not merely passed beyond that to the opposite extreme of insubstantial reflection of self into self, but beyond this too. It has not merely lost its essential and concrete life, it is also conscious of this loss and of the transitory finitude characteristic of its content. Turning away from the husks it has to feed on, and confessing that it lies in wickedness and sin, it reviles itself for so doing, and now desires from philosophy not so much to bring it to a knowledge of what it is, as to obtain once again through philosophy the restoration of that sense of solidity and substantiality of existence it has lost. Philosophy is thus expected not so much to meet this want by opening up the compact solidity of substantial existence, and bringing this to the light and level of self-consciousness—is not so much to bring chaotic conscious life back to the orderly ways of

---

[1] Hegel has in mind the views of Jacobi and the Romantics, Schlegel and Schleiermacher. [J.B.B.]

thought, and the simplicity of the notion, as to run together what thought has divided asunder, suppress the notion with its distinctions, and restore the *feeling* of existence. What it wants from philosophy is not so much insight as edification. The beautiful, the holy, the eternal, religion, love—these are the bait required to awaken the desire to bite: not the notion, but ecstasy, not the march of cold necessity in the subject-matter, but ferment and enthusiasm—these are to be the ways by which the wealth of the concrete substance is to be stored and increasingly extended.

With this demand there goes the strenuous effort, almost perfervidly zealous in its activity, to rescue mankind from being sunken in what is sensuous, vulgar, and of fleeting importance, and to raise men's eyes to the stars; as if men had quite forgotten the divine, and were on the verge of finding satisfaction, like worms, in mud and water. Time was when man had a heaven, decked and fitted out with endless wealth of thoughts and pictures. The significance of all that is, lay in the thread of light by which it was attached to heaven; instead of dwelling in the present as it is here and now, the eye glanced away over the present to the Divine, away, so to say, to a present that lies beyond. The mind's gaze had to be directed under compulsion to what is earthly, and kept fixed there; and it has needed a long time to introduce that clearness, which only celestial realities had, into the crassness and confusion shrouding the sense of things earthly, and to make attention to the immediate present as such, which was called Experience, of interest and of value. Now we have apparently the need for the opposite of all this; man's mind and interest are so deeply rooted in the earthly that we require a like power to have them raised above that level. His spirit shows such poverty of nature that it seems to long for the mere pitiful feeling of the divine in the abstract, and to get refreshment from that, like a wanderer in the desert craving for the merest mouthful of water. By the little which can thus satisfy the needs of the human spirit we can measure the extent of its loss.

This easy contentment in receiving, or stinginess in giving, does not suit the character of science. The man who only seeks edification, who wants to envelop in mist the manifold diversity of his earthly existence and thought, and craves after the vague enjoyment of this vague and indeterminate Divinity—he may look where he likes to find this: he will easily find for himself the means to procure something he can rave over and puff himself up withal. But philosophy must beware of wishing to be edifying.

Still less must this kind of contentment, which holds science in contempt, take upon itself to claim that raving obscurantism of this sort is something higher than science. These apocalyptic utterances pretend to occupy the very centre and the deepest depths; they look askance at all definiteness and preciseness of meaning; and they deliberately hold back from conceptual thinking and the constraining necessities of thought, as being the sort of reflection which, they say, can only feel at home in the sphere of finitude. But just as there is a breadth which is emptiness, there is a depth which is empty too: as we may have an extension of substance which over-flows into finite multiplicity without the power of keeping the manifold to-gether, in the same way we may have an insubstantial intensity which, keeping itself in as mere force without actual expression, is no better than superficiality. The force of mind is only as great as its expression; its depth only as deep as its power to expand and lose itself when spending and giv-ing out its substance. Moreover, when this unreflective emotional knowl-edge makes a pretence of having immersed its own very self in the depths of the absolute Being, and of philosophizing in all holiness and truth, it hides from itself the fact that instead of devotion to God, it rather, by this contempt for all measurable precision and definiteness, simply attests in its own case the fortuitous character of its content, and in the other endows God with its own caprice. When such minds commit themselves to the un-restrained ferment of sheer emotion, they think that, by putting a veil over self-consciousness, and surrendering all understanding, they are thus God's beloved ones to whom He gives His wisdom in sleep. This is the reason, too, that in point of fact what they do conceive and bring forth in sleep is dreams.

For the rest it is not difficult to see that our epoch is a birth-time, and a period of transition. The spirit of man has broken with the old order of things hitherto prevailing, and with the old ways of thinking, and is in the mind to let them all sink into the depths of the past and to set about its own transformation. It is indeed never at rest, but carried along the stream of progress ever onward. But it is here as in the case of the birth of a child; after a long period of nutrition in silence, the continuity of the gradual growth in size, of quantitative change, is suddenly cut short by the first breath drawn—there is a break in the process, a qualitative change—and the child is born. In like manner the spirit of the time, growing slowly and quietly ripe for the new form it is to assume, disintegrates one fragment after another of the structure of its previous world. That it is tottering to its fall is indicated only by symptoms here and there. Frivolity and again ennui, which are spreading in the established order of things, the undefined foreboding of something unknown—all these betoken that there is some-thing else approaching. This gradual crumbling to pieces, which did not alter the general look and aspect of the whole, is interrupted by the sunrise, which, in a flash and at a single stroke, brings to view the form and structure of the new world.

But this new world is perfectly realized just as little as the new-born child; and it is essential to bear this in mind. It comes on the stage to begin with in its immediacy, in its bare generality. A building is not finished when its foundation is laid; and just as little is the attainment of a general notion of a whole the whole itself. When we want to see an oak with all its vigour of trunk, its spreading branches, and mass of foliage, we are not satisfied to be shown an acorn instead. In the same way science, the crowning glory of a spiritual world, is not found complete in its initial stages. The beginning of the new spirit is the outcome of a widespread revolution in manifold forms of spiritual culture; it is the reward which comes after a chequered and devious course of development, and after much struggle and effort. It is a whole which, after running its course and laying bare all its content, returns again to itself; it is the resultant abstract notion of the whole. But the actual realization of this abstract whole is only found when those previous shapes and forms, which are now reduced to ideal moments of the whole, are developed anew again, but developed and shaped within this new medium, and with the meaning they have thereby acquired.

While the new world makes its first appearance merely in general outline, merely as a whole lying concealed and hidden within a bare abstraction, the wealth of the bygone life, on the other hand, is still consciously present in recollection. Consciousness misses in the new form the detailed expanse of content; but still more the developed expression of form by which distinctions are definitely determined and arranged in their precise relations. Without this last feature science has no general intelligibility, and has the appearance of being an esoteric possession of a few individuals— an esoteric possession, because in the first instance it is only the essential principle or notion of science, only its inner nature that is to be found; and a possession of few individuals, because, at its first appearance, its content is not elaborated and expanded in detail, and thus its existence is turned into something particular. Only what is perfectly determinate in form is at the same time exoteric, comprehensible, and capable of being learned and possessed by everybody. Intelligibility is the form in which science is offered to everyone, and is the open road to it made plain for all. To reach rational knowledge by our intelligence is the just demand of the mind which comes to science. For intelligence, understanding (*Verstand*), is thinking, pure activity of the self in general; and what is intelligible (*Verständige*) is something from the first familiar and common to the scientific and unscientific mind alike, enabling the unscientific mind to enter the domain of science.

Science, at its commencement, when as yet it has reached neither detailed completeness nor perfection of form, is exposed to blame on that account. But it would be as unjust to suppose this blame to attach to its essential nature, as it is inadmissible not to be ready to recognize the demand for that further development in fuller detail. In the contrast and opposition between these two aspects (the initial and the developed stages of science) seems to lie the critical knot which scientific culture at present struggles to loosen, and about which so far it is not very clear. One side parades the wealth of its material and the intelligibility of its ideas; the other pours contempt at any rate on the latter, and makes a parade of the immediate intuitive rationality and divine quality of its content. Although the first is reduced to silence, perhaps by the inner force of truth alone, perhaps, too, by the noisy bluster of the other side, and even though having regard to the reason and nature of the case it did feel overborne, yet it does not therefore feel satisfied as regards those demands for greater development; for those demands are just, but still unfulfilled. Its silence is due only in part to the victory of the other side; it is half due to that weariness and indifference which are usually the consequence when expectations are being constantly awakened by promises which are not followed up by performance.

The other side [2] no doubt at times makes an easy enough matter of having a vast expanse of content. They haul on to their territory a lot of material, that, namely, which is already familiar and arranged in order; and since they are concerned more especially about what is exceptional, strange, and curious, they seem all the more to be in possession of the rest, which knowledge in its own way was finished and done with, as well as to have control over what was unregulated and disorderly. Hence everything appears brought within the compass of the Absolute Idea, which seems thus to be recognized in everything, and to have succeeded in becoming a system *in extenso* of scientific knowledge. But if we look more closely at this expanded system we find that it has not been reached by one and the same principle taking shape in diverse ways; it is the shapeless repetition of one and the same idea, which is applied in an external fashion to different material, the wearisome reiteration of it keeping up the semblance of diversity. The Idea, which by itself is no doubt the truth, really never gets any farther than just where it began, as long as the development of it consists in nothing else than such a repetition of the same formula. If the knowing subject carries round everywhere the one inert abstract form, taking up in external fashion whatever material comes his way, and dipping it into this element, then this comes about as near to fulfilling what is wanted—viz. a self-origination of the wealth of detail, and a self-determining distinction of shapes and forms—as any chance fancies about the content in question. It is rather a monochrome formalism, which only arrives at distinction in the matter it has to deal with, because this is already prepared and well known.

This monotonousness and abstract universality are maintained to be the Absolute. This formalism insists that to be dissatisfied therewith argues an incapacity to grasp the standpoint of the Absolute, and keep a firm hold on it. If it was once the case that the bare possibility of thinking of something in some other fashion was sufficient to refute a given idea, and the naked possibility, the bare general thought, possessed and passed for the entire substantive value of actual knowledge; similarly we find here all the value ascribed to the general idea in this bare form without concrete realization; and we see here, too, the style and method of speculative contemplation identified with dissipating and resolving what is determinate and distinct, or rather with hurling it down, without more ado and without any justification, into the abyss of vacuity. To consider any specific fact as it is in the Absolute, consists here in nothing else than saying about it that, while it is now doubtless spoken of as something specific, yet in the Abso-

---

[2] Schelling and his school. [J.B.B.]

lute, in the abstract identity A = A, there is no such thing at all, for everything is there all one. To pit this single assertion, that "in the Absolute all is one," against the organized whole of determinate and complete knowledge, or of knowledge which at least aims at and demands complete development—to give out its Absolute as the night in which, as we say, all cows are black—that is the very *naïveté* of emptiness of knowledge.

The formalism which has been deprecated and despised by recent philosophy, and which has arisen once more in philosophy itself, will not disappear from science, even though its inadequacy is known and felt, till the knowledge of absolute reality has become quite clear as to what its own true nature consists in. Having in mind that the general idea of what is to be done, if it precedes the attempt to carry it out, facilitates the comprehension of this process, it is worth while to indicate here some rough idea of it, with the hope at the same time that this will give us the opportunity to set aside certain forms whose habitual presence is a hindrance in the way of speculative knowledge.

In my view—a view which the developed exposition of the system itself can alone justify—everything depends on grasping and expressing the ultimate truth not as Substance but as Subject as well. At the same time we must note that concrete substantiality implicates and involves the universal or the immediacy of knowledge itself, as well as that immediacy which is being, or immediacy *qua* object *for* knowledge. If the generation which heard God spoken of as the One Substance [Spinoza] was shocked and revolted by such a characterization of his nature, the reason lay partly in the instinctive feeling that in such a conception self-consciousness was simply submerged, and not preserved. But partly, again, the opposite position, which maintains thinking to be merely subjective thinking, abstract universality as such, is exactly the same bare uniformity, is undifferentiated, unmoved substantiality [Kant and Fichte]. And even if, in the third place, thought combines with itself the being of substance, and conceives immediacy or intuition (*Anschauung*) as thinking, it is still a question whether this intellectual intuition does not fall back into that inert, abstract simplicity, and exhibit and expound reality itself in an unreal manner [Schelling].

The living substance, further, is that being which is truly subject, or, what is the same thing, is truly realized and actual (*wirklich*) solely in the process of positing itself, or in mediating with its own self its transitions from one state or position to the opposite. As subject it is pure and simple negativity, and just on that account a process of splitting up what is simple and undifferentiated, a process of duplicating and setting factors in opposition, which [process] in turn is the negation of this indifferent diversity and of the opposition of factors it entails. True reality is merely this process of reinstating self-identity, of reflecting into its own self in and from its other, and is not an original and primal unity as such, not an immediate unity as such. It is the process of its own becoming, the circle which presupposes its end as its purpose, and has its end for its beginning; it becomes concrete and actual only by being carried out, and by the end it involves.

The life of God and divine intelligence, then, can, if we like, be spoken of as love disporting with itself; but this idea falls into edification, and even sinks into insipidity, if it lacks the seriousness, the suffering, the patience, and the labour of the negative. *Per se* the divine life is no doubt undisturbed identity and oneness with itself, which finds no serious obstacle in otherness and estrangement, and none in the surmounting of this estrangement. But this "per se" is abstract generality, where we abstract from its real nature, which consists in its being objective to itself, conscious of itself on its own account (*für sich zu sein*); and where consequently we neglect altogether the self-movement which is the formal character of its activity. If the form is declared to correspond to the essence, it is just for that reason a misunderstanding to suppose that knowledge can be content with the *"per se"*, the essence, but can do without the form, that the absolute principle, or absolute intuition, makes the carrying out of the former, or the development of the latter, needless. Precisely because the form is as necessary to the essence as the essence to itself, absolute reality must not be conceived of and expressed as essence alone, i.e. as immediate substance, or as pure self-intuition of the Divine, but as form also, and with the entire wealth of the developed form. Only then is it grasped and expressed as really actual.

The truth is the whole. The whole, however, is merely the essential nature reaching its completeness through the process of its own development. Of the Absolute it must be said that it is essentially a result, that only at the end is it what it is in very truth; and just in that consists its nature, which is to be actual, subject, or self-becoming, self-development. Should it appear contradictory to say that the Absolute has to be conceived essentially as a result, a little consideration will set this appearance of contradiction in its true light. The beginning, the principle, or the Absolute, as at first or immediately expressed, is merely the universal. If we say "all animals," that does not pass for zoology; for the same reason we see at once that the words absolute, divine, eternal, and so on do not express what is implied in them; and only mere words like these, in point of fact, express intuition as the immediate. Whatever is more than a word like that, even the mere transition to a proposition, is a form of mediation, contains a process towards another state from which we must return once more. It is this process of mediation, however, that is rejected with horror, as if absolute knowledge were being surrendered when more is made of mediation than merely the assertion that it is nothing absolute, and does not exist in the Absolute.

This horrified rejection of mediation, however, arises as a fact from want of acquaintance with its nature, and with the nature of absolute knowledge itself. For mediating is nothing but self-identity working itself out through an active self-directed process; or, in other words, it is reflection into self, the aspect in which the ego is for itself, objective to itself. It is pure negativity, or, reduced to its utmost abstraction, the process of bare and simple becoming. The ego, or becoming in general, this process of mediating, is, because of its being simple, just immediacy coming to be, and is immediacy itself. We misconceive therefore the nature of reason if we exclude reflection or mediation from ultimate truth, and do not take it to be a positive moment of the Absolute. It is reflection which constitutes truth the final result, and yet at the same time does away with the contrast between result and the process of arriving at it. For this process is likewise simple, and therefore not distinct from the form of truth, which consists in appearing as simple in the result; it is indeed just this restoration and return to simplicity. While the embryo is certainly, in itself, implicitly a human being, it is not so explicitly, it is not by itself a human being (*für sich*); man is explicitly man only in the form of developed and cultivated reason, which has made itself to be what it is implicitly. Its actual reality is first found here. But this result arrived at is itself simple immediacy; for it is self-conscious freedom, which is at one with itself, and has not set aside the opposition it involves and left it there, but has made its account with it and become reconciled to it.

What has been said may also be expressed by saying that reason is purposive activity. The exaltation of so-called nature at the expense of thought misconceived, and more especially the rejection of external purposiveness, have brought the idea of purpose in general into disrepute. All the same, in the sense in which Aristotle, too, characterizes nature as purposive activity, purpose is the immediate, the undisturbed, the unmoved which is self-moving; as such it is subject. Its power of moving, taken abstractly, is its existence for itself, or pure negativity. The result is the same as the beginning solely because the beginning is purpose. Stated otherwise, what is actual and concrete is the same as its inner principle or notion simply because the immediate *qua* purpose contains within it the self or pure actuality. The realized purpose, or concrete actuality, is movement and development unfolded. But this very unrest is the self; and it is one and the same with that immediacy and simplicity characteristic of the beginning just for the reason that it is the result, and has returned upon itself—while this latter again is just the self, and the self is self-referring and self-relating identity and simplicity.

The need to think of the Absolute as subject, has led men to make use of statements like "God is the eternal," the "moral order of the world," or "love," etc. In such propositions the truth is just barely stated to be Subject, but not set forth as the process of reflectively mediating itself with itself. In a proposition of that kind we begin with the word God. By itself this is a meaningless sound, a mere name; the predicate says afterwards *what* it is, gives it content and meaning: the empty beginning becomes real knowledge only when we thus get to the end of the statement. So far as that goes, why not speak alone of the eternal, of the moral order of the world, etc., or, like the ancients, of pure conceptions such as being, the one, etc., i.e. of what gives the meaning without adding the meaningless sound at all?

But this word just indicates that it is not a being or essence or universal in general that is put forward, but something reflected into self, a subject. Yet at the same time this acceptance of the Absolute as Subject is merely anticipated, not really affirmed. The subject is taken to be a fixed point, and to it as their support the predicates are attached, by a process falling within the individual knowing about it, but not looked upon as belonging to the point of attachment itself; only by such a process, however, could the content be presented as subject. Constituted as it is, this process cannot belong to the subject; but when that point of support is fixed to start with, this process cannot be otherwise constituted, it can only be external. The anticipation that the Absolute is subject is therefore not merely not the realization of this conception; it even makes realization impossible. For it makes out the notion to be a static point, while its actual reality is self-movement, self-activity.

Among the many consequences that follow from what has been said, it is of importance to emphasize this, that knowledge is only real and can only be set forth fully in the form of science, in the form of system; and further, that a so-called fundamental proposition or first principle of philosophy, even if it is true, is yet none the less false just because and in so far as it is merely a fundamental proposition, merely a first principle. It is for that reason easily refuted. The refutation consists in bringing out its defective character; and it *is* defective because it is merely the universal, merely a principle, the beginning. If the refutation is complete and thorough, it is derived and developed from the nature of the principle itself, and not accomplished by bringing in from elsewhere other counter assurances and chance fancies. It would be strictly the development of the principle, and thus the completion of its deficiency, were it not that it misunderstands its own purport by taking account solely of the negative aspect of what it seeks to do, and is not conscious of the positive character of its process and result. The really positive working out of the beginning is at the same time just as much the very reverse, it is a negative attitude towards the principle we start from, negative, that is to say, of its one-sided form, which consists in being primarily immediate, a mere purpose. It may therefore be regarded as a refutation of what constitutes the basis of the system, but more correctly it should be looked at as a demonstration that the *basis* or principle of the system is in point of fact merely its *beginning*.

That the truth is only realized in the form of system, that substance is essentially subject, is expressed in the idea which represents the Absolute as Spirit (*Geist*)—the grandest conception of all, and one which is due to modern times and its religion. Spirit is alone Reality. It is the inner being of the world, that which essentially is, and is *per se;* it assumes objective, determinate form, and enters into relations with itself—it is externality (otherness), and exists for self; yet, in this determination, and in its otherness, it is still one with itself—it is self-contained and self-complete, in itself and for itself at once. This self-containedness, however, is first something known by us, it is implicit in its nature (*an sich*); it is Substance spiritual. It has to become self-contained *for itself*, on its own account; it must be knowledge of spirit, and must be consciousness of itself as spirit. This means, it must be presented to itself as an object, but at the same time straightway annul and transcend this objective form; it must be its own object in which it finds itself reflected. So far as its spiritual content is produced by its own activity, it is only *we* [the thinkers] who know spirit to be for itself, to be objective to itself; but in so far as spirit knows itself to be for itself, then this self-production, the pure notion, is the sphere and element in which its objectification takes effect, and where it gets its existential form. In this way it is in its existence aware of itself as an object in which its own self is reflected. Mind, which, when thus developed, knows itself to be mind, is science. Science is its realization, and the kingdom it sets up for itself in its own native element.

A self having knowledge purely of itself in the absolute antithesis of itself, this pure ether as such, is the very soil where science flourishes, is knowledge in universal form. The beginning of philosophy presupposes or demands from consciousness that it should feel at home in this element. But this element only attains its perfect meaning and acquires transparency through the process of gradually developing it. It is pure spirituality as the universal which assumes the shape of simple immediacy; and this simple element, existing as such, is the field of science, is thinking, which can be only in mind. Because this medium, this immediacy of mind, is the mind's substantial nature in general, it is the transfigured essence, reflection which itself is simple, which is aware of itself as immediacy; it is being, which is reflection into itself. Science on its side requires the individual self-consciousness to have risen into this high ether, in order to be able to live with science, and in science, and really to feel alive there. Conversely the individual has the right to demand that science shall hold the ladder to help him to get at least as far as this position, shall show him that he has in himself this ground to stand on. His right rests on his absolute independence, which he knows he possesses in every type and phase of knowledge; for in every phase, whether recognized by science or not, and whatever be the content, his right as an individual is the absolute and final form, i.e. he is the immediate certainty of self, and thereby is unconditioned being, were this expression preferred. If the position taken up by consciousness, that of knowing about objective things as opposed to itself, and about itself as opposed to them, is held by science to be the very opposite of what science is: if, when in knowing it keeps within itself and never goes beyond itself, science holds this state to be rather the loss of mind altogether—on the other hand the element in which *science* consists is looked at by consciousness as a remote and distant region, in which consciousness is no longer in possession of itself. Each of these two sides takes the other to be the perversion of the truth. For the naïve consciousness, to give itself up completely and straight away to science is to make an attempt, induced by some unknown influence, all at once to walk on its head. The compulsion to take up this attitude and move about in this position, is a constraining force it is urged to fall in with, without ever being prepared for it and with no apparent necessity for doing so. Let science be *per se* what it likes, in its relation to naïve immediate self-conscious life it presents the appearance of being a reversal of the latter; or, again, because naïve self-consciousness finds the principle of its reality in the certainty of itself, science bears the character of unreality, since consciousness "for itself" is a state quite outside of science. Science has for that reason to combine that other element of self-certainty with its own, or rather to show that the other element belongs to itself, and how it does so. When devoid of that sort of reality, science is merely the content of mind *qua* something implicit or potential (*an sich*); purpose, which at the start is no more than something internal; not spirit, but at first merely spiritual substance. This implicit moment (*Ansich*) has to find external expression, and become objective on its own account. This means nothing else than that this moment has to establish self-consciousness as one with itself.

It is this process by which science in general comes about, this gradual development of knowing, that is set forth here in the *Phenomenology of Mind*. Knowing, as it is found at the start, mind in its immediate and primitive stage, is without the essential nature of mind, is sense-consciousness. To reach the stage of genuine knowledge, or produce the element where science is found—the pure conception of science itself—a long and laborious journey must be undertaken. This process towards science, as regards the content it will bring to light and the forms it will assume in the course of its progress, will not be what is primarily imagined by leading the unscientific consciousness up to the level of science: it will be something different, too, from establishing and laying the foundations of science; and anyway something else than the sort of ecstatic enthusiasm which starts straight off with absolute knowledge, as if shot out of a pistol, and makes short work of other points of view simply by explaining that it is to take no notice of them.

The task of conducting the individual mind from its unscientific standpoint to that of science had to be taken in its general sense; we had to contemplate the formative development (*Bildung*) of the universal [or general] individual, of self-conscious spirit. As to the relation between these two [the particular and general individual], every moment, as it gains concrete form and its own proper shape and appearance, finds a place in the life of the universal individual. The particular individual is incomplete mind, a concrete shape in whose existence, taken as a whole, one determinate characteristic predominates, while the others are found only in blurred outline. In that mind which stands higher than another the lower concrete form of existence has sunk into an obscure moment; what was formerly an objective fact (*die Sache selbst*) is now only a single trace: its definite shape has been veiled, and become simply a piece of shading. The individual, whose substance is mind at the higher level, passes through these past forms, much in the way that one who takes up a higher science goes through those preparatory forms of knowledge, which he has long made his own, in order to call up their content before him; he brings back the recollection of them without stopping to fix his interest upon them. The particular individual, so far as content is concerned, has also to go through the stages through which the general mind has passed, but as shapes once assumed by mind and now laid aside, as stages of a road which has been worked over and levelled out. Hence it is that, in the case of various kinds of knowledge, we find that what in former days occupied the energies of men of mature mental ability sinks to the level of information, exercises, and even pastimes, for children; and in this educational progress we can see the history of the world's culture delineated in faint outline. This by-gone mode of existence has already become an acquired possession of the general mind, which constitutes the substance of the individual, and, by thus appearing externally to him, furnishes his inorganic nature. In this respect culture or development of mind (*Bildung*), regarded from the side of the individual, consists in his acquiring what lies at his hand ready for him, in making its inorganic nature organic to himself, and taking possession of it for himself. Looked at, however, from the side of universal mind *qua* general spiritual substance, culture means nothing else than that this substance gives itself its own self-consciousness, brings about its own inherent process and its own reflection into self.

Science lays before us the morphogenetic process of this cultural development in all its detailed fullness and necessity, and at the same time shows it to be something that has already sunk into the mind as a moment of its being and become a possession of mind. The goal to be reached is the mind's insight into what knowing is. Impatience asks for the impossible, wants to reach the goal without the means of getting there. The length of the journey has to be borne with, for every moment is necessary; and again we must halt at every stage, for each is itself a complete individual form, and is fully and finally considered only so far as its determinate character is taken and dealt with as a rounded and concrete whole, or only so far as the whole is looked at in the light of the special and peculiar character which this determination gives it. Because the substance of individual mind, nay, more, because the universal mind at work in the world (*Weltgeist*), has had the patience to go through these forms in the long stretch of time's extent, and to take upon itself the prodigious labour of the world's history, where it bodied forth in each form the entire content of itself, as each is capable of presenting it; and because by nothing less could that all-pervading mind ever manage to become conscious of what itself is—for that reason, the individual mind, in the nature of the case, cannot expect by less toil to grasp what its own subtance contains. All the same, its task has meanwhile been made much lighter, because this has historically been implicitly (*an sich*) accomplished, the content is one where reality is already cancelled for spiritual possibilities, where immediacy has been overcome and brought under the control of reflection, the various forms and shapes have been already reduced to their intellectual abbreviations, to determinations of thought (*Gedankenbestimmung*) pure and simple. Being now a thought, the content is the property of the substance of mind; existence has no more to be changed into the form of what is inherent and implicit (*Ansichseins*), but only the implicit—no longer merely something primitive, nor lying hidden within existence, but already present as a recollection —into the form of what is explicit, of what is objective to self (*Fürsichseins*).

We have to state more exactly the way this is done. At the point at which we here take up this movement, we are spared, in connexion with the whole, the process of cancelling and transcending the stage of mere existence. This process has already taken place. What is still to be done and needs a higher kind of transformation, is to transcend the forms as ideally presented and made familiar to our minds. By that previous negative process, existence, having been withdrawn into the mind's substance, is, in the first instance, transferred to the life of self only in an immediate way. The property the self has thereby acquired, has still the same character of uncomprehended immediacy, of passive indifference, which existence itself had; existence has in this way merely passed into the form of an ideal presentation. At the same time, by so doing, it is something familiar to us, something "well-known", something which the existent mind has finished and done with, and hence takes no more to do with and no further interest in. While the activity that is done with the existent is itself merely the process of the particular mind, of mind which is not comprehending itself, on the other hand, *knowledge* is directed against this ideal presentation which has hereby arisen, against this "being-familiar" and "well-known"; it is an action of *universal* mind, the concern of *thought*.

What is "familiarly known" is not properly known, just for the reason that it is "familiar." When engaged in the process of knowing, it is the commonest form of self-deception, and a deception of other people as well, to assume something to be familiar, and give assent to it on that very account. Knowledge of that sort, with all its talk, never gets from the spot, but has no idea that this is the case. Subject and object, and so on, God, nature, understanding, sensibility, etc., are uncritically presupposed as familiar and something valid, and become fixed points from which to start and to which to return. The process of knowing flits between these secure points, and in consequence goes on merely along the surface. Apprehending and proving consist similarly in seeing whether everyone finds what is said corresponding to his idea too, whether it is familiar and seems to him so and so or not.

Analysis of an idea, as it used to be carried out, did in fact consist in nothing else than doing away with its character of familiarity. To break up an idea into its ultimate elements means returning upon its moments, which at least do not have the form of the given idea when found, but are the immediate property of the self. Doubtless this analysis only arrives at thoughts which are themselves familiar elements, fixed inert determinations. But what is thus separated, and in a sense is unreal, is itself an essential moment; for just because the concrete fact is self-divided, and turns into unreality, it is something self-moving, self-active. The action of separating the elements is the exercise of the force of Understanding, the most astonishing and greatest of all powers, or rather the absolute power. The circle, which is self-enclosed and at rest, and, *qua* substance, holds its own moments, is an immediate relation, the immediate, continuous relation of elements with their unity, and hence arouses no sense of wonderment. But that an accident as such, when cut loose from its containing circumference —that what is found and held by something else and actual only by being connected with it—should obtain an existence all its own, gain freedom and independence on its own account—this is the portentous power of the negative; it is the energy of thought, of pure ego. Death, as we may call that unreality, is the most terrible thing, and to keep and hold fast what is dead demands the greatest force of all. Beauty, powerless and helpless, hates understanding, because the latter exacts from it what it cannot perform. But the life of mind is not one that shuns death, and keeps clear of destruction; it endures death and in death maintains its being. It only wins to its truth when it finds itself utterly torn asunder. It is this mighty power, not by being a positive which turns away from the negative, as when we say of anything it is nothing or it is false, and, being then done with it, pass off to something else: on the contrary, mind is this power only by looking the negative in the face, and dwelling with it. This dwelling beside it is the magic power that converts the negative into being. That power is just what we spoke of above as subject, which by giving determinateness a place in its substance, cancels abstract immediacy, i.e. immediacy which merely *is,* and, by so doing, becomes the true substance, becomes being or immediacy that does not have mediation outside it, but is this mediation itself.

This process of making what is objectively presented a possession of pure self-consciousness, of raising it to the level of universality in general, is merely one aspect of mental development; spiritual evolution is not yet completed. The manner of study in ancient times is distinct from that of the modern world, in that the former consisted in the cultivation and perfecting of the natural mind. Testing life carefully at all points, philosophizing about everything it came across, the former created an experience permeated through and through by universals. In modern times, however, an individual finds the abstract form ready made. In straining to grasp it and make it his own, he rather strives to bring forward the inner meaning alone, without any process of mediation; the production of the universal is abridged, instead of the universal arising out of the manifold detail of concrete existence. Hence nowadays the task before us consists not so much in getting the individual clear of the stage of sensuous immediacy, and making him a substance that thinks and is grasped in terms of thought, but rather the very opposite: it consists in actualizing the universal, and giving it spiritual vitality, by the process of breaking down and superseding fixed and determinate thoughts. But it is much more difficult to make fixed and definite thoughts fuse with one another and form a continuous whole than to bring sensuous existence into this state. The reason lies in what was said before. Thought determinations get their substance and the element of their existence from the ego, the power of the negative, or pure reality; while determinations of sense find this in impotent abstract immediacy, in mere being as such. Thoughts become fluent and interfuse, when thinking pure and simple, this inner immediacy, knows itself as a moment, when pure certainty of self abstracts from itself. It does not "abstract" in the sense of getting away from itself and setting itself on one side, but of surrendering the fixed quality of its self-affirmation, and giving up both the fixity of the purely concrete—which is the ego as contrasted with the variety of its content—and the fixity of all those distinctions [the various thought-functions, principles, etc.] which are present in the element of pure thought and share that absoluteness of the ego. In virtue of this process pure thoughts become notions, concepts, and are then what they are in truth, self-moving functions, circles, are what their substance consists in, are spiritual entities.

This movement of the spiritual entities constitutes the nature of scientific procedure in general. Looked at as the concatenation of their content, this movement is the necessitated development and expansion of that content into an organic systematic whole. By this movement, too, the road, which leads to the notion of knowledge, becomes itself likewise a necessary and complete evolving process (*Werden*). This preparatory stage thus ceases to consist of casual philosophical reflections, referring to objects here and there, to processes and thoughts of the undeveloped mind as chance may direct; and it does not try to establish the truth by miscellaneous ratiocinations, inferences, and consequences drawn from circumscribed thoughts. The road to science, by the very movement of the notion itself, will compass the entire objective world of conscious life in its rational necessity.

Further, a systematic exposition like this constitutes the first part of science, because the positive existence of mind, *qua* primary and ultimate, is nothing but the immediate aspect of mind, the beginning; the beginning, but not yet its return to itself. The characteristic feature distinguishing this part of science [Phenomenology] from the others is the element of positive immediate existence. The mention of this distinction leads us to discuss certain established ideas that usually come to notice in this connexion.

The mind's immediate existence, conscious life, has two aspects—cognition and objectivity which is opposed to or negative of the subjective function of knowing. Since it is in the medium of consciousness that mind is developed and brings out its various moments, this opposition between the factors of conscious life is found at each stage in the evolution of mind, and all the various moments appear as modes or forms (*Gestalten*) of consciousness. The scientific statement of the course of this development is a science of the experience through which consciousness passes; the substance and its process are considered as the object of consciousness. Consciousness knows and comprehends nothing but what falls within its experience; for what is found in experience is merely spiritual substance, and, moreover, object of its self. Mind, however, becomes object, for it consists in the process of becoming an other to itself, i.e. an object for its own self, and in transcending this otherness. And experience is called this very process by which the element that is immediate, unexperienced, i.e. abstract —whether it be in the form of sense or of a bare thought—externalizes itself, and then comes back to itself from this state of estrangement, and by so doing is at length set forth in its concrete nature and real truth, and becomes too a possession of consciousness.

The dissimilarity which obtains in consciousness between the ego and the substance constituting its object, is their inner distinction, the factor of negativity in general. We may regard it as the defect of both opposites, but it is their very soul, their moving spirit. It was on this account that certain thinkers [3] long ago took the void to be the principle of movement, when they conceived the moving principle to be the negative element, though they had not as yet thought of it as self. While this negative factor appears in the first instance as a dissimilarity, as an inequality, between ego and object, it is just as much the inequality of the substance with itself. What seems to take place outside it, to be an activity directed against it, is its own doing, its own activity; and substance shows that it is in reality subject. When it has brought out this completely, mind has made its existence adequate to and one with its essential nature. Mind is object to itself just as it *is,* and the abstract element of immediacy, of the separation between knowing and the truth, is overcome. Being is entirely mediated; it is a substantial content, that is likewise directly in the possession of the ego, has the character of self, is notion. With the attainment of this the *Phenomenology of Mind* concludes. What mind prepares for itself in the course of its phenomenology is the element of true knowledge. In this element the moments of mind are now set out in the form of thought pure and simple, which knows its object to be itself. They no longer involve the opposition between being and knowing; they remain within the undivided simplicity of the knowing function; they are the truth in the form of truth, and their diversity is merely diversity of the content of truth. The process by which they are developed into an organically connected whole is Logic or Speculative Philosophy.

Now, because the systematic statement of the mind's experience em-

---

[3] Leucippus and Democritus. [J.B.B.]

braces merely its ways of appearing, it may well seem that the advance from that to the science of ultimate truth in the form of truth is merely negative; and we might readily be content to dispense with the negative process as something altogether false, and might ask to be taken straight to the truth at once: why meddle with what is false at all? The point formerly raised, that we should have begun with science at once, may be answered here by considering the character of negativity in general regarded as something false. The usual ideas on this subject particularly obstruct the approach to the truth. The consideration of this point will give us an opportunity to speak about mathematical knowledge, which non-philosophical knowledge looks upon as the idea which philosophy ought to try to attain, but has so far striven in vain to reach.

Truth and falsehood as commonly understood belong to those sharply defined ideas which claim a completely fixed nature of their own, one standing in solid isolation on this side, the other on that, without any community between them. Against that view it must be pointed out, that truth is not like stamped coin that is issued ready from the mint and so can be taken up and used. Nor, again, *is* there something false, any more than there *is* something evil. Evil and falsehood are indeed not so bad as the devil, for in the form of the devil they get the length of being particular subjects; *qua* false and evil they are merely universals, though they have a nature of their own with reference to one another. Falsity (that is what we are dealing with here) would be *otherness*, the negative aspect of the substance, which [substance], *qua* content of knowledge, is truth. But the substance is itself essentially the negative element, partly as involving distinction and determination of content, partly as being a process of distinguishing pure and simple, i.e. as being self and knowledge in general. Doubtless we can know in a way that is false. To know something falsely means that knowledge is not adequate to, is not on equal terms with, its substance. Yet this very dissimilarity is the process of distinction in general, the essential moment in knowing. It is, in fact, out of this active distinction that its harmonious unity arises, and this identity, when arrived at, is truth. But it is not truth in a sense which would involve the rejection of the discordance, the diversity, like dross from pure metal; nor, again, does truth remain detached from diversity, like a finished article from the instrument that shapes it. Difference itself continues to be an immediate element within truth as such, in the form of the principle of negation, in the form of the activity of Self. All the same, we cannot for that reason say that falsehood is a moment or forms even a constituent part of truth. That "in every case of falsity there is something true" is an expression in which they are taken to be like oil and water, which do not mix and are merely united externally. Just in the interest of their real meaning, precisely because we want to designate the aspect or moment of complete otherness, the terms true and false must no longer be used where their otherness has been cancelled and superseded. Just as the expressions "unity of subject and object," of "finite and infinite," of "being and thought," etc., are clumsy when subject and object, etc., are taken to mean what they are *outside* their unity, and are thus in that unity not meant to be what its very expression conveys; in the same way falsehood is not, *qua* false, any longer a moment of truth.

Dogmatism as a way of thinking, whether in ordinary knowledge or in the study of philosophy, is nothing else but the view that truth consists in a proposition, which is a fixed and final result, or again which is directly known. To questions like, "When was Caesar born?", "How many feet make a furlong?", etc., a straight answer ought to be given; just as it is absolutely true that the square of the hypotenuse is equal to the sum of the squares of the other two sides of a right-angled triangle. But the nature of a so-called truth of that sort is different from the nature of philosophical truth.

As regards truth in matters of historical fact—to deal briefly with this subject—so far as we consider the purely historical element, it will be readily granted that they have to do with the sphere of particular existence, with a content in its contingent and arbitrary aspects, features that have no necessity. But even bare truths of the kind, say, like those mentioned, are impossible without the activity of self-consciousness. In order to know any one of them, there has to be a good deal of comparison, books must be consulted, or in some way or other inquiry has to be made. Even in a case of direct perception, only when we know it along with the reasons behind it, is it held to be something of real value; although it is merely the naked fact itself that we are, properly speaking, supposed to be concerned about.

As to mathematical truths, we should be still less inclined to consider anyone a geometer who had got Euclid's theorems by heart (*auswendig*) without knowing the proofs, without, if we may say so by way of contrast, getting them into his head (*inwendig*). Similarly, if anyone came to know by measuring many right-angled triangles that their sides are related in the way everybody knows, we should regard knowledge so obtained as unsatisfactory. All the same, while proof is essential in the case of mathematical knowledge, it still does not have the significance and nature of being a moment in the result itself; the proof is over when we get the result, and has disappeared. *Qua* result the theorem is, no doubt, one that is seen to be true. But this eventuality has nothing to do with its content, but only with its relation to the knowing subject. The process of mathematical proof does not belong to the object; it is a function that takes place outside the matter in hand. Thus, the nature of a right-angled triangle does not break itself up into factors in the manner set forth in the mathematical construction which is required to prove the proposition expressing the relation of its parts. The entire process of producing the result is an affair of knowledge which takes its own way of going about it. In philosophical knowledge, too, the way existence, *qua* existence, comes about (*Werden*) is different from that whereby the essence or inner nature of the fact comes into being. But philosophical knowledge, for one thing, contains both, while mathematical knowledge sets forth merely the way an existence comes about, i.e. the way the nature of the fact gets to *be* in the sphere of knowledge as such. For another thing, too, philosophical knowledge unites both these particular movements. The inward rising into being, the process of substance, is an unbroken transition into outwardness, into existence or being for another; and conversely, the coming of existence into being is withdrawal into the inner essence. The movement is the twofold process in which the whole comes to be, and is such that each at the same time posits the other, and each on that account has in it both as its two aspects. Together they make the whole, through their resolving each other, and making themselves into moments of the whole.

In mathematical knowledge the insight required is an external function so far as the subject-matter dealt with is concerned. It follows that the actual fact is thereby altered. The means taken, construction and proof, contain, no doubt, true propositions; but all the same we are bound to say that the content is false. The triangle in the above example is taken to pieces, and its parts made into other figures to which the construction in the triangle gives rise. It is only at the end that we find again reinstated the triangle we are really concerned with; it was lost sight of in the course of the construction, and was present merely in fragments, that belonged to other wholes. Thus we find negativity of content coming in here too, a negativity which would have to be called falsity, just as much as in the case of the movement of the notion where thoughts that are taken to be fixed pass away and disappear.

The real defect of this kind of knowledge, however, affects its process of knowing as much as its material. As to that process, in the first place we do not see any necessity in the construction. The necessity does not arise from the nature of the theorem: it is imposed; and the injunction to draw just these lines, an infinite number of others being equally possible, is blindly acquiesced in, without our knowing anything further, except that, as we fondly believe, this will serve our purpose in producing the proof. Later on this design then comes out too, and is therefore merely external in character, just because it is only after the proof is found that it comes to be known. In the same way, again, the proof takes a direction that begins anywhere we like, without our knowing as yet what relation this beginning has to the result to be brought out. In its course, it takes up certain specific elements and relations and lets others alone, without its being directly obvious what necessity there is in the matter. An external purpose controls this process.

The evidence peculiar to this defective way of knowing—an evidence on the strength of which mathematics plumes itself and proudly struts before philosophy—rests solely on the poverty of its purpose and the defectiveness of its material, and is on that account of a kind that philosophy must scorn to have anything to do with. Its purpose or principle is quantity. This is precisely the relationship that is non-essential, alien to the character of the notion. The process of knowledge goes on, therefore, on the surface, does not affect the concrete fact itself, does not touch its inner nature or notion, and is hence not a conceptual way of comprehending. The material which provides mathematics with these welcome treasures of truth consists of space and numerical units (*das Eins*). Space is that kind of existence wherein the concrete notion inscribes the diversity it contains, as in an empty, lifeless element in which its differences likewise subsist in passive, lifeless form. What is concretely actual is not something spatial, such as is treated of in mathematics. With unrealities like the things mathematics takes account of, neither concrete sensuous perception nor philosophy has anything to do. In an unreal element of that sort we find, then, only unreal truth, fixed lifeless propositions. We can call a halt at any of them; the next begins of itself *de novo,* without the first having led up to the one that follows, and without any necessary connexion having in this way arisen from the nature of the subject-matter itself. So, too—and herein consists the formal character of mathematical evidence—because of that principle and the element where it applies, knowledge advances along the lines of bare equality, of abstract identity. For what is lifeless, not being self-moved, does not bring about distinction within its essential nature; does not attain to essential opposition or unlikeness; and hence involves no transition of one opposite element into its other, no qualitative, immanent movement, no *self*-movement. It is quantity, a form of difference that does not touch the essential nature, which alone mathematics deals with. It abstracts from the fact that it is the notion which separates space into its dimensions, and determines the connexions between them and in them. It does not consider, for example, the relation of line to surface, and when it compares the diameter of a circle with its circumference, it runs up against their incommensurability, i.e. a relation in terms of the notion, an infinite element, that escapes mathematical determination.

Immanent or so-called pure mathematics, again, does not oppose time *qua* time to space, as a second subject-matter for consideration. Applied mathematics, no doubt, treats of time, as also of motion, and other concrete things as well; but it picks up from experience synthetic propositions—i.e. statements of their relations, which are determined by their conceptual nature—and merely applies its formulae to those propositions assumed to start with. That the so-called proofs of propositions like that concerning the equilibrium of the lever, the relation of space and time in gravitation, etc., which applied mathematics frequently gives, should be taken and given as proofs, is itself merely a proof of how great the need is for knowledge to have a process of proof, seeing that, even where proof is not to be had, knowledge yet puts a value on the mere semblance of it, and gets thereby a certain sense of satisfaction. A criticism of those proofs would be as instructive as it would be significant, if the criticism could strip mathematics of this artificial finery, and bring out its limitations, and thence show the necessity for another type of knowledge.

As to time, which, it is to be presumed, would, by way of the counterpart to space, constitute the object-matter of the other division of pure mathematics, this is the notion itself in the form of existence. The principle of quantity, of difference which is not determined by the notion, and the principle of equality, of abstract, lifeless unity, are incapable of dealing with that sheer restlessness of life and its absolute and inherent process of differentiation. It is therefore only in an arrested, paralysed form, only in the form of the quantitative unit, that this essentially negative activity becomes the second object-matter of this way of knowing, which, itself an external operation, degrades what is self-moving to the level of mere matter, in order thus to get an indifferent, external, lifeless content.

Philosophy, on the contrary, does not deal with a determination that is non-essential, but with a determination so far as it is an essential factor. The abstract or unreal is not its element and content, but the real, what is self-establishing, has life within itself, existence in its very notion. It is the process that creates its own moments in its course, and goes through them all; and the whole of this movement constitutes its positive content and its truth. This movement includes, therefore, within it the negative factor as well, the element which would be named falsity if it could be considered one from which we had to abstract. The element that disappears has rather to be looked at as itself essential, not in the sense of being something fixed, that has to be cut off from truth and allowed to lie outside it, heaven knows where; just as similarly the truth is not to be held to stand on the other side as an immovable lifeless positive element. Appearance is the process of arising into being and passing away again, a process that itself does not arise and does not pass away, but is *per se,* and constitutes reality and the life-movement of truth. The truth is thus the bacchanalian revel, where not a member is sober; and because every member no sooner becomes detached than it *eo ipso* collapses straightway, the revel is just as much a state of transparent unbroken calm. Judged by that movement, the particular shapes which mind assumes do not indeed subsist any more than do determinate thoughts or ideas; but they are, all the same, as much positive and necessary moments, as negative and transitory. In the entirety of the movement, taken as an unbroken quiescent whole, that which obtains distinctness in the course of its process and secures specific existence, is preserved in the form of a self-recollection, in which existence is self-knowledge, and self-knowledge, again, is immediate existence.

It might well seem necessary to state at the outset the chief points in connexion with the *method* of this process, the way in which science operates. Its nature, however, is to be found in what has already been said, while the proper systematic exposition of it is the special business of Logic, or rather is Logic itself. For the method is nothing else than the structure of the whole in its pure and essential form. In regard, however, to what has been hitherto currently held on this point, we must be sensible that the system of ideas bearing on the question of philosophical method, belongs also to a stage of mental culture that has now passed away. This may perhaps seem somewhat boastful or revolutionary; and I am far from adopting an attitude of that sort; but it is significant that the scientific régime bequeathed by mathematics—a régime of explanations, divisions, axioms, an array of theorems, with proofs, principles, and the consequences and conclusions drawn from them—all this has already come to be generally considered as at any rate out of date. Even though there is no clear idea why it is unsuitable, yet little or no use is made of it any longer; and even though it is not condemned outright, it is all the same not in favour. And we must be so far prejudiced in favour of what is excellent to believe that it can turn itself to practical account, and make itself acceptable. But it is not difficult to see that the method of propounding a proposition, producing reasons for it and then refuting its opposite by reasons too, is not the form in which truth can appear. Truth moves itself by its very nature; but the method just mentioned is a form of knowledge external to its material. Hence it is peculiar to mathematics and must be left to mathematics, which, as already indicated, takes for its principle the relation of quantity, a relation alien to the notion, and gets its material from lifeless space, and the equally lifeless numerical unit. Or, again, such a method, adopting a freer style, one involving more of arbitrariness and chance, may have a place in ordinary life, in a conversation, or in supplying matter-of-fact instruction for the satisfaction of curiosity rather than knowledge, very much as a preface does. In every-day life the mind finds its content in different kinds of knowledge, experiences of various sorts, concrete facts of sense, thoughts, too, and principles, and, in general, in whatever lies ready to hand, or passes for a solid stable entity, or real being. The mind follows wherever this leads, sometimes interrupting the connexion by an unrestrained caprice in dealing with the content, and takes up the attitude of determining and handling it in quite an external fashion. It runs the content back to some touchstone of certainty or other, even though it be but the feeling of the moment; and conviction is satisfied if it reaches some familiar resting-place.

But when the necessity of the notion banishes from its realm the loose procedure of the *"raisonnements"* [reasonings] of conversation, as well as the pedantic style of scientific pomposity, its place, as we have already mentioned, must not be taken by the disconnected utterance of presageful surmise and inspiration, and the arbitrary caprice of prophetic utterance; for this does not merely despise that particular form of scientific procedure, but contemns scientific procedure altogether.

Now that the triplicity, adopted in the system of Kant—a method rediscovered, to begin with, by instinctive insight, but left lifeless and uncomprehended—has been raised to its significance as an absolute method, true form is thereby set up in its true content, and the conception of science has come to light. But the use this form has been put to in certain quarters has no right to the name of science. For we see it there reduced to a lifeless schema, to nothing better than a mere shadow, and scientific organization to a synoptic table. This formalism—about which we spoke before in general terms, and whose procedure we wish here to state more fully—thinks it has comprehended and expressed the nature and life of a given form when it proclaims a determination of the schema to be its predicate. The predicate may be subjectivity or objectivity, or again magnetism, electricity, and so on, contraction or expansion, East or West, and such like—a form of predication that can be multiplied indefinitely, because according to this way of working each determination, each mode, can be applied as a form or schematic element in the case of every other, and each will thankfully perform the same service for any other. With a circle of reciprocities of this sort it is impossible to make out what the real fact in question is, or what the one or the other is. We find there sometimes constituents of sense picked up from ordinary intuition, determinate elements which to be sure should mean something else than they say; at other times what is inherently significant, viz. pure determinations of thought—like subject, object, substance, cause, universality, etc.—these are applied just as uncritically and unreflectingly as in every-day life, are used much as people employ the terms strong and weak, expansion and contraction. As a result that type of metaphysics is as unscientific as those ideas of sense.

Instead of the inner activity and self-movement of its own actual life, such a simple determination of direct intuition (*Anschauung*)—which means here sense-knowledge—is predicated in accordance with a superficial analogy, and this external and empty application of the formula is called "construction." The same thing happens here, however, as in the case of every kind of formalism. A man's head must be indeed dull if he could not in a quarter of an hour get up the theory that there are enervating, innervating, and indirectly enervating diseases and as many cures, and who could not—since not so long ago instruction of that sort sufficed for the purpose—in as short a time be turned from being a man who works by rule of thumb into a theoretical physician. Formalism in the case of speculative Philosophy of Nature (*Naturphilosophie*) takes the shape of teaching that understanding is electricity, animals are nitrogen, or equivalent to South or North and so on. When it does this, whether as badly as it is here expressed or even concocted with more terminology, such forceful procedure brings and holds together elements to all appearance far removed from one another; the violence done to stable inert sense-elements by connecting them in this way, confers on them merely the semblance of a conceptual unity, and spares itself the trouble of doing what is after all the important thing—expressing the notion itself, the meaning that underlies sense-ideas. All this sort of thing may strike anyone who has no experience with admiration and wonder. He may be awed by the profound genius he thinks it displays, and be delighted at the happy ingenuity of such characterizations, since they fill the place of the abstract notion with something tangible and sensuous, and so make it more pleasing; and he may congratulate himself on feeling an instinctive mental affinity for that glorious way of proceeding. The trick of wisdom of that sort is as quickly acquired as it is easy to practise. Its repetition, when once it is familiar, becomes as boring as the repetition of any bit of sleight-of-hand once we see through it. The instrument for producing this monotonous formalism is no more difficult to handle than the palette of a painter, on which lie only two colours, say red and green, the former for colouring the surface when we want a historical piece, the latter when we want a bit of landscape. It would be difficult to settle which is greater in all this, the agreeable ease with which everything in heaven and earth and under the earth is plastered with that botch of colour, or the conceit that prides itself on the excellence of its means for every conceivable purpose; the one lends support to the other. What results from the use of this method of sticking on to everything in heaven and earth, to every kind of shape and form, natural and spiritual, the pair of determinations from the general schema, and filing everything in this manner, is no less than an "account as clear as noonday" of the organized whole of the universe. It is, that is to say, a synoptic index, like a skeleton with tickets stuck all over it, or like the rows of boxes kept shut and labelled in a grocer's stall; and is as intelligible as either the one or the other. It has lost hold of the living nature of concrete fact; just as in the former case we have merely dry bones with flesh and blood all gone, and in the latter, there is shut away in those boxes something equally lifeless too. We have already remarked that the final outcome of this style of thinking is, at the same time, to paint entirely in one kind of colour; for it turns with contempt from the distinctions in the schematic table, looks on them as belonging to the activity of mere reflection, and lets them drop out of sight in the void of the Absolute, and there reinstates pure identity, pure formless whiteness. Such uniformity of colouring in the schema with its lifeless determinations, this absolute identity, and the transition from one to the other—these are the one as well as the other, the expression of inert lifeless understanding, and equally an external process of knowledge.

Not only can what is excellent not escape the fate of being thus devitalized and despiritualized and excoriated of seeing its skin paraded about by lifeless knowledge and the conceit such knowledge engenders; but rather, such a fate lets us realize the power the "excellent" exercises over the heart (*Gemüth*), if not over the mind (*Geist*). Moreover, we recognize thereby, too, the constructive unfolding into universality and determinateness of form which marks the complete attainment of excellence, and which alone makes it possible that this universality can be turned to superficial uses.

Science can become an organic system only by the inherent life of the notion. In science the determinateness, which was taken from the schema and stuck on to existing facts in external fashion, is the self-directing inner soul of the concrete content. The movement of what is partly consists in becoming another to itself, and thus developing explicitly into its own immanent content; partly, again, it takes this evolved content, this existence it assumes, back into itself, i.e. makes *itself* into a moment, and reduces itself to simple determinateness. In the first stage of the process negativity lies in the function of distinguishing and establishing existence; in this latter return into self, negativity consists in the bringing about of determinate simplicity. It is in this way that the content shows its specific characteristic not to be received from something else, and stuck on externally; the content gives itself this determinate characteristic, appoints itself of its own initiative to the rank of a moment and to a place in the whole. The pigeonholing process of understanding retains for itself the necessity and the notion controlling the content, that which constitutes the concrete element, the actuality and living process of the subject-matter which it labels: or rather, understanding does not retain this for itself, on the contrary, understanding fails to know it. For if it had as much insight as that, it would surely show that it had. It is not even aware of the need for such insight; if it were, it would drop its schematizing process, or at least would no longer be satisfied to know by way of a mere table of contents. A table of contents is all that understanding gives, the content itself it does not furnish at all.

If the specific determination (say even one like magnetism) is one that in itself is concrete or actual, it all the same gets degraded into something lifeless and inert, since it is merely predicated of another existing entity, and not known as an immanent living principle of this existence; nor is there any comprehension of how in this entity its intrinsic and peculiar way of expressing and producing itself takes effect. This, the very kernel of the matter, formal understanding leaves to others to add later on. Instead of making its way into the inherent content of the matter in hand, understanding always takes a survey of the whole, assumes a position above the particular existence about which it is speaking, i.e. it does not see it at all. True scientific knowledge, on the contrary, demands abandonment to the very life of the object, or, which means the same thing, claims to have before it the inner necessity controlling the object, and to express this only. Steeping itself in its object, it forgets to take that general survey, which is merely a turning of knowledge away from the content back into itself. But being sunk into the material in hand, and following the course that such material takes, true knowledge returns back into itself, yet not before the content in its fullness is taken into itself, is reduced to the simplicity of being a determinate characteristic, drops to the level of being one aspect of an existing entity, and passes over into its higher truth. By this process the whole as such, surveying its entire content, itself emerges out of the wealth wherein its process of reflection seemed to be lost.

In general, in virtue of the principle that, as we expressed it before, substance is implicitly and in itself subject, all content makes its reflection into itself in its own special way. The subsistence or substance of anything that exists is its self-identity; for its want of identity, or oneness with itself, would be its dissolution. But self-identity is pure abstraction; and this is just thinking. When I say Quality, I state simple determinateness; by means of its quality one existence is distinguished from another or is an "existence"; it is for itself, something on its own account, or subsists with itself because of this simple characteristic. But by doing so it is essentially Thought.

Here we find contained the principle that Being is Thought: here is exercised that insight which usually tends to deviate from the ordinary non-conceptual way of speaking of the identity of thought and being. In virtue, further, of the fact that subsistence on the part of what exists is self-identity or pure abstraction, it is the abstraction of itself from itself, in other words, is itself its own want of identity with itself and dissolution—its own proper inwardness and retraction into self—its process of becoming.

Owing to the nature which being thus has, and so far as what is has this nature from the point of view of knowledge, this thinking is not an activity which treats the content as something alien and external; it is not reflection into self away from the content. Science is not that kind of Idealism which stepped into the place of the Dogmatism of mere assertion and took the shape of a Dogmatism of mere assurance, the Dogmatism of mere self-certainty. Rather, since knowledge sees the content go back into its own proper inner nature, the activity of knowledge is absorbed in that content —for it (the activity) is the immanent self of the content—and is also at the same time returned into itself, for this activity is pure self-identity in otherness. In this way the knowing activity is the artful device which, while seeming to refrain from activity, looks on and watches how specific determinateness with its concrete life, just where it believes it is working out its own self-preservation and its own private interest, is, in point of fact, doing the very opposite, is doing what brings about its own dissolution and makes itself a moment in the whole.

While, in the foregoing, the significance of Understanding was stated from the point of view of the self-consciousness of substance; by what has been here stated we can see clearly its significance from the point of view of substance *qua* being. Existence is Quality, self-identical determinateness, or determinate simplicity, determinate thought: this is existence from the point of view of Understanding. On this account it is νοῦς, as Anaxagoras first thought reality to be. Those who succeeded him grasped the nature of existence in a more determinate way as εἶδος or ἰδέα, i.e. as determinate or specific universality, kind or species. The term species or kind seems indeed too ordinary and inadequate for Ideas, for beauty, holiness, eternal, which are the vogue in these days. As a matter of fact, however, idea means neither more nor less than kind, species. But we often find nowadays that a term which exactly designates a conception is despised and rejected, and another preferred to it which hides and obscures the conception, and thus sounds more edifying, even though this is merely due to its being expressed in a foreign language.

Precisely for the reason that existence is designated a species or kind, it is a naked simple thought; νοῦς, simplicity, is substance. It is on account of its simplicity, its self-identity, that it appears steady, fixed, and permanent. But this self-identity is likewise negativity; hence that fixed and stable existence carries the process of its own dissolution within itself. The determinateness appears at first to be so solely through its relation to something else; and its process seems imposed and forced upon it externally. But its having its own otherness within itself, and the fact of its being a self-initiated process—these are implied in the very simplicity of thought itself. For this is self-moving thought, thought that distinguishes, is inherent inwardness, the pure notion. Thus, then, it is the very nature of understanding to be a process; and being a process it is Rationality.

In the nature of existence as thus described—to be its own notion and being in one—consists logical necessity in general. This alone is what is rational, the rhythm of the organic whole: it is as much knowledge of content as that content is notion and essential nature. In other words, this alone is the sphere and element of speculative thought. The concrete shape of the content is resolved by its own inherent process into a simple determinate quality. Thereby it is raised to logical form, and its being and essence coincide; its concrete existence is merely this process that takes place, and is *eo ipso* logical existence. It is therefore needless to apply a formal scheme to the concrete content in an external fashion; the content is in its very nature a transition into a formal shape, which, however, ceases to be formalism of an external kind, because the form is the indwelling process of the concrete content itself.

This nature of scientific method, which consists partly in being inseparable from the content, and partly in determining the rhythm of its movement by its own agency, finds, as we mentioned before, its peculiar systematic expression in speculative philosophy. What is here stated describes in effect the essential principle; but cannot stand for more at this stage than an assertion or assurance by way of anticipation. The truth it contains is not to be found in this exposition, which is in part historical in character. And just for that reason, too, it is not in the least refuted if anyone assures us on the contrary that this is not so, that the process instead is here so and so; if ideas we are all used to, being truths accepted or settled and familiar to everyone, are brought to mind and recounted; or, again, if something new is served up and guaranteed as coming from the inner sanctuaries of inspired intuition.

Such a view is bound to meet with opposition. The first instinctive reaction on the part of knowing, when offered something that was unfamiliar, is usually to resist it. It seeks by that means to save freedom and native insight, to secure its own inherent authority—against alien authority—for that is the way anything apprehended for the first time appears. This attitude is adopted, too, in order to do away with the semblance of a kind of disgrace which would lie in the fact that something has had to be learnt. In like manner, again, when the unfamiliar or unknown is received with applause, the reaction is in the same way an exaltation of freedom and native authority. It consists in something analogous to ultra-revolutionary declamation and action.

Hence the important thing for the student of science is to make himself undergo the strenuous toil of conceptual reflection, of thinking in the form of the notion. This demands concentrated attention on the notion as such, on simple and ultimate determinations like being-in-itself, being-for-itself, self-identity, and so on; for these are elemental, pure, self-determined functions of a kind we might call souls, were it not that their conceptual nature denotes something higher than that term contains. The interruption by conceptual thought of the habit of always thinking in figurative ideas (*Vorstellungen*) is as annoying and troublesome to this way of thinking as to that process of formal intelligence which in its reasoning rambles about with no real thoughts to reason with. The former, the habit, may be called materialized thinking, a fortuitous mental state, one that is absorbed in what is material, and hence finds it very distasteful at once to lift its self clear of this matter and be with itself alone. The latter, the process of *raisonnement,* is, on the other hand, detachment from all content, and conceited superiority to it. What is wanted here is the effort and struggle to give up this kind of freedom, and instead of being a merely arbitrary principle directing the content anyhow, this freedom should sink into and pervade the content, should let it be directed and controlled by its own proper nature, i.e. by the self as its own self, and should observe this process taking place. We must abstain from interrupting the immanent rhythm of the movement of conceptual thought; we must refrain from arbitrarily interfering with it, and introducing ideas and reflections that have been obtained elsewhere. Restraint of this sort is itself an essential condition of attending to and getting at the real nature of the notion.

There are two aspects in the case of that ratiocinative procedure which mark its contrast from conceptual thinking and call for further notice. *Raisonnement,* in the first place, adopts a negative attitude towards the content apprehended; knows how to refute it and reduce it to nothingness. To see what the content is *not* is merely a negative process; it is a dead halt, which does not of itself go beyond itself, and proceed to a new content; it has to get hold of something else from somewhere or other in order to have once more a content. It is reflection upon and into the empty ego, the vanity of its own knowledge. Conceit of this kind brings out not only that this content is vain and empty, but also that to see this is itself fatuity too: for it is negation with no perception of the positive element within it. In that this reflection does not even have its own negativity as its content, it is not inside actual fact at all, but for ever away outside it. On that account it imagines that by asserting mere emptiness it is going much farther than insight that embraces and reveals a wealth of content. On the other hand, in the case of conceptual thinking, as was above indicated, the negative aspect falls within the content itself, and is the positive substance of that content, as well as being its inherent character and moving principle as by being the entirety of what these are. Looked at as a result, it is determinate specific negation, the negative which is the outcome of this process, and consequently is a positive content as well.

In view of the fact that ratiocinative thinking has a content, whether of images or thoughts or a mixture of both, there is another side to its process which makes conceptual comprehension difficult for it. The peculiar nature of this aspect is closely connected with the essential meaning of the idea above described, in fact, expresses the idea in the way this appears as the process of thinking apprehension. For just as ratiocinative thinking in its negative reference, which we have been describing, is nothing but the self into which the content returns; in the same way, on the other hand, in its positive cognitive process the self is an ideally presented subject to which the content is related as an accident and predicate. This subject constitutes the basis to which the content is attached and on which the process moves to and fro. Conceptual thinking goes on in quite a different way. Since the concept or notion is the very self of the object, manifesting itself as the development of the object, it is not a quiescent subject, passively supporting accidents: it is a self-determining active concept which takes up its determinations and makes them its own. In the course of this process that inert passive subject really disappears; it enters into the different constituents and pervades the content; instead of remaining in inert antithesis to determinateness of content, it constitutes, in fact, that very specificity, i.e. the content as differentiated along with the process of bringing this about. Thus the solid basis, which ratiocination found in an inert subject, is shaken to its foundations, and the only object is this very movement of the subject. The subject supplying the concrete filling to its own content ceases to be something transcending this content, and cannot have further predicates or accidents. Conversely, again, the scattered diversity of the content is brought under the control of the self, and so bound together; the content is not a universal that can be detached from the subject, and adapted to several indifferently. Consequently the content is in truth no longer predicate of the subject; it is the very substance, is the inmost reality, and the very principle of what is being considered. Ideational thinking (*vorstellen*), since its nature consists in dealing with accidents or predicates, and in exercising the right to transcend them because they are nothing more than predicates and accidents—this way of thinking is checked in its course, since that which has in the proposition the form of a predicate is itself the substance of the statement. It is met by a counter-thrust, as we may say. Starting from the subject, as if this were a permanent base on which to proceed, it discovers, by the predicate being in reality the substance, that the subject has passed into the predicate, and has thereby ceased to be subject: and since in this way what seems to be predicate has become the entire mass of the content, whole and complete, thinking cannot wander and ramble about at will, but is restrained and controlled by this weight of content.

Usually the subject is first set down as the fixed and objective self; from this fixed position the necessary process passes on to the multiplicity of determinations or predicates. Here the knowing ego takes the place of that subject and is the function of knitting or combining the predicates one with another, and is the subject holding them fast. But since the former subject enters into the determinate constituents themselves, and is their very life, the subject in the second case—viz. the knowing subject—finds that the former—which it is supposed to be done with and which it wants to transcend, in order to return into itself—is still there in the predicate: and instead of being able to be the determining agency in the process of resolving the predicate—reflectively deciding whether this or that predicate should be attached to the former subject—it has really to deal with the self of the content, is not allowed to be something on its own account (*für sich*), but has to exist along with this content.

What has been said can be expressed in a formal manner by saying that the nature of judgment or the proposition in general, which involves the distinction of subject and predicate, is subverted and destroyed by the speculative judgment; and the identical proposition, which the former becomes [by uniting subject and predicate], implies the rejection and repudiation of the above relation between subject and predicate. This conflict between the form of a proposition in general and the unity of the notion which destroys that form, is similar to what we find between metre and accent in the case of rhythm. Rhythm is the result of what hovers between and unites both. So in the case of the speculative or philosophical judgment; the identity of subject and predicate is not intended to destroy their distinction, as expressed in propositional form; their unity is to arise as a harmony of the elements. The form of the judgment is the way the specific sense appears, or is made manifest, the accent which differentiates the meaning it contains: that the predicate expresses the substance, and the subject itself falls within the universal, is however the unity wherein that accent dies away.

To explain what has been said by examples let us take the proposition God is Being. The predicate is "being": it has substantive significance, and thus absorbs the meaning of the subject within it. Being is meant to be here not predicate but the essential nature. Thereby, God seems to cease to be what he was when the proposition was put forward, viz. a fixed subject. Thinking [i.e. ordinary reflection], instead of getting any farther with the transition from subject to predicate, in reality finds its activity checked through the loss of the subject, and it is thrown back on the thought of the subject because it misses this subject. Or again, since the predicate has itself been pronounced to be a subject, to be *the* being, to be the essential reality, which exhausts the nature of the subject, thinking finds the subject directly present in the predicate too: and now, instead of having, in the predicate, gone into *itself,* and preserved the freedom characteristic of ratiocination, it is absorbed in the content all the while, or, at any rate is required to be so.

Similarly, when it is said: "the real is the universal," the real, *qua* subject, passes away in its predicate. The universal is not only meant to have the significance of a predicate, as if the proposition stated that the real is universal: the universal is meant to express the essential nature of the real. Thinking therefore loses that fixed objective basis which it had in the subject, just as much as in the predicate it is thrown back on the subject, and therein returns not into itself but into the subject underlying the content.

This unaccustomed restraint imposed upon thought is for the most part the cause of the complaints concerning the unintelligibility of philosophical writings, when otherwise the individual has in him the requisite mental cultivation for understanding them. In what has been said we see the reason for the specific charge often made against them, that a good deal has to be read repeatedly before it can be understood—an accusation which is meant to convey something improper in the extreme, and one which if granted to be sound admits of no further reply. It is obvious from the above what is the state of the case here. The philosophical proposition, being a proposition, calls up the accepted view of the usual relation of subject and predicate, and suggests the idea of the customary procedure which takes place in knowledge. Its philosophical content destroys this way of proceeding and the ordinary view taken of this process. The common view discovers that the statement is intended in another sense than it is thinking of, and this correction of its opinion compels knowledge to recur to the proposition and take it now in some other sense.

There is a difficulty which might well be avoided. It consists in mixing up the methods of procedure followed by speculation and ratiocination, when what is said of the subject has at one time the significance of its conceptual principle, and at another time the meaning of its predicate or accidental quality. The one mode of thinking invalidates the other; and only that philosophical exposition can manage to become plastic in character which resolutely sets aside and has nothing to do with the ordinary way of relating the parts of a proposition.

As a matter of fact, non-speculative thinking has its rights too, which are justifiable, but are disregarded in the speculative way of stating a proposition. Abolishing the form of the proposition must not take place only in an immediate manner, through the mere content of the proposition. On the contrary, we must give explicit expression to this cancelling process; it must be not only that internal restraining and confining of thought within its own substance; this turning of the conception back into itself has to be expressly brought out and stated. This process, which constitutes what formerly had to be accomplished by proof, is the internal dialectical movement of the proposition itself. This alone is the concrete speculative element, and only the explicit expression of this is a speculative systematic exposition. *Qua* proposition, the speculative aspect is merely the internal restriction of thought within its own substance where the return of the essential principle into itself is not yet brought out. Hence we often find philosophical expositions referring us to the inner intuition, and thus dispensing with the systematic statement of the dialectical movement of the proposition, which is what we wanted all the while. The proposition ought to express *what* the truth is: in its essential nature the truth is subject: being so, it is merely the dialectical movement, this self-producing course of activity, maintaining its advance by returning back into itself. In the case of knowledge in other spheres this aspect of expressly stating the internal nature of the content is constituted by proof. When dialectic, however, has been separated from proof, the idea of philosophical demonstration as a matter of fact has vanished altogether.

On this point it may be mentioned that the dialectical process likewise consists of parts or elements which are propositions. The difficulty indicated seems therefore to recur continually, and seems to be a difficulty inherent in the nature of the case. This is like what happens in the ordinary process of proving anything; the grounds it makes use of need themselves to be based on other grounds again, and so on *ad infinitum*. This manner of furnishing grounds and conditions, however, concerns that type of proof from which the dialectical movement is distinct and hence belongs to the process of external knowledge. As to what this movement is, its element is the bare concept; this furnishes a content which is through and through subject *impliciter* and *per se*. There is to be found, therefore, no sort of content standing in a relation, as it were, to an underlying subject, and getting its significance by being attached to this as a predicate. The proposition as it appears is a mere empty form.

Apart from the sensuously apprehended or ideally presented (*vorgestellten*) self, it is in the main the mere name *qua* name which denotes the subject pure and simple, the empty unit without any conceptual character. For this reason it would e.g. be expedient to avoid the name "God," because this word is not in its primary use a conception as well, but the special name of an underlying subject, its fixed resting-place; while, on the other hand, being or the one, singleness, subject, etc., themselves directly indicate conceptions. Furthermore, if speculative truths are stated about that subject [God], even then their content is devoid of the immanent notion, because that content is merely present in the form of a passive subject, and owing to this the speculative truths easily take on the character of mere edification. From this side, too, the obstacle, arising from the habit of putting the speculative predicate in the form of a proposition, instead of taking it as an inherent essential conception, is capable of being made greater or less by the mere way philosophical truths are put forward. Philosophical exposition, faithfully following its insight into the nature of speculative truth, must retain the dialectical form, and exclude everything which is not grasped conceptually and is conception.

Just as much as in the procedure of ratiocination, the study of philosophy finds obstruction, too, in the unreasoning conceit that builds itself on well-established truths, which the possessor considers he has no need to return upon and reconsider, but rather takes to be fundamental, and thinks he can by means thereof propound as well as decide and pass sentence. In this regard, it is especially needful to make once again a serious business of philosophy. In all spheres of science, art, skill, and handicraft it is never doubted that, in order to master them, a considerable amount of trouble must be spent in learning and in being trained. As regards philosophy, on the contrary, there seems still an assumption prevalent that, though every one with eyes and fingers is not on that account in a position to make shoes if he only has leather and a last, yet everybody understands how to philosophize straight away, and pass judgment on philosophy, simply because he possesses the criterion for doing so in his natural reason—as if he did not in the same way possess the standard for shoemaking too in his own foot. It seems as if the possession of philosophy lay just in the want of knowledge and study, as if philosophy left off where the latter began. It is commonly held to be a formal kind of knowledge devoid of all substantial content. There is a general failure to perceive that, in the case of any knowledge and any science, what is taken for truth, even as regards content, can only deserve the name of "truth" when philosophy has had a hand in its production. Let the other sciences try as much as they like to get along by ratiocination or *raisonnement* without philosophy, they are unable to keep alive without it, or to have any spiritual significance and truth in them.

As regards philosophy in its proper and genuine sense, we find put forward without any hesitation, as an entirely sufficient equivalent for the long course of mental discipline—for that profound and fruitful process through which the human spirit attains to knowledge—the direct revelation of the divine and the healthy common sense of mankind, unconcerned with and undisciplined by any other knowledge or by proper philosophical reflection. These are held to be a good substitute for real philosophy, much in the way that chicory is lauded as a substitute for coffee. It is not a very pleasing spectacle to observe uncultivated ignorance and crudity of mind, with neither form nor taste, without the capacity to concentrate its thoughts on an abstract proposition, still less on a connected statement of such propositions, confidently proclaiming itself to be intellectual freedom and toleration, and even the inspiration of genius. This last used once upon a time, as everyone knows, to be all the vogue in the case of poetry, as it is now in philosophy. Instead of poetry, however, the efforts of this form of inspiration, when it had any sense at all, resulted in the production of trivial prose, or, if it went beyond that, it produced raving harangues. In the same way here in the case of philosophy; philosophizing by the light of nature, which thinks itself too good for conceptual thinking, and, because of the want of it, takes itself to have direct intuitive ideas and poetical thoughts, —such philosophizing trades in arbitrary combinations of an imagination merely disorganized through thinking—fictitious creations that are neither fish nor flesh, neither poetry nor philosophy.

On the other hand again, when instinctive philosophy follows the more secure course prescribed by healthy common sense, it treats us to a rhetorical *mélange* of commonplace truths. When it is charged with the triviality of what it offers, it assures us, in reply, that the fullness and richness of its meaning lie deep down in its own heart, and that others must feel this too, since with such phrases as the "heart's natural innocence," "purity of conscience," and so on, it supposes it has expressed things that are ultimate and final, to which no one can take exception, and about which nothing further can be required. But the very problem in hand was just that the best must not be left behind hidden away in secret, but be brought out of the depths and set forth in the light of day. It could quite well from the start have spared itself the trouble of bringing forward ultimate and final truths of that sort; they were long since to be found, say, in the Catechism, in popular proverbs, etc. It is an easy matter to grasp such truths in their indefinite and crooked inaccurate form, and in many cases to point out that the mind convinced of them is conscious of the very opposite truths. When it struggles to get itself out of the mental embarrassment thereby produced, it will tumble into further confusion, and possibly burst out with the assertion that in short and in fine the matter is settled, the truth is so and so, and anything else is mere "sophistry"—a password used by plain common sense against cultivated critical reason, like the phrase "visionary dreaming," by which those ignorant of philosophy sum up its character once for all. Since the man of common sense appeals to his feeling, to an oracle within his breast, he is done with any one who does not agree. He has just to explain that he has no more to say to any one who does not find and feel the same as himself. In other words, he tramples the roots of humanity underfoot. For the nature of humanity is to impel men to agree with one another, and its very existence lies simply in the explicit realization of a community of conscious life. What is anti-human, the condition of mere animals, consists in keeping within the sphere of feeling pure and simple, and in being able to communicate only by way of feeling-states.

When a man asks for a royal road to science, no more convenient and comfortable way can be mentioned to him than to put his trust in "healthy common sense." And for the rest, to keep abreast of the times and advance with philosophy, let him read reviews of philosophical works, and even go the length of reading the prefaces and first paragraphs of the works themselves; for the latter give the general principles on which everything turns, while the reviews along with the historical notice provide over and above the critical judgment and appreciation, which, being a judgment passed on the work, goes farther than the work that is judged. This common way a man can take in his dressing-gown. But spiritual elation in the eternal, the sacred, the infinite, moves along the highway of truth in the robes of the high priest—a road that, from the first, is itself immediate being in its innermost, the inspiration of profound and original ideas and flashes of elevated thought. All the same, those depths do not yet reveal the well-spring of inner reality; nor, again, are these sky-rockets the empyrean. True thoughts and scientific insight can only be won by the labour of the notion. Conceptions alone can produce universality in the knowing process. This universality is critically developed and completely finished knowledge. It is not the common indefiniteness and inadequacy of ordinary intelligence. Nor, again, is it that extraordinary kind of universality where the powers and potencies of reason are spoiled and ruined by genius through indolence and self-conceit. It is truth which has successfully reached its own inherent native form. It is this universality which is capable of being the property of every self-conscious reason.

Since I have taken the self-development of the notion to be the medium wherein science really exists, and since in those respects to which I have drawn attention, as well as in others, current ideas about the nature of truth and the shape it assumes deviate from my view, and indeed are quite opposed to my position, the consideration of this divergence of view does not seem to promise well for a favourable reception of an attempt to expound the system of science in this sense. In the meantime, I may call to mind that while e.g. the supreme merit of Plato's philosophy has sometimes been held to consist in his myths which are scientifically valueless, there have also been times, spoken of even as times of mere sentimental enthusiasm, when the Aristotelian philosophy has been respected on account of its speculative depth of insight, and when the *Parmenides* of Plato—perhaps the greatest literary product of ancient dialectic—has been taken to be the positive expression of the divine life, the unveiling and disclosing of its inmost truth. I may reflect, too, that notwithstanding much cloudy obscurity which was the product of ecstasy, this misunderstood ecstasy was in point of fact meant to be nothing else than the activity of the pure notion; furthermore, that what is best in the philosophy of our time takes its value to lie in its scientific character; and that, even though others take a different view, it is only in virtue of its scientific character that recent philosophy really gains validity and acceptance. Thus, then, I may hope too that this attempt to justify the claim of science to be a conceptual process, and systematically to develop and present science in this its own peculiar medium, will manage to make a way for itself by the inherent truth of the result accomplished. We may rest assured that it is the nature of truth to force its way to recognition when the time comes, and that it only appears when its time has come, and hence never appears too soon, and never finds a public that is not ripe to receive it. And, further, we may be sure that the individual thinker requires this result to take place, in order to give him confidence in regard to what is no more as yet than a matter for himself singly and alone, and in order to find his assurance, which in the first instance merely belongs to a particular individual, realized as something universal. In this connection, however, it is very often necessary to distinguish the public from those who take upon themselves to be its representatives and spokesmen. The public takes up an attitude in many respects quite different from the latter, indeed, even opposed to them. Whereas the public good-naturedly and generously will rather take the blame upon itself when a philosophical work is not quite acceptable or intelligible to it, these "representatives," on the contrary, convinced of their own competence, put all the blame on the authors. The influence of the work on the public is more silent than the action of those "representatives," who are like the dead burying their dead. While the general level of insight at the present time is in the main more highly cultivated, its curiosity more quickened and alert, and its judgment more swiftly made up and pronounced, so that the feet of those who will carry you out are already at the door: at the same time we have often to distinguish from all this the slower and more gradual effect which rectifies the direction of attention caught and compelled by imposing assurances, corrects, too, contemptuous censure, and after a little provides a contemporary audience for one part, while another after a temporary vogue finds no audience with posterity any longer.

For the rest, at a time when the universal nature of spiritual life has become so very much emphasized and strengthened, and the mere individual aspect has become, as it should be, correspondingly a matter of indifference, when, too, that universal aspect holds, by the entire range of its substance, the full measure of the wealth it has built up, and lays claim to it all, the share in the total work of mind that falls to the activity of any particular individual can only be very small. Because this is so, the individual must all the more forget himself, as in fact the very nature of science implies and requires that he should; and he must, moreover, become and do what he can. But all the less must be demanded of him, just as he can expect the less from himself, and may ask the less for himself.

QUESTIONS FOR STUDY AND DISCUSSION

1. Hegel has been accused of making the history of philosophy into philosophy itself. Is there any justification for this statement?
2. How does Hegel conceive of truth?
3. What does it mean to talk of reason as purposive activity?
4. How does "process" enter into Hegel's concept of science?
5. What is the point of the remark that "everything depends on grasping and expressing the ultimate truth not as Substance but as Subject as well"?

The Role of Thought in Religion

It has appeared to me to be necessary to make religion by itself the object of philosophical consideration, and to add on this study of it, in the form of a special part, to philosophy as a whole. By way of introduction I shall, however, first of all (A) give some account of the severance or division of consciousness, which awakens the need our science has to satisfy, and describe the relation of this science to philosophy and religion, as also to the prevalent principles of the religious consciousness. Then, after I have (B) touched upon some preliminary questions which follow from those relations, I shall give (C) the division of the subject.

To begin with, it is necessary to recollect generally what object we have before us in the Philosophy of Religion, and what is our ordinary idea of religion. We know that in religion we withdraw ourselves from what is temporal, and that religion is for our consciousness that region in which all the enigmas of the world are solved, all the contradictions of deeper-reaching thought have their meaning unveiled, and where the voice of the heart's pain is silenced—the region of eternal truth, of eternal rest, of eternal peace. Speaking generally, it is through thought, concrete thought, or, to put it more definitely, it is by reason of his being Spirit, that man is man; and from man as Spirit proceed all the many developments of the sciences and arts, the interests of political life, and all those conditions which have reference to man's freedom and will. But all these manifold forms of human relations, activities, and pleasures, and all the ways in which these are intertwined; all that has worth and dignity for man, all wherein he seeks his happiness, his glory, and his pride, finds its ultimate centre in religion, in the thought, the consciousness, and the feeling of God. Thus God is the beginning of all things, and the end of all things. As all things proceed from this point, so all return back to it again. He is the centre which gives life and quickening to all things, and which animates and preserves in existence all the various forms of being. In religion man places himself in a relation to this centre, in which all other relations concentrate themselves, and in so doing he rises up to the highest level of consciousness and to the region which is free from relation to what is other than itself, to something which is absolutely self-sufficient, the unconditioned, what is free, and is its own object and end.

Religion, as something which is occupied with this final object and end,

From pp. 1–48 of G. W. F. Hegel, *Lectures on the Philosophy of Religion, Together with a Work on the Proofs of the Existence of God*, vol. I, translated by E. B. Speirs and J. Burdon Sanderson. © 1962 by Humanities Press, Inc. Reprinted by permission of the publisher.

is therefore absolutely free, and is its own end; for all other aims converge in this ultimate end, and in presence of it they vanish and cease to have value of their own. No other aim can hold its ground against this, and here alone all find their fulfilment. In the region where the spirit occupies itself with this end, it unburdens itself of all finiteness, and wins for itself final satisfaction and deliverance; for here the spirit relates itself no longer to something that is other than itself, and that is limited, but to the unlimited and infinite, and this is an infinite relation, a relation of freedom, and no longer of dependence. Here its consciousness is absolutely free, and is indeed true consciousness, because it is consciousness of absolute truth. In its character as feeling, this condition of freedom is the sense of satisfaction which we call blessedness, while as activity it has nothing further to do than to manifest the honour of God and to reveal His glory, and in this attitude it is no longer with himself that man is concerned—with his own interests or his empty pride—but with the absolute end. All the various peoples feel that it is in the religious consciousness they possess truth, and they have always regarded religion as constituting their true dignity and the Sabbath of their life. Whatever awakens in us doubt and fear, all sorrow, all care, all the limited interests of finite life, we leave behind on the shores of time; and as from the highest peak of a mountain, far away from all definite view of what is earthly, we look down calmly upon all the limitations of the landscape and of the world, so with the spiritual eye man, lifted out of the hard realities of this actual world, contemplates it as something having only the semblance of existence, which seen from this pure region bathed in the beams of the spiritual sun, merely reflects back its shades of colour, its varied tints and lights, softened away into eternal rest. In this region of spirit flow the streams of forgetfulness from which Psyche drinks, and in which she drowns all sorrow, while the dark things of this life are softened away into a dream-like vision, and become transfigured until they are a mere framework for the brightness of the Eternal.

This image of the Absolute may have a more or less present vitality and certainty for the religious and devout mind, and be a present source of pleasure; or it may be represented as something longed and hoped for, far off, and in the future. Still it always remains a certainty, and its rays stream as something divine into this present temporal life, giving the consciousness of the active presence of truth, even amidst the anxieties which torment the soul here in this region of time. Faith recognises it as the truth, as the substance of actual existing things; and what thus forms the essence of religious contemplation, is the vital force in the present world, makes itself actively felt in the life of the individual, and governs his entire conduct. Such is the general perception, sensation, consciousness, or however we may designate it, of religion. To consider, to examine, and to comprehend its nature is the object of the present lectures.

We must first of all, however, definitely understand, in reference to the end we have in view, that it is not the concern of philosophy to produce religion in any individual. Its existence is, on the contrary, presupposed as forming what is fundamental in every one. So far as man's essential nature is concerned, nothing new is to be introduced into him. To try to do this would be as absurd as to give a dog printed writings to chew, under the idea that in this way you could put mind into it. He who has not extended his spiritual interests beyond the hurry and bustle of this finite world, nor succeeded in lifting himself above this life through aspiration, through the anticipation, through the feeling of the Eternal, and who has not gazed upon the pure ether of the soul, does not possess in himself that element which it is our object here to comprehend.

It may happen that religion is awakened in the heart by means of philosophical knowledge, but it is not necessarily so. It is not the purpose of philosophy to edify, and quite as little is it necessary for it to make good its claims by showing in any particular case that it must produce religious feeling in the individual. Philosophy, it is true, has to develop the necessity of religion in and for itself, and to grasp the thought that Spirit must of necessity advance from the other modes of its will in conceiving and feeling to this absolute mode; but it is the universal destiny of Spirit which is thus accomplished. It is another matter to raise up the individual subject to this height. The self-will, the perversity, or the indolence of individuals may interfere with the necessity of their universal spiritual nature; individuals may deviate from it, and attempt to get for themselves a standpoint of their own, and hold to it. This possibility of letting oneself drift, through inertness, to the standpoint of untruth, or of lingering there consciously and purposely, is involved in the freedom of the subject, while planets, plants, animals, cannot deviate from the necessity of their nature—from their truth—and become what they ought to be. But in human freedom what is and what ought to be are separate. This freedom brings with it the power of free choice, and it is possible for it to sever itself from its necessity, from its laws, and to work in opposition to its true destiny. Therefore, although philosophical knowledge should clearly perceive the necessity of the religious standpoint, and though the will should learn in the sphere of reality the nullity of its separation, all this does not hinder the will from being able to persist in its obstinacy, and to stand aloof from its necessity and truth.

There is a common and shallow manner of arguing against cognition or philosophical knowledge, as when, for instance, it is said that such and such a man has a knowledge of God, and yet remains far from religion, and has not become godly. It is not, however, the aim of knowledge to lead to this, nor is it meant to do so. What knowledge must do is to know religion as something which already exists. It is neither its intention nor its duty to induce this or that person, any particular empirical subject, to be religious if he has not been so before, if he has nothing of religion in himself, and does not wish to have.

But the fact is, no man is so utterly ruined, so lost, and so bad, nor can we regard any one as being so wretched that he has no religion whatever in him, even if it were only that he has the fear of it, or some yearning after it, or a feeling of hatred towards it. For even in this last case he is inwardly occupied with it, and cannot free himself from it. As man, religion is essential to him, and is not a feeling foreign to his nature. Yet the essential question is the relation of religion to his general theory of the universe, and it is with this that philosophical knowledge connects itself, and upon which it essentially works. In this relation we have the source of the division which arises in opposition to the primary absolute tendency of the spirit toward religion, and here, too, all the manifold forms of consciousness, and their most widely differing connections with the main interest of religion, have sprung up. Before the Philosophy of Religion can sum itself up in its own peculiar conception, it must work itself through all those ramifications of the interests of the time which have at present concentrated themselves in the widely-extended sphere of religion. At first the movement of the principles of the time has its place outside of philosophical study, but this movement pushes on to the point at which it comes into contact, strife, and antagonism with philosophy. We shall consider this opposition and its solution when we have examined the opposition as it still maintains itself outside of philosophy, and have seen it develop until it reaches that completed state where it involves philosophical knowledge in itself.

A

THE RELATION OF THE PHILOSOPHY OF RELIGION TO ITS PRESUPPOSITIONS AND TO THE PRINCIPLES OF THE TIME

I. THE SEVERANCE OF RELIGION FROM THE FREE WORLDLY CONSCIOUSNESS

a. In the relation in which religion, even in its immediacy, stands to the other forms of the consciousness of man, there already lie germs of division, since both sides are conceived of as in a condition of separation relatively to each other. In their simple relation they already constitute two kinds of pursuits, two different regions of consciousness, and we pass to and fro from the one to the other *alternately* only. Thus man has in his actual worldly life a number of working days during which he occupies himself with his own special interests, with worldly aims in general, and with the satisfaction of his needs; and then he has a Sunday, when he lays all this aside, collects his thoughts, and, released from absorption in finite occupations, lives to himself and to the higher nature which is in him, to his true essential being. But into this separateness of the two sides there directly enters a double modification.

Let us consider first of all the religion of the godly man; that is, of one who truly deserves to be so called. Faith is still presupposed as existing irrespective of, and without opposition to, anything else. To believe in God is thus in its simplicity, something different from that where a man, with reflection and with the consciousness that something else stands opposed to this faith, says, "I *believe* in God." Here the need of justification, of inference, of controversy, has already come in. Now that religion of the simple, godly man is not kept shut off and divided from the rest of his existence and life, but, on the contrary, it breathes its influence over all his feelings and actions, and his consciousness brings *all* the aims and objects of his worldly life into relation to God, as to its infinite and ultimate source. Every moment of his finite existence and activity, of his sorrow and joy, is lifted up by him out of his limited sphere, and by being thus lifted up produces in him the idea and sense of his eternal nature. The rest of his life, in like manner, is led under the conditions of confidence, of custom, of dutifulness, of habit; he *is* that which circumstances and nature have made him, and he takes his life, his circumstances, and rights as he receives everything, namely, as a lot or destiny which he does not understand. *It is so.* In regard to God, he either takes what is His and gives thanks, or else he offers it up to Him freely as a gift of free grace. The rest of his conscious life is thus subordinated, without reflection, to that higher region.

From the worldly side, however, the distinction involved in this relation develops until it becomes opposition. It is true that the development of this side does not seem to affect religion injuriously, and all action seems to limit itself strictly to that side in the matter. Judging from what is expressly acknowledged, religion is still looked upon as what is highest; but as a matter of fact it is not so, and starting from the worldly side, ruin and disunion creep over into religion. The development of this distinction may be generally designated as the maturing of the understanding and of human aims. While understanding awakens in human life and in science, and reflection has become independent, the will sets before itself absolute aims; for example, justice, the state, objects which are to have absolute worth, to be in and for themselves. Thus research recognises the laws, the constitution, the order, and the peculiar characteristics of natural things, and of the activities and productions of Spirit. Now these experiences and forms of knowledge, as well as the willing and actual carrying out of these aims, is a work of man, both of his understanding and will. In them he is in presence of *what is his own.* Although he sets out from what *is,* from what he finds, yet he *is* no longer merely one who knows, who *has* these rights; but what he *makes* out of that which is given in knowledge and in will is *his* affair, *his* work, and he has the consciousness that he has produced it. Therefore these productions constitute his glory and his pride, and provide for him an immense, an infinite wealth—that world of his intelligence, of his knowledge, of his external possession, of his rights and deeds.

Thus the spirit has entered into the condition of opposition—as yet, it is true, artlessly, and without at first knowing it—but the opposition comes to be a conscious one, for the spirit now moves between two sides, of which the distinction has actually developed itself. The one side is that in which the spirit knows itself to be its own, where it lives in its own aims and interests, and determines itself on its own authority as independent and self-sustaining. The other side is that where the spirit recognises a higher Power—absolute duties, duties without rights belonging to them, and what the spirit receives for the accomplishment of its duties is always regarded as grace alone. In the first instance it is the independence of the spirit which is the foundation, here its attitude is that of humility and dependence. Its religion is accordingly distinguished from what we have in that region of independence by this, that it restricts knowledge, science, to the *worldly side,* and leaves for the sphere of religion, feeling and faith.

Notwithstanding, that aspect of independence involves this also, that its action is conditioned, and knowledge and will must have experience of the fact that it is thus conditioned. Man demands his right; whether or not he actually gets it, is something independent of his efforts, and he is referred in the matter to an Other. In the act of knowledge he sets out from the organisation and order of nature, and this is something *given*. The content of his sciences is a material outside of him. Thus the two sides, that of independence and that of conditionality, enter into relation with each other, and this relation leads man to the avowal that everything is made by God—all things which constitute the content of his knowledge, which he takes possession of, and uses as means for his ends, as well as he himself, the spirit and the spiritual faculties of which he, as he says, makes use, in order to attain to that knowledge.

But this admission is cold and lifeless, because that which constitutes the vitality of this consciousness, in which it is "at home with itself," and is self-consciousness, this insight, this knowledge are wanting in it. All that is determined comes, on the contrary, to be included in the sphere of knowledge, and of human, self-appointed aims, and here, too, it is only the activity belonging to self-consciousness which is present. Therefore that admission is unfruitful too, because it does not get beyond the abstract-universal, that is to say, it stops short at the thought that all is a work of God, and with regard to objects which are absolutely different (as, for example, the course of the stars and their laws, ants, or men), that relation continues for it fixed at one and the same point, namely this, that God has made all. Since this religious relation of particular objects is always expressed in the same monotonous manner, it would become tedious and burdensome if it were repeated in reference to each individual thing. Therefore the matter is settled with the *one* admission, that God has made everything, and this religious side is thereby satisfied *once for all,* and then in the progress of knowledge and the pursuit of aims nothing further is thought of the matter. It would accordingly appear that this admission is made simply and solely in order to get rid of the whole business, or perhaps it may be to get protection for the religious side as it were relatively to what is without. In short, such expressions may be used either in earnest or not.

Piety does not weary of lifting up its eyes to God on all and every occasion, although it may do so daily and hourly in the same manner. But as religious feeling, it really rests *in singleness* or single instances; it is in every moment *wholly* what it is, and is without reflection and the consciousness which compares experiences. It is here, on the contrary, where knowledge and self-determination are concerned, that this comparison, and the consciousness of that sameness, are essentially present, and then a general proposition is enunciated once for all. On the one side we have understanding playing its part, while over against it is the religious feeling of dependence.

b. Even piety is not exempt from the fate of falling into a state of division or dualism. On the contrary, division is already present in it implicitly, in that its actual content is only a manifold, accidental one. These two attitudes, namely, that of piety and of the understanding that compares, however different they seem to be, have this in common, that in them the relation of God to the other side of consciousness is undetermined and general. The second of these attitudes has indicated and pronounced this unhesitatingly in the expression already quoted, "God has created all things."

The manner of looking at things, however, which is followed by the religious man, and whereby he gives a greater completeness to his reflection, consists in the contemplation of the constitution and arrangement of things according to the *relations of ends,* and similarly in the regarding all the circumstances of individual life, as well as the great events of history, as proceeding from Divine purposes, or else as directed and leading back to such. The universal divine relation is thus not adhered to here. On the contrary, this becomes a definite relation, and consequently a more strictly defined content is introduced—for the manifold materials are placed in relation to one another, and God is then considered as the one who brings about these relations. Animals and their surroundings are accordingly regarded as beings definitely regulated, in that they have food, nurture their young, are provided with weapons as a defence against what is hurtful, stand the winter, and can protect themselves against enemies. In human life it is seen how man is led to happiness, whether it be eternal or temporal, by means of this or that apparent accident, or perhaps misfortune. In short, the action, the will of God, is contemplated here in definite dealings, conditions of nature, occurrences, and such-like.

But this content itself, these ends, representing thus a finite content, are accidental, are taken up only for the moment, and even directly disappear in an inconsistent and illogical fashion. If, for example, we admire the wisdom of God in nature because we see how animals are provided with weapons, partly to obtain their food and partly to protect them against enemies, yet it is presently seen in experience that these weapons are of no avail, and that those creatures which have been considered as ends are made use of by others as means.

It is therefore really progressive knowledge which has depreciated and supplanted this external contemplation of ends; that higher knowledge, namely, which, to begin with, at least demands *consistency,* and recognises ends of this kind, which are taken as Divine ends, as subordinate and finite—as something which proves itself in the very same experience and observation to be worthless, and not to be an object of the eternal, divine Will.

If that manner of looking at the matter be accepted, and if, at the same time, its inconsistency be disregarded, yet it still remains indefinite and superficial, for the very reason that all and every content—no matter what it be—may be included in it; for there is nothing, no arrangement of nature, no occurrence, which, regarded in some aspect or other, might not be shown to have some use. Religious feeling is, in short, here no longer present in its naïve and experimental character. On the contrary, it proceeds from the universal thought of an end, of a good, and makes inferences, inasmuch as it subsumes present things under these universal thoughts. But this argumentation, this inferential process, brings the religious man into a condition of perplexity, because however much he may point to what serves a purpose, and is useful in this immediate world of natural things, he sees, in contrast to all this, just as much that does not serve a purpose, and is injurious. What is profitable to one person is detrimental to another, and therefore does not serve a purpose. The preservation of life and of the interests bound up with existence, which in the one case is promoted, is in the other case just as much endangered and put a stop to. Thus an implicit dualism or division is involved here, for in contradiction to God's eternal manner of operation, finite things are elevated to the rank of essential ends. The idea of God and of His manner of operation as universal and necessary is contradicted by this inconsistency, which is even destructive of that universal character.

Now, if the religious man considers external ends and the externality of the whole matter in accordance with which these things are profitable for an Other, the natural determinateness, which is the point of departure, appears indeed to be only *for an Other*. But this, more closely considered, is its own relation, its own nature, the immanent nature of what is related, its necessity, in short. Thus it is that the actual transition to the other side, which was formerly designated as the moment of selfness, comes about for ordinary religious thought.

Religious feeling, accordingly, is forced to abandon its argumentative process; and now that a beginning has once been made with thought, and with the relations of thought, it becomes necessary, above all things to thought, to demand and to look for that which belongs to itself; namely, first of all consistency and necessity, and to place itself in opposition to that standpoint of contingency. And with this, the principle of selfness at once develops itself completely. "I," as simple, universal, as thought, am really relation; since I am for myself, am self-consciousness, the relations too are to be for me. To the thoughts, ideas which I make my own, I give the character which I myself am. I am this simple point, and that which is for me I seek to apprehend in this unity.

Knowledge so far aims at that which *is,* and the *necessity* of it, and apprehends this in the relation of cause and effect, reason and result, power and manifestation; in the relation of the Universal, of the species and of the individual existing things which are included in the sphere of contingency. Knowledge, science, in this manner places the manifold material in mutual relation, takes away from it the contingency which it has through its immediacy, and while contemplating the relations which belong to the wealth of finite phenomena, encloses the world of finiteness in itself so as to form a system of the universe, of such a kind that knowledge requires nothing for this system outside of the system itself. For what a thing *is,* what it is in its essential determinate character, is disclosed when it is perceived and made the subject of observation. From the constitution of things, we proceed to their connections in which they stand in relation to an Other; not, however, in an accidental, but in a determinate relation, and in which they point back to the original source from which they are a deduction. Thus we inquire after the reasons and causes of things; and the meaning of inquiry here is, that what is desired is to know the *special* causes. Thus it is no longer sufficient to speak of God as the cause of the lightning, or of the downfall of the Republican system of government in Rome, or of the French Revolution; here it is perceived that this cause is only an entirely general one, and does not yield the desired explanation. What we wish to know regarding a natural phenomenon, or regarding this or that law as effect or result, is, the reason as the reason of this particular phenomenon, that is to say, not the reason which applies to all things, but only and exclusively to this definite thing. And thus the reason must be that of such special phenomena, and such reason or ground must be the most immediate, must be sought and laid hold of in the *finite,* and must itself be a finite one. Therefore this knowledge does not go above or beyond the sphere of the finite, nor does it desire to do so, since it is able to apprehend all in its finite sphere, is conversant with everything, and knows its course of action. In this manner science forms a universe of knowledge, to which God is not necessary, which lies outside of religion, and has absolutely nothing to do with it. In this kingdom, knowledge spreads itself out in its relations and connections, and in so doing has all determinate material and content on its side; and for the other side, the side of the infinite and the eternal, nothing whatever is left.

Thus both sides have developed themselves completely in their opposition. On the side of religion the heart is filled with what is Divine, but without freedom, or self-consciousness, and without consistency in regard to what is determinate, this latter having, on the contrary, the form of contingency. Consistent connection of what is determinate belongs to the side of knowledge, which is at home in the finite, and moves freely in the thought-determinations of the manifold connections of things, but can only create a system which is without absolute substantiality—without God. The religious side gets the absolute material and purpose, but only as something abstractly positive. Knowledge has taken possession of all finite material and drawn it into its territory, all determinate content has fallen to its share; but although it gives it a necessary connection, it is still unable to give it the absolute connection. Since finally science has taken possession of knowledge, and is the consciousness of the necessity of the finite, religion has become devoid of knowledge, and has shrivelled up into simple feeling, into the contentless or empty elevation of the spiritual to the Eternal. It can, however, affirm nothing regarding the Eternal, for all that could be regarded as knowledge would be a drawing down of the Eternal into the sphere of the finite, and of finite connections of things.

Now when two aspects of thought, which are so developed in this way, enter into relation with one another, their attitude is one of mutual distrust. Religious feeling distrusts the finiteness which lies in knowledge, and it brings against science the charge of futility, because in it the subject clings to itself, is in itself, and the "I" as the knowing subject is independent in relation to all that is external. On the other hand, knowledge has a distrust of the totality in which feeling entrenches itself, and in which it confounds together all extension and development. It is afraid to lose its freedom should it comply with the demand of feeling, and unconditionally recognise a truth which it does not definitely understand. And when religious feeling comes out of its universality, sets ends before itself, and passes over to the determinate, knowledge can see nothing but arbitrariness in this, and if it were to pass in a similar way to anything definite, would feel itself given over to mere contingency. When, accordingly, reflection is fully developed, and has to pass over into the domain of religion, it is unable to hold out in that region, and becomes impatient with regard to all that peculiarly belongs to it.

c. Now that the opposition has arrived at this stage of development, where the one side, whenever it is approached by the other, invariably thrusts it away from it as an enemy, the necessity for an adjustment comes in, of such a kind that the infinite shall appear in the finite, and the finite in the infinite, and each no longer form a separate realm. This would be the reconciliation of religious, genuine simple feeling, with knowledge and intelligence. This reconciliation must correspond with the highest demands of *knowledge,* and of the Notion, for these can surrender nothing of their dignity. But just as little can anything of the absolute content be given up, and that content be brought down into the region of finiteness; and when face to face with it knowledge must give up its finite form.

In the Christian religion, more than in other religions, the need of this reconciliation has of necessity come into prominence, for the following reasons:—

1. The Christian religion has its very beginning in absolute dualism or division, and starts from that sense of suffering in which it rends the natural unity of the spirit asunder, and destroys natural peace. In it man appears as evil from his birth, and is thus in his innermost life in contradic-

tion with himself, and the spirit, as it is driven back into itself, finds itself separated from the infinite, absolute Essence.

2. The Reconciliation, the need of which is here intensified to the uttermost degree, appears in the first place for Faith, but not in such a way as to allow of faith being of a merely ingenuous kind. For the spirit has left its natural simplicity behind, and entered upon an internal conflict; it is, as sinful, an Other in opposition to the truth; it is withdrawn, estranged from it. "I," in this condition of schism, am not the truth, and this is therefore given as an independent content of ordinary thought, and the truth is in the first instance put forward upon authority.

3. When, however, by this means I am transplanted into an intellectual world in which the nature of God, the characteristics and modes of action which belong to God, are presented to knowledge, and when the truth of these rests on the witness and assurance of others, yet I am at the same time referred *into myself,* for thought, knowledge, reason are *in me,* and in the feeling of sinfulness, and in reflection upon this, my freedom is plainly revealed to me. Rational knowledge, therefore, is an essential element in the Christian religion itself.

In the Christian religion I am to retain my freedom or rather, in it I am to become free. In it the subject, the salvation of the soul, the redemption of the individual as an individual, and not only the species, is an essential end. This subjectivity, this *selfness* (not selfishness) is just the principle of rational knowledge itself.

Rational knowledge being thus a fundamental characteristic in the Christian religion, the latter gives development to its content, for the ideas regarding its general subject-matter are implicitly or in themselves thoughts, and must as such develop themselves. On the other hand, however, since the content is something which exists essentially for the mind as forming ideas, it is distinct from unreflecting opinion and sense-knowledge, and as it were passes right beyond the distinction. In short, it has in relation to subjectivity the value of an absolute content existing in and for itself. The Christian religion therefore touches the antithesis between feeling and immediate perception on the one hand, and reflection and knowledge on the other. It contains rational knowledge as an essential element, and has supplied to this rational knowledge the occasion for developing itself to its full logical issue as Form and as a world of form, and has thus at the same time enabled it to place itself in opposition to this content as it appears in the shape of given truth. It is from this that the discord which characterises the thought of the present day arises.

Hitherto we have considered the progressive growth of the antitheses only in the form in which they have not yet developed into actual philosophy, or in which they still stand outside of it. Therefore the questions which primarily come before us are these: 1. How does philosophy in general stand related to religion? 2. How does the Philosophy of Religion stand related to philosophy? and 3. What is the relation of the philosophical study of religion to positive religion?

II. THE POSITION OF THE PHILOSOPHY OF RELIGION RELATIVELY TO PHILOSOPHY AND TO RELIGION

The Attitude of Philosophy to Religion Generally

In saying above that philosophy makes religion the subject of consideration, and when further this consideration of it appears to be in the position of something which is different from its object, it would seem as if we are still occupying that attitude in which both sides remain mutually independent and separate. In taking up such an attitude in thus considering the subject, we should accordingly come out of that region of devotion and enjoyment which religion is, and the object and the consideration of it as the movement of thought would be as different as, for example, the geometrical figures in mathematics are from the mind which considers them. Such is only the relation, however, as it at first appears, when knowledge is still severed from the religious side, and is finite knowledge. On the contrary, when we look more closely, it becomes apparent that as a matter of fact the content, the need, and the interest of philosophy represent something which it has in common with religion.

The object of religion as well as of philosophy is eternal truth in its objectivity, God and nothing but God, and the explication of God. Philosophy is not a wisdom of the world, but is knowledge of what is not of the world; it is not knowledge which concerns external mass, or empirical existence and life, but is knowledge of that which is eternal, of what God is, and what flows out of His nature. For this His nature must reveal and develop itself. Philosophy, therefore, only unfolds itself when it unfolds religion, and in unfolding itself it unfolds religion. As thus occupied with eternal truth which exists on its own account, or is in and for itself, and, as in fact, a dealing on the part of the thinking spirit, and not of individual caprice and particular interest, with this object, it is the same kind of activity as religion is. The mind in so far as it thinks philosophically immerses itself with like living interest in this object, and renounces its particularity in that it permeates its object, in the same way, as religious consciousness does, for the latter also does not seek to have anything of its own, but desires only to immerse itself in this content.

Thus religion and philosophy come to be one. Philosophy is itself, in fact, worship; it is religion, for in the same way it renounces subjective notions and opinions in order to occupy itself with God. Philosophy is thus identical with religion, but the distinction is that it is so in a peculiar manner, distinct from the manner of looking at things which is commonly called religion as such. What they have in common is, that they are religion; what distinguishes them from each other is merely the kind and manner of religion we find in each. It is in the peculiar way in which they both occupy themselves with God that the distinction comes out. It is just here, however, that the difficulties lie which appear so great, that it is even regarded as an impossibility that philosophy should be one with religion. Hence comes the suspicion with which philosophy is looked upon by theology, and the antagonistic attitude of religion and philosophy. In accordance with this antagonistic attitude (as theology considers it to be) philosophy seems to act injuriously, destructively, upon religion, robbing it of its sacred character, and the way in which it occupies itself with God seems to be absolutely different from religion. Here, then, is the same old opposition and contradiction which had already made its appearance among the Greeks. Among that free democratic people, the Athenians, philosophical writings were burnt, and Socrates was condemned to death; now, however, this opposition is held to be an acknowledged fact, more so than that unity of religion and philosophy just asserted.

Old though this opposition is, however, the combination of philosophy and religion is just as old. Already to the neo-Pythagoreans and neo-Platonists, who were as yet within the heathen world, the gods of the people were not gods of imagination, but had become gods of thought. That combination had a place, too, among the most eminent of the Fathers of the Church, who in their religious life took up an essentially intellectual attitude inasmuch as they set out from the presupposition that theology is religion together with conscious thought and comprehension. It is to their philosophical culture that the Christian Church is indebted for the first beginnings of a content of Christian doctrine.

This union of religion and philosophy was carried out to a still greater extent in the Middle Ages. So little was it believed that the knowledge which seeks to comprehend is hurtful to faith, that it was even held to be essential to the further development of faith itself. It was by setting out from philosophy that those great men, Anselm and Abelard, further developed the essential characteristics of faith.

Knowledge in constructing its world for itself, without reference to religion, had only taken possession of the finite contents; but since it has developed into the true philosophy, it has the same content as religion.

If we now look provisionally for the distinction between religion and philosophy as it presents itself in this unity of content, we find it takes the following form:—

a. A speculative philosophy is the consciousness of the Idea, so that everything is apprehended as Idea; the Idea, however, is the True in thought, and not in mere sensuous contemplation or in ordinary conception. The True in thought, to put it more precisely, means that it is something concrete, posited as divided in itself, and in such a way, indeed, that the two sides of what is divided are *opposed characteristics of thought,* and the Idea must be conceived of as the unity of these. To think speculatively means to resolve anything real into its parts, and to oppose these to each other in such a way that the distinctions are set in opposition in accordance with the characteristics of thought, and the object is apprehended as unity of the two.

In sense-perception or picture-thought we have the object before us as a whole, our reflection distinguishes, apprehends different sides, recognises the diversity in them, and severs them. In this act of distinguishing, reflection does not keep firm hold of their unity. Sometimes it forgets the wholeness, sometimes the distinctions; and if it has both before it, it yet separates the properties from the object, and so places both that that in which the two are one becomes a third, which is different from the object and its properties. In the case of mechanical objects which appear in the region of externality, this relation may have a place, for the object is only the lifeless substratum for the distinctions, and the quality of oneness is the gathering together of external aggregates. In the true object, however, which is not merely an aggregate, an externally united multiplicity, the object is one, although it has characteristics which are distinguished from it, and it is speculative thought which first gets a grasp of the unity in this very antithesis as such. It is in fact the business of speculative thought to apprehend all objects of pure thought, of nature and of Spirit, in the form of thought, and thus as the unity of the difference.

b. Religion, then, is itself the standpoint of the consciousness of the True, which is in and for itself, and is consequently the stage of Spirit at which the speculative content generally, is object for consciousness. Religion is not consciousness of this or that truth in individual objects, but of the absolute truth, of truth as the Universal, the All-comprehending, outside of which there lies nothing at all. The content of its consciousness is further the Universally True, which exists on its own account or in and for itself, which determines itself, and is not determined from without. While the finite required an Other for its determinateness, the True has its determinateness, the limit, its end in itself; it is not limited through an Other, but the Other is found in itself. It is this speculative element which comes to consciousness in religion. Truth is, indeed, contained in every other sphere, but not the highest absolute truth, for this exists only in perfect universality of characterisation or determination, and in the fact of being determined in and for itself, which is not simple determinateness having reference to an Other, but contains the Other, the difference in its very self.

c. Religion is accordingly this speculative element in the form, as it were, of a state of consciousness, of which the aspects are not simple qualities of thought, but are concretely filled up. These moments can be no other than the moment of Thought, active universality, thought in operation, and reality as immediate, particular self-consciousness.

Now, while in philosophy the rigidity of these two sides loses itself through reconciliation in thought, because both sides are thoughts, and the one is not pure universal thought, and the other of an empirical and individual character, religion only arrives at the enjoyment of unity by lifting these two rigid extremes out of this state of severance, by rearranging them, and bringing them together again. But by thus stripping off the form of dualism from its extremes, rendering the opposition in the element of Universality fluid, and bringing it to reconciliation, religion remains always akin to thought, even in its form and movement; and philosophy, as simply active thought, and thought which unites opposed elements, has approached closely to religion.

The contemplation of religion in thought has thus raised the determinate moments of religion to the rank of thoughts, and the question is how this contemplation of religion in thought is related generally to philosophy as forming an organic part in its system.

The Relation of the Philosophy of Religion to the System of Philosophy

a. In philosophy, the Highest is called the Absolute, the Idea; it is superfluous to go further back here, and to mention that this Highest was in the Wolfian[1] Philosophy called *ens,* Thing; for that at once proclaims itself an abstraction, which corresponds very inadequately to our idea of God. In the more recent philosophy, the Absolute is not so complete an abstraction, but yet it has not on that account the same signification as is implied in the term, God. In order even to make the difference apparent, we must in the first place consider what the word signify itself signifies. When we ask, "What does this or that signify?" we are asking about two kinds of things, and, in fact, about things which are opposed. In the first place, we call what we are thinking of, the meaning, the end or intention, the general thought of this or that expression, work of art, &c.; if we ask about its intrinsic character, it is essentially the *thought* that is in it of which we wish to have an idea. When we thus ask "What is God?" "What does the expression God signify?" it is the thought involved in it that we desire to know; the idea we possess already. Accordingly, what is signified here is that we have got to specify the Notion, and thus it follows that the *Notion* is the signification; it is the Absolute, the nature of God as grasped by thought, the logical knowledge of this, to which we desire to attain. This, then is the one signification of signification, and so far, that which we call the Absolute has a meaning identical with the expression God.

b. But we put the question again, in a second sense, according to which it is the opposite of this which is sought after. When we begin to occupy ourselves with pure thought-determinations, and not with outward ideas, it may be that the mind does not feel satisfied, is not at home, in these, and asks what this pure thought-determination signifies. For example, every one can understand for himself what is meant by the terms unity,

---

[1] After Christian Wolff (1679–1754), whose metaphysics influenced Kant, Hume, and other eighteenth-century thinkers. [T.N.M.]

objective, subjective, &c., and yet it may very well happen that the specific form of thought we call the unity of subjective and objective, the unity of real and ideal, is not understood. What is asked for in such a case is the meaning in the very opposite sense from that which was required before. Here it is an idea or a pictorial conception of the thought-determination which is demanded, an example of the content, which has as yet only been given in thought. If we find a thought-content difficult to understand, the difficulty lies in this, that we possess no pictorial idea of it; it is by means of an example that it becomes clear to us, and that the mind first feels at home with itself in this content. When, accordingly, we start with the ordinary conception of God, the Philosophy of Religion has to consider its signification—this, namely, that God is the Idea, the Absolute, the Essential Reality which is grasped in thought and in the Notion, and this it has in common with logical philosophy; the logical Idea is God as He is in Himself. But it is just the nature of God that He should not be implicit or in Himself only. He is as essentially for Himself, the Absolute Spirit, not only the Being who keeps Himself within thought, but who also manifests himself, and gives Himself objectivity.

c. Thus, in contemplating the Idea of God, in the Philosophy of Religion, we have at the same time to do with the manner of His manifestation or presentation to us; He simply makes Himself apparent, represents Himself to Himself. This is the aspect of the determinate being or existence of the Absolute. In the Philosophy of Religion we have thus the Absolute as object; not, however, merely in the form of thought, but also in the form of its manifestation. The universal Idea is thus to be conceived of with the purely concrete meaning of essentiality in general, and is to be regarded from the point of view of its activity in displaying itself, in appearing, in revealing itself. Popularly speaking, we say God is the Lord of the natural world and of the realm of Spirit. He *is* the absolute harmony of the two, and it is He who produces and carries on this harmony. Here neither thought and Notion nor their manifestation—determinate being or existence—are wanting. This aspect, thus represented by determinate being, is itself, however, to be grasped again in thought, since we are here in the region of philosophy.

Philosophy to begin with contemplates the Absolute as logical Idea, the Idea as it is in thought, under the aspect in which its content is constituted by the specific forms of thought. Further, philosophy exhibits the Absolute in its activity, in its creations. This is the manner in which the Absolute becomes actual or "for itself," becomes Spirit, and God is thus the result of philosophy. It becomes apparent, however, that this is not merely a result, but is something which eternally creates itself, and is that which precedes all else. The onesidedness of the result is abrogated and absorbed in the very result itself.

Nature, finite Spirit, the world of consciousness, of intelligence, and of will, are embodiments of the divine Idea, but they are definite shapes, special modes of the appearance of the Idea, forms, in which the Idea has not yet penetrated to itself, so as to be absolute Spirit.

In the Philosophy of Religion, however, we do not contemplate the implicitly existing logical Idea merely, in its determinate character as pure thought, nor in those finite determinations where its mode of appearance is a finite one, but as it is in itself or implicitly in thought, and at the same time as it appears, manifests itself, and thus in infinite manifestation as Spirit, which reflects itself in itself; for Spirit which does not appear, *is* not. In this characteristic of appearance *finite* appearance is also included—that is, the world of nature, and the world of finite spirit,—but Spirit is regarded as the power or force of these worlds, as producing them out of itself, and out of them producing itself.

This, then, is the position of the Philosophy of Religion in relation to the other parts of philosophy. Of the other parts, God is the result; here, this End is made the Beginning, and becomes our special Object, as the simply concrete Idea, with its infinite manifestations; and this characteristic concerns the content of the Philosophy of Religion. We look at this content, however, from the point of view of rational thought, and this concerns the form, and brings us to consider the position of the Philosophy of Religion with regard to religion as this latter appears in the shape of positive religion.

The Relation of the Philosophy of Religion to Positive Religion

It is well known that the faith of the Church, more especially of the Protestant Church, has taken a fixed form as a system of doctrine. This content has been universally accepted as truth; and as the description of what God is, and of what man is in relation to God, it has been called the *Creed,* that is, in the subjective sense that which is believed, and objectively, what is to be known as content, in the Christian Church, and what God has revealed Himself to be. Now as universal established doctrine this content is partly laid down in the Apostolic *Symbolum* or Apostles' Creed, partly in later symbolical books. And moreover, in the Protestant Church the Bible has always been characterised as the essential foundation of doctrine.

a. Accordingly, in the apprehension and determination of the content of doctrine, the influence of reason, as "argumentation" has made itself felt. At first indeed, this was so much the case that the doctrinal content, and the Bible as its positive foundation, were to remain unquestioned, and thought was only to take up the thoughts of the Bible as Exegesis. But as a matter of fact understanding had previously established its opinions and its thoughts for itself, and then attention was directed towards observing how the words of Scripture could be explained in accordance with these. The words of the Bible are a statement of truth which is not systematic; they are Christianity as it appeared in the beginning; it is Spirit which grasps the content, which unfolds its meaning. This exegesis having thus taken counsel with reason, the result has been that a so-called Theology of Reason has now come into existence, which is put in opposition to that doctrinal system of the Church, partly by this theology itself, and partly by that doctrinal system to which it is opposed. At the same time, exegesis takes possession of the written word, interprets it, and pretends only to lay stress on the understanding of the word, and to desire to remain faithful to it.

But whether it be chiefly to save appearances, or whether it is really and in downright earnest that the Bible is made the foundation, it is inherent in the very nature of an explanation which interprets, that thought should have its part in it. Thought explicitly contains categories, principles, premises, which must make their influence felt in the work of interpretation. If interpretation be not mere explanation of words but explanation of the sense, the thoughts of the interpreter must necessarily be put into the words which constitute the foundation. Mere word-interpretation can only amount to this, that for one word another co-extensive in meaning is substituted; but in the course of explanation further categories of thought are combined with it. For a development is advance to further thoughts. In appearance the sense is adhered to, but in reality further thoughts are developed. Commentaries on the Bible do not so much make us acquainted with the content of the Scriptures, as rather with the manner in which things were conceived in the age in which they were written. It is, indeed, the sense contained in the words which is supposed to be given. The giving of the sense means, however, the bringing forward of the sense into consciousness, into the region of ideas; and these ideas, which get determinate character elsewhere, then assert their influence in the exposition of the sense supposed to be contained in the words. It is the case even in the presentation of a philosophical system which is already fully developed, as, for example, that of Plato or of Aristotle, that the presentation takes a different form, according to the definite kind of idea which those who undertake thus to expound it have already formed themselves. Accordingly, the most contradictory meanings have been exegetically demonstrated by means of Theology out of the Scriptures, and thus the so-called Holy Scriptures have been made into a nose of wax. All heresies have, in common with the Church, appealed to the Scriptures.

b. The Theology of Reason, which thus came into existence, did not, however, limit itself to being merely an exegesis which kept to the Bible as its foundation, but in its character as free, rational knowledge assumed a certain relation to religion and its content generally. In this more general relation the dealing with the subject and result can amount to nothing more than to the taking possession by such knowledge of all that, in religion, has a determinate character. For the doctrine concerning God goes on to that of the characteristics, the attributes, and the actions of God. Such knowledge takes possession of this determinate content, and would make it appear that it belongs to it. It, on the one hand, conceives of the Infinite in its own finite fashion, as something which has a determinate character, as an *abstract* infinite, and then on the other hand finds that all special attributes are inadequate to this Infinite. By such a mode of proceeding the religious content is annihilated, and the absolute object reduced to complete poverty. The finite and determinate which this knowledge has drawn into its territory, points indeed to a Beyond as existing for it, but even this Beyond is conceived of by it in a *finite* manner, as an abstract, supreme Being, possessing no character at all. "Enlightenment"—which is that consummation of finite knowledge just described—intends to place God very high when it speaks of Him as the Infinite, with regard to which all predicates are inadequate, and are unwarranted anthropomorphisms. In reality, however, it has, in conceiving God as the supreme Being, made Him hollow, empty, and poor.

c. If it should now seem as if the Philosophy of Religion rested on the same basis as this Theology of Reason, or Theology of Enlightenment, and was consequently in the same condition of opposition to the content of religion, further reflection shows that this is merely an appearance of resemblance which vanishes directly it is examined into.

For God was conceived by that rationalistic way of looking at religion, which was only the abstract metaphysic of the understanding, as an abstraction which is empty ideality, and as against which the finite stands in an external fashion, and thus too from this point of view morals constituted, as a special science, the knowledge of that which was held to belong to the actual subject as regards general actions and conduct. The fact of the relation of man to God, which represents the one side, occupied a separate and independent position. Thinking reason, on the contrary, which is no longer abstract, but which sets out from the faith of man in the dignity of his spirit, and is actuated by the courage of truth and freedom, grasps the truth as something *concrete,* as fulness of content, as Ideality, in which determinateness—the finite—is contained as a moment. Therefore, to thinking reason, God is not emptiness, but Spirit; and this characteristic of Spirit does not remain for it a word only, or a superficial characteristic; on the contrary, the nature of Spirit unfolds itself for rational thought, inasmuch as it apprehends God as essentially the Triune God. Thus God is conceived of as making Himself an object to Himself, and further, the object remains in this distinction in identity with God; in it God loves Himself. Without this characteristic of Trinity, God would not be Spirit, and Spirit would be an empty word. But if God be conceived as Spirit, then this conception includes the *subjective* side in itself or even develops itself so as to reach to that side, and the Philosophy of Religion, as the contemplation of religion by thought, binds together again the determinate content of religion in its entirety.

With regard, however, to that form of contemplation in thought, which adheres to the words of Holy Scripture, and asserts that it explains them by the aid of reason, it is only in appearance that the Philosophy of Religion stands on the same basis with it. For that kind of contemplation by its own sovereign power lays down *its* argumentations as the foundation of Christian doctrine; and although it still leaves the Biblical words standing, yet the particular meaning remains as the principal determination, and to this the assumed Biblical truth must subordinate itself. This argumentation accordingly *retains* its assumptions, and moves within the relations of the Understanding, which belong to Reflection, without subjecting these to criticism. But the Philosophy of Religion, as being rational knowledge, is opposed to the arbitrariness of this argumentative process, and is the Reason of the Universal, which presses forward to unity.

Philosophy is therefore very far removed from being on the common highway on which this Theology of Reason and this exegetical argumentative process move, the truth rather being that it is these tendencies chiefly which combat it, and seek to bring it under suspicion. They protest against philosophy, but only in order to reserve to themselves the arbitrariness of their argumentative process. Philosophy is called something special and particular, although it is nothing else than rational, truly universal thought. Philosophy is regarded as a something ghostly, of which we know nothing, and about which there is something uncanny; but this idea only shows that these rationalistic theologians find it more convenient to keep to their unregulated arbitrary reflections, to which philosophy attaches no validity. If, then, those theologians, who busy themselves with their argumentations in exegesis, and appeal to the Bible in connection with all their notions, when they deny as against philosophy the possibility of knowledge, have brought matters to such a pass, and have so greatly depreciated the reputation of the Bible, that if the truth were as they say, and if according to the true explanation of the Bible, no knowledge of the nature of God were possible—the spirit would be compelled to look for another source in order to acquire such truth as should be substantial or full of content.

The Philosophy of Religion cannot, therefore, in the fashion of that metaphysic of the Understanding, and exegesis of inferences, put itself in opposition to positive religion, and to such doctrine of the Church as has still preserved its content. On the contrary, it will become apparent that it stands infinitely nearer to positive doctrine than it seems at first sight to do. Indeed, the re-establishment of the doctrines of the Church, reduced to a minimum by the Understanding, is so truly the work of philosophy, that it is decried by that so-called Theology of Reason, which is merely a Theology of the Understanding, as a darkening of the mind, and this just because of the true content possessed by it. The fears of the Understanding, and its hatred of philosophy, arise from a feeling of apprehension, based on the fact that it perceives how philosophy carries back its reflecting process to its foundation, that is, to the affirmative in which it perishes, and yet that philosophy arrives at a content, and at a knowledge of the nature of God, after all content seemed to be already done away with. Every content appears to this negative tendency to be a darkening of the mind, its only desire being to continue in that nocturnal darkness which it calls enlightenment, and hence the rays of the light of knowledge must be necessarily regarded by it as hostile.

It is sufficient here merely to observe regarding the supposed opposition of the Philosophy of Religion and positive religion, that there cannot be two kinds of reason and two kinds of Spirit; there cannot be a Divine reason and a human, there cannot be a Divine Spirit and a human, which are *absolutely different.* Human reason—the consciousness of one's being—is indeed reason; it is the divine in man, and Spirit, in so far as it is the Spirit of God, is not a spirit beyond the stars, beyond the world. On the contrary, God is present, omnipresent, and exists as Spirit in all spirits. God is a living God, who is acting and working. Religion is a product of the Divine Spirit; it is not a discovery of man, but a work of divine operation and creation in him. The expression that God as reason rules the world, would be irrational if we did not assume that it has reference also to religion, and that the Divine Spirit works in the special character and form assumed by religion. But the development of reason as perfected in thought does not stand in opposition to this Spirit, and consequently it cannot be absolutely different from the work which the Divine Spirit has produced in religion. The more a man in thinking rationally lets the true thing or fact itself hold sway with him, renounces his particularity, acts as universal consciousness, while his reason does not seek its own in the sense of something special, the less will he, as the embodiment of this reason, get into that condition of opposition; for it, namely, reason, is itself the essential fact or thing, the spirit, the Divine Spirit. The Church or the theologians may disdain this aid, or may take it amiss when their doctrine is made reasonable; they may even repel the exertions of philosophy with proud irony, though these are not directed in a hostile spirit against religion, but, on the contrary, seek to fathom its truth; and they may ridicule the "manufactured" truth— but this scorn is no longer of any avail, and is, in fact, idle when once the need of true rational knowledge, and the sense of discord between it and religion, have been awakened. The intelligence has here its rights, which can in no way be longer denied to it, and the triumph of knowledge is the reconciliation of the opposition.

Although then, philosophy, as the Philosophy of Religion, is so very different from those tendencies of the understanding, which are at bottom hostile to religion, and is in no way such a spectral thing as it has usually been represented to be, yet even at the present day we still see the belief in the absolute opposition between philosophy and religion made one of the shibboleths of the time. All those principles of the religious consciousness which have been developed at the present time, however widely distinguished their forms may be from one another, yet agree in this, that they are at enmity with philosophy, and endeavour at all hazards to prevent it from occupying itself with religion; and the work that now lies before us is to consider philosophy in its relation to these *principles of the time*. From this consideration of the subject we may confidently promise ourselves success, all the more that it will become apparent how, in presence of all that enmity which is shown to philosophy, from however many sides it may come —indeed, it comes from almost every side of consciousness in its present form—the time has nevertheless arrived when philosophy can, partly in an unprejudiced and partly in a favourable and successful manner, occupy itself with religion. For the opposition takes one or other of those forms of the divided consciousness which we considered above. They occupy partly the standpoint of the metaphysic of the Understanding, for which God is emptiness, and content has vanished, partly the standpoint of feeling, which after the loss of absolute content has withdrawn itself into its empty subjectivity, but is in accord with that metaphysic in coming to the result that every characterisation is inadequate to the eternal content—for this indeed is only an abstraction. Or we may even see that the assertions of the opponents of philosophy contain nothing else than what philosophy itself contains as its principle, and as the foundation of its principle. This contradiction, namely, that the opponents of philosophy are the opponents of religion who have been overcome by it, and that they yet implicitly possess the principle of philosophical knowledge in their reflections, has its foundation in this, that they represent the historical element out of which philosophical thought in its complete shape has been formed.

III. THE RELATION OF THE PHILOSOPHY OF RELIGION TO THE
CURRENT PRINCIPLES OF THE RELIGIOUS CONSCIOUSNESS

If at the present day philosophy be an object of enmity because it occupies itself with religion, this cannot really surprise us when we consider the general character of the time. Every one who attempts to take to do with the knowledge of God, and by the aid of thought to comprehend His nature, must be prepared to find, that either no attention will be paid to him, or that people will turn against him and combine to oppose him.

The more the knowledge of finite things has increased—and the increase is so great that the extension of the sciences has become almost boundless, and all regions of knowledge are enlarged to an extent which makes a comprehensive view impossible—so much the more has the sphere of the knowledge of God become contracted. There was a time when all knowledge was knowledge of God. Our own time, on the contrary, has the distinction of knowing about all and everything, about an infinite number of subjects, but nothing at all of God. Formerly the mind found its supreme interest in knowing God, and searching into His nature. It had and it found no rest unless in thus occupying itself with God. When it could not satisfy this need it felt unhappy. The spiritual conflicts to which the knowledge of God gives rise in the inner life were the highest which the spirit knew and experienced in itself, and all other interests and knowledge were lightly esteemed. Our own time has put this need, with all its toils and conflicts, to silence; we have done with all this, and got rid of it. What Tacitus said of the ancient Germans, that they were *securi adversus deos,* we have once more become in regard to knowledge, *securi adversus deum.*

It no longer gives our age any concern that it knows nothing of God; on the contrary, it is regarded as a mark of the highest intelligence to hold that such knowledge is not even possible. What is laid down by the Christian religion as the supreme, absolute commandment, "Ye shall know God," is regarded as a piece of folly. Christ says, "Be ye perfect, as My Father in heaven is perfect." This lofty demand is to the wisdom of our time an empty sound. It has made of God an infinite phantom, which is far from us, and in like manner has made human knowledge a futile phantom of finiteness, or a mirror upon which fall only shadows, only phenomena. How, then, are we any longer to respect the commandment, and grasp its meaning, when it says to us, "Be ye perfect, as your Father in heaven is perfect," since we know nothing of the Perfect One, and since our knowing and willing are confined solely and entirely to appearance, and the truth is to be and to remain absolutely and exclusively a something beyond the present? And what, we must further ask, what else would it be worth while to comprehend, if God is incomprehensible?

This standpoint must, judged by its content, be considered as the last stage of the degradation of man, in which at the same time he is, it is true, all the more arrogant inasmuch as he thinks he has proved to himself that this degradation is the highest possible state, and is his true destiny. Such a point of view is, indeed, directly opposed to the lofty nature of the Christian religion, for according to this we ought to know God, His nature, and His essential Being, and to esteem this knowledge as something which is the highest of all. (The distinction as to whether this knowledge is brought to us by means of faith, authority, revelation, or reason, is here of no importance.) But although this is the case, and although this point of view has come to dispense both with the content which revelation gives of the Divine nature, and with what belongs to reason, yet it has not shrunk, after all its abject gropings, in that blind arrogance which is proper to it, from turning against philosophy. And yet it is philosophy which is the liberation of the spirit from that shameful degradation, and which has once more brought religion out of the stage of intense suffering which it had to experience when occupying the standpoint referred to. Even the theologians, who are on their own ground in that region of vanity, have ventured to charge philosophy with its destructive tendency—theologians who have no longer anything left of that substantial element which could possibly be destroyed. In order to repel these not merely groundless, but, what is more, frivolous and unprincipled objections, we need only observe cursorily how theologians have, on the contrary, done everything in their power to do away with what is definite in religion, in that they have (1) thrust dogmas into the background, or pronounced them to be unimportant; or (2) consider them only as extraneous definitions given by others, and as mere phenomena of a past history. When we have reflected in this manner upon the aspect presented by the content, and have seen how this last is re-established by philosophy, and placed in safety from the devastations of theology, we shall (3) reflect upon the form of that standpoint, and shall see here how the tendency which, taking its departure from the form, is at enmity with philosophy, is so ignorant of what it is, that it does not even know that it contains in itself the very principle of philosophy.

Philosophy and the Prevalent Indifference to Definite Dogmas

If, then, it be made a reproach to philosophy in its relation to religion that the content of the doctrine of revealed positive religion, and more expressly of the Christian religion, is depreciated by it, and that it subverts and destroys its dogmas, yet this hindrance is taken out of the way, and by the new theology itself, in fact. There are very few dogmas of the earlier system of Church confessions left which have any longer the importance formerly attributed to them, and in their place no other dogmas have been set up. It is easy to convince oneself, by considering what is the real value now attached to ecclesiastical dogmas, that into the religious world generally there has entered a widespread, almost universal, indifference towards what in earlier times were held to be essential doctrines of the faith. A few examples will prove this.

Christ still indeed continues to be made the central point of faith, as Mediator, Reconciler, and Redeemer; but what was known as the work of redemption has received a very prosaic and merely psychological significimcation, so that although the edifying words have been retained, the very thing that was essential in the old doctrine of the Church has been expunged.

"Great energy of character, steadfast adherence to conviction for the sake of which He regarded not His life"—these are the common categories through which Christ is brought down, not indeed to the plane of ordinary everyday life, but to that of human action in general and moral designs, and into a moral sphere into which even heathens like Socrates were capable of entering. Even though Christ be for many the central point of faith and devotion in the deeper sense, yet Christian life as a whole restricts itself to this devotional bent, and the weighty doctrines of the Trinity, of the resurrection of the body, as also the miracles in the Old and New Testaments, are neglected as matters of indifference, and have lost their importance. The divinity of Christ, dogma, what is peculiar to the Christian religion is set aside, or else reduced to something of merely general nature. It is not only by "enlightenment" that Christianity has been thus treated, but even by pious theologians themselves. These latter join with the men of enlightenment in saying that the Trinity was brought into Christian doctrine by the Alexandrian school, by the neo-Platonists. But even if it must be conceded that the fathers of the Church studied Greek philosophy, it is in the first instance a matter of no importance whence that doctrine may have come; the only question is, whether it be essentially, inherently, true; but that is a point which is not examined into, and yet that doctrine is the key-note of the Christian religion.

If an opportunity was given to a large number of these theologians to lay their hand on their heart, and say whether they consider faith in the Trinity to be indispensably necessary to salvation, and whether they believe that the absence of such faith leads to damnation, there can be no doubt what the answer would be.

Even the words eternal happiness and eternal damnation are such as cannot be used in good society; such expressions are regarded as words which one shrinks from uttering. Even although a man should not wish to deny these doctrines, he would, in case of his being directly appealed to, find it very difficult to express himself in an affirmative way.

In the doctrinal teaching of these theologians, it will be found that dogmas have become very thin and shrunken, although they are talked about a great deal.

If any one were to take a number of religious books, or collections of sermons, in which the fundamental doctrines of the Christian religion are supposed to be set forth, and attempt to sift the greater part of those writings conscientiously in order to ascertain whether, in a large proportion of such literature, the fundamental doctrines of Christianity are to be found contained and stated in the orthodox sense, without ambiguity or evasion, the answer is again not a doubtful one.

It would appear that the theologians themselves, in accordance with the general training which most of them have received, only attribute that importance which they formerly assigned to the principle and doctrines of positive Christianity—when these were still regarded as such—to these doctrines when they are veiled in a misty indefiniteness. Thus if philosophy has always been regarded as the opponent of the doctrines of the Church, it cannot any longer be such, since these doctrines, which it seemed to threaten with destruction, are no longer regarded by general conviction as of importance. A great part of the danger which threatens philosophy from this side when she considers these dogmas in order to comprehend them ought to be thus taken away, and so philosophy can take up a more untrammelled attitude with regard to dogmas which have so much sunk in interest with theologians themselves.

The Historical Treatment of Dogmas

The strongest indication, however, that the importance of these dogmas has declined, is to be perceived in the fact that they are treated principally in an historical manner, and are regarded in the light of convictions which belong to *others,* as matters of history, which do not go on in our own mind as such, and which do not concern the needs of our spirit. The real interest here is to find out how the matter stands so far as others are concerned, what part others have played, and centres in this accidental origin and appearance of doctrine. The question as to what is a man's own personal conviction only excites astonishment. The absolute manner of the origin of these doctrines out of the depth of Spirit, and thus the necessity, the truth, which they have for *our* spirits too, is shoved on one side by this historical treatment. It brings much zeal and erudition to bear on these doctrines; it is not with their essential substance, however, that it is occupied, but with the externalities of the controversies about them, and with the passions which have gathered around this external mode of the origin of truth. Thus Theology is by her own act put in a low enough position. If the philosophical knowledge of religion is conceived of as something to be reached historically only, then we should have to regard the theologians who have brought it to this point as clerks in a mercantile house, who have only to keep an account of the wealth of strangers, who only act for others without obtaining any property for themselves. They do, indeed, receive salary, but their reward is only to serve, and to register that which is the property of others. Theology of this kind has no longer a place at all in the domain of thought; it has no longer to do with infinite thought in and for itself, but only with it as a finite fact, as opinion, ordinary thought, and so on. History occupies itself with truths which *were* truths—namely, for others, not with such as would come to be the possession of those who are occupied with them. With the true content, with the knowledge of God, such theologians have no concern. They know as little of God as a blind man sees of a painting, even though he handles the frame. They only know how a certain dogma was established by this or that council; what grounds those present at such a council had for establishing it, and how this or that opinion came to predominate. And in all this, it is indeed religion that is in question, and yet it is not religion itself which here comes under consideration. Much is told us of the history of the painter of the picture, and of the fate of the picture itself, what price it had at different times, into what hands it came, but we are never permitted to see anything of the picture itself.

It is essential in philosophy and religion, however, that the spirit should *itself* enter with supreme interest into an inner relation, should not only occupy itself with a thing that is foreign to it, but should draw its content from that which is essential, and should regard itself as worthy of such knowledge. For here it is with the value of his *own* spirit that man is concerned, and he is not at liberty humbly to remain outside and to wander about at a distance.

Philosophy and Immediate Knowledge

In consequence of the emptiness of the standpoint just considered, it might appear as if we only mentioned the reproaches which it casts upon philosophy in order to pronounce expressly against such a point of view, and that our aim, which we do not relinquish, is to do the opposite of that which it holds to be highest of all aims—namely, to know God. Yet this standpoint has an aspect belonging to its form in which it must really have a rational interest for us, and regarded from this side, the recent attitude of theology is more favourable for philosophy. For with the thought that all objective determinateness has converged in the inwardness of subjectivity, the conviction is bound up that God gives revelation in an immediate way in man; that religion consists just in this, that man has immediate knowledge of God. This immediate knowing is called reason, and also faith, but in a sense other than that in which the Church takes faith. All knowledge, all conviction, all piety, regarded from the point of view which we are considering, is based on the principle that in the spirit, as such, the consciousness of God exists immediately with the consciousness of its self.

a. This statement taken in a direct sense, and as not implying that any polemical attitude has been taken up to philosophy, passes for one which needs no proof, no confirmation. This universal idea, which is now matter of assumption, contains this essential principle—namely, that the highest, the religious content shows itself in the spirit itself, that Spirit manifests itself in Spirit, and in fact *in this my spirit,* that this faith has its source, its root in my deepest personal being, and that it is what is most peculiarly my own, and as such is inseparable from the consciousness of pure spirit.

Inasmuch as this knowledge exists immediately in myself, all external authority, all foreign attestation is cast aside; what is to be of value to me must have its verification in my own spirit, and in order that I may believe I must have the witness of my spirit. It may indeed come to me from without, but any such external origin is a matter of indifference; if it is to be valid, this validity can only build itself up upon the foundation of all truth, in the *witness of the Spirit.*

This principle is the simple principle of philosophical knowledge itself, and philosophy is so far from rejecting it that it constitutes a fundamental characteristic in it itself. Thus it is to be regarded as a gain, a kind of happy circumstance, that fundamental principles of philosophy live even in general popular conceptions, and have become general assumptions, for in this way the philosophical principle may expect the more easily to obtain the general consent of the educated. As a result of this general disposition of the spirit of our time, philosophy has not only won a position which is externally favourable—with what is external it is never concerned, and least of all where it, and active interest in it, takes the form of an institution of the State—but is favoured inwardly, since its principle already lives in the minds and in the hearts of men as an assumption. For philosophy has this in common with the form of culture referred to, that reason is regarded as that part of the spirit in which God reveals himself to man.

b. But the principle of immediate knowledge does not rest satisfied with this simple determinateness, this natural and ingenuous content; it does not only express itself affirmatively, but takes up a directly polemical attitude to philosophical knowledge, and directs its attacks especially against the philosophical knowledge and comprehension of God. Not only does it teach that we are to believe and to know in an immediate manner, not only is it maintained that the consciousness of God is bound up with the consciousness of self, but that the relation to God is *only* an immediate one. The immediateness of the connection is taken as excluding the other characteristic of mediateness, and philosophy, because it is mediated knowledge, is said to be only a finite knowledge of that which is finite.

Thus this knowledge in its immediacy is to get no further than this, that we know that God is, but not what He is; the content, the filling up of the idea of God, is negated. By philosophical knowledge or cognition, we mean not only that we know that an object is, but also what it is; and that to know what it is, is not to know it to the extent of possessing a certain knowledge, certainty, of what it is; but more than this, this knowledge must relate to its characteristics, to its content, and it must be complete and full and proved knowledge, in which the necessary connection of these characteristics is a matter of knowledge.

If we consider more closely what is involved in the assertion of immediate knowledge, it is seen to mean that the consciousness so relates itself to its content that it itself and this content—God—are inseparable. It is this relation, in fact—knowledge of God—and this inseparableness of consciousness from this content, which we call religion. Further, however, it is of the essence of this assertion that we are to limit ourselves to the consideration of religion as such, and to keep strictly to the consideration of the relation to God, and are not to proceed to the knowledge of God, that is, of the divine content—of what the divine content essentially is in itself.

In this sense it is stated, further, that we can only know our relation to God, not what God Himself is; and that it is only our relation to God which is embraced in what is generally called religion. Thus it happens that at the present time we only hear religion spoken of, and do not find that investigation is made regarding the nature of God, what He is in Himself, and how the nature of God must be determined. God, as God, is not even made an object of thought; knowledge does not trench upon that object, and does not exhibit distinct attributes in Him, so as to make it possible that He Himself should be conceived of as constituting the relation of these attributes, and as relation in Himself. God is not before us as an object of knowledge, but only our relation with God, our relation to Him; and while discussions of the nature of God have become fewer and fewer, it is now only required of a man that he should be religious, that he should abide by religion, and we are told that we are not to proceed further to get a knowledge of any divine content.

c. If, however, we bring out what is inherent in the principle of immediate knowing, that is, what is directly affirmed in it, we find it to be just this, that God is spoken of in relation to consciousness in such a way that this relation is something inseparable, or, in other words, that we must of necessity contemplate *both*. It implies, in the first place, the essential distinction which the conception of religion contains; on the one side, subjective consciousness, and on the other, God recognised as Object in Himself, or implicitly. At the same time, however, it is stated that there is an essential relation between the two, and that it is this inseparable relation of religion which is the real point, and not the notions which one may have concerning God.

What is really contained in this position, and really constitutes its true kernel, is the philosophical Idea itself, only that this Idea is confined by immediate knowledge within limitations which are abolished by philosophy, and which are by it exhibited in their onesidedness and untruth. According to the philosophical conception, God is Spirit, is concrete; and if we inquire more closely what Spirit is, we find that the whole of religious doctrine consists in the development of the fundamental conception of Spirit. For the present, however, it may suffice to say that Spirit is essentially self-manifestation—its nature is *to be for Spirit*. Spirit is for Spirit, and not, be it observed, only in an external, accidental manner. On the contrary, Spirit is only Spirit in so far as it is for Spirit; this constitutes the conception or notion of Spirit itself. Or, to express it more theologically, God is essentially Spirit, so far as He is in His Church. It has been said that the world, the material universe, must have spectators, and must be for Spirit or mind; how much more, then, must God be for Spirit.

We cannot, consequently, view the matter in a onesided way, and consider the subject merely according to its finiteness, to its contingent life, but inasmuch too as it has the infinite absolute object as its content. For if the Subject be considered by itself it is considered within the limits of finite knowledge, of knowledge which concerns the finite. It is also maintained, on the other hand, that God, in like manner, must not be considered for Himself, for man only knows of God in relation to consciousness; and thus the unity and inseparability of the two determinations—of the knowledge of God and self-consciousness—even presupposes what is expressed in identity, and that dreaded identity itself is contained in it.

As a matter of fact, we thus find the fundamental conception which belongs to philosophy already existing as an universal element in the cultured thought of the present day. And here it becomes apparent, too, that philosophy does not stand above its age as if it were something absolutely different from the general character of the time, but that it is One Spirit which pervades both the actual world and philosophical thought, and that this last is only the true self-comprehension of what is actual. Or, in other words, it is one movement upon which both the age and its philosophy are borne, the distinction being only that the character of the time still appears to present itself as accidental, and is not rationally justified, and may thus even stand in an unreconciled, hostile attitude towards the truly essential content; while philosophy, as the justification of principles, is at the same time the universal peace-bringer and universal reconciliation. As the Lutheran Reformation carried faith back to the first centuries, so the principle of immediate knowledge has carried Christian knowledge back to the primary elements. If, however, this process at first causes the essential content to evaporate, yet it is philosophy which recognises this very principle of immediate knowledge as representing content, and as being such carries it forward to its true expansion within itself.

The want of sound sense which marks the arguments advanced against philosophy knows no bounds. The very opinions which are supposed by those who hold them to militate against philosophy, and to be in the sharpest antagonism to it, upon examination of their content exhibit essential agreement with that which they combat. Thus the result of the study of philosophy is that these walls of separation, which are supposed to divide absolutely, become transparent; and that when we go to the root of things we find that there is absolute accordance where it was believed that there was the greatest opposition.

QUESTIONS FOR STUDY AND DISCUSSION

1. Where does religion fit into Hegel's thought?
2. Is philosophical knowledge opposed to religious knowledge? Explain.
3. How is "rational knowledge" an "essential element in the Christian religion itself"?
4. What is the relationship, if any, of the Absolute to God?
5. What does Hegel mean by the "theology of reason"? Why does he oppose it?

Marxism: Friedrich Engels and Karl Marx

KARL MARX was born in Trier (Trèves) in 1818 and studied at Bonn and later at Berlin, where he was influenced by the radical group of Young Hegelians. Having received his doctorate in philosophy in 1841, he edited the *Rheinische Zeitung,* a left-wing newspaper, until its suppression in 1843. After his marriage that summer, he moved to Paris, where he first met FRIEDRICH ENGELS, and collaborated with Arnold Ruge in the publication of the *Deutsch-Französische Jahrbücher.* Engels was born in Barmen in 1820 but left to work in Manchester when he was twenty-four. When Marx broke with Ruge in 1844 and was expelled from France, he went to Brussels. He was joined there by Engels, who became his constant collaborator even while still working in Manchester. In 1847 they produced the well-known *Communist Manifesto.* During the revolutionary years, 1848–49, Marx was back in Germany editing a radical newspaper. But having been expelled again, he joined Engels in London, where he lived in dire poverty until his death in 1883. The first volume of *Capital* was published during his lifetime in 1867. Volumes II and III were finished by Engels, who continued his writing until he died in 1895.

Dialectics

(The general nature of dialectics to be developed as the science of interconnections, in contrast to metaphysics.)

It is, therefore, from the history of nature and human society that the laws of dialectics are abstracted. For they are nothing but the most general laws of these two aspects of historical development, as well as of thought itself. And indeed they can be reduced in the main to three:

> The law of the transformation of quantity into quality and *vice versa;*
> The law of the interpenetration of opposites;
> The law of the negation of the negation.

All three are developed by Hegel in his idealist fashion as mere laws of *thought:* the first, in the first part of his *Logic,* in the Doctrine of Being;

From pp. 83–88 of Friedrich Engels, *Dialectics of Nature.* Copyright 1954 by Foreign Languages Publishing House, Moscow. Reprinted by permission of the publisher.

the second fills the whole of the second and by far the most important part of his *Logic,* the Doctrine of Essence; finally the third figures as the fundamental law for the construction of the whole system. The mistake lies in the fact that these laws are foisted on nature and history as laws of thought, and not deduced from them. This is the source of the whole forced and often outrageous treatment; the universe, willy-nilly, has to conform to a system of thought which itself is only the product of a definite stage of evolution of human thought. If we turn the thing round, then everything becomes simple, and the dialectical laws that look so extremely mysterious in idealist philosophy at once become simple and clear as noonday.

Moreover, anyone who is even only slightly acquainted with Hegel will be aware that in hundreds of passages Hegel is capable of giving the most striking individual illustrations of the dialectical laws from nature and history.

We are not concerned here with writing a handbook of dialectics, but only with showing that the dialectical laws are real laws of development of nature, and therefore are valid also for theoretical natural science. Hence we cannot go into the inner inter-connection of these laws with one another.

1. The law of the transformation of quantity into quality and *vice versa.* For our purpose, we can express this by saying that in nature, in a manner exactly fixed for each individual case, qualitative changes can only occur by the quantitative addition or quantitative subtraction of matter or motion (so-called energy).

All qualitative differences in nature rest on differences of chemical composition or on different quantities or forms of motion (energy) or, as is almost always the case, on both. Hence it is impossible to alter the quality of a body without addition or subtraction of matter or motion, i.e., without quantitative alteration of the body concerned. In this form, therefore, Hegel's mysterious principle appears not only quite rational but even rather obvious.

It is surely hardly necessary to point out that the various allotropic and aggregational states of bodies, because they depend on various groupings of the molecules, depend on greater or lesser amounts of motion communicated to the bodies.

But what about change of form of motion, or so-called energy? If we change heat into mechanical motion or *vice versa,* is not the quality altered while the quantity remains the same? Quite correct. But it is with change of form of motion as with Heine's vices; anyone can be virtuous by himself, for vices two are always necessary. Change of form of motion is always a process that takes place between at least two bodies, of which one loses a definite amount of motion of one quality (e.g., heat), while the other gains a corresponding quantity of motion of another quality (mechanical motion, electricity, chemical decomposition). Here, therefore, quantity and quality mutually correspond to each other. So far it has not been found possible to convert motion from one form to another inside a single isolated body.

We are concerned here in the first place with non-living bodies; the same law holds for living bodies, but it operates under very complex conditions and at present quantitative measurement is still often impossible for us.

If we imagine any non-living body cut up into smaller and smaller portions, at first no qualitative change occurs. But this has a limit: if we succeed, as by evaporation, in obtaining the separate molecules in the free state, then it is true that we can usually divide these still further, yet only with a complete change of quality. The molecule is decomposed into its separate atoms, which have quite different properties from those of the molecule. In the case of molecules composed of different chemical elements, atoms or molecules of these elements themselves make their appearance in the place of the compound molecule; in the case of molecules of elements, the free atoms appear, which exert quite distinct qualitative effects: the free atoms of nascent oxygen are easily able to effect what the atoms of atmospheric oxygen, bound together in the molecule, can never achieve.

But the molecule is also qualitatively different from the mass of the body to which it belongs. It can carry out movements independently of this mass and while the latter remains apparently at rest, e.g., heat vibrations; by means of a change of position and of connection with neighbouring molecules it can change the body into an allotrope or a different state of aggregation.

Thus we see that the purely quantitative operation of division has a limit at which it becomes transformed into a qualitative difference: the mass consists solely of molecules, but it is something essentially different from the molecule, just as the latter is different from the atom. It is this difference that is the basis for the separation of mechanics, as the science of heavenly and terrestrial masses, from physics, as the mechanics of molecules, and from chemistry, as the physics of atoms.

In mechanics, no qualities occur; at most, states such as equilibrium, motion, potential energy, which all depend on measurable transference of motion and are themselves capable of quantitative expression. Hence, in so far as qualitative change takes place here, it is determined by a corresponding quantitative change.

In physics, bodies are treated as chemically unalterable or indifferent; we have to do with changes of their molecular states and with the change of form of motion, which in all cases, at least on one of the two sides, brings the molecule into action. Here every change is a transformation of quantity into quality, a consequence of the quantitative change of the amount of motion of one form or another that is inherent in the body or communicated to it. "Thus the temperature of water is, in the first place, a point of no consequence in respect to its liquidity; still with the increase or diminution of the temperature of liquid water, there comes a point where this state of cohesion alters and the water is converted into steam or ice." Similarly, a definite minimum current strength is required to cause the platinum wire of an electric incandescent lamp to glow; and every metal has its temperature of incandescence and fusion, every liquid its definite freezing and boiling point at a given pressure—in so far as our means allow us to produce the temperature required; finally also every gas has its critical point at which it can be liquefied by pressure and cooling. In short, the so-called physical constants are for the most part nothing but designations of the nodal points at which quantitative [change] addition or substraction of motion produces qualitative change in the state of the body concerned, at which, therefore, quantity is transformed into quality.

The sphere, however, in which the law of nature discovered by Hegel celebrates its most important triumphs is that of chemistry. Chemistry can be termed the science of the qualitative changes of bodies as a result of changed quantitative composition. That was already known to Hegel himself. As in the case of oxygen: if three atoms unite into a molecule, instead of the usual two, we get ozone, a body which is very considerably different from ordinary oxygen in its odour and reactions. And indeed the various proportions in which oxygen combines with nitrogen or sulphur, each of which produces a substance qualitatively different from any of the others! How different is laughing gas (nitrogen monoxide N_2O) from nitric anhydride (nitrogen pentoxide, N_2O_5)! The first is a gas, the second at ordinary temperatures a solid crystalline substance. And yet the whole difference in composition is that the second contains five times as much oxygen as the first, and between the two of them are three more oxides of nitrogen (NO, N_2O_3, NO_2), each of which is qualitatively different from the first two and from one another.

FOR STUDY AND DISCUSSION

What does Engels want to prove in his discussion of the law of the transformation of quantity into quality? Why?

The Significance of Hegel

But precisely therein lay the true significance and the revolutionary character of the Hegelian philosophy (to which, as the close of the whole movement since Kant, we must here confine ourselves), that it once for all dealt

From pp. 362–71 of Friedrich Engels, *Feuerbach and the End of Classical German Philosophy*, in *Selected Works of Marx and Engels*, vol. II. Copyright 1958 by Foreign Languages Publishing House, Moscow. Reprinted by permission of the publisher.

the death blow to the finality of all products of human thought and action. Truth, the cognition of which is the business of philosophy, was in the hands of Hegel no longer an aggregate of finished dogmatic statements, which, once discovered, had merely to be learned by heart. Truth lay now in the process of cognition itself, in the long historical development of science, which mounts from lower to ever higher levels of knowledge without ever reaching, by discovering so-called absolute truth, a point at which it can proceed no further, where it would have nothing more to do than to fold its hands and gaze with wonder at the absolute truth to which it had attained. And what holds good for the realm of philosophical knowledge holds good also for that of every other kind of knowledge and also for practical action. Just as knowledge is unable to reach a complete conclusion in a perfect, ideal condition of humanity, so is history unable to do so; a perfect society, a perfect "state," are things which can only exist in imagination. On the contrary, all successive historical systems are only transitory stages in the endless course of development of human society from the lower to the higher. Each stage is necessary, and therefore justified for the time and conditions to which it owes its origin. But in the face of new, higher conditions which gradually develop in its own womb, it loses its validity and justification. It must give way to a higher stage which will also in its turn decay and perish. Just as the bourgeoisie by large-scale industry, competition and the world market dissolves in practice all stable time-honoured institutions, so this dialectical philosophy dissolves all conceptions of final, absolute truth and of absolute states of humanity corresponding to it. For it [dialectical philosophy] nothing is final, absolute, sacred. It reveals the transitory character of everything and in everything; nothing can endure before it except the uninterrupted process of becoming and of passing away, of endless ascendancy from the lower to the higher. And dialectical philosophy itself is nothing more than the mere reflection of this process in the thinking brain. It has, of course, also a conservative side: it recognizes that definite stages of knowledge and society are justified for their time and circumstances; but only so far. The conservatism of this mode of outlook is relative; its revolutionary character is absolute—the only absolute dialectical philosophy admits.

It is not necessary, here, to go into the question of whether this mode of outlook is thoroughly in accord with the present state of natural science, which predicts a possible end even for the earth, and for its habitability a fairly certain one: which therefore recognizes that for the history of mankind, too, there is not only an ascending but also a descending branch. At any rate we still find ourselves a considerable distance from the turning-point at which the historical course of society becomes one of descent, and we cannot expect Hegelian philosophy to be concerned with a subject which natural science, in its time, had not at all placed upon the agenda as yet.

But what must, in fact, be said here is this: that in Hegel the views developed above are not so sharply delineated. They are a necessary conclusion from his method, but one which he himself never drew with such explicitness. And this, indeed, for the simple reason that he was compelled to make a system and, in accordance with traditional requirements, a system of philosophy must conclude with some sort of absolute truth. Therefore, however much Hegel, especially in his *Logic,* emphasized that this eternal truth is nothing but the logical, or, the historical, process itself, he nevertheless finds himself compelled to supply this process with an end, just because he has to bring his system to a termination at some point or other. In his *Logic* he can make this end a beginning again, since here the point of conclusion, the absolute idea—which is only absolute in so far as he has absolutely nothing to say about it—"alienates," that is, transforms, itself into nature and comes to itself again later in the mind, that is, in thought and in history. But at the end of the whole philosophy a similar return to the beginning is possible only in one way. Namely, by conceiving of the end of history as follows: mankind arrives at the cognition of this selfsame absolute idea, and declares that this cognition of the absolute idea is reached in Hegelian philosophy. In this way, however, the whole dogmatic content of the Hegelian system is declared to be absolute truth, in contradiction to his dialectical method, which dissolves all dogmatism. Thus the revolutionary side is smothered beneath the overgrowth of the conservative side. And what applies to philosophical cognition applies also to historical practice. Mankind, which, in the person of Hegel, has reached the point of working out the absolute idea, must also in practice have gotten so far that it can carry out this absolute idea in reality. Hence the practical political demands of the absolute idea on contemporaries may not be stretched too far. And so we find at the conclusion of the *Philosophy of Right* that the absolute idea is to be realized in that monarchy based on social estates which Frederick William III so persistently but vainly promised to his subjects, that is, in a limited, moderate, indirect rule of the possessing classes suited to the petty-bourgeois German conditions of that time; and, moreover, the necessity of the nobility is demonstrated to us in a speculative fashion.

The inner necessities of the system are, therefore, of themselves sufficient to explain why a thoroughly revolutionary method of thinking produced an extremely tame political conclusion. As a matter of fact the specific form of this conclusion springs from this, that Hegel was a German, and like his contemporary Goethe had a bit of the Philistine's queue dangling behind. Each of them was an Olympian Zeus in his own sphere, yet neither of them ever quite freed himself from German Philistinism.

But all this did not prevent the Hegelian system from covering an incomparably greater domain than any earlier system, nor from developing in this domain a wealth of thought which is astounding even today. The phenomenology of mind (which one may call a parallel of the embryology and palaeontology of the mind, a development of individual consciousness through its different stages, set in the form of an abbreviated reproduction of the stages through which the consciousness of man has passed in the course of history), logic, natural philosophy, philosophy of mind, and the latter worked out in its separate, historical subdivisions: philosophy of history, of right, of religion, history of philosophy, aesthetics, etc.—in all these different historical fields Hegel laboured to discover and demonstrate the pervading thread of development. And as he was not only a creative genius but also a man of encyclopaedic erudition, he played an epoch-making role in every sphere. It is self-evident that owing to the needs of the "system" he very often had to resort to those forced constructions about which his pigmy opponents make such a terrible fuss even today. But these constructions are only the frame and scaffolding of his work. If one does not loiter here needlessly, but presses on farther into the immense building, one finds innumerable treasures which today still possess undiminished value. With all philosophers it is precisely the "system" which is perishable; and for the simple reason that it springs from an imperishable desire of the human mind—the desire to overcome all contradictions. But if all contradictions are once for all disposed of, we shall have arrived at so-called absolute truth—world history will be at an end. And yet it has to continue, although there is nothing left for it to do—hence, a new, insoluble contradiction. As soon as we have once realized—and in the long run no one has helped us to realize it more than Hegel himself—that the task of philosophy thus stated means nothing but the task that a single philosopher should accomplish that which can only be accomplished by the entire human race in its progressive development—as soon as we realize that, there is an end to all philosophy in the hitherto accepted sense of the word. One leaves alone "absolute truth," which is unattainable along this path or by any single individual; instead, one pursues attainable relative truths along the path of the positive sciences, and the summation of their results by means of dialectical thinking. At any rate, with Hegel philosophy comes to an end: on the one hand, because in his system he summed up its whole development in the most splendid fashion; and on the other hand, because, even though unconsciously, he showed us the way out of the labyrinth of systems to real positive knowledge of the world.

One can imagine what a tremendous effect this Hegelian system must have produced in the philosophy-tinged atmosphere of Germany. It was a triumphal procession which lasted for decades and which by no means came to a standstill on the death of Hegel. On the contrary, it was precisely from 1830 to 1840 that "Hegelianism" reigned most exclusively, and to a greater or lesser extent infected even its opponents. It was precisely in this period that Hegelian views, consciously or unconsciously, most extensively penetrated the most diversified sciences and leavened even popular literature and the daily press, from which the average "educated consciousness" derives its mental pabulum. But this victory along the whole front was only the prelude to an internal struggle.

As we have seen, the doctrine of Hegel, taken as a whole, left plenty of room for giving shelter to the most diverse practical party views. And in the theoretical Germany of that time, two things above all were practical: religion and politics. Whoever placed the chief emphasis on the Hegelian *system* could be fairly conservative in both spheres; whoever regarded the dialectical *method* as the main thing could belong to the most extreme opposition, both in politics and religion. Hegel himself, despite the fairly frequent outbursts of revolutionary wrath in his works, seemed on the whole to be more inclined to the conservative side. Indeed, his system had cost him much more "hard mental plugging" than his method. Towards the end of the thirties, the cleavage in the school became more and more apparent. The Left wing, the so-called Young Hegelians, in their fight with the pietist orthodox and the feudal reactionaries, abandoned bit by bit that philosophical-genteel reserve in regard to the burning questions of the day which up to that time had secured state toleration and even protection for their teachings. And when, in 1840, orthodox pietism and absolutist feudal reaction ascended the throne with Frederick William IV, open partisanship became unavoidable. The fight was still carried on with philosophical weapons, but no longer for abstract philosophical aims. It turned directly on the destruction of traditional religion and of the existing state. And while in the *Deutsche Jahrbücher* [1] the practical ends were still predominantly put forward in philosophical disguise, in the *Rheinische Zeitung* of 1842 the Young Hegelian school revealed itself directly as the philosophy of the aspiring radical bourgeoisie and used the meagre cloak of philosophy only to deceive the censorship.

At that time, however, politics was a very thorny field, and hence the main fight came to be directed against religion; this fight, particularly since 1840, was indirectly also political. Strauss' *Life of Jesus,* published in 1835, had provided the first impulse. The theory therein developed of the formation of the gospel myths was combated later by Bruno Bauer with proof that a whole series of evangelic stories had been fabricated by the authors themselves. The controversy between these two was carried out in the philosophical disguise of a battle between "self-consciousness" and "substance." The question whether the miracle stories of the gospels came into being through unconscious-traditional myth-creation within the bosom of the community or whether they were fabricated by the evangelists themselves was magnified into the question whether, in world history, "substance" or "self-consciousness" was the decisive operative force. Finally

---

[1] The *Deutsche Jahrbücher für Wissenschaft und Kunst* [*German Annals of Science and Art*]: Organ of the Young Hegelians edited by A. Ruge and T. Echtermeyer, and published in Leipzig from 1841 to 1843. [Editor of Foreign Languages Publishing House—FLPH.]

came Stirner, the prophet of contemporary anarchism—Bakunin has taken a great deal from him—and capped the sovereign "self-consciousness" by his sovereign "ego." [2]

We will not go further into this side of the decomposition process of the Hegelian school. More important for us is the following: the main body of the most determined Young Hegelians was, by the practical necessities of its fight against positive religion, driven back to Anglo-French materialism. This brought them into conflict with their school system. While materialism conceives nature as the sole reality, nature in the Hegelian system represents merely the " alienation" of the absolute idea, so to say, a degradation of the idea. At all events, thinking and its thought-product, the idea, is here the primary, nature the derivative, which only exists at all by the condescension of the idea. And in this contradiction they floundered as well or as ill as they could.

Then came Feuerbach's *Essence of Christianity*.[3] With one blow it pulverized the contradiction, in that without circumlocutions it placed materialism on the throne again. Nature exists independently of all philosophy. It is the foundation upon which we human beings, ourselves products of nature, have grown up. Nothing exists outside nature and man, and the higher beings our religious fantasies have created are only the fantastic reflection of our own essence. The spell was broken; the "system" was exploded and cast aside, and the contradiction, shown to exist only in our imagination was dissolved. One must himself have experienced the liberating effect of this book to get an idea of it. Enthusiasm was general; we all became at once Feuerbachians. How enthusiastically Marx greeted the new conception and how much—in spite of all critical reservations—he was influenced by it, one may read in *The Holy Family*.

Even the shortcomings of the book contributed to its immediate effect. Its literary, sometimes even high-flown, style secured for it a large public and was at any rate refreshing after long years of abstract and abstruse Hegelianizing. The same is true of its extravagant deification of love, which, coming after the now intolerable sovereign rule of "pure reason," had its excuse, if not justification. But what we must not forget is that it was precisely these two weaknesses of Feuerbach that "true Socialism," which had been spreading like a plague in "educated" Germany since 1844, took as its starting-point, putting literary phrases in the place of scientific knowledge, the liberation of mankind by means of "love" in place of the emancipation of the proletariat through the economic transformation of production—in short, losing itself in the nauseous fine writing and ecstasies of love typified by Herr Karl Grün.

Another thing we must not forget is this: the Hegelian school disinte-

---

[2] Engels refers to Max Stirner's (pseudonym for Kaspar Schmidt) *Der Einzige und sein Eigentum* [*The Ego and His Own*], which appeared in 1845. [FLPH.]

[3] Feuerbach's *Das Wesen des Christentums* [*The Essence of Christianity*] appeared in Leipzig in 1841. [FLPH.]

grated, but Hegelian philosophy was not overcome through criticism; Strauss and Bauer each took one of its sides and set it polemically against the other. Feuerbach broke through the system and simply discarded it. But a philosophy is not disposed of by the mere assertion that it is false. And so powerful a work as Hegelian philosophy, which had exercised so enormous an influence on the intellectual development of the nation, could not be disposed of by simply being ignored. It had to be "sublated" in its own sense, that is, in the sense that while its form had to be annihilated through criticism, the new content which had been won through it had to be saved. How this was brought about we shall see below.

But in the meantime the Revolution of 1848 thrust the whole of philosophy aside as unceremoniously as Feuerbach had thrust aside Hegel. And in the process Feuerbach himself was also pushed into the background.

The great basic question of all philosophy, especially of more recent philosophy, is that concerning the relation of thinking and being. From the very early times when men, still completely ignorant of the structure of their own bodies, under the stimulus of dream apparitions [4] came to believe that their thinking and sensation were not activities of their bodies, but of a distinct soul which inhabits the body and leaves it at death—from this time men have been driven to reflect about the relation between this soul and the outside world. If upon death it took leave of the body and lived on, there was no occasion to invent yet another distinct death for it. Thus arose the idea of its immortality, which at that stage of development appeared not at all as a consolation but as a fate against which it was no use fighting, and often enough, as among the Greeks, as a positive misfortune. Not religious desire for consolation, but the quandary arising from the common universal ignorance of what to do with this soul, once its existence had been accepted, after the death of the body, led in a general way to the tedious notion of personal immortality. In an exactly similar manner the first gods arose through the personification of natural forces. And these gods in the further development of religions assumed more and more an extra-mundane form, until finally by a process of abstraction, I might almost say of distillation, occurring naturally in the course of man's intellectual development, out of the many more or less limited and mutually limiting gods there arose in the minds of men the idea of the one exclusive God of the monotheistic religions.

Thus the question of the relation of thinking to being, the relation of the spirit to nature—the paramount question of the whole of philosophy —has, no less than all religion, its roots in the narrow-minded and ignorant

---

[4] Among savages and lower barbarians the idea is still universal that the human forms which appear in dreams are souls which have temporarily left their bodies; the real man is, therefore, held responsible for acts committed by his dream apparition against the dreamer. Thus Imthurn found this belief current, for example, among the Indians of Guiana in 1884. [F.E.]

notions of savagery. But this question could for the first time be put forward in its whole acuteness, could achieve its full significance, only after humanity in Europe had awakened from the long hibernation of the Christian Middle Ages. The question of the position of thinking in relation to being, a question which, by the way, had played a great part also in the scholasticism of the Middle Ages, the question: which is primary, spirit or nature—that question, in relation to the church, was sharpened into this: Did God create the world or has the world been in existence eternally?

The answers which the philosophers gave to this question split them into two great camps. Those who asserted the primacy of spirit to nature and, therefore, in the last instance, assumed world creation in some form or other—and among the philosophers, Hegel, for example, this creation often becomes still more intricate and impossible than in Christianity—comprised the camp of idealism. The others, who regarded nature as primary, belong to the various schools of materialism.

These two expressions, idealism and materialism, originally signify nothing else but this; and here too they are not used in any other sense. What confusion arises when some other meaning is put into them will be seen below.

But the question of the relation of thinking and being has yet another side: in what relation do our thoughts about the world surrounding us stand to this world itself? Is our thinking capable of the cognition of the real world? Are we able in our ideas and notions of the real world to produce a correct reflection of reality? In philosophical language this question is called the question of the identity of thinking and being, and the overwhelming majority of philosophers give an affirmative answer to this question. With Hegel, for example, its affirmation is self-evident; for what we cognize in the real world is precisely its thought-content—that which makes the world a gradual realization of the absolute idea, which absolute idea has existed somewhere from eternity, independent of the world and before the world. But it is manifest without further proof that thought can know a content which is from the outset a thought-content. It is equally manifest that what is to be proved here is already tacitly contained in the premises. But that in no way prevents Hegel from drawing the further conclusion from his proof of the identity of thinking and being that his philosophy, because it is correct for his thinking, is therefore the only correct one, and that the identity of thinking and being must prove its validity by mankind immediately translating his philosophy from theory into practice and transforming the whole world according to Hegelian principles. This is an illusion which he shares with well-nigh all philosophers.

QUESTIONS FOR STUDY AND DISCUSSION

1. How does Engels characterize dialectical philosophy?
2. What does Engels think Hegel meant by "system"?

3. What role does Engels assign to Feuerbach in the development of Marxism?
4. Evaluate Engels' definition of nature.
5. For Engels, what is the basic philosophical problem?

Marxist Methodology

I was taking up law, which discipline, however, I only pursued as a subordinate subject along with philosophy and history. In the year 1842–43, as editor of the *Rheinische Zeitung*,[1] I experienced for the first time the embarrassment of having to take part in discussions on so-called material interests. The proceedings of the Rhenish Landtag on thefts of wood and parcelling of landed property, the official polemic which Herr von Schaper, then *Oberpräsident* of the Rhine Province, opened against the *Rheinische Zeitung* on the conditions of the Moselle peasantry, and finally debates on free trade and protective tariffs provided the first occasions for occupying myself with economic questions. On the other hand, at that time when the good will "to go further" greatly outweighed knowledge of the subject, a philosophically weakly tinged echo of French socialism and communism made itself audible in the *Rheinische Zeitung*. I declared myself against this amateurism, but frankly confessed at the same time in a controversy with the *Allgemeine Augsburger Zeitung*[2] that my previous studies did not permit me even to venture any judgement on the content of the French tendencies. Instead, I eagerly seized on the illusion of the managers of the *Rheinische Zeitung*, who thought that by a weaker attitude on the part of the paper they could secure a remission of the death sentence passed upon it, to withdraw from the public stage into the study.

The first work which I undertook for a solution of the doubts which assailed me was a critical review of the Hegelian philosophy of right, a work the introduction to which appeared in 1844 in the *Deutsch-Französische Jahrbücher*,[3] published in Paris. My investigation led to the result that legal relations as well as forms of state are to be grasped neither from

---

[1] *Rheinische Zeitung* [*Rhenish Gazette*]: A daily radical newspaper published in Cologne in 1842–43. [FLPH.]

[2] Marx has in mind his article, "Der Kommunismus und die *Augsburger Allgemeine Zeitung*" [Communism and the *Augsburg General Journal*], *Marx-Engels Gesamtausgabe*, Abt. I, B. I, Halbband I, Frankfurt a. M. 1927, S. 260–65. [FLPH.]

[3] *Deutsch-Französische Jahrbücher* [German-French Annuals]: Organ of revolutionary and communist propaganda published by Marx in Paris in 1844. [FLPH.]

From pp. 361–65 of Karl Marx, the Preface to *A Contribution to the Critique of Political Economy*, in *Selected Works of Marx and Engels*, vol. I. Copyright 1958 by Foreign Languages Publishing House, Moscow. Reprinted by permission of the publisher.

themselves nor from the so-called general development of the human mind, but rather have their roots in the material conditions of life, the sum total of which Hegel, following the example of the Englishmen and Frenchmen of the eighteenth century, combines under the name of "civil society," that, however, the anatomy of civil society is to be sought in political economy. The investigation of the latter, which I began in Paris, I continued in Brussels, whither I had emigrated in consequence of an expulsion order of M. Guizot. The general result at which I arrived and which, once won, served as a guiding thread for my studies, can be briefly formulated as follows: In the social production of their life, men enter into definite relations that are indispensable and independent of their will, relations of production which correspond to a definite stage of development of their material productive forces. The sum total of these relations of production constitutes the economic structure of society, the real foundation, on which rises a legal and political superstructure and to which correspond definite forms of social consciousness. The mode of production of material life conditions the social, political and intellectual life process in general. It is not the consciousness of men that determines their being, but, on the contrary, their social being that determines their consciousness. At a certain stage of their development, the material productive forces of society come in conflict with the existing relations of production, or—what is but a legal expression for the same thing—with the property relations within which they have been at work hitherto. From forms of development of the productive forces these relations turn into their fetters. Then begins an epoch of social revolution. With the change of the economic foundation the entire immense superstructure is more or less rapidly transformed. In considering such transformations a distinction should always be made between the material transformation of the economic conditions of production, which can be determined with the precision of natural science, and the legal, political, religious, aesthetic or philosophic—in short, ideological forms in which men become conscious of this conflict and fight it out. Just as our opinion of an individual is not based on what he thinks of himself, so can we not judge of such a period of transformation by its own consciousness; on the contrary, this consciousness must be explained rather from the contradictions of material life, from the existing conflict between the social productive forces and the relations of production. No social order ever perishes before all the productive forces for which there is room in it have developed; and new, higher relations of production never appear before the material conditions of their existence have matured in the womb of the old society itself. Therefore mankind always sets itself only such tasks as it can solve; since, looking at the matter more closely, it will always be found that the task itself arises only when the material conditions for its solution already exist or are at least in the process of formation. In broad outlines Asiatic, ancient, feudal, and modern bourgeois modes of production can be designated as progressive epochs in the economic formation of society. The bourgeois relations of production are the last antagonistic form of the social process of production—antagonistic not in the sense of individual antagonism, but of one arising from the social conditions of life of the individuals; at the same time the productive forces developing in the womb of bourgeois society create the material conditions for the solution of that antagonism. This social formation brings, therefore, the prehistory of human society to a close.

Friedrich Engels, with whom, since the appearance of his brilliant sketch on the criticism of the economic categories (in the *Deutsch-Französische Jahrbücher*), I maintained a constant exchange of ideas by correspondence, had by another road (compare his *The Condition of the Working Class in England in 1844*) arrived at the same result as I, and when in the spring of 1845 he also settled in Brussels, we resolved to work out in common the opposition of our view to the ideological view of German philosophy, in fact, to settle accounts with our erstwhile philosophical conscience. The resolve was carried out in the form of a criticism of post-Hegelian philosophy. The manuscript, two large octavo volumes,[4] had long reached its place of publication in Westphalia when we received the news that altered circumstances did not allow of its being printed. We abandoned the manuscript to the gnawing criticism of the mice all the more willingly as we had achieved our main purpose—self-clarification. Of the scattered works in which we put our views before the public at that time, now from one aspect, now from another, I will mention only the *Manifesto of the Communist Party,* jointly written by Engels and myself, and *Discours sur le libre échange*[5] published by me. The decisive points of our view were first scientifically, although only polemically, indicated in my work published in 1847 and directed against Proudhon: *Misère de la Philosophie,*[6] etc. A dissertation written in German on *Wage Labour,* in which I put together my lectures on this subject delivered in the Brussels German Workers' Society, was interrupted, while being printed, by the February Revolution and my consequent forcible removal from Belgium.

The editing of the *Neue Rheinische Zeitung* in 1848 and 1849, and the subsequent events, interrupted my economic studies which could only be resumed in the year 1850 in London. The enormous material for the history of political economy which is accumulated in the British Museum, the favourable vantage point afforded by London for the observation of bourgeois society, and finally the new stage of development upon which the latter appeared to have entered with the discovery of gold in California and Australia, determined me to begin afresh from the very beginning and to work through the new material critically. These studies led partly of themselves into apparently quite remote subjects on which I had to dwell for a shorter or longer period. Especially, however, was the time at my disposal curtailed by the imperative necessity of earning my living. My contribu-

---

[4] The reference is to *The German Ideology.* [FLPH.]

[5] *Discourse on Free Trade.* [FLPH.]

[6] *The Poverty of Philosophy.* [FLPH.]

tions, during eight years now, to the first English-American newspaper, the *New York Tribune*,[7] compelled an extraordinary scattering of my studies, since I occupy myself with newspaper correspondence proper only in exceptional cases. However, articles on striking economic events in England and on the Continent constituted so considerable a part of my contributions that I was compelled to make myself familiar with practical details which lie outside the sphere of the actual science of political economy.

This sketch of the course of my studies in the sphere of political economy is intended only to show that my views, however they may be judged and however little they coincide with the interested prejudices of the ruling classes, are the result of conscientious investigation lasting many years. But at the entrance to science, as at the entrance to hell, the demand must be posted:

> *Qui si convien lasciare ogni sospetto;*
> *Ogni viltà convien che qui sia morta.*[8]

QUESTIONS FOR STUDY AND DISCUSSION

1. How does Marx conceive his position in relation to Hegel?
2. What is a superstructure?
3. Does Marx distinguish clearly between a condition and a determination?
4. How does Marx define an ideology?
5. Explain the doctrine of economic determinism.

The Opposition of the Materialistic and Idealistic Outlook

As we hear from German ideologists, Germany has in the last few years gone through an unparalleled revolution. The decomposition of the Hegelian philosophy, which began with Strauss, has developed into a universal ferment into which all the "powers of the past" are swept. In the general chaos mighty empires have arisen only to meet with immediate doom,

---

[7] *The New York Daily Tribune:* Democratic daily newspaper, which appeared in New York from 1841 to 1924 and to which Marx contributed from 1851 to 1862. [FLPH.]
[8] Here all mistrust must be abandoned
And here must perish every craven thought. (Dante, *The Divine Comedy*.) [FLPH.]

From pp. 3–27 of Karl Marx, *Feuerbach*, in *The German Ideology*, edited by R. Pascal. Copyright 1947 by International Publishers Co., Inc. By permission of International Publishers Co., Inc.

heroes have emerged momentarily only to be hurled into obscurity by bolder and stronger rivals. It was a revolution beside which the French Revolution was child's play, a world struggle beside which the struggles of the Diadochi appear insignificant. Principles ousted one another, heroes of the mind overthrew each other with unheard-of rapidity, and in the three years 1842–1845 more of the past was swept away than normally in three centuries.

All this is supposed to have taken place in the realm of pure thought.

Certainly it is an interesting event we are dealing with: the putrescence of the absolute spirit. When the last spark of its life had failed, the various components of this *caput mortuum* began to decompose, entered on new combinations and formed new substances. The industrialists of philosophy, who till then had lived on the exploitation of the absolute spirit, now seized upon the new combinations. Each with all possible zeal set about retailing his apportioned share. This naturally gave rise to competition, which, to start with, was carried on in moderately staid bourgeois fashion. Later when the German market was glutted, and the commodity in spite of all efforts found no response in the world-market, the business was spoiled in the usual German manner by fake and shoddy production, deterioration in quality, adulteration of the raw materials, falsification of labels, fake purchases, bill-jobbing and a credit-system devoid of any real basis. The competition turned into a bitter struggle, which is now being extolled and interpreted to us as a revolution of world significance, the begetter of the most prodigious results and achievements.

If we wish to rate at its true value this philosophic charlatanry, which awakens even in the breast of the honest German citizen a glow of national pride, if we wish to bring out clearly the pettiness, the parochial narrowness of this whole Young-Hegelian movement and the tragi-comic contrast between the illusions of these heroes about their achievements and the actual achievements themselves, we must look at the whole spectacle from a standpoint beyond the frontiers of Germany.

IDEOLOGY IN GENERAL, GERMAN IDEOLOGY IN PARTICULAR

German criticism has, right up to its latest efforts, never quitted the realm of philosophy. Far from examining its general philosophic premises, the whole body of its inquiries has actually sprung from the soil of a definite philosophical system, that of Hegel. Not only in their answers but in their very questions there was a mystification. This dependence on Hegel is the reason why not one of these modern critics has ever attempted a comprehensive criticism of the Hegelian system, however much each professes to have advanced beyond Hegel. Their polemics against Hegel and against one another are confined to this—each extracts one side of the Hegelian system and turns this against the whole system as well as against the sides extracted by the others. To begin with they extracted pure unfalsified Hegelian categories such as "substance" and "self-consciousness," later they desecrated these categories with more secular names such as "species," "the unique," "man," etc.

The entire body of German philosophical criticism from Strauss to Stirner is confined to criticism of religious conceptions. The critics started from real religion and actual theology. What religious consciousness and a religious conception really meant was determined variously as they went along. Their advance consisted in subsuming the allegedly dominant metaphysical, political, juridical, moral and other conceptions under the class of religious or theological conceptions; and similarly in pronouncing political, juridical, moral consciousness as religious or theological, and the political, juridical, moral man—"man" in the last resort—as religious. The dominance of religion was taken for granted. Gradually every dominant relationship was pronounced a religious relationship and transformed into a cult, a cult of law, cult of the State, etc. On all sides it was only a question of dogmas and belief in dogmas. The world was sanctified to an ever-increasing extent till at last our venerable Saint Max[1] was able to canonize it *en bloc* and thus dispose of it once for all.

The Old Hegelians had *comprehended* everything as soon as it was reduced to an Hegelian logical category. The Young Hegelians *criticized* everything by attributing to it religious conceptions or by pronouncing it a theological matter. The Young Hegelians are in agreement with the Old Hegelians in their belief in the rule of religion, of concepts, of an abstract general principle in the existing world. Only, the one party attacks this dominion as usurpation, while the other extols it as legitimate.

Since the Young Hegelians consider conceptions, thoughts, ideas, in fact all the products of consciousness, to which they attribute an independent existence, as the real chains of men (just as the Old Hegelians declared them the true bonds of human society) it is evident that the Young Hegelians have to fight only against these illusions of the consciousness. Since, according to their fantasy, the relationships of men, all their doings, their chains and their limitations are products of their consciousness, the Young Hegelians logically put to men the moral postulate of exchanging their present consciousness for human, critical or egoistic consciousness, and thus of removing their limitations. This demand to change consciousness amounts to a demand to interpret reality in another way, i.e. to accept it by means of another interpretation. The Young-Hegelian ideologists, in spite of their allegedly "world-shattering" statements, are the staunchest conservatives. The most recent of them have found the correct expression for their activity when they declare they are only fighting against "phrases." They forget, however, that to these phrases they themselves are only oppos-

---

[1] Max Stirner (1806–56): his work, *The Individual and His Individuality* (1844), was bitterly attacked by Marx as "spiritual history." Stirner advocated a liberation of the individual (a society of isolated individuals, Marx called it) and an acceptance of the world as it is. [T.N.M.]

ing other phrases, and that they are in no way combating the real existing world when they are merely combating the phrases of this world. The only results which this philosophic criticism could achieve were a few (and at that thoroughly one-sided) elucidations of Christianity from the point of view of religious history; all the rest of their assertions are only further embellishments of their claim to have furnished, in these unimportant elucidations, discoveries of universal importance.

It has not occurred to any one of these philosophers to inquire into the connection of German philosophy with German reality, the relation of their criticism to their own material surroundings.

. . .

The premises from which we begin are not arbitrary ones, not dogmas, but real premises from which abstraction can only be made in the imagination. They are the real individuals, their activity and the material conditions under which they live, both those which they find already existing and those produced by their activity. These premises can thus be verified in a purely empirical way.

The first premise of all human history is, of course, the existence of living human individuals. Thus the first fact to be established is the physical organization of these individuals and their consequent relation to the rest of nature. Of course, we cannot here go either into the actual physical nature of man, or into the natural conditions in which man finds himself —geological, orohydrographical, climatic and so on. The writing of history must always set out from these natural bases and their modification in the course of history through the action of man.

Men can be distinguished from animals by consciousness, by religion or anything else you like. They themselves begin to distinguish themselves from animals as soon as they begin to *produce* their means of subsistence, a step which is conditioned by their physical organization. By producing their means of subsistence men are indirectly producing their actual material life.

The way in which men produce their means of subsistence depends first of all on the nature of the actual means they find in existence and have to reproduce. This mode of production must not be considered simply as being the reproduction of the physical existence of the individuals. Rather it is a definite form of activity of these individuals, a definite form of expressing their life, a definite *mode of life* on their part. As individuals express their life, so they are. What they are, therefore, coincides with their production, both with *what* they produce and with *how* they produce. The nature of individuals thus depends on the material conditions determining their production.

This production only makes its appearance with the increase of population. In its turn this presupposes the intercourse of individuals with one another. The form of this intercourse is again determined by production.

The relations of different nations among themselves depend upon the extent to which each has developed its productive forces, the division of labour and internal intercourse. This statement is generally recognized. But not only the relation of one nation to others, but also the whole internal structure of the nation itself depends on the stage of development reached by its production and its internal and external intercourse. How far the productive forces of a nation are developed is shown most manifestly by the degree to which the division of labour has been carried. Each new productive force, in so far as it is not merely a quantitative extension of productive forces already known (for instance the bringing into cultivation of fresh land), brings about a further development of the division of labour.

The division of labour inside a nation leads at first to the separation of industrial and commercial from agricultural labour, and hence to the separation of town and country and a clash of interests between them. Its further development leads to the separation of commercial from industrial labour. At the same time through the division of labour there develop further, inside these various branches, various divisions among the individuals co-operating in definite kinds of labour. The relative position of these individual groups is determined by the methods employed in agriculture, industry and commerce (patriarchalism, slavery, estates, classes). These same conditions are to be seen (given a more developed intercourse) in the relations of different nations to one another.

The various stages of development in the division of labour are just so many different forms of ownership; i.e. the existing stage in the division of labour determines also the relations of individuals to one another with reference to the material, instrument, and product of labour.

The first form of ownership is tribal ownership. It corresponds to the undeveloped stage of production, at which a people lives by hunting and fishing, by the rearing of beasts or, in the highest stage, agriculture. In the latter case it presupposes a great mass of uncultivated stretches of land. The division of labour is at this stage still very elementary and is confined to a further extension of the natural division of labour imposed by the family. The social structure is therefore limited to an extension of the family; patriarchal family chieftains; below them the members of the tribe; finally slaves. The slavery latent in the family only develops gradually with the increase of population, the growth of wants, and with the extension of external relations, of war or of trade.

The second form is the ancient communal and State ownership which proceeds especially from the union of several tribes into a city by agreement or by conquest, and which is still accompanied by slavery. Beside communal ownership we already find movable, and later also immovable, private property developing, but as an abnormal form subordinate to communal ownership. It is only as a community that the citizens hold power over their labouring slaves, and on this account alone, therefore, they are bound to the form of communal ownership. It is the communal private property which compels the active citizens to remain in this natural form of association over against their slaves. For this reason the whole structure of society based on this communal ownership, and with it the power of the people, decays in the same measure as immovable private property evolves. The division of labour is already more developed. We already find the antagonism of town and country; later the antagonism between those states which represent town interests and those which represent country, and inside the towns themselves the antagonism between industry and maritime commerce. The class relation between citizens and slaves is now completely developed.

This whole interpretation of history appears to be contradicted by the fact of conquest. Up till now violence, war, pillage, rape and slaughter, etc. have been accepted as the driving force of history. Here we must limit ourselves to the chief points and take therefore only a striking example—the destruction of an old civilization by a barbarous people and the resulting formation of an entirely new organization of society. (Rome and the barbarians; Feudalism and Gaul; the Byzantine Empire and the Turks.) With the conquering barbarian people war itself is still, as hinted above, a regular form of intercourse, which is the more eagerly exploited as the population increases, involving the necessity of new means of production to supersede the traditional and, for it, the only possible, crude mode of production. In Italy it was, however, otherwise. The concentration of landed property (caused not only by buying-up and indebtedness but also by inheritance, since loose living being rife and marriage rare, the old families died out and their possessions fell into the hands of a few) and its conversion into grazing-land (caused not only by economic forces still operative to-day but by the importation of plundered and tribute-corn and the resultant lack of demand for Italian corn) brought about the almost total disappearance of the free population. The very slaves died out again and again, and had constantly to be replaced by new ones. Slavery remained the basis of the whole productive system. The plebeians, mid-way between freemen and slaves, never succeeded in becoming more than a proletarian rabble. Rome indeed never became more than a city; its connection with the provinces was almost exclusively political and could therefore easily be broken again by political events.

With the development of private property, we find here for the first time the same conditions which we shall find again, only on a more extensive scale, with modern private property. On the one hand the concentration of private property, which began very early in Rome (as the Licinian agrarian law proves), and proceeded very rapidly from the time of the civil wars and especially under the Emperors; on the other hand, coupled with this, the transformation of the plebeian small peasantry into a proletariat, which, however, owing to its intermediate position between propertied citizens and slaves, never achieved an independent development.

The third form of ownership is feudal or estate-property. If antiquity started out from the town and its little territory, the Middle Ages started out from the country. This different starting-point was determined by the sparseness of the population at that time, which was scattered over a large area and which received no large increase from the conquerors. In contrast to Greece and Rome, feudal development therefore extends over a much wider field, prepared by the Roman conquests and the spread of agriculture at first associated with it. The last centuries of the declining Roman Empire and its conquest by the barbarians destroyed a number of productive forces; agriculture had declined, industry had decayed for want of a market, trade had died out or been violently suspended, the rural and urban population had decreased. From these conditions and the mode of organization of the conquest determined by them, feudal property developed under the influence of the Germanic military constitution. Like tribal and communal ownership, it is based again on a community; but the directly producing class standing over against it is not, as in the case of the ancient community, the slaves, but the enserfed small peasantry. As soon as feudalism is fully developed, there also arises antagonism to the towns. The hierarchical system of land ownership, and the armed bodies of retainers associated with it, gave the nobility power over the serfs. This feudal organization was, just as much as the ancient communal ownership, an association against a subjected producing class; but the form of association and the relation to the direct producers were different because of the different conditions of production.

This feudal organization of land-ownership had its counterpart in the towns in the shape of corporative property, the feudal organization of trades. Here property consisted chiefly in the labour of each individual person. The necessity for association against the organized robber-nobility, the need for communal covered markets in an age when the industrialist was at the same time a merchant, the growing competition of the escaped serfs swarming into the rising towns, the feudal structure of the whole country: these combined to bring about the guilds. Further, the gradually accumulated capital of individual craftsmen and their stable numbers, as against the growing population, evolved the relation of journeyman and apprentice, which brought into being in the towns a hierarchy similar to that in the country.

Thus the chief form of property during the feudal epoch consisted on the one hand of landed property with serf-labour chained to it, and on the other of individual labour with small capital commanding the labour of journeymen. The organization of both was determined by the restricted conditions of production—the small-scale and primitive cultivation of the land, and the craft type of industry. There was little division of labour in the heyday of feudalism. Each land bore in itself the conflict of town and country and the division into estates was certainly strongly marked; but apart from the differentiation of princes, nobility, clergy and peasants in the country, and masters, journeymen, apprentices and soon also the rabble of casual labourers in the towns, no division of importance took place. In agriculture it was rendered difficult by the strip-system, beside which the cottage industry of the peasants themselves emerged as another factor. In industry there was no division of labour at all in the individual trades themselves, and very little between them. The separation of industry and commerce was found already in existence in older towns; in the newer it only developed later, when the towns entered into mutual relations.

The grouping of larger territories into feudal kingdoms was a necessity for the landed nobility as for the towns. The organization of the ruling class, the nobility, had, therefore, everywhere a monarch at its head.

The fact is, therefore, that definite individuals who are productively active in a definite way enter into these definite social and political relations. Empirical observation must in each separate instance bring out empirically, and without any mystification and speculation, the connection of the social and political structure with production. The social structure and the State are continually evolving out of the life-process of definite individuals, but of individuals, not as they may appear in their own or other people's imagination, but as they really are; i.e. as they are effective, produce materially, and are active under definite material limits, presuppositions and conditions independent of their will.

The production of ideas, of conceptions, of consciousness, is at first directly interwoven with the material activity and the material intercourse of men, the language of real life. Conceiving, thinking, the mental intercourse of men, appear at this stage as the direct efflux of their material behaviour. The same applies to mental production as expressed in the language of the politics, laws, morality, religion, metaphysics of a people. Men are the producers of their conceptions, ideas, etc.—real, active men, as they are conditioned by a definite development of their productive forces and of the intercourse corresponding to these, up to its furthest forms. Consciousness can never be anything else than conscious existence, and the existence of men is their actual life-process. If in all ideology men and their circumstances appear upside down as in a *camera obscura*,[2] this phenomenon arises just as much from their historical life-process as the inversion of objects on the retina does from their physical life-process.

In direct contrast to German philosophy which descends from heaven to earth, here we ascend from earth to heaven. That is to say, we do not set out from what men say, imagine, conceive, nor from men as narrated, thought of, imagined, conceived, in order to arrive at men in the flesh. We set out from real, active men, and on the basis of their real life-process we demonstrate the development of the ideological reflexes and echoes of this life-process. The phantoms formed in the human brain are also, necessarily, sublimates of their material life-process, which is empirically verifiable and bound to material premises. Morality, religion, metaphysics, all the

---

[2] *Camera obscura:* a darkened room or enclosure with an aperture through which light from external objects enters to form a reversed image of the object on the opposite surface. [T.N.M.]

rest of ideology and their corresponding forms of consciousness, thus no longer retain the semblance of independence. They have no history, no development; but men, developing their material production and their material intercourse, alter, along with this their real existence, their thinking and the products of their thinking. Life is not determined by consciousness, but consciousness by life. In the first method of approach the starting-point is consciousness taken as the living individual; in the second it is the real living individuals themselves, as they are in actual life, and consciousness is considered solely as *their* consciousness.

This method of approach is not devoid of premises. It starts out from the real premises and does not abandon them for a moment. Its premises are men, not in any fantastic isolation or abstract definition, but in their actual, empirically perceptible process of development under definite conditions. As soon as this active life-process is described, history ceases to be a collection of dead facts as it is with the empiricists (themselves still abstract), or an imagined activity of imagined subjects, as with the idealists.

Where speculation ends—in real life—there real, positive science begins: the representation of the practical activity, of the practical process of development of men. Empty talk about consciousness ceases, and real knowledge has to take its place. When reality is depicted, philosophy as an independent branch of activity loses its medium of existence. At the best its place can only be taken by a summing-up of the most general results, abstractions which arise from the observation of the historical development of men. Viewed apart from real history, these abstractions have in themselves no value whatsoever. They can only serve to facilitate the arrangement of historical material, to indicate the sequence of its separate strata. But they by no means afford a recipe or schema, as does philosophy, for neatly trimming the epochs of history. On the contrary, our difficulties begin only when we set about the observation and the arrangement—the real depiction—of our historical material, whether of a past epoch or of the present. The removal of these difficulties is governed by premises which it is quite impossible to state here, but which only the study of the actual life-process and the activity of the individuals of each epoch will make evident. We shall select here some of these abstractions, which we use to refute the ideologists, and shall illustrate them by historical examples.

History

Since we are dealing with the Germans, who do not postulate anything, we must begin by stating the first premise of all human existence, and therefore of all history, the premise namely that men must be in a position to live in order to be able to "make history." But life involves before everything else eating and drinking, a habitation, clothing and many other things. The first historical act is thus the production of the means to satisfy these needs, the production of material life itself. And indeed this is an historical act, a fundamental condition of all history, which to-day, as thousands of years ago, must daily and hourly be fulfilled merely in order to sustain human life. Even when the sensuous world is reduced to a minimum, to a stick as with Saint Bruno,[3] it presupposes the action of producing the stick. The first necessity therefore in any theory of history is to observe this fundamental fact in all its significance and all its implications and to accord it its due importance. This, as is notorious, the Germans have never done, and they have never therefore had an earthly basis for history and consequently never a historian. The French and the English, even if they have conceived the relation of this fact with so-called history only in an extremely one-sided fashion, particularly as long as they remained in the toils of political ideology, have nevertheless made the first attempts to give the writing of history a materialistic basis by being the first to write histories of civil society, of commerce and industry.

The second fundamental point is that as soon as a need is satisfied (which implies the action of satisfying, and the acquisition of an instrument), new needs are made; and this production of new needs is the first historical act. Here we recognize immediately the spiritual ancestry of the great historical wisdom of the Germans who, when they run out of positive material and when they can serve up neither theological nor political nor literary rubbish, do not write history at all, but invent the "prehistoric era." They do not, however, enlighten us as to how we proceed from this nonsensical "prehistory" to history proper; although, on the other hand, in their historical speculation they seize upon this "prehistory" with especial eagerness because they imagine themselves safe there from interference on the part of "crude facts," and, at the same time, because there they can give full rein to their speculative impulse and set up and knock down hypotheses by the thousand.

The third circumstance which, from the very first, enters into historical development, is that men, who daily remake their own life, begin to make other men, to propagate their kind: the relation between man and wife, parents and children, the *family*. The family which to begin with is the only social relationship, becomes later, when increased needs create new social relations and the increased population new needs, a subordinate one (except in Germany), and must then be treated and analysed according to the existing empirical data,[4] not according to "the concept of the family,"

---

[3] Bruno Bauer (1809–82). [T.N.M.]

[4] The building of houses. With savages each family has of course its own cave or hut like the separate family tent of the nomads. This separate domestic economy is made only the more necessary by the further development of private property. With the agricultural peoples a communal domestic economy is just as impossible as a communal cultivation of the soil. A great advance was the building of towns. In all previous periods, however, the abolition of individual economy, which is inseparable from the abolition of private property, was impossible for the simple reason that the material conditions governing it were not present. The setting-up of a communal domestic economy presupposes the development of machinery, of the use of natural forces and of many other productive forces—e.g. of water-supplies, of gas-lighting, steam-heating, etc., the removal of the antagonism of town and country. Without

as is the custom in Germany. These three aspects of social activity are not of course to be taken as three different stages, but just, as I have said, as three aspects or, to make it clear to the Germans, three "moments," which have existed simultaneously since the dawn of history and the first men, and still assert themselves in history to-day.

The production of life, both of one's own in labour and of fresh life in procreation, now appears as a double relationship: on the one hand as a natural, on the other as a social relationship. By social we understand the co-operation of several individuals, no matter under what conditions, in what manner and to what end. It follows from this that a certain mode of production, or industrial stage, is always combined with a certain mode of co-operation, or social stage, and this mode of co-operation is itself a "productive force." Further, that the multitude of productive forces accessible to men determines the nature of society, hence that the "history of humanity" must always be studied and treated in relation to the history of industry and exchange. But it is also clear now in Germany it is impossible to write this sort of history, because the Germans lack not only the necessary power of comprehension and the material but also the "evidence of their senses," for across the Rhine you cannot have any experience of these things since history has stopped happening. Thus it is quite obvious from the start that there exists a materialistic connection of men with one another, which is determined by their needs and their mode of production, and which is as old as men themselves. This connection is ever taking on new forms, and thus presents a "history" independently of the existence of any political or religious nonsense which would hold men together on its own.

Only now, after having considered four moments, four aspects of the fundamental historical relationships, do we find that man also possesses "consciousness"; but, even so, not inherent, not "pure" consciousness. From the start the "spirit" is afflicted with the curse of being "burdened" with matter, which here makes its appearance in the form of agitated layers of air, sounds, in short of language. Language is as old as consciousness, language is practical consciousness, as it exists for other men, and for that reason is really beginning to exist for me personally as well; for language, like consciousness, only arises from the need, the necessity, of intercourse with other men. Where there exists a relationship, it exists for me: the animal has no "relations" with anything, cannot have any. For the animal, its relation to others does not exist as a relation. Consciousness is therefore from the very beginning a social product, and remains so as long as men

---

these conditions a communal economy would not in itself form a new productive force; lacking any material basis and resting on a purely theoretical foundation, it would be a mere freak and would end in nothing more than a monastic economy.— What was possible can be seen in the formation of towns and the erection of communal buildings for various definite purposes (prisons, barracks, etc.). That the abolition of individual economy is inseparable from the abolition of the family is self-evident. [K.M.]

exist at all. Consciousness is at first, of course, merely consciousness concerning the immediate sensuous environment and consciousness of the limited connection with other persons and things outside the individual who is growing self-conscious. At the same time it is consciousness of nature, which first appears to men as a completely alien, all powerful and unassailable force, with which men's relations are purely animal and by which they are overawed like beasts; it is thus a purely animal consciousness of nature (natural religion).

We see here immediately: this natural religion or animal behaviour towards nature is determined by the form of society and *vice versa*. Here, as everywhere, the identity of nature and man appears in such a way that the restricted relation of men to nature determines their restricted relation to one another, and their restricted relation to one another determines men's restricted relation to nature, just because nature is as yet hardly modified historically; and, on the other hand, man's consciousness of the necessity of associating with the individuals around him is the beginning of the consciousness that he is living in society at all. This beginning is as animal as social life itself at this stage. It is mere herd-consciousness, and at this point man is only distinguished from sheep by the fact that with him consciousness takes the place of instinct or that his instinct is a conscious one.

This sheep-like or tribal consciousness receives its further development and extension through increased productivity, the increase of needs, and, what is fundamental to both of these, the increase of population. With these there develops the division of labour, which was originally nothing but the division of labour in the sexual act, then that division of labour which develops spontaneously or "naturally" by virtue of natural predisposition (e.g. physical strength), needs, accidents, etc., etc. Division of labour only becomes truly such from the moment when a division of material and mental labour appears. From this moment onwards consciousness *can* really flatter itself that it is something other than consciousness of existing practice, that it is *really* conceiving something without conceiving something *real;* from now on consciousness is in a position to emancipate itself from the world and to proceed to the formation of "pure" theory, theology, philosophy, ethics, etc. But even if this theory, theology, philosophy, ethics, etc. comes into contradiction with the existing relations, this can only occur as a result of the fact that existing social relations have come into contradiction with existing forces of production; this, moreover, can also occur in a particular national sphere of relations through the appearance of the contradiction, not within the national orbit, but between this national consciousness and the practice of other nations, i.e. between the national and the general consciousness of a nation.

Moreover, it is quite immaterial what consciousness starts to do on its own: out of all such muck we get only the one inference that these three moments, the forces of production, the state of society, and consciousness, can and must come into contradiction with one another, because the division of labour implies the possibility, nay the fact that intellectual and material activity—enjoyment and labour, production and consumption—devolve on different individuals, and that the only possibility of their not coming into contradiction lies in the negation in its turn of the division of labour. It is self-evident, moreover, that "spectres," "bonds," "the higher being," "concept," "scruple," are merely the idealistic, spiritual expression, the conception apparently of the isolated individual, the image of very empirical fetters and limitations, within which the mode of production of life, and the form of intercourse coupled with it, move.

With the division of labour, in which all these contradictions are implicit, and which in its turn is based on the natural division of labour in the family and the separation of society into individual families opposed to one another, is given simultaneously the distribution, and indeed the unequal distribution (both quantitative and qualitative), of labour and its products, hence property: the nucleus, the first form, of which lies in the family, where wife and children are the slaves of the husband. This latent slavery in the family, though still very crude, is the first property, but even at this early stage it corresponds perfectly to the definition of modern economists who call it the power of disposing of the labour-power of others. Division of labour and private property are, moreover, identical expressions: in the one the same thing is affirmed with reference to activity as is affirmed in the other with reference to the product of the activity.

Further, the division of labour implies the contradiction between the interest of the separate individual or the individual family and the communal interest of all individuals who have intercourse with one another. And indeed, this communal interest does not exist merely in the imagination, as "the general good," but first of all in reality, as the mutual interdependence of the individuals among whom the labour is divided. And finally, the division of labour offers us the first example of how, as long as man remains in natural society, that is as long as a cleavage exists between the particular and the common interest, as long therefore as activity is not voluntarily, but naturally, divided, man's own deed becomes an alien power opposed to him, which enslaves him instead of being controlled by him. For as soon as labour is distributed, each man has a particular, exclusive sphere of activity, which is forced upon him and from which he cannot escape. He is a hunter, a fisherman, a shepherd, or a critical critic, and must remain so if he does not want to lose his means of livelihood; while in communist society, where nobody has one exclusive sphere of activity but each can become accomplished in any branch he wishes, society regulates the general production and thus makes it possible for me to do one thing to-day and another to-morrow, to hunt in the morning, fish in the afternoon, rear cattle in the evening, criticize after dinner, just as I have a mind, without ever becoming hunter, fisherman, shepherd or critic.

This crystallization of social activity, this consolidation of what we ourselves produce into an objective power above us, growing out of our control, thwarting our expectations, bringing to naught our calculations, is one of the chief factors in historical development up till now. And out of this very contradiction between the interest of the individual and that of the community the latter takes an independent form as the STATE, divorced from the real interests of individual and community, and at the same time as an illusory communal life, always based, however, on the real ties existing in every family and tribal conglomeration (such as flesh and blood, language, division of labour on a larger scale, and other interests) and especially, as we shall enlarge upon later, on the classes, already determined by the division of labour, which in every such mass of men separate out, and of which one dominates all the others. It follows from this that all struggles within the State, the struggle between democracy, aristocracy and monarchy, the struggle for the franchise, etc., etc., are merely the illusory forms in which the real struggles of the different classes are fought out among one another (of this the German theoreticians have not the faintest inkling, although they have received a sufficient introduction to the subject in *The German-French Annals* and *The Holy Family*).

Further, it follows that every class which is struggling for mastery, even when its domination, as is the case with the proletariat, postulates the abolition of the old form of society in its entirety and of mastery itself, must first conquer for itself political power in order to represent its interest in turn as the general interest, a step to which in the first moment it is forced. Just because individuals seek *only* their particular interest, i.e. that not coinciding with their communal interest (for the "general good" is the illusory form of communal life), the latter will be imposed on them as an interest "alien" to them, and "independent" of them, as in its turn a particular, peculiar "general interest"; or they must meet face to face in this antagonism, as in democracy. On the other hand too, the *practical* struggle of these particular interests, which constantly *really* run counter to the communal and illusory communal interests, make *practical* intervention and control necessary through the illusory "general-interest" in the form of the State. The social power, i.e. the multiplied productive force, which arises through the co-operation of different individuals as it is determined within the division of labour, appears to these individuals, since their co-operation is not voluntary but natural, not as their own united power but as an alien force existing outside them, of the origin and end of which they are ignorant, which they thus cannot control, which on the contrary passes through a peculiar series of phases and stages independent of the will and the action of man, nay even being the prime governor of these.

This "estrangement" (to use a term which will be comprehensible to the philosophers) can, of course, only be abolished given two *practical* premises. For it to become an "intolerable" power, i.e. a power against which men make a revolution, it must necessarily have rendered the great mass of humanity "propertyless," and produced, at the same time, the contradiction of an existing world of wealth and culture, both of which conditions presuppose a great increase in productive power, a high degree of its development. And, on the other hand, this development of productive forces (which itself implies the actual empirical existence of men in their *world-historical,* instead of local, being) is absolutely necessary as a practical premise: firstly, for the reason that without it only *want* is made general, and with want the struggle for necessities and all the old filthy business would necessarily be reproduced; and secondly, because only with this universal development of productive forces is a *universal* intercourse between men established, which produces in all nations simultaneously the phenomenon of the "propertyless" mass (universal competition), makes each nation dependent on the revolutions of the others, and finally has put *world-historical,* empirically universal individuals in place of local ones. Without this, (1) Communism could only exist as a local event; (2) The forces of intercourse themselves could not have developed as universal, hence intolerable powers: they would have remained homebred superstitious conditions; and (3) Each extension of intercourse would abolish local communism. Empirically, communism is only possible as the act of the dominant peoples "all at once" or simultaneously, which presupposes the universal development of productive forces and the world-intercourse bound up with them. How otherwise could property have had a history at all, have taken on different forms, and landed property, for instance, according to the different premises given, have proceeded in France from parcellation to centralization in the hands of a few, in England from centralization in the hands of a few to parcellation, as is actually the case today? Or how does it happen that trade, which after all is nothing more than the exchange of products of various individuals and countries, rules the whole world through the relation of supply and demand—a relation which, as an English economist says, hovers over the earth like the Fate of the Ancients, and with invisible hand allots fortune and misfortune to men, sets up empires and overthrows empires, causes nations to rise and to disappear—while with the abolition of the basis of private property, with the communistic regulation of production (and, implicit in this, the destruction of the alien relation between men and what they themselves produce), the power of the relation of supply and demand is dissolved into nothing, and men get exchange, production, the mode of their mutual relation, under their own control again?

Communism is for us not a stable state which is to be established, an *ideal* to which reality will have to adjust itself. We call communism the *real* movement which abolishes the present state of things. The conditions of this movement result from the premises now in existence. Besides, the world-market is presupposed by the mass of propertyless workers—labour-power cut off as a mass from capital or from even a limited satisfaction—and therefore no longer by the mere precariousness of labour, which, not giving an assured livelihood, is often lost through competition. The proletariat can thus only exist *world-historically,* just as communism, its movement, can only have a "world-historical" existence. World-historical existence of individuals, i.e. existence of individuals which is directly linked up with world history.

The form of intercourse determined by the existing productive forces at all previous historical stages, and in its turn determining these, is *civil society*. This, as is clear from what we have said above, has as its premises and basis the simple family and the multiple, the so-called tribe, the more precise determinants of which are enumerated in our remarks above. Already here we see how this civil society is the true source and theatre of all history, and how nonsensical is the conception of history held hitherto, which neglects the real relationships and confines itself to high-sounding dramas of princes and states. Civil society embraces the whole material intercourse of individuals within a definite stage of the development of productive forces. It embraces the whole commercial and industrial life of this stage and, in so far, transcends the State and the nation, though, on the other hand again, it must assert itself towards foreign peoples as nationality, and inwardly must organize itself as State. The word "civil society" emerged in the eighteenth century, when property relationships had already extricated themselves from the ancient and medieval communal society. Civil society as such only develops with the bourgeoisie; the social organization evolving directly out of production and commerce, which in all ages forms the basis of the State and of the rest of the idealistic superstructure, has, however, always been designated by the same name.

QUESTIONS FOR STUDY AND DISCUSSION

1. Is Marx justified in his idea of Hegelian comprehension?
2. Evaluate his argument for the connection between man's nature and production.
3. Has Marx grounds for his position on the development of morality, religion, and metaphysics?
4. Can one justify the claim that "consciousness is at first . . . merely consciousness concerning the immediate, sensuous environment"?
5. How does one substantiate the statement that nature "first appears to man as a completely alien, all-powerful, and unassailable force"?
6. Do we have any evidence for another view of the State?

Religion as an Ideology

We will now in addition deal only briefly with religion, since the latter stands furthest away from material life and seems to be most alien to it. Religion arose in very primitive times from erroneous, primitive conceptions of men about their own nature and external nature surrounding them. Every ideology, however, once it has arisen, develops in connection with the given concept-material, and develops this material further; otherwise it would not be an ideology, that is, occupation with thoughts as with independent entities, developing independently and subject only to their own laws. That the material life conditions of the persons inside whose heads this thought process goes on in the last resort determine the course of this process remains of necessity unknown to these persons, for otherwise there would be an end to all ideology. These original religious notions, therefore, which in the main are common to each group of kindred peoples, develop, after the group separates, in a manner peculiar to each people, according to the conditions of life falling to their lot. For a number of groups of peoples, and particularly for the Aryans (so-called Indo-Europeans) this process has been shown in detail by comparative mythology. The gods thus fashioned within each people were national gods, whose domain extended no farther than the national territory which they were to protect; on the other side of its boundaries other gods held undisputed sway. They could continue to exist, in imagination, only as long as the nation existed; they fell with its fall. The Roman world empire, the economic conditions of whose origin we do not need to examine here, brought about this downfall of the old nationalities. The old national gods decayed, even those of the Romans, which also were patterned to suit only the narrow confines of the city of Rome. The need to complement the world empire by means of a world religion was clearly revealed in the attempts made to provide in Rome recognition and altars for all the foreign gods to the slightest degree respectable alongside of the indigenous ones. But a new world religion is not to be made in this fashion, by imperial decree. The new world religion, Christianity, had already quietly come into being, out of a mixture of generalized Oriental, particularly Jewish, theology, and vulgarized Greek, particularly Stoic, philosophy. What it originally looked like has to be first laboriously discovered, since its official form, as it has been handed down to us, is merely that in which it became the state religion to which purpose

From pp. 397–400 of Friedrich Engels, *Feuerbach and the End of Classical German Philosophy,* in *Selected Works of Marx and Engels,* vol. II. Copyright 1958 by Foreign Languages Publishing House, Moscow. Reprinted by permission of the publisher.

it was adapted by the Council of Nicaea. The fact that already after 250 years it became the state religion suffices to show that it was the religion in correspondence with the conditions of the time. In the Middle Ages, in the same measure as feudalism developed, Christianity grew into the religious counterpart to it, with a corresponding feudal hierarchy. And when the burghers began to thrive, there developed, in opposition to feudal Catholicism, the Protestant heresy, which first appeared in Southern France, among the Albigenses, at the time the cities there reached the highest point of their florescence. The Middle Ages had attached to theology all the other forms of ideology—philosophy, politics, jurisprudence—and made them subdivisions of theology. It thereby constrained every social and political movement to take on a theological form. The sentiments of the masses were fed with religion to the exclusion of all else; it was therefore necessary to put forward their own interests in a religious guise in order to produce an impetuous movement. And just as the burghers from the beginning brought into being an appendage of propertyless urban plebeians, day labourers, and servants of all kinds, belonging to no recognized social estate, precursors of the later proletariat, so likewise heresy soon became divided into a burgher-moderate heresy and a plebeian-revolutionary one, the latter an abomination to the burgher heretics themselves.

The ineradicability of the Protestant heresy corresponded to the invincibility of the rising burghers. When these burghers had become sufficiently strengthened, their struggle against the feudal nobility, which till then had been predominantly local, began to assume national dimensions. The first great action occurred in Germany—the so-called Reformation. The burghers were neither powerful enough nor sufficiently developed to be able to unite under their banner the remaining rebellious estates—the plebians of the towns, the lower nobility and the peasants on the land. At first the nobles were defeated; the peasants rose in a revolt which formed the peak of the whole revolutionary struggle; the cities left them in the lurch, and thus the revolution succumbed to the armies of the secular princes who reaped the whole profit. Thenceforward Germany disappears for three centuries from the ranks of countries playing an independent active part in history. But beside the German Luther appeared the Frenchman Calvin. With true French acuity he put the bourgeois character of the Reformation in the forefront, republicanized and democratized the Church. While the Lutheran Reformation in Germany degenerated and reduced the country to rack and ruin, the Calvinist Reformation served as a banner for the republicans in Geneva, in Holland and in Scotland, freed Holland from Spain and from the German Empire and provided the ideological costume for the second act of the bourgeois revolution, which was taking place in England. Here Calvinism justified itself as the true religious disguise of the interests of the bourgeoisie of that time, and on this account did not attain full recognition when the revolution ended in 1689 in a compromise between one part of the nobility and the bourgeoisie. The English state

Church was re-established; but not in its earlier form of a Catholicism which had the king for its pope, being, instead, strongly Calvinized. The old state Church had celebrated the merry Catholic Sunday and had fought against the dull Calvinist one. The new, bourgeoisified Church introduced the latter, which adorns England to this day.

In France, the Calvinist minority was suppressed in 1685 and either Catholicized or driven out of the country. But what was the good? Already at that time the freethinker Pierre Bayle was at the height of his activity, and in 1694 Voltaire was born. The forcible measures of Louis XIV only made it easier for the French bourgeoisie to carry through its revolution in the irreligious, exclusively political form which alone was suited to a developed bourgeoisie. Instead of Protestants, freethinkers took their seats in the national assemblies. Thereby Christianity entered into its final stage. It had become incapable for the future of serving any progressive class as the ideological garb of its aspirations. It became more and more the exclusive possession of the ruling classes and these apply it as a mere means of government, to keep the lower classes within bounds. Moreover, each of the different classes uses its own appropriate religion: the landed nobility—Catholic Jesuitism or Protestant orthodoxy; the liberal and radical bourgeoisie—rationalism; and it makes little difference whether these gentlemen themselves believe in their respective religions or not.

We see, therefore: religion, once formed, always contains traditional material, just as in all ideological domains tradition forms a great conservative force. But the transformations which this material undergoes spring from class relations, that is to say, out of the economic relations of the people who execute these transformations. And here that is sufficient.

FOR STUDY AND DISCUSSION

Criticize the evidence Engels offers for his view of religion.

TOPICS FOR DISCUSSION AND TERM PAPERS

A.

1. What does philosophy mean for Hegel? for Marx and Engels?
2. Are these thinkers metaphysical in the traditional sense? If not, what meaning should be attached to their use of the word "metaphysics"? What does Hegel say about being, cause, and substance?
3. What does Hegel mean by truth? Show how his notion differs from Kant's idea of knowledge.
4. What do we emphasize when we talk about the "dialectical tradition" in philosophy?
5. How does the Marxist dialectic differ from the Hegelian?
6. Explain the role of history in dialectical thought.
7. On what grounds can Marxist thought be classified as a dialectical materialism?
8. Is there an opposition between idealistic and materialistic thinking? Explain your answer.
9. What is the place of religion in Hegelian thought?
10. How might the Christian reply to the Marxist "economic analysis" of religion?

B.

1. Is there a relationship between Hegel's insistence that philosophical thought be a union of form with content and Aquinas's notion that Being and Truth are convertible?
2. What does a "process" metaphysics owe to Hegel?
3. Is it fair to say that naturalists have falsely assumed that Hegel took over uncriticized Kantian-type categories, and have thus obscured his notion of "the Absolute"?
4. Is it possible to have anything but an abstract metaphysics without dialectical thought?
5. What does Sartre's *en soi–pour soi* owe to Hegel?
6. What does Sartre mean when he says that the only philosophy today is Marxism, whereas existentialism is one of many subordinate ideologies?

RECOMMENDED READINGS

Primary Sources

Hegel, G. W. F. *Phenomenology of Mind,* 2nd ed. Trans. and with Introd. and notes by J. B. Baillie. New York: Macmillan Co., 1931.

————. *Reason in History: A General Introduction to the Philosophy of History.* Trans. and with Introd. by Robert S. Hartman. New York: Liberal Arts Press, 1953. This short paperback is an application of Hegel's dialectical method in the areas of human liberty and the State, and in the general movement of history.

Kant, Immanuel. *Critique of Practical Reason, and Other Writings in Moral Philosophy.* Trans., ed., and with Introd. by L. W. Beck. Chicago: University of Chicago Press, 1949.

————. *Prolegomena to Any Future Metaphysics.* Trans. and ed. by Paul Carus. La Salle, Ill.: Open Court Publishing Co., 1933. An abridged popularization of the difficult *Critique of Pure Reason.*

Marx, Karl, and Friedrich Engels. *Selected Works of Marx and Engels.* 2 vols. Moscow: Foreign Languages Publishing House, 1958.

Commentaries

Berlin, Isaiah. *Karl Marx: His Life and Environment,* 2nd ed. London: Oxford University Press, 1948. Eminently clear and readable, without heavy philosophical discussion.

Cornu, Auguste. *Origins of Marxian Thought,* Springfield, Ill.: Charles C. Thomas, 1957. A Marxian-inclined presentation of the formative influences on Marx's thought: rationalism, romanticism, Hegel, the Hegelian Left.

Dupré, Louis. *The Philosophical Foundations of Marxism.* New York: Harcourt, Brace & World, 1966. A direct introduction to Marx's texts, this analytical commentary familiarizes the reader with the philosopher's concepts, terminology, and method of thinking. Chapters 1 and 2 show the development of Hegel's social theory and give a detailed discussion of the *Philosophy of Right.*

Findlay, J. N. *Hegel: A Reexamination.* New York: Collier Books, 1962. Pages 27–33 offer the reader biographical and literary data. In general, a cursory glance at Hegel's entire system, aimed principally at an unsympathetic British audience.

Hook, Sidney. *From Hegel to Marx: Studies in the Intellectual Development of Karl Marx.* Ann Arbor, Mich.: University of Michigan Press, 1962. A bit out of date and weighted in favor of Marx but interesting reading and not difficult.

Kaufmann, Walter. *Hegel: Reinterpretation, Texts, and Commentary.* Garden City, N.Y.: Doubleday & Co., 1965. The beginner will find the chronology, pp. 21–25, helpful, and also the discussion of the influence of Schiller and Goethe on Hegel, pp. 44–58. The section on Hegel's terminology, pp. 158–62, is brief but useful. Prof. Kaufmann has made some important changes in Baillie's translation of the Preface in his translation, pp. 369–465; his commentary will be useful on certain points. In general, the beginner should be warned that an apodictic style does not change *an* interpretation into *the* interpretation.

Koerner, S. *Kant.* Baltimore: Penguin Books, 1955. A clear presentation of the purpose and principal arguments of the three *Critiques.*

Kroner, Richard. "Hegel's Philosophical Development," the Introduction to Hegel's *Early Theological Writings.* Trans. by T. M. Knox. New York: Harper & Row, 1961. This is an excellent presentation of the genesis and thrust of Hegel's thought.

Loewenberg, Jacob. *Hegel's Phenomenology: Dialogues on the Life of Mind.* La Salle, Ill.: Open Court Publishing Co., 1965. A commentary on the *Phenomenology* written in an urbane style. The author attempts to bring out some of the issues of the *Phenomenology,* but the beginner might be confused by a rather formal vocabulary.

Löwith, Karl. *From Hegel to Nietzsche: The Revolution in Nineteenth-Century Thought.* Trans. from the 3rd German ed. by David E. Green. New York: Holt, Rinehart & Winston, 1964. Not always easy reading, but an excellent coverage of intellectual history, with special reference to the problems of man, of history, and of Christianity from Goethe to Nietzsche.

Marcuse, Herbert. "The Foundations of Hegel's Philosophy," Part I, in *Reason and Revolution: Hegel and the Rise of Social Theory,* 2nd ed. New York: Humanities Press, 1955. Pp. 8–248. This covers the same ground as Kroner.

McKeon, Richard. *Freedom and History: The Semantics of Philosophical Controversies and Ideological Conflicts.* New York: Farrar, Straus & Giroux, 1952. Although the work is not devoted to Hegel, pp. 19–68 afford a good idea of the dialectical mode of thought. The student might supplement this with Findlay's treatment of Hegel in the above-cited work, Ch. 3, "The Dialectical Method," pp. 58–82.

Mehring, Franz. *Karl Marx: The Story of His Life.* Trans. by Edward Fitzgerald. Ann Arbor, Mich.: University of Michigan Press, 1962. A popular presentation, easily readable.

Mure, G. R. G. *The Philosophy of Hegel.* Oxford: Oxford University Press, 1965. A short, very readable, and comprehensive view of Hegel, for the beginner.

Stace, W. T. *The Philosophy of Hegel: A Systematic Exposition.* New York: Dover Publications, 1955. This book is dated and most contemporary Hegelian scholars would not consider it wholly reliable. However, the student might profitably read "Greek Idealism and Hegel," pp. 3–31.

Tucker, Robert C. *Philosophy and Myth in Karl Marx.* Cambridge, Eng.: Cambridge University Press, 1961. "Marx in Changing Perspective," pp. 11–27. A glimpse into the problem of the "different" look at Marx today.

Walsh, W. H. *Philosophy of History: An Introduction.* New York: Harper & Bros., 1960. "Speculative Philosophy of History," pp. 137–54. A brief, clear presentation, although the scholar might cavil about certain points.

Wetter, Gustave A. *Dialectical Materialism: A Historical and Systematic Survey of Philosophy in the Soviet Union.* Trans. from the German by Peter Heath. London: Routledge & Kegan Paul, 1958. After a brief but adequate historical presentation of Marx, Wetter opens the door in a clear but magisterial way to Marxism as it has developed in the Soviet Union.

PART THREE

AMERICAN PRAGMATIC-NATURALIST THOUGHT:

James
Peirce
Dewey

EDITED BY

Robert J. Roth, S.J.

FORDHAM UNIVERSITY

AMERICAN PRAGMATIC-NATURALIST THOUGHT:
James
Peirce
Dewey

Introduction

Historical Background

At the outset, one might well ask: Is there such a discipline as a pragmatic-naturalist metaphysics? If we heed the most outspoken among men of this tradition, the answer would be clearly and emphatically in the negative. It would not be straying too far from the truth to say that the development of American philosophy from the late nineteenth century has been in large measure a polemic against metaphysics, which in the traditional Aristotelian sense can be roughly defined as the knowledge or science of being as being.

On the other hand, in spite of frequent disclaimers, we find the word "metaphysics" occurring often in the literature of the pragmatists and naturalists. In this they follow the lead of John Dewey who was willing to accept the term, provided that it be understood as "cognizance of the generic traits of existence." [1] Actually this is a definition that could be susceptible of an Aristotelian interpretation, though, as we shall see, the differences between the two traditions are considerable. [2]

We could better understand what the pragmatist and naturalist mean by metaphysics if we see why they reacted against metaphysics in the Aristotelian sense. In the early nineteenth century America became increasingly

---

[1] *Experience and Nature* (New York: W. W. Norton & Co., 1929), p. 51. See also p. 412.

[2] Some American naturalists have attempted to interpret Aristotle in terms of process metaphysics. See, for example, the references to John Herman Randall, Jr., and George Boas in the bibliography.

interested in science.[3] Conditions in America stimulated this interest since the growing nation was continually facing problems in the areas of engineering, commerce, and industry that demanded solutions only science could provide. It was natural that military, educational, and government agencies should concern themselves with preparing men to fill the needs created by these problems. Existing colleges and universities reshaped their academic departments and curricula to give more attention to science, while new institutions for scientific research and training sprang into being.

Scientific interest affected philosophical thinking as well; in fact some of the leading philosophers had strong scientific backgrounds. For example, William James (1842–1910), an outstanding figure in the pragmatist movement, received an early training in medicine and later became the "father of American psychology." Charles Sanders Peirce (1839–1914), only recently recognized as one of our greatest philosophers, was actually a philosopher of science, for he did original and pioneering work in the fields of logical and mathematical analysis, yet still had time to become proficient in geodesy and meteorology, psychophysics and photometry. John Dewey (1859–1952), our most influential naturalist philosopher, was familiar with the main scientific currents though he was not a scientist.

William James in 1906 summed up the influence of science and the empirical spirit when he said: "Never were as many men of a decidedly empiricist proclivity in existence as there are at the present day. Our children, one may say, are almost born scientific." [4] The thesis of John Dewey's *Reconstruction in Philosophy* (1920) and *Experience and Nature* (1925) is that philosophy must be entirely rethought, for "modern science, modern industry and politics, have presented us with an immense amount of material foreign to, often inconsistent with, the most prized intellectual and moral heritage of the western world." [5]

Influence of Empiricism

The American philosophers of this period took as their models the empiricist philosophers of an earlier era. The works of men like Francis Bacon (1561–1626) and David Hume (1711–76) became sources for inspiration and guidance. Though pragmatists and naturalists have differed with these British empiricists on many points, they took from them the empirical method which was to become their model in both philosophy and science. For such a method, the only criterion for our knowledge of reality is sense experience, and this becomes the starting point as well as the limit for all knowledge. Anything that goes beyond such experience is either denied or at least considered as unknowable and consequently irrelevant. This immediately undercuts many of those objects that have traditionally

---

[3] Merle Curti, *The Growth of American Thought* (New York: Harper & Bros., 1943), pp. 318–43.

[4] *Pragmatism* (New York: Longmans, Green & Co., 1907), p. 14.

[5] *Experience and Nature*, p. ii.

been considered to be within the scope of metaphysics. Such objects would be substance, nature and essence, cause and finality. Finally, the whole of natural theology is rejected, since by limiting knowledge to sense experience one also gives up all possibility of arriving at rational knowledge of a transcendent being or God.

Moreover, the empirical method adopts the fundamental position that every conclusion reached in a line of thought or reasoning is merely a hypothesis—it is always subject to further test and experiment. One can never say that he has come to the end of inquiry, for every position adopted is merely tentative. It may serve as a guide for thought and conduct, but further investigation may dictate that it be changed or even rejected. This again leads to the position that there are no absolute, unchanging principles, whether in the field of knowledge, reality, or morals.

A second result of the rise of science was to shift the emphasis of metaphysical inquiry. According to the pragmatist and naturalist, Aristotelian metaphysics had stressed the permanent aspect of reality almost to the exclusion of everything else. With the Greeks, philosophical inquiry had taken its rise in the effort to reconcile permanence and change. The former was emphasized with Parmenides (530–444 B.C.), while the latter became the exclusive category for Heraclitus (c. 540–475 B.C.). The attempt of Plato (c. 427–347 B.C.) to harmonize the two succeeded only in giving prominence again to the eternal and fixed, while change, though recognized, was relegated to a position of minor importance. Aristotle (384–322 B.C.) gave place to both with his distinction between act and potency, form and matter; but in the eyes of pragmatists and naturalists both Aristotle and the whole Aristotelian tradition as absorbed into the scholasticism of the Middle Ages became almost exclusively a search for permanence and stability. Fixed norms and absolute principles, whether in the order of logic or of reality, had become the all-absorbing preoccupation. To the degree to which permanence and stability were stressed, change and instability were ignored.

To the pragmatist and the naturalist who began to feel the first fresh breezes of science, this seemed to be a rather curious situation. The most obvious, and for the scientist the most exciting, aspect of reality was not permanence but change. With improved instruments and techniques for research and experiment, nature revealed itself in ways never before known. Objects could be subjected to new conditions that would produce new changes, thus enabling the scientist to expand his knowledge of the material universe.

In addition, not only could new relations *within* things be discovered, but more importantly new relations *between* things could be instituted. In this manner, objects could be brought together in novel ways giving rise to whole new series of activities and whole new categories of scientific objects. In fact, the scientist came to realize that an object could not be truly understood in isolation but only in relation to other things. And when it was discovered that there was almost no limit to the ways in which things could be combined and recombined, the possibilities of fresh combinations became almost infinite.

In a sense, America was discovering in the late nineteenth and early twentieth centuries what Europe had discovered as early as the sixteenth and seventeenth centuries. But the impact was perhaps even greater. For one thing America did not have to go through the scientific awakening in slow stages. As soon as conditions were favorable, she had only to avail herself of advances that had already been made in other times and places. Moreover, America had at its disposal almost limitless and untapped natural resources from which to draw, and when the knowledge and techniques were mastered, the materials were at hand with which to fashion an advanced stage of science, industry, and technology. It is small wonder that the men of the times were intoxicated with the prospects of a scientific age that would surpass the highest hopes of the post-medieval scientists.

The Resulting Metaphysics

These new currents of thought could not but have an effect upon philosophical thinking. Philosophers of the pragmatic-naturalist tradition felt that Aristotelian metaphysics, with what they took to be its emphasis on permanence and stability to the neglect and even distrust of change, was totally inadequate for the new trend that science had initiated. For them, the older metaphysics was dead because it was essentially a "static metaphysics." They were in favor of discarding it altogether, but, as we have seen, one could still speak of it since interest would center upon what Dewey called the "generic traits" of reality. However, the metaphysics of the future was to be a "process metaphysics," namely, one that would do away with substance as primary category and give prominence to relations, events, and interactions, with room for surprises and novelties in nature.

From this point of view, reality is not made up of static and disconnected objects; rather, it comprises interactions, or things in relation. This challenged the stress that traditional metaphysics had placed upon the "ontological status" of objects, as though one knows what a thing is when he can define it in terms of substance, nature, essence, and accident. The process metaphysician maintains that we neither begin our knowledge of external objects nor complete such knowledge by defining them as being "out there," in isolation, as it were, from other things.

This point of view has profound implications for one's whole approach to knowledge. For example, what does it mean to say that we "know" an object? The pragmatist and naturalist claim that traditional epistemologies have adopted a "spectator" theory of knowledge, in which knowledge becomes merely the blank staring at reality in order to reproduce it in some cognitive way. According to the new approach, however, we do not know objects by reproducing them but by interacting with them. An object is said to be "hard" if it is resistant to the touch; we explain what we mean by a chair when we show how we act toward it. Digestion can be understood only in terms of how it interacts with food. Even the word "food" is meaningless except in relation to a digestive system. The primary category, then, for the process metaphysician is "interaction" or "transaction." This relational theory of metaphysics sees meaning in things as they interact, not as they are viewed in isolation.

In all this the process metaphysician feels that he is being faithful to the data of science. The physicist has gradually altered his view of the material universe, seeing it first as inert matter, then as matter in motion, and finally as matter in action and reaction. The biologist has appreciated the importance of the organism's interaction with the environment. A living being ceases to be an organism if torn from its environment. Once the roots of a tree, for example, are taken from the soil, the tree withers and dies.

But there is more to it than this. Interaction between organism and environment is necessary, not only for the continued existence of the living being but also for its continued growth. In fact, if the organism ceases to grow, it will die. Life means essentially growth and development; these in turn mean interaction with environment. The living being is not something there, in static equilibrium. It is something in action, or in interaction. Further, the living being is not something that simply *is*—that is, ontologically complete. It is rather something that is *becoming,* or in process. As long as the organism lives, it is changing and developing, and we can never say at any one moment that it is finished. To do so would be to attempt intellectually to wrench the being from its whole context, without which it is meaningless.

Evolution has given added significance to this concept, for it is a process, a coming-to-be of new forms of living beings. Had organisms repeated the same cycle of birth, growth, and decay, evolution would never have taken place. As a process evolution is possible because living beings are not static but are able to take new turns and new steps, to break out of routine patterns into novelties so that new forms of life could emerge. Even now one cannot say that evolution is finished, for as human intelligence understands and controls the secrets of the living cell, the development of new organisms becomes more possible.

Psychology has verified on the human level what has been discovered on the level of physics and biology. Theories of personality have stressed the fact that the human being becomes a person only to the extent to which he interacts with his environment. The human being must find outside himself interests that engage his attention, his striving, and his efforts. In a manner analogous to that of the biological organism, the human being needs the environment that for him includes the world of matter, and especially the world of people and social institutions.

From this viewpoint, a person cannot merely be thought of ontologically, that is, as finished and completed, as though external conditions affect him peripherally or not at all. So long as the human being exists, he is in process of change and growth. He is what he is by reason of his past strivings and actions, and what he will be tomorrow will depend on his present interaction with his surroundings.

The process metaphysician, then, sees all evidence pointing toward the emphasis on change and development. Of all characteristics of real things, this seems to be the most general; it becomes for him the primary category. In many cases, of course, he will explicitly deny that there is anything beyond change and hence will reject what the traditional metaphysician has called substance, essence, or nature. In most cases, however, he will simply say that by reason of his methodology these cannot be discovered; hence they are meaningless and, by reason of their failure to answer the pressing questions raised by a scientific age, irrelevant.

Pragmatic-Naturalist Metaphysics

With this as background, it is possible to outline the key metaphysical problems of the pragmatic-naturalist tradition. We will begin with American naturalism. Naturalists admit that their position is not so much a set of doctrines as an outlook on life. Moreover, on the academic philosophical level at least, naturalism did not grow in conscious, orderly stages. Rather it was the product of slow development in the minds of philosophers who had the same insights and who came to agree on the same basic points, even though they developed them in their own way. It is possible, however, to set down the following as included among the "generic traits of existence" mentioned by Dewey.

1. Naturalism as a metaphysics is limited to reality that can be known by the senses. This is characteristic of the British empirical method and results in a denial of those objects that are usually associated with Aristotelian metaphysics. Also it is intramundane, that is, it excludes anything that transcends finite reality.

2. The primary interest of the naturalist was in the universe as changing. Change is the most prominent trait; in fact, it is the only trait that leads to genuine knowledge of the world in which we live. In this respect, the naturalist had assumed the serious task of constructing a metaphysics that would adequately describe reality in terms of change.

On the level of the living being, evolution has served to join together these characteristics of naturalistic metaphysics into a coherent system. It accounts for two things. First, it explains the interaction of organisms with environment, leading not only to the development of the individual living being but also to the onward progress of evolution as a whole. Whether viewed at any one point or considered as a continuing process, evolution includes the basic elements of a process metaphysics on the organic level —interaction, change, growth, and novelties.

Second, evolution gives a unified picture of all living beings: it proposes that all organisms, including man, come from nature, develop in nature, and find their ultimate fulfillment in nature. Naturalism recognizes that animals are superior to plants, and men to animals, but considers this superiority as one of complexity of operation, with no essential difference or transcendence of one over the other. Evolution presents a continuous picture of all material beings, from inorganic matter to man.

Although naturalism is emphatic in its assertion that reality is confined to material things and that all material reality including man is strictly continuous, this does not mean that reality is reduced to the "atoms-in-motion" theory of the late nineteenth century. The new science stresses the quantitative aspect of reality; it was precisely in the joining of material phenomena with mathematics that science was able to accelerate at such an astounding rate. The late 1800s saw the high-water mark of mechanistic determinism in the attempt to reduce all reality to the interaction of physicochemical laws.

No one resisted this tendency more than the naturalist. He objected to an exclusively quantitative view of reality. Though in agreement with the mechanistic emphasis on sense experience as the criterion of knowledge and on the general scientific methodology of test and hypothesis, he refused to screen out the qualitative from reality. In this he agreed with traditional philosophies that attempt to preserve the natural values all men cherish —love, freedom, patriotism, friendship, loyalty, and self-sacrifice.

This profoundly affected his view of the human person. The naturalist in no sense reduced man to a high-grade vegetable. He regarded the human person as worthy of respect, as a being who has the ability to determine his own destiny and to develop a culture and civilization that includes science, technology, art, and political and social institutions for the enrichment of man.

It is on the level of the human that the naturalist saw the most fruitful application of the category of interaction. As we have seen, the naturalist viewed things as metaphysically in relation with other things. A being in separation is unintelligible. A living being in isolation ceases to be alive and consequently there is an end to all possibility of development. The same applies to the human level. Naturalism stands for a sincere regard for and interest in matter and the universe as possibilities for human growth and development. It maintains that man can be truly human only through participation in interests that concern his earthly existence.

Many men of the late nineteenth and early twentieth centuries had discovered this insight into the importance of matter through their studies in biology, evolution, and psychology. These sciences taught the same lesson —the living organism, from the most primitive cell to man, can grow and develop only to the extent to which it engages in active interaction with the environment. The complexity of the environment will vary with the complexity of the organism until we reach the human person. Man, then, has in his environment all those things that make for true human growth: science and technology, education, politics, social and economic institutions. The naturalist saw that all these conditions were necessary for man to develop his potentialities as a human being. In this insight the naturalist proposed to offer a corrective to idealist philosophies. The idealist took man from interaction with nature and seriously hindered possibilities for growth of personality by emphasizing values that are above and outside nature, and by looking upon the world of matter and natural values as detrimental.

What has been said so far has referred explicitly to naturalism, but on almost all these points the pragmatist would be in agreement. In fact, it is difficult to distinguish naturalism from pragmatism as these two developed in America.

The word "pragmatism" was coined by Charles Sanders Peirce, but it was popularized and brought into the mainstream of American philosophy by William James. Its influence has been enormous; there is scarcely an aspect of American philosophy that has not felt the effects of pragmatism, particularly as a method of arriving at truth. Since this aspect of pragmatism is more pertinent to the philosophy of man than to metaphysics, it will not be treated in this volume.[6] We should note, however, that although Jamesian pragmatism contains other elements, some of which have been severely criticized, it is as a criterion of truth and indeed as a new meaning of truth that pragmatism has survived and has exerted its greatest influence.

As we have already pointed out, pragmatism and naturalism are in general agreement on the points thus far developed. In regard to the problem of God, or what might loosely be called "natural theology," we shall see the important differences between the two.

Natural Theology

Natural theology is the discipline that attempts to demonstrate God's existence, essence, and relation to the universe. It is an extension of metaphysics, its culmination and supreme moment.

From our previous discussions the reader can surmise that the pragmatist and naturalist ruled out any possibility of a natural theology and consequently any proof for God's existence through human reason. This followed from the methodology that limits human knowledge to what can be grasped by sense experience. Anything transcending such experience was immediately dismissed as nonexistent, or at least as unknowable.

More particularly, the principle of causality plays a key role in any metaphysical proof for God's existence. Hume had constructed the classi-

---

[6] See Part III of *Reflections on Man*, also in this series.

cal empirical argument against this principle and thereby set the trend for practically all future empiricism. Immanuel Kant (1724–1804) attempted to answer Hume's critique and to reinstate causality in the universe. But he was still enough of an empiricist to deny that causality applies to things beyond our sensory experience.

Critique of the Absolute

In this regard, the pragmatist and the naturalist were heirs of both Hume and Kant. They accepted Hume's basic empiricism regarding the limitation of knowledge to what can be perceived by the senses, and, while not going as far as Hume's philosophical scepticism, particularly in his critique of causality, they agreed with Kant that knowledge cannot be applied to immaterial or extramundane beings. In so doing, they cut off the possibility of a metaphysical proof for the existence of a first cause, an Absolute, a God.

Furthermore, this tradition leveled a frontal attack against the very notion of God as it had been treated by the various philosophical schools. For one thing, it reacted against all forms of idealism, whether of the German, British, or American variety, that considered God under the title of the "absolute." To the pragmatic-naturalist mind idealism reduced God to an "all-explainer" who could reconcile all seeming inconsistencies in nature. In a derogatory sense, God was looked upon as a tent that covers over everything, unifies everything, and gives meaning to everything, no matter how irrational or disorganized reality might seem to be.

William James continually criticized the idealist position. He chided Gottfried Wilhelm Leibniz (1646–1716) for attempting to show that the suffering of souls in hell is greatly offset by experiencing all the goods of our best possible world.[7] He showed in sharp terms his displeasure at Leibniz' utter disregard for the contingencies and inconsistencies in the world. He had strong criticism, too, for the British type of idealism as exemplified by F. H. Bradley (1846–1924), and in the Hibbert Lectures given in 1908 at Manchester College, Oxford, and published as a book entitled *A Pluralistic Universe* (1909), James developed his own philosophy to show that the affairs of the world are not neatly tied together by some cold and disinterested Absolute.

John Dewey, the leading spokesman in America for naturalism, likewise took up the attack against all forms of idealism. In his early philosophical development he was attracted to G. W. F. Hegel (1770–1831). Dewey felt within himself an intense craving for unity against separations in both philosophy and religion, "divisions by way of isolation of self from the world, of soul from body, of nature from God."[8] For a time, Hegel's Absolute supplied the unity he needed. But his gradual dissatisfaction with

---

[7] *Pragmatism,* pp. 23–27.
[8] "From Absolutism to Experimentalism," in *Contemporary American Philosophy,* ed. by George P. Adams and William P. Montague (New York: Macmillan Co., 1930), II, 13–27.

all forms of theism, and the discovery of the unity of things in natural relationships, caused him to substitute interactions between objects in the universe. He did not feel it necessary any longer to unite things artificially by
an all-embracing Absolute; things were already unified in interactions. For
this reason Sidney Hook states that Dewey naturalized Hegel; [9] he substituted the natural unity of interactions for the divine unity of an Absolute.

The pragmatists and naturalists also had difficulty with the notion of
God as developed by Aristotelian and Scholastic metaphysics. Notions
such as aseity, immutability, infinity, and necessity were simply beyond
minds and temperaments geared to the concrete human needs of daily living. God and religion for James had to be relevant: God had to touch the
wellsprings of human wants and religion had to bind up all aspects of life
to give them meaning and purpose. The notions as developed in treatises of
natural theology were too much the product of "logical machines," [10] and
though fit for the lecture hall they were incapable of touching daily life.

Alfred North Whitehead (1861–1947) also had extreme difficulty in
ordering his own ideas about God. The struggle that went on in his mind in
the attempt to adopt a position that was intellectually acceptable is reflected
in the fact that his natural theology is perhaps the most difficult and least
satisfying part of his philosophy. He faced the problem of reconciling seemingly contradictory notions—for example, God's creative action and immutability.

The problems which James, Dewey, and Peirce faced in working out a
philosophy of God are neither easy nor superficial. They have vexed metaphysicians of all ages. These American philosophers, in confronting traditional difficulties, did not have the traditional metaphysical tools to cope
with them and they found it necessary to strike out afresh. While disagree-
ing with their conclusions, one cannot deny that the problems they faced
are serious ones.

Although both pragmatists and naturalists were in agreement in their
denial of any rational proof of God's existence, not all of them denied the
possibility of arriving at a belief in God. To see the various positions on
this point, we shall turn to a discussion of William James, Charles Sanders
Peirce, and John Dewey. The first two came to a belief in God, while the
third steadfastly denied the possibility.

The Theism of James

As a pragmatist and an empiricist, William James held to sense experience
as the criterion of knowledge. Applying this criterion to the existence of
God, he maintained that the resulting evidence could not definitely prove

---

[9] *John Dewey: An Intellectual Portrait* (New York: John Day Co., 1939), p. 14.

[10] *The Varieties of Religious Experience* (New York: Longmans, Green & Co., 1902),
p. 446.

either side of the question. He then adopted a position directly opposed to the opinion that prevailed in scientific circles at the time and that has continued to hold sway to the present. James boldly stated that until sense experience definitely decides the issue of God's existence one way or the other, one is free to appeal to the evidence of internal experience. He utterly refused to allow science to put limits upon sources of evidence; he felt that although sense knowledge is the ultimate arbiter, one can still learn from what one's inner promptings indicate. Thus, when sense experience does not decide the issue, it is perfectly legitimate to turn to inner experience.

James contended that one of the most pressing facts of human existence is the drive of the human person for fulfillment. Science is one very evident and concrete example of this drive. Interest in science is motivated by the desire of the human mind to explore and solve the natural mysteries of the universe. Man cannot be content with folding his arms and putting an end to scientific inquiry. As long as the world exists, there will be further facts to uncover and problems to solve. To men of scientific inclinations, this is an exhilarating experience that makes them impatient with the lack of interest of nonscientists.

The drive for human fulfillment, however, is not limited to the scientific level, nor even to the intellectual level. It is one of those "generic traits" that Dewey classed under metaphysics, and that James believed cut through every aspect of human experience. Man longs for the completion of his aspirations on every level, and his capacity for fulfillment seems almost infinite. James denied that such satisfaction could be found in this world.

It is not that James was a pessimist at heart; in fact, the opposite was true. He enjoyed the prospect of battle and the uncertainty of outcome. A world without risks was to him a drab world, and a cause without dangers was not worth fighting for. He was not afraid of frustrations and disappointments which he knew are the lot of every normal life. But at the same time he could not reconcile himself to a universe that is ultimately meaningless or to a life that will not eventually achieve the ultimate fulfillment of its expectations. At the very core of human existence is the yearning for the final completion of human ambitions.

James was not satisfied with the meliorism of other pragmatists and naturalists. That position professes to stand midway between optimism and pessimism by claiming that we must take the world as it is, with its disappointments and frustrations, and strive to make it better by human effort. Though James was not unaffected by such an outlook and was willing to follow it in many of the aspects of daily life, he openly scorned the cold consolation that it offers. If anything, he would call it a pessimism that does not look further for the meaning of human existence and human striving.

To James, the choice was clear. When empirical evidence does not decide the issue, man can choose one of two positions. First, he can refuse to accept the existence of God or at least withhold assent, which in James's view is equivalent to a refusal. But then one gives up hope of making life meaningful. One can strive to find satisfaction in leaving behind the works of his hands or in working for the betterment of future generations. This to James is an unhappy compromise. What good is it to leave behind one's works when the very person is faced with destruction? And what motivation for life and action is given in the prospect of laboring for future generations that appear now only as a dim blur on the horizon? One then has to settle for ultimate frustration and disillusionment.

For James, the second choice—to believe in the existence of God—can be the only one if life is to be at all meaningful. He was willing to admit that this belief does not rest on clear-cut empirical evidence and that the commitment does not have the force of certainty. But he decisively asserted his freedom to believe, first because empirical evidence does not dictate the contrary, and second because belief has in its favor the imperious demands of inner experience that the world and life itself be meaningful. For him this evidence is sufficient to invite, but not compel, assent. In assenting, he felt that he was being more "rational" than those who withhold or refuse such belief.

In this we see a very important side of James's whole approach to belief in God and religion. Belief for him is not as clear as a mathematical formula or the conclusion to a scientific problem. It is not the click of a machine that comes from pressing a button after the appropriate data has been fed into it. Belief is a human and personal affair where one feels that he is free in such an act, but that once made, it need not be for all time. It demands a recommitment on the part of the person in the light of changing circumstances and even in the face of uncertainty.

We see, then, that James resented two types of individuals: first, the absolutist philosopher who claims to draw irrefutable proofs which every mind must accept and whose God could serenely absorb into a mysterious All the inconsistencies of daily human existence; second, the scientist who rules out all but empirical evidence and who refuses to admit the inner demands of concrete human experience. James did not wish to be cramped by any one approach to knowledge. He was willing to listen to the most humble and ordinary experience for whatever it could teach him about himself, the world, or something beyond the world.

Though later pragmatists have followed James in his criterion of truth, few, if any, have been willing to accept his approach to God. To them, it seems like a traitorous desertion of the empirical method, for it questions the supremacy of sense experience as the arbiter of truth and seems to accept what transcends sense experience. In addition, it appears to be altogether too subjective for the scientific mind inasmuch as it appeals to inner experience. This seems like a denial of the objectivity of empirical knowledge.

In general, James's whole philosophy is an answer to this criticism, for it is a defense of the validity of human experience in all its aspects. As much as he favored the scientific method, he still felt that there are dimensions of experience that are not subject to scientific handling.

More particularly, James maintained that he had no intention of deserting the criterion of sense experience. He urged that men press their inquiry to the empirical level to see if the theistic position is valid. He had confidence that the existence of God would some day be verified by scientific evidence, but in the meantime he reserved the right to believe on the strength of the evidence supplied by inner experience.

The charge of subjectivism is one that inevitably appears when James's theism is discussed. It is an indictment that is understandable but unjustified. James was not always careful about exact terminology since his works were originally given in the form of popular lectures. In appealing to an inner proof for the existence of God he spoke about "passional nature." Since James was also a psychologist, the conclusion usually drawn is that he was speaking of personal feelings and emotions.

This, however, is a complete misunderstanding of his position. By passional nature James never meant merely feelings and emotions. It was rather the inner cry of the whole human person, with all its hopes and anticipations, for completion on the level of personality. To reduce passional nature to an organic or emotional drive is to distort the surge of the whole person toward that which can completely fulfill his highest aspirations.

Neither was James speaking of personal, individual elements. He believed that the experience he described was characteristic of himself and of a large number of human beings. He also felt that if properly explored, it would be seen to lie at the root of the human person and hence to be a universal characteristic. Such an exploration, however, could not be forced on anyone, for that would be to return to the approach of the absolutist whom he severely criticized. Each one must make this investigation for himself; he must listen to the voice of his own inner experience and then make his commitment or refusal on the strength of that evidence. No one can assume the responsibility for anyone else. The investigation and the choice must be one's own. All James asked, both for himself and for others, was the right to believe on terms that he considered to be neither unwarranted nor irrational.

The Theism of Peirce

Charles Sanders Peirce, one of William James's closest friends, was another great American philosopher who could find a place for God. Although science dominated his thought, as is evident from the bulk of his scientific writings, what he had to say about religion reveals the soul of a man who tried desperately to find a place in his life for God. In reviewing the main lines of his argument for God, we shall notice striking similarities with the approach of James.[11]

Peirce's starting point is the assertion that scientists should not block the road to inquiry by placing arbitrary restrictions on our sources of evidence. This position is interesting in view of the fact that Peirce, as he himself stated, was saturated with the spirit of the physical sciences and spent his whole life in scientific pursuits. But when it was a question of seeking evidence for the existence of God, he refused to be hedged in by scientific presuppositions.

Peirce's main argument for God's existence is long and sometimes obscure, and the discussion here is only a brief sketch of its main lines. Peirce first recognized in man a latent tendency to believe in God. He compared it to instinct in animals, which enables them to make judgments regarding what is required for their survival and well-being. Though the comparison with animal instinct is explicit, Peirce did not necessarily reduce the human tendency to mere instinct.

The tendency in man to believe in God will find stimulation if man will look at the universe. Everywhere he will see the handiwork of the creator: in the marvelous complexity and unity of the material universe from our terrestrial globe to the stars and heavenly bodies; in the natural beauty of flowers, animals, and sunsets; in the progressive development of living beings from inorganic matter to man. In seeing these things the human mind will come to realize how impossible it would be to explain them by the forces of physicochemical laws alone. The beauty and complexity of the universe can find their cause only in a God without whom the world would be unintelligible.

But the ultimate criterion for belief in the existence of God is the influence that this belief has on the conduct of life and on man's highest growth. Peirce recognized, as did James, that man demands continued development and fulfillment. It is both a fact of one's inner experience and the ultimate motivation for action. If the possibility of ultimate fulfillment is removed, all motivation to develop human potentialities is also removed.

Since Peirce was not willing to admit that human existence is meaningless, he too defended his right to believe in God. For him, it was the only hypothesis that satisfied the drive in man to find explanation for the material universe and the imperious demand of the human person for completion. Without God, Peirce had the feeling of alienation and incompleteness.

Peirce viewed God as a being who enters intimately into the affairs of men, who can be found in the simple things of nature and the "miserable littlenesses" of everyday affairs as well as in the great problems that perplex the man of science. On the more personal level, contact with God is made in prayer, which means not the artificiality of exaggerated ceremonial

---

[11] For a more detailed discussion of Peirce's religious philosophy and its similarities with that of James, see my article, "Is Peirce Anti-Jamesian?" in *International Philosophical Quarterly*, V, 4 (Dec., 1965), 541–63.

but the close relationship of father to son. Finally, in Peirce's view the divine is found most of all in love which binds the individual to God and draws all men to one another in their common love for God.

The Naturalism of Dewey

We come now to John Dewey—educator, philosopher, philosopher of science, logician, psychologist, political and social theorist, all at once. It would seem that in him we have finally reached the age that is thought to be typically American. For Dewey rejected a God and religion in the traditional sense, and he became our official spokesman for naturalism, which strives to limit the hopes and dreams of men within the confines of the present world. The naturalism of Dewey, with its rejection of God and religion and its attempt to work out a theory of morals and religious experience exclusively within the framework of this world, began a movement that was to have profound influence in many areas of America's intellectual and practical life.

Two forces were at work in Dewey's approach to God. One was the insight into the importance of matter that he shared with all pragmatists and naturalists. The other was his critique of organized religions. The former has been discussed above. We need only add that perhaps of all the men of his time, Dewey had the deepest sense of the importance of involvement in the affairs of the material universe for human growth and development. He gave priority to the demand of the human person for fulfillment, and in a sense all other philosophies or theologies had to respect this demand. If they in any way hindered or prevented human development, they were ruled out as viable outlooks on man and the universe.

In the light of this insight, Dewey confronted what he felt to be the universal opposition of all religions to the world and all that it stands for. In his eyes, religion by its very nature orients the soul to God and this orientation involves a hatred of material things and institutions. Dewey then felt that the religious man is put in an impossible situation; by reason of his religious ties he is forced to despise the very things that make for his human growth. It was not through a frantic hatred of God and religion that Dewey rejected them, but out of the fear that by committing himself to religion he would to that extent cease to be human.

If the issue is placed on these grounds, one cannot blame the naturalist for his position. For the most part, of course, he simply did not understand traditional religions. John Herman Randall, Jr. (b. 1899), one of the leading contemporary naturalist philosophers, admitted that "Dewey criticized the husk of American religious life without penetrating to the core of Christianity." [12] But Dewey, and naturalists generally, took religion as they

---

[12] Randall, review of Robert J. Roth, *John Dewey and Self-Realization, Thought,* XXXIX, 155 (Winter, 1964), 630.

knew it, and as they knew it religion represented an open hostility to the world and all that it contains.

Although Dewey abandoned God and religion, he did not abandon what he called "religious experience." Like James and Peirce, he too began with the inner experience of men testifying to the need for self-realization. But by reason of his opposition to God and religion in the traditional sense, he held that the object that would satisfy that need would have to come from this world. Dewey also felt that man has natural tendencies to self-lessness and sympathy for others. He proposed that man could find the fulfillment of his highest human potentialities by directing his thought and action to the betterment of mankind. Religious experience then becomes the fulfillment that one achieves when he realizes that whatever he does will further the human interests of present and future generations. Man will become more fully a person when his interests go beyond merely personal concerns and unite with the hopes and strivings of all men, present and future, in a fellowship of friendship and love. To draw apart from the solidarity of mankind will mean the disillusionment of the individual, while union with it will lead to man's consummation.

Notes on the Readings

Such is the pragmatic-naturalist viewpoint on metaphysics and natural theology. Although much more could be said on the subject, an attempt was made to adhere to the essentials. The readings that follow should help to fill in further details.

It will be noted that the readings have been taken almost entirely from James and Dewey. It seemed preferable to concentrate on these two authors since—until very recently—they have been America's best-known and most influential philosophers. A good grasp of their thought will enable the student to understand more readily the philosophy of other American pragmatists and naturalists.

The first chapter of William James's *Pragmatism* shows his approach to philosophy, while the last consciously relates pragmatism to his theism. For an understanding of James's theory of truth, one could profitably read the second chapter of *Pragmatism,* "What Pragmatism Means." In any case, a reading of any part of this work will show his mastery of style.

It is difficult to select from Peirce's works any sizable sections that give the main lines of his metaphysics and natural theology. He has literally worked out a new language to convey new ideas, and this language must be mastered in order to understand his thought. Hence the selection taken from this author is limited in length, but it is hoped that what is given will indicate the orientation of his thought on the topics under discussion.

John Dewey's *Reconstruction in Philosophy* is not one of his best books because it shows that he was not always a good historian of philosophy. But the chapter on the scientific factor points up the impact that science made on philosophy.

The sections from *Logic: The Theory of Inquiry* and *Art as Experience* show how key concepts of process metaphysics are applied by emphasizing the necessity of interaction with environment for growth of the living organism. Moreover, *Art as Experience* is actually more than a work on art criticism. Dewey considers it essential for the understanding of his whole philosophy. In it he tries to show that every experience can be consummatory, esthetic, and hence conducive to human self-realization and that the primary characteristic of personality is change and growth.

Experience and Nature is Dewey's most definitive philosophical work and ranks among the most important of all his works. Unfortunately it is difficult to read, for it is long, repetitious, frequently obscure, and occasionally disconnected. But it is the core of his philosophy and the key to the understanding of his writing in all other fields. It must eventually be read by anyone seriously interested in Dewey and in American naturalism. The chapter selected in the readings gives a good sampling of his metaphysical position.

A Common Faith is one of Dewey's more important and readable books. It is only eighty-seven pages long but it pulls together into one volume his theory of religious experience.

Glossary

ABSOLUTE:
    In theistic terms, a transcendent being as ultimate principle of the existence and intelligibility of all reality. In pragmatic-naturalist terms, a being completely separate from the world and human experience, and hence unattainable by man.

EMPIRICAL METHOD:
    In contemporary philosophy and science, empirical method is equivalent to scientific method in the broad sense, namely, the use of the senses as the source of knowledge where every conclusion is tentative and subject to the test of future sense experience.

EMPIRICISM:
    Emphasis on sense experience as a means of understanding reality. In an exclusive meaning empiricism admits no other form of knowledge.

IDEALISM:
    Emphasis on spiritual reality to the minimizing and even exclusion of sensible reality. The sensible aspects of the universe are considered to be only appearances.

MECHANISTIC DETERMINISM:

The position that all activities—inorganic, organic, and human—can be reduced to the operations of matter and energy according to physical and chemical laws.

METAPHYSICS:

In scholastic terms, the science of being as such. In pragmatic-naturalist terms, the knowledge of the general traits of nature. "Static" metaphysics: one that emphasizes permanence and stability. "Process" metaphysics: one that emphasizes change.

NATURAL THEOLOGY:

A science that demonstrates God's existence, essence, and attributes through human reason.

NATURALISM:

In American philosophy, an outlook on reality characterized by the empirical method and by an emphasis on the importance of matter. Naturalists such as John Dewey also reject God and religion in the traditional sense.

PRAGMATISM:

A philosophy that attempts to interpret truth and reality in terms of significance for human experience.

William James

WILLIAM JAMES, brother of the distinguished novelist, playwright, and critic, Henry James, was born in New York City in 1842. He was educated in England and on the Continent, and also studied in the Lawrence Scientific School at Harvard University. He received a medical degree from Harvard in 1869 but never practiced medicine. From 1873 until 1907 he taught physiology, psychology, and philosophy at Harvard, and in 1875 organized the first laboratory of psychological experimentation in the United States. A master stylist, he published his famous *Principles of Psychology* in 1890 and *The Varieties of Religious Experience* in 1902. His most noted work, *Pragmatism,* appeared in 1907. The Hibbert Lectures, which he delivered at Oxford in 1908, were published in 1909 under the title *A Pluralistic Universe*. James died in Chocorua, New Hampshire, in 1910.

The Present Dilemma in Philosophy

In the preface to that admirable collection of essays of his called "Heretics," Mr. Chesterton writes these words: "There are some people—and I am one of them—who think that the most practical and important thing about a man is still his view of the universe. We think that for a landlady considering a lodger it is important to know his income, but still more important to know his philosophy. We think that for a general about to fight an enemy it is important to know the enemy's numbers, but still more important to know the enemy's philosophy. We think the question is not whether the theory of the cosmos affects matters, but whether in the long run anything else affects them."

I think with Mr. Chesterton in this matter. I know that you, ladies and gentlemen, have a philosophy, each and all of you, and that the most interesting and important thing about you is the way in which it determines the perspective in your several worlds. You know the same of me. And yet I confess to a certain tremor at the audacity of the enterprise which I am about to begin. For the philosophy which is so important in each of us is not a technical matter; it is our more or less dumb sense of what life honestly and deeply means. It is only partly got from books; it is our individual way of just seeing and feeling the total push and pressure of the cosmos. I have no right to assume that many of you are students of the cosmos in the classroom sense, yet here I stand desirous of interesting you in a philosophy which to no small extent has to be technically treated. I wish to fill you with sympathy with a contemporaneous tendency in which I profoundly believe, and yet I have to talk like a professor to you who are not students. Whatever universe a professor believes in must at any rate be a universe that lends itself to lengthy discourse. A universe definable in two sentences is something for which the professorial intellect has no use. No faith in anything of that cheap kind! I have heard friends and colleagues try to popularize philosophy in this very hall, but they soon grew dry, and then technical, and the results were only partially encouraging. So my enterprise is a bold one. The founder of pragmatism himself recently gave a course of lectures at the Lowell Institute with that very word in its title,—flashes of brilliant light relieved against Cimmerian darkness! None of us, I fancy, understood *all* that he said—yet here I stand, making a very similar venture.

I risk it because the very lectures I speak of *drew*—they brought good audiences. There is, it must be confessed, a curious fascination in hearing deep things talked about, even though neither we nor the disputants understand them. We get the problematic thrill, we feel the presence of the vastness. Let a controversy begin in a smoking-room anywhere, about free-will or God's omniscience, or good and evil, and see how every one in the place pricks up his ears. Philosophy's results concern us all most vitally, and philosophy's queerest arguments tickle agreeably our sense of subtlety and ingenuity.

Believing in philosophy myself devoutly, and believing also that a kind of new dawn is breaking upon us philosophers, I feel impelled, *per fas aut nefas,*[1] to try to impart to you some news of the situation.

Philosophy is at once the most sublime and the most trivial of human pursuits. It works in the minutest crannies and it opens out the widest vistas. It "bakes no bread," as has been said, but it can inspire our souls with courage; and repugnant as its manners, its doubting and challenging, its quibbling and dialectics, often are to common people, no one of us can get along without the far-flashing beams of light it sends over the world's perspectives. These illuminations at least, and the contrast-effects of darkness and mystery that accompany them, give to what it says an interest that is much more than professional.

The history of philosophy is to a great extent that of a certain clash of human temperaments. Undignified as such a treatment may seem to some of my colleagues, I shall have to take account of this clash and explain a good many of the divergencies of philosophers by it. Of whatever tempera-

---

[1] *Per fas aut nefas:* by fair means or foul. [R.J.R.]

ment a professional philosopher is, he tries, when philosophizing, to sink the fact of his temperament. Temperament is no conventionally recognized reason, so he urges impersonal reasons only for his conclusions. Yet his temperament really gives him a stronger bias than any of his more strictly objective premises. It loads the evidence for him one way or the other, making for a more sentimental or a more hard-hearted view of the universe, just as this fact or that principle would. He *trusts* his temperament. Wanting a universe that suits it, he believes in any representation of the universe that does suit it. He feels men of opposite temper to be out of key with the world's character, and in his heart considers them incompetent and "not in it," in the philosophic business, even though they may far excel him in dialectical ability.

Yet in the forum he can make no claim, on the bare ground of his temperament, to superior discernment or authority. There arises thus a certain insincerity in our philosophic discussions: the potentest of all our premises is never mentioned. I am sure it would contribute to clearness if in these lectures we should break this rule and mention it, and I accordingly feel free to do so.

Of course I am talking here of very positively marked men, men of radical idiosyncracy, who have set their stamp and likeness on philosophy and figure in its history. Plato, Locke, Hegel, Spencer, are such temperamental thinkers. Most of us have, of course, no very definite intellectual temperament, we are a mixture of opposite ingredients, each one present very moderately. We hardly know our own preferences in abstract matters; some of us are easily talked out of them, and end by following the fashion or taking up with the beliefs of the most impressive philosopher in our neighborhood, whoever he may be. But the one thing that has *counted* so far in philosophy is that a man should *see* things, see them straight in his own peculiar way, and be dissatisfied with any opposite way of seeing them. There is no reason to suppose that this strong temperamental vision is from now onward to count no longer in the history of man's beliefs.

Now the particular difference of temperament that I have in mind in making these remarks is one that has counted in literature, art, government, and manners as well as in philosophy. In manners we find formalists and free-and-easy persons. In government, authoritarians and anarchists. In literature, purists or academicals, and realists. In art, classics and romantics. You recognize these contrasts as familiar; well, in philosophy we have a very similar contrast expressed in the pair of terms "rationalist" and "empiricist," "empiricist" meaning your lover of facts in all their crude variety, "rationalist" meaning your devotee to abstract and eternal principles. No one can live an hour without both facts and principles, so it is a difference rather of emphasis; yet it breeds antipathies of the most pungent character between those who lay the emphasis differently; and we shall find it extraordinarily convenient to express a certain contrast in men's ways of taking their universe, by talking of the "empiricist" and of the "rationalist" temper. These terms make the contrast simple and massive.

More simple and massive than are usually the men of whom the terms are predicated. For every sort of permutation and combination is possible in human nature; and if I now proceed to define more fully what I have in mind when I speak of rationalists and empiricists, by adding to each of those titles some secondary qualifying characteristics, I beg you to regard my conduct as to a certain extent arbitrary. I select types of combination that nature offers very frequently, but by no means uniformly, and I select them solely for their convenience in helping me to my ulterior purpose of characterizing pragmatism. Historically we find the terms "intellectualism" and "sensationalism" used as synonyms of "rationalism" and "empiricism." Well, nature seems to combine most frequently with intellectualism an idealistic and optimistic tendency. Empiricists on the other hand are not uncommonly materialistic, and their optimism is apt to be decidedly conditional and tremulous. Rationalism is always monistic. It starts from wholes and universals, and makes much of the unity of things. Empiricism starts from the parts, and makes of the whole a collection—is not averse therefore to calling itself pluralistic. Rationalism usually considers itself more religious than empiricism, but there is much to say about this claim, so I merely mention it. It is a true claim when the individual rationalist is what is called a man of feeling, and when the individual empiricist prides himself on being hard-headed. In that case the rationalist will usually also be in favor of what is called free-will, and the empiricist will be a fatalist —I use the terms most popularly current. The rationalist finally will be of dogmatic temper in his affirmations, while the empiricist may be more sceptical and open to discussion.

I will write these traits down in two columns. I think you will practically recognize the two types of mental make-up that I mean if I head the columns by the titles "tender-minded" and "tough-minded" respectively.

THE TENDER-MINDED	THE TOUGH-MINDED
Rationalistic (going by "principles")	Empiricist (going by "facts")
Intellectualistic	Sensationalistic
Idealistic	Materialistic
Optimistic	Pessimistic
Religious	Irreligious
Free-willist	Fatalistic
Monistic	Pluralistic
Dogmatical	Sceptical

Pray postpone for a moment the question whether the two contrasted mixtures which I have written down are each inwardly coherent and self-consistent or not—I shall very soon have a good deal to say on that point. It suffices for our immediate purpose that tender-minded and tough-minded people, characterized as I have written them down, do both exist. Each of you probably knows some well-marked example of each type, and you know what each example thinks of the example on the other side of the line. They have a low opinion of each other. Their antagonism, whenever as individuals their temperaments have been intense, has formed in all ages a part of the philosophic atmosphere of the time. It forms a part of the philosophic atmosphere to-day. The tough think of the tender as sentimentalists and soft-heads. The tender feel the tough to be unrefined, callous, or brutal. Their mutual reaction is very much like that that takes place when Bostonian tourists mingle with a population like that of Cripple Creek. Each type believes the other to be inferior to itself; but disdain in the one case is mingled with amusement, in the other it has a dash of fear.

Now, as I have already insisted, few of us are tender-foot Bostonians pure and simple, and few are typical Rocky Mountain toughs, in philosophy. Most of us have a hankering for the good things on both sides of the line. Facts are good, of course—give us lots of facts. Principles are good—give us plenty of principles. The world is indubitably one if you look at it in one way, but as indubitably is it many, if you look at it in another. It is both one and many—let us adopt a sort of pluralistic monism. Everything of course is necessarily determined, and yet of course our wills are free: a sort of free-will determinism is the true philosophy. The evil of the parts is undeniable, but the whole can't be evil: so practical pessimism may be combined with metaphysical optimism. And so forth—your ordinary philosophic layman never being a radical, never straightening out his system, but living vaguely in one plausible compartment of it or another to suit the temptations of successive hours.

But some of us are more than mere laymen in philosophy. We are worthy of the name of amateur athletes, and are vexed by too much inconsistency and vacillation in our creed. We cannot preserve a good intellectual conscience so long as we keep mixing incompatibles from opposite sides of the line.

And now I come to the first positively important point which I wish to make. Never were as many men of a decidedly empiricist proclivity in existence as there are at the present day. Our children, one may say, are almost born scientific. But our esteem for facts has not neutralized in us all religiousness. It is itself almost religious. Our scientific temper is devout. Now take a man of this type, and let him be also a philosophic amateur, unwilling to mix a hodge-podge system after the fashion of a common layman, and what does he find his situation to be, in this blessed year of our Lord 1906? He wants facts; he wants science; but he also wants a religion. And being an amateur and not an independent originator in philosophy he naturally looks for guidance to the experts and professionals whom he finds already in the field. A very large number of you here present, possibly a majority of you, are amateurs of just this sort.

Now what kinds of philosophy do you find actually offered to meet your need? You find an empirical philosophy that is not religious enough, and a religious philosophy that is not empirical enough for your purpose. If you look to the quarter where facts are most considered you find the whole tough-minded program in operation, and the "conflict between science and religion" in full blast. Either it is that Rocky Mountain tough of a Haeckel with his materialistic monism, his ether-god and his jest at your God as a "gaseous vertebrate"; or it is Spencer treating the world's history as a redistribution of matter and motion solely, and bowing religion politely out at the front door:—she may indeed continue to exist, but she must never show her face inside the temple.

For a hundred and fifty years past the progress of science has seemed to mean the enlargement of the material universe and the diminution of man's importance. The result is what one may call the growth of naturalistic or positivistic feeling. Man is no lawgiver to nature, he is an absorber. She it is who stands firm; he it is who must accommodate himself. Let him record truth, inhuman though it be, and submit to it! The romantic spontaneity and courage are gone, the vision is materialistic and depressing. Ideals appear as inert by-products of physiology; what is higher is explained by what is lower and treated forever as a case of "nothing but"— nothing but something else of a quite inferior sort. You get, in short, a materialistic universe, in which only the tough-minded find themselves congenially at home.

If now, on the other hand, you turn to the religious quarter for consolation, and take counsel of the tender-minded philosophies, what do you find?

Religious philosophy in our day and generation is, among us English-reading people, of two main types. One of these is more radical and aggressive, the other has more the air of fighting a slow retreat. By the more radical wing of religious philosophy I mean the so-called transcendental idealism of the Anglo-Hegelian school, the philosophy of such men as Green, the Cairds, Bosanquet, and Royce. This philosophy has greatly influenced the more studious members of our protestant ministry. It is pantheistic, and undoubtedly it has already blunted the edge of the traditional theism in protestantism at large.

That theism remains, however. It is the lineal descendant, through one stage of concession after another, of the dogmatic scholastic theism still taught rigorously in the seminaries of the catholic church. For a long time it used to be called among us the philosophy of the Scottish school. It is what I meant by the philosophy that has the air of fighting a slow retreat. Between the encroachments of the Hegelians and other philosophers of the "Absolute," on the one hand, and those of the scientific evolutionists and agnostics, on the other, the men that give us this kind of a philosophy, James Martineau, Professor Bowne, Professor Ladd and others, must feel themselves rather tightly squeezed. Fair-minded and candid as you like, this philosophy is not radical in temper. It is eclectic, a thing of compromises, that seeks a *modus vivendi* above all things. It accepts the facts of Darwinism, the facts of cerebral physiology, but it does nothing active or enthusiastic with them. It lacks the victorious and aggressive note. It lacks *prestige* in consequence; whereas absolutism has a certain *prestige* due to the more radical style of it.

These two systems are what you have to choose between if you turn to the tender-minded school. And if you are the lovers of facts I have supposed you to be, you find the trail of the serpent of rationalism, of intellectualism, over everything that lies on that side of the line. You escape indeed the materialism that goes with the reigning empiricism; but you pay for your escape by losing contact with the concrete parts of life. The more absolutistic philosophers dwell on so high a level of abstraction that they never even try to come down. The absolute mind which they offer us, the mind that makes our universe by thinking it, might, for aught they show us to the contrary, have made any one of a million other universes just as well as this. You can deduce no single actual particular from the notion of it. It is compatible with any state of things whatever being true here below. And the theistic God is almost as sterile a principle. You have to go to the world which he has created to get any inkling of his actual character: he is the kind of god that has once for all made that kind of a world. The God of the theistic writers lives on as purely abstract heights as does the Absolute. Absolutism has a certain sweep and dash about it, while the usual theism is more insipid, but both are equally remote and vacuous. What *you* want is a philosophy that will not only exercise your powers of intellectual abstraction, but that will make some positive connexion with this actual world of finite human lives.

You want a system that will combine both things, the scientific loyalty to facts and willingness to take account of them, the spirit of adaptation and accommodation, in short, but also the old confidence in human values and the resultant spontaneity, whether of the religious or of the romantic type. And this is then your dilemma: you find the two parts of your *quaesitum* hopelessly separated. You find empiricism with inhumanism and irreligion; or else you find a rationalistic philosophy that indeed may call itself religious, but that keeps out of all definite touch with concrete facts and joys and sorrows.

I am not sure how many of you live close enough to philosophy to realize fully what I mean by this last reproach, so I will dwell a little longer on that unreality in all rationalistic systems by which your serious believer in facts is so apt to feel repelled.

I wish that I had saved the first couple of pages of a thesis which a student handed me a year or two ago. They illustrated my point so clearly that I am sorry I can not read them to you now. This young man, who was a graduate of some Western college, began by saying that he had always taken for granted that when you entered a philosophic classroom you had to open relations with a universe entirely distinct from the one you left behind you in the street. The two were supposed, he said, to have so little to do with each other, that you could not possibly occupy your mind with them at the same time. The world of concrete personal experiences to which the street belongs is multitudinous beyond imagination, tangled, muddy, painful and perplexed. The world to which your philosophy-professor introduces you is simple, clean and noble. The contradictions of real life are absent from it. Its architecture is classic. Principles of reason trace its outlines, logical necessities cement its parts. Purity and dignity are what it most expresses. It is a kind of marble temple shining on a hill.

In point of fact it is far less an account of this actual world than a clear addition built upon it, a classic sanctuary in which the rationalist fancy may take refuge from the intolerably confused and gothic character which mere facts present. It is no *explanation* of our concrete universe, it is another thing altogether, a substitute for it, a remedy, a way of escape.

Its temperament, if I may use the word temperament here, is utterly alien to the temperament of existence in the concrete. *Refinement* is what characterizes our intellectualist philosophies. They exquisitely satisfy that craving for a refined object of contemplation which is so powerful an appetite of the mind. But I ask you in all seriousness to look abroad on this colossal universe of concrete facts, on their awful bewilderments, their surprises and cruelties, on the wildness which they show, and then to tell me whether "refined" is the one inevitable descriptive adjective that springs to your lips.

Refinement has its place in things, true enough. But a philosophy that breathes out nothing but refinement will never satisfy the empiricist temper of mind. It will seem rather a monument of artificiality. So we find men of science preferring to turn their backs on metaphysics as on something altogether cloistered and spectral, and practical men shaking philosophy's dust off their feet and following the call of the wild.

Truly there is something a little ghastly in the satisfaction with which a pure but unreal system will fill a rationalist mind. Leibnitz [2] was a rationalist mind, with infinitely more interest in facts than most rationalist minds can show. Yet if you wish for superficiality incarnate, you have only to read that charmingly written "Théodicée" of his, in which he sought to justify the ways of God to man, and to prove that the world we live in is the best of possible worlds. Let me quote a specimen of what I mean.

Among other obstacles to his optimistic philosophy, it falls to Leibnitz to consider the number of the eternally damned. That it is infinitely greater, in our human case, than that of those saved, he assumes as a premise from the theologians, and then proceeds to argue in this way. Even then, he says:

"The evil will appear as almost nothing in comparison with the good, if

---

[2] Gottfried Wilhelm Leibnitz (1646–1716): German mathematician and philosopher. His name is more usually spelled Leibniz. [R.J.R.]

we once consider the real magnitude of the City of God. Coelius Secundus Curio has written a little book, 'De Amplitudine Regni Coelestis,' which was reprinted not long ago. But he failed to compass the extent of the kingdom of the heavens. The ancients had small ideas of the works of God. . . . It seemed to them that only our earth had inhabitants, and even the notion of our antipodes gave them pause. The rest of the world for them consisted of some shining globes and a few crystalline spheres. But to-day, whatever be the limits that we may grant or refuse to the Universe we must recognize in it a countless number of globes, as big as ours or bigger, which have just as much right as it has to support rational inhabitants, tho it does not follow that these need all be men. Our earth is only one among the six principal satellites of our sun. As all the fixed stars are suns, one sees how small a place among visible things our earth takes up, since it is only a satellite of one among them. Now all these suns *may* be inhabited by none but happy creatures; and nothing obliges us to believe that the number of damned persons is very great; for *a very few instances and samples suffice for the utility which good draws from evil.* Moreover, since, there is no reason to suppose that there are stars everywhere, may there not be a great space beyond the region of the stars? And this immense space, surrounding all this region, . . . may be replete with happiness and glory. . . . What now becomes of the consideration of our Earth and of its denizens? Does it not dwindle to something incomparably less than a physical point, since our Earth is but a point compared with the distance of the fixed stars. Thus the part of the Universe which we know, being almost lost in nothingness compared with that which is unknown to us, but which we are yet obliged to admit; and all the evils that we know lying in this almost-nothing; it follows that the evils may be almost-nothing in comparison with the goods that the Universe contains."

Leibnitz continues elsewhere:

"There is a kind of justice which aims neither at the amendment of the criminal, nor at furnishing an example to others, nor at the reparation of the injury. This justice is founded in pure fitness, which finds a certain satisfaction in the expiation of a wicked deed. The Socinians [3] and Hobbes [4] objected to this punitive justice, which is properly vindictive justice, and which God has reserved for himself at many junctures. . . . It is always founded in the fitness of things, and satisfies not only the offended party, but all wise lookers-on, even as beautiful music or a fine piece of architecture satisfies a well-constituted mind. It is thus that the torments of the damned continue, even tho they serve no longer to turn any one away from sin, and that the rewards of the blest continue, even tho they confirm no one in good ways. The damned draw to themselves ever new penalties by their continuing sins, and the blest attract ever fresh joys by their unceasing

---

[3] Socinians: followers of Socinus, sixteenth-century Protestant reformer. [R.J.R.]
[4] Thomas Hobbes (1588–1679): British philosopher. [R.J.R.]

progress in good. Both facts are founded on the principle of fitness, . . . for God has made all things harmonious in perfection as I have already said."

Leibnitz's feeble grasp of reality is too obvious to need comment from me. It is evident that no realistic image of the experience of a damned soul had ever approached the portals of his mind. Nor had it occurred to him that the smaller is the number of "samples" of the genus "lost-soul" whom God throws as a sop to the eternal fitness, the more unequitably grounded is the glory of the blest. What he gives us is a cold literary exercise, whose cheerful substance even hell-fire does not warm.

And do not tell me that to show the shallowness of rationalist philosophizing I have had to go back to a shallow wigpated age. The optimism of present-day rationalism sounds just as shallow to the fact-loving mind. The actual universe is a thing wide open, but rationalism makes systems, and systems must be closed. For men in practical life perfection is something far off and still in process of achievement. This for rationalism is but the illusion of the finite and relative: the absolute ground of things is a perfection eternally complete.

I find a fine example of revolt against the airy and shallow optimism of current religious philosophy in a publication of that valiant anarchistic writer Morrison I. Swift. Mr. Swift's anarchism goes a little farther than mine does, but I confess that I sympathize a good deal, and some of you, I know, will sympathize heartily with his dissatisfaction with the idealistic optimisms now in vogue. He begins his pamphlet on "Human Submission" with a series of city reporter's items from newspapers (suicides, deaths from starvation, and the like) as specimens of our civilized régime. For instance:

"After trudging through the snow from one end of the city to the other in the vain hope of securing employment, and with his wife and six children without food and ordered to leave their home in an upper east-side tenement-house because of non-payment of rent, John Corcoran, a clerk, to-day ended his life by drinking carbolic acid. Corcoran lost his position three weeks ago through illness, and during the period of idleness his scanty savings disappeared. Yesterday he obtained work with a gang of city snow-shovelers, but he was too weak from illness, and was forced to quit after an hour's trial with the shovel. Then the weary task of looking for employment was again resumed. Thoroughly discouraged, Corcoran returned to his home last night to find his wife and children without food and the notice of dispossession on the door. On the following morning he drank the poison.

"The records of many more such cases lie before me [Mr. Swift goes on]; an encyclopedia might easily be filled with their kind. These few I cite as an interpretation of the Universe. 'We are aware of the presence of God in his world,' says a writer in a recent English review. [The very presence of ill in the temporal order is the condition of the perfection of the eternal

order, writes Professor Royce (*The World and the Individual,* II, 385).]
'The Absolute is the richer for every discord and for all the diversity which
it embraces,' says F. H. Bradley (*Appearance and Reality,* 204). He
means that these slain men make the universe richer, and that is philosophy. But while Professors Royce and Bradley [5] and a whole host of guile-
less thoroughfed thinkers are unveiling Reality and the Absolute and explaining away evil and pain, this is the condition of the only beings known
to us anywhere in the universe with a developed consciousness of what the
universe is. What these people experience *is* Reality. It gives us an absolute
phase of the universe. It is the personal experience of those best qualified in
our circle of knowledge to *have* experience, to tell us *what is.* Now what
does *thinking about* the experience of these persons come to, compared to
directly and personally feeling it as they feel it? The philosophers are dealing in shades, while those who live and feel know truth. And the mind of
mankind—not yet the mind of philosophers and of the proprietary class—
but of the great mass of the silently thinking men and feeling men, is
coming to this view. They are judging the universe as they have hitherto
permitted the hierophants of religion and learning to judge *them.* . . .

"This Cleveland workingman, killing his children and himself [another
of the cited cases] is one of the elemental stupendous facts of this modern
world and of this universe. It cannot be glozed over or minimized away by
all the treatises on God, and Love, and Being, helplessly existing in their
monumental vacuity. This is one of the simple irreducible elements of this
world's life, after millions of years of opportunity and twenty centuries of
Christ. It is in the mental world what atoms or sub-atoms are in the physical, primary, indestructible. And what it blazons to man is the imposture of
all philosophy which does not see in such events the consummate factor of
all conscious experience. These facts invincibly prove religion a nullity.
Man will not give religion two thousand centuries or twenty centuries more
to try itself and waste human time. Its time is up; its probation is ended; its
own record ends it. Mankind has not æons and eternities to spare for trying out discredited systems."

Such is the reaction of an empiricist mind upon the rationalist bill of
fare. It is an absolute "No, I thank you." "Religion," says Mr. Swift, "is
like a sleep-walker to whom actual things are blank." And such, tho possibly less tensely charged with feeling, is the verdict of every seriously inquiring amateur in philosophy to-day who turns to the philosophy-professors
for the wherewithal to satisfy the fullness of his nature's needs. Empiricist
writers give him a materialism, rationalists give him something religious,
but to that religion "actual things are blank." He becomes thus the judge of
us philosophers. Tender or tough, he finds us wanting. None of us may

---

[5] Josiah Royce (1855–1916) and F. H. Bradley (1846–1924): American and British
idealist philosophers, respectively. [R.J.R.]

treat his verdicts disdainfully, for after all, his is the typically perfect mind, the mind the sum of whose demands is greatest, the mind whose criticisms and dissatisfactions are fatal in the long run.

It is at this point that my own solution begins to appear. I offer the oddly-named thing pragmatism as a philosophy that can satisfy both kinds of demand. It can remain religious like the rationalisms, but at the same time, like the empiricisms, it can preserve the richest intimacy with facts. I hope I may be able to leave many of you with as favorable an opinion of it as I preserve myself. Yet, as I am near the end of my hour, I will not introduce pragmatism bodily now. I will begin with it on the stroke of the clock next time. I prefer at the present moment to return a little on what I have said.

If any of you here are professional philosophers, and some of you I know to be such, you will doubtless have felt my discourse so far to have been crude in an unpardonable, nay, in an almost incredible degree. Tender-minded and tough-minded, what a barbaric disjunction! And, in general, when philosophy is all compacted of delicate intellectualities and subtleties and scrupulosities, and when every possible sort of combination and transition obtains within its bounds, what a brutal caricature and reduction of highest things to the lowest possible expression is it to represent its field of conflict as a sort of rough-and-tumble fight between two hostile temperaments! What a childishly external view! And again, how stupid it is to treat the abstractness of rationalist systems as a crime, and to damn them because they offer themselves as sanctuaries and places of escape, rather than as prolongations of the world of facts. Are not all our theories just remedies and places of escape? And, if philosophy is to be religious, how can she be anything else than a place of escape from the crassness of reality's surface? What better thing can she do than raise us out of our animal senses and show us another and a nobler home for our minds in that great framework of ideal principles subtending all reality, which the intellect divines? How can principles and general views ever be anything but abstract outlines? Was Cologne cathedral built without an architect's plan on paper? Is refinement in itself an abomination? Is concrete rudeness the only thing that's true?

Believe me, I feel the full force of the indictment. The picture I have given is indeed monstrously over-simplified and rude. But like all abstractions, it will prove to have its use. If philosophers can treat the life of the universe abstractly, they must not complain of an abstract treatment of the life of philosophy itself. In point of fact the picture I have given is, however coarse and sketchy, literally true. Temperaments with their cravings and refusals do determine men in their philosophies, and always will. The details of systems may be reasoned out piecemeal, and when the student is working at a system, he may often forget the forest for the single tree. But when the labor is accomplished, the mind always performs its big summarizing act, and the system forthwith stands over against one like a living thing, with that strange simple note of individuality which haunts our memory, like the wrath of the man, when a friend or enemy of ours is dead.

Not only Walt Whitman could write "who touches this book touches a man." The books of all the great philosophers are like so many men. Our sense of an essential personal flavor in each one of them, typical but indescribable, is the finest fruit of our own accomplished philosophic education. What the system pretends to be is a picture of the great universe of God. What it is,—and oh so flagrantly!—is the revelation of how intensely odd the personal flavor of some fellow creature is. Once reduced to these terms (and all our philosophies get reduced to them in minds made critical by learning) our commerce with the systems reverts to the informal, to the instinctive human reaction of satisfaction or dislike. We grow as peremptory in our rejection or admission, as when a person presents himself as a candidate for our favor; our verdicts are couched in as simple adjectives of praise or dispraise. We measure the total character of the universe as we feel it, against the flavor of the philosophy proffered us, and one word is enough.

.   .   .

Our work over the details of his system is indeed what gives us our resultant impression of the philosopher, but it is on the resultant impression itself that we react. Expertness in philosophy is measured by the definiteness of our summarizing reactions, by the immediate perceptive epithet with which the expert hits such complex objects off. But great expertness is not necessary for the epithet to come. Few people have definitely articulated philosophies of their own. But almost every one has his own peculiar sense of a certain total character in the universe, and of the inadequacy fully to match it of the peculiar systems that he knows. They don't just cover *his* world. One will be too dapper, another too pedantic, a third too much of a job-lot of opinions, a fourth too morbid, and a fifth too artificial, or what not. At any rate he and we know off-hand that such philosophies are out of plumb and out of key and out of "whack," and have no business to speak up in the universe's name. Plato, Locke, Spinoza, Mill, Caird,[6] Hegel—I prudently avoid names nearer home!—I am sure that to many of you, my hearers, these names are little more than reminders of as many curious personal ways of falling short. It would be an obvious absurdity if such ways of taking the universe were actually true.

We philosophers have to reckon with such feelings on your part. In the last resort, I repeat, it will be by them that all our philosophies shall ultimately be judged. The finally victorious way of looking at things will be the most completely *impressive* way to the normal run of minds.

One word more—namely about philosophies necessarily being abstract

---

[6] John Stuart Mill (1806–73): English philosopher and radical reformer; Edward Caird (1835–1908): British idealist philosopher. [R.J.R.]

outlines. There are outlines and outlines, outlines of buildings that are *fat,* conceived in the cube by their planner, and outlines of buildings invented flat on paper, with the aid of ruler and compass. These remain skinny and emaciated even when set up in stone and mortar, and the outline already suggests that result. An outline in itself is meagre, truly, but it does not necessarily suggest a meagre thing. It is the essential meagreness of *what is suggested* by the usual rationalistic philosophies that moves empiricists to their gesture of rejection. The case of Herbert Spencer's system is much to the point here. Rationalists feel his fearful array of insufficiencies. His dry schoolmaster temperament, the hurdy-gurdy monotony of him, his preference for cheap makeshifts in argument, his lack of education even in mechanical principles, and in general the vagueness of all his fundamental ideas, his whole system wooden, as if knocked together out of cracked hemlock boards—and yet the half of England wants to bury him in Westminster Abbey.

Why? Why does Spencer call out so much reverence in spite of his weakness in rationalistic eyes? Why should so many educated men who feel that weakness, you and I perhaps, wish to see him in the Abbey notwithstanding?

Simply because we feel his heart to be *in the right place* philosophically. His principles may be all skin and bone, but at any rate his books try to mould themselves upon the particular shape of this particular world's carcase. The noise of facts resounds through all his chapters, the citations of fact never cease, he emphasizes facts, turns his face towards their quarter; and that is enough. It means the right *kind* of thing for the empiricist mind.

QUESTIONS FOR STUDY AND DISCUSSION

1. Show how the question of theism forms the starting point of James's pragmatism.
2. What does James mean by the "tender-minded" and the "tough-mnded"?
3. How does pragmatism try to reconcile rationalism and empiricism?

Pragmatism and Religion

At the close of the last lecture I reminded you of the first one, in which I had opposed tough-mindedness to tender-mindedness and recommended pragmatism as their mediator. Tough-mindedness positively rejects tender-

From pp. 273–301 of William James, *Pragmatism.* Copyright 1907 by William James. Reprinted by permission of Paul R. Reynolds, Inc.

mindedness's hypothesis of an eternal perfect edition of the universe coexisting with our finite experience.

On pragmatic principles we can not reject any hypothesis if consequences useful to life flow from it. Universal conceptions, as things to take account of, may be as real for pragmatism as particular sensations are. They have, indeed, no meaning and no reality if they have no use. But if they have any use they have that amount of meaning. And the meaning will be true if the use squares well with life's other uses.

Well, the use of the Absolute is proved by the whole course of men's religious history. The eternal arms are then beneath. . . .

It is always best to discuss things by the help of concrete examples. Let me read therefore some of those verses entitled "To You" by Walt Whitman—"You" of course meaning the reader or hearer of the poem whosoever he or she may be.

Whoever you are, now I place my hand upon you that you be my poem;
I whisper with my lips close to your ear,
I have loved many men and women and men, but I love none better than you.

O I have been dilatory and dumb;
I should have made my way to you long ago;
I should have blabbed nothing but you, I should have chanted nothing but you.

I will leave all and come and make the hymns of you;
None have understood you, but I understand you;
None have done justice to you—you have not done justice to yourself;
None but have found you imperfect—I only find no imperfection in you.

O I could sing such glories and grandeurs about you;
You have not known what you are—you have slumbered upon yourself all your
    life;
What you have done returns already in mockeries.

But the mockeries are not you;
Underneath them and within them, I see you lurk;
I pursue you where none else has pursued you.
Silence, the desk, the flippant expression, the night, the accustomed routine, if
    these conceal you from others, or from yourself, they do not conceal you
    from me;
The shaved face, the unsteady eye, the impure complexion, if these balk others,
    they do not balk me;
The pert apparel, the deformed attitude, drunkenness, greed, premature death,
    all these I part aside.

There is no endowment in man or woman that is not tallied in you;
There is no virtue, no beauty, in man or woman, but as good is in you;
No pluck nor endurance in others, but as good is in you;
No pleasure waiting for others, but an equal pleasure waits for you.

Whoever you are! claim your own at any hazard!
These shows of the east and west are tame, compared with you;

These immense meadows—these interminable rivers—you are immense and
  interminable as they;
You are he or she who is master or mistress over them,
Master or mistress in your own right over Nature, elements, pain, passion, dissolution.

The hopples fall from your ankles—you find an unfailing sufficiency;
Old or young, male or female, rude, low, rejected by the rest whatever you are
  promulgates itself;
Through birth, life, death, burial, the means are provided, nothing is scanted;
Through angers, losses, ambition, ignorance, ennui, what you are picks its way.

Verily a fine and moving poem, in any case, but there are two ways of
taking it, both useful.

One is the monistic way, the mystical way of pure cosmic emotion. The
glories and grandeurs, they are yours absolutely, even in the midst of your
defacements. Whatever may happen to you, whatever you may appear to
be, inwardly you are safe. Look back, *lie* back, on your true principle of
being! This is the famous way of quietism, of indifferentism. Its enemies
compare it to a spiritual opium. Yet pragmatism must respect this way, for
it has massive historic vindication.

But pragmatism sees another way to be respected also, the pluralistic
way of interpreting the poem. The you so glorified, to which the hymn is
sung, may mean your better possibilities phenomenally taken, or the specific redemptive effects even of your failures, upon yourself or others. It
may mean your loyalty to the possibilities of others whom you admire and
love so that you are willing to accept your own poor life, for it is that
glory's partner. You can at least appreciate, applaud, furnish the audience, of so brave a total world. Forget the low in yourself, then, think only
of the high. Identify your life therewith; then, through angers, losses, ignorance, ennui, whatever you thus make yourself, whatever you thus most
deeply are, picks its way.

In either way of taking the poem, it encourages fidelity to ourselves.
Both ways satisfy; both sanctify the human flux. Both paint the portrait of
the *you* on a gold background. But the background of the first way is the
static One, while in the second way it means possibles in the plural, genuine possibles, and it has all the restlessness of that conception.

Noble enough is either way of reading the poem; but plainly the pluralistic way agrees with the pragmatic temper best, for it immediately suggests
an infinitely larger number of the details of future experience to our mind.
It sets definite activities in us at work. Altho this second way seems prosaic
and earth-born in comparison with the first way, yet no one can accuse it of
tough-mindedness in any brutal sense of the term. Yet if, as pragmatists,
you should positively set up the second way *against* the first way, you
would very likely be misunderstood. You would be accused of denying
nobler conceptions, and of being an ally of tough-mindedness in the worst
sense.

You remember the letter from a member of this audience from which I read some extracts at our previous meeting. Let me read you an additional extract now. It shows a vagueness in realizing the alternatives before us which I think is very widespread.

"I believe," writes my friend and correspondent, "in pluralism; I believe that in our search for truth we leap from one floating cake of ice to another, on an infinite sea, and that by each of our acts we make new truths possible and old ones impossible; I believe that each man is responsible for making the universe better, and that if he does not do this it will be in so far left undone.

"Yet at the same time I am willing to endure that my children should be incurably sick and suffering (as they are not) and I myself stupid and yet with brains enough to see my stupidity, only on one condition, namely, that through the construction, in imagination and by reasoning, of a *rational unity of all things,* I can conceive my acts and my thoughts and my troubles as *supplemented by all the other phenomena of the world, and as forming—when thus supplemented—a scheme which I approve and adopt as my own;* and for my part I refuse to be persuaded that we can not look beyond the obvious pluralism of the naturalist and pragmatist to a logical unity in which they take no interest or stock."

Such a fine expression of personal faith warms the heart of the hearer. But how much does it clear his philosophic head? Does the writer consistently favor the monistic, or the pluralistic, interpretation of the world's poem? His troubles become atoned for *when thus supplemented,* he says, supplemented, that is, by all the remedies that *the other phenomena* may supply. Obviously here the writer faces forward into the particulars of experience, which he interprets in a pluralistic-melioristic way.

But he believes himself to face backward. He speaks of what he calls the rational *unity* of things, when all the while he really means their possible empirical *unification.* He supposes at the same time that the pragmatist, because he criticises rationalism's abstract One, is cut off from the consolation of believing in the saving possibilities of the concrete many. He fails in short to distinguish between taking the world's perfection as a necessary principle, and taking it only as a possible *terminus ad quem.*

I regard the writer of the letter as a genuine pragmatist, but as a pragmatist *sans le savoir.* He appears to me as one of that numerous class of philosophic amateurs whom I spoke of in my first lecture, as wishing to have all the good things going, without being too careful as to how they agree or disagree. "Rational unity of all things" is so inspiring a formula, that he brandishes it off-hand, and abstractly accuses pluralism of conflicting with it (for the bare names do conflict), altho concretely he means by it just the pragmatistically unified and ameliorated world. Most of us remain in this essential vagueness, and it is well that we should; but in the interest of clearheadedness it is well that some of us should go farther, so I will try now to focus a little more discriminatingly on this particular religious point.

Is then this you of yous, this absolutely real world, this unity that yields the moral inspiration and has the religious value, to be taken monistically or pluralistically? Is it *ante rem* or *in rebus?* Is it a principle or an end, an absolute or an ultimate, a first or a last? Does it make you look forward or lie back? It is certainly worth while not to clump the two things together, for if discriminated, they have decidedly diverse meanings for life.

Please observe that the whole dilemma revolves pragmatically about the notion of the world's possibilities. Intellectually, rationalism invokes its absolute principle of unity, as a ground of possibility for the many facts. Emotionally, it sees it as a container and limiter of possibilities, a guarantee that the upshot shall be good. Taken in this way, the absolute makes all good things certain, and all bad things impossible (in the eternal, namely), and may be said to transmute the entire category of possibility into categories more secure. One sees at this point that the great religious difference lies between the men who insist that the world *must and shall be,* and those who are contented with believing that the world *may be,* saved. The whole clash of rationalistic and empiricist religion is thus over the validity of possibility. It is necessary therefore to begin by focusing upon that word. What may the word "possible" definitely mean? To unreflecting men it means a sort of third estate of being, less real than existence, more real than non-existence, a twilight realm, a hybrid status, a limbo into which and out of which realities ever and anon are made to pass.

Such a conception is of course too vague and nondescript to satisfy us. Here, as elsewhere, the only way to extract a term's meaning is to use the pragmatic method on it. When you say that a thing is possible, what difference does it make? It makes at least this difference that if any one calls it impossible you can contradict him, if any one calls it actual you can contradict *him,* and if any one calls it necessary you can contradict him too.

But these privileges of contradiction don't amount to much. When you say a thing is possible, does not that make some farther difference in terms of actual fact?

It makes at least this negative difference that if the statement be true, it follows that *there is nothing extant capable of preventing* the possible thing. The absence of real grounds of interference may thus be said to make things *not impossible,* possible therefore in the *bare* or *abstract* sense.

But most possibles are not bare, they are concretely grounded, or well-grounded, as we say. What does this mean pragmatically? It means not only that there are no preventive conditions present, but that some of the conditions of production of the possible thing actually are here. Thus a concretely possible chicken means: (1) that the idea of chicken contains no essential self-contradiction; (2) that no boys, skunks, or other enemies are about; and (3) that at least an actual egg exists. Possible chicken means actual egg—plus actual sitting hen, or incubator, or what not. As the actual conditions approach completeness the chicken becomes a better-and-better-grounded possibility. When the conditions are entirely complete, it ceases to be a possibility, and turns into an actual fact.

Let us apply this notion to the salvation of the world. What does it pragmatically mean to say that this is possible? It means that some of the conditions of the world's deliverance do actually exist. The more of them there are existent, the fewer preventing conditions you can find, the better-grounded is the salvation's possibility, the more *probable* does the fact of the deliverance become.

So much for our preliminary look at possibility.

Now it would contradict the very spirit of life to say that our minds must be indifferent and neutral in questions like that of the world's salvation. Any one who pretends to be neutral writes himself down here as a fool and a sham. We all do wish to minimize the insecurity of the universe; we are and ought to be unhappy when we regard it as exposed to every enemy and open to every life-destroying draft. Nevertheless there are unhappy men who think the salvation of the world impossible. Theirs is the doctrine known as pessimism.

Optimism in turn would be the doctrine that thinks the world's salvation inevitable.

Midway between the two there stands what may be called the doctrine of meliorism, tho it has hitherto figured less as a doctrine than as an attitude in human affairs. Optimism has always been the regnant *doctrine* in European philosophy. Pessimism was only recently introduced by Schopenhauer [1] and counts few systematic defenders as yet. Meliorism treats salvation as neither necessary nor impossible. It treats it as a possibility, which becomes more and more of a probability the more numerous the actual conditions of salvation become.

It is clear that pragmatism must incline towards meliorism. Some conditions of the world's salvation are actually extant, and she can not possibly close her eyes to this fact: and should the residual conditions come, salvation would become an accomplished reality. Naturally the terms I use here are exceedingly summary. You may interpret the word "salvation" in any way you like, and make it as diffuse and distributive, or as climacteric and integral a phenomenon as you please.

Take, for example, any one of us in this room with the ideals which he cherishes and is willing to live and work for. Every such ideal realized will be one moment in the world's salvation. But these particular ideals are not bare abstract possibilities. They are grounded, they are *live* possibilities, for we are their live champions and pledges, and if the complementary conditions come and add themselves, our ideals will become actual things. What now are the complementary conditions? They are first such a mixture

---

[1] Arthur Schopenhauer (1788–1860): German philosopher. [R.J.R.]

of things as will in the fulness of time give us a chance, a gap that we can spring into, and, finally, *our act*.

Does our act then *create* the world's salvation so far as it makes room for itself, so far as it leaps into the gap? Does it create, not the whole world's salvation of course, but just so much of this as itself covers of the world's extent?

Here I take the bull by the horns, and in spite of the whole crew of rationalists and monists, of whatever brand they be, I ask *why not?* Our acts, our turning-places, where we seem to ourselves to make ourselves and grow, are the parts of the world to which we are closest, the parts of which our knowledge is the most intimate and complete. Why should we not take them at their face-value? Why may they not be the actual turning-places and growing-places which they seem to be, of the world—why not the workshop of being, where we catch fact in the making, so that nowhere may the world grow in any other kind of way than this?

Irrational! we are told. How can new being come in local spots and patches which add themselves or stay away at random, independently of the rest? There must be a reason for our acts, and where in the last resort can any reason be looked for save in the material pressure or the logical compulsion of the total nature of the world? There can be but one real agent of growth, or seeming growth, anywhere, and that agent is the integral world itself. It may grow all-over, if growth there be, but that single parts should grow *per se* is irrational.

But if one talks of rationality—and of reasons for things, and insists that they can't just come in spots, what *kind* of a reason can there ultimately be why anything should come at all? Talk of logic and necessity and categories and the absolute and the contents of the whole philosophical machine-shop as you will, the only *real* reason I can think of why anything should ever come is that *some one wishes it to be here*. It is *demanded*, —demanded, it may be, to give relief to no matter how small a fraction of the world's mass. This is *living reason*, and compared with it material causes and logical necessities are spectral things.

In short the only fully rational world would be the world of wishing-caps, the world of telepathy, where every desire is fulfilled instanter, without having to consider or placate surrounding or intermediate powers. This is the Absolute's own world. He calls upon the phenomenal world to be, and it *is*, exactly as he calls for it, no other condition being required. In our world, the wishes of the individual are only one condition. Other individuals are there with other wishes and they must be propitiated first. So Being grows under all sorts of resistances in this world of the many, and, from compromise to compromise, only gets organized gradually into what may be called secondarily rational shape. We approach the wishing-cap type of organization only in a few departments of life. We want water and we turn a faucet. We want a kodak-picture and we press a button. We want information and we telephone. We want to travel and we buy a ticket. In these and similar cases, we hardly need to do more than the wishing—the world is rationally organized to do the rest.

But this talk of rationality is a parenthesis and a digression. What we were discussing was the idea of a world growing not integrally but piecemeal by the contributions of its several parts. Take the hypothesis seriously and as a live one. Suppose that the world's author put the case to you before creation, saying: "I am going to make a world not certain to be saved, a world the perfection of which shall be conditional merely, the condition being that each several agent does its own 'level best.' I offer you the chance of taking part in such a world. Its safety, you see, is unwarranted. It is a real adventure, with real danger, yet it may win through. It is a social scheme of co-operative work genuinely to be done. Will you join the procession? Will you trust yourself and trust the other agents enough to face the risk?"

Should you in all seriousness, if participation in such a world were proposed to you, feel bound to reject it as not safe enough? Would you say that, rather than be part and parcel of so fundamentally pluralistic and irrational a universe, you preferred to relapse into the slumber of nonentity from which you had been momentarily aroused by the tempter's voice?

Of course if you are normally constituted, you would do nothing of the sort. There is a healthy-minded buoyancy in most of us which such a universe would exactly fit. We would therefore accept the offer—"*Top! und schlag auf schlag!*" It would be just like the world we practically live in; and loyalty to our old nurse Nature would forbid us to say no. The world proposed would seem "rational" to us in the most living way.

Most of us, I say, would therefore welcome the proposition and add our *fiat* to the *fiat* of the creator. Yet perhaps some would not; for there are morbid minds in every human collection, and to them the prospect of a universe with only a fighting chance of safety would probably make no appeal. There are moments of discouragement in us all, when we are sick of self and tired of vainly striving. Our own life breaks down, and we fall into the attitude of the prodigal son. We mistrust the chances of things. We want a universe where we can just give up, fall on our father's neck, and be absorbed into the absolute life as a drop of water melts into the river or the sea.

The peace and rest, the security desiderated at such moments is security against the bewildering accidents of so much finite experience. Nirvana means safety from this everlasting round of adventures of which the world of sense consists. The hindoo and the buddhist, for this is essentially their attitude, are simply afraid, afraid of more experience, afraid of life.

And to men of this complexion, religious monism comes with its consoling words: "All is needed and essential—even you with your sick soul and heart. All are one with God, and with God all is well. The everlasting arms are beneath, whether in the world of finite appearance you seem to fail or to succeed." There can be no doubt that when men are reduced to their last sick extremity absolutism is the only saving scheme. Pluralistic moralism simply makes their teeth chatter, it refrigerates the very heart within their breast.

So we see concretely two types of religion in sharp contrast. Using our old terms of comparison, we may say that the absolutistic scheme appeals to the tender-minded while the pluralistic scheme appeals to the tough. Many persons would refuse to call the pluralistic scheme religious at all. They would call it moralistic, and would apply the word religious to the monistic scheme alone. Religion in the sense of self-surrender, and moralism in the sense of self-sufficingness, have been pitted against each other as incompatibles frequently enough in the history of human thought.

We stand here before the final question of philosophy. I said in my fourth lecture that I believed the monistic-pluralistic alternative to be the deepest and most pregnant question that our minds can frame. Can it be that the disjunction is a final one? that only one side can be true? Are a pluralism and monism genuine incompatibles? So that, if the world were really pluralistically constituted, if it really existed distributively and were made up of a lot of eaches, it could only be saved piecemeal and *de facto* as the result of their behavior, and its epic history in no wise short-circuited by some essential oneness in which the severalness were already "taken up" beforehand and eternally "overcome"? If this were so, we should have to choose one philosophy or the other. We could not say "yes, yes" to both alternatives. There would have to be a "no" in our relations with the possible. We should confess an ultimate disappointment: we could not remain healthy-minded and sick-minded in one indivisible act.

Of course as human beings we can be healthy minds on one day and sick souls on the next; and as amateur dabblers in philosophy we may perhaps be allowed to call ourselves monistic pluralists, or free-will determinists, or whatever else may occur to us of a reconciling kind. But as philosophers aiming at clearness and consistency, and feeling the pragmatistic need of squaring truth with truth, the question is forced upon us of frankly adopting either the tender or the robustious type of thought. In particular *this* query has always come home to me: May not the claims of tender-mindedness go too far? May not the notion of a world already saved *in toto* anyhow, be too saccharine to stand? May not religious optimism be too idyllic? Must *all* be saved? Is *no* price to be paid in the work of salvation? Is the last word sweet? Is all "yes, yes" in the universe? Doesn't the fact of "no" stand at the very core of life? Doesn't the very "seriousness" that we attribute to life mean that ineluctable noes and losses form a part of it, that there are genuine sacrifices somewhere, and that something permanently drastic and bitter always remains at the bottom of its cup?

I can not speak officially as a pragmatist here; all I can say is that my own pragmatism offers no objection to my taking sides with this more moralistic view, and giving up the claim of total reconciliation. The possibility of this is involved in the pragmatistic willingness to treat pluralism as a serious hypothesis. In the end it is our faith and not our logic that decides such questions, and I deny the right of any pretended logic to veto my own faith. I find myself willing to take the universe to be really dangerous and adventurous, without therefore backing out and crying "no play." I am willing to think that the prodigal-son attitude, open to us as it is in many vicissitudes, is not the right and final attitude towards the whole of life. I am willing that there should be real losses and real losers, and no total preservation of all that is. I can believe in the ideal as an ultimate, not as an origin, and as an extract, not the whole. When the cup is poured off, the dregs are left behind for ever, but the possibility of what is poured off is sweet enough to accept.

As a matter of fact countless human imaginations live in this moralistic and epic kind of a universe, and find its disseminated and strung-along successes sufficient for their rational needs. There is a finely translated epigram in the Greek anthology which admirably expresses this state of mind, this acceptance of loss as unatoned for, even though the lost element might be one's self:

> A shipwrecked sailor, buried on this coast,
>> Bids you set sail.
> Full many a gallant bark, when we were lost,
>> Weathered the gale.

Those puritans who answered "yes" to the question: Are you willing to be damned for God's glory? were in this objective and magnanimous condition of mind. The way of escape from evil on this system is *not* by getting it "*aufgehoben*," or preserved in the whole as an element essential but "overcome." *It is by dropping it out altogether, throwing it overboard and getting beyond it, helping to make a universe that shall forget its very place and name.*

It is then perfectly possible to accept sincerely a drastic kind of a universe from which the element of "seriousness" is not to be expelled. Whoso does so, it seems to me, a genuine pragmatist. He is willing to live on a scheme of uncertified possibilities which he trusts; willing to pay with his own person, if need be, for the realization of the ideals which he frames.

What now actually *are* the other forces which he trusts to co-operate with him, in a universe of such a type? They are at least his fellow men, in the stage of being which our actual universe has reached. But are there not superhuman forces also, such as religious men of the pluralistic type we have been considering have always believed in? Their words may have sounded monistic when they said "there is no God but God"; but the original polytheism of mankind has only imperfectly and vaguely sublimated itself into monotheism, and monotheism itself, so far as it was religious and not a scheme of classroom instruction for the metaphysicians, has always viewed God as but one helper, *primus inter pares,* in the midst of all the shapers of the great world's fate.

I fear that my previous lectures, confined as they have been to human and humanistic aspects, may have left the impression on many of you that pragmatism means methodically to leave the superhuman out. I have shown small respect indeed for the Absolute, and I have until this moment spoken of no other superhuman hypothesis but that. But I trust that you see sufficiently that the Absolute has nothing but its superhumanness in common with the theistic God. On pragmatistic principles, if the hypothesis of God works satisfactorily in the widest sense of the word, it is true. Now whatever its residual difficulties may be, experience shows that it certainly does work, and that the problem is to build it out and determine it so that it will combine satisfactorily with all the other working truths. I can not start upon a whole theology at the end of this last lecture; but when I tell you that I have written a book on men's religious experience, which on the whole has been regarded as making for the reality of God, you will perhaps exempt my own pragmatism from the charge of being an atheistic system. I firmly disbelieve, myself, that our human experience is the highest form of experience extant in the universe. I believe rather that we stand in much the same relation to the whole of the universe as our canine and feline pets do to the whole of human life. They inhabit our drawing-rooms and libraries. They take part in scenes of whose significance they have no inkling. They are merely tangent to curves of history the beginnings and ends and forms of which pass wholly beyond their ken. So we are tangent to the wider life of things. But, just as many of the dog's and cat's ideals coincide with our ideals, and the dogs and cats have daily living proof of the fact, so we may well believe, on the proofs that religious experience affords, that higher powers exist and are at work to save the world on ideal lines similar to our own.

You see that pragmatism can be called religious, if you allow that religion can be pluralistic or merely melioristic in type. But whether you will finally put up with that type of religion or not is a question that only you yourself can decide. Pragmatism has to postpone dogmatic answer, for we do not yet know certainly which type of religion is going to work best in the long run. The various overbeliefs of men, their several faith-ventures, are in fact what are needed to bring the evidence in. You will probably make your own ventures severally. If radically tough, the hurly-burly of the sensible facts of nature will be enough for you, and you will need no religion at all. If radically tender, you will take up with the more monistic form of religion: the pluralistic form, with its reliance on possibilities that are not necessities, will not seem to afford you security enough.

But if you are neither tough nor tender in an extreme and radical sense, but mixed as most of us are, it may seem to you that the type of pluralistic and moralistic religion that I have offered is as good a religious synthesis as you are likely to find. Between the two extremes of crude naturalism on the one hand and transcendental absolutism on the other, you may find that what I take the liberty of calling the pragmatistic or melioristic type of theism is exactly what you require.

QUESTIONS FOR STUDY AND DISCUSSION

1. Show how James applies his theory of pragmatism to the salvation of the world.
2. What does James mean when he says that pragmatism is a doctrine of meliorism?
3. Show how James by his pragmatism tries to justify a belief in theism.

Charles Sanders Peirce

CHARLES SANDERS PEIRCE, son of the distinguished mathematician and
Harvard professor Benjamin Peirce, was born in 1839 in Cambridge,
Massachusetts. He was graduated from Harvard in 1859 and received
his M.A. in chemistry from the Lawrence Scientific School at Harvard
in 1862. In 1861 he joined the staff of the United States Coastal and
Geodetic Survey with which he was associated for thirty years. Peirce
taught logic at the Johns Hopkins University from 1879 until 1884 and
also lectured at Harvard and at the Lowell Institute in Boston.
Mathematician, logician, and philosopher of science, Peirce had a far-
reaching influence on contemporary philosophy. His writings are
contained in the *Collected Papers of Charles Sanders Peirce,* edited by
Charles Hartshorne, Paul Weiss, and Arthur Burks. He died in Cambridge in 1914.

A Neglected Argument
for the Reality of God

Of the three Universes of Experience familiar to us all, the first comprises
all mere Ideas, those airy nothings to which the mind of poet, pure mathematician, or another *might* give local habitation and a name within that
mind. Their very airy-nothingness, the fact that their Being consists in mere
capability of getting thought, not in anybody's Actually thinking them, saves
their Reality. The second Universe is that of the Brute Actuality of things
and facts. I am confident that their Being consists in reactions against
Brute forces, notwithstanding objections redoubtable until they are closely
and fairly examined. The third Universe comprises everything whose being
consists in active power to establish connections between different objects,
especially between objects in different Universes. Such is everything which
is essentially a Sign—not the mere body of the Sign, which is not essentially such, but, so to speak, the Sign's Soul, which has its Being in its
power of serving as intermediary between its Object and a Mind. Such, too,

Reprinted by permission of the publishers from pp. 312–19 of Charles Hartshorne
and Paul Weiss (eds.), *Collected Papers of Charles Sanders Peirce,* vol. VI. Cambridge, Mass.: The Belknap Press of Harvard University Press. Copyright 1935, 1963
by the President and Fellows of Harvard College.

is a living consciousness, and such the life, the power of growth, of a plant. Such is a living constitution—a daily newspaper, a great fortune, a social "movement."

An "Argument" is any process of thought reasonably tending to produce a definite belief. An "Argumentation" is an Argument proceeding upon definitely formulated premisses.

If God Really be, and be benign, then, in view of the generally conceded truth that religion, were it but proved, would be a good outweighing all others, we should naturally expect that there would be some Argument for His Reality that should be obvious to all minds, high and low alike, that should earnestly strive to find the truth of the matter; and further, that this Argument should present its conclusion, not as a proposition of metaphysical theology, but in a form directly applicable to the conduct of life, and full of nutrition for man's highest growth. What I shall refer to as the N.A.—the Neglected Argument—seems to me best to fulfill this condition, and I should not wonder if the majority of those whose own reflections have harvested belief in God must bless the radiance of the N.A. for that wealth. Its persuasiveness is no less than extraordinary; while it is not unknown to anybody. Nevertheless, of all those theologians (within my little range of reading) who, with commendable assiduity, scrape together all the sound reasons they can find or concoct to prove the first proposition of theology, few mention this one, and they most briefly. They probably share those current notions of logic which recognize no other Arguments than Argumentations.

There is a certain agreeable occupation of mind which, from its having no distinctive name, I infer is not as commonly practiced as it deserves to be; for indulged in moderately—say through some five to six per cent of one's waking time, perhaps during a stroll—it is refreshing enough more than to repay the expenditure. Because it involves no purpose save that of casting aside all serious purpose, I have sometimes been half-inclined to call it reverie with some qualification; but for a frame of mind so antipodal to vacancy and dreaminess such a designation would be too excruciating a misfit. In fact, it is Pure Play. Now, Play, we all know, is a lively exercise of one's powers. Pure Play has no rules, except this very law of liberty. It bloweth where it listeth. It has no purpose, unless recreation. The particular occupation I mean—a *petite bouchée* with the Universes—may take either the form of æsthetic contemplation, or that of distant castle-building (whether in Spain or within one's own moral training), or that of considering some wonder in one of the Universes, or some connection between two of the three, with speculation concerning its cause. It is this last kind—and I will call it "Musement" on the whole—that I particularly recommend, because it will in time flower into the N.A. One who sits down with the purpose of becoming convinced of the truth of religion is plainly not inquiring in scientific singleness of heart, and must always suspect himself of rea-

soning unfairly. So he can never attain the entirety even of a physicist's belief in electrons, although this is avowedly but provisional. But let religious
meditation be allowed to grow up spontaneously out of Pure Play without
any breach of continuity, and the Muser will retain the perfect candour
proper to Musement.

If one who had determined to make trial of Musement as a favorite
recreation were to ask me for advice, I should reply as follows: The dawn
and the gloaming most invite one to Musement; but I have found no watch
of the nychthemeron that has not its own advantages for the pursuit. It
begins passively enough with drinking in the impression of some nook in
one of the three Universes. But impression soon passes into attentive observation, observation into musing, musing into a lively give and take of
communion between self and self. If one's observations and reflections are
allowed to specialize themselves too much, the Play will be converted into
scientific study; and that cannot be pursued in odd half hours.

I should add: Adhere to the one ordinance of Play, the law of liberty. I
can testify that the last half century, at least, has never lacked tribes of Sir
Oracles, colporting brocards to bar off one or another roadway of inquiry;
and a Rabelais would be needed to bring out all the fun that has been
packed in their airs of infallibility. Auguste Comte, notwithstanding his
having apparently produced some unquestionably genuine thinking, was
long the chief of such a band. The vogue of each particular maxim of theirs
was necessarily brief. For what distinction can be gained by repeating saws
heard from all mouths? No bygone fashion seems more grotesque than a
panache of obsolete wisdom. I remember the days when a pronouncement
all the rage was that no science must borrow the methods of another; the
geologist must not use a microscope, nor the astronomer a spectroscope.
Optics must not meddle with electricity, nor logic with algebra. But twenty
years later, if you aspired to pass for a commanding intellect, you would
have to pull a long face and declare that "It is not the business of science
to search for origins." This maxim was a masterpiece, since no timid soul,
in dread of being thought naïve, would dare inquire what "origins" were,
albeit the secret confessor within his breast compelled the awful self-
acknowledgment of his having no idea into what else than "origins" of phenomena (in some sense of that indefinite word) man can inquire. That
human reason can comprehend some causes is past denial, and once we are
forced to recognize a given element in experience, it is reasonable to await
positive evidence before we complicate our acknowledgment with qualifications. Otherwise, why venture beyond direct observation? Illustrations of
this principle abound in physical science. Since, then, it is certain that man
is able to understand the laws and the causes of some phenomena, it is reasonable to assume, in regard to any given problem, that it would get rightly
solved by man, if a sufficiency of time and attention were devoted to it.
Moreover, those problems that at first blush appear utterly insoluble re-

ceive, in that very circumstance, as Edgar Poe remarked [1] in his "The Murders in the Rue Morgue," their smoothly-fitting keys. This particularly adapts them to the Play of Musement.

Forty or fifty minutes of vigorous and unslackened analytic thought bestowed upon one of them usually suffices to educe from it all there is to educe, its general solution. There is no kind of reasoning that I should wish to discourage in Musement; and I should lament to find anybody confining it to a method of such moderate fertility as logical analysis. Only, the Player should bear in mind that the higher weapons in the arsenal of thought are not playthings but edge-tools. In any mere Play they can be used by way of exercise alone; while logical analysis can be put to its full efficiency in Musement. So, continuing the counsels that had been asked of me, I should say, "Enter your skiff of Musement, push off into the lake of thought, and leave the breath of heaven to swell your sail. With your eyes open, awake to what is about or within you, and open conversation with yourself; for such is all meditation." It is, however, not a conversation in words alone, but is illustrated, like a lecture, with diagrams and with experiments.

Different people have such wonderfully different ways of thinking that it would be far beyond my competence to say what courses Musements might not take; but a brain endowed with automatic control, as man's indirectly is, is so naturally and rightly interested in its own faculties that some psychological and semi-psychological questions would doubtless get touched; such, in the latter class, as this: Darwinians, with truly surprising ingenuity, have concocted, and with still more astonishing confidence have accepted as proved, one explanation for the diverse and delicate beauties of flowers, another for those of butterflies, and so on; but why is all nature —the forms of trees, the compositions of sunsets—suffused with such beauties throughout, and not nature only, but the other two Universes as well? Among more purely psychological questions, the nature of pleasure and pain will be likely to attract attention. Are they mere qualities of feeling, or are they rather motor instincts attracting us to some feelings and repelling others? Have pleasure and pain the same sort of constitution, or are they contrasted in this respect, pleasure arising upon the forming or strengthening of an association by resemblance, and pain upon the weakening or disruption of such a habit or conception?

Psychological speculations will naturally lead on to musings upon metaphysical problems proper, good exercise for a mind with a turn for exact thought. It is here that one finds those questions that at first seem to offer no handle for reason's clutch, but which readily yield to logical analysis. But problems of metaphysics will inevitably present themselves that logical analysis will not suffice to solve. Some of the best will be motived by

---

[1] "It appears to me that this mystery is considered insoluble for the very reason which should cause it to be regarded as easy of solution. I mean the *outré* character of its features." [C.S.P.]

a desire to comprehend universe-wide aggregates of unformulated but partly experienced phenomena. I would suggest that the Muser be not too impatient to analyze these, lest some significant ingredient be lost in the process; but that he begin by pondering them from every point of view, until he seems to read some truth beneath the phenomena.

At this point a trained mind will demand that an examination be made of the truth of the interpretation; and the first step in such examination must be a logical analysis of the theory. But strict examination would be a task a little too serious for the Musement of hour fractions, and if it is postponed there will be ample remuneration even in the suggestions that there is not time to examine; especially since a few of them will appeal to reason as all but certain.

Let the Muser, for example, after well appreciating, in its breadth and depth, the unspeakable variety of each Universe, turn to those phenomena that are of the nature of homogeneities of connectedness in each; and what a spectacle will unroll itself! As a mere hint of them I may point out that every small part of space, however remote, is bounded by just such neighbouring parts as every other, without a single exception throughout immensity. The matter of Nature is in every star of the same elementary kinds, and (except for variations of circumstance), what is more wonderful still, throughout the whole visible universe, about the same proportions of the different chemical elements prevail. Though the mere catalogue of known carbon-compounds alone would fill an unwieldy volume, and perhaps, if the truth were known, the number of amino-acids alone is greater, yet it is unlikely that there are in all more than about 600 elements, of which 500 dart through space too swiftly to be held down by the earth's gravitation, coronium being the slowest-moving of these. This small number bespeaks comparative simplicity of structure. Yet no mathematician but will confess the present hoplessness of attempting to comprehend the constitution of the hydrogen-atom, the simplest of the elements that can be held to earth.

From speculations on the homogeneities of each Universe, the Muser will naturally pass to the consideration of homogeneities and connections between two different Universes, or all three. Especially in them all we find one type of occurrence, that of growth, itself consisting in the homogeneities of small parts. This is evident in the growth of motion into displacement, and the growth of force into motion. In growth, too, we find that the three Universes conspire; and a universal feature of it is provision for later stages in earlier ones. This is a specimen of certain lines of reflection which will inevitably suggest the hypothesis of God's Reality. It is not that such phenomena might not be capable of being accounted for, in one sense, by the action of chance with the smallest conceivable dose of a higher element; for if by God be meant the *Ens necessarium,* that very hypothesis requires that such should be the case. But the point is that that sort of explanation leaves a mental explanation just as needful as before. Tell me, upon sufficient authority, that all cerebration depends upon movements of neurites that strictly obey certain physical laws, and that thus all expressions of thought, both external and internal, receive a physical explanation, and I shall be ready to believe you. But if you go on to say that this explodes the theory that my neighbour and myself are governed by reason, and are thinking beings, I must frankly say that it will not give me a high opinion of your intelligence. But however that may be, in the Pure Play of Musement the idea of God's Reality will be sure sooner or later to be found an attractive fancy, which the Muser will develop in various ways. The more he ponders it, the more it will find response in every part of his mind, for its beauty, for its supplying an ideal of life, and for its thoroughly satisfactory explanation of his whole threefold environment.

THE HYPOTHESIS OF GOD

The hypothesis of God is a peculiar one, in that it supposes an infinitely incomprehensible object, although every hypothesis, as such, supposes its object to be truly conceived in the hypothesis. This leaves the hypothesis but one way of understanding itself; namely, as vague yet as true so far as it is definite, and as continually tending to define itself more and more, and without limit. The hypothesis, being thus itself inevitably subject to the law of growth, appears in its vagueness to represent God as so, albeit this is directly contradicted in the hypothesis from its very first phase. But this apparent attribution of growth to God, since it is ineradicable from the hypothesis, cannot, according to the hypothesis, be flatly false. Its implications concerning the Universes will be maintained in the hypothesis, while its implications concerning God will be partly disavowed, and yet held to be less false than their denial would be. Thus the hypothesis will lead to our thinking of features of each Universe as purposed; and this will stand or fall with the hypothesis. Yet a purpose essentially involves growth, and so cannot be attributed to God. Still it will, according to the hypothesis, be less false to speak so than to represent God as purposeless.

Assured as I am from my own personal experience that every man capable of so controlling his attention as to perform a little exact thinking will, if he examines Zeno's argument about Achilles and the tortoise, come to think, as I do, that it is nothing but a contemptible catch, I do not think that I either am or ought to be less assured, from what I know of the effects of Musement on myself and others, that any normal man who considers the three Universes in the light of the hypothesis of God's Reality, and pursues that line of reflection in scientific singleness of heart, will come to be stirred to the depths of his nature by the beauty of the idea and by its august practicality, even to the point of earnestly loving and adoring his strictly hypothetical God, and to that of desiring above all things to shape the whole conduct of life and all the springs of action into conformity with that hypothesis. Now to be deliberately and thoroughly prepared to shape one's conduct into conformity with a proposition is neither more nor less than the state of mind called Believing that proposition, however long the conscious classification of it under that head be postponed.

QUESTIONS FOR STUDY AND DISCUSSION

1. What does Peirce mean by "Musement"?
2. Show how this leads "to the hypothesis of God's reality."
3. How does Peirce indicate his opposition to dogmatism in science?

John Dewey

JOHN DEWEY was born in Burlington, Vermont, in 1859. He was graduated from the University of Vermont in 1879 and received the doctorate of philosophy from the Johns Hopkins University in 1884. From 1888 to 1904 he taught at the Universities of Michigan and Chicago and while at Chicago gained national renown as Director of the Laboratory School. From 1904 until his retirement in 1930 he was professor of Philosophy at Columbia University and then served as professor emeritus in residence until 1939. One of America's most distinguished and controversial philosophers, Dewey exerted profound influence not only in contemporary philosophy but also in education, psychology, and social theory. He was a prolific writer and among his most important works are *Reconstruction in Philosophy* (1920), *Experience and Nature* (1925), *Art as Experience* (1934), *A Common Faith* (1934), and *Logic: The Theory of Inquiry* (1938). Dewey died in New York City in 1952.

The Scientific Factor

Philosophy starts from some deep and wide way of responding to the difficulties life presents, but it grows only when material is at hand for making this practical response conscious, articulate and communicable. Accompanying the economic, political and ecclesiastical changes which were alluded to in an earlier lecture, was a scientific revolution enormous in scope and leaving unchanged almost no detail of belief about nature, physical and human. In part this scientific transformation was produced by just the change in practical attitude and temper. But as it progressed, it furnished that change an appropriate vocabulary, congenial to its needs, and made it articulate. The advance of science in its larger generalizations and in its specific detail of fact supplied precisely that intellectual equipment of ideas and concrete fact that was needed in order to formulate, precipitate, communicate and propagate the new disposition. Today, accordingly, we shall deal with those contrasting conceptions of the structure and constitution of

From pp. 53–76 of John Dewey, *Reconstruction in Philosophy*. Reprinted by permission of the Beacon Press. Copyright 1920 by Henry Holt and Company, enlarged edition copyright 1948 by Beacon Press.

Nature, which when they are accepted on the authority of science (alleged or real), form the intellectual framework of philosophy.

Contrasting conceptions of ancient and modern science have been selected. For I see no way in which the truly philosophic import of the picture of the world painted by modern science can be appreciated except to exhibit it in contrast with that earlier picture which gave classic metaphysics its intellectual foundation and confirmation. The world in which philosophers once put their trust was a closed world, a world consisting internally of a limited number of fixed forms, and having definite boundaries externally. The world of modern science is an open world, a world varying indefinitely without the possibility of assignable limit in its internal make-up, a world stretching beyond any assignable bounds externally. Again, the world in which even the most intelligent men of olden times thought they lived was a fixed world, a realm where changes went on only within immutable limits of rest and permanence, and a world where the fixed and unmoving was, as we have already noted, higher in quality and authority than the moving and altering. And in the third place, the world which men once saw with their eyes, portrayed in their imaginations and repeated in their plans of conduct, was a world of a limited number of classes, kinds, forms, distinct in quality (as kinds and species must be distinct) and arranged in a graded order of superiority and inferiority.

It is not easy to recall the image of the universe which was taken for granted in the world tradition. In spite of its dramatic rendering (as in Dante), of the dialectical elaborations of Aristotle and St. Thomas, in spite of the fact that it held men's minds captive until the last three hundred years, and that its overthrow involved a religious upheaval, it is already dim, faded and remote. Even as a separate and abstract thing of theory it is not easy to recover.

As something pervasive, interwoven with all the details of reflection and observation, with the plans and rules of behavior, it is impossible to call it back again. Yet, as best we can, we need to put before our minds a definitely enclosed universe, something which can be called a universe in a literal and visible sense, having the earth at its fixed and unchanging centre and at a fixed circumference the heavenly arch of fixed stars moving in an eternal round of divine ether, hemming in all things and keeping them forever at one and in order. The earth, though at the centre, is the coarsest, grossest, most material, least significant and good (or perfect) of the parts of this closed world. It is the scene of maximum fluctuation and vicissitude. It is the least rational, and therefore the least notable, or knowable; it offers the least to reward contemplation, provoke admiration and govern conduct. Between this grossly material centre and the immaterial, spiritual and eternal heavens lie a definite series of regions of moon, planets, sun, etc., each of which gains in rank, value, rationality and true being as it is farther from earth and nearer the heavens. Each of these regions is composed of its own appropriate stuff of earth, water, air, fire in its own dominant degree, until we reach the heavenly firmament which transcends all these principles, being constituted, as was just said, of that immaterial, in-alterable energy called ether.

Within this tight and pent in universe, changes take place of course. But they are only of a small number of fixed kinds; and they operate only within fixed limits. Each kind of stuff has its own appropriate motion. It is the nature of earthly things to be heavy, since they are gross, and hence to move downward. Fire and superior things are light and hence move upward to their proper place; air rises only to the plane of the planets, where it then takes its back and forth motion which naturally belongs to it, as is evident in the winds and in respiration. Ether being the highest of all physical things has a purely circular movement. The daily return of the fixed stars is the closest possible approximation to eternity, and to the self-involved revolution of mind upon its own ideal axis of reason. Upon the earth in vir-tue of its earthly nature—or rather its lack of virtue—is a scene of mere change. Mere flux, aimless and meaningless, starts at no definite point and arrives at nothing, amounts to nothing. Mere changes of quantity, all purely mechanical changes, are of this kind. They are like the shiftings of the sands by the sea. They may be sensed, but they cannot be "noted" or understood; they lack fixed limits which govern them. They are contempti-ble. They are casual, the sport of accident.

Only changes which lead to some defined or fixed outcome of form are of any account and can have any account—any *logos* or reason—made of them. The growth of plants and animals illustrates the highest kind of change which is possible in the sublunary or mundane sphere. They go from one definite fixed form to another. Oaks generate only oaks, oysters only oysters, man only man. The material factor of mechanical production enters in, but enters in as accident to prevent the full consummation of the type of the species, and to bring about the meaningless variations which diversify various oaks or oysters from one another; or in extreme cases to produce freaks, sports, monsters, three-handed or four-toed men. Aside from accidental and undesirable variations, each individual has a fixed ca-reer to pursue, a fixed path in which to travel. Terms which sound modern, words like potentiality and development abound in Aristotelian thought, and have misled some into reading into his thought modern meanings. But the significance of these words in classic and medieval thought is rigidly determined by their context. Development holds merely of the course of changes which takes place within a particular member of the species. It is only a name for the predetermined movement from the acorn to the oak tree. It takes place not in things generally but only in some one of the numerically insignificant members of the oak species. Development, evolu-tion, never means, as in modern science, origin of new forms, a mutation from an old species, but only the monotonous traversing of a previously plotted cycle of change. So potentiality never means, as in modern life, the possibility of novelty, of invention, of radical deviation, but only that principle in virtue of which the acorn becomes the oak. Technically, it is the capacity for movement between opposites. Only the cold can become hot; only the dry can become wet; only the babe can become a man; the seed the full-grown wheat and so on. Potentiality instead of implying the emergence of anything novel means merely the facility with which a particular thing repeats the recurrent processes of its kind, and thus becomes a specific case of the eternal forms in and through which all things are constituted.

In spite of the almost infinite numerical diversity of individuals, there are only a limited number of species, kinds or sorts. And the world is essentially a world which falls into sorts; it is pre-arranged into distinct classes. Moreover, just as we naturally arrange plants and animals into series, ranks and grades, from the lower to the highest, so with all things in the universe. The distinct classes to which things belong by their very nature form a hierarchical order. There are castes in nature. The universe is constituted on an aristocratic, one can truly say a feudal, plan. Species, classes do not mix or overlap—except in cases of accident, and to the result of chaos. Otherwise, everything belongs in advance to a certain class, and the class has its own fixed place in the hierarchy of Being. The universe is indeed a tidy spot whose purity is interfered with only by those irregular changes in individuals which are due to the presence of an obdurate matter that refuses to yield itself wholly to rule and form. Otherwise it is a universe with a fixed place for everything and where everything knows its place, its station and class, and keeps it. Hence what are known technically as final and formal causes are supreme, and efficient causes are relegated to an inferior place. The so-called final cause is just a name for the fact that there is some fixed form characteristic of a class or sort of things which governs the changes going on, so that they tend toward it as their end and goal, the fulfilment of their true nature. The supralunar region is the end or final cause of the proper movements of air and fire; the earth of the motions of crass, heavy things; the oak of the acorn; the mature form in general of the germinal.

The "efficient cause," that which produces and instigates a movement, is only some external change as it accidentally gives a kind of push to an immature, imperfect being and starts it moving toward its perfected or fulfilled form. The final cause is the perfected form regarded as the *explanation or reason* of prior changes. When it is not taken in reference to the changes completed and brought to rest in it, but in itself it is the "formal cause": The inherent *nature* or character which "makes" or constitutes a thing *what it is* so far as it truly *is,* namely, what it is so far as it does not change. Logically and practically all of the traits which have been enumerated cohere. Attack one and you attack all. When any one is undermined all go. This is the reason why the intellectual modification of the last few centuries may truly be called a revolution. It has substituted a conception of the world differing at every point. It makes little matter at what point you commence to trace the difference, you find yourself carried into all other points.

Instead of a closed universe, science now presents us with one infinite in space and time having no limits here or there, at this end, so to speak, or at that, and as infinitely complex in internal structure as it is infinite in extent. Hence it is also an open world, an infinitely variegated one, a world which in the old sense can hardly be called a universe at all; so multiplex and far-reaching that it cannot be summed up and grasped in any one formula. And change rather than fixity is now a measure of "reality" or energy of being; change is omnipresent. The laws in which the modern man of science is interested are laws of motion, of generation and consequence. He speaks of law where the ancients spoke of kind and essence, because what he wants is a correlation of changes, an ability to detect one change occurring in correspondence with another. He does not try to define and delimit something remaining constant *in* change. He tries to describe a constant order *of* change. And while the word "constant" appears in both statements, the meaning of the word is not the same. In one case, we are dealing with something constant in *existence,* physical or metaphysical; in the other case, with something constant in *function* and operation. One is a form of independent being; the other is a formula of description and calculation of interdependent changes.

In short, classic thought accepted a feudally arranged order of classes or kinds, each "holding" from a superior and in turn giving the rule of conduct and service to an inferior. This trait reflects and parallels most closely the social situation we were considering at the last hour. We have a fairly definite notion of society as organized upon the feudal basis. The family principle, the principle of kinship is strong, and especially is this true as we ascend in the social scale. At the lower end, individuals may be lost more or less in the mass. Since all are parts of the common herd, there is nothing especial to distinguish their birth. But among the privileged and ruling class the case is quite different. The tie of kinship at once marks a group off externally and gives it distinction, and internally holds all its members together. Kinship, kind, class, genus are synonymous terms, starting from social and concrete facts and going to the technical and abstract. For kinship is a sign of a common nature, of something universal and permanent running through all particular individuals, and giving them a real and objective unity. Because such and such persons are kin they are *really,* and not merely conventionally, marked off into a class having something unique about it. All contemporary members are bound into an objective unity which includes ancestors and descendants and excludes all who belong to another kin or kind. Assuredly this parcelling out of the world into separate kinds, each having its qualitatively distinct nature in contrast with other species, binding numerically distinct individuals together, and preventing their diversities from exceeding fixed bounds, may without exaggeration be called a projection of the family principle into the world at large.

In a feudally organized society, moreover, each kinship group or species occupies a definite place. It is marked by the possession of a specific *rank* higher or lower with respect to other grades. This position confers upon it certain privileges, enabling it to enforce certain claims upon those lower in the scale and entailing upon it certain services and homage to be rendered to superiors. The relationship of causation, so to speak, is up and down. Influence, power, proceeds from above to below; the activities of the inferior are performed with respect, quite literally, to what is above. Action and reaction are far from being equal and in opposite directions. All action is of one sort, of the nature of lordship, and proceeds from the higher to the lower. Reaction is of the nature of subjection and deference and proceeds from lower to higher. The classic theory of the constitution of the world corresponds point by point to this ordering of classes in a scale of dignity and power.

A third trait assigned by historians to feudalism is that the ordering of ranks centres about armed service and the relationship of armed defense and protection. I am afraid that what has already been said about the parallelism of ancient cosmology with social organization may seem a fanciful analogy; and if a comparison is also drawn in this last regard, there will be no doubt in your minds that a metaphor is being forced. Such is truly the case if we take the comparison too literally. But not so, if we confine our attention to the notion of rule and command implied in both. Attention has already been called to the meaning that is now given the term law—a constant relationship among changes. Nevertheless, we often hear about laws which "govern" events, and it often seems to be thought that phenomena would be utterly disorderly were there not laws to keep them in order. This way of thinking is a survival of reading social relationships into nature—not necessarily a feudal relationship, but the relation of ruler and ruled, sovereign and subject. Law is assimilated to a command or order. If the factor of personal will is eliminated (as it was in the best Greek thought) still the idea of law or universal is impregnated with the sense of a guiding and ruling influence exerted from above on what is naturally inferior to it. The universal governs as the end and model which the artisan has in mind "governs" his movements. The Middle Ages added to this Greek idea of control the idea of a command proceeding from a superior will; and hence thought of the operations of nature as if they were a fulfilment of a task set by one who had authority to direct action.

The traits of the picture of nature drawn by modern science fairly spring by contrast into high relief. Modern science took its first step when daring astronomers abolished the distinction of high, sublime and ideal forces operating in the heavens from lower and material forces actuating terrestrial events. The supposed heterogeneity of substances and forces between heaven and earth was denied. It was asserted that the same laws hold everywhere, that there is homogeneity of material and process everywhere throughout nature. The remote and esthetically sublime is to be scientifically described and explained in terms of homely familiar events and forces. The material of direct handling and observation is that of which we are surest; it is the better known. Until we can convert the grosser and more superficial observations of far-away things in the heavens into elements identical with those of things directly at hand, they remain blind and not understood. Instead of presenting superior worth, they present only problems. They are not means of enlightenment but challenges. The earth is not superior in rank to sun, moon and stars, but it is equal in dignity, and its occurrences give the key to the understanding of celestial existences. Being *at* hand, they are also capable of being brought *under* our hand; they can be manipulated, broken up, resolved into elements which can be managed, combined at will in old and new forms. The net result may be termed, I think, without any great forcing, the substitution of a democracy of individual facts equal in rank for the feudal system of an ordered gradation of general classes of unequal rank.

One important incident of the new science was the destruction of the idea that the earth is the centre of the universe. When the idea of a fixed centre went, there went with it the idea of a closed universe and a circumscribing heavenly boundary. To the Greek sense, just because its theory of knowing was dominated by esthetic considerations, the finite was the perfect. Literally, the finite was the finished, the ended, the completed, that with no ragged edges and unaccountable operations. The infinite or limitless was lacking in character just because it was in-finite. Being everything, it was nothing. It was unformed and chaotic, uncontrolled and unruly, source of incalculable deviations and accidents. Our present feeling that associates infinity with boundless power, with capacity for expansion that knows no end, with the delight in a progress that has no external limit, would be incomprehensible were it not that interest has shifted from the esthetic to the practical; from interest in beholding a harmonious and complete scene to interest in transforming an inharmonious one. One has only to read the authors of the transition period, say Giordano Bruno,[1] to realize what a pent-in, suffocating sensation they associated with a closed, finite world, and what a feeling of exhilaration, expansion and boundless possibility was aroused in them by the thought of a world infinite in stretch of space and time, and composed internally of infinitesimal infinitely numerous elements. That which the Greeks withdrew from with repulsion they welcomed with an intoxicated sense of adventure. The infinite meant, it was true, something forever untraversed even by thought, and hence something forever unknown—no matter how great attainment in learning. But this "forever unknown" instead of being chilling and repelling was now an inspiring challenge to ever-renewed inquiry, and an assurance of inexhaustible possibilities of progress.

The student of history knows well that the Greeks made great progress

---

[1] Giordano Bruno (1548–1600): Italian philosopher of nature. [R.J.R.]

in the science of mechanics as well as of geometry. At first sight, it appears strange that with this advance in mechanics so little advance was made in the direction of modern science. The seeming paradox impels us to ask why it was that mechanics remained a separate science, why it was not used in description and explanation of natural phenomena after the manner of Galileo and Newton. The answer is found in the social parallelism already mentioned. Socially speaking, machines, tools, were devices employed by artisans. The science of mechanics had to do with the kind of things employed by human mechanics, and mechanics were base fellows. They were at the lower end of the social scale, and how could light on the heavens, the highest, be derived from them? The application of considerations of mechanics to natural phenomena would moreover have implied an interest in the practical control and utilization of phenomena which was totally incompatible with the importance attached to final causes as fixed determiners of nature. All the scientific reformers of the sixteenth and seventeenth centuries strikingly agree in regarding the doctrine of final causes as *the* cause of the failure of science. Why? Because this doctrine taught that the processes of nature are held in bondage to certain fixed ends which they must tend to realize. Nature was kept in leading strings; it was cramped down to production of a limited number of stereotyped results. Only a comparatively small number of things could be brought into being, and these few must be similar to the ends which similar cycles of change had effected in the past. The scope of inquiry and understanding was limited to the narrow round of processes eventuating in the fixed ends which the observed world offered to view. At best, invention and production of new results by use of machines and tools must be restricted to articles of transient dignity and bodily, not intellectual, use.

When the rigid clamp of fixed ends was taken off from nature, observation and imagination were emancipated, and experimental control for scientific and practical purposes enormously stimulated. Because natural processes were no longer restricted to a fixed number of immovable ends or results, anything might conceivably happen. It was only a question of what elements could be brought into juxtaposition so that they would work upon one another. Immediately, mechanics ceased to be a separate science and became an organ for attacking nature. The mechanics of the lever, wheel, pulley and inclined plane told accurately what happens when things in space are used to move one another during definite periods of time. The whole of nature became a scene of pushes and pulls, of cogs and levers, of motions of parts or elements to which the formulae of movements produced by well-known machines were directly applicable.

The banishing of ends and forms from the universe has seemed to many an ideal and spiritual impoverishment. When nature was regarded as a set of mechanical interactions, it apparently lost all meaning and purpose. Its glory departed. Elimination of differences of quality deprived it of beauty. Denial to nature of all inherent longings and aspiring tendencies toward ideal ends removed nature and natural science from contact with poetry, religion and divine things. There seemed to be left only a harsh, brutal despiritualized exhibition of mechanical forces. As a consequence, it has seemed to many philosophers that one of their chief problems was to reconcile the existence of this purely mechanical world with belief in objective rationality and purpose—to save life from a degrading materialism. Hence many sought to re-attain by way of an analysis of the process of knowing, or epistemology, that belief in the superiority of Ideal Being which had anciently been maintained on the basis of cosmology. But when it is recognized that the mechanical view is determined by the requirements of an experimental control of natural energies, this problem of reconciliation no longer vexes us. Fixed forms and ends, let us recall, mark fixed limits to change. Hence they make futile all human efforts to produce and regulate change except within narrow and unimportant limits. They paralyze constructive human inventions by a theory which condemns them in advance to failure. Human activity can conform only to ends already set by nature. It was not till ends were banished from nature that purposes became important as factors in human minds capable of reshaping existence. A natural world that does not subsist for the sake of realizing a fixed set of ends is relatively malleable and plastic; it may be used for this end *or* that. That nature can be known through the application of mechanical formulae is the prime condition of turning it to human account. Tools, machines are means to be utilized. Only when nature is regarded as mechanical, is systematic invention and construction of machines relevant to nature's activities. Nature is subdued to human purpose because it is no longer the slave of metaphysical and theological purpose.

Bergson [2] has pointed out that man might well be called *Homo Faber*. He is distinguished as the tool-making animal. This has held good since man was man; but till nature was construed in mechanical terms, the making of tools with which to attack and transform nature was sporadic and accidental. Under such circumstances it would not have occurred even to a Bergson that man's tool-making capacity was so important and fundamental that it could be used to define him. The very things that make the nature of the mechanical-physical scientist esthetically blank and dull are the things which render nature amenable to human control. When qualities were subordinated to quantitative and mathematical relationships, color, music and form disappeared from the object of the scientist's inquiry as such. But the remaining properties of weight, extension, numerable velocity of movement and so on were just the qualities which lent themselves to the substitution of one thing for another, to the conversion of one form of energy into another; to the effecting of transformations. When chemical fertilizers can be used in place of animal manures, when improved grain and

---

[2] Henri Bergson (1859–1941): French philosopher. [R.J.R.]

cattle can be purposefully bred from inferior animals and grasses, when mechanical energy can be converted into heat and electricity into mechanical energy, man gains power to manipulate nature. Most of all he gains power to frame *new* ends and aims and to proceed in regular system to their actualization. Only indefinite substitution and convertibility regardless of quality render nature manageable. The mechanization of nature is the condition of a practical and progressive idealism in action.

It thus turns out that the old, old dread and dislike of matter as something opposed to mind and threatening it, to be kept within the narrowest bounds of recognition; something to be denied so far as possible lest it encroach upon ideal purposes and finally exclude them from the real world, is as absurd practically as it was impotent intellectually. Judged from the only scientific standpoint, what it does and how it functions, matter means conditions. To respect matter means to respect the conditions of achievement; conditions which hinder and obstruct and which have to be changed, conditions which help and further and which can be used to modify obstructions and attain ends. Only as men have learned to pay sincere and persistent regard to matter, to the conditions upon which depends negatively and positively the success of all endeavor, have they shown sincere and fruitful respect for ends and purposes. To profess to have an aim and then neglect the means of its execution is self-delusion of the most dangerous sort. Education and morals will begin to find themselves on the same road of advance that say chemical industry and medicine have found for themselves when they too learn fully the lesson of wholehearted and unremitting attention to means and conditions—that is, to what mankind so long despised as material and mechanical. When we take means for ends we indeed fall into moral materialism. But when we take ends without regard to means we degenerate into sentimentalism. In the name of the ideal we fall back upon mere luck and chance and magic or exhortation and preaching; or else upon a fanaticism that will force the realization of preconceived ends at any cost.

I have touched in this lecture upon many things in a cursory way. Yet there has been but one point in mind. The revolution in our conceptions of nature and in our methods of knowing it has bred a new temper of imagination and aspiration. It has confirmed the new attitude generated by economic and political changes. It has supplied this attitude with definite intellectual material with which to formulate and justify itself.

In the first lecture it was noted that in Greek life prosaic matter of fact or empirical knowledge was at a great disadvantage as compared with the imaginative beliefs that were bound up with special institutions and moral habitudes. Now this empirical knowledge has grown till it has broken its low and limited sphere of application and esteem. It has itself become an organ of inspiring imagination through introducing ideas of boundless possibility, indefinite progress, free movement, equal opportunity irrespective of fixed limits. It has reshaped social institutions, and in so far developed a new morale. It has achieved ideal values. It is convertible into creative and constructive philosophy.

Convertible, however, rather than already converted. When we consider how deeply embedded in customs of thought and action the classic philosophy came to be and how congenial it is to man's more spontaneous beliefs, the throes that attended its birth are not to be wondered at. We should rather wonder that a view so upsetting, so undermining, made its way without more persecutions, martyrdoms and disturbances. It certainly is not surprising that its complete and consistent formulation in philosophy has been long delayed. The main efforts of thinkers were inevitably directed to minimizing the shock of change, easing the strains of transition, mediating and reconciling. When we look back upon almost all of the thinkers of the seventeenth and eighteenth centuries, upon all excepting those who were avowedly sceptical and revolutionary, what strikes us is the amount of traditional subject-matter and method that is to be found even among those who were regarded as most advanced. Men cannot easily throw off their old habits of thinking, and never can throw off all of them at once. In developing, teaching and receiving new ideas we are compelled to use some of the old ones as tools of understanding and communication. Only piecemeal, step-by-step, could the full import of the new science be grasped. Roughly speaking, the seventeenth century witnessed its application in astronomy and general cosmology; the eighteenth century in physics and chemistry; the nineteenth century undertook an application in geology and the biological sciences.

It was said that it has now become extremely difficult to recover the view of the world which universally obtained in Europe till the seventeenth century. Yet after all we need only recur to the science of plants and animals as it was before Darwin and to the ideas which even now are dominant in moral and political matters to find the older order of conceptions in full possession of the popular mind. Until the dogma of fixed unchangeable types and species, of arrangement in classes of higher and lower, of subordination of the transitory individual to the universal or kind had been shaken in its hold upon the science of life, it was impossible that the new ideas and method should be made at home in social and moral life. Does it not seem to be the intellectual task of the twentieth century to take this last step? When this step is taken the circle of scientific development will be rounded out and the reconstruction of philosophy be made an accomplished fact.

QUESTIONS FOR STUDY AND DISCUSSION

1. Explain the two different pictures of the world as given by ancient and modern science.
2. In describing the older view of the universe, Dewey says: "There are castes in nature." What does he mean?

3. Show the contrasting views of "change" as given by ancient and modern science.
4. Give Dewey's critique of "fixed ends."
5. What does Dewey mean by "respect for matter"?

The Existential Matrix of Inquiry: Biological

If one denies the supernatural, then one has the intellectual responsibility of indicating how the logical may be connected with the biological in a process of continuous development. This point deserves emphasis, for if the following discussion fails to fulfil the task of pointing out satisfactorily the continuous path, then that failure becomes, for those who accept the naturalistic postulate, but a challenge to perform the task better.

Whatever else organic life is or is not, it is a process of activity that involves an environment. It is a transaction extending beyond the spatial limits of the organism. An organism does not live *in* an environment; it lives by means of an environment. Breathing, the ingestion of food, the ejection of waste products, are cases of *direct* integration; the circulation of the blood and the energizing of the nervous system are relatively *indirect*. But every organic function is an interaction of intra-organic and extra-organic energies, either directly or indirectly. For life involves expenditure of energy and the energy expended can be replenished only as the activities performed succeed in making return drafts upon the environment—the only source of restoration of energy. Not even a hibernating animal can live indefinitely upon itself. The energy that is drawn is not forced in from without; it is a consequence of energy expended. If there is a surplus balance, growth occurs. If there is a deficit balance, degeneration commences. There are things in the world that are indifferent to the life-activities of an organism. But they are not parts of *its* environment, save potentially. The processes of living are enacted by the environment as truly as by the organism; for they *are* an integration.

It follows that with every differentiation of structure the environment expands. For a new organ provides a new way of interacting in which things in the world that were previously indifferent enter into life-functions. The environment of an animal that is locomotor differs from that of a sessile plant; that of a jelly fish differs from that of a trout, and the environment of any fish differs from that of a bird. So, to repeat what was just said, the difference is not just that a fish lives *in* the water and a bird *in* the air, but that the characteristic functions of these animals are what they are

From pp. 25–29 of John Dewey, *Logic: The Theory of Inquiry.* Copyright 1938, Holt, Rinehart and Winston, Inc. Reprinted by permission.

because of the special way in which water and air enter into their respective activities.

With differentiation of interactions comes the need of maintaining a balance among them; or, in objective terms, a unified environment. The balance has to be maintained by a mechanism that responds both to variations that occur within the organism and in surroundings. For example, such an apparently self-contained function as that of respiration is kept constant by means of active exchanges between the alkaline and carbon dioxide contents of changing pressures exerted by the blood and the carbon dioxide in the lungs. The lungs in turn are dependent upon interactions effected by kidneys and liver, which effect the interactions of the circulating blood with materials of the digestive tract. This whole system of accurately timed interchanges is regulated by changes in the nervous system.

The effect of this delicate and complex system of internal changes is the maintenance of a fairly uniform integration with the environment, or—what amounts to the same thing—a fairly unified environment. The interactions of inanimate things with their surroundings are not such as to maintain a stable relation between the things involved. The blow of a hammer, for example, breaks a stone into bits. But as long as life normally continues, the interactions in which organic and environmental energies enter are such as to maintain the conditions in both of them needed for later interactions. The processes, in other words, are self-maintaining, in a sense in which they are not in the case of the interactions of non-living things.

Capacity for maintenance of a constant form of interaction between organism and environment is not confined to the individual organism. It is manifested also, in the reproduction of similar organisms. The stone is presumably indifferent as to how it reacts mechanically and chemically (within the limits of its potentialities) to other things. The stone may lose its individuality but basic mechanical and chemical processes go on uninterruptedly. As long as life continues, its processes are such as continuously to maintain and restore the enduring relationship which is characteristic of the life-activities of a given organism.

Each particular activity prepares the way for the activity that follows. These form not a mere succession but a series. This seriated quality of life activities is effected through the delicate balance of the complex factors in each particular activity. When the balance within a given activity is disturbed—when there is a proportionate excess or deficit in some factor—then there is exhibited need, search and fulfilment (or satisfaction) in the objective meaning of those terms. The greater the differentiation of structures and their corresponding activities becomes, the more difficult it is to keep the balance. Indeed, living may be regarded as a continual rhythm of disequilibrations and recoveries of equilibrium. The "higher" the organism, the more serious become the disturbances and the more energetic (and often more prolonged) are the efforts necessary for its reestablishment. The state of disturbed equilibration constitutes *need*. The movement towards its restoration is search and exploration. The recovery is fulfilment or satisfaction.

Hunger, for example, is a manifestation of a state of imbalance between organic and environmental factors in that integration which is life. This disturbance is a consequence of lack of full responsive adaptation to one another of various organic functions. The function of digestion fails to meet the demands made upon it directly by the circulatory system which carries replenishing nutritive material to all the organs concerned in the performance of other functions, and the demands indirectly made by motor activities. A state of tension is set up which is an actual state (not mere feeling) of organic uneasiness and restlessness. This state of tension (which defines need) passes into search for material that will restore the condition of balance. In the lower organisms it is expressed in the bulgings and retractions of parts of the organism's periphery so that nutritive material is ingested. The matter ingested initiates activities throughout the rest of the animal that lead to a restoration of balance, which, as the outcome of the state of previous tension, is fulfilment.

Rignano, in an instructive discussion of the biological basis of thinking, says that every organism strives to stay in a stationary state. He gives evidence from the activity of lower organisms which shows that activities occurring when their state is disturbed are such as tend to restore the former stationary condition. He also states that "a prior physiological state cannot be perfectly reestablished and made to persist in normal activity until an animal by its movements has succeeded in getting again into an environment identical with its old one." His position may be interpreted so that what is said in this text is in agreement with it. But as his treatment stands, it emphasizes *restoration* of the previous *state* of the *organism* rather than the institution of an integrated *relation*. The establishment of the latter relation is compatible with definite changes in both the organism and the environment; it does not require that old and new states of either the organism or the environments be identical with one another. Hence the difference in the two views is of considerable theoretical importance.

If we take as an example the search for food found in connection with the higher organisms, it appears clear that the very search often leads the organism into an environment that differs from the old one, and that the appropriation of food under new conditions involves a modified state of the organism. The *form* of the relationship, of the interaction, is reinstated, not the identical conditions. Unless this fact is recognized, development becomes an abnormal or an unusual matter rather than the normal feature of life activities. Need remains a constant factor but it changes its quality. With change in need comes a change in exploratory and searching activities; and that change is followed by a changed fulfilment or satisfaction. The conservative tendency is doubtless strong; there is a tendency to get *back*. But in at least the more complex organisms, the activity of search involves modification of the old environment, if only by a change in the connection of the organism with it. Ability to make and retain a changed mode of adaptation in response to new conditions is the source of that more extensive development called organic evolution. Of human organisms it is especially true that activities carried on for satisfying needs so change the environment that new needs arise which demand still further change in the activities of the organism by which they are satisfied; and so on in a potentially endless chain.

In the lower organisms, interaction between organic and environ-energies takes place for the most part through direct contact. The tension in the organism is that between its surface and its interior. In the organisms that have distance receptors and special organs of locomotion, the serial nature of life behavior demands that earlier acts in the series be such as to prepare the way for the later. The time between the occurrence of need and the occurrence of its satisfaction inevitably becomes longer when the interaction is not one of direct contact. For the attainment of an integral relation is then dependent upon establishing connections with the things at a distance which arouse exploratory activity through stimulation of eye and ear. A definite order of initial, of intermediate, and of final or closing activities, is thus instituted. The *terminus a quo* is fixed by such a condition of imbalance in the organism that integration of organic factors cannot be attained by any material with which the organism is in direct contact. Certain of its activities tend in one direction; others move in a different direction. More particularly, its existing contact-activities and those aroused by its distance-receptors, are at odds with each other, and the outcome of this tension is that the latter activities dominate. A satiated animal is not stirred by the sight or smell of the prey that moves him when he is hungry. In the hungry creature activities of search become a definite intervening or intermediate series. At each intermediate stage there is still tension between contact activities and those responsive to stimuli through distance-receptors. Movement continues until integration is established between contact and visual and motor activities, as in the consummatory act of devouring food.

QUESTIONS FOR STUDY AND DISCUSSION

1. What does Dewey mean by "organic life"?
2. Explain the need-striving-satisfaction relationship in organic life.

The Existential Matrix of Inquiry: Cultural

The environment in which human beings live, act and inquire, is not simply physical. It is cultural as well. Problems which induce inquiry grow out of the relations of fellow beings to one another, and the organs for dealing with these relations are not only the eye and ear, but the meanings which have developed in the course of living, together with the ways of forming and transmitting culture with all its constituents of tools, arts, institutions, traditions and customary beliefs.

To a very large extent the ways in which human beings respond even to physical conditions are influenced by their cultural environment. Light and fire are physical facts. But the occasions in which a human being responds to things as merely physical in purely physical ways are comparatively rare. Such occasions are the act of jumping when a sudden noise is heard, withdrawing the hand when something hot is touched, blinking in the presence of a sudden increase of light, animal-like basking in sunshine, etc. Such reactions are on the biological plane. But the typical cases of human behavior are not represented by such examples. The *use* of sound in speech and listening to speech, making and enjoying music; the kindling and tending of fire to cook and to keep warm; the production of light to carry on and regulate occupations and social enjoyments:—these things are representative of distinctively human activity.

To indicate the full scope of cultural determination of the conduct of living one would have to follow the behavior of an individual throughout at least a day; whether that of a day laborer, of a professional man, artist or scientist, and whether the individual be a growing child or a parent. For the result would show how thoroughly saturated behavior is with conditions and factors that are of cultural origin and import. Of distinctively human behavior it may be said that the strictly physical environment is so incorporated in a cultural environment that our interactions with the former, the problems that arise with reference to it, and our ways of dealing with these problems, are profoundly affected by incorporation of the physical environment in the cultural.

Man, as Aristotle remarked, is a *social* animal. This fact introduces him into situations and originates problems and ways of solving them that have no precedent upon the organic biological level. For man is social in another sense than the bee and ant, since his activities are encompassed in an environment that is culturally transmitted, so that what man does and

From pp. 42–45 of John Dewey, *Logic: The Theory of Inquiry.* Copyright 1938, Holt, Rinehart and Winston, Inc. Reprinted by permission, how he acts, is determined not by organic structure and physical heredity alone but by the influence of cultural heredity, embedded in traditions, institutions, customs and the purposes and beliefs they both carry and inspire. Even the neuro-muscular structures of individuals are modified through the influence of the cultural environment upon the activities performed. The acquisition and understanding of language with proficiency in the arts (that are foreign to other animals than men) represent an incorporation within the physical structure of human beings of the effects of cultural conditions, an interpenetration so profound that resulting activities are as direct and seemingly "natural" as are the first reactions of an infant. To speak, to read, to exercise any art, industrial, fine or political, are instances of modifications wrought *within* the biological organism by the cultural environment.

This modification of organic behavior in and by the cultural environment accounts for, or rather is, the transformation of purely organic behavior into behavior marked by intellectual properties with which the present discussion is concerned. Intellectual operations are foreshadowed in behavior of the biological kind, and the latter prepares the way for the former. But to foreshadow is not to exemplify and to prepare is not to fulfil. Any theory that rests upon a naturalistic postulate must face the problem of the extraordinary differences that mark off the activities and achievements of human beings from those of other biological forms. It is these differences that have led to the idea that man is completely separated from other animals by properties that come from a non-natural source. The conception to be developed in the present chapter is that the development of language (in its widest sense) out of prior biological activities is, in its connection with wider cultural forces, the key to this transformation. The problem, so viewed, is not the problem of the transition of organic behavior into something wholly discontinuous with it—as is the case when, for example, Reason, Intuition and the *A priori* are appealed to for explanation of the difference. It is a special form of the general problem of continuity of change and the emergence of new modes of activity—the problem of development at any level.

Viewing the problem from this angle, its constituents may be reduced to certain heads, three of which will be noted. Organic behavior is centered in *particular* organisms. This statement applies to inferring and reasoning as existential activities. But if inferences made and conclusions reached are to be valid, the subject-matter dealt with and the operations employed must be such as to yield identical results for all who infer and reason. If the same evidence leads different persons to different conclusions, then either the evidence is only speciously the same, or one conclusion (or both) is wrong. The *special* constitution of an individual organism which plays such a role in biological behavior is so irrelevant in controlled inquiry that it has to be discounted and mastered.

Another phase of the problem is brought out by the part played in human judgments by emotion and desire. These *personal* traits cook the evidence and determine the result that is reached. That is, upon the level of organic factors (which are the actively determining forces in the type of cases just mentioned), the individual with his individual peculiarities, whether native or acquired, is an active participant in producing ideas and beliefs, and yet the latter are logically grounded only when such peculiarities are deliberately precluded from taking effect. This point restates what was said in connection with the first point, but it indicates another phase of the matter. If, using accepted terminology, we say that the first difference is that between the singular and the general, the present point may be formulated as the difference between the subjective and the objective. To be intellectually "objective" is to discount and eliminate merely personal factors in the operations by which a conclusion is reached.

Organic behavior is a strictly temporal affair. But when behavior is *intellectually* formulated, in respect both to general ways of behavior and the special environing conditions in which they operate, propositions result and the terms of a proposition do not sustain a temporal relation to one another. It was a temporal event when someone landed on Robinson Crusoe's island. It was a temporal event when Crusoe found the footprint on the sands. It was a temporal event when Crusoe inferred the presence of a possibly dangerous stranger. But while the proposition was *about* something temporal, the *relation* of the observed fact as evidential to the inference drawn from it is non-temporal. The same holds of every logical relation in and of propositions.

QUESTIONS FOR STUDY AND DISCUSSION

1. What does Dewey mean by the "cultural environment"?
2. Do you think that Dewey reduces human activity to that of a biological organism? Explain.

Existence as Precarious and as Stable

It was suggested in the last chapter that experience has its equivalents in such affairs as history, life, culture. Reference to these other affairs enables us to put to one side the reminiscences which so readily give the word experience a sectarian and provincial content. According to Tylor, culture is "that complex whole which includes knowledge, belief, art, morals, custom, and any other capabilities acquired by a man as a member of society." It is, in some sense, a whole, but it is a complex, a diversified whole. It is differentiated into religion, magic, law, fine and useful art, science, philosophy, language, domestic, and political relations, etc. Consider the following words of an anthropologist and ask if they do not fairly define the problem of philosophy, although intended for another purpose. "Cultural reality is never wholly deterministic nor yet wholly accidental, never wholly psychological nor yet wholly objective, never wholly of yesterday nor yet wholly of today, but combines all of these in its existential reality. . . . A reconstructive synthesis re-establishes the synthetic unity necessarily lost in the process of analytic dismemberment." [1] I do not mean that philosophy is to be merged in an anthropological view of culture. But in a different context and by a different method, it has the task of analytic dismemberment and synthetic reconstruction of experience; the phenomena of culture as presented by the anthropologist provide, moreover, precious material to aid the performance of this office, material more pertinent to the task of philosophizing than that of psychology isolated from a theory of culture.

A feature of existence which is emphasized by cultural phenomena is the precarious and perilous. Sumner refers to Grimm as authority for the statement that the Germanic tribes had over a thousand distinct sayings, proverbs and apothegms, concerning luck. Time is brief, and this statement must stand instead of the discourse which the subject deserves. Man finds himself living in an aleatory world; his existence involves, to put it baldly, a gamble. The world is a scene of risk; it is uncertain, unstable, uncannily unstable. Its dangers are irregular, inconstant, not to be counted upon as to their times and seasons. Although persistent, they are sporadic, episodic. It is darkest just before dawn; pride goes before a fall; the moment of greatest prosperity is the moment most charged with ill-omen, most opportune for the evil eye. Plague, famine, failure of crops, disease, death, defeat in battle, are always just around the corner, and so are abundance, strength, victory, festival and song. Luck is proverbially both good and bad in its distributions. The sacred and the accursed are potentialities of the same situation; and there is no category of things which has not embodied the sacred and accursed: persons, words, places, times, directions in space, stones, winds, animals, stars.

Anthropologists have shown incontrovertibly the part played by the precarious aspect of the world in generating religion with its ceremonies, rites, cults, myths, magic; and it has shown the pervasive penetration of these affairs into morals, law, art, and industry. Beliefs and dispositions connected with them are the background out of which philosophy and secular morals slowly developed, as well as more slowly those late inventions, art for art's sake, and business is business. Interesting and instructive as is this fact, it is not the ramifications which here concern us. We must not be

---

[1] Alexander A. Goldenweiser (1880–1940): American anthropologist and sociologist. [J.D.]

diverted to consider the consequences for philosophy, even for doctrines reigning today, of facts concerning the origin of philosophies. We confine ourselves to one outstanding fact: the evidence that the world of empirical things includes the uncertain, unpredictable, uncontrollable, and hazardous.

It is an old saying that the gods were born of fear. The saying is only too likely to strengthen a misconception bred by confirmed subjective habits. We first endow man in isolation with an instinct of fear and then we imagine him irrationally ejecting that fear into the environment, scattering broadcast as it were, the fruits of his own purely personal limitations, and thereby creating supersitition. But fear, whether an instinct or an acquisition, is a function of the environment. Man fears because he exists in a fearful, an awful world. The *world* is precarious and perilous. It is as easily accessible and striking evidence of this fact that primitive experience is cited. The voice is that of early man; but the hand is that of nature, the nature in which we still live. It was not fear of gods that created the gods.

For if the life of early man is filled with expiations and propitiations, if in his feats and festivals what is enjoyed is gratefully shared with his gods, it is not because a belief in supernatural powers created a need for expiatory, propitiatory and communal offerings. Everything that man achieves and possesses is got by actions that may involve him in other and obnoxious consequences in addition to those wanted and enjoyed. His acts are trespasses upon the domain of the unknown; and hence atonement, if offered in season, may ward off direful consequences that haunt even the moment of prosperity—or that most haunt that moment. While unknown consequences flowing from the past dog the present, the future is even more unknown and perilous; the present by that fact is ominous. If unknown forces that decide future destiny can be placated, the man who will not study the methods of securing their favor is incredibly flippant. In enjoyment of present food and companionship, nature, tradition and social organization have coöperated, thereby supplementing our own endeavors so petty and so feeble without this extraneous reinforcement. Goods are by grace not of ourselves. He is a dangerous churl who will not gratefully acknowledge by means of free-will offerings the help that sustains him.

These things are as true today as they were in the days of early culture. It is not the facts which have changed, but the methods of insurance, regulation and acknowledgment. Herbert Spencer [2] sometimes colored his devotion to symbolic experiences with a fact of dire experience. When he says that every fact has two opposite sides, "the one its near or visible side and the other its remote or invisible side," he expresses a persistent trait of every object in experience. The visible is set in the invisible; and in the end what is unseen decides what happens in the seen; the tangible rests precari-

---

[2] Herbert Spencer (1820–1903): British philosopher and champion of evolution in America. [R.J.R.]

ously upon the untouched and ungrasped. The contrast and the potential maladjustment of the immediate, the conspicuous and focal phase of things, with those indirect and hidden factors which determine the origin and career of what is present, are indestructible features of any and every experience. We may term the way in which our ancestors dealt with the contrast superstitious, but the contrast is no superstition. It is a primary datum in any experience.

We have substituted sophistication for superstition, at least measurably so. But the sophistication is often as irrational and as much at the mercy of words as the superstition it replaces. Our magical safeguard against the uncertain character of the world is to deny the existence of chance, to mumble universal and necessary law, the ubiquity of cause and effect, the uniformity of nature, universal progress, and the inherent rationality of the universe. These magic formulae borrow their potency from conditions that are not magical. Through science we have secured a degree of power of prediction and of control; through tools, machinery and an accompanying technique we have made the world more conformable to our needs, a more secure abode. We have heaped up riches and means of comfort between ourselves and the risks of the world. We have professionalized amusement as an agency of escape and forgetfulness. But when all is said and done, the fundamentally hazardous character of the world is not seriously modified, much less eliminated. Such an incident as the last war and preparations for a future war remind us that it is easy to overlook the extent to which, after all, our attainments are only devices for blurring the disagreeable recognition of a fact, instead of means of altering the fact itself.

What has been said sounds pessimistic. But the concern is not with morals but with metaphysics, with, that is to say, the nature of the existential world in which we live. It would have been as easy and more comfortable to emphasize good luck, grace, unexpected and unwon joys, those unsought for happenings which we so significantly call happiness. We might have appealed to good fortune as evidence of this important trait of hazard in nature. Comedy is as genuine as tragedy. But it is traditional that comedy strikes a more superficial note than tragedy. And there is an even better reason for appealing to misfortunes and mistakes as evidence of the precarious nature of the world. The problem of evil is a well recognized problem, while we rarely or never hear of a problem of good. Goods we take for granted; they are as they should be; they are natural and proper. The good is a recognition of our deserts. When we pull out a plum we treat it as evidence of the *real* order of cause and effect in the world. For this reason it is difficult for the goods of existence to furnish as convincing evidence of the uncertain character of nature as do evils. It is the latter we term accidents, not the former, even when their adventitious character is as certain.

What of it all, it may be asked? In the sense in which an assertion is true that uncontrolled distribution of good and evil is evidence of the precarious, uncertain nature of existence, it is a truism, and no problem is forwarded by its reiteration. But it is submitted that just this predicament of the inextricable mixture of stability and uncertainty gives rise to philosophy, and that it is reflected in all its recurrent problems and issues. If classic philosophy says so much about unity and so little about unreconciled diversity, so much about the eternal and permanent, and so little about change (save as something to be resolved into combinations of the permanent), so much about necessity and so little about contingency, so much about the comprehending universal and so little about the recalcitrant particular, it may well be because the ambiguousness and ambivalence of reality are actually so pervasive. Since these things form the problem, solution is more apparent (although not more actual), in the degree in which whatever of stability and assurance the world presents is fastened upon and asserted.

Upon their surface, the reports of the world which form our different philosophies are various to the point of stark contrariness. They range from spiritualism to materialism, from absolutism to relativistic phenomenalism, from transcendentalism to positivism, from rationalism to sensationalism, from idealism to realism, from subjectivism to bald objectivism, from Platonic realism to nominalism. The array of contradictions is so imposing as to suggest to sceptics that the mind of man has tackled an impossible job, or that philosophers have abandoned themselves to vagary. These radical oppositions in philosophers suggest however another consideration. They suggest that all their different philosophies have a common premise, and that their diversity is due to acceptance of a common premise. Variant philosophies may be looked at as different ways of supplying recipes for denying to the universe the character of contingency which it possesses so integrally that its denial leaves the reflecting mind without a clue, and puts subsequent philosophising at the mercy of temperament, interest and local surroundings.

Quarrels among conflicting types of philosophy are thus family quarrels. They go on within the limits of a too domestic circle, and can be settled only by venturing further afield, and out of doors. Concerned with imputing complete, finished and sure character to the world of real existence, even if things have to be broken into two disconnected pieces in order to accomplish the result, the character desiderated can plausibly be found in reason or in mechanism; in rational conceptions like those of mathematics, or brute things like sensory data; in atoms or in essences; in consciousness or in a physical externality which forces and overrides consciousness.

As against this common identification of reality with what is sure, regular and finished, experience in unsophisticated forms gives evidence of a different world and points to a different metaphysics. We live in a world which is an impressive and irresistible mixture of sufficiencies, tight completenesses, order, recurrences which make possible prediction and control, and singularities, ambiguities, uncertain possibilities, processes going on to consequences as yet indeterminate. They are mixed not mechanically but vitally like the wheat and tares of the parable. We may recognize them separately but we cannot divide them, for unlike wheat and tares they grow from the same root. Qualities have defects as necessary conditions of their excellencies; the instrumentalities of truth are the causes of error; change gives meaning to permanence and recurrence makes novelty possible. A world that was wholly risky would be a world in which adventure is impossible, and only a living world can include death. Such facts have been celebrated by thinkers like Heraclitus and Lotze; they have been greeted by theologians as furnishing occasions for exercise of divine grace; they have been elaborately formulated by various schools under a principle of relativity, so defined as to become itself final and absolute. They have rarely been frankly recognized as fundamentally significant for the formation of a naturalistic metaphysics.

Aristotle perhaps came the nearest to a start in that direction. But his thought did not go far on the road, though it may be used to suggest the road which he failed to take. Aristotle acknowledges contingency, but he never surrenders his bias in favor of the fixed, certain and finished. His whole theory of forms and ends is a theory of the superiority in Being of rounded-out fixities. His physics is a fixation of ranks or grades of necessity and contingency so sorted that necessity measures dignity and equals degree of reality, while contingency and change measure degrees of deficiency of Being. The empirical impact and sting of the mixture of universality and singularity and chance is evaded by parcelling out the regions of space so that they have their natural abode in different portions of nature. His logic is one of definition and classification, so that its task is completed when changing and contingent things are distinguished from the necessary, universal and fixed, by attribution to inferior species of things. Chance appears in thought not as a calculus of probabilities in predicting the observable occurrence of any and every event, but as marking an inferior type of syllogism. Things that move are intrinsically different from things that exhibit eternal regularity. Change is honestly recognized as a genuine feature of *some* things, but the point of the recognition is avoided by imputing alteration to inherent deficiency of Being over against complete Being which never changes. Changing things belong to a purgatorial realm, where they wander aimlessly until redeemed by love of finality of form, the acquisition of which lifts them to a paradise of self-sufficient Being. With slight exaggeration, it may be said that the thoroughgoing way in which Aristotle defined, distinguished and classified rest and movement, the finished and the incomplete, the actual and potential, did more to fix tradition, *the* genteel tradition one is tempted to add, which identifies the fixed and regular with reality of Being and the changing and hazardous with deficiency of Being than ever was accomplished by those who took the shorter path of asserting that change is illusory.

His philosophy was closer to empirical facts than most modern philosophies, in that it was neither monistic nor dualistic but openly pluralistic. His plurals fall however, within a grammatical system, to each portion of which a corresponding cosmic status is allotted. Thus his pluralism solved the problem of how to have your cake and eat it too, for a classified and hierarchically ordered set of pluralities, of variants, has none of the sting of the miscellaneous and uncoördinated plurals of our actual world. In this classificatory scheme of separation he has been followed, though perhaps unwittingly, by many philosophers of different import. Thus Kant assigns all that is manifold and chaotic to one realm, that of sense, and all that is uniform and regular to that of reason. A single and all embracing dialectic problem of the combination of sense and thought is thereby substituted for the concrete problems that arise through the mixed and varied union in existence of the variable and the constant, the necessary and that which proceeds uncertainly.

The device is characteristic of a conversion such as has already been commented upon of a moral insight to be made good in action into an antecedent metaphysics of existence or a general theory of knowledge. The striving to make stability of meaning prevail over the instability of events is the main task of intelligent human effort. But when the function is dropped from the province of art and treated as a property of given things, whether cosmological or logical, effort is rendered useless, and a premium is put upon the accidental good-fortune of a class that happens to be furnished by the toil of another class with products that give to life its dignity and leisurely stability.

The argument is not forgetful that there are, from Heraclitus to Bergson, philosophies, metaphysics, of change. One is grateful to them for keeping alive a sense of what classic, orthodox philosophies have whisked out of sight. But the philosophies of flux also indicate the intensity of the craving for the sure and fixed. They have deified change by making it universal, regular, sure. To say this is not, I hope, verbal by-play. Consider the wholly eulogistic fashion in which Hegel and Bergson, and the professedly evolutionary philosophers of becoming, have taken change. With Hegel becoming is a rational process which defines logic although a new and strange logic, and an absolute, although new and strange, God. With Spencer, evolution is but the transitional process of attaining a fixed and universal equilibrium of harmonious adjustment. With Bergson, change is the creative operation of God, or *is* God—one is not quite sure which. The change of change is not only cosmic pyrotechnics, but is a process of divine, spiritual, energy. We are here in the presence of prescription, not description. Romanticism is an evangel in the garb of metaphysics. It sidesteps the painful, toilsome labor of understanding and of control which change sets us, by glorifying it for its own sake. Flux is made something to revere, something profoundly akin to what is best within ourselves, will and creative energy. It is not, as it is in experience, a call to effort, a challenge to investigation, a potential doom of disaster and death.

If we follow classical terminology, philosophy is love of wisdom, while metaphysics is cognizance of the generic traits of existence. In this sense of metaphysics, incompleteness and precariousness is a trait that must be given footing of the same rank as the finished and fixed. Love of wisdom is concerned with finding its implications for the conduct of life, in devotion to what is good. On the cognitive side, the issue is largely that of measure, of the ratio one bears to others in the situations of life. On the practical side, it is a question of the use to be made of each, of turning each to best account. Man is naturally philosophic, rather than metaphysical or coldly scientific, noting and describing. Concerned with prudence if not with what is honorifically called wisdom, man naturally prizes knowledge only for the sake of its bearing upon success and failure in attaining goods and avoiding evils. This is a fact of our structure and nothing is gained by recommending it as an ideal truth, and equally nothing is gained by attributing to intellect an intrinsic relationship to pure truth for its own sake or bare fact on its own account. The first method encourages dogma, and the second expresses a myth. The love of knowledge for its own sake is an ideal of morals; it is an integral condition of the wisdom that rightly conceives and effectually pursues the good. For wisdom as to ends depends upon acquaintance with conditions and means, and unless the acquaintance is adequate and fair, wisdom becomes a sublimated folly of self-deception.

Denial of an inherent relation of mind to truth or fact for its own sake, apart from insight into what the fact or truth exacts of us in behavior and imposes upon us in joy and suffering, and simultaneous affirmation that devotion to fact, to truth, is a necessary moral demand, involve no inconsistency. Denial relates to natural events as independent of choice and endeavor; affirmation relates to choice and action. But choice and the reflective effort involved in it are themselves such contingent events and so bound up with the precarious uncertainty of other events, that philosophers have too readily assumed that metaphysics, and science of fact and truth, are themselves wisdom, thinking thus to avoid the necessity of either exercising or recognizing choice. The consequence is that conversion of unavowed morals or wisdom into cosmology, and into a metaphysics of nature, which was termed in the last chapter *the* philosophic fallacy. It supplies the formula of the technique by which thinkers have relegated the uncertain and unfinished to an invidious state of unreal being, while they have systematically exalted the assured and complete to the rank of true Being.

Upon the side of wisdom, as human beings interested in good and bad things in their connection with human conduct, thinkers are concerned to mitigate the instability of life, to introduce moderation, temper and economy, and when worst comes to worst to suggest consolations and compensations. They are concerned with rendering more stable good things, and more unstable bad things; they are interested in how changes may be turned to account in the consequences to which they contribute. The facts of the ungoing, unfinished and ambiguously potential world give point and poignancy to the search for absolutes and finalities. Then when philosophers have hit in reflection upon a thing which is stably good in quality and hence worthy of persistent and continued choice, they hesitate, and withdraw from the effort and struggle that choice demands:—namely, from the effort to give it some such stability in observed existence as it possesses in quality when thought of. Thus it becomes a refuge, an asylum for contemplation, or a theme for dialectical elaboration, instead of an ideal to inspire and guide conduct.

Since thinkers claim to be concerned with knowledge of existence, rather than with imagination, they have to make good the pretention to knowledge. Hence they transmute the imaginative perception of the stably good object into a definition and description of true reality in contrast with lower and specious existence, which, being precarious and incomplete, alone involves us in the necessity of choice and active struggle. Thus they remove from actual existence the very traits which generate philosophic reflection and which give point and bearing to its conclusions. In briefest formula, "reality" becomes what we wish existence to be, after we have analyzed its defects and decided upon what would remove them; "reality" is what existence would be if our reasonably justified preferences were so completely established in nature as to exhaust and define its entire being and thereby render search and struggle unnecessary. What is left over (and since trouble, struggle, conflict, and error still empirically exist, something *is* left over), being excluded by definition from full reality, is assigned to a grade or order of being which is asserted to be metaphysically inferior; and order variously called appearance, illusion, mortal mind, or the merely empirical, against what really and truly is. Then the problem of metaphysics alters: instead of being a detection and description of the generic traits of existence, it becomes an endeavor to adjust or reconcile to each other two separate realms of being. Empirically we have just what we started with: the mixture of the precarious and problematic with the assured and complete. But a classificatory device, based on desire and elaborated in reflective imagination, has been introduced by which the two traits are torn apart, one of them being labelled reality and the other appearance. The genuinely moral problem of mitigating and regulating the troublesome factor by active employment of the stable factor then drops out of sight. The dialectic problem of logical reconciliation of two notions has taken its place.

The most widespread of these classificatory devices, the one of greatest popular appeal, is that which divides existence into the supernatural and the natural. Men may fear the gods but it is axiomatic that the gods have nothing to fear. They lead a life of untroubled serenity, the life that pleases them. There is a long story between the primitive forms of this division of objects of experience and the dialectical imputation to the divine of omnipotence, omniscience, eternity and infinity, in contrast with the attribution to man and experienced nature of finitude, weakness, limitation, struggle and change. But in the make-up of human psychology the later history is implicit in the early crude division. One realm is the home of assured appropriation and possession; the other of striving, transiency and frustration. How many persons are there today who conceive that they have disposed of ignorance, struggle and disappointment by pointing to man's "finite" nature as if finitude signifies anything else but an abstract classificatory naming of certain concrete and discriminable traits of nature itself—traits of nature which generate ignorance, arbitrary appearance and disappearance, failure and striving. It pleases man to substitute the dialectic exercise of showing how the "finite" can exist with or within the "infinite" for the problem of dealing with the contingent, thinking to solve the problem by distinguishing and naming its factors. Failure of the exercise is certain, but the failure can be flourished as one more proof of the finitude of man's intellect, and the needlessness because impotency of endeavor of "finite" creatures to attack ignorance and oppressive fatalities. Wisdom then consists in administration of the temporal, finite and human in its relation to the eternal and infinite, by means of dogma and cult, rather than in regulation of the events of life by understanding of actual conditions.

It does not demand great ingenuity to detect the inversion here. The starting point is precisely the existing mixture of the regular and dependable and the unsettled and uncertain. There are a multitude of recipes for obtaining a vicarious possession of the stable and final without getting involved in the labor and pain of intellectual effort attending regulation of the conditions upon which these fruits depend.

This situation is worthy of remark as an exemplification of how easy it is to arrive at a description of existence via a theory of wisdom, of reflective insight into goods. It has a direct bearing upon a metaphysical doctrine which is not popular, like the division into the supernatural and natural, but which is learned and technical. The philosopher may have little esteem for the crude forms assumed by the popular metaphysics of earth and heaven, of God, nature, and man. But the philosopher has often proceeded in a manner analogous to that which resulted in this popular metaphysics; some of the most cherished metaphysical distinctions seem to be but learned counterparts, dependent upon an elaborate intellectual technique, for these rough, crude notions of supernatural and natural, divine and human, in popular belief. I refer to such things as the Platonic division into ideal archetypes and physical events; the Aristotelian division into form which is actuality and matter which is potential, when that is understood as a distinction of ranks of reality; the noumenal things, things-in-themselves of Kant in contrast with natural objects as phenomenal; the distinction, current among contemporary absolute idealists, of reality and appearance.

The division however is not confined to philosophers with leanings toward spiritualistic philosophies. There is some evidence that Plato got the term Idea, as a name for essential form, from Democritus. Whether this be the case or no, the Idea of Democritus,[3] though having a radically diverse structure from the Platonic Idea, had the same function of designating a finished, complete, stable, wholly unprecarious reality. Both philosophers craved solidity and both found it; corresponding to the Platonic phenomenal flux are the Democritean things as they are in custom or ordinary experience: corresponding to the ideal archetypes are substantial indivisible atoms. Corresponding, again to the Platonic theory of Ideas is the modern theory of mathematical structures which are alone independently real, while the empirical impressions and suggestions to which they give rise is the counterpart of his realm of phenomena.

Apart from the materialistic and spiritualistic schools, there is the Spinozistic [4] division into attributes and modes; the old division of essence and existence, and its modern counterpart subsistence and existence. It is impossible to force Mr. Bertrand Russell into any one of the pigeon-holes of the cabinet of conventional philosophic schools. But moral, or philosophical, motivation is obvious in his metaphysics when he says that mathematics takes us "into the region of absolute necessity, to which not only the actual world but every possible world must conform." Indeed with his usual lucidity, he says, mathematics "finds a habitation eternally standing, where our ideals are fully satisfied and our best hopes are not thwarted." When he adds that contemplation of such objects is the "chief means of overcoming the terrible sense of impotence, of weakness, of exile amid hostile power, which is too apt to result from acknowledging the all but omnipotence of alien forces," the presence of moral origin is explicit.

No modern thinker has pointed out so persuasively as Santayana [5] that "every phase of the ideal world emanates from the natural," that "sense, art, religion, society express nature exuberantly." And yet unless one reads him wrong, he then confounds his would-be disciples and confuses his critics by holding that nature is *truly* presented only in an esthetic contemplation of essences reached by physical science, an envisagement reached through a dialectic which "is a transubstantiation of matter, a passage from existence to eternity." This passage moreover is so utter that there is no road back. The stable ideal meanings which are the fruit of nature are forbidden, in the degree in which they are its highest and truest fruits, from dropping seeds in nature to its further fructification.

The perception of genetic continuity between the dynamic flux of nature and an eternity of static ideal forms thus terminates in a sharp division, in reiteration of the old tradition. Perhaps it is a caricature to say that the ultimate of reason is held to be ability to behold nature as a complete mechanism which generates and sustains the beholding of the mechanism, but the caricature is not wilful. If the separation of contingency and necessity is abandoned, what is there to exclude a belief that science, while it is

---

[3] Democritus (*c.* 460–370 B.C.): Greek philospher. [R.J.R.]

[4] Benedict Spinoza (1632–77): Jewish philosopher who lived and wrote in Holland. [R.J.R.]

[5] George Santayana (1863–1952): American philosopher. [R.J.R.]

grasp of the regular and stable mechanism of nature, is also an organ of regulating and enriching, through its own expansion, the more exuberant and irregular expressions of nature in human intercourse, the arts, religion, industry, and politics?

To follow out the latter suggestion would take us to a theme reserved for later consideration. We are here concerned with the fact that it is the intricate mixture of the stable and the precarious, the fixed and the unpredictably novel, the assured and the uncertain, in existence which sets mankind upon that love of wisdom which forms philosophy. Yet too commonly, although in a great variety of technical modes, the result of the search is converted into a metaphysics which denies or conceals from acknowledgment the very characters of existence which initiated it, and which give significance to its conclusions. The form assumed by the denial is, most frequently, that striking division into a superior true realm of being and lower illusory, insignificant or phenomenal realm which characterizes metaphysical systems as unlike as those of Plato and Democritus, St. Thomas and Spinoza, Aristotle and Kant, Descartes and Comte,[6] Haeckel [7] and Mrs. Eddy.[8]

The same jumble of acknowledgment and denial attends the conception of Absolute Experience: as if any experience could be more absolutely experience than that which marks the life of humanity. This conception constitutes the most recent device for first admitting and then denying the combinedly stable and unstable nature of the world. Its plaintive recognition of our experience as finite and temporal, as full of error, conflict and contradiction, is an acknowledgment of the precarious uncertainty of the objects and connections that constitute nature as it emerges in history. Human experience however has also the pathetic longing for truth, beauty and order. There is more than the longing: there are moments of achievement. Experience exhibits ability to possess harmonious objects. It evinces an ability, within limits, to safeguard the excellent objects and to deflect and reduce the obnoxious ones. The concept of an absolute experience which is only and always perfect and good, first explicates these desirable implications of things of actual experience, and then asserts that they alone are real. The experienced occurrences which give poignancy and pertinency to the longing for a better world, the experimental endeavors and plans which make possible actual betterments within the objects of actual experience, are thus swept out of real Being into a limbo of appearances.

The notion of Absolute Experience thus serves as a symbol of two facts. One is the ineradicable union in nature of the relatively stable and the relatively contingent. The division of the movement and leadings of things which are experienced into two parts, such that one set constitutes and

---

[6] Auguste Comte (1798–1857): French positivist philosopher. [R.J.R.]
[7] Ernst Haeckel (1834–1919): German biologist and philosopher. [R.J.R.]
[8] Mary Baker Eddy (1821–1910): founder of Christian Science Church. [R.J.R.]

defines absolute and eternal experience, while the other set constitutes and defines finite experience, tells us nothing about absolute experience. It tells us a good deal about experience as it exists: namely, that it is such as to involve permanent and general objects of reference as well as temporally changing events; the possibility of truth as well as error; conclusive objects and goods as well as things whose purport and nature is determinable only in an indeterminate future. Nothing is gained—except the delights of a dialectic problem—in labelling one assortment absolute experience and the other finite experience. Since the appeal of the adherents of the philosophy of absolute and phenomenal experience is to a logical criterion, namely, to the implication in every judgment, however erroneous, of a standard of consistency which excludes any possibility of contradictoriness, the inherent logical contradictions in the doctrine itself are worth noting.

In the first place, the contents as well as the form of ultimate Absolute Experience are derived from and based upon the features of actual experience, the very experience which is then relegated to unreality by the supreme reality derived from its unreality. It is "real" just long enough to afford a spring-board into ultimate reality and to afford a hint of the essential contents of the latter and then it obligingly dissolves into mere appearance. If we start from the standpoint of the Absolute Experience thus reached, the contradiction is repeated from its side. Although absolute, eternal, all-comprehensive, and pervasively integrated into a whole so logically perfect that no separate patterns, to say nothing of seams and holes, can exist in it, it proceeds to play a tragic joke upon itself—for there is nothing else to be fooled—by appearing in a queer combination of rags and glittering gew-gaws, in the garb of the temporal, partial and conflicting things, mental as well as physical, of ordinary experience. I do not cite these dialectic contradictions as having an inherent importance. But the fact that a doctrine which avowedly takes logical consistence for its method and criterion, whose adherents are noteworthy for dialectic acumen in specific issues, should terminate in such thoroughgoing contradictions may be cited as evidence that after all the doctrine is merely engaged in an arbitrary sorting out of characters of things which in nature are always present in conjunction and interpenetration.

The union of the hazardous and the stable, of the incomplete and the recurrent, is the condition of all experienced satisfaction as truly as of our predicaments and problems. While it is the source of ignorance, error and failure of expectation, it is the source of the delight which fulfillments bring. For if there were nothing in the way, if there were no deviations and resistances, fulfillment would be at once, and in so being would fulfill nothing, but merely be. It would not be in connection with desire or satisfaction. Moreover when a fulfillment comes and is pronounced good, it is *judged* good, distinguished and asserted, simply because it is in jeopardy, because it occurs amid indifferent and divergent things. Because of this mixture of the regular and that which cuts across stability, a good object once experienced acquires ideal quality and attracts demand and effort to itself. A particular ideal may be an illusion, but having ideals is no illusion. It embodies features of existence. Although imagination is often fantastic it is also an organ of nature; for it is the appropriate phase of indeterminate events moving toward eventualities that are now but possibilities. A purely stable world permits of no illusions, but neither is it clothed with ideals. It just exists. To be good is to be better than; and there can be no better except where there is shock and discord combined with enough assured order to make attainment of harmony possible. Better objects when brought into existence are existent not ideal; they retain ideal quality only retrospectively as commemorative of issue from prior conflict and prospectively, in contrast with forces which make for their destruction. Water that slakes thirst, or a conclusion that solves a problem have ideal character as long as thirst or problem persists in a way which qualifies the result. But water that is not a satisfaction of need has no more ideal quality than water running through pipes into a reservoir; a solution ceases to be a solution and becomes a bare incident of existence when its antecedent generating conditions of doubt, ambiguity and search are lost from its context. While the precarious nature of existence is indeed the source of all trouble, it is also an indispensable condition of ideality, becoming a sufficient condition when conjoined with the regular and assured.

We long, amid a troubled world, for perfect being. We forget that what gives meaning to the notion of perfection is the events that create longing, and that, apart from them, a "perfect" world would mean just an unchanging brute existential thing. The ideal significance of esthetic objects is no exception to this principle. Their satisfying quality, their power to compose while they arouse, is not dependent upon definite prior desire and effort as is the case with the ideally satisfying quality of practical and scientific objects. It is part of their peculiar satisfying quality to be gratuitous, not purchased by endeavor. The contrast to other things of this detachment from toil and labor in a world where most realizations have to be bought, as well as the contrast to trouble and uncertainty, give esthetic objects their peculiar traits. If all things came to us in the way our esthetic objects do, none of them would be a source of esthetic delight.

Some phases of recent philosophy have made much of need, desire and satisfaction. Critics have frequently held that the outcome is only recurrence to an older subjective empiricism, though with substitution of affections and volitional states for cognitive sensory states. But need and desire are exponents of natural being. They are, if we use Aristotelian phraseology, actualizations of its contingencies and incompletenesses; as such nature itself is wistful and pathetic, turbulent and passionate. Were it not, the existence of wants would be a miracle. In a world where everything is complete, nothing requires anything else for its completion. A world in which events can be carried to a finish only through the coinciding assistance of other transitory events, is already necessitous, a world of begging as well as of beggarly elements. If human experience is to express and reflect this world, it must be marked by needs; in becoming aware of the needful and needed quality of things it must project satisfactions or completions. For irrespective of whether a satisfaction is conscious, a satisfaction or non-satisfaction is an objective thing with objective conditions. It means fulfill-ment of the demands of objective factors. Happiness may *mark* an aware-ness of such satisfaction, and it may *be* its culminating form. But satisfac-tion is not subjective, private or personal: it is conditioned by objective partialities and defections and made real by objective situations and com-pletions.

By the same logic, necessity implies the precarious and contingent. A world that was all necessity would not be a world of necessity; it would just be. For in its being, nothing would be necessary for anything else. But where some things are indigent, other things are necessary if demands are to be met. The common failure to note the fact that a world of complete being would be a world in which necessity is meaningless is due to a rapid shift from one universe of discourse to another. First we postulate a whole of Being; then we shift to a part; now since a "part" is logically dependent as such in its existence and its properties, it is necessitated by other parts. But we have unwittingly introduced contingency in the very fact of marking off something as just a part. If the logical implications of the original no-tion are held to firmly, a part is already a part-of-a-whole. Its being what it is, is not necessitated by the whole or by other parts: its being what it is, is just a name for the whole being what it is. Whole and parts alike are but names for existence there as just what it is. But wherever we can say *if* so-and-so, then something else, there is necessity, because partialities are im-plied which are not just parts-of-a-whole. A world of "ifs" is alone a world of "musts"—the "ifs" express real differences; the "musts" real connec-tions. The stable and recurrent is needed for the fulfillment of the possible; the doubtful can be settled only through its adaptation to stable objects. The necessary is always necessary for, not necessary in and of itself; it is conditioned by the contingent, although itself a condition of the full deter-mination of the latter.

One of the most striking phases of the history of philosophic thought is the recurrent grouping together of unity, permanence (or "the eternal"), completeness and rational thought, while upon another side full multiplic-ity, change and the temporal, the partial, defective, sense and desire. This division is obviously but another case of violent separation of the precari-ous and unsettled from the regular and determinate. One aspect of it how-ever, is worthy of particular attention: the connection of thought and unity. Empirically, all reflection sets out from the problematic and confused. Its aim is to clarify and ascertain. When thinking is successful, its career closes in transforming the disordered into the orderly, the mixed-up into the dis-tinguished or placed, the unclear and ambiguous into the defined and un-equivocal, the disconnected into the systematized. It is empirically assured that the goal of thinking does not remain a mere ideal, but is attained often enough so as to render reasonable additional efforts to achieve it.

In these facts we have, I think, the empirical basis of the philosophic doctrines which assert that reality is really and truly a rational system, a coherent whole of relations that cannot be conceived otherwise than in terms of intellect. Reflective inquiry moves in each particular case from differences toward unity; from indeterminate and ambiguous position to clear determination, from confusion and disorder to system. When thought in a given case has reached its goal of organized totality, of definite relations of distinctly placed elements, its object is the accepted starting point, the defined subject matter, of further experiences; antecedent and outgrown conditions of darkness and of unreconciled differences are dismissed as a transitory state of ignorance and inadequate apprehensions. Retain connection of the goal with the thinking by which it is reached, and then identify it with true reality in contrast with the merely phenomenal, and the outline of the logic of rational and "objective" idealisms is before us. Thought like Being, has two forms, one real; the other phenomenal. It is compelled to take on *reflective* form, it involves doubt, inquiry and hypothesis, because it sets out from a subject-matter conditioned by sense, a fact which proves that thought, intellect, is not pure in man, but restricted by an animal organism that is but one part linked with other parts, of nature. But the conclusion of reflection affords us a pattern and guarantee of thought which is *constitutive;* one with the system of objective reality. Such in outline is the procedure of all ontological logics.

A philosophy which accepts the denotative or empirical method accepts at full value the fact that reflective thinking transforms confusion, ambiguity and discrepancy into illumination, definiteness and consistency. But it also points to the contextual situation in which thinking occurs. It notes that the starting point is the actually *problematic,* and that the problematic phase resides in some actual and specifiable situation.

It notes that the means of converting the dubious into the assured, and the incomplete into the determinate, is use of assured and established things, which are just as empirical and as indicative of the nature of experienced things as is the uncertain. It thus notes that thinking is no different in kind from the use of natural materials and energies, say fire and tools, to refine, re-order, and shape other natural materials, say ore. In both cases, there are matters which as they stand are unsatisfactory and there are also adequate agencies for dealing with them and connecting them. At no point or place is there any jump outside empirical, natural objects and their relations. Thought and reason are not specific powers. They consist of the procedures intentionally employed in the application to each other of the unsatisfactorily confused and indeterminate on one side and the regular and stable on the other. Generalizing from such observations, empirical philosophy perceives that thinking is a continuous process of temporal reorganization within one and the same world of experienced things, not a jump from the latter world into one of objects constituted once for all by thought. It discovers thereby the empirical basis of rational idealism, and the point at which it empirically goes astray. Idealism fails to take into account the specified or concrete character of the uncertain situation in which thought occurs; it fails to note the empirically concrete nature of the subject-matter, acts, and tools by which determination and consistency are reached; it fails to note that the conclusive eventual objects having the latter properties are themselves as many as the situations dealt with. The conversion of the logic of reflection into an ontology of rational being is thus due to arbitrary conversion of an eventual natural function of unification into a causal antecedent reality; this in turn is due to the tendency of the imagination working under the influence of emotion to carry unification from an actual, objective and experimental enterprise, limited to particular situations where it is needed, into an unrestricted, wholesale movement which ends in an all-absorbing dream.

The occurrence of reflection is crucial for dualistic metaphysics as well as for idealistic ontologies. Reflection occurs only in situations qualified by uncertainty, alternatives, questioning, search, hypotheses, tentative trials or experiments which test the worth of thinking. A naturalistic metaphysics is bound to consider reflection as itself a natural event occurring *within* nature because of traits of the latter. It is bound to inference from the empirical traits of thinking in precisely the same way as the sciences make inferences from the happening of suns, radio-activity, thunder-storms or any other natural event. Traits of reflection are as truly indicative or evidential of the traits of *other* things as are the traits of these events. A theory of the nature of the occurrence and career of a sun reached by denial of the obvious traits of the sun, or by denial that these traits are so connected with the traits of other natural events that they can be used as evidence concerning the nature of these other things, would hardly possess scientific standing. Yet philosophers, and strangely enough philosophers who call themselves realists, have constantly held that the traits which are characteristic of thinking, namely, uncertainty, ambiguity, alternatives, inquiring, search, selection, experimental reshaping of external conditions, do not possess the same existential character as do the objects of valid knowledge. They have denied that these traits are evidential of the character of the world within which thinking occurs. They have not, as realists, asserted that these traits are mere appearances; but they have often asserted and implied that such things are only personal or psychological in contrast with a world of objective nature. But the interests of empirical and denotative method and of naturalistic metaphysics wholly coincide. The world must actually be such as to generate ignorance and inquiry; doubt and hypothesis, trial and temporal conclusions; the latter being such that they develop out of existences which while wholly "real" are not as satisfactory, as good, or as significant, as those into which they are eventually re-organized. The ultimate evidence of genuine hazard, contingency, irregularity and indeterminateness in nature is thus found in the occurrence of thinking. The traits of natural existence which generate the fears and adorations of superstitious barbarians generate the scientific procedures of disciplined civilization. The superiority of the latter does not consist in the fact that they are based on "real" existence, while the former depend wholly upon a human nature different from nature in general. It consists in the fact that scientific inquiries reach *objects* which are better, because reached by method which controls them and which adds greater control to life itself, method which mitigates accident, turns contingency to account, and releases thought and other forms of endeavor.

The conjunction of problematic and determinate characters in nature renders every existence, as well as every idea and human act, an experiment in fact, even though not in design. To be intelligently experimental is but to be conscious of this intersection of natural conditions so as to profit by it instead of being at its mercy. The Christian idea of this world and this life as a probation is a kind of distorted recognition of the situation; distorted because it applied wholesale to one stretch of existence in contrast with another, regarded as original and final. But in truth anything which can exist at any place and at any time occurs subject to tests imposed upon it by surroundings, which are only in part compatible and reinforcing. These surroundings test its strength and measure its endurance. As we can discourse of change only in terms of velocity and acceleration which involve relations to other things, so assertion of the permanent and enduring is comparative. The stablest thing we can speak of is not free from conditions set to it by other things. That even the solid earth mountains, the emblems of constancy, appear and disappear like the clouds is an old theme of moralists and poets. The fixed and unchanged being of the Democritean atom is now reported by inquirers to possess some of the traits of his non-being, and to embody a temporary equilibrium in the economy of nature's compromises and adjustments. A thing may endure *secula seculorum* and yet not be everlasting; it will crumble before the gnawing tooth of time, as it exceeds a certain measure. Every existence is an event.

This fact is nothing at which to repine and nothing to gloat over. It is something to be noted and used. If it is discomfiting when applied to good things, to our friends, possessions and precious selves, it is consoling also to know that no evil endures forever; that the longest lane turns sometime, and that the memory of loss of nearest and dearest grows dim in time. The eventful character of all existences is no reason for consigning them to the realm of mere appearance any more than it is a reason for idealizing flux into a deity. The important thing is measure, relation, ratio, knowledge of the comparative tempos of change. In mathematics some variables are constants in some problems; so it is in nature and life. The rate of change of some things is so slow, or is so rhythmic, that these changes have all the advantages of stability in dealing with more transitory and irregular happenings—if we know enough. Indeed, if any one thing that concerns us is subject to change, it is fortunate that all other things change. A thing "absolutely" stable and unchangeable would be out of the range of the principle of action and reaction, of resistance and leverage as well as of friction. Here it would have no applicability, no potentiality of use as measure and control of other events. To designate the slower and the regular rhythmic events structure, and more rapid and irregular ones process, is sound practical sense. It expresses the function of one in respect to the other.

But spiritualistic idealism and materialism alike treat this relational and functional distinction as something fixed and absolute. One doctrine finds structure in a framework of ideal forms, the other finds it in matter. They agree in supposing that structure has some superlative reality. This supposition is another form taken by preference for the stable over the precarious and uncompleted. The fact is that all structure is structure *of* something; anything defined as structure is a character of *events,* not something intrinsic and *per se.* A set of traits is called structure, because of its limiting function in relation to other traits of events. A house has a structure; in comparison with the disintegration and collapse that would occur without its presence, this structure is fixed. Yet it is not something external to which the changes involved in building and using the house have to submit. It is rather an arrangement of changing events such that properties which change slowly, limit and direct a series of quick changes and give them an order which they do not otherwise possess. Structure is constancy of means, of things used for consequences, not of things taken by themselves or absolutely. Structure is what makes construction possible and cannot be discovered or defined except in some realized construction, construction being, of course, an evident order of changes. The isolation of structure from the changes whose stable ordering it is, renders it mysterious—something that is metaphysical in the popular sense of the word, a kind of ghostly queerness.

The "matter" of materialists and the "spirit" of idealists is a creature similar to the constitution of the United States in the minds of unimaginative persons. Obviously the real constitution is certain basic relationships among the activities of the citizens of the country; it is a property or phase of these processes, so connected with them as to influence their rate and direction of change. But by literalists it is often conceived of as something external to them; in itself fixed, a rigid framework to which *all* changes must accommodate themselves. Similarly what we call matter is that character of natural events which is so tied up with changes that are sufficiently rapid to be perceptible as to give the latter a characteristic rhythmic order, the causal sequence. It is no cause or source of events or processes; no absolute monarch; no principle of explanation; no substance behind or underlying changes—save in that sense of substance in which a man well fortified with this world's goods, and hence able to maintain himself through vicissitudes of surroundings, is a man of substance. The name designates a character in operation, not an entity.

That structure, whether of the kind called material or of the kind summed up in the word mental, is stable or permanent relationally and in its office, may be shown in another way. There is no action without reaction; there is no exclusively one-way exercise of conditioning power, no mode of regulation that operates wholly from above to below or from within outwards or from without inwards. Whatever influences the changes of other things is itself changed. The idea of an activity proceeding only in one direction, of an unmoved mover, is a survival of Greek physics. It has been banished from science, but remains to haunt philosophy. The vague and mysterious properties assigned to mind and matter, the very conceptions of mind and matter in traditional thought, are ghosts walking underground. The notion of matter actually found in the practice of science has nothing in common with the matter of materialists—and almost everybody is still a materialist as to matter, to which he merely adds a second rigid structure which he calls mind. The matter of science is a character of natural events and changes as they change; their character of regular and stable order.

Natural events are so complex and varied that there is nothing surprising in their possession of different characterizations, characters so different that they can be easily treated as opposites.

Nothing but unfamiliarity stands in the way of thinking of both mind and matter as different characters of natural events, in which matter expresses their sequential order, and mind the order of their meanings in their logical connections and dependencies. Processes may be eventful for functions which taken in abstract separation are at opposite poles, just as physiological processes eventuate in both anabolic and katabolic functions. The idea that matter and mind are two sides or "aspects" of the same things, like the convex and the concave in a curve, is literally unthinkable.

A curve is an intelligible object and concave and convex are defined in terms of this object; they are indeed but names for properties involved in its meaning. We do not start with convexity and concavity as two independent things and then set up an unknown *tertium quid* to unite two disparate things. In spite of the literal absurdity of the comparison, it may be understood however in a way which conveys an inkling of the truth. That to which both mind and matter belong is the complex of events that constitute nature. This becomes a mysterious *tertium quid,* incapable of designation, only when mind and matter are taken to be static structures instead of functional characters. It is a plausible prediction that if there were an interdict placed for a generation upon the use of mind, matter, consciousness as nouns, and we were obliged to employ adjectives and adverbs, conscious and consciously, mental and mentally, material and physically, we should find many of our problems much simplified.

We have selected only a few of the variety of the illustrations that might be used in support of the idea that the significant problems and issues of life and philosophy concern the rate and mode of the conjunction of the precarious and the assured, the incomplete and the finished, the repetitious and the varying, the safe and sane and the hazardous. If we trust to the evidence of experienced things, these traits, and the modes and tempos of their interaction with each other, are fundamental features of natural existence. The experience of their various consequences, according as they are relatively isolated, unhappily or happily combined, is evidence that wisdom, and hence that love of wisdom which is philosophy, is concerned with choice and administration of their proportioned union. Structure and process, substance and accident, matter and energy, permanence and flux, one and many, continuity and discreteness, order and progress, law and liberty, uniformity and growth, tradition and innovation, rational will and impelling desires, proof and discovery, the actual and the possible, are names given to various phases of their conjunction, and the issue of living depends upon the art with which these things are adjusted to each other.

While metaphysics may stop short with noting and registering these traits, man is not contemplatively detached from them. They involve him in his perplexities and troubles, and are the source of his joys and achievements. The situation is not indifferent to man, because it forms man as a desiring, striving, thinking, feeling creature. It is not egotism that leads man from contemplative registration of these traits to interest in managing them, to intelligence and purposive art. Interest, thinking, planning, striving, consummation and frustration are a drama enacted by these forces and conditions. A particular choice may be arbitrary; this is only to say that it does not approve itself to reflection. But choice is not arbitrary, not in a universe like this one, a world which is not finished and which has not consistently made up its mind where it is going and what it is going to do. Or, if we call it arbitrary, the arbitrariness is not ours but that of existence itself. And to call existence arbitrary or by any moral name, whether disparaging or honorific, is to patronize nature. To assume an attitude of condescension toward existence is perhaps a natural human compensation for the straits of life. But it is an ultimate source of the covert, uncandid and cheap in philosophy. This compensatory disposition it is which forgets that reflection exists to guide choice and effort. Hence its love of wisdom is but an unlaborious transformation of existence by dialectic, instead of an opening and enlarging of the ways of nature in man. A true wisdom, devoted to the latter task, discovers in thoughtful observation and experiment the method of administering the unfinished processes of existence so that frail goods shall be substantiated, secure goods be extended, and the precarious promises of good that haunt experienced things be more liberally fulfilled.

QUESTIONS FOR STUDY AND DISCUSSION

1. What are the features of existence emphasized by cultural phenomena?
2. In contrast, what is the common premise of all philosophies?

3. What is the position of Aristotle regarding the universe?
4. Though Dewey admits that there have been philosophies of change, what in his opinion is their basic weakness?
5. What does Dewey mean by the empirical method?

The Live Creature

The comparison of the emergence of works of art out of ordinary experiences to the refining of raw materials into valuable products may seem to some unworthy, if not an actual attempt to reduce works of art to the status of articles manufactured for commercial purposes. The point, however, is that no amount of ecstatic eulogy of finished works can of itself assist the understanding or the generation of such works. Flowers can be enjoyed without knowing about the interactions of soil, air, moisture, and seeds of which they are the result. But they cannot be *understood* without taking just these interactions into account—and theory is a matter of understanding. Theory is concerned with discovering the nature of the production of works of art and of their enjoyment in perception. How is it that the everyday making of things grows into that form of making which is genuinely artistic? How is it that our everyday enjoyment of scenes and situations develops into the peculiar satisfaction that attends the experience which is emphatically esthetic? These are the questions theory must answer. The answers cannot be found, unless we are willing to find the germs and roots in matters of experience that we do not currently regard as esthetic. Having discovered these active seeds, we may follow the course of their growth into the highest forms of finished and refined art.

It is a commonplace that we cannot direct, save accidentally, the growth and flowering of plants, however lovely and enjoyed, without understanding their causal conditions. It should be just a commonplace that esthetic understanding—as distinct from sheer personal enjoyment—must start with the soil, air, and light out of which things esthetically admirable arise. And these conditions are the conditions and factors that make an ordinary experience complete. The more we recognize this fact, the more we shall find ourselves faced with a problem rather than with a final solution. *If* artistic and esthetic quality is implicit in every normal experience, how shall we explain how and why it so generally fails to become explicit? Why is it that to multitudes art seems to be an importation into experience from a foreign country and the esthetic to be a synonym for something artificial?

We cannot answer these questions any more than we can trace the development of art out of everyday experience, unless we have a clear and coherent idea of what is meant when we say "normal experience." Fortunately, the road to arriving at such an idea is open and well marked. The nature of experience is determined by the essential conditions of life. While man is other than bird and beast, he shares basic vital functions with them and has to make the same basal adjustments if he is to continue the process of living. Having the same vital needs, man derives the means by which he breathes, moves, looks and listens, the very brain with which he coördinates his senses and his movements, from his animal forbears. The organs with which he maintains himself in being are not of himself alone, but by the grace of struggles and achievements of a long line of animal ancestry.

Fortunately a theory of the place of the esthetic in experience does not have to lose itself in minute details when it starts with experience in its elemental form. Broad outlines suffice. The first great consideration is that life goes on in an environment; not merely *in* it but because of it, through interaction with it. No creature lives merely under its skin; its subcutaneous organs are means of connection with what lies beyond its bodily frame, and to which, in order to live, it must adjust itself, by accommodation and defense but also by conquest. At every moment, the living creature is exposed to dangers from its surroundings, and at every moment, it must draw upon something in its surroundings to satisfy its needs. The career and destiny of a living being are bound up with its interchanges with its environment, not externally but in the most intimate way.

The growl of a dog crouching over his food, his howl in time of loss and loneliness, the wagging of his tail at the return of his human friend are expressions of the implication of a living in a natural medium which includes man along with the animal he has domesticated. Every need, say hunger for fresh air or food, is a lack that denotes at least a temporary absence of adequate adjustment with surroundings. But it is also a demand, a reaching out into the environment to make good the lack and to restore adjustment by building at least a temporary equilibrium. Life itself consists of phases in which the organism falls out of step with the march of surrounding things and then recovers unison with it—either through effort or by some happy chance. And, in a growing life, the recovery is never mere return to a prior state, for it is enriched by the state of disparity and resistance through which it has successfully passed. If the gap between organism and environment is too wide, the creature dies. If its activity is not enhanced by the temporary alienation it merely subsists. Life grows when a temporary falling out is a transition to a more extensive balance of the energies of the organism with those of the conditions under which it lives.

These biological commonplaces are something more than that; they reach to the roots of the esthetic in experience. The world is full of things that are indifferent and even hostile to life; the very processes by which life is maintained tend to throw it out of gear with its surroundings. Nevertheless, if life continues and if in continuing it expands, there is an overcoming of factors of opposition and conflict; there is a transformation of them into differentiated aspects of a higher powered and more significant life. The marvel of organic, of vital, adaptation through expansion (instead of by contraction and passive accommodation) actually takes place. Here in germ are balance and harmony attained through rhythm. Equilibrium comes about not mechanically and inertly but out of, and because of, tension.

There is in nature, even below the level of life, something more than mere flux and change. Form is arrived at whenever a stable, even though moving, equilibrium is reached. Changes interlock and sustain one another. Wherever there is this coherence there is endurance. Order is not imposed from without but is made out of the relations of harmonious interactions that energies bear to one another. Because it is active (not anything static because foreign to what goes on) order itself develops. It comes to include within its balanced movement a greater variety of changes.

Order cannot but be admirable in a world constantly threatened with disorder—in a world where living creatures can go on living only by taking advantage of whatever order exists about them, incorporating it into themselves. In a world like ours, every living creature that attains sensibility welcomes order with a response of harmonious feeling whenever it finds a congruous order about it.

For only when an organism shares in the ordered relations of its environment does it secure the stability essential to living. And when the participation comes after a phase of disruption and conflict, it bears within itself the germs of a consummation akin to the esthetic.

The rhythm of loss of integration with environment and recovery of union not only persists in man but becomes conscious with him; its conditions are material out of which he forms purposes. Emotion is the conscious sign of a break, actual or impending. The discord is the occasion that induces reflection. Desire for restoration of the union converts mere emotion into interest in objects as conditions of realization of harmony. With the realization, material of reflection is incorporated into objects as their meaning. Since the artists cares in a peculiar way for the phase of experience in which union is achieved, he does not shun moments of resistance and tension. He rather cultivates them, not for their own sake but because of their potentialities, bringing to living consciousness an experience that is unified and total. In contrast with the person whose purpose is esthetic, the scientific man is interested in problems, in situations wherein tension between the matter of observation and of thought is marked. Of course he cares for their resolution. But he does not rest in it; he passes on to another problem using an attained solution only as a stepping stone from which to set on foot further inquiries.

The difference between the esthetic and the intellectual is thus one of the place where emphasis falls in the constant rhythm that marks the interaction of the live creature with his surroundings. The ultimate matter of both emphases in experience is the same, as is also their general form. The odd notion that an artist does not think and a scientific inquirer does nothing else is the result of converting a difference of tempo and emphasis into a difference in kind. The thinker has his esthetic moment when his ideas cease to be mere ideas and become the corporate meanings of objects. The artist has his problems and thinks as he works. But his thought is more immediately embodied in the object. Because of the comparative remoteness of his end, the scientific worker operates with symbols, words and mathematical signs. The artist does his thinking in the very qualitative media he works in, and the terms lie so close to the object that he is producing that they merge directly into it.

The live animal does not have to project emotions into the objects experienced. Nature is kind and hateful, bland and morose, irritating and comforting, long before she is mathematically qualified or even a congeries of "secondary" qualities like colors and their shapes. Even such words as long and short, solid and hollow, still carry to all, but those who are intellectually specialized, a moral and emotional connotation. The dictionary will inform any one who consults it that the early use of words like sweet and bitter was not to denote qualities of sense as such but to discriminate things as favorable and hostile. How could it be otherwise? Direct experience comes from nature and man interacting with each other. In this interaction, human energy gathers, is released, dammed up, frustrated and victorious. There are rhythmic beats of want and fulfillment, pulses of doing and being withheld from doing.

All interactions that effect stability and order in the whirling flux of change are rhythms. There is ebb and flow, systole and diastole: ordered change. The latter moves within bounds. To overpass the limits that are set is destruction and death, out of which, however, new rhythms are built up. The proportionate interception of changes establishes an order that is spatially, not merely temporally patterned: like the waves of the sea, the ripples of sand where waves have flowed back and forth, the fleecy and the black-bottomed cloud. Contrast of lack and fullness, of struggle and achievement, of adjustment after consummated irregularity, form the drama in which action, feeling, and meaning are one. The outcome is balance and counterbalance. These are not static nor mechanical. They express power that is intense because measured through overcoming resistance. Environing objects avail and counteravail.

There are two sorts of possible worlds in which esthetic experience would not occur. In a world of mere flux, change would not be cumulative; it would not move toward a close. Stability and rest would have no being. Equally is it true, however, that a world that is finished, ended, would have no traits of suspense and crisis, and would offer no opportunity for resolution. Where everything is already complete, there is no fulfillment. We envisage with pleasure Nirvana and a uniform heavenly bliss only because they are projected upon the background of our present world of stress and conflict. Because the actual world, that in which we live, is a combination of movement and culmination, of breaks and re-unions, the experience of a living creature is capable of esthetic quality. The live being recurrently loses and reëstablishes equilibrium with his surroundings. The moment of passage from disturbance into harmony is that of intensest life. In a finished world, sleep and waking could not be distinguished. In one wholly perturbed, conditions could not even be struggled with. In a world made after the pattern of ours, moments of fulfillment punctuate experience with rhythmically enjoyed intervals.

Inner harmony is attained only when, by some means, terms are made with the environment. When it occurs on any other than an "objective" basis, it is illusory—in extreme cases to the point of insanity. Fortunately for variety in experience, terms are made in many ways—ways ultimately decided by selective interest. Pleasures may come about through chance contact and stimulation; such pleasures are not to be despised in a world full of pain. But happiness and delight are a different sort of thing. They come to be through a fulfillment that reaches to the depths of our being— one that is an adjustment of our whole being with the conditions of existence. In the process of living, attainment of a period of equilibrium is at the same time the initiation of a new relation to the environment, one that brings with it potency of new adjustments to be made through struggle. The time of consummation is also one of beginning anew. Any attempt to perpetuate beyond its term the enjoyment attending the time of fulfillment and harmony constitutes withdrawal from the world. Hence it marks the lowering and loss of vitality. But, through the phases of perturbation and conflict, there abides the deep-seated memory of an underlying harmony, the sense of which haunts life like the sense of being founded on a rock.

Most mortals are conscious that a split often occurs between their present living and their past and future. Then the past hangs upon them as a burden; it invades the present with a sense of regret, of opportunities not used, and of consequences we wish undone. It rests upon the present as an oppression, instead of being a storehouse of resources by which to move confidently forward. But the live creature adopts its past; it can make friends with even its stupidities, using them as warnings that increase present wariness. Instead of trying to live upon whatever may have been achieved in the past, it uses past successes to inform the present. Every living experience owes its richness to what Santayana well calls "hushed reverberations."

To the being fully alive, the future is not ominous but a promise; it surrounds the present as a halo. It consists of possibilities that are felt as a possession of what is now and here. In life that is truly life, everything overlaps and merges. But all too often we exist in apprehensions of what the future may bring, and are divided within ourselves. Even when not overanxious, we do not enjoy the present because we subordinate it to that which is absent. Because of the frequency of this abandonment of the present to the past and future, the happy periods of an experience that is now complete because it absorbs into itself memories of the past and anticipations of the future, come to constitute an esthetic ideal. Only when the past ceases to trouble and anticipations of the future are not perturbing is a being wholly united with his environment and therefore fully alive. Art celebrates with peculiar intensity the moments in which the past reënforces the present and in which the future is a quickening of what now is.

To grasp the sources of esthetic experience it is, therefore, necessary to have recourse to animal life below the human scale. The activities of the fox, the dog, and the thrush may at least stand as reminders and symbols of that unity of experience which we so fractionize when work is labor, and thought withdraws us from the world. The live animal is fully present, all there, in all of its actions: in its wary glances, its sharp sniffings, its abrupt cocking of ears. All senses are equally on the *qui vive*. As you watch, you see motion merging into sense and sense into motion—constituting that animal grace so hard for man to rival. What the live creature retains from the past and what it expects from the future operate as directions in the present. The dog is never pedantic nor academic; for these things arise only when the past is served in consciousness from the present and is set up as a model to copy or a storehouse upon which to draw. The past absorbed into the present carries on; it presses forward.

There is much in the life of the savage that is sodden. But, when the savage is most alive, he is most observant of the world about him and most taut with energy. As he watches what stirs about him, he, too, is stirred. His observation is both action in preparation and foresight of the future. He is as active through his whole being when he looks and listens as when he stalks his quarry or stealthily retreats from a foe. His senses are sentinels of immediate thought and outposts of action, and not, as they so often are with us, mere pathways along which material is gathered to be stored away for a delayed and remote possibility.

It is mere ignorance that leads then to the supposition that connection of art and esthetic perception with experience signifies a lowering of their significance and dignity. Experience in the degree in which it *is* experience is heightened vitality. Instead of signifying being shut up within one's own private feelings and sensations, it signifies active and alert commerce with the world; at its height it signifies complete interpenetration of self and the world of objects and events. Instead of signifying surrender to caprice and disorder, it affords our sole demonstration of a stability that is not stagnation but is rhythmic and developing. Because experience is the fulfillment of an organism in its struggles and achievements in a world of things, it is art in germ. Even in its rudimentary forms, it contains the promise of that delightful perception which is esthetic experience.

1. Dewey attempts to remove the difference between art and human experience. Explain.
2. Dewey states that the future is a promise. What does he mean?
3. Show how he relates his analysis of esthetic experience to biological life.

The Live Creature and "Etherial Things"

Why is the attempt to connect the higher and ideal things of experience with basic vital roots so often regarded as betrayal of their nature and denial of their value? Why is there repulsion when the high achievements of fine art are brought into connection with common life, the life that we share with all living creatures? Why is life thought of as an affair of low appetite, or at its best a thing of gross sensation, and ready to sink from its best to the level of lust and harsh cruelty? A complete answer to the question would involve the writing of a history of morals that would set forth the conditions that have brought about contempt for the body, fear of the senses, and the opposition of flesh to spirit.

One aspect of this history is so relevant to our problem that it must receive at least passing notice. The institutional life of mankind is marked by disorganization. This disorder is often disguised by the fact that it takes the form of static division into classes, and this static separation is accepted as the very essence of order as long as it is so fixed and so accepted as not to generate open conflict. Life is compartmentalized and the institutionalized compartments are classified as high and as low; their values as profane and spiritual, as material and ideal. Interests are related to one another externally and mechanically, through a system of checks and balances. Since religion, morals, politics, business has each its own compartment, within which it is fitting each should remain, art, too, must have its peculiar and private realm. Compartmentalization of occupations and interests brings about separation of that mode of activity commonly called "practice" from insight, of imagination from executive doing, of significant purpose from work, of emotion from thought and doing. Each of these has, too, its own place in which it must abide. Those who write the anatomy of experience then suppose that these divisions inhere in the very constitution of human nature.

Of much of our experience as it is actually lived under present economic and legal institutional conditions, it is only too true that these sepa-

Reprinted by permission of G. P. Putnam's Sons from pp. 20–39 of *Art as Experience* by John Dewey. Copyright © 1934 by John Dewey. Capricorn Edition.

rations hold. Only occasionally in the lives of many are the senses fraught with the sentiment that comes from deep realization of intrinsic meanings. We undergo sensations as mechanical stimuli or as irritated stimulations, without having a sense of the reality that is in them and behind them: in much of our experience our different senses do not unite to tell a common and enlarged story. We see without feeling; we hear, but only a second-hand report, second hand because not reënforced by vision. We touch, but the contact remains tangential because it does not fuse with qualities of senses that go below the surface. We use the senses to arouse passion but not to fulfill the interest of insight, not because that interest is not potentially present in the exercise of sense but because we yield to conditions of living that force sense to remain an excitation on the surface. Prestige goes to those who use their minds without participation of the body and who act vicariously through control of the bodies and labor of others.

Under such conditions, sense and flesh get a bad name. The moralist, however, has a truer sense of the intimate connections of sense with the rest of our being than has the professional psychologist and philosopher, although his sense of these connections takes a direction that reverses the potential facts of our living in relation to the environment. Psychologist and philosopher have in recent times been so obsessed with the problem of knowledge that they have treated "sensations" as mere elements of knowledge. The moralist knows that sense is allied with emotion, impulse and appetition. So he denounces the lust of the eye as part of the surrender of spirit to flesh. He identifies the sensuous with the sensual and the sensual with the lewd. His moral theory is askew, but at least he is aware that the eye is not an imperfect telescope designed for intellectual reception of material to bring about knowledge of distant objects.

"Sense" covers a wide range of contents: the sensory, the sensational, the sensitive, the sensible, and the sentimental, along with the sensuous. It includes almost everything from bare physical and emotional shock to sense itself—that is, the meaning of things present in immediate experience. Each term refers to some real phase and aspect of the life of an organic creature as life occurs through sense organs. But sense, as meaning so directly embodied in experience as to be its own illuminated meaning, is the only signification that expresses the function of sense organs when they are carried to full realization. The senses are the organs through which the live creature participates directly in the ongoings of the world about him. In this participation the varied wonder and splendor of this world are made actual for him in the qualities he experiences. This material cannot be opposed to action, for motor apparatus and "will" itself are the means by which this participation is carried on and directed. It cannot be opposed to "intellect," for mind is the means by which participation is rendered fruitful through sense; by which meanings and values are extracted, retained, and put to further service in the intercourse of the live creature with his surroundings.

Experience is the result, the sign, and the reward of that interaction of organism and environment which, when it is carried to the full, is a transformation of interaction into participation and communication. Since sense-organs with their connected motor apparatus are the means of this participation, any and every derogation of them, whether practical or theoretical, is at once effect and cause of a narrowed and dulled life-experience. Oppositions of mind and body, soul and matter, spirit and flesh all have their origin, fundamentally, in fear of what life may bring forth. They are marks of contraction and withdrawal. Full recognition, therefore, of the continuity of the organs, needs and basic impulses of the human creature with his animal forbears, implies no necessary reduction of man to the level of the brutes. On the contrary, it makes possible the drawing of a ground-plan of human experience upon which is erected the superstructure of man's marvelous and distinguishing experience. What is distinctive in man makes it possible for him to sink below the level of the beasts. It also makes it possible for him to carry to new and unprecedented heights that unity of sense and impulse, of brain and eye and ear, that is exemplified in animal life, saturating it with the conscious meanings derived from communication and deliberate expression.

Man excels in complexity and minuteness of differentiations. This very fact constitutes the necessity for many more comprehensive and exact relationships among the constituents of his being. Important as are the distinctions and relations thus made possible, the story does not end here. There are more opportunities for resistance and tension, more drafts upon experimentation and invention, and therefore more novelty in action, greater range and depth of insight and increase of poignancy in feeling. As an organism increases in complexity, the rhythms of struggle and consummation in its relation to its environment are varied and prolonged, and they come to include within themselves an endless variety of sub-rhythms. The designs of living are widened and enriched. Fulfillment is more massive and more subtly shaded.

Space thus becomes something more than a void in which to roam about, dotted here and there with dangerous things and things that satisfy the appetite. It becomes a comprehensive and enclosed scene within which are ordered the multiplicity of doings and undergoings in which man engages. Time ceases to be either the endless and uniform flow or the succession of instantaneous points which some philosophers have asserted it to be. It, too, is the organized and organizing medium of the rhythmic ebb and flow of expectant impulse, forward and retracted movement, resistance and suspense, with fulfillment and consummation. It is an ordering of growth and maturations—as James said, we learn to skate in summer after having commenced in winter. Time as organization in change is growth, and growth signifies that a varied series of change enters upon intervals of pause and rest; of completions that become the initial points of new processes of development. Like the soil, mind is fertilized while it lies fallow, until a new burst of bloom ensues.

When a flash of lightning illumines a dark landscape, there is a momentary recognition of objects. But the recognition is not itself a mere point in time. It is the focal culmination of long, slow processes of maturation. It is the manifestation of the continuity of an ordered temporal experience in a sudden discrete instant of climax. It is as meaningless in isolation as would be the drama of Hamlet were it confined to a single line or word with no context. But the phrase "the rest is silence" is infinitely pregnant as the conclusion of a drama enacted through development in time; so may be the momentary perception of a natural scene. Form, as it is present in the fine arts, is the art of making clear what is involved in the organization of space and time prefigured in every course of a developing life-experience.

Moments and places, despite physical limitation and narrow localization, are charged with accumulations of long-gathering energy. A return to a scene of childhood that was left long years before floods the spot with a release of pent-up memories and hopes. To meet in a strange country one who is a casual acquaintance at home may arouse a satisfaction so acute as to bring a thrill. Mere recognitions occur only when we are occupied with something else than the object or person recognized. It marks either an interruption or else an intent to use what is recognized as a means for something else. To see, to perceive, is more than to recognize. It does not identify something present in terms of a past disconnected from it. The past is carried into the present so as to expand and deepen the content of the latter. There is illustrated the translation of bare continuity of external time into the vital order and organization of experience. Identification nods and passes on. Or it defines a passing moment in isolation, it marks a dead spot in experience that is merely filled in. The extent to which the process of living in any day or hour is reduced to labeling situations, events, and objects as "so-and-so" in mere succession marks the cessation of a life that is a conscious experience. Continuities realized in an individual, discrete, form are the essence of the latter.

Art is thus prefigured in the very processes of living. A bird builds its nest and a beaver its dam when internal organic pressures coöperate with external materials so that the former are fulfilled and the latter are transformed in a satisfying culmination. We may hesitate to apply the word "art," since we doubt the presence of directive intent. But all deliberation, all conscious intent, grows out of things once performed organically through the interplay of natural energies. Were it not so, art would be built on quaking sands, nay, on unstable air. The distinguishing contribution of man is consciousness of the relations found in nature. Through consciousness, he converts the relations of cause and effect that are found in nature into relations of means and consequence. Rather, consciousness itself is the inception of such a transformation. What was mere shock becomes an invitation; resistance becomes something to be used in changing existing arrangements of matter; smooth facilities become agencies for executing an idea. In these operations, an organic stimulation becomes the bearer of meanings, and motor responses are changed into instruments of expression and communication; no longer are they mere means of locomotion and direct reaction. Meanwhile, the organic substratum remains as the quickening and deep foundation. Apart from relations of cause and effect in nature, conception and invention could not be. Apart from the relation of processes of rhythmic conflict and fulfillment in animal life, experience would be without design and pattern. Apart from organs inherited from animal ancestry, idea and purpose would be without a mechanism of realization. The primeval arts of nature and animal life are so much the material, and, in gross outline, so much the model for the intentional achievements of man, that the theologically minded have imputed conscious intent to the structure of nature—as man, sharing many activities with the ape, is wont to think of the latter as imitating his own performances.

The existence of art is the concrete proof of what has just been stated abstractly. It is proof that man uses the materials and energies of nature with intent to expand his own life, and that he does so in accord with the structure of his organism—brain, sense-organs, and muscular system. Art is the living and concrete proof that man is capable of restoring consciously, and thus on the plane of meaning, the union of sense, need, impulse and action characteristic of the live creature. The intervention of consciousness adds regulation, power of selection, and redisposition. Thus it varies the arts in ways without end. But its intervention also leads in time to the *idea* of art as a conscious idea—the greatest intellectual achievement in the history of humanity.

The variety and perfection of the arts in Greece led thinkers to frame a generalized conception of art and to project the ideal of an art of organization of human activities as such—the art of politics and morals as conceived by Socrates and Plato. The ideas of design, plan, order, pattern, purpose emerged in distinction from and relation to the materials employed in their realization. The conception of man as the being that uses art became at once the ground of the distinction of man from the rest of nature and of the bond that ties him to nature. When the conception of art as the distinguishing trait of man was made explicit, there was assurance that, short of complete relapse of humanity below even savagery, the possibility of invention of new arts would remain, along with use of old arts, as the guiding ideal of mankind. Although recognition of the fact still halts, because of traditions established before the power of art was adequately recognized, science itself is but a central art auxiliary to the generation and utilization of other arts.[1]

---

[1] I have developed this point in *Experience and Nature,* in Chapter 9, on "Experience, Nature and Art." As far as the present point is concerned, the conclusion is contained in the statement that "art, the mode of activity that is charged with

It is customary, and from some points of view necessary, to make a distinction between fine art and useful or technological art. But the point of view from which it is necessary is one that is extrinsic to the work of art itself. The customary distinction is based simply on acceptance of certain existing social conditions. I suppose the fetiches of the negro sculptor were taken to be useful in the highest degree to his tribal group, more so even than spears and clothing. But now they are fine art, serving in the twentieth century to inspire renovations in arts that had grown conventional. But they are fine art only because the anonymous artist lived and experienced so fully during the process of production. An angler may eat his catch without thereby losing the esthetic satisfaction he experienced in casting and playing. It is this degree of completeness of living in the experience of making and of perceiving that makes the difference between what is fine or esthetic in art and what is not. Whether the thing made is put to use, as are bowls, rugs, garments, weapons, is, *intrinsically* speaking, a matter of in-difference. That many, perhaps most, of the articles and utensils made at present for use are not genuinely esthetic happens, unfortunately, to be true. But it is true for reasons that are foreign to the relation of the "beauti-ful" and "useful" as such. Wherever conditions are such as to prevent the act of production from being an experience in which the whole creature is alive and in which he possesses his living through enjoyment, the product will lack something of being esthetic. No matter how useful it is for special and limited ends, it will not be useful in the ultimate degree—that of con-tributing directly and liberally to an expanding and enriched life. The story of the severance and final sharp opposition of the useful and the fine is the history of that industrial development through which so much of production has become a form of postponed living and so much of consumption a super-imposed enjoyment of the fruits of the labors of others.

Usually there is a hostile reaction to a conception of art that connects it with the activities of a live creature in its environment. This hostility to as-sociation of fine art with normal processes of living is a pathetic, even a tragic, commentary on life as it is ordinarily lived. Only because that life is usually so stunted, aborted, slack, or heavy laden, is the idea entertained that there is some inherent antagonism between the process of normal living and creation and enjoyment of works of esthetic art. After all, even though "spiritual" and "material" are separated and set in opposition to one another, there must be conditions through which the ideal is capable of embodiment and realization—and this is all, fundamentally, that "matter" signifies. The very currency which the opposition has acquired testifies, therefore, to a widespread operation of forces that convert what might be means of executing liberal ideas into oppressive burdens and that cause

---

meanings capable of immediately enjoyed possession, is the complete culmination of nature, and that science is properly a handmaiden that conducts natural events to this happy issue." [J.D.]

392 / JOHN DEWEY

ideals to be loose aspirations in an uncertain and ungrounded atmosphere.

While art itself is the best proof of the existence of a realized and there-fore realizable, union of material and ideal, there are general arguments that support the thesis in hand. Wherever continuity is possible, the burden of proof rests upon those who assert opposition and dualism. Nature is the mother and the habitat of man, even if sometimes a stepmother and an un-friendly home. The fact that civilization endures and culture continues—and sometimes advances—is evidence that human hopes and purposes find a basis and support in nature. As the developing growth of an individual from embryo to maturity is the result of interaction of organism with sur-roundings, so culture is the product not of efforts of men put forth in a void or just upon themselves, but of prolonged and cumulative interaction with environment. The depth of the responses stirred by works of art shows *their* continuity with the operations of this enduring experience. The works and the responses they evoke are continuous with the very processes of liv-ing as these are carried to unexpected happy fulfillment.

As to absorption of the esthetic in nature, I cite a case duplicated in some measure in thousands of persons, but notable because expressed by an artist of the first order, W. H. Hudson. "I feel when I am out of sight of living, growing grass, and out of the sound of birds' voices and all rural sounds, that I am not properly alive." He goes on to say, ". . . when I hear people say that they have not found the world and life so agreeable and interesting as to be in love with it, or that they look with equanimity to its end, I am apt to think that they have never been properly alive, nor seen with clear vision the world they think so meanly of or anything in it—not even a blade of grass." The mystic aspect of acute esthetic surrender, that renders it so akin as an experience to what religionists term ecstatic com-munion, is recalled by Hudson from his boyhood life. He is speaking of the effect the sight of acacia trees had upon him. "The loose feathery foliage on moonlight nights had a peculiar hoary aspect that made this tree seem more intensely alive than others, more conscious of me and of my pres-ence. . . . Similar to a feeling a person would have if visited by a super-natural being if he was perfectly convinced that it was there in his presence, albeit silent and unseen, intently regarding him and divining every thought in his mind." Emerson is often regarded as an austere thinker. But it was Emerson as an adult who said, quite in the spirit of the passage quoted from Hudson: "Crossing a bare common, in snow puddles, at twilight, under a clouded sky, without having in my thought any occurrence of spe-cial good fortune, I have enjoyed a perfect exhilaration. I am glad to the brink of fear."

I do not see any way of accounting for the multiplicity of experiences of this kind (something of the same quality being found in every spontane-ous and uncoerced esthetic response), except on the basis that there are stirred into activity resonances of dispositions acquired in primitive rela-tionships of the living being to its surroundings, and irrecoverable in distinct or intellectual consciousness. Experiences of the sort mentioned take us to a further consideration that testifies to natural continuity. There is no limit to the capacity of immediate sensuous experience to absorb into itself meanings and values that in and of themselves—that is in the abstract— would be designated "ideal" and "spiritual." The animistic strain of religious experience, embodied in Hudson's memory of his childhood days, is an instance on one level of experience. And the poetical, in whatever medium, is always a close kin of the animistic. And if we turn to an art that in many ways is at the other pole, architecture, we learn how ideas, wrought out at first perhaps in highly technical thought like that of mathematics, are capable of direct incorporation in sensuous form. The sensible surface of things is never merely a surface. One can discriminate rock from flimsy tissue-paper by the surface alone, so completely have the resistances of touch and the solidities due to stresses of the entire muscular system been embodied in vision. The process does not stop with incarnation of other sensory qualities that give depth of meaning to surface. Nothing that a man has ever reached by the highest flight of thought or penetrated by any probing insight is inherently such that it may not become the heart and core of sense.

The same word, "symbol," is used to designate expressions of abstract thought, as in mathematics, and also such things as a flag, crucifix, that embody deep social value and the meaning of historic faith and theological creed. Incense, stained glass, the chiming of unseen bells, embroidered robes accompany the approach to what is regarded as divine. The connection of the origin of many arts with primitive rituals becomes more evident with every excursion of the anthropologist into the past. Only those who are so far removed from the earlier experiences as to miss their sense will conclude that rites and ceremonies were merely technical devices for securing rain, sons, crops, success in battle. Of course they had this magical intent, but they were enduringly enacted, we may be sure, in spite of all practical failures, because they were immediate enhancements of the experience of living. Myths were something other than intellectualistic essays of primitive man in science. Uneasiness before any unfamiliar fact doubtless played its part. But delight in the story, in the growth and rendition of a good yarn, played its dominant part then as it does in the growth of popular mythologies today. Not only does the direct sense element—and emotion is a mode of sense—tend to absorb all ideational matter but, apart from special discipline enforced by physical apparatus, it subdues and digests all that is merely intellectual.

The introduction of the supernatural into belief and the all too human easy reversion to the supernatural is much more an affair of the psychology that generates works of art than of effort at scientific and philosophic explanation. It intensifies emotional thrill and punctuates the interest that belongs to all break in familiar routine. Were hold of the supernatural on human thought an exclusively—or even mainly—intellectual matter, it would be comparatively insignificant. Theologies and cosmogonies have laid hold of imagination because they have been attended with solemn processions, incense, embroidered robes, music, the radiance of colored lights, with stories that stir wonder and induce hypnotic admiration. That is, they have come to man through a direct appeal to sense and to sensuous imagination. Most religions have identified their sacraments with the highest reaches of art, and the most authoritative beliefs have been clothed in a garb of pomp and pageantry that gives immediate delight to eye and ear and that evokes massive emotions of suspense, wonder, and awe. The flights of physicists and astronomers today answer to the esthetic need for satisfaction of the imagination rather than to any strict demand of unemotional evidence for rational interpretation.

Henry Adams made it clear that the theology of the middle ages is a construction of the same intent as that which wrought the cathedrals. In general this middle age, popularly deemed to express the acme of Christian faith in the western world, is a demonstration of the power of sense to absorb the most highly spiritualized ideas. Music, painting, sculpture, architecture, drama and romance were handmaidens of religion, as much as were science and scholarship. The arts hardly had a being outside of the church, and the rites and ceremonies of the church were arts enacted under conditions that gave them the maximum possible of emotional and imaginative appeal. For I do not know what would give the spectator and auditor of the manifestation of the arts a more poignant surrender than the conviction that they were informed with the necessary means of eternal glory and bliss.

The following words of Pater are worth quoting in this connection. "The Christianity of the middle ages made its way partly by its esthetic beauty, a thing so profoundly felt by the Latin hymn writers, *who for one moral or spiritual sentiment had a hundred sensuous images.* A passion of which the outlets are sealed begets a tension of nerve in which the sensible world comes to one with a reinforced brilliancy and relief—all redness turned into blood, all water into tears. Hence a wild convulsed sensuousness in all the poetry of the middle ages, in which the things of nature began to play a strange delirious part. Of the things of nature, the medieval mind had a deep sense; but its sense of them was not objective, no real escape to the world without us."

In his autobiographical essay, *The Child in the House,* he generalizes what is implicit in his passage. He says: "In later years he came upon philosophies which occupied him much in the estimate of the proportions of the sensuous and ideal elements in human knowledge, the relative parts they bear in it; and, in his intellectual scheme, was led to assign very little to the abstract thought, and much to its sensible vehicle or occasion." The latter "became the necessary concomitant of any perception of things, real enough to have any weight or reckoning, in his house of thought. . . . He came more and more to be unable to care for, or think of soul but as in an actual body, or of any world but that wherein are water and trees, and where men and women look, so or so, and press actual hands." The elevation of the ideal above and beyond immediate sense has operated not only to make it pallid and bloodless, but it has acted, like a conspirator with the sensual mind, to impoverish and degrade all things of direct experience.

In the title of this chapter I took the liberty of borrowing from Keats the word "etherial" to designate the meanings and values that many philosophers and some critics suppose are inaccessible to sense, because of their spiritual, eternal and universal characters—thus exemplifying the common dualism of nature and spirit. Let me re-quote his words. The artist may look "upon the Sun, the Moon, the Stars, and the Earth and its contents as material to form greater things, that is etherial things—greater things than the Creator himself made." In making this use of Keats, I had also in mind the fact that he identified the attitude of the artist with that of the live creature; and did so not merely in the implicit tenor of his poetry but in reflection expressed the idea explicitly in words. As he wrote in a letter to his brother: "The greater part of men make their way with the same instinctiveness, the same unwandering eye from their purposes as the Hawk. The Hawk wants a mate, so does the man—look at them both, they set about and procure one in the same manner. They both want a nest and they both set about it in the same manner—they get their food in the same manner. The noble animal Man for his amusement smokes his pipe—the Hawk balances about in the clouds—this is the only difference of their leisures. This is that which makes the amusement of Life to a speculative mind. I go out among the Fields and catch a glimpse of a Stoat or a field mouse hurrying along—to what? The creature has a purpose and his eyes are bright with it. I go amongst the buildings of a city and a Man hurrying along—to what? The Creature has a purpose and his eyes are bright with it. . . .

"Even here though I am pursuing the same instinctive course as the veriest human animal I can think of [though] I am, however young, writing at random straining at particles of light in the midst of great darkness, without knowing the bearing of any assertion, of any one opinion. Yet may I not in this be free from sin? May there not be superior beings amused with any graceful, though instinctive, attitude my mind may fall into as I am entertained with the alertness of a Stoat or the anxiety of a Deer? Though a quarrel in the streets is to be hated, the energies displayed in it are fine; the commonest Man has a grace in his quarrel. Seen by a supernatural Being our reasonings may take the same tone—though erroneous, they may be fine. *This is the very thing in which consists poetry.* There may be reasonings, but when they take an instinctive form, like that of animal forms and movements, they are poetry, they are fine; they have grace."

In another letter he speaks of Shakespeare as a man of enormous "Negative Capability"; as one who was "capable of being in uncertainties, mysteries, doubts, without any irritable reaching after fact and reason." He contrasts Shakespeare in this respect with his own contemporary Coleridge, who would let a poetic insight go when it was surrounded with obscurity, because he could not intellectually justify it; could not, in Keats' language, be satisfied with *"half*-knowledge." I think the same idea is contained in what he says, in a letter to Bailey, that he "never yet has been able to perceive how anything can be known for truth by consecutive reasoning. . . . Can it be that even the greatest Philosopher ever arrived at his Goal without putting aside numerous objections": asking, in effect, Does not the reasoner have also to trust to his "intuitions," to what come upon him in his immediate sensuous and emotional experiences, even against objections that reflection presents to him. For he goes on to say "the simple imaginative mind may have its rewards in the repetitions of its own silent workings coming continually on the Spirit with a fine suddenness"—a remark that contains more of the psychology of productive thought than many treatises.

In spite of the elliptical character of Keats' statements two points emerge. One of them is his conviction that "reasonings" have an origin like that of the movements of a wild creature toward its goal, and they may become spontaneous, "instinctive," and when they become instinctive are sensuous and immediate, poetic. The other side of this conviction is his belief that no "reasoning" as reasoning, that is, as excluding imagination and sense, can reach truth. Even "the greatest philosopher" exercises an animal-like preference to guide his thinking to its conclusions. He selects and puts aside as his imaginative sentiments move. "Reason" at its height cannot attain complete grasp and a self-contained assurance. It must fall back upon imagination—upon the embodiment of ideas in emotionally charged sense.

There has been much dispute as to what Keats meant in his famous lines:

> *Beauty is truth, truth beauty—that is all*
> *Ye know on earth, and all ye need to know,*

and what he meant in the cognate prose statement—"What imagination seizes as beauty must be truth." Much of the dispute is carried on in ignorance of the particular tradition in which Keats wrote and which gave the term "truth" its meaning. In this tradition, "truth" never signifies correctness of intellectual statements about things, or truth as its meaning is now influenced by science. It denotes the wisdom by which men live, especially "the lore of good and evil." And in Keats' mind it was particularly connected with the question of justifying good and trusting to it in spite of the evil and destruction that abound. "Philosophy" is the attempt to answer this question rationally. Keats' belief that even philosophers cannot deal with the question without depending on imaginative intuitions receives an independent and positive statement in his identification of "beauty" with "truth"—the particular truth that solves for man the baffling problem of destruction and death—which weighed so constantly on Keats—in the very

realm where life strives to assert supremacy. Man lives in a world of surmise, of mystery, of uncertainties. "Reasoning" must fail man—this of
course is a doctrine long taught by those who have held to the necessity of
a divine revelation. Keats did not accept this supplement and substitute for
reason. The insight of imagination must suffice. "This is all ye know on
earth and all ye need to know." The critical words are "on earth"—that is
amid a scene in which "irritable reaching after fact and reason" confuses
and distorts instead of bringing us to the light. It was in moments of most
intense esthetic perception that Keats found his utmost solace and his
deepest convictions. This is the fact recorded at the close of his Ode. Ultimately there are but two philosophies. One of them accepts life and experience in all its uncertainty, mystery, doubt, and half-knowledge and turns
that experience upon itself to deepen and intensify its own qualities—to
imagination and art. This is the philosophy of Shakespeare and Keats.

. . .

Experience occurs continuously, because the interaction of live creature and environing conditions is involved in the very process of living.
Under conditions of resistance and conflict, aspects and elements of the self
and the world that are implicated in this interaction qualify experience with
emotions and ideas so that conscious intent emerges. Oftentimes, however,
the experience had is inchoate. Things are experienced but not in such a
way that they are composed into *an* experience. There is distraction and
dispersion; what we observe and what we think, what we desire and what
we get, are at odds with each other. We put our hands to the plow and turn
back; we start and then we stop, not because the experience has reached
the end for the sake of which it was initiated but because of extraneous
interruptions or of inner lethargy.

In contrast with such experience, we have *an* experience when the material experienced runs its course to fulfillment. Then and then only is it
integrated within and demarcated in the general stream of experience from
other experiences. A piece of work is finished in a way that is satisfactory;
a problem receives its solution; a game is played through; a situation,
whether that of eating a meal, playing a game of chess, carrying on a conversation, writing a book, or taking part in a political campaign, is so
rounded out that its close is a consummation and not a cessation. Such an
experience is a whole and carries with it its own individualizing quality and
self-sufficiency. It is *an* experience.

Philosophers, even empirical philosophers, have spoken for the most
part of experience at large. Idiomatic speech, however, refers to experiences each of which is singular, having its own beginning and end. For life
is no uniform uninterrupted march or flow. It is a thing of histories, each
with its own plot, its own inception and movement toward its close, each
having its own particular rhythmic movement; each with its own unre-
peated quality pervading it throughout. A flight of stairs, mechanical as it

is, proceeds by individualized steps, not by undifferentiated progression, and an inclined plane is at least marked off from other things by abrupt discreteness.

Experience in this vital sense is defined by those situations and episodes that we spontaneously refer to as being "real experiences"; those things of which we say in recalling them, "that *was* an experience." It may have been something of tremendous importance—a quarrel with one who was once an intimate, a catastrophe finally averted by a hair's breadth. Or it may have been something that in comparison was slight—and which perhaps because of its very slightness illustrates all the better what is to be an experience. There is that meal in a Paris restaurant of which one says "that *was* an experience." It stands out as an enduring memorial of what food may be. Then there is that storm one went through in crossing the Atlantic —the storm that seemed in its fury, as it was experienced, to sum up in itself all that a storm can be, complete in itself, standing out because marked out from what went before and what came after.

In such experiences, every successive part flows freely, without seam and without unfilled blanks, into what ensues. At the same time there is no sacrifice of the self-identity of the parts. A river, as distinct from a pond, flows. But its flow gives a definiteness and interest to its successive portions greater than exist in the homogeneous portions of a pond. In an experience, flow is from something to something. As one part leads into another and as one part carries on what went before, each gains distinctness in itself. The enduring whole is diversified by successive phases that are emphases of its varied colors.

Because of continuous merging, there are no holes, mechanical junctions, and dead centers when we have *an* experience. There are pauses, places of rest, but they punctuate and define the quality of movement. They sum up what has been undergone and prevent its dissipation and idle evaporation. Continued acceleration is breathless and prevents parts from gaining distinction. In a work of art, different acts, episodes, occurrences melt and fuse into unity, and yet do not disappear and lose their own character as they do so—just as in a genial conversation there is a continuous interchange and blending, and yet each speaker not only retains his own character but manifests it more clearly than is his wont.

An experience has a unity that gives it its name, *that* meal, that storm, that rupture of friendship. The existence of this unity is constituted by a single *quality* that pervades the entire experience in spite of the variation of its constituent parts. This unity is neither emotional, practical, nor intellectual, for these terms name distinctions that reflection can make within it. In discourse *about* an experience, we must make use of these adjectives of interpretation. In going over an experience in mind *after* its occurrence, we may find that one property rather than another was sufficiently dominant so that it characterizes the experience as a whole. There are absorbing inquiries and speculations which a scientific man and philosopher will recall as "experiences" in the emphatic sense. In final import they are intellectual. But in their actual occurrence they were emotional as well; they were purposive and volitional. Yet the experience was not a sum of these different characters; they were lost in it as distinctive traits. No thinker can ply his occupation save as he is lured and rewarded by total integral experiences that are intrinsically worth while. Without them he would never know what it is really to think and would be completely at a loss in distinguishing real thought from the spurious article. Thinking goes on in trains of ideas, but the ideas form a train only because they are much more than what an analytic psychology calls ideas. They are phases, emotionally and practically distinguished, of a developing underlying quality; they are its moving variations, not separate and independent like Locke's and Hume's so-called ideas and impressions, but are subtle shadings of a pervading and developing hue.

We say of an experience of thinking that we reach or draw a conclusion. Theoretical formulation of the process is often made in such terms as to conceal effectually the similarity of "conclusion" to the consummating phase of every developing integral experience. These formulations apparently take their cue from the separate propositions that are premises and the proposition that is the conclusion as they appear on the printed page. The impression is derived that there are first two independent and ready-made entities that are then manipulated so as to give rise to a third. In fact, in an experience of thinking, premises emerge only as a conclusion becomes manifest. The experience, like that of watching a storm reach its height and gradually subside, is one of continuous movement of subject-matters. Like the ocean in the storm, there are a series of waves; suggestions reaching out and being broken in a clash, or being carried onwards by a coöperative wave. If a conclusion is reached, it is that of a movement of anticipation and cumulation, one that finally comes to completion. A "conclusion" is no separate and independent thing; it is the consummation of a movement.

Hence *an* experience of thinking has its own esthetic quality. It differs from those experiences that are acknowledged to be esthetic, but only in its materials. The material of the fine arts consists of qualities; that of experience having intellectual conclusion are signs or symbols having no intrinsic quality of their own, but standing for things that may in another experience be qualitatively experienced. The difference is enormous. It is one reason why the strictly intellectual art will never be popular as music is popular. Nevertheless, the experience itself has a satisfying emotional quality because it possesses internal integration and fulfillment reached through ordered and organized movement. This artistic structure may be immediately felt. In so far, it is esthetic. What is even more important is that not only is this quality a significant motive in undertaking intellectual inquiry and in keeping it honest, but that no intellectual activity is an integral event (is *an* experience), unless it is rounded out with this quality. Without it, thinking is inconclusive. In short, esthetic cannot be sharply marked off from intellectual experience since the latter must bear an esthetic stamp to be itself complete.

The same statement holds good of a course of action that is dominantly practical, that is, one that consists of overt doings. It is possible to be efficient in action and yet not have a conscious experience. The activity is too automatic to permit of a sense of what it is about and where it is going. It comes to an end but not to a close or consummation in consciousness. Obstacles are overcome by shrewd skill, but they do not feed experience. There are also those who are wavering in action, uncertain, and inconclusive like the shades in classic literature. Between the poles of aimlessness and mechanical efficiency, there lie those courses of action in which through successive deeds there runs a sense of growing meaning conserved and accumulating toward an end that is felt as accomplishment of a process. Successful politicians and generals who turn statesmen like Caesar and Napoleon have something of the showman about them. This of itself is not art, but it is, I think, a sign that interest is not exclusively, perhaps not mainly, held by the result taken by itself (as it is in the case of mere efficiency), but by it as the outcome of a process. There is interest in completing an experience. The experience may be one that is harmful to the world and its consummation undesirable. But it has esthetic quality.

QUESTIONS FOR STUDY AND DISCUSSION

1. What are the historic reasons cited by Dewey for the rise of the compartmental conception of fine art?
2. What does Dewey mean when he says that "life goes on in an environment"? Show the connection between this statement and his basic metaphysics.
3. What does Dewey mean by "an experience"?
4. How does his notion of experience lead into his meaning of esthetic experience? Do you think these two are different? Explain.

Religion Versus the Religious

It is widely supposed that a person who does not accept any religion is thereby shown to be a non-religious person. Yet it is conceivable that the present depression in religion is closely connected with the fact that religions now prevent, because of their weight of historic encumbrances, the religious quality of experience from coming to consciousness and finding the expression that is appropriate to present conditions, intellectual and moral. I believe that such is the case. I believe that many persons are so repelled from what exists as a religion by its intellectual and moral implications, that they are not even aware of attitudes in themselves that if they came to fruition would be genuinely religious. I hope that this remark may help make clear what I mean by the distinction between "religion" as a noun substantive and "religious" as adjectival.

To be somewhat more explicit, a religion (and as I have just said there is no such thing as religion in general) always signifies a special body of beliefs and practices having some kind of institutional organization, loose or tight. In contrast, the adjective "religious" denotes nothing in the way of a specifiable entity, either institutional or as a system of beliefs. It does not denote anything to which one can specifically point as one can point to this and that historic religion or existing church. For it does not denote anything that can exist by itself or that can be organized into a particular and distinctive form of existence. It denotes attitudes that may be taken toward every object and every proposed end or ideal.

Before, however, I develop my suggestion that realization of the distinction just made would operate to emancipate the religious quality from encumbrances that now smother or limit it, I must refer to a position that in some respects is similar in words to the position I have taken, but that in fact is a whole world removed from it. I have several times used the phrase "religious elements of experience." Now at present there is much talk, especially in liberal circles, of religious experience as vouching for the authenticity of certain beliefs and the desirability of certain practices, such as particular forms of prayer and worship. It is even asserted that religious experience is the ultimate basis of religion itself. The gulf between this position and that which I have taken is what I am now concerned to point out.

Those who hold to the notion that there is a definite kind of experience which is itself religious, by that very fact make out of it something specific, as a kind of experience that is marked off from experience as æsthetic, scientific, moral, political; from experience as companionship and friendship. But "religious" as a quality of experience signifies something that may belong to all these experiences. It is the polar opposite of some type of experience that can exist by itself. The distinction comes out clearly when it is noted that the concept of this distinct kind of experience is used to validate a belief in some special kind of object and also to justify some special kind of practice.

For there are many religionists who are now dissatisfied with the older "proofs" of the existence of God, those that go by the name of ontological, cosmological and teleological. The cause of the dissatisfaction is perhaps not so much the arguments that Kant used to show the insufficiency of these alleged proofs, as it is the growing feeling that they are too formal to offer any support to religion in action. Anyway, the dissatisfaction exists.

Moreover, these religionists are moved by the rise of the experimental method in other fields. What is more natural and proper, accordingly, than that they should affirm they are just as good empiricists as anybody else—indeed, as good as the scientists themselves? As the latter rely upon certain kinds of experience to prove the existence of certain kinds of objects, so the religionists rely upon a certain kind of experience to prove the existence of the object of religion, especially the supreme object, God.

The discussion may be made more definite by introducing, at this point, a particular illustration of this type of reasoning. A writer says: "I broke down from overwork and soon came to the verge of nervous prostration. One morning after a long and sleepless night . . . I resolved to stop drawing upon myself so continuously and begin drawing upon God. I determined to set apart a quiet time every day in which I could relate my life to its ultimate source, regain the consciousness that in God I live, move and have my being. That was thirty years ago. Since then I have had literally not one hour of darkness or despair."

This is an impressive record. I do not doubt its authenticity nor that of the experience related. It illustrates a religious aspect of experience. But it illustrates also the use of that quality to carry a superimposed load of a particular religion. For having been brought up in the Christian religion, its subject interprets it in the terms of the personal God characteristic of that religion. Taoists, Buddhists, Moslems, persons of no religion including those who reject all supernatural influence and power, have had experiences similar in their effect. Yet another author commenting upon the passage says: "The religious expert can be more sure that this God exists than he can of either the cosmological God of speculative surmise or the Christ-like God involved in the validity of moral optimism," and goes on to add that such experiences "mean that God the savior, the power that gives victory over sin on certain conditions that man can fulfill, is an existent, accessible and scientifically knowable reality." It should be clear that this inference is sound only if the conditions, of whatever sort, that produce the effect are called "God." But most readers will take the inference to mean that the existence of a particular Being, of the type called "God" in the Christian religion, is proved by a method akin to that of experimental science.

In reality, the only thing that can be said to be "proved" is the existence of some complex of conditions that have operated to effect an adjustment in life, an orientation, that brings with it a sense of security and peace. The particular interpretation given to this complex of conditions is not inherent in the experience itself. It is derived from the culture with which a particular person has been imbued. A fatalist will give one name to it; a Christian Scientist another, and the one who rejects all supernatural being still another. The determining factor in the interpretation of the experience is the particular doctrinal apparatus into which a person has been inducted. The emotional deposit connected with prior teaching floods the whole situation. It may readily confer upon the experience such a peculiarly sacred preciousness that all inquiry into its causation is barred. The stable outcome is so invaluable that the cause to which it is referred is usually nothing but a reduplication of the thing that has occurred, plus some name that has acquired a deeply emotional quality.

The intent of this discussion is not to deny the genuineness of the result nor its importance in life. It is not, save incidentally, to point out the possibility of a purely naturalistic explanation of the event. My purpose is to indicate what happens when religious experience is already set aside as something *sui generis*. The actual religious quality in the experience described is the *effect* produced, the better adjustment in life and its conditions, not the manner and cause of its production. The way in which the experience operated, its function, determines its religious value. If the reorientation actually occurs, it, and the sense of security and stability accompanying it, are forces on their own account. It takes place in different persons in a multitude of ways. It is sometimes brought about by devotion to a cause; sometimes by a passage of poetry that opens a new perspective; sometimes as was the case with Spinoza—deemed an atheist in his day—through philosophical reflection.

The difference between an experience having a religious force because of what it does in and to the processes of living and religious experience as a separate kind of thing gives me occasion to refer to a previous remark. If this function were rescued through emancipation from dependence upon specific types of beliefs and practices, from those elements that constitute a religion, many individuals would find that experiences having the force of bringing about a better, deeper and enduring adjustment in life are not so rare and infrequent as they are commonly supposed to be. They occur frequently in connection with many significant moments of living. The idea of invisible powers would take on the meaning of all the conditions of nature and human association that support and deepen the sense of values which carry one through periods of darkness and despair to such an extent that they lose their usual depressive character.

I do not suppose for many minds the dislocation of the religious from a religion is easy to effect. Tradition and custom, especially when emotionally charged, are a part of the habits that have become one with our very being But the possibility of the transfer is demonstrated by its actuality. Let us then for the moment drop the term "religious," and ask what are the attitudes that lend deep and enduring support to the processes of living. I have, for example, used the words "adjustment" and "orientation." What do they signify?

While the words "accommodation," "adaptation," and "adjustment" are frequently employed as synonyms, attitudes exist that are so different that for the sake of clear thought they should be discriminated. There are conditions we meet that cannot be changed. If they are particular and limited, we modify our own particular attitudes in accordance with them. Thus we accommodate ourselves to changes in weather, to alterations in income when we have no other recourse. When the external conditions are lasting we become inured, habituated, or, as the process is now often called, conditioned. The two main traits of this attitude, which I should like to call accommodation, are that it affects *particular* modes of conduct, not the entire self, and that the process is mainly *passive*. It may, however, become general and then it becomes fatalistic resignation or submission. There are other attitudes toward the environment that are also particular but that are more active. We re-act against conditions and endeavor to change them to meet our wants and demands. Plays in a foreign language are "adapted" to meet the needs of an American audience. A house is rebuilt to suit changed conditions of the household; the telephone is invented to serve the demand for speedy communication at a distance; dry soils are irrigated so that they may bear abundant crops. Instead of accommodating ourselves to conditions, we modify conditions so that they will be accommodated to our wants and purposes. This process may be called adaptation.

Now both of these processes are often called by the more general name of adjustment. But there are also changes in ourselves in relation to the world in which we live that are much more inclusive and deep seated. They relate not to this and that want in relation to this and that condition of our surroundings, but pertain to our being in its entirety. Because of their scope, this modification of ourselves is enduring. It lasts through any amount of vicissitude of circumstances, internal and external. There is a composing and harmonizing of the various elements of our being such that, in spite of changes in the special conditions that surround us, these conditions are also arranged, settled, in relation to us. This attitude includes a note of submission. But it is voluntary, not externally imposed; and as voluntary it is something more than a mere Stoical resolution to endure unperturbed throughout the buffetings of fortune. It is more outgoing, more ready and glad, than the latter attitude, and it is more active than the former. And in calling it voluntary, it is not meant that it depends upon a particular resolve or volition. It is a change *of* will conceived as the organic plenitude of our being, rather than any special change *in* will.

It is the claim of religions that they effect this generic and enduring change in attitude. I should like to turn the statement around and say that whenever this change takes place there is a definitely religious attitude. It is not *a* religion that brings it about, but when it occurs, from whatever cause and by whatever means, there is a religious outlook and function. As I have said before, the doctrinal or intellectual apparatus and the institutional accretions that grow up are, in a strict sense, adventitious to the intrinsic quality of such experiences. For they are affairs of the traditions of the culture with which individuals are inoculated. Mr. Santayana has connected the religious quality of experience with the imaginative, as that is expressed in poetry. "Religion and poetry," he says, "are identical in essence, and differ merely in the way in which they are attached to practical affairs. Poetry is called religion when it intervenes in life, and religion, when it merely supervenes upon life, is seen to be nothing but poetry." The difference between intervening *in* and supervening *upon* is as important as is the identity set forth. Imagination may play upon life or it may enter profoundly into it. As Mr. Santayana puts it, "poetry has a universal and a moral function," for "its highest power lies in its relevance to the ideals and purposes of life." Except as it intervenes, "all observation is observation of brute fact, all discipline is mere repression, until these facts digested and this discipline embodied in humane impulses become the starting point for a creative movement of the imagination, the firm basis for ideal constructions in society, religion, and art."

If I may make a comment upon this penetrating insight of Mr. Santayana, I would say that the difference between imagination that only supervenes and imagination that intervenes is the difference between one that completely interpenetrates all the elements of our being and one that is interwoven with only special and partial factors. There actually occurs extremely little observation of brute facts merely for the sake of the facts, just as there is little discipline that is repression and nothing but repression. Facts are usually observed with reference to some practical end and purpose, and that end is presented only imaginatively. The most repressive discipline has some end in view to which there is at least imputed an ideal quality; otherwise it is purely sadistic. But in such cases of observation and discipline imagination is limited and partial. It does not extend far; it does not permeate deeply and widely.

The connection between imagination and the harmonizing of the self is closer than is usually thought. The idea of a whole, whether of the whole personal being or of the world, is an imaginative, not a literal, idea. The limited world of our observation and reflection becomes the Universe only through imaginative extension. It cannot be apprehended in knowledge nor realized in reflection. Neither observation, thought, nor practical activity can attain that complete unification of the self which is called a whole. The *whole* self is an ideal, an imaginative projection. Hence the idea of a thoroughgoing and deepseated harmonizing of the self with the Universe (as a name for the totality of conditions with which the self is connected) operates only through imagination—which is one reason why this composing of the self is not voluntary in the sense of an act of special volition or resolution. An "adjustment" possesses the will rather than is its express product. Religionists have been right in thinking of it as an influx from sources beyond conscious deliberation and purpose—a fact that helps explain, psychologically, why it has so generally been attributed to a supernatural source and that, perhaps, throws some light upon the reference of it by William James to unconscious factors. And it is pertinent to note that the unification of the self throughout the ceaseless flux of what it does, suffers, and achieves, cannot be attained in terms of itself. The self is always directed toward something beyond itself and so its own unification depends upon the idea of the integration of the shifting scenes of the world into that imaginative totality we call the Universe.

The intimate connection of imagination with ideal elements in experience is generally recognized. Such is not the case with respect to its connection with faith. The latter has been regarded as a substitute for knowledge, for sight. It is defined, in the Christian religion, as *evidence* of things not seen. The implication is that faith is a kind of anticipatory vision of things that are now invisible because of the limitations of our finite and erring nature. Because it is a substitute for knowledge, its material and object are intellectual in quality. As John Locke summed up the matter, faith is "assent to a proposition . . . on the credit of its proposer." Religious faith is then given to a body of propositions as true on the credit of their supernatural author, reason coming in to demonstrate the reasonableness of giving such credit. Of necessity there results the development of theologies, or bodies of systematic propositions, to make explicit in organized form the content of the propositions to which belief is attached and assent given. Given the point of view, those who hold that religion necessarily implies a theology are correct.

But belief or faith has also a moral and practical import. Even devils, according to the older theologians, believe—and tremble. A distinction was made, therefore, between "speculative" or intellectual belief and an act called "justifying" faith. Apart from any theological context, there is a difference between belief that is a conviction that some end should be supreme over conduct, and belief that some object or being exists as a truth for the intellect. Conviction in the moral sense signifies being conquered, vanquished, in our active nature by an ideal end; it signifies acknowledgment of its rightful claim over our desires and purposes. Such acknowledgment is practical, not primarily intellectual. It goes beyond evidence that can be presented to *any* possible observer. Reflection, often long and arduous, may be involved in arriving at the conviction, but the import of thought is not exhausted in discovery of evidence that can justify intellectual assent. The authority of an ideal over choice and conduct is the authority of an ideal, not of a fact, of a truth guaranteed to intellect, not of the status of the one who propounds the truth.

Such moral faith is not easy. It was questioned of old whether the Son of Man should find faith on the earth in his coming. Moral faith has been bolstered by all sorts of arguments intended to prove that its object is not ideal and that its claim upon us is not primarily moral or practical, since the ideal in question is already embedded in the existent frame of things. It is argued that the ideal is already the final reality at the heart of things that exist, and that only our senses or the corruption of our natures prevent us from apprehending its prior existential being. Starting, say, from such an idea as that justice is more than a moral ideal because it is embedded in the very make-up of the actually existent world, men have gone on to build up vast intellectual schemes, philosophies, and theologies, to prove that ideals are real not as ideals but as antecedently existing actualities. They have failed to see that in converting moral realities into matters of intellectual assent they have evinced lack of *moral* faith. Faith that something should be in existence as far as lies in our power is changed into the intellectual belief that it is already in existence. When physical existence does not bear out the assertion, the physical is subtly changed into the metaphysical. In this way, moral faith has been inextricably tied up with intellectual beliefs about the supernatural.

The tendency to convert ends of moral faith and action into articles of an intellectual creed has been furthered by a tendency of which psychologists are well aware. What we ardently desire to have thus and so, we tend to believe is already so. Desire has a powerful influence upon intellectual beliefs. Moreover, when conditions are adverse to realization of the objects of our desire—and in the case of significant ideals they are extremely adverse—it is an easy way out to assume that after all they are already embodied in the ultimate structure of what is, and that appearances to the contrary are *merely* appearances. Imagination then merely supervenes and is freed from the responsibility for intervening. Weak natures take to reverie as a refuge as strong ones do to fanaticism. Those who dissent are mourned over by the first class and converted through the use of force by the second.

What has been said does not imply that all moral faith in ideal ends is by virtue of that fact religious in quality. The religious is "morality touched by emotion" only when the ends of moral conviction arouse emotions that are not only intense but are actuated and supported by ends so inclusive that they unify the self. The inclusiveness of the end in relation to both self and the "universe" to which an inclusive self is related is indispensable. According to the best authorities, "religion" comes from a root that means being bound or tied. Originally, it meant being bound by vows to a particular way of life—as *les religieux* were monks and nuns who had assumed certain vows. The religious attitude signifies something that is bound through imagination to a *general* attitude. This comprehensive attitude, moreover, is much broader than anything indicated by "moral" in its usual sense. The quality of attitude is displayed in art, science and good citizenship.

If we apply the conception set forth to the terms of the definition earlier quoted, these terms take on a new significance. An unseen power controlling our destiny becomes the power of an ideal. All possibilities, as possibilities, are ideal in character. The artist, scientist, citizen, parent, as far as they are actuated by the spirit of their callings, are controlled by the unseen. For all endeavor for the better is moved by faith in what is possible, not by adherence to the actual. Nor does this faith depend for its moving power upon intellectual assurance or belief that the things worked for must surely prevail and come into embodied existence. For the authority of the object to determine our attitude and conduct, the right that is given it to claim our allegiance and devotion is based on the intrinsic nature of the ideal. The outcome, given our best endeavor, is not with us. The inherent vice of all intellectual schemes of idealism is that they convert the idealism of action into a system of beliefs about antecedent reality. The character assigned this reality is so different from that which observation and reflection lead to and support that these schemes inevitably glide into alliance with the supernatural.

All religions, marked by elevated ideal quality, have dwelt upon the power of religion to introduce perspective into the piecemeal and shifting episodes of existence. Here too we need to reverse the ordinary statement and say that whatever introduces genuine perspective is religious, not that religion is something that introduces it. There can be no doubt (referring to the second element of the definition) of our dependence upon forces beyond our control. Primitive man was so impotent in the face of these forces that, especially in an unfavorable natural environment, fear became a dominant attitude, and, as the old saying goes, fear created the gods.

With increase of mechanisms of control, the element of fear has, relatively speaking, subsided. Some optimistic souls have even concluded that the forces about us are on the whole essentially benign. But every crisis, whether of the individual or of the community, reminds man of the precarious and partial nature of the control he exercises. When man, individually and collectively, has done his uttermost, conditions that at different times and places have given rise to the ideas of Fate and Fortune, of Chance and Providence, remain. It is the part of manliness to insist upon the capacity of mankind to strive to direct natural and social forces to humane ends. But unqualified absolutistic statements about the omnipotence of such endeavors reflect egoism rather than intelligent courage.

The fact that human destiny is so interwoven with forces beyond human control renders it unnecessary to suppose that dependence and the humility that accompanies it have to find the particular channel that is prescribed by traditional doctrines. What is especially significant is rather the form which the sense of dependence takes. Fear never gave stable perspective in the life of anyone. It is dispersive and withdrawing. Most religions have in fact added rites of communion to those of expiation and propitiation. For our dependence is manifested in those relations to the environment that support our undertakings and aspirations as much as it is in the defeats inflicted upon us. The essentially unreligious attitude is that which attributes human achievement and purpose to man in isolation from the world of physical nature and his fellows. Our successes are dependent upon the coöperation of nature. The sense of the dignity of human nature is as religious as is the sense of awe and reverence when it rests upon a sense of human nature as a coöperating part of a larger whole. Natural piety is not of necessity either a fatalistic acquiescence in natural happenings or a romantic idealization of the world. It may rest upon a just sense of nature as the whole of which we are parts, while it also recognizes that we are parts that are marked by intelligence and purpose, having the capacity to strive by their aid to bring conditions into greater consonance with what is humanly desirable. Such piety is an inherent constituent of a just perspective in life.

Understanding and knowledge also enter into a perspective that is religious in quality. Faith in the continued disclosing of truth through directed coöperative human endeavor is more religious in quality than is any faith in a completed revelation. It is of course now usual to hold that revelation is not completed in the sense of being ended. But religions hold that the essential framework is settled in its significant moral features at least, and that new elements that are offered must be judged by conformity to this framework. Some fixed doctrinal apparatus is necessary for *a* religion. But faith in the possibilities of continued and rigorous inquiry does not limit access to truth to any channel or scheme of things. It does not first say that truth is universal and then add there is but one road to it. It does not depend for assurance upon subjection to any dogma or item of doctrine. It trusts that the natural interactions between man and his environment will breed more intelligence and generate more knowledge provided the scientific methods that define intelligence in operation are pushed further into the mysteries of the world, being themselves promoted and improved in the operation. There is such a thing as faith in intelligence becoming religious in quality—a fact that perhaps explains the efforts of some religionists to disparage the possibilities of intelligence as a force. They properly feel such faith to be a dangerous rival.

Lives that are consciously inspired by loyalty to such ideals as have been mentioned are still comparatively infrequent to the extent of that comprehensiveness and intensity which arouse an ardor religious in function. But before we infer the incompetency of such ideals and of the actions they inspire, we should at least ask ourselves how much of the existing situation is due to the fact that the religious factors of experience have been drafted into supernatural channels and thereby loaded with irrelevant encumbrances. A body of beliefs and practices that are apart from the common and natural relations of mankind must, in the degree in which it is influential, weaken and sap the force of the possibilities inherent in such relations. Here lies one aspect of the emancipation of the religious from religion.

Any activity pursued in behalf of an ideal end against obstacles and in spite of threats of personal loss because of conviction of its general and enduring value is religious in quality. Many a person, inquirer, artist, philanthropist, citizen, men and women in the humblest walks of life, have achieved, without presumption and without display, such unification of themselves and of their relations to the conditions of existence. It remains to extend their spirit and inspiration to ever wider numbers. If I have said anything about religions and religion that seems harsh, I have said those things because of a firm belief that the claim on the part of religions to possess a monopoly of ideals and of the supernatural means by which alone, it is alleged, they can be furthered, stands in the way of the realization of distinctively religious values inherent in natural experience. For that reason, if for no other, I should be sorry if any were misled by the frequency with which I have employed the adjective "religious" to conceive of what I have said as a disguised apology for what have passed as religions. The opposition between religious values as I conceive them and religions is not to be bridged. Just because the release of these values is so important, their identification with the creeds and cults of religions must be dissolved.

QUESTIONS FOR STUDY AND DISCUSSION

1. Explain Dewey's distinction between "religion" and "religious."
2. How does Dewey explain religious experience in terms of adjustment? What is the precise nature of that adjustment?

Faith and Its Object

The conception that faith is the best available substitute for knowledge in our present estate still attaches to the notion of the symbolic character of the materials of faith; unless by ascribing to them a symbolic nature we mean that these materials stand for something that is verifiable in general and public experience.

Were we to adopt the latter point of view, it would be evident not only that the intellectual articles of a creed must be understood to be symbolic of moral and other ideal values, but that the facts taken to be historic and used as concrete evidence of the intellectual articles are themselves symbolic. These articles of a creed present events and persons that have been made over by the idealizing imagination in the interest, at their best, of moral ideals. Historic personages in their divine attributes are materializations of the ends that enlist devotion and inspire endeavor. They are symbolic of the reality of ends moving us in many forms of experience. The ideal values that are thus symbolized also mark human experience in science and art and the various modes of human association: they mark almost everything in life that rises from the level of manipulation of conditions as they exist. It is admitted that the objects of religion are ideal in contrast with our present state. What would be lost if it were also admitted that they have authoritative claim upon conduct just because they are ideal? The assumption that these objects of religion exist already in some realm of Being seems to add

From pp. 40–57 of John Dewey, *A Common Faith*. Copyright 1934 by Yale University Press. Reprinted by permission of the publisher.

nothing to their force, while it weakens their claim over us as ideals, in so far as it bases that claim upon matters that are intellectually dubious. The question narrows itself to this: Are the ideals that move us genuinely ideal or are they ideal only in contrast with our present estate?

The import of the question extends far. It determines the meaning given to the word "God." On one score, the word can mean only a particular Being. On the other score, it denotes the unity of all ideal ends arousing us to desire and actions. Does the unification have a claim upon our attitude and conduct because it is already, apart from us, in realized existence, or because of its own inherent meaning and value? Suppose for the moment that the word "God" means the ideal ends that at a given time and place one acknowledges as having authority over his volition and emotion, the values to which one is supremely devoted, as far as these ends, through imagination, take on unity. If we make this supposition, the issue will stand out clearly in contrast with the doctrine of religions that "God" designates some kind of Being having prior and therefore non-ideal existence.

The word "non-ideal" is to be taken literally in regard to some religions that have historically existed, to all of them as far as they are neglectful of moral qualities in their divine beings. It does not apply in the same *literal* way to Judaism and Christianity. For they have asserted that the Supreme Being has moral and spiritual attributes. But it applies to them none the less in that these moral and spiritual characters are thought of as properties of a particular existence and are thought to be of religious value for us because of this embodiment in such an existence. Here, as far as I can see, is the ultimate issue as to the difference between *a* religion and the religious as a function of experience.

The idea that "God" represents a unification of ideal values that is essentially imaginative in origin when the imagination supervenes in conduct is attended with verbal difficulties owing to our frequent use of the word "imagination" to denote fantasy and doubtful reality. But the reality of ideal ends as ideals is vouched for by their undeniable power in action. An ideal is not an illusion because imagination is the organ through which it is apprehended. For *all* possibilities reach us through the imagination. In a definite sense the only meaning that can be assigned the term "imagination" is that things unrealized in fact come home to us and have power to stir us. The unification effected through imagination is not fanciful, for it is the reflex of the unification of practical and emotional attitudes. The unity signifies not a single Being, but the unity of loyalty and effort evoked by the fact that many ends are one in the power of their ideal, or imaginative, quality to stir and hold us.

We may well ask whether the power and significance in life of the traditional conceptions of God are not due to the ideal qualities referred to by them, the hypostatization of them into an existence being due to a conflux of tendencies in human nature that converts the object of desire into an antecedent reality (as was mentioned in the previous chapter) with beliefs that have prevailed in the cultures of the past. For in the older cultures the idea of the supernatural was "natural," in the sense in which "natural" signifies something customary and familiar. It seems more credible that religious persons have been supported and consoled by the reality with which ideal values appeal to them than that they have been upborne by sheer matter of fact existence. That, when once men are inured to the idea of the union of the ideal and the physical, the two should be so bound together in emotion that it is difficult to institute a separation, agrees with all we know of human psychology.

The benefits that will accrue, however, from making the separation are evident. The dislocation frees the religious values of experience once for all from matters that are continually becoming more dubious. With that release there comes emancipation from the necessity of resort to apologetics. The reality of ideal ends and values in their authority over us is an undoubted fact. The validity of justice, affection, and that intellectual correspondence of our ideas with realities that we call truth, is so assured in its hold upon humanity that it is unnecessary for the religious attitude to encumber itself with the apparatus of dogma and doctrine. Any other conception of the religious attitude, when it is adequately analyzed, means that those who hold it care more for force than for ideal value—since all that an Existence can add is force to establish, to punish, and to reward. There are, indeed, some persons who frankly say that their own faith does not require any guarantee that moral values are backed up by physical force, but who hold that the masses are so backward that ideal values will not affect their conduct unless in the popular belief these values have the sanction of a power that can enforce them and can execute justice upon those who fail to comply.

There are some persons, deserving of more respect, who say: "We agree that the beginning must be made with the primacy of the ideal. But why stop at this point? Why not search with the utmost eagerness and vigor for all the evidence we can find, such as is supplied by history, by presence of design in nature, which may lead on to the belief that the ideal is already extant in a Personality having objective existence?"

One answer to the question is that we are involved by this search in all the problems of the existence of evil that have haunted theology in the past and that the most ingenious apologetics have not faced, much less met. If these apologists had not identified the existence of ideal goods with that of a Person supposed to originate and support them—a Being, moreover, to whom omnipotent power is attributed—the problem of the occurrence of evil would be gratuitous. The significance of ideal ends and meanings is, indeed, closely connected with the fact that there are in life all sorts of things that are evil to us because we would have them otherwise. Were existing conditions wholly good, the notion of possibilities to be realized would never emerge.

But the more basic answer is that while if the search is conducted upon a strictly empirical basis there is no reason why it should not take place, as a matter of fact it is always undertaken in the interest of the supernatural. Thus it diverts attention and energy from ideal values and from the exploration of actual conditions by means of which they may be promoted. History is testimony to this fact. Men have never fully used the powers they possess to advance the good in life, because they have waited upon some power external to themselves and to nature to do the work they are responsible for doing. Dependence upon an external power is the counterpart of surrender of human endeavor. Nor is emphasis on exercising our own powers for good an egoistical or a sentimentally optimistic recourse. It is not the first, for it does not isolate man, either individually or collectively, from nature. It is not the second, because it makes no assumption beyond that of the need and responsibility for human endeavor, and beyond the conviction that, if human desire and endeavor were enlisted in behalf of natural ends, conditions would be bettered. It involves no expectation of a millennium of good.

Belief in the supernatural as a necessary power for apprehension of the ideal and for practical attachment to it has for its counterpart a pessimistic belief in the corruption and impotency of natural means. That is axiomatic in Christian dogma. But this apparent pessimism has a way of suddenly changing into an exaggerated optimism. For according to the terms of the doctrine, if the faith in the supernatural is of the required order, regeneration at once takes place. Goodness, in all essentials, is thereby established; if not, there is proof that the established relation to the supernatural has been vitiated. This romantic optimism is one cause for the excessive attention to individual salvation characteristic of traditional Christianity. Belief in a sudden and complete transmutation through conversion and in the objective efficacy of prayer, is too easy a way out of difficulties. It leaves matters in general just about as they were before; that is, sufficiently bad so that there is additional support for the idea that only supernatural aid can better them. The position of natural intelligence is that there exists a *mixture* of good and evil, and that reconstruction in the direction of the good which is indicated by ideal ends, must take place, if at all, through continued coöperative effort. There is at least enough impulse toward justice, kindliness, and order so that if it were mobilized for action, not expecting abrupt and complete transformation to occur, the disorder, cruelty, and oppression that exist would be reduced.

The discussion has arrived at a point where a more fundamental objection to the position I am taking needs consideration. The misunderstanding upon which this objection rests should be pointed out. The view I have advanced is sometimes treated as if the identification of the divine with ideal ends left the ideal wholly without roots in existence and without support from existence. The objection implies that my view commits one to such a separation of the ideal and the existent that the ideal has no chance to find lodgment even as a seed that might grow and bear fruit. On the contrary, what I have been criticizing is the *identification* of the ideal with a particular Being, especially when that identification makes necessary the conclusion that this Being is outside of nature, and what I have tried to show is that the ideal itself has its roots in natural conditions; it emerges when the imagination idealizes existence by laying hold of the possibilities offered to thought and action. There are values, goods, actually realized upon a natural basis—the goods of human association, of art and knowledge. The idealizing imagination seizes upon the most precious things found in the climacteric moments of experience and projects them. We need no external criterion and guarantee for their goodness. They are had, they exist as good, and out of them we frame our ideal ends.

Moreover, the ends that result from our projection of experienced goods into objects of thought, desire and effort exist, only they exist *as* ends. Ends, purposes, exercise determining power in human conduct. The aims of philanthropists, of Florence Nightingale, of Howard, of Wilberforce, of Peabody, have not been idle dreams. They have modified institutions. Aims, ideals, do not exist simply in "mind"; they exist in character, in personality and action. One might call the roll of artists, intellectual inquirers, parents, friends, citizens who are neighbors, to show that purposes exist in an *operative* way. What I have been objecting to, I repeat, is not the idea that ideals are linked with existence and that they themselves exist, through human embodiment, as forces, but the idea that their authority and value depend upon some prior complete embodiment—as if the efforts of human beings in behalf of justice, or knowledge or beauty, depended for their effectiveness and validity upon assurance that there already existed in some supernal region a place where criminals are humanely treated, where there is no serfdom or slavery, where all facts and truths are already discovered and possessed, and all beauty is eternally displayed in actualized form.

The aims and ideals that move us are generated through imagination. But they are not made out of imaginary stuff. They are made out of the hard stuff of the world of physical and social experience. The locomotive did not exist before Stevenson, nor the telegraph before the time of Morse. But the conditions for their existence were there in physical material and energies and in human capacity. Imagination seized hold upon the idea of a rearrangement of existing things that would evolve new objects. The same thing is true of a painter, a musician, a poet, a philanthropist, a moral prophet. The new vision does not arise out of nothing, but emerges through seeing, in terms of possibilities, that is, of imagination, old things in new relations serving a new end which the new end aids in creating.

Moreover the process of creation is experimental and continuous. The artist, scientific man, or good citizen, depends upon what others have done before him and are doing around him. The sense of new values that become ends to be realized arises first in dim and uncertain form. As the values are dwelt upon and carried forward in action they grow in definiteness and coherence. Interaction between aim and existent conditions improves and tests the ideal; and conditions are at the same time modified. Ideals change as they are applied in existent conditions. The process endures and advances with the life of humanity. What one person and one group accomplish becomes the standing ground and starting point of those who succeed them. When the vital factors in this natural process are generally acknowledged in emotion, thought and action, the process will be both accelerated and purified through elimination of that irrelevant element that culminates in the idea of the supernatural. When the vital factors attain the religious force that has been drafted into supernatural religions, the resulting reinforcement will be incalculable.

These considerations may be applied to the idea of God, or, to avoid misleading conceptions, to the idea of the divine. This idea is, as I have said, one of ideal possibilities unified through imaginative realization and projection. But this idea of God, or of the divine, is also connected with all the natural forces and conditions—including man and human association—that promote the growth of the ideal and that further its realization. We are in the presence neither of ideals completely embodied in existence nor yet of ideals that are mere rootless ideals, fantasies, utopias. For there are forces in nature and society that generate and support the ideals. They are further unified by the action that gives them coherence and solidity. It is this *active* relation between ideal and actual to which I would give the name "God." I would not insist that the name *must* be given. There are those who hold that the associations of the term with the supernatural are so numerous and close that any use of the word "God" is sure to give rise to misconception and be taken as a concession to traditional ideas.

They may be correct in this view. But the facts to which I have referred are there, and they need to be brought out with all possible clearness and force. There exist concretely and experimentally goods—the values of art in all its forms, of knowledge, of effort and of rest after striving, of education and fellowship, of friendship and love, of growth in mind and body. These goods are there and yet they are relatively embryonic. Many persons are shut out from generous participation in them; there are forces at work that threaten and sap existent goods as well as prevent their expansion. A clear and intense conception of a union of ideal ends with actual conditions is capable of arousing steady emotion. It may be fed by every experience, no matter what its material.

In a distracted age, the need for such an idea is urgent. It can unify interests and energies now dispersed; it can direct action and generate the heat of emotion and the light of intelligence. Whether one gives the name "God" to this union, operative in thought and action, is a matter for individual decision. But the *function* of such a working union of the ideal and actual seems to me to be identical with the force that has in fact been attached to the conception of God in all the religions that have a spiritual content; and a clear idea of that function seems to me urgently needed at the present time.

The sense of this union may, with some persons, be furthered by mystical experiences, using the term "mystical" in its broadest sense. That result depends largely upon temperament. But there is a marked difference between the union associated with mysticism and the union which I had in mind. There is nothing mystical about the latter; it is natural and moral. Nor is there anything mystical about the perception or consciousness of such union. Imagination of ideal ends pertinent to actual conditions represents the fruition of a disciplined mind. There is, indeed, even danger that resort to mystical experiences will be an escape, and that its result will be the passive feeling that the union of actual and ideal is already accomplished. But in fact this union is active and practical; it is a *uniting,* not something given.

One reason why personally I think it fitting to use the word "God" to denote that uniting of the ideal and actual which has been spoken of, lies in the fact that aggressive atheism seems to me to have something in common with traditional supernaturalism. I do not mean merely that the former is mainly so negative that it fails to give positive direction to thought, though that fact is pertinent. What I have in mind especially is the exclusive preoccupation of both militant atheism and supernaturalism with man in isolation. For in spite of supernaturalism's reference to something beyond nature, it conceives of this earth as the moral center of the universe and of man as the apex of the whole scheme of things. It regards the drama of sin and redemption enacted within the isolated and lonely soul of man as the one thing of ultimate importance. Apart from man, nature is held either accursed or negligible. Militant atheism is also affected by lack of natural piety. The ties binding man to nature that poets have always celebrated are passed over lightly. The attitude taken is often that of man living in an indifferent and hostile world and issuing blasts of defiance. A religious attitude, however, needs the sense of a connection of man, in the way of both dependence and support, with the enveloping world that the imagination feels is a universe. Use of the words "God" or "divine" to convey the union of actual with ideal may protect man from a sense of isolation and from consequent despair or defiance.

In any case, whatever the name, the meaning is selective. For it involves no miscellaneous worship of everything in general. It selects those factors in existence that generate and support our idea of good as an end to be striven for. It excludes a multitude of forces that at any given time are irrelevant to this function. Nature produces whatever gives reinforcement and direction but also what occasions discord and confusion. The "divine" is thus a term of human choice and aspiration. A humanistic religion, if it excludes our relation to nature, is pale and thin, as it is presumptuous, when it takes humanity as an object of worship. Matthew Arnold's conception of a "power not ourselves" is too narrow in its reference to operative and sustaining conditions. While it is selective, it is too narrow in its basis of selection—righteousness. The conception thus needs to be widened in two ways. The powers that generate and support the good as experienced and as ideal, work *within* as well as without. There seems to be a reminiscence of an external Jehovah in Arnold's statement. And the powers work to enforce other values and ideals than righteousness. Arnold's sense of an opposition between Hellenism and Hebraism resulted in exclusion of beauty, truth, and friendship from the list of the consequences toward which powers work within and without.

In the relation between nature and human ends and endeavors, recent science has broken down the older dualism. It has been engaged in this task for three centuries. But as long as the conceptions of science were strictly mechanical (mechanical in the sense of assuming separate things acting upon one another purely externally by push and pull), religious apologists had a standing ground in pointing out the differences between man and physical nature. The differences could be used for arguing that something supernatural had intervened in the case of man. The recent acclaim, however, by apologists for religion of the surrender by science of the classic type of mechanicalism [1] seems ill-advised from their own point of view. For the change in the modern scientific view of nature simply brings man and nature nearer together. We are no longer compelled to choose between explaining away what is distinctive in man through reducing him to another form of a mechanical model and the doctrine that something literally supernatural marks him off from nature. The less mechanical—in its older sense—physical nature is found to be, the closer is man to nature.

In his fascinating book, *The Dawn of Conscience,* James Henry Breasted refers to Haeckel as saying that the question he would most wish to have answered is this: Is the universe friendly to man? The question is an ambiguous one. Friendly to man in what respect? With respect to ease and comfort, to material success, to egoistic ambitions? Or to his aspiration to inquire and discover, to invent and create, to build a more secure order for human existence? In whatever form the question be put, the answer cannot in all honesty be an unqualified and absolute one. Mr. Breasted's answer, as a historian, is that nature has been friendly to the emergence and development of conscience and character. Those who will have all or nothing cannot be satisfied with this answer. Emergence and growth are not enough for them. They want something more than growth accompanied by toil and pain. They want final achievement. Others who are less absolutist may be content to think that, morally speaking, growth is a higher value and ideal than is sheer attainment. They will remember also that growth has not been confined to conscience and character; that it extends also to

---

[1] I use this term because science has not abandoned its beliefs in working mechanisms in giving up the idea that they are of the nature of a strictly mechanical contact of discrete things. [J.D.]

discovery, learning and knowledge, to creation in the arts, to furtherance of ties that hold men together in mutual aid and affection. These persons at least will be satisfied with an intellectual view of the religious function that is based on continuing choice directed toward ideal ends.

For, I would remind readers in conclusion, it is the intellectual side of the religious attitude that I have been considering. I have suggested that the religious element in life has been hampered by conceptions of the supernatural that were imbedded in those cultures wherein man had little control over outer nature and little in the way of sure method of inquiry and test. The crisis today as to the intellectual content of religious belief has been caused by the change in the intellectual climate due to the increase of our knowledge and our means of understanding. I have tried to show that this change is not fatal to the religious values in our common experience, however adverse its impact may be upon historic religions. Rather, provided that the methods and results of intelligence at work are frankly adopted, the change is liberating.

It clarifies our ideals, rendering them less subject to illusion and fantasy. It relieves us of the incubus of thinking of them as fixed, as without power of growth. It discloses that they develop in coherence and pertinency with increase of natural intelligence. The change gives aspiration for natural knowledge a definitely religious character, since growth in understanding of nature is seen to be organically related to the formation of ideal ends. The same change enables man to select those elements in natural conditions that may be organized to support and extend the sway of ideals. All purpose is selective, and all intelligent action includes deliberate choice. In the degree in which we cease to depend upon belief in the supernatural, selection is enlightened and choice can be made in behalf of ideals whose inherent relations to conditions and consequences are understood. Were the naturalistic foundations and bearings of religion grasped, the religious element in life would emerge from the throes of the crisis in religion. Religion would then be found to have its natural place in every aspect of human experience that is concerned with estimate of possibilities, with emotional stir by possibilities as yet unrealized, and with all action in behalf of their realization. All that is significant in human experience falls within this frame.

QUESTIONS FOR STUDY AND DISCUSSION

1. What does Dewey understand by the word "God"?
2. Dewey is opposed to the traditional meaning of God because it separates man from nature and thus prevents human growth. Explain.
3. Show how this opposition is in accord with his basic metaphysics.

TOPICS FOR DISCUSSION AND TERM PAPERS

A.

1. Can it be said with justice that the naturalists and pragmatists have no regard for tradition? Is it their aim to dismiss the past as simply irrelevant to the present or do they see a proper use for traditional knowledge? If so, precisely what is that role?
2. Do the pragmatists have a metaphysical theory? If so, in what sense can it be described? Is it, for instance, a form of empiricism?
3. What reasons can you give for the opposition of such philosophers as James and Dewey to the rationalistic idealism of the late nineteenth century?
4. What aspects of the philosophy of Dewey show the very great influence of Charles Darwin's evolutionary theory?
5. A principal theme in Dewey is the biological nature of the interaction between the live creature and its environment. Does Dewey think of environment as something static or indifferent here? Explain.
6. Does the evolutionary theory of Peirce leave room for the reality of God? If so, is Peirce a naturalistic philosopher? Can one be a naturalist and a theist?
7. Dewey opts for an empirical method in philosophy. Specify some of the details and attitudes of that empirical method.
8. Does William James think of pragmatism as a philosophical doctrine with fixed content or does he see it as open to any content because it is a method primarily?
9. How would you distinguish between the instrumentalism of Dewey and the pragmatism of James?

B.

1. Can you give any reason why Bacon's axiom that knowledge is power is a welcome statement to a philosopher such as Dewey?
2. Do you think the charge correct that naturalism is so concerned with "public" inquiry that the unique existing person is left out of account? If so, do you think the philosophy of Sartre or Marcel more relevant to you?
3. Dewey began his philosophic career as a Hegelian. Are there any elements of Hegelianism that can be found in the selections just read?
4. Does the work of the pragmatists and naturalists in seeking an empirical method suggest any similarity to the logical positivists?
5. Aristotle developed a theory of act and potency to explain the striving of beings toward perfection. Is this theme of perfective change toward self-fulfillment present in Dewey?

RECOMMENDED READINGS

Primary Sources

Dewey, John. "Antinaturalism in Extremis," in Krikorian. (See *Commentaries.*)

Dewey, John. *Art as Experience*. New York: Minton, Balch & Co., 1934. Chapters 1–5 and 11–14 present Dewey's philosophy of experience. The middle chapters could be appreciated by those interested in art criticism.

————. *A Common Faith*. New Haven: Yale University Press, 1934.

————. *Experience and Nature*. New York: W. W. Norton & Co., 1929. Dewey's most important philosophical work. Chapters 1, 2, and 4 contain his metaphysics.

————. *Reconstruction in Philosophy,* 2d ed. rev. Boston: Beacon Press, 1948. Although weak on the history of philosophy, this book offers a good view of how modern problems have influenced the naturalists. See especially the Introduction and Chs. 1–3.

————, Sidney Hook, and Ernest Nagel. "Are Naturalists Materialists?" *Journal of Philosophy,* XLII, 19 (Sept. 13, 1945), 515–30. An answer to Sheldon's critique, this article is a good attempt on the part of three leading naturalists to draw a compromise between idealism and mechanistic materialism.

James, William. *Pragmatism*. New York: Longmans, Green & Co., 1907. This whole book is a good example of how James synthesized pragmatism and religion.

————. *The Will to Believe, and Other Essays in Popular Philosophy*. New York: Longmans, Green & Co., 1912. Contains the much-discussed and often criticized article, "The Will to Believe." Also see chapters entitled "Is Life Worth Living?" "The Sentiment of Rationality," "Reflex Action and Theism," and "The Moral Philosopher and the Moral Life."

Peirce, Charles Sanders. *Collected Papers of Charles Sanders Peirce*. 8 vols. Ed. by Charles Hartshorne and Paul Weiss (vols. I–VI) and Arthur W. Burks (vols. VII–VIII). Cambridge, Mass.: Harvard University Press, 1931–58. These volumes constitute the most complete and authoritative collection of Peirce's works.

————. *Essays in the Philosophy of Science*. Ed. by Vincent Tomas. New York: Liberal Arts Press, 1957. This volume includes the more important essays of Peirce in the *Philosophy of Science*. Especially recommended are Chs. 1, 2, 6, 9, and 13.

————. *Philosophical Writings*. Ed. by J. Buchler. New York: Dover Publications, 1940. Especially recommended are Chs. 2, 3, 4, 11, 16–19, and 26–28.

————. *Values in a Universe of Chance: Selected Writings of Charles S. Peirce*. Ed. by Philip P. Wiener. Garden City, N.Y.: Doubleday & Co., 1958. Covers wider variety of topics than found in other anthologies of Peirce's works. Especially valuable is the topic entitled "A Neglected Argument for the Reality of God"; also recommended are Chs. 3, 5, 6, 10, and 11.

Commentaries

Blewett, John, ed. *John Dewey: His Thought and Influence*. New York: Fordham University Press, 1960. Especially recommended are the chapters by James Collins, "The Genesis of Dewey's Naturalism," and Robert C. Pollock, "Process and Experience."

Boas, George. Review of Randall's *Nature and Historical Experience, Journal of Philosophy,* LVI, 2 (Jan. 15, 1959), 72–76. A generally favorable review, although Boas criticizes Randall for trying to interpret Aristotle's notion of substance in terms of process.

Gallie, W. B. *Peirce and Pragmatism*. Harmondsworth, Eng.: Penguin Books, 1952. A good discussion of Peirce's pragmatism and metaphysics; especially helpful are Chs. 1–4, 8, and 9.

Goudge, T. A. *The Thought of C. S. Peirce*. Toronto: University of Toronto Press, 1950. A reliable introduction into Peirce's thought, though other works have gone beyond it.

Hook, Sidney. *The Quest for Being, and Other Studies in Naturalism and Humanism*. New York: St. Martin's Press, 1961. Essays by one of our leading naturalists. Of special note are "The New Failure of Nerve," "Modern Knowledge and the Concept of God," "The Quest for Being," "Naturalism and First Principles," and "Scientific Knowledge and Philosophical 'Knowledge.'"

Krikorian, Yervant H., ed. *Naturalism and the Human Spirit*. New York: Columbia University Press, 1944. The best single work on American naturalism; includes a series of essays of leading naturalists. Especially recommended are chapters by Dewey, Lamprecht, Larrabee, and Randall.

Lamont, Corliss. "New Light on Dewey's *Common Faith*," *Journal of Philosophy*, LVIII, 1 (Jan. 5, 1961), 21–28. Lamont maintains that although Dewey continued to use the word "God," he remained a thoroughgoing naturalist.

Lamprecht, Sterling P. "Naturalism and Religion," in Krikorian. A faithful presentation of the naturalist's theory of religion.

Larrabee, Harold A. "Naturalism in America," in Krikorian. A good discussion of the development of naturalism in America from earliest times.

Murphey, Murray G. *The Development of Peirce's Philosophy*. Cambridge, Mass.: Harvard University Press, 1961. A technical discussion of Peirce's thought that can be understood only after considerable preliminary work has been done on Peirce. It contains, however, the best biographical study of Peirce that has as yet appeared.

Olafsen, F. A. Review of Hook's *The Quest for Being, Journal of Philosophy*, LIX, 13 (June 21, 1962), 355–59.

Randall, John Herman, Jr. *Aristotle*. New York: Columbia University Press, 1960. A naturalist's attempt to interpret Aristotle in terms of process metaphysics.

————. "Epilogue: The Nature of Naturalism," in Krikorian.

————. *Nature and Historical Experience*. New York: Columbia University Press, 1958. See Ch. 5, "The Nature of Metaphysics: Its Function, Criteria, and Method," and Ch. 6, "Substance as a Cooperation of Processes: A Metaphysical Analysis."

Roth, Robert J., "The Challenge of American Naturalism," *Thought*, XXXIX, 155 (Winter, 1964), 559–84. Attempts to show the origin and main elements of American naturalism as well as its challenge to Christian thought.

————. "Charles Sanders Peirce—1839–1914," *America*, CXI, 5 (Aug. 1, 1964), 108–10. A discussion of Peirce's religious thought and its implications for modern Christianity.

————. "The Importance of Matter," *America*, CIX, 25 (Dec. 21–28, 1963), 792–94. A comparison between American experience and the thought of Pierre Teilhard de Chardin regarding the importance of involvement in the world for human growth.

Roth, Robert J. "Is Peirce Anti-Jamesian?" *International Philosophical Quarterly,* V, 4 (Dec., 1965), 541–63. A comparison between the religious philosophies of Peirce and James shows their similarities.

————. *John Dewey and Self-Realization.* Englewood Cliffs, N.J.: Prentice-Hall, 1963. An attempt to show that the aim of Dewey's whole philosophical enterprise was to help the human person achieve self-realization through engagement in the world. Especially helpful for present purposes are Chs. 1, 2, 3, 6, 7, and 8.

Sheldon, W. H. "Critique of Naturalism," *Journal of Philosophy,* XLII, 10 (May 10, 1945), 253–70. A review of Krikorian's *Naturalism and the Human Spirit.* Sheldon maintains that the naturalism developed in this volume differs not at all from the old materialism, but is only a softer name for it; hence the authors failed to reconcile idealism and materialism as they claimed. Sheldon focuses the issues involved in an attempt to avoid the extremes of idealism and mechanistic materialism.

Smith, John E., "The Course of American Philosophy," *Review of Metaphysics,* XI, 2 (Dec., 1957), 279–303. A good review of the main trends of American philosophy with some evaluation of its present status and future development.

————. *The Spirit of American Philosophy.* New York: Oxford University Press, 1963. A treatment of the five men who make up the so-called golden age of American philosophy: Peirce, James, Royce, Dewey, and Whitehead. See especially Ch. 6, "Retrospect and Prospect," which gives an evaluation of past and future.

PART FOUR

ANALYTIC-POSITIVIST THOUGHT:

Hume

Russell

Carnap

Tarski

Ayer

EDITED BY

Jerzy A. Wojciechowski

UNIVERSITY OF OTTAWA

ANALYTIC-POSITIVIST THOUGHT:
Hume
Russell
Carnap
Tarski
Ayer

Introduction

Historical Setting

We shall be concerned in this section with the eighteenth-century philosophy of David Hume (1711–76) and with two schools of twentieth-century thought: analytic philosophy and logical empiricism, also known as logical positivism. These philosophies are all forms of empiricism, an important doctrine of modern philosophy that reduces all knowledge to and explains it in terms of sense perception. The way for empiricism was prepared by the nominalism of William of Ockham (c. 1280–1349) and by the idealism of René Descartes (1596–1650).

Students who are already familiar with examples of classical metaphysics will not find in this section anything similar to the writings of Plato or Aristotle, St. Augustine or Aquinas. Empiricism is antimetaphysical by design; if anything, its metaphysics is of a negative type. To search in the writings of the empiricists for well-developed metaphysical doctrines is futile, for there is a conspicuous absence of books, or even chapters, devoted to the discussion of traditional problems of being. If these problems are mentioned, it is only to criticize them and to declare them meaningless or incongruous.

What then, one may ask, is the purpose of including a chapter on empiricism in a book on metaphysics. There are two reasons: first, the present volume is intended to acquaint the reader with various solutions to metaphysical problems, positive or negative; second, empiricism has definite metaphysical views, although most of them can be reduced to negations of traditional doctrines. There is such a thing as an antimetaphysical metaphysics, and empiricism specializes in this theory. Of course, a negation necessarily presupposes an affirmation. Empiricism can therefore develop only in the wake of some positive doctrines about the nature of being and the nature of knowledge. Moreover, a negation cannot be fully understood without some knowledge of the affirmation that it rejects. Consequently, if one wants to grasp the full import of empiricism, one must first become acquainted with the doctrines that preceded it and against which empiricism reacted so violently.

Philosophical endeavor, like every other rational activity, carries the imprint of the epoch to which it belongs. Since philosophy is an attempt to face up to the most fundamental problems man can think of, it tries to solve them in light of and with the aid of the knowledge that man has at his disposal at any given time. If we want to understand a philosophical system and evaluate its role and its influence, we have to place it in its proper historical setting. We must be aware of the main problems and trends of the time, as well as know the preceding theories and points of view. We will be able to appreciate a philosophy if we compare it with philosophies that preceded it and with its contemporaries.

David Hume: Forerunner of Analytic-Positivist Thought

Many of the doctrines held by logical positivists and linguistic analysts can be traced back to the ideas expressed by David Hume. The brilliant Scot was the most extreme and the most powerful British empiricist. He may rightly be considered as the forefather and spiritual patron of the twentieth-century philosophies with which we shall be concerned. Largely self-educated and endowed with a powerful, logical, and analytic mind, Hume was not afraid to challenge even the best established opinions and beliefs. He was able and willing to draw the most extreme conclusions from premises he considered to be true. The independence of his mind predestined him to play the role of the great critic of traditional philosophy and of the eighteenth-century belief in reason.

Hume's Theory of Knowledge

Like René Descartes before him and many after him, Hume was convinced that philosophy was in need of major corrections. Much of what commonly passed for philosophy he thought to be simple mind-wandering, a pretentious abuse of profound-sounding words. The source of corruption in philosophy is the indulgence in abstruse (i.e., metaphysical) fundamental questions and the use of vague terms. If philosophizing is to be made a valid and meaningful mode of thinking, the illicit methods and problems must be weeded out.

> The only method of freeing learning, at once, from the abstruse questions, is to inquire seriously into the nature of human understanding, and show, from an exact analysis of its powers and capacity, that it is by no means fitted for such remote and abstruse subjects. We must submit to this fatigue, in order to live at ease ever after.

This passage, taken from the first section of *An Enquiry Concerning Human Understanding* (1748), clearly expresses Hume's philosophical creed. His philosophy, which is concerned with the analysis of knowledge and directed toward the solution of such practical problems as may be found in ethics or psychology, is antimetaphysical.

It would be false to think that to achieve his aim Hume occupied himself with empirical research. Faithful to the tradition of empiricism, he studied not the concrete things that make up the universe, but our ideas of these things. His philosophical empiricism must be sharply distinguished from empirical researches of natural scientists. The first and foremost duty of the philosopher, according to Hume, is to find an adequate theory of knowledge. Once in the possession of such theory, the thinker will be able to classify all problems into two categories: those with which he may profitably employ himself, that is, concrete practical ones, or those that he will dismiss as abstruse and transcending his intellectual powers, that is, as not conducive to precise, meaningful solutions.

Two theses underlie this doctrine. The first, inherited from Descartes, is the principle of clarity that may be described as the principle of rational evidence: what is true must be grasped as a clear, precise, and fully intelligible idea. The second is the basic tenet of empiricism that all meaningful ideas come from sense perceptions. Consequently, the meaning of ideas is founded upon the sense data. The philosophy built on these affirmations is a system of empiricism consistent to a fault with its fundamental affirmations, and verging on scepticism. Hume was not the first or the only empiricist. In England he was preceded by John Locke (1632–1704) and George Berkeley (1685–1753), and he had a distant precursor in the Middle Ages in Nicolas d'Autrecourt (1300–50). But Hume is the most important of all the empiricists—his analysis of knowledge the most incisive and far-reaching. Moreover, his belief that the problem of the nature and value of knowledge must be solved before all other problems expresses perfectly the attitude of modern philosophy. In contradistinction to ancient philosophy, which on the whole accepted the very fact of knowledge and the value of cognition as indubitable, modern philosophy adopted a critical attitude toward knowledge. Knowledge had to be explained and justified; its value had to be proven.

"It is evident that all the sciences have a relation, greater or less, to human nature," Hume wrote in the Introduction to *A Treatise of Human Nature* (1739). He was logical with himself when a little further he stated:

> There is no question of importance whose decision is not comprised in the science of man; and there is none which can be decided with any certainty, before we become acquainted with that science. In pretending therefore to explain the principles of human nature, we in effect propose a complete system of the sciences, built on a foundation almost entirely new, and the only one which they can stand with any security.

It is this bold, grand design, from which Hume tried to dissociate himself in his later years, that has captivated the imagination of generations of thinkers and has assured Hume a prominent place in the history of philosophy.

There are, generally speaking, two aspects to the problem of knowledge: How does knowledge arise, and how true is our knowledge? Any theory of knowledge that does not inquire into and try to account for the origin and value of knowledge is highly inadequate. Hume's merit was to recognize and distinguish clearly the psychological and the epistemological problems of knowledge and, moreover, to suggest very definite solutions that have become classical theses accepted with slight variations by all subsequent empiricists. In order to understand his theories fully we must keep in mind that Hume reacted at the same time against decadent forms of scholasticism and against Continental rationalism arising out of Descartes' idealism. He wanted to save philosophy from the abusive rationalistic belief in reason and free it from empty verbosity. He saw the solution in making the meaning of ideas dependent upon underlying sense data, "impressions," as he called them. In this respect he followed Locke and Berkeley. Having solved, as he thought, the psychological question, he felt free to deal with the epistemological aspect of the problem of knowledge. The solution which he suggested may rightly be said to be his major contribution to philosophy and his principal claim to glory.

Hume first distinguished two objects of knowledge: *relations of ideas* and *matters of fact*. The latter are singular, concrete, and changing; the former are abstract, universal, and unchanging. What we would call today physical phenomena is the world perceived as a series of matters of fact, while mathematical relations are relations of ideas. With regard to statements about matters of fact, the principle of contradiction cannot be applied so as to prove by pure reasoning the truth or the falsity of these statements. For instance, no amount of logical ingenuity will allow us to demonstrate the truth or the falsity of the proposition "this table is round," without recourse to direct perception. On the other hand mathematical relations can be demonstrated by proper logical procedures to be true or false. In this case full use of the principle of contradiction can be made, and there is no need of sense evidence to support the conclusion. "Propositions of this kind are discoverable by the mere operation of thought, without dependence on what is anywhere existent in the universe," said Hume.

If Hume's distinction between the two objects of knowledge is accepted, then the question arises: How can one justify propositions about matters of fact that cannot be adequately verified—for example, future events, or generalizations from observed facts such as scientific laws? Is there anything in our perceptions that justifies this type of proposition? The question is fundamental and Hume's answer has far-reaching consequences. According to him there is nothing in any particular perception to justify a general statement or a proposition about a future event. However, these statements are made on the basis of the principle of causality. Do we perceive causal relations? In Hume's view *we do not*. What then is the source of the notion of causality? According to Hume this notion is based on the habit of perceiving certain phenomena as apparently connected or as following each other. For instance, every time I expose myself to the sun my skin darkens; consequently, I presume that if I expose myself again, the same effect will take place. I therefore generalize the observation and state: Whenever one exposes oneself to the sun, his skin will darken.

Although habit explains the origin of such a statement, Hume was convinced that it does not justify it objectively. In other words, these propositions do not reveal anything objectively true about the nature of things. What I really know are my "impressions" and the order in which they appear. To induce from this knowledge the knowledge of objective reality is a great and common mistake. The consequence of this subjectivistic theory is the conviction "that nature has kept us at a great distance from all her secrets."

Hume's Rejection of Metaphysics

Since the conclusions of the theory of knowledge have far-reaching consequences for other parts of the unified system of philosophy, we shall present briefly the conclusions Hume drew from his epistemology that are pertinent to our study. The first and foremost is his denial of metaphysics. If objective reality is unknowable, then all that was said in the past about "being" and its nature is simply meaningless. In particular, the notion of substance becomes "nothing but a collection of simple ideas, that are united by the imagination, and have a particular name assigned to them." There is no possible justification of this notion other than convenience.

The second major consequence is the denial of the value of theoretical sciences based on experience. This is the result of the rejection of the objective principle of causality. No generations involving the presumed relation of cause and effect can be objectively justified. Consequently the only two modes of knowledge that find justification in Hume's eyes are purely practical knowledge and mathematics. The former he called "moral reasoning," the latter "demonstrative reasoning." The destruction of metaphysics leads to the destruction of natural theology. Hume did not reject revelation or its contents but declared that nothing religion teaches about the supernatural can be rationally proven. Consequently, he also rejected contemporary theories of presumably philosophically demonstrable, rational religion. On the other hand, he defended religion against the attacks of atheists as a psychological necessity.

The Intellectual Climate
of Twentieth-Century Philosophy

Analytic philosophy and logical empiricism (logical positivism) are of particular interest to students of philosophy because they are unmistakably the products of the twentieth century. Perennial problems, as well as new ones, resulting from the general progress of science are dealt with in the light of present-day knowledge. The two schools had many common characteristics: they both flourished in the first half of this century; they exercised profound influence on each other; they were expressly antimetaphysical, empirical, and analytic. The analysts and the positivists officially renounced the building of philosophical systems, insisted on the importance of language, and considered the analysis of language a major task of philosophy. They were convinced that for the twentieth century a new philosophy was needed and believed they knew what this philosophy should be and how to develop it. Since their efforts were products of a particular epoch, we shall review briefly the general intellectual climate of the twentieth century, as well as the philosophies of the nineteenth century that prepared the way for analytic-positivist thought.

The twentieth century is the period of the most intense intellectual activity in human history. Rapid expansion of factual knowledge has led to revolutionary theories in the sciences of nature, to an unprecedented widening of intellectual horizons, and to ever more massive influence of science on the life of man. During the nineteenth century, science had amply proven its theoretical and practical value. Scientific method revealed itself as the most fruitful way of studying physical reality. To understand analytic and logico-positivistic philosophy one must constantly bear in mind the overwhelming success of science and the promise of mastery over nature, which science seems to inspire.

Reaction Against Nineteenth-Century Idealism

Compared with this tangible intellectual fertility, traditional forms of philosophizing seemed to be nothing more than sterile mind-wandering, unable to further our knowledge, incapable of solving once and for always any serious problem. Since science was new and philosophy old, it was easy to conclude that philosophy belonged to the past and science to the future. The contempt for traditional philosophy was common not only among scientists but also among analytic and positivistic philosophers. The latter could not, of course, reject philosophy as a whole. Instead, they officially dissociated themselves, as we shall see, from metaphysics as a way of philosophizing and from philosophical tradition that recognized metaphysics as a central element of philosophy. The negative attitude toward philosophy in general and metaphysics in particular was prompted not only by the success of science but also by the kind of philosophy that was prevalent in the nineteenth century, namely, idealism. The two thinkers most responsible for this situation were Immanuel Kant (1724–1804) and G. W. F. Hegel (1770–1831). Their theories and their style of philosophizing largely dominated the intellectual scene for a century. Much of what happened in the beginning of the twentieth century was largely the result of a violent reaction against the various forms of Kantianism and Hegelianism, and we will not fully understand the analytic philosophies if we do not understand this reaction. This in turn requires some knowledge of the theories against which the reaction was directed.

The Philosophy of Kant

Kant's philosophy is mainly an attempt to rethink critically the problem of knowledge in the wake of Hume's denial of the objective value of perceptions. Hume dismissed Newton's mechanics as meaningless. In Kant's time, the progress of science and the success of Newtonian mechanics no longer allowed the high-handed treatment of Hume. Before becoming professor of Philosophy, Kant taught physics and mathematics. He accepted science as an established fact, and his explicit intention was to explain and to justify the scientific mode of knowledge and its success.

The theory of knowledge which Kant developed is to a large extent the consequence of the fundamental question he asked concerning the value of perception, that is, its role as a source of information. The question may be formulated in three parts: *Do* sense images inform us about objective reality? *How* do they inform us? *To what extent* do they inform us? Agreeing with Hume, he rejected the objective value of sense perception and constructed a consistent, subjectivistic theory of knowledge. The following assertions underlie his theory: Knowledge is a subjective (i.e., immanent) activity entirely contained within the knower. The contents of the cognitive act, be it sensation or intellection, are not determined by the outside object but by the subjective a priori forms of knowledge. The knower actually shapes the contents of knowledge. The forms of sense and of intellectual knowledge are the same for all humans, but have no relation with the outside world. Consequently, this external reality remains for always unknowable, a "noumenon." The image of things that we form, the "phenomenon," is a subjective product of the forms of knowledge.

Sense perception is determined by the a priori forms of time and space. That I see things as having three dimensions and as continuing in time is not because of their really being extended in space and time but because of the a priori forms of my perception. Since these forms are common to all people, it is possible to arrive at propositions acceptable and verifiable by everybody who cares to make the verification. If, for instance, a physicist measures the atmospheric pressure at different elevations, anyone else using the appropriate apparatus can confirm his results. However, the confirmation and the agreement thus reached concerning the results of measurements do not tell us anything about the objective reality. Confirmation of measurements and of scientific hypothesis and the resulting agreement are intrasubjective acts, unrelated to the outside world. Consequently, science is not a knowledge of the material being. The nature and the success of science are explicable in terms of the subjective mode of knowledge. What science says is not determined by the nature of things material but by the mode of our knowledge.

It is commonly agreed that scientific knowledge is the most certain and efficient way of studying material nature. However, if science cannot tell us anything objective about the outside world, then philosophy, being a speculative, nonexperimental knowledge, is even less suited to reveal the true nature of objective being. If this is the case, and Kant thought it was, metaphysics is impossible. Metaphysics, in the traditional sense of this word, is the most fundamental analysis of the general characteristics of being, and there is simply no possibility for such a study according to Kantian theory of knowledge. All metaphysical systems developed by various philosophers tell us absolutely nothing about objective reality and never will.

CLASSIFICATION OF JUDGMENTS. A further consequence of the subjectivistic theory of knowledge is the all-important classification of judgments. The classification is the result of the conviction that perception, subjective as Kant thought it to be, cannot account for or justify the existence of judgments expressing a universal, necessary relation—for instance; "The whole is bigger than the part" or "Two plus two equals four." These judgments are therefore nonempirical and a priori. On the contrary, perception is the cause of particular, contingent judgments such as: "John is tall" or "It rained last Sunday." These judgments can be formed only as a result of concrete perceptions and are a posteriori. Thus Kant classified all judgments in relation to perception as a priori (those that come before) and a posteriori (those that come after perception).

The second classification divides judgments into analytic and synthetic. Analytic judgments are those whose predicate is contained in the definition of the subject. The predicate can therefore be found and the judgment formed by mere analysis of the meaning of the given subject without any recourse to experience. As a result, analytic judgments are always a priori. Moreover they express a necessary and universal relation between the subject and the predicate. Consequently analytic judgments are by their very nature universal. In synthetic judgments, the predicate is not contained in the definition of the subject. These judgments cannot be formed in the process of mere analysis of the meaning of the subject. From the combination of the two classifications, three types of judgment result: (1) analytic a priori (man is a rational animal; body is an extended substance); (2) synthetic a priori (two plus two equals four; the sum of angles of a triangle equals two right angles); (3) synthetic a posteriori (I am cold; Mary wore a green dress yesterday).

Analytic a priori and synthetic a posteriori types of judgments were known before, if by other names. It is the discovery of the synthetic a priori judgment that Kant considered his greatest contribution to the theory of knowledge, for this type of judgment forms the backbone of mathematics and mathematical physics. Its value lies in combining the necessity and the universality of a priori judgments with the nature of synthetic judgments. Synthetic judgments, in contrast to analytic judgments, contribute to the progress of knowledge because they express facts about the subject that cannot be obtained by mere analysis of the notion of the subject. Mathematics and mathematical physics based on synthetic a priori judgments further our knowledge of the perceptible and at the same time transcend the realm of perceptions and reveal whatever necessary order there may be in this realm.

For all its ingenuity and powerful analysis, Kant's theory of knowledge had one basic weakness: it could not explain why all humans have the same set of the a priori forms of knowledge. It must be remembered that the principle of subjectivism accepted by Kant limits the knower to his own subjective perceptions and does not allow him any knowledge of objective reality. Consequently, for each knower the nature of other knowers remains unknowable. What then is the value of the claim that all humans have the same set of a priori forms of knowledge? Moreover how can there be any question of communication with others, not to mention confirmation of scientific results and agreement concerning them?

Kant unwittingly presupposed a specific human nature in order to explain the possibility of communication between men and the existence of scientific knowledge. The existence of such nature justifies the identity of the knowing structure in all humans, but this tacit admission contradicts the principle of subjectivism.

Transcendental Idealism: The System of Hegel

In order to remedy the inconveniences created by the Kantian theory of knowledge, Hegel developed a powerful system known as spiritualistic monism. Being is one all-embracing spirit. Materiality and multiplicity are exteriorizations of this unique spiritual reality. The Spirit of the world, as he calls it, is pure thought. *Being is thought; thought is being.* The Absolute contemplates itself and in this process realizes all its possibilities. The mind of every man is a part of the Absolute, the universal Spirit. Thus human knowledge partakes in the absolute knowledge and is therefore anterior to things that are the object of thought. The intellect does not have to conform to the object, but, vice versa, the object to the intellect. The Absolute is the cause of all finite modes of being. Thought is prior to and more important than matter; it transcends the matter. The belief in the superiority of the spiritual over the material allows Hegel to proclaim the principle of transcendence of the mind over the object, the universal over the singular, and the abstract over the concrete. Thought not only transcends matter but the very process of thinking is the cause of the structure of the world. The Absolute contemplates itself and realizes the inexhaustible potentialities of its being. The process of realization of the potentialities is *the* history of the Absolute. Since the Absolute and the world are one and the same thing, the history of the Absolute is identical to the process of becoming of all things—the history of this world.

THE LAW OF DIALECTICS.   According to Hegel, thought and becoming are both governed by the same strict law of the dialectical movement: thesis, antithesis, and synthesis. This is the famous law of dialectics, one of the most important and far-reaching doctrines in the history of philosophy. In order to understand it we must remember that thought and being are identified so that ideas and judgments are taken to be identical with that which they express. The dialectical process begins with a thesis, that is, an affirmation. It is a process because the intellect can never satisfy itself with any one affirmation. No affirmation is the expression of the totality of reality. An affirmation is either universal or particular. If it is universal it leaves out the determinations of the singulars; for instance, when I say "bodies are extended," I say nothing about the variety of bodies or about their other properties. If the judgment is particular, it is limited to one or a few individuals. To overcome the limitation of the initial affirmation I must form the antithesis, which represents the other side of the picture. The two judgments together contain a more complete truth, which I express in a new affirmation called synthesis, which in turn becomes a new thesis, and the dialectical movement continues.

A good illustration of the dialectical process is the first trilogy: being, non-being, becoming. The thesis, "being is," expresses a *common* property of all things but none of the distinctions and limitations found in them. Besides participating in the common denominator of being, each singular being implies a *negation* of another singular being: a stone is *not* a tree, this table is *not* that table, and in general this thing is not that thing. This aspect of being forms the antithesis: "being is non-being," that is, this being is not that being. The combination of the thesis and the antithesis gives us the synthesis: "being becomes," which expresses the process of realization of being and the fact that no particular manifestation or aspect of being realizes the plenitude of being.

Hegel's philosophy is the high-water mark of rationalism, a powerful expression of faith in the unlimited capacities of reason and in the fundamental intelligibility of reality. Its consequences are multiple and far-reaching, and in the twentieth century provoked the violent reaction of the analytic and logical-positivist movements. The overconfidence in the powers of reason resulted in a high-handed treatment of concrete facts and in an overindulgence in abstract speculations. Post-Hegelian idealism became a very dry, remote, abstruse, formal play of profound-sounding notions. It turned away as much as possible from the consideration of tangible, contingent, imperfect reality and delved into the necessary and the ideal. The a posteriori knowledge of the humble observation of facts and of the painstaking confrontation of theories with reality was rejected in the name of an a priori analysis of "pure" notions and relations between those notions. The more abstract the reasoning, the better—because of its abstractness it was thought to be above the need of verification by way of confrontation with facts. As a consequence, philosophers of this orientation held themselves and their mode of thinking in high esteem, while the other modes of more concrete, "pedestrian" knowledge (the physical sciences, for instance) were allotted a secondary position. Only mathematics, thought to be the study of absolute, necessary relations, was treated with due respect. What mattered to these thinkers was not to find out how things really are but to elucidate the ideal conditions, the necessary principles. The question was not how does it look or how does it behave, but rather how must it be. In short, philosophy was identified with aprioristic metaphysics.

The Rise of Logical Positivism and Analytic Philosophy

If this type of philosophy had been developed several centuries earlier, it might not have produced so violent a reaction as it did in the present century. Triumphant science simply swept aside this mode of thinking, or so it seemed. As is often the case, a reaction to one extreme takes the form of another extreme. Logical positivism and analytic philosophy are good examples of this law of compensation. They are meant to be the perfect antithesis of post-Hegelian idealism. It would, however, be wrong to believe that the negation was in fact as radical as it was meant to be. We shall see that the new philosophies have some points in common with the rejected systems. By the fact that they were conceived as reactions to a definite set of affirmations, they were to a certain extent determined by the negated doctrines.

In contrast to nineteenth-century idealism, the founders of the two new systems renounced the claim to the autonomy and to the superiority of philosophy with regard to the sciences. Abstract speculations and aprioristic metaphysical considerations of the Absolute were to them sterile verbal exercises devoid of concrete meaning and leading nowhere. The conceptual analysis of notions resulted merely in the creation of pompous phraseology, but it did not help to further our knowledge of this world. To remedy this situation the new thinkers decided to turn away from the study of concepts to the study of facts. To them the abstract, the universal, became highly suspicious. To save thought from the pitfalls of verbosity, they accepted the empiricist theory of knowledge. According to this theory, the only valid source of information is sense knowledge. Sensation reveals to us singular objects as singular. The intellect unavoidably universalizes these sense data, but there is no objective justification for this universalization. Concepts in themselves do not add anything positive to our knowledge of facts. Their abstractness and universality are themselves imperfections, blurrings of distinctions and simplifications, incapable of furthering our knowledge or of revealing anything above and beyond what is contained in sense images.

Logical Empiricism

Logical empiricism, or logical positivism, is largely the product of a collective effort of a group of thinkers associated with the University of Vienna, known as the Vienna Circle. The Circle and its philosophy evolved in the early 1920s from the philosophical seminar led by Moritz Schlick (1882–1936). It is interesting to note that besides professional philosophers such as Schlick and Rudolf Carnap (b. 1891), the organizers of the Circle included representatives of other disciplines such as Philip Frank (b. 1884, physicist), Hans Hahn (1879–1924, mathematician), Otto Neurath (1882–1945, economist, sociologist), and Felix Kaufmann (1895–1949, lawyer). All these thinkers were animated by a common dislike for the majority of the philosophical systems of their time and by the ardent desire to find an intellectual attitude fit for the scientific age. The philosophy that they knew and rejected was the post-Hegelian, German idealism, which, though condemned, left more than a trace on their thought. They opposed spiritualistic monism of the Hegelian type with "scientific" monism; they exchanged a self-sufficient, universal philosophy for a self-sufficient, universal science.

Logical empiricists recognized Hume, Auguste Comte (1798–1857), and Ernst Mach (1838–1916) as their predecessors. Among their contemporaries, English analytic philosophers and mathematical logicians were considered as their closest allies. The clearest and the most extreme expression of the philosophy of logical empiricism is contained in the famous *Vienna Manifesto* (1929). Written on behalf of the Circle by Hahn, Neurath, and Carnap, this work is a belligerent and triumphant proclamation of the philosophy of scientism in its most drastic form: the only meaningful knowledge is of the scientific type. An enumeration of the most important theses of the *Vienna Manifesto* will give us an idea of the convictions of the Vienna Circle.

The Vienna Circle—A Scientific World View

The general aim of the Vienna Circle was the creation of a "unified science" through the collective work of various specialists. It was believed that all meaningful knowledge is essentially of one kind best exemplified by the physical sciences: empirical, quantitative knowledge of measurable phenomena. Useful propositions are either synthetic statements of scientific facts or analytic propositions of logic or mathematics. Philosophy in the ordinary sense was declared useless. Other sciences that had not yet achieved the rigor and the degree of mathematization proper to physics were invited to do so.

The belief in a unified science was aided by the conviction that the whole of reality is accessible to man. Everything is essentially observable and measurable. In science "there is no depth, everything is surface," and there are no insoluble problems. *Reality is intelligible.* Given the proper method, everything can be discovered and understood. Hegel would have no difficulty understanding these last two affirmations. And yet his metaphysics was rejected together with that of the Scholastics as meaningless.

Although metaphysics as a valid mode of knowledge was unacceptable to the proponents of scientism, their philosophy was not entirely bereft of metaphysical statements. The most important one was the definition of reality: *Real is that which conforms to the general structure of experience.* There is no doubt that the definition was meant to be in agreement with the basic thesis of empiricism that all meaningful knowledge comes from experience. But so defined, reality became a function of perception and in turn perception—that is, in the final analysis the knower himself—assumed the role of the criterion of reality. It may seem surprising to see a contemporary version of the claim of the Sophists of Ancient Greece that "Man is the measure of all things" in a work extolling the virtues of scientific knowledge. But we ought to remember that all empiricism, whether classical or contemporary, is basically a form of subjectivism.

Among the multiple consequences of the definition of reality, the following are especially worth noting. Only two types of concepts are meaningful: those that express an empirical content, that is, a sense-datum, and those that are reducible to them. Of course, meaningful judgments must be expressed by means of them. The reduction of concepts to those having an immediate empirical content must occur according to a set of precise rules, which forms a system of reductionistic analysis. Adequate logical "tools" are necessary for the precise formulation and expression of these rules. Aristotelian or, more properly speaking, traditional logic is inadequate for this purpose and must be replaced by more sophisticated forms of logistic. Logic thus becomes an inherent and important part of the epistemology of logical empiricism.

The system of reductionistic analysis is composed of two levels of elements. At the basis of the whole system are personal experiences and qualities—perceptions such as long, hard, heavy, or white. On the second level are physical objects, experience of other minds, and events and situations of the social order studied by the social sciences. Although it is not clearly stated, this enumeration of the types of elements is in fact a classification of the supreme modes of being, to use the Aristotelian terminology; but the underlying principle of classification is a subjective one based on the modes of knowledge and not on those of objective existence as in the philosophy of Aristotle.

Another extremely important consequence of the definition of reality is the far-reaching affirmation that science studies only the structure of reality, not its content. In other words, true meaningful knowledge is solely concerned with and expresses only the form and not the matter of things. In this way a justification is given to the mathematization of knowledge and to the formalized and if possible axiomatized treatment of methods of reasoning, best exemplified in advanced mathematics and in mathematical logic. At the same time an explanation is found for the general, abstract nature of logical and mathematical formulas, which otherwise are incompatible with the principle of classical empiricism.

In view of the fact that there is only one valid mode of knowledge, that of the sciences, there cannot be a valid mode of philosophical knowledge of reality that would stand aside from or above the various branches of scientific knowledge. There is only one meaningful explanation of reality—the scientific one. In this situation philosophy is reduced to the status of the servant and helper of science. The purpose of philosophy is to analyze and to clarify the logical structure of science, to investigate the methods of science, and to analyze language as the means of communication and a tool of science. In all its investigations, philosophy must look up to science as to the supreme form of knowledge and accept it as a measure that delineates the limits of meaningful cognition. Philosophy must never transgress these limits.

It would be wrong to believe that all these rigorous theses are an expression of abstruse, detached minds content with purely intellectual pursuits. The role and the purpose of the "scientific world view" as expounded in the *Vienna Manifesto* is more than mere philosophizing. This doctrine is a concrete attitude toward life and reality, a definite and radical choice in regard to the basic problems facing man. It has moral, sociological, and even theological implications. Some of the consequences were clearly spelled out, while others were merely implied. Logical empiricism wanted to be not only a way of thought but also a way of life. In this respect, notwithstanding its intended antitraditional character, it conformed to the great philosophical tradition.

In the course of years the philosophy of the Vienna Circle developed and underwent several transformations. At least three stages of development may be distinguished: logical atomism, logical syntax, semantics. This evolution was the result of both internal and external criticism. The first period, dominated by Schlick, was characterized by the belief in the existence of absolutely elementary, independent (i.e., atomic) propositions forming the basis of meaningful knowledge, from which meaningful language was constructed solely with the use of the laws of logic. The philosopher became a logician, and logical analysis of language became the aim of philosophy.

Logical Syntax

With the publication of the *Vienna Manifesto* and the two important works by Carnap, "The Logical Construction of the World" and "The Apparent Problems of Philosophy" (both in 1928), began the second and most radical period of logical positivism. Physical science was proclaimed the most perfect mode of knowledge (physicalism). Only empirically verifiable propositions were accepted as meaningful. Out of the verifiability criterion of meaning came a subjectivistic theory of knowledge. The verification was identified with sense perception. In this situation the knower is reduced to solipsism; he knows only his own perceptions and has no possibility of objectively knowing the external world. An example of these views is provided by Carnap's paper included in the readings section.

To avoid the problem of objective reality and the dilemma of solipsism, Carnap accepted as the only purpose of philosophy the logical study of the syntax of scientific language. To be consistent he renounced all consideration of the relation between scientific language and reality. In this situation the traditional definition of truth as an adequation of judgment and object had to be abandoned and in turn replaced by the criterion of logical consistency of reasoning. It soon became evident that science could not be adequately analyzed within the narrow framework of logical syntax. Alfred Tarski (b. 1902), an eminent member of the Polish school of mathematical logic, demonstrated in his famous paper, "The Concept of Truth in Formalized Languages" (1933), that it was impossible to explain the concept of truth without considering the relation between the judgment and the object. The relation between language (i.e., knowledge) and the objective reality had to be taken into consideration.

Semantics

Under the influence of Tarski's critique, Carnap developed after 1936 a new theory. Philosophy was to be concerned with semantics, the study of the meaning of language. The mode of signifying of words was scrutinized and the relation of words to what they stand for was analyzed. This third stage of logical empiricism was less extreme than the second, less exclusive, and more mindful of the complexity of problems facing philosophers interested in the problem of knowledge. It would be wrong to believe that logical empiricists have abandoned all their original convictions. What has not changed throughout the years is the insistence on the importance of the study of language and of the formal aspects of thought, that is, logic. In these fields logical empiricists have made their most important and lasting contributions.

Carnap's paper, "Empiricism, Semantics and Ontology" (1950), is an example of the third, semantic stage of development of logical empiricism. In it Carnap posits one of the fundamental questions with which semantics has to deal, namely, whether expressions designate entities other than concrete, material things. In his opinion this very question is meaningless. It stems from the incorrect use of language.

To explain his point of view, Carnap begins the article by outlining the semantic theory of meaning. According to this theory, the meaning of terms depends on the rules of speaking, that is, on the rules according to which words are used in the given language. The set of rules forms the semantic "framework." Since semantics does not deal with the world of things but with the universe of language, the ordinary understanding of the word "real" is not acceptable to semanticists. For them, real is what fits into the framework of other events "according to the rules of the framework." Of course, this definition must be understood as applying to the elements of language and not to anything outside the language.

The language in question is not necessarily identical with what is normally understood by "language," English or French, for instance. Carnap cites several examples of semantic frameworks including "the thing language" expressing perceptions, "the system of numbers," and "the framework of propositions." Each framework defines a kind of language, and the acceptance of a framework requires the introduction of new forms of usage proper to this particular language.

After these preliminary explanations, Carnap is ready to discuss the problem of abstract entities in semantics. The problem is essentially this: Can the use of the universals such as "red," "color," or "five" be justified or not? Nominalists and strict empiricists claim that a term has a meaning only if it represents a singular object. Consequently, they deny meaning to the universals that they do not think represent any concrete entities. This, however, is not Carnap's opinion, although it is not in the name of a realistic solution that he disagrees with the nominalistic thesis. He contends that the question of accepting or rejecting abstract entities is a practical problem, not a theoretical one. If these entities are useful for the purpose of analyzing a language, if they are efficient as instruments of explanation and communication, then they should be accepted. If they do not serve any useful purpose, they should be rejected.

The acceptance of universals does not mean an automatic affirmation of some objective entities that these universals supposedly represent. Carnap neither accepts nor rejects the existence of such entities. In his opinion the question concerning their existence is not a legitimate one, but results from a wrong use of language; it is "a metaphysical pseudo-statement" and as such is meaningless. This conclusion will be less surprising if one remembers that semantics is more than just a method of analyzing language. To understand semantics properly, one must take it for what it is for Carnap: a new form of antimetaphysical positivism.

That semantics need not be necessarily a system of crusading antimetaphysical positivism can readily be seen from the well-known paper of Alfred Tarski, "The Semantic Conception of Truth" (1943). Semantics is strictly a method of analysis of problems of meaning, that is, problems of relations between language and what it expresses. It is not to be mistaken for a complete system of philosophy or for a substitute for such a system. In this particular case, semantical analysis is applied to the notion of truth. The purpose of the paper is to give a definition of truth that will satisfy the requirements of precision of contemporary logical analysis. The definition will be satisfactory if it explains the conditions implicit in the traditional definition of truth, which have not yet been fully elucidated. It must be stressed that it is not the author's intention to invent a new definition of truth; he is content with Aristotle's that truth is the adequation of the proposition and what it affirms. This definition suits semantics because it allows the establishment of a correspondence between the verbal form of a sentence and what it stands for. So understood, truth becomes a property of sentences and is "related to the more general problem of setting up the foundations of theoretical semantics."

In order to analyze the conditions of the definition of truth, it is necessary to specify exactly the structure of language according to the rules of definition (used in the language), the criteria for distinguishing sentences from other linguistic elements, the axioms or basic propositions of the language, and the rules of inference (rules of proof). Using the antinomy of the liar as an occasion for furthering the analysis of the definition of truth, Tarski explains the notion of semantically closed languages, that is, perfectly defined languages.

Everyday language has no exactly specified structure, nor is it suitable to discuss the antinomy of the liar or the definition of truth in a semantically closed language. The solution of the antinomy requires two levels of language: the first, *object-language,* is that in which the definition of truth is given, while the second, *meta-language,* is formed by the language in which we talk about the first language ("We wish . . . to construct the definition of truth for the first language"). The antinomy can be solved and the definition of truth given if the meta-language is essentially richer than the object-language. This condition is fulfilled if the meta-language allows us to formulate more complex logical relations than the object-language.

It is possible to construct the definition of truth using the notion of satisfaction. In semantics, satisfaction denotes a relation between sentential functions, such as "*x* is white" or "*x* is greater than *y,*" and arbitrary objects. If by substituting the objects for the free variables *x* and *y* we obtain true sentences such as "snow is white," then these objects satisfy the sentential functions. Consequently the semantical definition of truth is as follows: "A sentence is true if it is satisfied by all objects and false otherwise."

Analytic Philosophy

The term "analytic philosophy" is a general one given to the philosophies of several twentieth-century British thinkers. In contradistinction to the logical empiricists, analytic philosophers did not form one closely knit team working together towards a common goal. The movement began around the year 1900 as a reaction to transcendental idealism developed in England mainly by F. H. Bradley (1846–1924), Bernard Bosanquet (1848–1923), and John McTaggart (1866–1925). The new school of thought renounced philosophizing in the grand manner of Hegel and his followers. Instead of sweeping generalizations and all-embracing syntheses it preferred precise analysis of particular problems. To idealism it opposed a common-sense realism, a predilection for clarity and linguistic and logical precision. It reintroduced the clear distinction between the knower and the object of knowledge and affirmed the objective existence of the latter. This realism was blended with traditional English empiricism. With time, the empirical point of view became more and more prevalent.

The first period of the new philosophy, lasting roughly some twenty years (1900–20), was dominated by George Edward Moore (1873–1958), the originator of this movement, and by Bertrand Russell (b. 1872). The two most outstanding works then published were Moore's *Principia Ethica* (1903) and the monumental *Principia Mathematica* (1910–13), written jointly by Russell and Alfred North Whitehead (1861–1947). This latter work, the culmination of over half a century of development of modern symbolic logic, endeavors to explain and to formulate the logical foundations of mathematics, and to transform mathematics into a coherent, axiomatic system—a system deducible from a few basic postulates. Although the *Principia Mathematica* is essentially a work of logic, its authors had to adopt a definite position on such fundamental problems as the nature of concepts, their relation to the things they stand for, and, in the final analysis, the structure of reality.

Atomistic View of Reality

Russell's paper "Logical Atomism" (1924), included in the readings, describes his philosophical convictions. "Logic is what is fundamental in philosophy," says Russell. In other words, philosophy should consist mainly of logical analysis of knowledge. Central among the philosophical problems he has to concern himself with is the question of the foundation of mathematics. This interest in logic does not prevent him, however, from having definite opinions about other problems. The paper clearly expresses his metaphysical ideas about the nature of reality, which are a new variation of the old nominalistic thesis: "Only the singular exists." This metaphysical conviction is coupled with the empiricist theory of knowledge. For Russell, the world is composed of singular, autonomous (i.e., independent from each other) fact-atoms of sense data. Sense data exist objectively but they are not substantial entities. Besides atomic data the mind perceives relations between data. Through the comparison of data, classes of facts are established, and thus an intelligible order emerges from the variety of things perceived.

It is essential for the proper understanding of Russell's thought to stress the importance that he attaches to the notion of class. This notion and the notion of logical relation become fundamental for the philosophical investigation of reality. Surprisingly enough, Russell is not quite clear in his mind whether classes and relations are objective entities or subjective ones. The uncertainty concerning their metaphysical status is not, however, a great hindrance for him. He studies the structure of classes and their relations mainly from the logical point of view, and thus avoids taking a definite stand concerning the underlying metaphysical problem. Moreover, Russell affirms in "Logical Atomism" that whenever we find that a group of objects has a common logical property, as in the case of all numbers divisible by two, "the supposed entities can be replaced by purely logical structures" (i.e., logical classes). The study of reality thus becomes a logical investigation. It is not surprising that for Russell "the business of philosophy . . . is essentially that of logical analysis."

Generally speaking, logic is the study of the form of reasoning. The concern with logic enhances, in Russell's eyes, the importance of the formal aspect of thought. Because the form is the source of intelligibility, other elements have to be subordinated to it in the process of correct reasoning. Russell warns against possible errors arising from an indiscriminate reliance on ordinary (i.e., logically imperfect) language. He declares invalid "inferences from the nature of language to the nature of the world . . . because they depend upon the logical defects of language." Another important consequence of the insistence on the importance of form is the conviction that: "In science, structure is the main study." As we have seen, this affirmation becomes one of the principal theses of logical empiricism. Thus the philosophy expounded in "Logical Atomism" may be considered as similar to and a source of inspiration for the Vienna Circle.

A Return to Empiricism

After 1920 a new era began for analytic philosophy. As a result of internal criticism and because of the influence of the Austrian philosopher Ludwig Wittgenstein (1889–1951), the initial common-sense realism was abandoned. In its place more critical and subjectivistic views of knowledge have become prevalent. Wittgenstein in his famous and obscure *Tractatus Logico-Philosophicus* (1921) accepted as the basis of his reflections Russell's atomistic view of reality. Since facts are singular, only singular propositions express facts. All universal judgments are merely "truth-functions" of the underlying singular propositions. They are products of the mind and as such do not represent any objective reality. Logical and mathematical laws and formulae are pure tautologies that do not further our factual knowledge of the world. The world is studied by empirical sciences. All logic and mathematics can do is tell us how to draw a conclusion from a premise in which it was already implicitly contained. Wittgenstein, like Russell, believed that philosophy should be essentially a logical analysis, and he concluded that philosophy has nothing to say about reality. The subject matter of philosophy is language, and the best philosophy can do is to subject language to a careful analysis.

Wittgenstein's theory of knowledge leads to a radical subjectivism verging on solipsism. While Wittgenstein in his later years moderated his epistemological views, British philosophers, to an extent under his influence, have abandoned realism and reverted to strong empiricism. In this new, yet old, epistemological setting, philosophy is denied the status of an independent and original study of reality. Science is declared the only legitimate and meaningful method of investigating the world. Philosophy has to be given a new task, the analysis of language. According to linguistic analysts, the only legitimate application of philosophy is to the study of language as a means of expressing and communicating thoughts. Since philosophy cannot form judgments about reality, it has to limit itself to the study of propositions about things formed by sciences. What can possibly be the purpose of this study? Briefly, the aim of the undertaking is the clarification of thoughts. "In philosophy we take the propositions we make in science and everyday life, and try to exhibit them in a logical system with primitive terms and definitions, etc." [1]

So conceived philosophy can be neither metaphysics, nor philosophy of nature, nor ethics, nor psychology in the traditional meaning of these terms. And yet philosophy is important, say the analysts, and its importance results from the importance of language. According to this school of thought, the role and the importance of language has never before been adequately stressed by philosophers. For language, they believe, impresses thought just as much as it expresses it. Language, like traditional philosophy, is full of great words like being, the absolute, and necessary truth, which seem to be meaningful but which in fact are empty sounds. When we use these pseudomeaningful words we mistake verbal structures for adequate explanations. True philosophy, analytic philosophy, owes its importance to the aim that it proposes for itself: to rid knowledge of meaningless words. If this task is successfully accomplished, then words will be classified into two categories, the meaningful and the meaningless, and we will be able to exclude all pseudoproblems and pseudoknowledge. In point of fact, it has been a much simpler task to announce the sweeping plans than

---

[1] Frank P. Ramsey, *The Foundations of Mathematics* (London: Routledge & Kegan Paul, 1954), p. 263.

to carry them out, simply because it is very difficult indeed to do philosophical analysis without explicitly or implicitly accepting some thesis about the nature of knowledge or the nature of reality.

Among the philosophers of the second period of analytic philosophy (after 1920), the most outspken and the most extreme is Alfred Jules Ayer (b. 1910). He is also closest of all British thinkers to the Vienna Circle and its positivism. Like the logical empiricists, Ayer condemns philosophy that is a deductive, a priori system, specifically the various forms of idealism that make unwarranted or unverifiable statements of the metaphysical type. According to Ayer there are two general sources of errors in these philosophies: first, the belief in the existence of a priori principles, and, second, the desire to talk about the whole of reality, that is, a pernicious tendency to sweeping generalizations. How can philosophy be cured of these deep-rooted ills? The answer is given by a phenomenalistic theory of meaning: Only that which is empirically verifiable is meaningful. This implies that besides verifiable personal experience, science is the only source of meaningful propositions. All meaningful knowledge is therefore scientific.

The Development of Linguistic Analysis

After the Second World War, a new form of analytic philosophy, namely, the philosophy of linguistic analysis, developed, to some extent under the influence of Wittgenstein's *Philosophical Investigations* (1953). The principal representatives of this philosophy are Gilbert Ryle (b. 1900), John Langshaw Austin (1911–60), John Wisdom (b. 1904), and Peter Frederick Strawson (b. 1919).

Even more than the earlier analytic philosophers, these thinkers renounce all metaphysical problems and, moreover, try to refrain from universal philosophical statements. One might say that their general philosophical opinion is that there is no general philosophical opinion. The majority of traditional philosophical problems are simply set aside. Instead of searching for some overall doctrines and solutions, linguistic analysts concentrate their attention on particular sentences and submit them to minute analysis. The purpose of their efforts is to clarify statements and, by way of eliminating wrong forms of expression, retain only the correct and meaningful propositions. It must be noted that the aim is not the knowledge of the world through language but the intelligibility of language for its own sake. Knowledge is identified with language and intelligibility with grammatical correctness. In this situation there exists a definite tendency to dissociate language from the reality that it is meant to represent and to treat language as if it were a self-contained and self-sufficient universe.

Linguistic analysis presupposes in fact an empiricist theory of perceptions; it believes that language has an essentially logical structure similar to that of mathematics and accepts the distinction between synthetic and analytic propositions as fundamental and final. It is assumed that the synthetic propositions are formed by empirical sciences, not by philosophy. What philosophy really does, as Wisdom claims, is to form verbal recommendations concerning language, devoid of factual content.

Linguistic analysts are inclined to think that even questions like the value of the verifiability theory of meaning smack of metaphysics. It is not astonishing therefore that one finds fewer metaphysical considerations in their writings than even in those of the logical empiricists. Consequently the present selection of readings does not contain examples of their writings.

Conclusion

Each philosophical system is a complex structure; to be fully appreciated it must be viewed from different angles. A system may be judged in the light of its own principles, stated aims, and actual achievements. Or, again, it may be compared with another system as to internal coherence, power of explanation, richness of ideas, and the soundness of conclusions. One must also consider the importance of a philosophy for philosophical thought in general, its place in the history of thought, and its relevance to the epoch to which it belongs. In this scientific age of ours, the last condition requires a comparison of a philosophy with the body of scientific knowledge. A philosophy will command attention and respect if it is able to tell us something significant, yet different from what science can tell us. It is of course easier to take stock of an old system firmly established in the history of thought and whose consequences are well known, than to judge a contemporary movement. In the latter case we lack distance necessary for viewing a philosophy in the proper perspective, and we cannot adequately foresee all its consequences.

In the light of these remarks what can we say about the philosophies considered in this section? Hume has a major and permanent place in the history of philosophy, and his ideas continue to exercise profound influence on philosophers in the Anglo-Saxon countries. Whether one agrees with him or not, his critique of the notion of perception, and in particular that of causality, has been a decisive factor in the development of the majority of great philosophical systems since his time. No one who is seriously interested in the problems of knowledge can afford to ignore his views. We now know that the theory of knowledge plays a fundamental role in the elaboration of a philosophy. Metaphysics, philosophy of nature, and the whole system as such depend on what the philosopher regards as the true nature of knowledge. In this sense, they are the results of the theory of knowledge.

Hume's philosophy is a perfect illustration of the central role of epistemology. If knowledge is what he thought it to be, namely, a radically subjective perception resulting from atomic stimuli, then there is no question of objective reality. Consequently, metaphysics, philosophy of nature, and even empirical sciences inasmuch they form universal laws must be dismissed as meaningless. Since intellection, with its universalizing mode of cognition, cannot be dismissed altogether, it is relegated to the realm of analytic judgments—to the elucidation of obvious or hidden tautologies. The atomic theory of perception destroys the objectivity of causality, and with it the traditional understanding of explanation.

With objective reality destroyed, objective causality denied, and knowledge reduced to subjective perception, the very value of knowledge becomes a major problem and a constant preoccupation of philosophers subscribing to the Humean doctrines. If there is no objective reality to study, a substitute must be found. This substitute is language. The twentieth century will witness, as we have seen, the prodigious development of philosophies studying language as this substitute.

It is no exaggeration to call these philosophies Humean. In more than one way they depend on the ideas of the brilliant Scot. They continue his empiricism and develop various consequences resulting from his theories. Of course it would be wrong simply to identify them with the philosophy of Hume. They are the product of the twentieth century, and were formed in a vastly different and richer framework of knowledge than that of the times of Hume. Logical empiricism and analytic philosophy developed in the wake of the transcendental idealism which has left on them a definite, even if unsolicited, mark.

The philosophers of the Vienna Circle have tried to take as full account as possible of sciences in general, and of physical sciences in particular. Although the philosophy of linguistic analysis is much less preoccupied with science, philosophers of this orientation accept as a foregone conclusion that science is the valid source of factual statements. At the basis of their theories lies the conviction in the atomicity of facts: whatever reality there is, is made up of singular facts. The only propositions that can adequately express physical reality are singular statements. Only they can be verified empirically; therefore only they can be meaningful. Universal propositions do not have an adequate foundation in the realm of facts and consequently do not represent any objective universality.

It is not astonishing that these thinkers reject metaphysics as meaningless and with it all search for common characteristics of being. Thinking for them can validly be concerned only with the empirical or singular data, or with logic and mathematics that belong to the realm of universal, analytic judgments. Philosophy loses its traditional status of an original and independent inquiry into the nature of reality, and is given a new role— either as helper of science (by logical empiricism) or as generalized logic (by early analytic philosophy and later logical empiricism) or as glorified grammar (by linguistic analysis).

In each case the ideal of knowledge which philosophy is called to serve is the old Cartesian ideal of absolute clarity, evidence, and certitude, best realized in mathematics and mathematical logic. In the light of this ideal, to further knowledge is to grasp the form, the determination, and to overcome all that is indetermination, irregularity, unintelligibility. It is assumed, whether stated explicitly or implicitly, that to serve this ideal is to advance on the path of truth. Truth and intelligibility are identified, and, in the final analysis, truth is subordinated to the all-powerful and ever present desire of intellectual certitude resulting from intelligibility.

The belief underlying this attitude is the belief common to all monism since the time of Parmenides, namely that reality is intelligible, that Being, as Hegel said, is thought. The thinkers we have studied belong unmistakably to the great tradition of Western thought, and their thought is another element in the great intellectual adventure that began in Ancient Greece.

Glossary

ANALYTIC PROPOSITION:
  A proposition in which the predicate is contained in the definition of the subject. For example, every husband has a wife; a square is four-sided. Analytic propositions are often called a priori propositions; they are opposed to synthetic propositions.

EMPIRICISM:
  The philosophical tradition that claims that the only genuine knowledge is that which is derivable from, reducible to, and verifiable in sense experience.

META-LANGUAGE:
  A language used primarily to talk about another language. (See *Object-language.*)

NOMINALISM:
  The philosophical position that disclaims the ability of the intellect to know or represent natures or essences in the order of knowledge. It asserts that the universal idea is universal in name only, rather than in nature.

OBJECT-LANGUAGE:
  Language in which the definition of truth is given.

PHENOMENALISM:
  The philosophical position that claims we can but know the appearances of things, and that implicitly questions the reality of anything beyond the appearances or sense data.

PHILOSOPHICAL ANALYSIS:
  The method of subjecting terms and propositions to language clarification in order to determine their meaning, significance, or lack thereof.

POSITIVISM:

The philosophy that accepts physical sciences as the most perfect and most genuine mode of knowledge and subordinates all other modes to it. Associated with Auguste Comte.

SEMANTICS:

The study of the meaning of words, or more currently, the meaning of meaning.

SUBJECTIVISM:

A philosophical attitude stressing the subject and all that pertains to him to the detriment of the object. A subordination of the object of knowledge to the knower.

SYNTHETIC PROPOSITION:

A proposition in which the predicate is never contained in the subject. Its attachment to the subject term cannot be made by analysis, but by reference to experience. For example, this oven is hot; some animals are vegetarians. Synthetic propositions are often called empirical propositions; they are opposed to analytic propositions.

TRANSCENDENTAL:

That which applies to everything and pertains to the realm of the absolute, the necessary. For Kant, that which is above and prior to experience.

David Hume

DAVID HUME, the most important British philosopher since William of Ockham, was born in Edinburgh, Scotland, in 1711. At his family's urging he studied law at Edinburgh University, but left without obtaining a degree. Self-educated as a philosopher, he went to France in 1734 and there spent three years writing his *Treatise of Human Nature*. It was finally published in 1739 but, as he says in his autobiography, it "fell dead born from the press without reaching such distinction as even to excite a murmur among the zealots." The next ten years he was engaged in varied activities—tutor, private secretary, and member of the British Ambassador's staff at the courts of Vienna and Turin. During this time he also published *Essays Moral and Political* (1742) and drastically reworked his *Treatise*. This work subsequently appeared in two versions: the first, in 1748, entitled *Philosophical Essays Concerning Human Understanding* (which Hume renamed in 1758 *An Enquiry Concerning Human Understanding*); the second, in 1751, entitled *An Enquiry Concerning the Principles of Morals*. Between 1754 and 1762 he published a *History of England* which gained for him more fame and income during his lifetime than any of his philosophical writings. After serving for two years as Undersecretary of State for Scotland, he retired to Edinburgh in 1769, where he became the center of literary society. He died in 1776.

Metaphysics Denied

SECTION II

OF THE ORIGINS OF IDEAS

Everyone will readily allow that there is a considerable difference between the perceptions of the mind, when a man feels the pain of excessive heat, or the pleasure of moderate warmth, and when he afterwards recalls to his memory this sensation, or anticipates it by his imagination. These faculties may mimic or copy the perceptions of the senses; but they never can entirely reach the force and vivacity of the original sentiment. The utmost we say of them, even when they operate with greatest vigor, is, that they repre-

From pp. 14–21 of David Hume, *An Enquiry Concerning Human Understanding*. Copyright 1960 by Henry Regnery Company.

451

sent their object in so lively a manner, that we could *almost* say we feel or see it: But, except the mind be disordered by disease or madness, they never can arrive at such a pitch of vivacity, as to render these perceptions altogether undistinguishable. All the colors of poetry, however splendid, can never paint natural objects in such a manner as to make the description be taken for a real landscape. The most lively thought is still inferior to the dullest sensation.

We may observe a like distinction to run through all the other perceptions of the mind. A man in a fit of anger, is actuated in a very different manner from one who only thinks of that emotion. If you tell me, that any person is in love, I easily understand your meaning, and form a just conception of his situation; but never can mistake that conception for the real disorders and agitations of the passion. When we reflect on our past sentiments and affections, our thought is a faithful mirror, and copies its objects truly; but the colors which it employs are faint and dull, in comparison of those in which our original perceptions were clothed. It requires no nice discernment or metaphysical head to mark the distinction between them.

Here therefore we may divide all the perceptions of the mind into two classes or species, which are distinguished by their different degrees of force and vivacity. The less forcible and lively are commonly denominated *thoughts* or *ideas*. The other species want a name in our langauge, and in most others; I suppose, because it was not requisite for any, but philosophical purposes, to rank them under a general term or appellation. Let us, therefore, use a little freedom and call them *impressions;* employing that word in a sense somewhat different from the usual. By the term *impression,* then, I mean all our more lively perceptions, when we hear, or see, or feel, or love, or hate, or desire, or will. And impressions are distinguished from ideas, which are the less lively perceptions, of which we are conscious, when we reflect on any of those sensations or movements above mentioned.

Nothing, at first view, may seem more unbounded than the thought of man, which not only escapes all human power and authority, but is not even restrained within the limits of nature and reality. To form monsters, and join incongruous shapes and appearances, costs the imagination no more trouble than to conceive the most natural and familiar objects. And while the body is confined to one planet, along which it creeps with pain and difficulty; the thought can in an instant transport us into the most distant regions of the universe; or even beyond the universe, into the unbounded chaos, where nature is supposed to lie in total confusion. What never was seen, or heard of, may yet be conceived; nor is anything beyond the power of thought, except what implies an absolute contradiction.

But though our thought seems to possess this unbounded liberty, we shall find, upon a nearer examination, that it is really confined within very narrow limits, and that all this creative power of the mind amounts to no more than the faculty of compounding, transposing, augmenting, or diminishing the materials afforded us by the senses and experience. When we think of a golden mountain, we only joint two consistent ideas, *gold* and *mountain,* with which we were formerly acquainted. A virtuous horse we can conceive; because, from our own feeling, we can conceive virtue; and this we may unite to the figure and shape of a horse, which is an animal familiar to us. In short, all the materials of thinking are derived either from our outward or inward sentiment: the mixture and composition of these belongs alone to the mind and will. Or, to express myself in philosophical language, all our ideas or more feeble perceptions are copies of our impressions or more lively ones.

To prove this, the two following arguments will, I hope, be sufficient. *First,* when we analyze our thoughts or ideas, however compounded or sublime, we always find that they resolve themselves into such simple ideas as were copied from a precedent feeling or sentiment. Even those ideas, which, at first view, seem the most wide of this origin, are found, upon a nearer scrutiny, to be derived from it. The idea of God, as meaning an infinitely intelligent, wise, and good Being, arises from reflecting on the operations of our own mind, and augmenting, without limit, those qualities of goodness and wisdom. We may prosecute this inquiry to what length we please; where we shall always find, that every idea which we examine is copied from a similar impression. Those who would assert that this position is not universally true nor without exception, have only one, and that an easy method of refuting it; by producing that idea, which, in their opinion, is not derived from this source. It will then be incumbent on us, if we would maintain our doctrine, to produce the impression, or lively perception, which corresponds to it.

Secondly, if it happen, from a defect of the organ, that a man is not susceptible of any species of sensation, we always find that he is as little susceptible of the correspondent ideas. A blind man can form no notion of colors; a deaf man of sounds. Restore either of them that sense in which he is deficient; by opening this new inlet for his sensations, you also open an inlet for the ideas; and he finds no difficulty in conceiving these objects. The case is the same, if the object, proper for exciting any sensation, has never been applied to the organ. A Laplander or Negro has no notion of the relish of wine. And though there are few or no instances of a like deficiency in the mind, where a person has never felt or is wholly incapable of a sentiment or passion that belongs to his species; yet we find the same observation to take place in a less degree. A man of mind manners can form no idea of inveterate revenge or cruelty; nor can a selfish heart easily conceive the heights of friendship and generosity. It is readily allowed, that other beings may possess many senses of which we can have no conception; because the ideas of them have never been introduced to us in the only manner by which an idea can have access to the mind, to wit, by the actual feeling and sensation.

There is, however, one contradictory phenomenon, which may prove that it is not absolutely impossible for ideas to arise, independent of their correspondent impressions. I believe it will readily be allowed, that the several distinct ideas of color, which enter by the eye, or those of sound, which are conveyed by the ear, are really different from each other; though, at the same time resembling. Now if this be true of different colors, it must be no less so of the different shades of the same color; and each shade produces a distinct idea, independent of the rest. For if this should be denied, it is possible, by the continued gradation of shades, to run a color insensibly into what is most remote from it; and if you will not allow any of the means to be different, you cannot, without absurdity, deny the extremes to be the same. Suppose, therefore, a person to have enjoyed his sight for thirty years, and to have become perfectly acquainted with colors of all kinds except one particular shade of blue, for instance, which it never has been his fortune to meet with. Let all the different shades of that color, except that single one, be placed before him, descending gradually from the deepest to the lightest; it is plain that he will perceive a blank, where that shade is wanting, and will be sensible that there is a greater distance in that place between the contiguous colors than in any other. Now I ask, whether it be possible for him, from his own imagination, to supply this deficiency, and raise up to himself the idea of that particular shade, though it had never been conveyed to him by his senses? I believe there are few but will be of opinion that he can: and this may serve as a proof that the simple ideas are not always, in every instance, derived from the correspondent impressions; though this instance is so singular, that it is scarcely worth our observing, and does not merit that for it alone we should alter our general maxim.

Here, therefore, is a proposition, which not only seems, in itself, simple and intelligible; but, if a proper use were made of it, might render every dispute equally intelligible, and banish all that jargon, which has so long taken possession of metaphysical reasonings, and drawn disgrace upon them. All ideas, especially abstract ones, are naturally faint and obscure: the mind has but a slender hold on them: they are apt to be confounded with other resembling ideas; and when we have often employed any term, though without a distinct meaning, we are apt to imagine it has a determinate idea annexed to it. On the contrary, all impressions, that is, all sensations, either outward or inward, are strong and vivid: the limits between them are more exactly determined: nor is it easy to fall into any error or mistake with regard to them. When we entertain, therefore, any suspicion that a philosophical term is employed without any meaning or idea (as is but too frequent), we need but inquire, *from what impression is that supposed idea derived?* And if it be impossible to assign any, this will serve to confirm our suspicion.[1] By bringing ideas into so clear a light we may rea-

---

[1] It is probable that no more was meant by those, who denied innate ideas, than that all ideas were copies of our impressions; though it must be confessed, that the terms, which they employed, were not chosen with such caution, nor so exactly defined, as to prevent all mistakes about their doctrine. For what is meant by *innate?* If innate

sonably hope to remove all dispute, which may arise, concerning their nature and reality.

SECTION III

OF THE ASSOCIATION OF IDEAS

It is evident that there is a principle of connection between the different thoughts or ideas of the mind, and that, in their appearance to the memory or imagination, they introduce each other with a certain degree of method and regularity. In our more serious thinking or discourse this is so observable that any particular thought, which breaks in upon the regular tract or chain of ideas, is immediately remarked and rejected. And even in our wildest and most wandering reveries, nay in our very dreams, we shall find, if we reflect, that the imagination ran not altogether at adventures, but that there was still a connection upheld among the different ideas, which succeeded each other. Were the loosest and freest conversation to be transcribed, there would immediately be observed something which connected it in all its transitions. Or where this is wanting, the person who broke the thread of discourse might still inform you, that there had secretly revolved in his mind a succession of thought, which had gradually led him from the subject of conversation. Among different languages, even where we cannot suspect the least connection or communication, it is found, that the words, expressive of ideas, the most compounded, do yet nearly correspond to each other, a certain proof that the simple ideas, comprehended in the compound ones, were bound together by some universal principle, which had an equal influence on all mankind.

Though it be too obvious to escape observation, that different ideas are connected together; I do not find that any philosopher has attempted to enumerate or class all the principles of association; a subject, however, that

---

be equivalent to natural, then all the perceptions and ideas of the mind must be allowed to be innate or natural, in whatever sense we take the latter word, whether in opposition to what is uncommon, artificial, or miraculous. If by innate be meant, contemporary to our birth, the dispute seems to be frivolous; nor is it worth while to inquire at what time thinking begins, whether before, at, or after our birth. Again, the word *idea,* seems to be commonly taken in a very loose sense, by Locke and others; as standing for any of our perceptions, or sensations and passions, as well as thoughts. Now in this sense, I should desire to know, what can be meant by asserting, that self-love, or resentment of injuries, or the passion between the sexes is not innate?

But admitting these terms, *impressions* and *ideas,* in the sense above explained, and understanding by *innate,* what is original or copied from no precedent perception, then may we assert that all our impressions are innate and our ideas not innate.

To be ingenuous, I must own it to be my opinion, that Locke was betrayed into this question by the schoolmen, who, making use of undefined terms, draw out their disputes to a tedious length, without ever touching the point in question. A like ambiguity and circumlocution seem to run through that philosopher's reasonings on this as well as most other subjects. [D.H.]

seems worthy of curiosity. To me, there appear to be only three principles of connection among ideas, namely, *resemblance, contiguity* in time or place, and *cause* or *effect*.

That these principles serve to connect ideas will not, I believe, be much doubted. A picture naturally leads our thoughts to the original: [2] the mention of one apartment in a building naturally introduces an inquiry or discourse concerning the others: [3] and if we think of a wound, we can scarcely forbear reflecting on the pain which follows it.[4] But that this enumeration is complete, and that there are no other principles of association except these, may be difficult to prove to the satisfaction of the reader, or even to a man's own satisfaction. All we can do, in such cases, is to run over several instances, and examine carefully the principle which binds the different thoughts to each other, never stopping till we render the principle as general as possible.[5] The more instances we examine, and the more care we employ, the more assurance shall we acquire, that the enumeration, which we form from the whole, is complete and entire.

SECTION IV

SCEPTICAL DOUBTS CONCERNING THE OPERATION OF THE UNDERSTANDING

Part I

All the objects of human reason or inquiry may naturally be divided into two kinds, to wit, *relations of ideas,* and *matters of fact.* Of the first kind are the sciences of geometry, algebra, and arithmetic; and in short, every affirmation which is either intuitively or demonstratively certain. *That the square of the hypothenuse is equal to the squares of the two sides,* is a proposition which expresses a relation between these figures. *That three times five is equal to the half of thirty,* expresses a relation between these numbers. Propositions of this kind are discoverable by the mere operation of thought, without dependence on what is anywhere existent in the universe. Though there never were a circle or triangle in nature, the truths demonstrated by Euclid would for ever retain their certainty and evidence.

Matters of fact, which are the second objects of human reason, are not ascertained in the same manner; nor is our evidence of their truth, however great, of a like nature with the foregoing. The contrary of every matter of fact is still possible; because it can never imply a contradiction, and is conceived by the mind with the same facility and distinctness, as if ever so

---

[2] Resemblance. [D.H.]

[3] Contiguity. [D.H.]

[4] Cause and effect. [D.H.]

[5] For instance, *contrast* or *contrariety* is also a connection among ideas but it may, perhaps, be considered as a mixture of *causation* and *resemblance.* Where two objects are contrary, the one destroys the other; that is, the cause of its annihilation and the idea of the annihilation of an object implies the idea of its former existence. [D.H.]

conformable to reality. *That the sun will not rise tomorrow* is no less intelligible a proposition, and implies no more contradiction than the affirmation, *that it will rise.* We should in vain, therefore, attempt to demonstrate its falsehood. Were it demonstratively false, it would imply a contradiction, and could never be distinctly conceived by the mind.

It may, therefore, be a subject worthy of curiosity, to inquire what is the nature of that evidence which assures us of any real existence and matter of fact, beyond the present testimony of our senses, or the records of our memory. This part of philosophy, it is observable, has been little cultivated, either by the ancients or moderns; and therefore our doubts and errors, in the prosecution of so important an inquiry, may be the more excusable; while we march through such difficult paths without any guide or direction. They may even prove useful, by exciting curiosity, and destroying that implicit faith and security, which is the bane of all reasoning and free inquiry. The discovery of defects in the common philosophy, if any such there be, will not, I presume, be a discouragement, but rather an incitement, as is usual, to attempt something more full and satisfactory than has yet been proposed to the public.

All reasonings concerning matter of fact seem to be founded on the relation of *cause and effect.* By means of that relation alone we can go beyond the evidence of our memory and senses. If you were to ask a man, why he believes any matter of fact, which is absent; for instance, that his friend is in the country, or in France; he would give you a reason; and this reason would be some other fact; as a letter received from him, or the knowledge of his former resolutions and promises. A man finding a watch or any other machine in a desert island, would conclude that there had once been men in that island. All our reasonings concerning fact are of the same nature. And here it is constantly supposed that there is a connection between the present fact and that which is inferred from it. Were there nothing to bind them together, the inference would be entirely precarious. The hearing of an articulate voice and rational discourse in the dark assures us of the presence of some person: Why? because these are the effects of the human make and fabric, and closely connected with it. If we anatomize all the other reasonings of this nature, we shall find that they are founded on the relation of cause and effect, and that this relation is either near or remote, direct or collateral. Heat and light are collateral effects of fire, and the one effect may justly be inferred from the other.

If we would satisfy ourselves, therefore, concerning the nature of that evidence, which assures us of matters of fact, we must inquire how we arrive at the knowledge of cause and effect.

I shall venture to affirm, as a general proposition, which admits of no exception, that the knowledge of this relation is not, in any instance, attained by reasonings *a priori;* but arises entirely from experience, when we find that any particular objects are constantly conjoined with each other. Let an object be presented to a man of ever so strong natural reason and abilities; if that object be entirely new to him, he will not be able, by the most accurate examination of its sensible qualities, to discover any of its causes or effects. Adam, though his rational faculties be supposed, at the very first, entirely perfect, could not have inferred from the fluidity and transparency of water that it would suffocate him, or from the light and warmth of fire that it would consume him. No object ever discovers, by the qualities which appear to the senses, either the causes which produced it, or the effects which will arise from it; nor can our reason, unassisted by experience, ever draw any inference concerning real existence and matter of fact.

This proposition, *that causes and effects are discoverable, not by reason but by experience,* will readily be admitted with regard to such objects, as we remember to have once been altogether unknown to us; since we must be conscious of the utter inability, which we then lay under, of foretelling what would arise from them. Present two smooth pieces of marble to a man who has no tincture of natural philosophy; he will never discover that they will adhere together in such a manner as to require great force to separate them in a direct line, while they make so small a resistence to a lateral pressure. Such events, as bear little analogy to the common course of nature, are also readily confessed to be known only by experience; nor does any man imagine that the explosion of gunpowder, or the attraction of a loadstone, could ever be discovered by arguments *a priori.* In like manner, when an effect is supposed to depend upon an intricate machinery or secret structure of parts, we make no difficulty in attributing all our knowledge of it to experience. Who will assert that he can give the ultimate reason, why milk or bread is proper nourishment for a man, not for a lion or a tiger?

But the same truth may not appear, at first sight, to have the same evidence with regard to events, which have become familiar to us from our first appearance in the world, which bear a close analogy to the whole course of nature, and which are supposed to depend on the simple qualities of objects, without any secret structure of parts. We are apt to imagine that we could discover these effects by the mere operation of our reason, without experience. We fancy, that were we brought on a sudden into this world, we could at first have inferred that one billiard ball would communicate motion to another upon impulse; and that we needed not to have waited for the event, in order to pronounce with certainty concerning it. Such is the influence of custom, that, where it is strongest, it not only covers our natural ignorance, but even conceals itself, and seems not to take place, merely because it is found in the highest degree.

But to convince us that all the laws of nature, and all the operations of bodies without exception, are known only by experience, the following reflections may, perhaps, suffice. Were any object presented to us, and were we required to pronounce concerning the effect, which will result from it, without consulting past observation; after what manner, I beseech you, must the mind proceed in this operation? It must invent or imagine some event, which it ascribes to the object as its effect; and it is plain that this invention must be entirely arbitrary. The mind can never possibly find the effect in the supposed cause, by the most accurate scrutiny and examination. For the effect is totally different from the cause, and consequently can never be discovered in it. Motion in the second billiard ball is a quite distinct event from motion in the first: nor is there anything in the one to suggest the smallest hint of the other. A stone or piece of metal raised into the air, and left without any support, immediately falls: but to consider the matter *a priori,* is there anything we discover in this situation which can beget the idea of a downward, rather than an upward, or any other motion, in the stone or metal?

And as the first imagination or invention of a particular effect, in all natural operations, is arbitrary, where we consult not experience; so must we also esteem the supposed tie or connection between the cause and effect, which binds them together, and renders it impossible that any other effect could result from the operation of that cause. When I see, for instance, a billiard ball moving in a straight line towards another; even suppose motion in the second ball should by accident be suggested to me, as the result of their contact or impulse; may I not conceive, that a hundred different events might as well follow from that cause? May not both these balls remain at absolute rest? May not the first ball return in a straight line, or leap off from the second in any line or direction? All these suppositions are consistent and conceivable. Why then should we give the preference to one, which is not more consistent or conceivable than the rest? All our reasonings *a priori* will never be able to show us any foundation for this preference.

In a word, then, every effect is a distinct event from its cause. It could not, therefore, be discovered in the cause, and the first invention or conception of it, *a priori,* must be entirely arbitrary. And even after it is suggested, the conjunction of it with the cause must appear equally arbitrary; since there are always many other effects, which, to reason, must seem fully as consistent and natural. In vain, therefore, should we pretend to determine any single event, or infer any cause or effect, without the assistance of observation and experience.

Hence we may discover the reason why no philosopher, who is rational and modest, has ever pretended to assign the ultimate cause of any natural operation, or to show distinctly the action of that power, which produces any single effect in the universe. It is confessed, that the utmost effort of human reason is to reduce the principles, productive of natural phenomena, to a great simplicity, and to resolve the many particular effects into a few general causes, by means of reasonings from analogy, experience, and observation. But as to the causes of these general causes, we should in vain attempt their discovery; nor shall we ever be able to satisfy ourselves, by any particular explication of them. These ultimate springs and principles are totally shut up from human curiosity and inquiry. Elasticity, gravity, cohesion of parts, communication of motion by impulse; these are probably the ultimate causes and principles which we ever discover in nature; and we may esteem ourselves sufficiently happy, if, by accurate inquiry and reasoning, we can trace up the particular phenomena to, or near to, these general principles. The most perfect philosophy of the natural kind only staves off our ignorance a little longer: as perhaps the most perfect philosophy of the moral or metaphysical kind serves only to discover larger portions of it. Thus the observation of human blindness and weakness is the result of all philosophy, and meets us at every turn, in spite of our endeavors to elude or avoid it.

Nor is geometry, when taken into the assistance of natural philosophy, ever able to remedy this defect, or lead us into the knowledge of ultimate causes, by all that accuracy of reasoning for which it is so justly celebrated. Every part of mixed mathematics proceeds upon the supposition that certain laws are established by nature in her operations; and abstract reasonings are employed, either to assist experience in the discovery of these laws, or to determine their influence in particular instances, where it depends upon any precise degree of distance and quantity. Thus, it is a law of motion, discovered by experience, that the moment or force of any body in motion is in the compound ratio or proportion of its solid contents and its velocity; and consequently, that a small force may remove the greatest obstacle or raise the greatest weight, if, by any contrivance or machinery, we can increase the velocity of that force, so as to make it an overmatch for its antagonist. Geometry assists us in the application of this law, by giving us the just dimensions of all the parts and figures which can enter into any species of machine; but still the discovery of the law itself is owing merely to experience, and all the abstract reasonings in the world could never lead us towards the knowledge of it. When we reason *a priori,* and consider merely any object or cause, as it appears to the mind, independent of all observation, it never could suggest to us the notion of any distinct object, such as its effect; much less, show us the inseparable and inviolable connection between them. A man must be very sagacious who could discover by reasoning that crystal is the effect of heat, and ice of cold, without being previously acquainted with the operation of these qualities.

Part II

But we have not yet attained any tolerable satisfaction with regard to the question first proposed. Each solution still gives rise to a new question as difficult as the foregoing, and leads us on to farther inquiries. When it is asked, *What is the nature of all our reasonings concerning matter of fact?* the proper answer seems to be, that they are founded on the relation of cause and effect. When again it is asked, *What is the foundation of all our reasonings and conclusions concerning that relation?* it may be replied in one word, *experience.* But if we still carry on our sifting humor, and ask,

What is the foundation of all conclusions from experience? this implies a new question, which may be of more difficult solution and explication. Philosophers, that give themselves airs of superior wisdom and sufficiency, have a hard task when they encounter persons of inquisitive dispositions, who push them from every corner to which they retreat, and who are sure at last to bring them to some dangerous dilemma. The best expedient to prevent this confusion, is to be modest in our pretensions; and even to discover the difficulty ourselves before it is objected to us. By this means, we may make a kind of merit of our very ignorance.

I shall content myself, in this section, with an easy task, and shall pretend only to give a negative answer to the question here proposed. I say then, that, even after we have experience of the operations of cause and effect, our conclusions from that experience are *not* founded on reasoning, or any process of the understanding. This answer we must endeavor both to explain and to defend.

It must certainly be allowed, that nature has kept us at a great distance from all her secrets, and has afforded us only the knowledge of a few superficial qualities of objects; while she conceals from us those powers and principles on which the influence of those objects entirely depends. Our senses inform us of the color, weight, and consistence of bread; but neither sense nor reason can ever inform us of those qualities which fit it for the nourishment and support of a human body. Sight or feeling conveys an idea of the actual motion of bodies; but as to that wonderful force of power, which would carry on a moving body for ever in a continued change of place, and which bodies never lose but by communicating it to others; of this we cannot form the most distant conception. But notwithstanding this ignorance of natural powers [6] and principles, we always presume, when we see like sensible qualities, that they have like secret powers, and expect that effects, similar to those which we have experienced, will follow from them. If a body of like color and consistence with that bread, which we have formerly eaten, be presented to us, we make no scruple of repeating the experiment, and foresee, with certainty, like nourishment and support. Now this is a process of the mind or thought, of which I would willingly know the foundation. It is allowed on all hands that there is no known connection between the sensible qualities and the secret powers; and consequently, that the mind is not led to form such a conclusion concerning their constant and regular conjunction, by anything which it knows of their nature. As to past *experience,* it can be allowed to give *direct* and *certain* information of those precise objects only, and that precise period of time, which fell under its cognizance: but why this experience should be extended to future times,

---

[6] The word, *power,* is here used in a loose and popular sense. The more accurate explication of it would give additional evidence to this argument. [D.H.]

For a more accurate explanation of the word "power," Hume refers the reader to Section 7 of the *Enquiry,* where he discusses the "idea of necessary connection." [J.A.W.]

and to other objects, which, for aught we know, may be only in appearance similar; this is the main question on which I would insist. The bread, which I formerly eat, nourished me; that is, a body of such sensible qualities was, at that time, endued with such secret powers: but does it follow, that other bread must also nourish me at another time, and that like sensible qualities must always be attended with like secret powers? The consequence seems no wise necessary. At least, it must be acknowledged that there is here a consequence drawn by the mind; that there is a certain step taken; a process of thought, and an inference, which wants to be explained. These two propositions are far from being the same, *I have found that such an object has always been attended with such an effect,* and *I foresee, that other objects, which are, in appearance, similar, will be attended with similar effects.* I shall allow, if you please, that the one proposition may justly be inferred from the other; I know, in fact, that it always is inferred. But if you insist that the inference is made by a chain of reasoning, I desire you to produce that reasoning. The connection between these propositions is not intuitive. There is required a medium, which may enable the mind to draw such an inference, if indeed it be drawn by reasoning and argument. What that medium is, I must confess, passes my comprehension; and it is incumbent on those to produce it, who assert that it really exists, and is the origin of all our conclusions concerning matter of fact.

This negative argument must certainly, in process of time, become altogether convincing, if many penetrating and able philosophers shall turn their inquiries this way and no one be ever able to discover any connecting proposition or intermediate step, which supports the understanding in this conclusion. But as the question is yet new, every reader may not trust so far to his own penetration, as to conclude, because an argument escapes his inquiry, that therefore it does not really exist. For this reason it may be requisite to venture upon a more difficult task; and enumerating all the branches of human knowledge, endeavor to show that none of them can afford such an argument.

All reasonings may be divided into two kinds, namely demonstrative reasoning, or that concerning relations of ideas, and moral reasoning, or that concerning relations of ideas, and moral reasoning, or that concerning matter of fact and existence. That there are no demonstrative arguments in the case seems evident; since it implies no contradiction that the course of nature may change, and that an object, seemingly like those which we have experienced, may be attended with different or contrary effects. May I not clearly and distinctly conceive that a body, falling from the clouds, and which, in all other respects, resembles snow, has yet the taste of salt or feeling of fire? Is there any more intelligible proposition than to affirm, that all the trees will flourish in December and January, and decay in May and June? Now whatever is intelligible, and can be distinctly conceived, implies no contradiction, and can never be proved false by any demonstrative argument or abstract reasoning *a priori.*

If we be, therefore, engaged by arguments to put trust in past experience, and make it the standard of our future judgment, these arguments must be probable only, or such as regard matter of fact and real existence, according to the division above mentioned. But that there is no argument of this kind, must appear, if our explication of that species of reasoning be admitted as solid and satisfactory. We have said that all arguments concerning existence are founded on the relation of cause and effect; that our knowledge of that relation is derived entirely from experience; and that all our experimental conclusions proceed upon the supposition that the future will be conformable to the past. To endeavor, therefore, the proof of this last supposition by probable arguments, or arguments regarding existence, must be evidently going in a circle, and taking that for granted, which is the very point in question.

In reality, all arguments from experience are founded on the similarity which we discover among natural objects, and by which we are induced to expect effects similar to those which we have found to follow from such objects. And though none but a fool or madman will ever pretend to dispute the authority of experience, or to reject that great guide of human life, it may surely be allowed a philosopher to have so much curiosity at least as to examine the principle of human nature, which gives this mighty authority to experience, and makes us draw advantage from that similarity which nature has placed among different objects. From causes which appear *similar* we expect similar effects. This is the sum of all our experimental conclusions. Now it seems evident that, if this conclusion were formed by reason, it would be as perfect at first, and upon one instance, as after ever so long a course of experience. But the case is far otherwise. Nothing so like as eggs; yet no one, on account of this appearing similarity, expects the same taste and relish in all of them. It is only after a long course of uniform experiments in any kind, that we attain a firm reliance and security with regard to a particular event. Now where is that process of reasoning which, from one instance, draws a conclusion, so different from that which it infers from a hundred instances that are nowise different from that single one? This question I propose as much for the sake of information, as with an intention of raising difficulties. I cannot find, I cannot imagine any such reasoning. But I keep my mind still open to instruction, if anyone will vouchsafe to bestow it on me.

Should it be said that, from a number of uniform experiments, we *infer* a connection between the sensible qualities and the secret powers; this, I must confess, seems the same difficulty, couched in different terms. The question still recurs, on what process of argument this *inference* is founded? Where is the medium, the interposing ideas, which join propositions so very wide of each other? It is confessed that the color, consistence, and other sensible qualities of bread appear not, of themselves, to have any connection with the secret powers of nourishment and support. For otherwise we could infer these secret powers from the first appearance of these sensible qualities, without the aid of experience; contrary to the sentiment of all philosophers, and contrary to plain matter of fact. Here, then, is our natural state of ignorance with regard to the powers and influence of all objects. How is this remedied by experience? It only shows us a number of uniform effects, resulting from certain objects, and teaches us that those particular objects, at that particular time, were endowed with such powers and forces. When a new object, endowed with similar sensible qualities, is produced we expect similar powers and forces, and look for a like effect. From a body of like color and consistence with bread we expect like nourishment and support. But this surely is a step or progress of the mind, which wants to be explained. When a man says, *I have found, in all past instances, such sensible qualities conjoined with such secret powers:* And when he says, *Similar sensible qualities will always be conjoined with similar secret powers,* he is not guilty of a tautology, nor are these propositions in any respect the same. You say that the one proposition is an inference from the other. But you must confess that the inference is not intuitive; neither is it demonstrative: Of what nature is it, then? To say it is experimental, is begging the question. For all inferences from experience suppose, as their foundation, that the future will resemble the past, and that similar powers will be conjoined with similar sensible qualities. If there be any suspicion that the course of nature may change, and that the past may be no rule for the future, all experience becomes useless, and can give rise to no inference or conclusion. It is impossible, therefore, that any arguments from experience can prove this resemblance of the past to the future; since all these arguments are founded on the supposition of that resemblance. Let the course of things be allowed hitherto ever so regular; that alone, without some new argument or inference, proves not that, for the future, it will continue so. In vain do you pretend to have learned the nature of bodies from your past experience. Their secret nature, and consequently all their effects and influence, may change, without any change in their sensible qualities. This happens sometimes, and with regard to some objects: Why may it not happen always, and with regard to all objects? What logic, what process of argument secures you against this supposition? My practice, you say, refutes my doubts. But you mistake the purport of my question. As an agent, I am quite satisfied in the point; but as a philosopher, who has some share of curiosity, I will not say scepticism, I want to learn the foundation of this inference. No reading, no inquiry has yet been able to remove my difficulty, or to give me satisfaction in a matter of such importance. Can I do better than propose the difficulty to the public, even though, perhaps, I have small hopes of obtaining a solution? We shall, at least, by this means, be sensible of our ignorance, if we do not augment our knowledge.

I must confess that a man is guilty of unpardonable arrogance who concludes, because an argument has escaped his own investigation, that therefore it does not really exist. I must also confess that, though all the learned, for several ages, should have employed themselves in fruitless search upon any subject, it may still, perhaps, be rash to conclude positively that the subject must, therefore, pass all human comprehension. Even though we examine all the sources of our knowledge, and conclude them unfit for such a subject, there may still remain a suspicion, that the enumeration is not complete, or the examination not accurate. But with regard to the present subject, there are some considerations which seem to remove all this accusation of arrogance or suspicion of mistake.

It is certain that the most ignorant and stupid peasants—nay infants, nay even brute beasts—improve by experience, and learn the qualities of natural objects, by observing the effects which result from them. When a child has felt the sensation of pain from touching the flame of a candle, he will be careful not to put his hand near any candle; but will expect a similar effect from a cause which is similar in its sensible qualities and appearance. If you assert, therefore that the understanding of the child is led into this conclusion by any process of argument or ratiocination, I may justly require you to produce that argument; nor have you any pretense to refuse so equitable a demand. You cannot say that the argument is abstruse, and may possibly escape your inquiry; since you confess that it is obvious to the capacity of a mere infant. If you hesitate, therefore, a moment, or if, after reflection, you produce any intricate or profound argument, you, in a manner, give up the question, and confess that it is not reasoning which engages us to suppose the past resembling the future, and to expect similar effects from causes which are, to appearance, similar. This is the proposition which I intended to enforce in the present section. If I be right, I pretend not to have made any mighty discovery. And if I be wrong, I must acknowledge myself to be indeed a very backward scholar; since I cannot now discover an argument which, it seems, was perfectly familiar to me long before I was out of my cradle.

QUESTIONS FOR STUDY AND DISCUSSION

1. Is the universality of ideas an advantage or a disadvantage?
2. Explain what Hume understands by association of ideas?
3. Is there any relation between Hume's theory concerning the origin of ideas and the distinction between "relations of ideas" and "matters of fact"?
4. Explain Hume's ideas about causality.
5. What is the role of experience in the knowledge of the world?
6. What is real knowledge for Hume and what is not?

Bertrand Russell

BERTRAND RUSSELL, the most celebrated and controversial of contemporary British philosophers, was born in 1872 of aristocratic parents. He was educated at Trinity College, Cambridge, and lectured there from 1910 to 1916. During World War I he was imprisoned for his pacifist activities, and since then his espousal of unpopular causes has frequently brought him into conflict with the authorities. In 1931 he succeeded to the peerage on the death of is brother, becoming the Third Earl of Russell. A prolific writer, he was awarded the Nobel prize for literature in 1950. His most important work is the *Principia Mathematica* (3 vols., 1910–13), which he wrote with Alfred North Whitehead. Other works include *Some Problems of Philosophy* (1912), *Our Knowledge of the External World* (1914), *The Analysis of Mind* (1921), *The Analysis of Matter* (1927), *An Inquiry into Meaning and Truth* (1940), and *Human Knowledge* (1948).

Logical Atomism

The philosophy which I advocate is generally regarded as a species of realism, and accused of inconsistency because of the elements in it which seem contrary to that doctrine. For my part, I do not regard the issue between realists and their opponents as a fundamental one; I could alter my view on this issue without changing my mind as to any of the doctrines upon which I wish to lay stress. I hold that logic is what is fundamental in philosophy, and that schools should be characterized rather by their logic than by their metaphysic. My own logic is atomic, and it is this aspect upon which I should wish to lay stess. Therefore I prefer to describe my philosophy as "logical atomism," rather than as "realism," whether with or without some prefixed adjective.

A few words as to historical development may be useful by way of preface. I came to philosophy through mathematics, or rather through the wish to find some reason to believe in the truth of mathematics. From early youth, I had an ardent desire to believe that there can be such a thing as knowledge, combined with a great difficulty in accepting much that passes

From pp. 323–43 of Bertrand Russell, *Logic and Knowledge, Essays 1901-1950,* edited by Robert Charles Marsh. © 1956 by George Allen and Unwin Ltd., London. Reprinted by permission of the publisher.

as knowledge. It seemed clear that the best chance of finding indubitable truth would be in pure mathematics, yet some of Euclid's axioms were obviously doubtful, and the infinitesimal calculus, as I was taught it, was a mass of sophisms, which I could not bring myself to regard as anything else. I saw no reason to doubt the truth of arithmetic, but I did not then know that arithmetic can be made to embrace all traditional pure mathematics. At the age of eighteen I read Mill's *Logic,* but was profoundly dissatisfied with his reasons for accepting arithmetic and geometry. I had not read Hume, but it seemed to me that pure empiricism (which I was disposed to accept) must lead to scepticism rather than to Mill's support of received scientific doctrines. At Cambridge I read Kant and Hegel, as well as Mr. Bradley's *Logic,* which influenced me profoundly. For some years I was a disciple of Mr. Bradley, but about 1898 I changed my views, largely as a result of arguments with G. E. Moore. I could no longer believe that knowing makes any difference to what is known. Also I found myself driven to pluralism. Analysis of mathematical propositions persuaded me that they could not be explained as even partial truths unless one admitted pluralism and the reality of relations. An accident led me at this time to study Leibniz, and I came to the conclusion (subsequently confirmed by Couturat's masterly researches) that many of his most characteristic opinions were due to the purely logical doctrine that every proposition has a subject and a predicate. This doctrine is one which Leibniz shares with Spinoza, Hegel, and Mr. Bradley; it seemed to me that, if it is rejected, the whole foundation for the metaphysics of all these philosophers is shattered. I therefore returned to the problem which had originally led me to philosophy, namely, the foundations of mathematics, applying to it a new logic derived largely from Peano and Frege, which proved (at least, so I believe) far more fruitful than that of traditional philosophy.

In the first place, I found that many of the stock philosophical arguments about mathematics (derived in the main from Kant) had been rendered invalid by the progress of mathematics in the meanwhile. Non-Euclidean geometry had undermined the argument of the transcendental aesthetic. Weierstrass had shown that the differential and integral calculus do not require the conception of the infinitesimal, and that, therefore, all that had been said by philosophers on such subjects as the continuity of space and time and motion must be regarded as sheer error. Cantor freed the conception of infinite number from contradiction, and thus disposed of Kant's antinomies as well as many of Hegel's. Finally Frege showed in detail how arithmetic can be deduced from pure logic, without the need of any fresh ideas or axioms, thus disproving Kant's assertion that "$7 + 5 = 12$" is synthetic at least in the obvious interpretation of that dictum. As all these results were obtained, not by any heroic method, but by patient detailed reasoning, I began to think it probable that philosophy had erred in adopting heroic remedies for intellectual difficulties, and that solutions were to be found merely by greater care and accuracy. This view I have come to hold more and more strongly as time went on, and it has led me to doubt whether philosophy, as a study distinct from science and possessed of a method of its own, is anything more than an unfortunate legacy from theology.

Frege's work was not final, in the first place because it applied only to arithmetic, not to other branches of mathematics; in the second place because his premises did not exclude certain contradictions to which all past systems of formal logic turned out to be liable. Dr. Whitehead and I in collaboration tried to remedy these two defects, in *Principia Mathematica,* which, however, still falls short of finality in some fundamental points (notably the axiom of reducibility). But in spite of its shortcomings I think that no one who reads this book will dispute its main contention, namely, that from certain ideas and axioms of formal logic, by the help of the logic of relations, all pure mathematics can be deduced, without any new undefined idea or unproved propositions. The technical methods of mathematical logic, as developed in this book, seem to me very powerful, and capable of providing a new instrument for the discussion of many problems that have hitherto remained subject to philosophic vagueness. Dr. Whitehead's *Concept of Nature* and *Principles of Natural Knowledge* may serve as an illustration of what I mean.

When pure mathematics is organized as a deductive system—i.e. as the set of all those propositions that can be deduced from an assigned set of premises—it becomes obvious that, if we are to believe in the truth of pure mathematics, it cannot be solely because we believe in the truth of the set of premises. Some of the premises are much less obvious than some of their consequences, and are believed chiefly because of their consequences. This will be found to be always the case when a science is arranged as a deductive system. It is not the logically simplest propositions of the system that are the most obvious, or that provide the chief part of our reasons for believing in the system. With the empirical sciences this is evident. Electrodynamics, for example, can be concentrated into Maxwell's equations, but these equations are believed because of the observed truth of certain of their logical consequences. Exactly the same thing happens in the pure realm of logic; the logically first principles of logic—at least some of them—are to be believed, not on their own account, but on account of their consequences. The epistemological question: "Why should I believe this set of propositions?" is quite different from the logical question: "What is the smallest and logically simplest group of propositions from which this set of propositions can be deduced?" Our reasons for believing logic and pure mathematics are, in part, only inductive and probable, in spite of the fact that, in their *logical* order, the propositions of logic and pure mathematics follow from the premises of logic by pure deduction. I think this point important, since errors are liable to arise from assimilating the logical to the epistemological order, and also, conversely, from assimilating the epistemological to the logical order. The only way in which work on mathematical logic throws light on the truth or falsehood of mathematics is by disproving the supposed antinomies. This shows that mathematics *may* be true. But to show that mathematics *is* true would require other methods and other considerations.

One very important heuristic maxim which Dr. Whitehead and I found, by experience, to be applicable in mathematical logic, and have since applied in various other fields, is a form of Ockham's razor. When some set of supposed entities has neat logical properties, it turns out, in a great many instances, that the supposed entities can be replaced by purely logical structures composed of entities which have not such neat properties. In that case, in interpreting a body of propositions hitherto believed to be about the supposed entities, we can substitute the logical structures without altering any of the detail of the body of propositions in question. This is an economy, because entities with neat logical properties are always inferred, and if the propositions in which they occur can be interpreted without making this inference, the ground for the inference fails, and our body of propositions is secured against the need of a doubtful step. The principle may be stated in the form: "Wherever possible, substitute constructions out of known entities for inferences to unknown entities."

The uses of this principle are very various, but are not intelligible in detail to those who do not know mathematical logic. The first instance I came across was what I have called "the principle of abstraction," or "the principle which dispenses with abstraction." This principle is applicable in the case of any symmetrical and transitive relation, such as equality. We are apt to infer that such relations arise from possession of some common quality. This may or may not be true; probably it is true in some cases and not in others. But all the formal purposes of a common quality can be served by membership of the group of terms having the said relation to a given term. Take magnitude, for example. Let us suppose that we have a group of rods, all equally long. It is easy to suppose that there is a certain quality, called their length, which they all share. But all propositions in which this supposed quality occurs will retain their truth-value unchanged if, instead of "length of the rod x" we take "membership of the group of all those rods which are as long as x". In various special cases—e.g. the definition of real numbers—a simpler construction is possible.

A very important example of the principle is Frege's definition of the cardinal number of a given set of terms as the class of all sets that are "similar" to the given set—where two sets are "similar" when there is a one-one relation whose domain is the one set and whose converse domain is the other. Thus a cardinal number is the class of all those classes which are similar to a given class. This definition leaves unchanged the truth-values of all propositions in which cardinal numbers occur, and avoids the inference to a set of entities called "cardinal numbers," which were never needed except for the purpose of making arithmetic intelligible, and are now no longer needed for that purpose.

Perhaps even more important is the fact that classes themselves can be dispensed with by similar methods. Mathematics is full of propositions which seem to require that a class or an aggregate should be in some sense a single entity—e.g. the proposition "the number of combinations of n things any number at a time is 2^n." Since 2^n is always greater than n, this proposition leads to difficulties if classes are admitted because the number of classes of entities in the universe is greater than the number of entities in the universe, which would be odd if classes were some among entities. Fortunately, all the propositions in which classes appear to be mentioned can be interpreted without supposing that there are classes. This is perhaps the most important of all the applications of our principle. (See *Principia Mathematica, *20.*)

Another important example concerns what I call "definite descriptions," i.e. such phrases as "the even prime," "the present King of England," "the present King of France." There has always been a difficulty in interpreting such propositions as "the present King of France does not exist." The difficulty arose through supposing that "the present King of France" is the subject of this proposition, which made it necessary to suppose that he subsists although he does not exist. But it is difficult to attribute even subsistence to "the round square" or "the even prime greater than 2." In fact, "the round square does not subsist" is just as true as "the present King of France does not exist." Thus the distinction between existence and subsistence does not help us. The fact is that, when the words "the so-and-so" occur in a proposition, there is no corresponding single constituent of the proposition, and when the proposition is fully analysed the words "the so-and-so" have disappeared. An important consequence of the theory of descriptions is that it is meaningless to say "A exists" unless "A" is (or stands for) a phrase of the form "the so-and-so." If the so-and-so exists, and x is the so-and-so, to say "x exists" is nonsense. Existence, in the sense in which it is ascribed to single entities, is thus removed altogether from the list of fundamentals. The ontological argument and most of its refutations are found to depend upon bad grammar. (See *Principia Mathematica, *14.*)

There are many other examples of the substitution of constructions for inferences in pure mathematics, for example, series, ordinal numbers, and real numbers. But I will pass on to the examples in physics.

Points and instants are obvious examples: Dr. Whitehead has shown how to construct them out of sets of events all of which have a finite extent and a finite duration. In relativity theory, it is not points or instants that we primarily need, but event-particles, which correspond to what, in older language, might be described as a point at an instant, or an instantaneous point. (In former days, a point of space endured throughout all time, and an instant of time pervaded all space. Now the unit that mathematical physics wants has neither spatial nor temporal extension.) Event-particles are constructed by just the same logical process by which points and instants were constructed. In such constructions, however, we are on a different plane from that of constructions in pure mathematics. The possibility of constructing an event-particle depends upon the existence of sets of events with certain properties; whether the required events exist can only be known empirically, if at all. There is therefore no *a priori* reason to expect continuity (in the mathematical sense), or to feel confident that event-particles can be constructed. If the quantum theory should seem to demand a discrete space-time, our logic is just as ready to meet its requirements as to meet those of traditional physics, which demands continuity. The question is purely empirical, and our logic is (as it ought to be) equally adapted to either alternative.

Similar considerations apply to a particle of matter, or to a piece of matter of finite size. Matter, traditionally, has two of those "neat" properties which are the mark of a logical construction; first, that two pieces of matter cannot be at the same place at the same time; secondly, that one piece of matter cannot be in two places at the same time. Experience in the substitution of constructions for inferences makes one suspicious of anything so tidy and exact. One cannot help feeling that impenetrability is not an empirical fact, derived from observation of billiard-balls, but is something logically necessary. This feeling is wholly justified, but it could not be so if matter were not a logical construction. An immense number of occurrences coexist in any little region of space-time; when we are speaking of what is not logical construction, we find no such property as impenetrability, but, on the contrary, endless overlapping of the events in a part of space-time, however small. The reason that matter is impenetrable is because our definitions make it so. Speaking roughly, and merely so as to give a notion of how this happens, we may say that a piece of matter is all that happens in a certain track in space-time, and that we construct the tracks called bits of matter in such a way that they do not intersect. Matter is impenetrable because it is easier to state the laws of physics if we make our constructions so as to secure impenetrability. Impenetrability is a logically necessary result of definition, though the fact that such a definition is convenient is empirical. Bits of matter are not among the bricks out of which the world is built. The bricks are events, and bits of matter are portions of the structure to which we find it convenient to give separate attention.

In the philosophy of mental occurrences there are also opportunities for the application of our principle of constructions *versus* inferences. The subject, and the relation of a cognition to what is known, both have that schematic quality that arouses our suspicions. It is clear that the subject, if it is to be preserved at all, must be preserved as a construction, not as an inferred entity; the only question is whether the subject is sufficiently useful to be worth constructing. The relation of a cognition to what is known, again, cannot be a straightforward single ultimate, as I at one time believed it to be. Although I do not agree with pragmatism, I think William James was right in drawing attention to the complexity of "knowing." It is impossible in a general summary, such as the present, to set out the reasons for this view. But whoever has acquiesced in our principle will agree that here is prima facie a case for applying it. Most of my *Analysis of Mind* consists of applications of this principle. But as psychology is scientifically much less perfected than physics, the opportunities for applying the principle are not so good. The principle depends, for its use, upon the existence of some fairly reliable body of propositions, which are to be interpreted by the logician in such a way as to preserve their truth while minimizing the element of inference to unobserved entities. The principle therefore presupposes a moderately advanced science, in the absence of which the logician does not know what he ought to construct. Until recently, it would have seemed necessary to construct geometrical points; now it is event-particles that are wanted. In view of such a change in an advanced subject like physics, it is clear that constructions in psychology must be purely provisional.

I have been speaking hitherto of what it is *not* necessary to assume as part of the ultimate constituents of the world. But logical constructions, like all other constructions, require materials, and it is time to turn to the positive question, as to what these materials are to be. This question, however, requires as a preliminary a discussion of logic and language and their relation to what they try to represent.

The influence of language on philosophy has, I believe, been profound and almost unrecognized. If we are not to be misled by this influence, it is necessary to become conscious of it, and to ask ourselves deliberately how far it is legitimate. The subject-predicate logic, with the substance-attribute metaphysic, are a case in point. It is doubtful whether either would have been invented by people speaking a non-Aryan language; certainly they do not seem to have arisen in China, except in connexion with Buddhism, which brought Indian philosophy with it. Again, it is natural, to take a different kind of instance, to suppose that a proper name which can be used significantly stands for a single entity; we suppose that there is a certain more or less persistent being called "Socrates," because the same name is applied to a series of occurrences which we are led to regard as appearances of this one being. As language grows more abstract, a new set of entities come into philosophy, namely, those represented by abstract words —the universals. I do not wish to maintain that there are no universals, but certainly there are many abstract words which do not stand for single universals—e.g. triangularity and rationality. In these respects language misleads us both by its vocabulary and by its syntax. We must be on our guard in both respects if our logic is not to lead to a false metaphysic.

Syntax and vocabulary have had different kinds of effects on philosophy. Vocabulary has most influence on common sense. It might be urged, conversely, that common sense produces our vocabulary. This is only partially true. A word is applied at first to things which are more or less similar, without any reflection as to whether they have any point of identity. But when once usage has fixed the objects to which the word is to be applied, common sense is influenced by the existence of the word, and tends to suppose that one word must stand for one object, which will be a universal in the case of an adjective or an abstract word. Thus the influence of vocabulary is towards a kind of platonic pluralism of things and ideas.

The influence of syntax, in the case of the Indo-European languages, is quite different. Almost any proposition can be put into a form in which it has a subject and a predicate, united by a copula. It is natural to infer that every fact has a corresponding form, and consists in the possession of a quality by a substance. This leads, of course, to monism, since the fact that there were several substances (if it were a fact) would not have the requisite form. Philosophers, as a rule, believe themselves free from this sort of influence of linguistic forms, but most of them seem to me to be mistaken in this belief. In thinking about abstract matters, the fact that the words for abstractions are no more abstract than ordinary words always makes it easier to think about the words than about what they stand for, and it is almost impossible to resist consistently the temptation to think about the words.

Those who do not succumb to the subject-predicate logic are apt to get only one step further, and admit relations of two terms, such as before-and-after, greater-and-less, right-and-left. Language lends itself to this extension of the subject-predicate logic, since we say "*A* precedes *B*," "*A* exceeds *B*," and so on. It is easy to prove that the fact expressed by a proposition of this sort cannot consist of the possession of a quality by a substance, or of the possession of two or more qualities by two or more substances. (See *Principia Mathematica,* § 214.) The extension of the subject-predicate logic is therefore right so far as it goes, but obviously a further extension can be proved necessary by exactly similar arguments. How far it is necessary to go up the series of three-term, four-term, five-term . . . relations I do not know. But it is certainly necessary to go beyond two-term relations. In projective geometry, for example, the order of points on a line or of planes through a line requires a four-term relation.

A very unfortunate effect of the peculiarities of language is in connexion with adjectives and relations. All words are of the same logical type; a word is a class of series, of noises or shapes according as it is heard or read. But the meanings of words are of various different types; an attribute (expressed by an adjective) is of a different type from the objects to which it can be (whether truly or falsely) attributed; a relation (expressed perhaps by a preposition, perhaps by a transitive verb, perhaps in some other way) is of a different type from the terms between which it holds or does not hold. The definition of a logical type is as follows: *A* and *B* are of the same logical type if, and only if, given any fact of which *A* is a constituent, there is a corresponding fact which has *B* as a constituent, which either results by substituting *B* for *A,* or is the negation of what so results. To take an illustration, Socrates and Aristotle are of the same type, because "Socrates was a philosopher" and "Aristotle was a philosopher" are both acts; Socrates and Caligula are of the same type, because "Socrates was a philosopher" and "Caligula was not a philosopher" are both facts. To love and to kill are of the same type, because "Plato loved Socrates" and "Plato did not kill Socrates" are both facts. It follows formally from the definition that, when two words have meanings of different types, the relations of the words to what they mean are of different types; that is to say, there is not one relation of meaning between words and what they stand for, but as many relations of meaning, each of a different logical type, as there are logical types among the objects for which there are words. This fact is a very potent source of error and confusion in philosophy. In particular, it has made it extraordinarily difficult to express in words any theory of relations which is logically capable of being true, because language cannot preserve the difference of type between a relation and its terms. Most of the arguments for and against the reality of relations have been vitiated through this source of confusion.

At this point, I propose to digress for a moment, and to say, as shortly as I can, what I believe about relations. My own views on the subject of relations in the past were less clear than I thought them, but were by no means the views which my critics supposed them to be. Owing to lack of clearness in my own thoughts, I was unable to convey my meaning. The subject of relations is difficult, and I am far from claiming to be now clear about it. But I think certain points are clear to me. At the time when I wrote *The Principles of Mathematics,* I had not yet seen the necessity of logical types. The doctrine of types profoundly affects logic, and I think shows what, exactly, is the valid element in the arguments of those who oppose "external" relations. But so far from strengthening their main position, the doctrine of types leads, on the contrary, to a more complete and radical atomism than any that I conceived to be possible twenty years ago. The question of relations is one of the most important that arise in philosophy, as most other issues turn on it: monism and pluralism; the question whether anything is wholly true except the whole of truth, or wholly real except the whole of reality; idealism and realism, in some of their forms; perhaps the very existence of philosophy as a subject distinct from science and possessing a method of its own. It will serve to make my meaning clear if I take a passage in Mr. Bradley's *Essays on Truth and Reality,* not for controversial purposes, but because it raises exactly the issues that ought to be raised. But first of all I will try to state my own view, without argument.[1]

Certain contradictions—of which the simplest and oldest is the one about Epimenides the Cretan, who said that all Cretans were liars, which may be reduced to the man who says "I am lying"—convinced me, after five years devoted mainly to this one question, that no solution is technically possible without the doctrine of types. In its technical form, this doc-

---

[1] I am much indebted to my friend Wittgenstein in this matter. See his *Tractatus Logico-Philosophicus,* Kegan Paul, 1922. I do not accept all his doctrines, but my debt to him will be obvious to those who read his book. [B.R.]

trine states merely that a word or symbol may form part of a significant proposition, and in this sense have meaning, without being always able to be substituted for another word or symbol in the same or some other proposition without producing nonsense. Stated in this way, the doctrine may seem like a truism. "Brutus killed Caesar" is significant, but "Killed killed Caesar" is nonsense, so that we cannot replace "Brutus" by "killed," although both words have meaning. This is plain common sense, but unfortunately almost all philosophy consists in an attempt to forget it. The following words, for example, by their very nature, sin against it: attribute, relation, complex, fact, truth, falsehood, not, liar, omniscience. To give a meaning to these words, we have to make a detour by way of words or symbols and the different ways in which they may mean; and even then, we usually arrive, not at one meaning, but at an infinite series of different meanings. Words, as we saw, are all of the same logical type; therefore when the meanings of two words are of different types, the relations of the two words to what they stand for are also of different types. Attribute-words and relation-words are of the same type, therefore we can say significantly "attribute-words and relation-words have different uses." But we cannot say significantly "attributes are not relations." By our definition of types, since relations are relations, the form of words "attributes are relations" must be not false, but meaningless, and the form of words "attributes are not relations," similarly, must be not true, but meaningless. Nevertheless, the statement "attribute-words are not relation-words" is significant and true.

We can now tackle the question of internal and external relations, remembering that the usual formulations, on both sides, are inconsistent with the doctrine of types. I will begin with attempts to state the doctrine of external relations. It is useless to say "terms are independent of their relations," because "independent" is a word which means nothing. Two events may be said to be causally independent when no causal chain leads from one to the other; this happens, in the special theory of relativity, when the separation between the events is space-like. Obviously this sense of "independent" is irrelevant. If, when we say "terms are independent of their relations," we mean "two terms which have a given relation would be the same if they did not have it," that is obviously false; for, being what they are, they have the relation, and therefore whatever does not have the relation is different. If we mean—as opponents of external relations suppose us to mean—that the relation is a third term which comes between the other two terms and is somehow hooked on to them, that is obviously absurd, for in that case the relation has ceased to be a relation, and all that is truly relational is the hooking of the relation to the terms. The conception of the relation as a third term between the other two sins against the doctrine of types, and must be avoided with the utmost care.

What, then, can we mean by the doctrine of external relations? Primarily this, that a relational proposition is not, in general, logically equivalent formally to one or more subject-predicate propositions. Stated more precisely: Given a relational propositional function "xRy," it is not in general the case that we can find predicates a, β, γ, such that, for all values of x and y, xRy is equivalent to xa, $y\beta$, $(x,y)\gamma$ (where (x,y) stands for the whole consisting of x and y), or to any one or two of these. This, and this only, is what I mean to affirm when I assert the doctrine of external relations; and this, clearly, is at least part of what Mr. Bradley denies when he asserts the doctrine of internal relations.

In place of "unities" or "complexes," I prefer to speak of "facts." It must be understood that the word "fact" cannot occur significantly in any position in a sentence where the word "simple" can occur significantly, nor can a fact occur where a simple can occur. We must not say "facts are not simples." We can say, "The symbol for a fact must not replace the symbol for a simple or vice versa, if significance is to be preserved." But it should be observed that, in this sentence, the word "for" has different meanings on the two occasions of its use. If we are to have a language which is to safeguard us from errors as to types, the symbol for a fact must be a proposition, not a single word or letter. Facts can be asserted or denied, but cannot be named. (When I say "facts cannot be named," this is, strictly speaking, nonsense. What can be said without falling into nonsense is: "The symbol for a fact is not a name.") This illustrates how meaning is a different relation for different types. The way to mean a fact is to assert it; the way to mean a simple is to name it. Obviously naming is different from asserting, and similar differences exist where more advanced types are concerned, though language has no means of expressing the differences.

There are many other matters in Mr. Bradley's examination of my views which call for reply. But as my present purpose is explanatory rather than controversial, I will pass them by, having, I hope, already said enough on the question of relations and complexes to make it clear what is the theory that I advocate. I will only add, as regards the doctrine of types, that most philosophers assume it now and then, and few would deny it, but that all (so far as I know) avoid formulating it precisely or drawing from it those deductions that are inconvenient for their systems.

I come now to some of Mr. Bradley's criticisms (*loc. cit.*, p. 280 ff.). He says:

"Mr. Russell's main position has remained to myself incomprehensible. On the one side I am led to think that he defends a strict pluralism, for which nothing is admissible beyond simple terms and external relations. On the other side Mr. Russell seems to assert emphatically, and to use throughout, ideas which such a pluralism surely must repudiate. He throughout stands upon unities which are complex and which cannot be analysed into terms and relations. These two positions to my mind are irreconcilable, since the second, as I understand it, contradicts the first flatly."

With regard to external relations, my view is the one I have just stated, not the one commonly imputed by those who disagree. But with regard to unities, the question is more difficult. The topic is one with which language, by its very nature, is peculiarly unfitted to deal. I must beg the reader, therefore, to be indulgent if what I say is not exactly what I mean, and to try to see what I mean in spite of unavoidable linguistic obstacles to clear expression.

To begin with, I do not believe that there are complexes or unities in the same sense in which there are simples. I did believe this when I wrote *The Principles of Mathematics,* but, on account of the doctrine of types, I have since abandoned this view. To speak loosely, I regard simples and complexes as always of different types. That is to say, the statements "There are simples" and "There are complexes" use the words "there are" in different senses. But if I use the words "there are" in the sense which they have in the statement "there are simples," then the form of words "there are not complexes" is neither true nor false, but meaningless. This shows how difficult it is to say clearly, in ordinary language, what I want to say about complexes. In the language of mathematical logic it is much easier to say what I want to say, but much harder to induce people to understand what I mean when I say it.

When I speak of "simples" I ought to explain that I am speaking of something not experienced as such, but known only inferentially as the limit of analysis. It is quite possible that, by greater logical skill, the need for assuming them could be avoided. A logical language will not lead to error if its simple symbols (i.e. those not having any parts that are symbols, or any significant structure) all stand for objects of some one type, even if these objects are not simple. The only drawback to such a language is that it is incapable of dealing with anything simpler than the objects which it represents by simple symbols. But I confess it seems obvious to me (as it did to Leibniz) that what is complex must be composed of simples, though the number of constituents may be infinite. It is also obvious that the logical uses of the old notion of substance (i.e. those uses which do not imply temporal duration) can only be applied, if at all, to simples; objects of other types do not have that kind of being which one associates with substances. The essence of a substance, from the symbolic point of view, is that it can only be named—in old-fashioned language, it never occurs in a proposition except as the subject or as one of the terms of a relation. If what we take to be simple is really complex, we may get into trouble by naming it, when what we ought to do is to assert it. For example, if Plato loves Socrates, there is not an entity "Plato's love for Socrates," but only the fact that Plato loves Socrates. And in speaking of this as "a fact," we are already making it more substantial and more of a unity than we have any right to do.

Attributes and relations, though they may be not susceptible of analysis, differ from substances by the fact that they suggest a structure, and that there can be no significant symbol which symbolizes them in isolation. All propositions in which an attribute or a relation *seems* to be the subject are only significant if they can be brought into a form in which the attribute is attributed or the relation relates. If this were not the case, there would be significant propositions in which an attribute or a relation would occupy a position appropriate to a substance, which would be contrary to the doctrine of types, and would produce contradictions. Thus the proper symbol for "yellow" (assuming for the sake of illustration that this is an attribute) is not the single word "yellow," but the propositional function "x is yellow," where the structure of the symbol shows the position which the word "yellow" must have if it is to be significant. Similarly the relation "precedes" must not be represented by this one word, but by the symbol "x precedes y," showing the way in which the symbol can occur significantly. (It is here assumed that values are not assigned to x and y when we are speaking of the attribute or relation itself.)

The symbol for the simplest possible kind of fact will still be of the form "x is yellow" or "x precedes y," only that "x" and "y" will be no longer undetermined variables, but names.

In addition to the fact that we do not experience simples as such, there is another obstacle to the actual creation of a correct logical language such as I have been trying to describe. This obstacle is vagueness. All our words are more or less infected with vagueness, by which I mean that it is not always clear whether they apply to a given object or not. It is of the nature of words to be more or less general, and not to apply only to a single particular, but that would not make them vague if the particulars to which they applied were a definite set. But this is never the case in practice. The defect, however, is one which it is easy to imagine removed, however difficult it may be to remove it in fact.

The purpose of the foregoing discussion of an ideal logical language (which would of course be wholly useless for daily life) is twofold: first, to prevent inferences from the nature of language to the nature of the world, which are fallacious because they depend upon the logical defects of language; secondly, to suggest, by inquiring what logic requires of a language which is to avoid contradiction, what sort of a structure we may reasonably suppose the world to have. If I am right, there is nothing in logic that can help us to decide between monism and pluralism, or between the view that there are ultimate relational facts and the view that there are none. My own decision in favour of pluralism and relations is taken on empirical grounds, after convincing myself that the *a priori* arguments to the contrary are invalid. But I do not think these arguments can be adequately refuted without a thorough treatment of logical types, of which the above is a mere sketch.

This brings me, however, to a question of method which I believe to be very important. What are we to take as data in philosophy? What shall we regard as having the greatest likelihood of being true, and what as proper to be rejected if it conflicts with other evidence? It seems to me that science has a much greater likelihood of being true in the main than any philosophy hitherto advanced (I do not, of course, except my own). In science there are many matters about which people are agreed; in philosophy there are none. Therefore, although each proposition in a science may be false, and it is practically certain that there are some that are false, yet we shall be wise to build our philosophy upon science, because the risk of error in philosophy is pretty sure to be greater than in science. If we could hope for certainty in philosophy the matter would be otherwise, but so far as I can see such a hope would be chimerical.

Of course those philosophers whose theories, *prima facie,* run counter to science always profess to be able to interpret science so that it shall remain true on its own level, with that minor degree of truth which ought to content the humble scientist. Those who maintain a position of this sort are bound—so it seems to me—to show in detail how the interpretation is to be effected. In many cases, I believe that this would be quite impossible. I do not believe, for instance, that those who disbelieve in the reality of relations (in some such sense as that explained above) can possibly interpret those numerous parts of science which employ asymmetrical relations. Even if I could see no way of answering the objections to relations raised (for example) by Mr. Bradley, I should still think it more likely than not that some answer was possible, because I should think an error in a very subtle and abstract argument more probable than so fundamental a falsehood in science. Admitting that everything we believe ourselves to know is doubtful, it seems, nevertheless, that what we believe ourselves to know in philosophy is more doubtful than the detail of science, though perhaps not more doubtful than its most sweeping generalizations.

The question of interpretation is of importance for almost every philosophy, and I am not at all inclined to deny that many scientific results require interpretation before they can be fitted into a coherent philosophy. The maxim of "constructions *versus* inferences" is itself a maxim of interpretation. But I think that any valid kind of interpretation ought to leave the detail unchanged, though it may give a new meaning to fundamental ideas. In practice, this means that *structure* must be preserved. And a test of this is that all the propositions of a science should remain, though new meanings may be found for their terms. A case in point, on a non-philosophical level, is the relation of the physical theory of light to our perceptions of colour. This provides different physical occurrences corresponding to different seen colours, and thus makes the structure of the physical spectrum the same as that of what we see when we look at a rainbow. Unless structure is preserved, we cannot validly speak of an interpretation. And structure is just what is destroyed by a monistic logic.

I do not mean, of course, to suggest that, in any region of science, the structure revealed at present by observation is exactly that which actually exists. On the contrary, it is in the highest degree probable that the actual structure is more fine-grained than the observed structure. This applies just as much to psychological as to physical material. It rests upon the fact that, where we perceive a difference (e.g. between two shades of colour), there is a difference, but where we do not perceive a difference it does not follow that there is not a difference. We have therefore a right, in all interpretation, to demand the preservation of observed differences, and the provision of room for hitherto unobserved differences, although we cannot say in advance what they will be, except when they can be inferentially connected with observed differences.

In science, structure is the main study. A large part of the importance of relativity comes from the fact that it has substituted a single four-dimensional manifold (space-time) for the two manifolds, three-dimensional space and one-dimensional time. This is a change of structure, and therefore has far-reaching consequences, but any change which does not involve a change of structure does not make much difference. The mathematical definition and study of structure (under the name of "relation-numbers") form Part IV of *Principia Mathematica*.

The business of philosophy, as I conceive it, is essentially that of logical analysis, followed by logical synthesis. Philosophy is more concerned than any special science with relations of different sciences and possible conflicts between them; in particular, it cannot acquiesce in a conflict between physics and psychology, or between psychology and logic. Philosophy should be comprehensive, and should be bold in suggesting hypotheses as to the universe which science is not yet in a position to confirm or confute. But these should always be presented *as* hypotheses, not (as is too often done) as immutable certainties like the dogmas of religion. Although, moreover, comprehensive construction is part of the business of philosophy, I do not believe it is the most important part. The most important part, to my mind, consists in criticizing and clarifying notions which are apt to be regarded as fundamental and accepted uncritically. As instances I might mention: mind, matter, consciousness, knowledge, experience, causality, will, time. I believe all these notions to be inexact and approximate, essentially infected with vagueness, incapable of forming part of any exact science. Out of the original manifold of events, logical structures can be built which will have properties sufficiently like those of the above common notions to account for their prevalence, but sufficiently unlike to allow a great deal of error to creep in through their acceptance as fundamental.

I suggest the following as an outline of a possible structure of the world; it is no more than an outline, and is not offered as more than possible.

The world consists of a number, perhaps finite, perhaps infinite, of entities which have various relations to each other, and perhaps also various qualities. Each of these entities may be called an "event"; from the point of view of old-fashioned physics, an event occupies a short finite time and a small finite amount of space, but as we are not going to have an old-fashioned space and an old-fashioned time, this statement cannot be taken at its face value. Every event has to a certain number of others a relation which may be called "compresence"; from the point of view of physics, a collection of compresent events all occupy one small region in space-time. One example of a set of compresent events is what would be called the contents of one man's mind at one time—i.e. all his sensations, images, memories, thoughts, etc., which can coexist temporally. His visual field has, in one sense, spatial extension, but this must not be confused with the extension of physical space-time; every part of his visual field is compresent with every other part, and with the rest of "the contents of his mind" at that time, and a collection of compresent events occupies a minimal region in space-time. There are such collections not only where there are brains, but everywhere. At any point in "empty space," a number of stars could be photographed if a camera were introduced; we believe that light travels over the regions intermediate between its source and our eyes, and therefore something is happening in these regions. If light from a number of different sources reaches a certain minimal region in space-time, then at least one event corresponding to each of these sources exists in this minimal region, and all these events are compresent.

We will define a set of compresent events as a "minimal region." We find that minimal regions form a four-dimensional manifold, and that, by a little logical manipulation, we can construct from them the manifold of space-time that physics requires. We find also that, from a number of different minimal regions, we can often pick out a set of events, one from each, which are closely similar when they come from neighbouring regions, and vary from one region to another according to discoverable laws. These are the laws of the propagation of light, sound, etc. We find also that certain regions in space-time have quite peculiar properties; these are the regions which are said to be occupied by "matter." Such regions can be collected, by means of the laws of physics, into tracks or tubes, very much more extended in one dimension of space-time than in the other three. Such a tube constitutes the "history" of a piece of matter; from the point of view of the piece of matter itself, the dimension in which it is most extended can be called "time," but it is only the private time of that piece of matter, because it does not correspond exactly with the dimension in which another piece of matter is most extended. Not only is space-time very peculiar within a piece of matter, but it is also rather peculiar in its neighbourhood, growing less so as the spatio-temporal distance grows greater; the law of this peculiarity is the law of gravitation.

All kinds of matter to some extent, but some kinds of matter (viz. nervous tissue) more particularly, are liable to form "habits," i.e. to alter their structure in a given environment in such a way that, when they are subsequently in a similar environment, they react in a new way, but if similar environments recur often, the reaction in the end becomes nearly uniform, while remaining different from the reaction on the first occasion.

(When I speak of the reaction of a piece of matter to its environment, I am thinking both of the constitution of the set of compresent events of which it consists, and of the nature of the track in space-time which constitutes what we should ordinarily call its motion; these are called a "reaction to the environment" in so far as there are laws correlating them with characteristics of the environment.) Out of habit, the peculiarities of what we call "mind" can be constructed; a mind is a track of sets of compresent events in a region of space-time where there is matter which is peculiarly liable to form habits. The greater the liability, the more complex and organized the mind becomes. Thus a mind and a brain are not really distinct, but when we speak of a mind we are thinking chiefly of the set of compresent events in the region concerned, and of their several relations to other events forming parts of other periods in the history of the spatio-temporal tube which we are considering, whereas when we speak of a brain we are taking the set of compresent events as a whole, and considering its external relations to other sets of compresent events, also taken as wholes; in a word, we are considering the shape of the tube, not the events of which each cross-section of it is composed.

The above summary hypothesis would, of course, need to be amplified and refined in many ways in order to fit in completely with scientific facts. It is not put forward as a finished theory, but merely as a suggestion of the kind of thing that may be true. It is of course easy to imagine other hypotheses which may be true, for example, the hypothesis that there is nothing outside the series of sets of events constituting my history. I do not believe that there is any method of arriving at one sole possible hypothesis, and therefore certainty in metaphysics seems to me unattainable. In this respect I must admit that many other philosophies have the advantage, since in spite of their differences *inter se,* each arrives at certainty of its own exclusive truth.

QUESTIONS FOR STUDY AND DISCUSSION

1. Explain the theory of descriptions.
2. What does Russell understand by the word "fact"?
3. How are the entities that form the world related to sense-data?
4. Discuss Russell's notion of "mind."
5. Would you say that Russell's metaphysical views are realistic, idealistic, nominalistic, or other?

Rudolf Carnap

RUDOLF CARNAP, born in Wuppertal, Germany, in 1891, joined the University of Vienna in 1926 where he exerted great influence in the founding and development of the Vienna Circle. He was coauthor, with Hans Hahn and Otto Neurath, of the famous *Vienna Manifesto* (1929), a section of which is included in the readings that follow. He also taught at the University of Prague before coming to the United States in 1936 to accept a position as professor of Philosophy at the University of Chicago, where he stayed until 1954. He then moved to the University of California at Los Angeles where he currently teaches. He has published widely in the fields of logic and semantics, and among his important works are "The Logical Structure of the World" (1928), *The Logical Syntax of Language* (1934), *Philosophy and Logical Syntax* (1935), *Foundations of Logic and Mathematics* (1939), and *Meaning and Necessity* (1947).

The Scientific World View

What characterizes the scientific view of the world is not so much a particular set of theses as a fundamental attitude, a point of view, a line of inquiry. The goal is a *unified science*. The effort is to unite and bring into accord the achievements of individual investigators in the various domains of science. It is the adoption of such a goal that accounts both for the stress on *collaboration* and the emphasis on that which can be understood intersubjectively. This also explains the quest for a neutral form of language—a symbolism free from the impurities that affect natural language—and for an overall system of concepts.

The scientific world view strives for clarity and exactness; it rejects the dim and the distant, the unfathomably deep. In science there are no "depths"; all is surface in the sense that all that is experienced forms a complex network—not always susceptible to being grasped as a whole, often intelligible only in detail. Everything is accessible to man, and man is the measure of all things. The kinship here is with the Sophists, not the Platonists, with the Epicureans, not the Pythagoreans, with all who

From Chs. 2, 3, and 4, of Rudolf Carnap, Hans Hahn, and Otto Neurath, *Wissenschaftliche Weltauffassung: Der Wiener Kreis* (*Vienna Manifesto*), translated especially for this volume by Albert E. Blumberg.

champion the temporal and the secular. The scientific conception of the world knows *no insoluble riddles.* The clarification of the traditional problems of philosophy results in part in their being unmasked as pseudoproblems, and in part in their being transformed into empirical problems and thus made subject to the judgment of empirical science. The philosophical enterprise consists in just this clarification of problems and propositions, not in the assertion of its own "philosophical" propositions. The method employed in clarification is that of *logical analysis,* which, as Bertrand Russell describes it,

> has gradually crept into philosophy through the critical scrutiny of mathematics. . . . It represents, I believe, the same kind of advance as was introduced into physics by Galileo: the substitution of piecemeal, detailed and verifiable results for large untested generalities recommended only by a certain appeal to the imagination.[1]

This *method of logical analysis* marks the *new* empiricism and positivism as essentially different from the earlier forms of these doctrines which were more biological and psychological in orientation. If someone asserts "There is a God" or "The Unconscious is the primitive ground of the world" or "Entelechies are the guiding principle of living beings," we do not say to him "What you say is false." Rather, we ask: "What do you mean by your statements?" It then becomes evident that a sharp dividing line exists between two kinds of statements. The first of these are the statements made in empirical science; their sense can be determined by logical analysis, or more exactly, by reducing them to the most simple assertions about the empirically given. The second, which include the examples cited above, turn out to be completely devoid of meaning if taken as the metaphysicians intend them to be taken. To be sure, such statements can often be given new interpretations that transform them into empirical statements; but then they lose that emotive content which, in general, is precisely what is essential for the metaphysician.

Metaphysicians and theologians believe, mistakenly, that their propositions say something, that they describe some state of affairs. Analysis shows, however, that these propositions do not signify anything; they are merely expressive of, say, an attitude toward life. Now giving expression to such attitudes may indeed be an important task in life; but for this the proper medium is art, for example lyric poetry or music. When, instead, attitudes are clothed in the linguistic garb of a theory, the danger arises that theoretical content will appear to be present where none in fact exists. If a metaphysician or theologian wishes to retain the usual forms of expression, then he must be clear himself and have it distinctly understood that what he is offering is not exposition but expression, not theory or informa-

---

[1] *Our Knowledge of the External World* (La Salle, Ill.: Open Court Publishing Co., 1914), p. 4. [J.A.W.]

tion but poetry or myth. When a mystic claims to have experiences that lie above or beyond all concepts, one cannot argue with him. But he cannot speak about these experiences; for to speak about something is to capture it in concepts, to reduce it to sets of facts that can be fitted into the body of science.

Accordingly, the scientific world view rejects metaphysical philosophy. But the question remains: How have the aberrant ways of metaphysics come into being? This question can be raised from different points of view —psychological, sociological, and logical. Studies of a psychological nature are still in their initial phase; a start has perhaps been made in the researches of Freudian psychoanalysis. The same situation holds for sociological investigations; here as a first step one can cite the theory of the "ideological superstructure." The field is thus still open for further profitable study.

Much more progress has been made in elucidating the *logical* origins of metaphysical aberrations, thanks especially to the work of Russell and Wittgenstein. The theories of metaphysics, indeed the very formulations of its problems, involve two basic errors. One of these is too close a tie to the form of the *natural languages,* and the other is a lack of clear understanding of the logical efficiency of thought. For instance, ordinary language uses the same verbal form, a substantive, for things ("apples"), properties ("hardness"), relations ("friendship"), and processes ("sleep"); we are thereby lured into viewing functional concepts as if they were things (hypostatization, substantialization). There are many other instances of how language misleads us, with consequences equally disastrous for philosophy.

The second fundamental error of metaphysics consists in the notion that *thought* can of itself generate new knowledge without using empirical material, or at least can derive new content from given data by means of deduction. Logical research, however, establishes that all valid reasoning or deduction consists simply in the passage from certain sentences to other sentences that contain nothing beyond what was already present in the first sentences (tautological transformation). It is therefore impossible to develop a metaphysics out of "pure thought."

Thus logical analysis renders obsolete not only classical metaphysics, in particular the systems of the scholastics and of German idealism, but also the veiled metaphysics of Kantian and modern *apriorism.* The scientific world view recognizes no unconditionally valid truths of pure reason, no "synthetic judgments a priori," such as lie at the base of the Kantian theory of knowledge and, for that matter, of all pre-Kantian and post-Kantian ontology and metaphysics. The judgments of arithmetic and geometry and certain principles of physics, which were taken by Kant as examples of a priori knowledge, will be discussed later. It is precisely the denial of the possibility of synthetic knowledge a priori that constitutes the basic thesis of modern empiricism. The scientific world view recognizes only empirical propositions about objects of various kinds, and the analytic propositions of logic and mathematics.

All supporters of a scientific conception of the world are united in rejecting metaphysics whether open or in the veiled form of apriorism. The Vienna Circle, however, goes further. It holds that even the assertions of (critical) *realism* and *idealism* about the reality or unreality of the external world and of other minds are metaphysical in character. For these assertions are subject to the very same objections raised against the assertions of the old metaphysics: they are without meaning because they are not verifiable and have no factual content. *To say that something is "real" is to say merely that it can be fitted into the total edifice of experience.*

Intuition, which is especially stressed by metaphysicians as a source of knowledge, is not altogether ruled out by the scientific world view. But every piece of intuitive knowledge must undergo a subsequent step-by-step rational vindication. All means are permitted those who search; but what they find must be able to withstand testing. What the scientific world view rejects is the notion that intuition is a more valuable, a more penetrating kind of knowledge, which goes beyond the contents of sense experience and need not be bound by the narrow fetters of conceptual thought.

We have characterized the *scientific view of the world,* essentially, by two features. First, it is both *empirical* and *positivist:* only empirical knowledge exists, and this rests on the immediately given. A boundary is thus drawn defining the content of legitimate science. Second, the scientific world view is distinguished by the use of a certain method, that of *logical* analysis. The endeavor in scientific work is to attain the goal of a unified science by applying logical analysis to the material of experience. It must be possible to specify the sense of any scientific statement by reducing that statement to one about the immediately given. Similarly, it must be possible to specify the sense of any scientific concept, no matter to which branch of science it belongs, by reducing it step by step to other concepts until we reach the concepts of the lowest level, those that refer directly to the given. Were this sort of analysis carried out for all concepts, they would then be arranged in a reduction system or "constitution system" (*Konstitutionssystem*). Studies directed toward such an end are called *"constitution (or construction) theory";* they form the framework within which the scientific world view applies logical analysis.

In conducting these studies, we very soon find that the traditional logic of Aristotle and the Scholastics is entirely inadequate. Only modern logic or "logistic" affords the rigor of statement and conceptual definition needed to formalize the intuitive reasoning of ordinary thought, that is, to reduce such reasoning to an exact form automatically controlled by signs and the rules for their use.

The inquiries undertaken by constitution theory show that concepts related to the experiences and qualities of one's own mind (*eigenpsychischer Erlebnisse und Qualitäten*) make up the lowest level of the constructed system. Next come physical objects, and from these in turn are constructed other minds and finally the objects studied by the social sciences. How the concepts of the various sciences fit into the constitution system is by now visible in broad outline; however, much remains to be done so far as the detailed execution of the program is concerned. The proof that an overall system of concepts is possible, together with the indication already offered of its form, also discloses the relationship of all assertions to the given —and thereby reveals the structural form of a *unified science.*

What enters into a scientific description is the structure or mode of arrangement of objects, not their "essence." The linguistic element that unites men consists of statements expressing structure; it is in these that the content of our common knowledge is presented. Subjectively experienced qualities, such as redness or pleasure, are strictly speaking experiences, not knowledge. There is nothing in physical optics, for example, which is not in principle intelligible even to a blind person.

PROBLEM AREAS

The Foundations of Arithmetic

The Vienna Circle, in its discussions and writings, deals with a mass of problems stemming from the different branches of science. The objective is to bring about a systematic unity in the attack upon the various groups of problems and thus to clarify their status.

The foundation problems of arithmetic have been of special historical significance for the growth of the scientific world view, since it was these problems that stimulated the unfolding of a new logic. Mathematics underwent an extraordinarily fruitful development during the eighteenth and nineteenth centuries, in the course of which attention was directed more to the wealth of new results than to the careful examination of conceptual foundations. Such an examination, however, could not long be postponed if the celebrated dependability of the mathematical structure was to be preserved. The need to scrutinize foundations assumed particular urgency with the appearance of certain contradictions—the "paradoxes of set theory." It soon became evident that what was involved were not merely difficulties in some special branch of mathematics, but *antinomies* or logical contradictions of a quite general nature, which pointed to essential defects in the foundations of the old logic.

The task of eliminating these contradictions acted as an especially strong stimulus to the further development of logic. At this point, efforts to *clarify the concept of number* merged with efforts to achieve an *internal reform of logic.* From the time of Leibniz and Lambert, the notion had persisted of mastering reality by means of an increased refinement of concepts and reasoning, and of attaining this greater refinement through a symbolism patterned after that of mathematics. After Boole, Venn, and others, it was in particular Frege (1884), Schröder (1890), and Peano

(1895) who considered the problem. On the basis of their preparatory studies, Russell and Whitehead (1910) were able to construct a system of logic in symbolic form ("logistic"), which not only avoided the contradictions of the old logic but far surpassed it in practical applicability. From this system they undertook to derive the basic concepts of arithmetic and analysis so as to furnish mathematics with a secure foundation in logic.

However, this attempt to overcome the crisis in the foundations of arithmetic (and set theory) left certain difficulties standing which to this day have not found a fully satisfactory solution. At present three opposing schools are in the field: besides the *logicism* of Russell and Whitehead, there are the *formalism* of Hilbert,[2] which regards arithmetic as a game of formulas played according to certain definite rules, and the *intuitionism* of Brouwer,[3] according to which knowledge of arithmetic rests on an irreducible, primordial intuition of "two-oneness." The Vienna Circle follows the debates among these three schools with the greatest of interest. In what direction the decision will finally lead cannot be foreseen; but whatever the outcome, it will also include a decision about the structure of logic. That is why this problem is so important for the scientific world view. Many students are of the opinion that the three schools are not as far apart as would seem. They surmise that essential features of the three will, in the course of further development, tend to converge and to be united in a definitive solution most probably utilizing the far-reaching ideas of Wittgenstein.

The conception of the tautological character of mathematics, which rests on the investigations of Russell and Wittgenstein, is also supported by the Vienna Circle. This view, it should be noted, is opposed not only to apriorism and intuitionism, but also to the older empiricism (that of John Stuart Mill, for example) which to a degree sought to derive logic and mathematics inductively.

Also connected with the problems of arithmetic and logic are studies that have been initiated concerning both the nature of the *axiomatic method* in general (such concepts as completeness, independence, and the like) and the construction of axiom systems for specific mathematical disciplines.

The Foundations of Physics

Originally, the chief concern of the Vienna Circle was with the methodological problems of empirical science. Influenced by the ideas of Mach, Poincaré,[4] and Duhem,[5] discussions centered on the problems of achiev-

---

[2] David Hilbert (1862–1943): German mathematician who developed the thesis of formalism: mathematical entities are symbols whose meanings are given by definitions. "In the beginning was the sign." [J.A.W.]

[3] Luitzen Egbert Jan Brouwer (b. 1881): Dutch mathematician who developed the thesis of intuitionism: mathematical entities are products of intuition. [J.A.W.]

[4] Henri Poincaré (1854–1912): French mathematician, physicist, and philosopher of science, who developed the thesis of conventionalism in which scientific propositions,

ing mastery over nature by means of scientific systems, in particular *systems of hypotheses and of axioms*. To begin with, an axiom system can be regarded, quite apart from any empirical application, as a system of implicit definitions: that is, as a system in which the axioms determine or in a sense define the concepts that occur in them not with respect to their content but solely with respect to their mutual relations. But such a system does not acquire meaning for reality until further definitions are added, the so-called coordinating definitions. Through these we specify just which real objects are to be regarded as the elements referred to by the axiom system. Empirical science, which aims at describing reality with the simplest and most unified network of concepts and judgments, can move forward, as history shows, in two different ways. Modifications made necessary as a result of new experiences may be effected either in the axioms or in the coordinating definitions. Here we encounter the problem of conventions, dealt with especially by Poincaré.

The methodological question of applying axiom systems to reality is in principle of importance to all branches of science. That the investigations undertaken thus far have been fruitful almost exclusively for physics is to be explained by the present stage in the historical development of science. In short, physics is far in advance of the other scientific disciplines as regards precision and refinement of concept formation.

Through epistemological analysis, the chief concepts of natural science have more and more been freed from the *metaphysical impurities* that have clung to them since the earliest times. The concepts of *space, time, substance, causality,* and *probability,* in particular, have been cleansed as a result of the work of Helmholtz,[6] Mach, Einstein, and others. The doctrines of absolute space and absolute time have been made obsolete by the theory of relativity. Space and time are no longer seen as absolute containers or receptacles, but as schemes of order of elementary processes. Material substance has been dissolved by atomic theory and field theory. Causality has been stripped of its anthropomorphic character of "influence" or "necessary connection," and has been reduced to a functional correlation or conditional relation. In addition, many laws of nature held to be deterministic have been replaced by statistical laws; indeed, quantum theory has made it increasingly doubtful whether the concept of a strictly causal law is applicable at all to phenomena in very small regions of space-time. The concept of probability has been reduced to the empirically intelligible concept of relative frequency.

---

whether laws, equations, or theories, are merely convenient conventional expressions; they do not represent objective reality. [J.A.W.]

[5] Pierre Duhem (1861–1916): French physicist, historian of science, and philosopher of science, author of the ten-volume *Système du Monde,* a history of cosmological doctrines from Plato to Copernicus. [J.A.W.]

[6] Hermann Ludwig Helmholtz (1821–94): German physiologist and physicist. [J.A.W.]

The application of the *axiomatic method* to these problems results in sorting out the empirical components of science from the purely conventional, the factual content from the definitions. No place is left for synthetic judgments a priori. Knowledge of the world is possible not because human reason imprints its form on the material of knowledge, but because the material itself is ordered in a certain way. The nature and extent of this ordering cannot be known in advance. The world might be much more or much less ordered than it is, without thereby ceasing to be knowable. Only empirical science, as it moves forward step by step, can tell us to what degree the world conforms to laws. The method of *induction*—the inference from yesterday to tomorrow, from here to there—is of course valid only if a conformity to law exists. But the method does not rest on any supposed a priori assumption of such conformity. Induction, whether satisfactorily grounded or not, may be applied wherever it leads to fruitful results; in no event does it afford certainty. But from the standpoint of epistemology, meaning may be ascribed to an inductive inference only in so far as it can be verified empirically. The scientific world view does not cast aside the result of a piece of research merely because it has been garnered by inadequate methods that lack the requisite logical clarity or empirical basis. It will, however, constantly strive for and insist on verification by means that have been fully clarified, namely, the direct or indirect reduction to what is experienced.

The Foundations of Geometry

In the last few decades, the question of *physical space* has gained a special importance among the foundations problems of physics. A century ago the work of Gauss (1816), Bolyai (1823), Lobachevsky (1835), and others led to the discovery of *non-Euclidean geometry*. The classic geometry of Euclid, which till then had reigned supreme, was shown to be but one of an infinite set of geometrical systems each enjoying the same logical justification. The question then arose: Which of these is the geometry of real space? Gauss had tried to answer this question by measuring the sum of the angles of a very large triangle. His effort marked the birth of *physical geometry* as an empirical science, a branch of physics. Later the problems in this area were carried further toward solution by Riemann (1868), Helmholtz (1868), and Poincaré (1904). In particular, Poincaré stressed the close ties between physical geometry and all the other branches of physics: the question as to the nature of real space is to be answered only in the context of an entire system of physics. Subsequently, Einstein discovered such a general system within which the question was answered; and the answer was expressed in the framework of a system of non-Euclidean geometry.

In consequence of this whole development, physical geometry came to be ever more clearly distinguished from purely *mathematical geometry*. Step by step, the latter became increasingly formalized through the further evolution of logical analysis. First, pure geometry was arithmetized, that is, interpreted as the theory of a particular number system. Then it was axiomatized, that is, presented by means of an axiom system that treated geometrical elements (points and the like) as undefined objects and specified only the mutual relations of these objects. And finally it was logicized, or exhibited as a theory of certain definite relational structures. Geometry thus became the most important sphere of application of the axiomatic method and of the general theory of relations. It thereby furnished the strongest impetus for the development of these two methods, which have since become so significant for the growth of logic itself and hence for the scientific world view in general.

Consideration of the relations between mathematical and physical geometry has led in a natural way to the problem of applying axiom systems to the real world. As indicated above, this problem plays a large role in the more general inquiries into the foundations of physics.

Foundations Problems of Biology and Psychology

Biology has long been marked out by the metaphysicians as a preferred domain. A reflection of this is the doctrine of vitalism, the belief in a special vital force. The modern advocates of this theory try to rid it of its past vague and hazy form, and give it a conceptually clear setting. The vital force is replaced by "dominants" (Reinke, 1899) or "entelechies" (Driesch, 1905). Since these concepts do not satisfy the requirement of being reducible to the given, the scientific world view rejects them as metaphysical. The same thing applies to "psycho-vitalism," which teaches that the soul intervenes, that "the mental plays a guiding role in the material." When one extracts the empirically intelligible kernel from metaphysical vitalism, one then has the thesis that organic processes take place in accordance with laws that cannot be reduced to the laws of physics. On closer analysis, this thesis is seen to be equivalent to the contention that certain domains of reality do not come under any unified, pervasive order.

It stands to reason that the scientific world view can produce clearer confirmation for its fundamental ideas in domains that have already attained conceptual precision, than in those that have not: the confirmation is clearer in physics than in psychology. The linguistic forms that we still use today in discussing mental phenomena were fashioned in ancient times on the basis of certain metaphysical conceptions of the soul. Concept formation in psychology is impeded above all by flaws in our language— metaphysical encumbrances and logical inconsistencies. In addition, there are a number of material and technical obstacles. The result is that up to now most of the concepts used in psychology have been defined in a very faulty way; in many cases it is not even determined whether the concepts are meaningful or whether they only seem to be meaningful because of linguistic usage. In this field, nearly everything remains to be done as far as epistemological analysis is concerned; and here, naturally, analysis is more difficult than in the physical domain. The behaviorist attempt to comprehend the mental as the behavior of bodies and hence at a level accessible to perception is, in its basic attitude, close to the scientific world view.

The Foundations of the Social Sciences

As we saw especially in the case of physics and mathematics, every branch of science at some time in its development comes up against the need to verify its epistemological foundations, to analyze logically its concepts. This is also true of the social sciences, above all history and political economy. A century or so ago, a process set in of eliminating metaphysical impurities in these fields. To be sure, the cleansing has not yet reached the same degree as in physics; but in the social sciences the task of purification is also perhaps less urgent. It seems that in these domains the metaphysical deposits, even in the heyday of metaphysics and theology, were not particularly heavy; this may have been because such concepts as war and peace or exports and imports are much closer to direct observation than concepts like atoms or the ether. It is not so very hard to drop such concepts as "national spirit" (*Volksgeist*) and instead to take groups of individuals of a specified sort as the object of study. Quesnay, Adam Smith, Ricardo, Comte, Marx, Menger, Walras, Müller-Lyer—to mention scholars of the most varied tendencies—have all worked in an empirical, antimetaphysical sense. The subject matter of history and political economy is constituted of people, things, and their disposition or arrangement.

RETROSPECT AND PROSPECT

It is from labors on such problems as these that the scientific world view has evolved. We have seen how physics in its endeavor to obtain tangible results—at first even with inadequate or insufficiently clarified scientific tools—found itself increasingly propelled toward methodological investigations. Thus arose the method of hypothesis construction, followed some time later by the axiomatic method and logical analysis; in this manner the formation of concepts acquired ever greater clarity and rigor.

The same methodological problems were raised, as we saw, by the development of research in the foundations of physical geometry, mathematical geometry, and arithmetic. These are the chief sources of the problems with which representatives of the scientific world view are most concerned today. As is to be expected, some of the various problem areas in the Vienna Circle still bear the marks of their origin. This often produces differences in interest and point of view, which in turn lead to differences in conception. What is distinctive, however, is that these differences are narrowed as a result of the striving for precise formulations, for the application of an exact logical language and symbolism, and for a clear distinction between the theoretical import of a proposition and the imagery associated with it. Thus step by step the stock of common views is enlarged. These form the kernel of the scientific world conception; and around this kernel are outer layers which exhibit greater subjective divergences.

As we look back, the *gist of the new scientific world view* as contrasted with traditional philosophy now becomes clear. The enterprise is not to establish "philosophical propositions" but to make propositions clear. And these propositions come from empirical science, as we have learned in connection with the various groups of problems discussed above. In order to emphasize even more strongly the contrast with systematic philosophy, many representatives of the scientific world view prefer not to apply the word "philosophy" at all to their work. But no matter how we designate such inquiries, one thing at any rate is certain: *There is no such thing as a philosophy that is a basic or universal science beside or above the various domains of empirical science itself.* There is no road to factual knowledge other than that of experience; there is no realm of ideas standing above or beyond experience. Yet the conduct of "philosophical" or "foundational" studies in the spirit of the scientific world view remains important. For the logical clarification of the concepts, propositions, and methods of science serves to free us from inhibiting prejudices. Logical and epistemological analysis is not intended to impose limits on scientific research; on the contrary, it puts at the disposal of science the most complete range of formal possibilities from which to select the one that accords with the given experience (for example, non-Euclidean geometry and relativity theory).

The advocates of the scientific world view stand firmly on the ground of simple human experience. They push ahead confidently with the task of removing the metaphysical and theological debris of the millennia—or, as some express it, of returning after a metaphysical interlude to a unified secular world picture such as, in a sense, lay at the basis of the theology-free, magical beliefs of an early epoch.

The growth of metaphysical and theological tendencies, manifest today in numerous societies and sects, books and periodicals, lectures and university courses, appears to be due to the present intense social and economic conflicts. One group of combatants, clinging to the past in social and economic affairs, also fosters the traditional attitudes of metaphysics and theology which with regard to content have long been rendered obsolete. The other group faces toward the present; it rejects these attitudes, especially in Central Europe, and takes its stand on the ground of empirical science. This development is connected with the growth of the modern production process, which is shaped more and more by machinery and technology and allows less and less room for metaphysical notions. Likewise, it reflects the disillusionment of broad masses with the actions of those who preach the received metaphysical and theological doctrines. So it is that in many countries the masses—far more consciously than ever before—reject these doctrines, and in the context of their socialist orientation tend toward a down-to-earth, empiricist view. Formerly, the term for this conception was *materialism;* in the meantime, however, modern empiricism evolved out of numerous inadequate versions, and in the *scientific world view* acquired a tenable and valid form.

The scientific world view is thus closely connected with the concerns of present-day life. It is indeed threatened with severe struggles and persecutions. Nonetheless, there are many who do not lose heart but, in the face of the present social situation, look forward to the future hopefully. Not all supporters of the scientific world view, of course, are fighters. Some of them, happy in their isolation, lead withdrawn lives on the icy peaks of logic; some perhaps even inveigh against any mingling with the masses and deplore the "oversimplification" that inevitably accompanies popularization. Yet the contributions of even these persons fit into the course of history. We see how the spirit of the scientific world view in growing measure permeates the forms of public and private life, of education, of architecture, and helps shape economic and social life according to rational principles. *The scientific world view serves life, and is being accepted by life.*

QUESTIONS FOR STUDY AND DISCUSSION

1. Describe the ideal of knowledge expounded by the *Manifesto.*
2. Why is the method of physical science considered as the most adequate for the furthering of knowledge?
3. What is the purpose of philosophy?
4. What is the purpose of the method of reduction?
5. Explain why great importance is attached to logic and to logical analysis?
6. Give the general characteristics of the philosophy of the *Manifesto.*

Language, the Key to Understanding

VERIFIABILITY

The problems of philosophy as usually dealt with are of very different kinds. From the point of view which I am here taking we may distinguish mainly three kinds of problems and doctrines in traditional philosophy. For the sake of simplicity we shall call these parts *Metaphysics, Psychology,* and *Logic.* Or, rather, there are not three distinct regions, but three sorts of

From "The Rejection of Metaphysics," in Rudolf Carnap, *Philosophy and Logical Syntax.* Copyright 1935 by Routledge and Kegan Paul, London. Reprinted by permission of Rudolf Carnap and the Orthological Institute of London.

components which in most theses and questions are combined: a metaphysical, a psychological, and a logical component.

The considerations that follow belong to the third region: we are here carrying out *Logical Analysis*. The function of logical analysis is to analyse all knowledge, all assertions of science and of everyday life, in order to make clear the sense of each such assertion and the connections between them. One of the principal tasks of the logical analysis of a given proposition is to find out the method of verification for that proposition. The question is: What reasons can there be to assert this proposition; or: How can we become certain as to its truth or falsehood? This question is called by the philosophers the epistemological question; epistemology or the philosophical theory of knowledge is nothing other than a special part of logical analysis, usually combined with some psychological questions concerning the process of knowing.

What, then, is the method of verification of a proposition? Here we have to distinguish between two kinds of verification: direct and indirect. If the question is about a proposition which asserts something about a present perception, *e.g.* "Now I see a red square on a blue ground," then the proposition can be tested directly by my present perception. If at present I do see a red square on a blue ground, the proposition is directly verified by this seeing; if I do not see that, it is disproved. To be sure, there are still some serious problems in connection with direct verification. We will however not touch on them here, but give our attention to the question of *indirect* verification, which is more important for our purposes. A proposition P which is not directly verifiable can only be verified by direct verification of propositions deduced from P together with other already verified propositions.

Let us take the proposition P_1: "This key is made of iron." There are many ways of verifying this proposition; *e.g.*: I place the key near a magnet; then I perceive that the key is attracted. Here the deduction is made in this way:

Premises: P_1: "This key is made of iron"; the proposition to be examined.

P_2: "If an iron thing is placed near a magnet, it is attracted"; this is a physical law, already verified.

P_3: "This object—a bar—is a magnet"; proposition already verified.

P_4: "The key is placed near the bar"; this is now directly verified by our observation.

From these four premises we can deduce the conclusion:

P_5: "The key will now be attracted by the bar."

This proposition is a prediction which can be examined by observation. If we look, we either observe the attraction or we do not. In the first case we have found a positive instance, an instance of verification of the proposition P_1 under consideration; in the second case we have a negative instance, an instance of disproof of P_1.

In the first case the examination of the proposition P_1 is not finished. We may repeat the examination by means of a magnet, *i.e.* we may deduce other propositions similar to P_5 by the help of the same or similar premises as before. After that, or instead of that, we may make an examination by electrical tests, or by mechanical, chemical, or optical tests, etc. If in these further investigations all instances turn out to be positive, the certainty of the proposition P_1 gradually grows. We may soon come to a degree of certainty sufficient for all practical purposes, but *absolute* certainty we can never attain. The number of instances deducible from P_1 by the help of other propositions already verified or directly verifiable is *infinite*. Therefore there is always a possibility of finding in the future a negative instance, however small its probability may be. Thus the proposition P_1 *can never be completely verified*. For this reason it is called an *hypothesis*.

So far we have considered an individual proposition concerning one single thing. If we take a general proposition concerning all things or events at whatever time and place, a so-called natural *law,* it is still clearer that the number of examinable instances is infinite and so the proposition is an hypothesis.

Every assertion P in the wide field of science has this character, that it either asserts something about present perceptions or other experiences, and therefore is verifiable by them, or that propositions about future perceptions are deducible from P together with some other already verified propositions. If a scientist should venture to make an assertion from which no perceptive propositions could be deduced, what should we say to that? Suppose, *e.g.,* he asserts that there is not only a gravitational field having an effect on bodies according to the known laws of gravitation, but also a *levitational field,* and on being asked what sort of effect this levitational field has, according to his theory, he answers that there is no observable effect; in other words, he confesses his inability to give rules according to which we could deduce perceptive propositions from his assertion. In that case our reply is: your assertion is no assertion at all; it does not speak about anything; it is nothing but a series of empty words; it is simply without sense.

It is true that he may have images and even feelings connected with his words. This fact may be of psychological importance; logically, it is irrelevant. What gives theoretical meaning to a proposition is not the attendant images and thoughts, but the possibility of deducing from it perceptive propositions, in other words, the possibility of verification. To give sense to a proposition the presence of images is not sufficient; it is not even necessary. We have no actual image of the electro-magnetic field, nor even, I should say, of the gravitational field. Nevertheless the propositions which physicists assert about these fields have a perfect sense, because perceptive propositions are deducible from them. I by no means object to the proposition just mentioned about a levitational field that we do not know how to imagine or conceive such a field. My only objection to that proposition is that we are not told how to verify it.

METAPHYSICS

What we have been doing so far is *logical analysis.* Now we are going to apply these considerations not to propositions of physics as before, but to propositions of *metaphysics.* Thus our investigation belongs to *logic,* to the third of the three parts of philosophy spoken about before, but the *objects* of this investigation belong to the first part.

I will call *metaphysical* all those propositions which claim to represent knowledge about something which is over or beyond all experience, *e.g.* about the real Essence of things, about Things in themselves, the Absolute, and such like. I do not include in metaphysics those theories—sometimes called metaphysical—whose object is to arrange the most general propositions of the various regions of scientific knowledge in a well-ordered system; such theories belong actually to the field of empirical science, not of philosophy, however daring they may be. The sort of propositions I wish to denote as metaphysical may most easily be made clear by some examples: "The Essence and Principle of the world is Water," said Thales; "Fire," said Heraclitus; "the Infinite," said Anaximander; "Number," said Pythagoras. "All things are nothing but shadows of eternal ideas which themselves are in a spaceless and timeless sphere," is a doctrine of Plato. From the Monists we learn: "There is only one principle on which all that is, is founded"; but the Dualists tell us: "There are two principles." The Materialists say: "All that is, is in its essence material"; but the Spiritualists say: "All that is, is spiritual." To metaphysics (in our sense of the word) belong the principal doctrines of Spinoza, Schelling, Hegel, and—to give at least one name of the present time—Bergson.

Now let us examine this kind of proposition from the point of view of *verifiability.* It is easy to realise that such propositions are not verifiable. From the proposition: "The Principle of the world is Water" we are not able to deduce any proposition asserting any perceptions or feelings or experiences whatever which may be expected for the future. Therefore the proposition, "The Principle of the world is Water," asserts nothing at all. It is perfectly analogous to the proposition in the fictive example above about the levitational field and therefore it has no more sense than that proposition. The Walter-Metaphysician—as we may call him—has no doubt many images connected with his doctrine; but they cannot give sense to the proposition, any more than they could in the case of the levitational field. Metaphysicians cannot avoid making their propositions non-verifiable, because if they made them verifiable, the decision about the truth or falsehood of their doctrines would depend upon experience and therefore belong to the region of empirical science. This consequence they wish to avoid, because they pretend to teach knowledge which is of a higher level than that of empirical science. Thus they are compelled to cut all connection between their propositions and experience; and precisely by this procedure they deprive them of any sense.

PROBLEMS OF REALITY

So far I have considered only examples of such propositions as are usually called metaphysical. The judgment I have passed on these propositions, namely, that they have no empirical sense, may perhaps appear not very astonishing, and even trivial. But it is to be feared that the reader will experience somewhat more difficulty in agreement when I now proceed to apply that judgment also to philosophical doctrines of the type which is usually called epistemological. I prefer to call them also metaphysical because of their similarity, in the point under consideration, to the propositions usually so called. What I have in mind are the doctrines of Realism, Idealism, Solipsism, Positivism and the like, taken in their traditional form as asserting or denying the Reality of something. The Realist asserts the Reality of the external world; the Idealist denies it. The Realist—usually at least— asserts also the Reality of other minds; the Solipsist—an especially radical Idealist—denies it, and asserts that only his own mind or consciousness is real. Have these assertions sense?

Perhaps it may be said that assertions about the reality or unreality of something occur also in empirical science, where they are examined in an empirical way, and that therefore they have sense. This is quite true. But we have to distinguish between two concepts of reality, one occurring in empirical propositions and the other occurring in the philosophical propositions just mentioned. When a zoologist asserts the reality of kangaroos, his assertion means that there are things of a certain sort which can be found and perceived at certain times and places; in other words that there are objects of a certain sort which are elements of the space-time system of the physical world. This assertion is of course verifiable; by empirical investigation every zoologist arrives at a positive verification, independent of whether he is a Realist or an Idealist. Between the Realist and the Idealist there is full agreement as to the question of the reality of things of such and such sort, *i.e.* of the possibility of locating elements of such and such sort in the system of the physical world. The disagreement begins only when the question about the Reality of the physical world as a whole is raised. But this question has no sense, because the reality of anything is nothing else than the possibility of its being placed in a certain system, in this case, in the space-time system of the physical world, and such a question has sense only if it concerns elements or parts, not if it concerns the system itself.

The same result is obtained by applying the criterion explained before: the possibility of deducing perceptive propositions. While from the assertion of the reality or the existence of kangaroos we *can* deduce perceptive propositions, from the assertion of the Reality of the physical world this is not possible; neither is it possible from the opposite assertion of the Unreality of the physical world. Therefore both assertions have no empirical content—no sense at all. It is to be emphasized that this criticism of having no sense applies equally to the assertion of Unreality. Sometimes the views of the *Vienna Circle* have been mistaken for a denial of the Reality of the physical world, but we make no such denial. It is true that we reject the thesis of the Reality of the physical world; but we do not reject it as false, but as having no sense, and its Idealistic *anti*-thesis is subject to exactly the same rejection. We neither assert nor deny these theses, we reject the whole question.

All the considerations which apply to the question of the Reality of the physical world apply also to the other philosophical questions of Reality, *e.g.* the Reality of other minds, the Reality of the given, the Reality of universals, the Reality of qualities, the Reality of relations, the Reality of numbers, etc. If any philosophical thesis answering any of these questions positively or negatively is added to the system of scientific hypotheses, this system will not in the least become more effective; we shall not be able to make any further prediction as to future experiences. Thus all these philosophical theses are deprived of empirical content, of theoretical sense; they are pseudo-theses.

If I am right in this assertion, the philosophical problems of Reality —as distinguished from the empirical problems of Reality—have the same logical character as the problems (or rather, pseudo-problems) of transcendental metaphysics earlier referred to. For this reason I call those problems of Reality not epistemological problems—as they usually are called—but metaphysical.

Among the metaphysical doctrines that have no theoretical sense I have also mentioned *Positivism,* although the *Vienna Circle* is sometimes designated as Positivistic. It is doubtful whether this designation is quite suitable for us. In any case we do not assert the thesis that only the Given is Real, which is one of the principal theses of traditional Positivism. The name Logical Positivism seems more suitable, but this also can be misunderstood. At any rate it is important to realize that our doctrine is a logical one and has nothing to do with metaphysical theses of the Reality or Unreality of anything whatever. What the character of a *logical* thesis is, will be made clear in the following chapters.

ETHICS

One division of philosophy, which by some philosophers is considered the most important, has not been mentioned at all so far, namely, the philosophy of values, with its main branch, moral philosophy or *Ethics.* The word "Ethics" is used in two different senses. Sometimes a certain empirical investigation is called "Ethics," *viz.* psychological and sociological investigations about the actions of human beings, especially regarding the origin of these actions from feelings and volitions and their effects upon other people. Ethics in this sense is an empirical, scientific investigation; it belongs to empirical science rather than to philosophy. Fundamentally different from this is ethics in the second sense, as the philosophy of moral values or moral norms, which one can designate normative ethics. This is not an investigation of facts, but a pretended investigation of what is good and what is evil, what it is right to do and what it is wrong to do. Thus the purpose of this philosophical, or normative, ethics is to state norms for human action or judgments about moral values.

It is easy to see that it is merely a difference of formulation, whether we state a norm or a value judgment. A norm or rule has an imperative form, for instance: "Do not kill!" The corresponding value judgment would be: "Killing is evil." This difference of formulation has become practically very important, especially for the development of philosophical thinking. The rule, "Do not kill," has grammatically the imperative form and will therefore not be regarded as an assertion. But the value statement, "Killing is evil," although, like the rule, it is merely an expression of a certain wish, has the grammatical form of an assertive proposition. Most philosophers have been deceived by this form into thinking that a value statement is really an assertive proposition, and must be either true or false. Therefore they give reasons for their own value statements and try to disprove those of their opponents. But actually a value statement is nothing else than a command in a misleading grammatical form. It may have effects upon the actions of men, and these effects may either be in accordance with our wishes or not; but it is neither true nor false. It does not assert anything and can neither be proved nor disproved.

This is revealed as soon as we apply to such statements our method of logical analysis. From the statement "Killing is evil" we cannot deduce any proposition about future experiences. Thus this statement is not verifiable and has no theoretical sense, and the same thing is true of all other value statements.

Perhaps somebody will contend in opposition that the following proposition is deducible: "If a person kills anybody he will have feelings of remorse." But this proposition is in no way deducible from the proposition "Killing is evil." It is deducible only from psychological propositions about the character and the emotional reactions of the person. These propositions are indeed verifiable and not without sense. They belong to psychology, not to philosophy; to psychological ethics (if one wishes to use this word), not to philosophical or normative ethics. The propositions of normative ethics, whether they have the form of rules or the form of value statements, have no theoretical sense, are not scientific propositions (taking the word scientific to mean any assertive proposition).

To avoid misunderstanding it must be said that we do not at all deny the possibility and importance of a scientific investigation of value statements as well as of acts of valuation. Both of these are acts of individuals and are, like all other kinds of acts, possible objects of empirical investigation. Historians, psychologists, and sociologists may give analyses and causal explanations of them, and such historical and psychological propositions about acts of valuation and about value statements are indeed meaningful scientific propositions which belong to ethics in the first sense of this word. But the value statements themselves are here only objects of investigation; they are not propositions in these theories, and have, here as elsewhere, no theoretical sense. Therefore we assign them to the realm of metaphysics.

METAPHYSICS AS EXPRESSION

Now we have analysed the propositions of metaphysics in a wide sense of this word, including not only transcendental metaphysics, but also the problems of philosophical Reality and lastly normative ethics. Perhaps many will agree that the propositions of all these kinds of metaphysics are not verifiable, *i.e.* that their truth cannot be examined by experience. And perhaps many will even grant that for this reason they have not the character of scientific propositions. But when I say that they are without sense, assent will probably seem more difficult. Someone may object: these propositions in the metaphysical books obviously have an effect upon the reader, and sometimes a very strong effect; therefore they certainly *express* something. That is quite true, they *do* express something, but nevertheless they have no sense, no theoretical content.

We have here to distinguish two functions of language, which we may call the expressive function and the representative function. Almost all the conscious and unconscious movements of a person, including his linguistic utterances, express something of his feelings, his present mood, his temporary or permanent dispositions to reaction, and the like. Therefore we may take almost all his movements and words as symptoms from which we can infer something about his feelings or his character. That is the expressive function of movements and words. But besides that, a certain portion of linguistic utterances (*e.g.* "this book is black"), as distinguished from other linguistic utterances and movements, has a second function: these utterances represent a certain state of affairs; they tell us that something is so and so; they assert something, they predicate something, they judge something.

In special cases, this asserted state may be the same as that which is inferred from a certain expressive utterance; but even in such cases we must sharply distinguish between the assertion and the expression. If, for instance, somebody is laughing, we may take this as a symptom of his merry mood; if on the other hand he tells us without laughing: "Now I am merry," we can learn from his words the same thing which we inferred in the first case from his laughing. Nevertheless, there is a fundamental difference between the laughter and the words: "I am merry now." This linguistic utterance *asserts* the merry mood, and therefore it is either true or false.

The laughter does not assert the merry mood but *expresses* it. It is neither true nor false, because it does not assert anything, although it may be either genuine or deceptive.

Now many linguistic utterances are analogous to laughing in that they have only an expressive function, no representative function. Examples of this are cries like "Oh, Oh" or, on a higher level, lyrical verses. The aim of a lyrical poem in which occur the words "sunshine" and "clouds," is not to inform us of certain meteorological facts, but to express certain feelings of the poet and to excite similar feelings in us. A lyrical poem has no assertional sense, no theoretical sense, it does not contain knowledge.

The meaning of our anti-metaphysical thesis may now be more clearly explained. This thesis asserts that metaphysical propositions—like lyrical verses—have only an expressive function, but no representative function. Metaphysical propositions are neither true nor false, because they assert nothing, they contain neither knowledge nor error, they lie completely outside the field of knowledge, of theory, outside the discussion of truth or falsehood. But they are, like laughing, lyrics, and music, expressive. They express not so much temporary feelings as permanent emotional or volitional dispositions. Thus, for instance, a metaphysical system of Monism may be an expression of an even and harmonious mode of life, a Dualistic system may be an expression of the emotional state of someone who takes life as an eternal struggle; an ethical system of Rigorism may be expressive of a strong sense of duty or perhaps of a desire to rule serverely. Realism is often a symptom of the type of constitution called by psychologists extroverted, which is characterized by easily forming connections with men and things; Idealism, of an opposite constitution, the so-called introverted type, which has a tendency to withdraw from the unfriendly world and to live within its own thoughts and fancies.

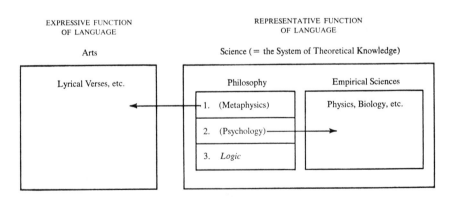

Thus we find a great similarity between metaphysics and lyrics. But there is one decisive difference between them. Both have no representative function, no theoretical content. A metaphysical proposition, however—as distinguished from a lyrical verse—*seems* to have some, and by this not only is the reader deceived, but the metaphysician himself. He believes that in his metaphysical treatise he has asserted something, and is led by this into argument and polemics against the propositions of some other metaphysician. A poet, however, does not assert that the verses of another are wrong or erroneous; he usually contents himself with calling them bad.

The non-theoretical character of metaphysics would not be in itself a defect; all arts have this non-theoretical character without thereby losing their high value for personal as well as for social life. The danger lies in the *deceptive* character of metaphysics; it gives the illusion of knowledge without actually giving any knowledge. This is the reason why we reject it.

PSYCHOLOGY

When we have eliminated metaphysical problems and doctrines from the region of knowledge or theory, there remain still two kinds of philosophical questions: psychological and logical. Now we shall eliminate the psychological questions also, not from the region of knowledge, but from philosophy. Then, finally, philosophy will be reduced to logic alone (in a wide sense of this word).

Psychological questions and propositions are certainly not without sense. From such propositions we can deduce other propositions about future experiences and by their help we can verify the psychological propositions. But the propositions of psychology belong to the region of empirical science in just the same way as do the propositions of chemistry, biology, history and the like. The character of psychology is by no means more philosophical than that of the other sciences mentioned. When we look at the historical development of the sciences we see that philosophy has been the mother of them all. One science after another has been detached from philosophy and has become an independent science. Only in our time has the umbilical cord between psychology and philosophy been cut. Many philosophers have not yet realized quite clearly that psychology is no longer an embryo, but an independent organism, and that psychological questions have to be left to empirical research.

Of course we have no objection to connecting psychological and logical investigations, any more than to connecting investigations of any scientific kind. We reject only the confusion of the two kinds of questions. We demand that they should be clearly distinguished even where in practice they are combined. The confusion sometimes consists in dealing with a logical question as if it were a psychological one. This mistake—called Psychologism—leads to the opinion that logic is a science concerning thinking, that is, either concerning the actual operation of thinking or the rules according to which thinking should proceed. But as a matter of fact the investigation of operations of thinking as they really occur is a task for psychology and has nothing to do with logic. And learning how to think *aright* is what we do in every other science as well as in logic. In astronomy we learn how to think aright about stars; in logic we learn how to think aright about the special objects of logic. What these special objects of logic are, will be seen in the next chapter. In any case thinking is not an object of logic, but of psychology.

Psychological questions concern all kinds of so-called psychic or mental events, all kinds of sensations, feelings, thoughts, images, etc., whether they are conscious or unconscious. These questions of psychology can be answered only by experience, not by philosophising.

LOGICAL ANALYSIS

The only proper task of *Philosophy* is *Logical Analysis*. And now the principal question to be answered here will be: *"What is logical analysis?"* In our considerations so far we have already practised logical analysis: we have tried to determine the character of physical hypotheses, of metaphysical propositions (or rather, pseudo-propositions), of psychological propositions. And now we have to apply logical analysis to logical analysis itself; we have to determine the character of the propositions of logic, of those propositions which are the results of logical analysis.

The opinion that metaphysical propositions have no sense because they do not concern any facts, has already been expressed by Hume. He writes in the last chapter of his *Enquiry Concerning Human Understanding* (published in the year 1748) as follows: "It seems to me, that the only objects of the abstract sciences or of demonstration, are quantity and number. . . . All other enquiries of men regard only matter of fact and existence; and these are evidently incapable of demonstration. . . . When we run over libraries, persuaded of these principles, what havoc must we make? If we take in our hand any volume, of divinity or school metaphysics, for instance; let us ask, Does it contain any abstract reasoning concerning quantity or number? No. Does it contain any experimental reasoning concerning matter of fact and existence? No. Commit it then to the flames: for it can contain nothing but sophistry and illusion." We agree with this view of Hume, which says—translated into our terminology—that only the propositions of mathematics and empirical science have sense, and that all other propositions are without sense.

But now it may perhaps be objected: "How about your own propositions? In consequence of your view your own writings, including this book, would be without sense, for they are neither mathematical nor empirical, that is, verifiable by experience." What answer can be given to this objection? What is the character of my propositions and in general of the propositions of logical analysis? This question is decisive for the consistency of the view which has been explained here.

An answer to the objection is given by Wittgenstein in his book *Tractatus Logico-Philosophicus*.[1] This author has developed most radically the

---

[1] Carnap is referring to the 1922 edition, published by Routledge & Kegan Paul, London. [J.A.W.]

view that the propositions of metaphysics are shown by logical analysis to be without sense. How does he reply to the criticism that in that case his own propositions are also without sense? He replies by agreeing with it. He writes: "The result of philosophy is not a number of 'philosophical propositions,' but to make propositions clear" (p. 77). "My propositions are elucidatory in this way: he who understands me finally recognizes them as senseless, when he has climbed out through them, on them, over them. (He must so to speak throw away the ladder, after he has climbed up on it.) He must surmount these propositions; then he sees the world rightly. Whereof one cannot speak, thereof one must be silent" (p. 189).

I, as well as my friends in the Vienna Circle, owe much to Wittgenstein, especially as to the analysis of metaphysics. But on the point just mentioned I cannot agree with him. In the first place he seems to me to be inconsistent in what he does. He tells us that one cannot state philosophical propositions and that whereof one cannot speak, thereof one must be silent; and then instead of keeping silent, he writes a whole philosophical book. Secondly, I do not agree with his statement that all his propositions are quite as much without sense as metaphysical propositions are. My opinion is that a great number of his propositions (unfortunately not all of them) have in fact sense; and that the same is true for all propositions of logical analysis.

QUESTIONS FOR STUDY AND DISCUSSION

1. What is the meaning and the role of linguistic frameworks?
2. Is there a relation between linguistic frameworks and objective reality?
3. What does an entity mean to Carnap?
4. How are questions classified into cognitive and noncognitive?
5. Are abstract entities admissible in semantics?
6. Explain Carnap's position with regard to nominalism.

Alfred Tarski

ALFRED TARSKI (b. 1902), a prominent member of the Polish school of mathematical logic, taught the philosophy of mathematics at the University of Warsaw. After the German invasion in 1939, he came to the United States, taught at Harvard and Princeton, and is currently professor of Mathematics at the University of California in Berkeley. Among his principal works are *Introduction to Logic and the Methodology of Deductive Sciences* (1936) and *Logic, Semantics and Mathematics* (1956).

Truth as a Linguistic Problem

This paper consists of two parts; the first has an expository character, and the second is rather polemical.*

In the first part I want to summarize in an informal way the main results of my investigations concerning the definition of truth and the more general problem of the foundations of semantics. These results have been embodied in a work which appeared in print several years ago.[1] Although my investigations concern concepts dealt with in classical philosophy, they happen to be comparatively little known in philosophical circles, perhaps because of their strictly technical character. For this reason I hope I shall be excused for taking up the matter once again.[2]

Since my work was published, various objections, of unequal value, have been raised to my investigations; some of these appeared in print, and others were made in public and private discussions in which I took part.[3] In the second part of the paper I should like to express my views regarding these objections. I hope that the remarks which will be made in this context will not be considered as purely polemical in character, but will be found to contain some constructive contributions to the subject.

In the second part of the paper I have made extensive use of material graciously put at my disposal by Dr. Marja Kokoszyńska (University of Lwów). I am especially indebted and grateful to Professors Ernest Nagel

---

* Tarski's footnote references will be found at the end of this selection.

From Alfred Tarski, "The Semantic Conception of Truth and the Foundations of Semantics." Reprinted with the authorization of the editors from *Philosophy and Phenomenological Research,* vol. IV, 1944, and by permission of the author.

(Columbia University) and David Rynin (University of California, Berkeley) for their help in preparing the final text and for various critical remarks.

EXPOSITION

1. The Main Problem—A Satisfactory Definition of Truth. Our discussion will be centered around the notion [4] of *truth.* The main problem is that of giving a *satisfactory definition* of this notion, i.e., a definition which is *materially adequate* and *formally correct.* But such a formulation of the problem, because of its generality, cannot be considered unequivocal, and requires some further comments.

In order to avoid any ambiguity, we must first specify the conditions under which the definition of truth will be considered adequate from the material point of view. The desired definition does not aim to specify the meaning of a familiar word used to denote a novel notion; on the contrary, it aims to catch hold of the actual meaning of an old notion. We must then characterize this notion precisely enough to enable anyone to determine whether the definition actually fulfills its task.

Secondly, we must determine on what the formal correctness of the definition depends. Thus, we must specify the words or concepts which we wish to use in defining the notion of truth; and we must also give the formal rules to which the definition should conform. Speaking more generally, we must describe the formal structure of the language in which the definition will be given.

The discussion of these points will occupy a considerable portion of the first part of the paper.

2. The Extension of the Term "True." We begin with some remarks regarding the extension of the concept of truth which we have in mind here.

The predicate *"true"* is sometimes used to refer to psychological phenomena such as judgments or beliefs, sometimes to certain physical objects, namely, linguistic expressions and specifically sentences, and sometimes to certain ideal entities called "propositions." By "sentence" we understand here what is usually meant in grammar by "declarative sentence"; as regards the term "proposition," its meaning is notoriously a subject of lengthy disputations by various philosophers and logicians, and it seems never to have been made quite clear and unambiguous. For several reasons its appears most convenient to *apply the term "true" to sentences,* and we shall follow this course.[5]

Consequently, we must always relate the notion of truth, like that of a sentence, to a specific language; for it is obvious that the same expression which is a true sentence in one language can be false or meaningless in another.

Of course, the fact that we are interested here primarily in the notion of truth for sentences does not exclude the possibility of a subsequent extension of this notion to other kinds of objects.

3. The Meaning of the Term "True." Much more serious difficulties are connected with the problem of the meaning (or the intension) of the concept of truth.

The word *"true,"* like other words from our everyday language, is certainly not unambiguous. And it does not seem to me that the philosophers who have discussed this concept have helped to diminish its ambiguity. In works and discussions of philosophers we meet many different conceptions of truth and falsity, and we must indicate which conception will be the basis of our discussion.

We should like our definition to do justice to the intuitions which adhere to the *classical Aristotelian conception of Truth*—intuitions which find their expression in the well-known words of Aristotle's *Metaphysics:*

> *To say of what is that it is not, or of what is not that it is, is false, while to say of what is that it is, or of what is not that it is not, is true.*

If we wished to adapt ourselves to modern philosophical terminology, we could perhaps express this conception by means of the familiar formula:

> *The truth of a sentence consists in its agreement with (or correspondence to) reality.*

(For a theory of truth which is to be based upon the latter formulation the term "correspondence theory" has been suggested.)

If, on the other hand, we should decide to extend the popular usage of the term *"designate"* by applying it not only to names, but also to sentences, and if we agreed to speak of the designata of sentences as "states of affairs," we could possibly use for the same purpose the following phrase:

> *A sentence is true if it designates an existing state of affairs.*[6]

However, all these formulations can lead to various misunderstandings, for none of them is sufficiently precise and clear (though this applies much less to the original Aristotelian formulation than to either of the others); at any rate, none of them can be considered a satisfactory definition of truth. It is up to us to look for a more precise expression of our intuitions.

4. A Criterion for the Material Adequacy of the Definition.[7] Let us start with a concrete example. Consider the sentence *"snow is white."* We ask the question under what conditions this sentence is true or false. It seems clear that if we base ourselves on the classical conception of truth, we shall say that the sentence is true if snow is white, and that it is false if snow is not white. Thus, if the definition of truth is to conform to our conception, it must imply the following equivalence:

> *The sentence "snow is white" is true if, and only if, snow is white.*

Let me point out that the phrase *"snow is white"* occurs on the left side of this equivalence in quotation marks, and on the right without quotation marks. On the right side we have the sentence itself, and on the left the name of the sentence. Employing the medieval logical terminology we could also say that on the right side the words *"snow is white"* occur in *suppositio formalis,* and on the left in *suppositio materialis.* It is hardly necessary to explain why we must have the name of the sentence, and not the sentence itself, on the left side of the equivalence. For, in the first place, from the point of view of the grammar of our language, an expression of the form *"X is true"* will not become a meaningful sentence if we replace in it *"X"* by a sentence or by anything other than a name—since the subject of a sentence may be only a noun or an expression functioning like a noun. And, in the second place, the fundamental conventions regarding the use of any language require that in any utterance we make about an object it is the name of the object which must be employed, and not the object itself. In consequence, if we wish to say something about a sentence, for example, that it is true, we must use the name of this sentence, and not the sentence itself.[8]

It may be added that enclosing a sentence in quotation marks is by no means the only way of forming its name. For instance, by assuming the usual order of letters in our alphabet, we can use the following expression as the name (the description) of the sentence *"snow is white":*

> *the sentence constituted by three words, the first of which consists of the 19th, 14th, 15th, and 23rd letters, the second of the 9th and 19th letters, and the third of the 23rd, 8th, 9th, 20th, and 5th letters of the English alphabet.*

We shall now generalize the procedure which we have applied above. Let us consider an arbitrary sentence; we shall replace it by the letter *"p."* We form the name of this sentence and we replace it by another letter, say *"X."* We ask now what is the logical relation between the two sentences *"X is true"* and *"p."* It is clear that from the point of view of our basic conception of truth these sentences are equivalent. In other words, the following equivalence holds:

(T)   *X is true if, and only if, p.*

We shall call any such equivalence (with *"p"* replaced by any sentence of the language to which the word *"true"* refers, and *"X"* replaced by a name of this sentence) an *"equivalence of the form* (T)*."*

Now at last we are able to put into a precise form the conditions under which we will consider the usage and the definition of the term *"true"* as adequate from the material point of view: we wish to use the term *"true"* in such a way that all equivalences of the form (T) can be asserted, and *we shall call a definition of truth "adequate" if all these equivalences follow from it.*

It should be emphasized that neither the expression (T) itself (which is not a sentence, but only a schema of a sentence) nor any particular instance of the form (T) can be regarded as a definition of truth. We can only say that every equivalence of the form (T) obtained by replacing *"p"* by a particular sentence, and *"X"* by a name of this sentence, may be considered a partial definition of truth, which explains wherein the truth of this one individual sentence consists. The general definition has to be, in a certain sense, a logical conjunction of these partial definitions.

(The last remark calls for some comments. A language may admit the construction of infinitely many sentences; and thus the number of partial definitions of truth referring to sentences of such a language will also be infinite. Hence to give our remark a precise sense we should have to explain what is meant by a "logical conjunction of infinitely many sentences"; but this would lead us too far into technical problems of modern logic.)

5. *Truth as a Semantic Concept.* I should like to propose the name *"the semantic conception of truth"* for the conception of truth which has just been discussed.

Semantics is a discipline which, speaking loosely, *deals with certain relations between expressions of a language and the objects* (or "states of affairs") *"referred to" by those expressions.* As typical examples of semantic concepts we may mention the concepts of *designation, satisfaction,* and *definition* as these occur in the following examples:

> the expression *"the father of his country"* designates (*denotes*) *George Washington;*
>
> snow satisfies the sentential function (*the condition*) *"x is white";*
>
> the equation *"2 · x = 1"* defines (*uniquely determines*) the number ½.

While the words *"designates," "satisfies,"* and *"defines"* express relations (between certain expressions and the objects "referred to" by these expressions), the word *"true"* is of a different logical nature: it expresses a property (or denotes a class) of certain expressions, viz., of sentences. However, it is easily seen that all the formulations which were given earlier and which aimed to explain the meaning of this word (cf. Sections 3 and 4) referred not only to sentences themselves, but also to objects "talked about" by these sentences, or possibly to "states of affairs" described by them. And, moreover, it turns out that the simplest and the most natural way of obtaining an exact definition of truth is one which involves the use of other semantic notions, e.g., the notion of satisfaction. It is for these reasons that we count the concept of truth which is discussed here among the concepts of semantics, and the problem of defining truth proves to be closely related to the more general problem of setting up the foundations of theoretical semantics.

It is perhaps worth while saying that semantics as it is conceived in this paper (and in former papers of the author) is a sober and modest discipline which has no pretentions of being a universal patent-medicine for all the ills and diseases of mankind, whether imaginary or real. You will not find in semantics any remedy for decayed teeth or illusions of grandeur or class conflicts. Nor is semantics a device for establishing that everyone except the speaker and his friends is speaking nonsense.

From antiquity to the present day the concepts of semantics have played an important rôle in the discussions of philosophers, logicians, and philologists. Nevertheless, these concepts have been treated for a long time with a certain amount of suspicion. From a historical standpoint, this suspicion is to be regarded as completely justified. For although the meaning of semantic concepts as they are used in everyday language seems to be rather clear and understandable, still all attempts to characterize this meaning in a general and exact way miscarried. And what is worse, various arguments in which these concepts were involved, and which seemed otherwise quite correct and based upon apparently obvious premises, led frequently to paradoxes and antinomies. It is sufficient to mention here the *antinomy of the liar,* Richard's *antinomy of definability* (by means of a finite number of words), and Grelling-Nelson's *antinomy of heterological terms.*[9]

I believe that the method which is outlined in this paper helps to overcome these difficulties and assures the possibility of a consistent use of semantic concepts.

6. *Languages with a Specified Structure.* Because of the possible occurrence of antinomies, the problem of specifying the formal structure and the vocabulary of a language in which definitions of semantic concepts are to be given becomes especially acute; and we turn now to this problem.

There are certain general conditions under which the structure of a language is regarded as *exactly specified.* Thus, to specify the structure of a language, we must characterize unambiguously the class of those words and expressions which are to be considered *meaningful.* In particular, we must indicate all words which we decide to use without defining them, and which are called *"undefined* (or *primitive) terms";* and we must give the so-called *rules of definition* for introducing new or *defined terms.* Furthermore, we must set up criteria for distinguishing within the class of expressions those which we call *"sentences."* Finally, we must formulate the conditions under which a sentence of the language can be *asserted.* In particular, we must indicate all *axioms* (or *primitive sentences*), i.e., those sentences which we decide to assert without proof; and we must give the so-called *rules of inference* (or *rules of proof*) by means of which we can deduce new asserted sentences from other sentences which have been previously asserted. Axioms, as well as sentences deduced from them by means of rules of inference, are referred to as *"theorems"* or *"provable sentences."*

If in specifying the structure of a language we refer exclusively to the form of the expressions involved, the language is said to be *formalized.* In such a language theorems are the only sentences which can be asserted.

At the present time the only languages with a specified structure are the formalized languages of various systems of deductive logic, possibly enriched by the introduction of certain non-logical terms. However, the field of application of these languages is rather comprehensive; we are able, theoretically, to develop in them various branches of science, for instance, mathematics and theoretical physics.

(On the other hand, we can imagine the construction of languages which have an exactly specified structure without being formalized. In such a language the assertability of sentences, for instance, may depend not always on their form, but sometimes on other, non-linguistic factors. It would be interesting and important actually to construct a language of this type, and specifically one which would prove to be sufficient for the development of a comprehensive branch of empirical science; for this would justify the hope that languages with specified structure could finally replace everyday language in scientific discourse.)

The problem of the definition of truth obtains a precise meaning and can be solved in a rigorous way only for those languages whose structure has been exactly specified. For other languages—thus, for all natural, "spoken" languages—the meaning of the problem is more or less vague, and its solution can have only an approximate character. Roughly speaking, the approximation consists in replacing a natural language (or a portion of it in which we are interested) by one whose structure is exactly specified, and which diverges from the given language "as little as possible."

7. *The Antinomy of the Liar.* In order to discover some of the more specific conditions which must be satisfied by languages in which (or for which) the definition of truth is to be given, it will be advisable to begin with a discussion of that antinomy which directly involves the notion of truth, namely, the antinomy of the liar.

To obtain this antinomy in a perspicuous form,[10] consider the following sentence:

The sentence printed in this paper on p. 512, l. 32, is not true.

For brevity we shall replace the sentence just stated by the letter "*s.*"

According to our convention concerning the adequate usage of the term "*true*," we assert the following equivalence of the form (T):

(1) "*s*" is true if, and only if, the sentence printed in this paper on p. 512, l. 32, is not true.

On the other hand, keeping in mind the meaning of the symbol "*s*," we establish empirically the following fact:

(2) "*s*" is identical with the sentence printed in this paper on p. 512, l. 32.

Now, by a familiar law from the theory of identity (Leibniz's law), it follows from (2) that we may replace in (1) the expression "*the sentence printed in this paper on p. 512, l. 32"* by the symbol " *'s.' "* We thus obtain what follows:

(3)   *"s" is true if, and only if, "s" is not true.*

In this way we have arrived at an obvious contradiction.

In my judgment, it would be quite wrong and dangerous from the standpoint of scientific progress to depreciate the importance of this and other antinomies, and to treat them as jokes or sophistries. It is a fact that we are here in the presence of an absurdity, that we have been compelled to assert a false sentence (since (3), as an equivalence between two contradictory sentences, is necessarily false). If we take our work seriously, we cannot be reconciled with this fact. We must discover its cause, that is to say, we must analyze premises upon which the antinomy is based; we must then reject at least one of these premises, and we must investigate the consequences which this has for the whole domain of our research.

It should be emphasized that antinomies have played a preëminent rôle in establishing the foundations of modern deductive sciences. And just as class-theoretical antinomies, and in particular Russell's antinomy (of the class of all classes that are not members of themselves), were the starting point for the successful attempts at a consistent formalization of logic and mathematics, so the antinomy of the liar and other semantic antinomies give rise to the construction of theoretical semantics.

8. *The Inconsistency of Semantically Closed Languages.*[7] If we now analyze the assumptions which lead to the antinomy of the liar, we notice the following:

(I) We have implicitly assumed that the language in which the antinomy is constructed contains, in addition to its expressions, also the names of these expressions, as well as semantic terms such as the term *"true"* referring to sentences of this language; we have also assumed that all sentences which determine the adequate usage of this term can be asserted in the language. A language with these properties will be called *"semantically closed."*

(II) We have assumed that in this language the ordinary laws of logic hold.

(III) We have assumed that we can formulate and assert in our language an empirical premise such as the statement (2) which has occurred in our argument.

It turns out that the assumption (III) is not essential, for it is possible to reconstruct the antinomy of the liar without its help.[11] But the assumptions (I) and (II) prove essential. Since every language which satisfies both of these assumptions is inconsistent, we must reject at least one of them.

It would be superfluous to stress here the consequences of rejecting the assumption (II), that is, of changing our logic (supposing this were possible) even in its more elementary and fundamental parts. We thus consider only the possibility of rejecting the assumption (I). Accordingly, we decide *not to use any language which is semantically closed* in the sense given.

This restriction would of course be unacceptable for those who, for reasons which are not clear to me, believe that there is only one "genuine" language (or, at least, that all "genuine" languages are mutually translatable). However, this restriction does not affect the needs or interests of science in any essential way. The languages (either the formalized languages or—what is more frequently the case—the portions of everyday language) which are used in scientific discourse do not have to be semantically closed. This is obvious in case linguistic phenomena and, in particular, semantic notions do not enter in any way into the subject-matter of a science; for in such a case the language of this science does not have to be provided with any semantic terms at all. However, we shall see in the next section how semantically closed languages can be dispensed with even in those scientific discussions in which semantic notions are essentially involved.

The problem arises as to the position of everyday language with regard to this point. At first blush it would seem that this language satisfies both assumptions (I) and (II), and that therefore it must be inconsistent. But actually the case is not so simple. Our everyday language is certainly not one with an exactly specified structure. We do not know precisely which expressions are sentences, and we know even to a smaller degree which sentences are to be taken as assertible. Thus the problem of consistency has no exact meaning with respect to this language. We may at best only risk the guess that a language whose structure has been exactly specified and which resembles our everyday language as closely as possible would be inconsistent.

9. Object-Language and Meta-Language. Since we have agreed not to employ semantically closed languages, we have to use two different languages in discussing the problem of the definition of truth and, more generally, any problems in the field of semantics. The first of these languages is the language which is "talked about" and which is the subject-matter of the whole discussion; the definition of truth which we are seeking applies to the sentences of this language. The second is the language in which we "talk about" the first language, and in terms of which we wish, in particular, to construct the definition of truth for the first language. We shall refer to the first language as *"the object-language,"* and to the second as *"the meta-language."*

It should be noticed that these terms "object-language" and "meta-language" have only a relative sense. If, for instance, we become interested in the notion of truth applying to sentences, not of our original object-language, but of its meta-language, the latter becomes automatically the object-language of our discussion; and in order to define truth for this language, we have to go to a new meta-language—so to speak, to a meta-language of a higher level. In this way we arrive at a whole hierarchy of languages.

The vocabulary of the meta-language is to a large extent determined by previously stated conditions under which a definition of truth will be considered materially adequate. This definition, as we recall, has to imply all equivalences of the form (T):

(T)   *X is true if, and only if, p.*

The definition itself and all the equivalences implied by it are to be formulated in the meta-language. On the other hand, the symbol "*p*" in (T) stands for an arbitrary sentence of our object-language. Hence it follows that every sentence which occurs in the object-language must also occur in the meta-language; in other words, the meta-language must contain the object-language as a part. This is at any rate necessary for the proof of the adequacy of the definition—even though the definition itself can sometimes be formulated in a less comprehensive meta-language which does not satisfy this requirement.

(The requirement in question can be somewhat modified, for it suffices to assume that the object-language can be translated into the meta-language; this necessitates a certain change in the interpretation of the symbol "*p*" in (T). In all that follows we shall ignore the possibility of this modification.)

Furthermore, the symbol "*X*" in (T) represents the name of the sentence which "*p*" stands for. We see therefore that the meta-language must be rich enough to provide possibilities of constructing a name for every sentence of the object-language.

In addition, the meta-language must obviously contain terms of a general logical character, such as the expression "if, and only if." [12]

It is desirable for the meta-language not to contain any undefined terms except such as are involved explicitly or implicitly in the remarks above, i.e.: terms of the object-language; terms referring to the form of the expressions of the object-language, and used in building names for these expressions; and terms of logic. In particular, we desire *semantic terms* (referring to the object-language) *to be introduced into the meta-language only by definition.* For, if this postulate is satisfied, the definition of truth, or of any other semantic concept, will fulfill what we intuitively expect from every definition; that is, it will explain the meaning of the term being defined in terms whose meaning appears to be completely clear and unequivocal. And, moreover, we have then a kind of guarantee that the use of semantic concepts will not involve us in any contradictions.

We have no further requirements as to the formal structure of the object-language and the meta-language; we assume that it is similar to that of other formalized languages known at the present time. In particular, we assume that the usual formal rules of definition are observed in the meta-language.

10. Conditions for a Positive Solution of the Main Problem. Now, we have already a clear idea both of the conditions of material adequacy to which the definition of truth is subjected, and of the formal structure of the language in which this definition is to be constructed. Under these circumstances the problem of the definition of truth acquires the character of a definite problem of a purely deductive nature.

The solution of the problem, however, is by no means obvious, and I would not attempt to give it in detail without using the whole machinery of contemporary logic. Here I shall confine myself to a rough outline of the solution and to the discussion of certain points of a more general interest which are involved in it.

The solution turns out to be sometimes positive, sometimes negative. This depends upon some formal relations between the object-language and its meta-language; or, more specifically, upon the fact whether the meta-language in its logical part is *"essentially richer"* than the object-language or not. It is not easy to give a general and precise definition of this notion of "essential richness." If we restrict ourselves to languages based on the logical theory of types, the condition for the meta-language to be "essentially richer" than the object-language is that it contain variables of a higher logical type than those of the object-language.

If the condition of "essential richness" is not satisfied, it can usually be shown that an interpretation of the meta-language in the object-language is possible; that is to say, with any given term of the meta-language a well-determined term of the object-language can be correlated in such a way that the assertible sentences of the one language turn out to be correlated with assertible sentences of the other. As a result of this interpretation, the hypothesis that a satisfactory definition of truth has been formulated in the meta-language turns out to imply the possibility of reconstructing in that language the antinomy of the liar; and this in turn forces us to reject the hypothesis in question.

(The fact that the meta-language, in its non-logical part, is ordinarily more comprehensive than the object-language does not affect the possibility of interpreting the former in the latter. For example, the names of expressions of the object-language occur in the meta-language, though for the most part they do not occur in the object-language itself; but, nevertheless, it may be possible to interpret these names in terms of the object-language.)

Thus we see that the condition of "essential richness" is necessary for the possibility of a satisfactory definition of truth in the meta-language. If we want to develop the theory of truth in a meta-language which does not satisfy this condition, we must give up the idea of defining truth with the exclusive help of those terms which were indicated above (in Section 8). We have then to include the term *"true,"* or some other semantic term, in the list of undefined terms of the meta-language, and to express fundamental properties of the notion of truth in a series of axioms. There is nothing essentially wrong in such an axiomatic procedure, and it may prove useful for various purposes.[13]

It turns out, however, that this procedure can be avoided. For *the con-*

dition of the "essential richness" of the meta-language proves to be, not only necessary, but also sufficient for the construction of a satisfactory definition of truth; i.e., if the meta-language satisfies this condition, the notion of truth can be defined in it. We shall now indicate in general terms how this construction can be carried through.

11. The Construction (in Outline) of the Definition.[14] A definition of truth can be obtained in a very simple way from that of another semantic notion, namely, of the notion of *satisfaction.*

Satisfaction is a relation between arbitrary objects and certain expressions called *"sentential functions."* These are expressions like *"x is white,"* *"x is greater than y,"* etc. Their formal structure is analogous to that of sentences; however, they may contain the so-called free variables (like *"x"* and *"y"* in *"x is greater than y"*), which cannot occur in sentences.

In defining the notion of a sentential function in formalized languages, we usually apply what is called a "recursive procedure"; i.e., we first describe sentential functions of the simplest structure (which ordinarily presents no difficulty), and then we indicate the operations by means of which compound functions can be constructed from simpler ones. Such an operation may consist, for instance, in forming the logical disjunction or conjunction of two given functions, i.e., by combining them by the word *"or"* or *"and."* A sentence can now be defined simply as a sentential function which contains no free variables.

As regards the notion of satisfaction, we might try to define it by saying that given objects satisfy a given function if the latter becomes a true sentence when we replace in it free variables by names of given objects. In this sense, for example, snow satisfies the sentential function *"x is white"* since the sentence *"snow is white"* is true. However, apart from other difficulties, this method is not available to us, for we want to use the notion of satisfaction in defining truth.

To obtain a definition of satisfaction we have rather to apply again a recursive procedure. We indicate which objects satisfy the simplest sentential functions; and then we state the conditions under which given objects satisfy a compound function—assuming that we know which objects satisfy the simpler functions from which the compound one has been constructed. Thus, for instance, we say that given numbers satisfy the logical disjunction *"x is greater than y or x is equal to y"* if they satisfy at least one of the functions *"x is greater than y"* or *"x is equal to y."*

Once the general definition of satisfaction is obtained, we notice that it applies automatically also to those special sentential functions which contain no free variables, i.e., to sentences. It turns out that for a sentence only two cases are possible: a sentence is either satisfied by all objects, or by no objects. Hence we arrive at a definition of truth and falsehood simply by saying that *a sentence is true if it is satisfied by all objects, and false otherwise.*[15]

(It may seem strange that we have chosen a roundabout way of defining the truth of a sentence, instead of trying to apply, for instance, a direct recursive procedure. The reason is that compound sentences are constructed from simpler sentential functions, but not always from simpler sentences; hence no general recursive method is known which applies specifically to sentences.)

From this rough outline it is not clear where and how the assumption of the "essential richness" of the meta-language is involved in the discussion; this becomes clear only when the construction is carried through in a detailed and formal way.[16]

12. Consequences of the Definition. The definition of truth which was outlined above has many interesting consequences.

In the first place, the definition proves to be not only formally correct, but also materially adequate (in the sense established in Section 4); in other words, it implies all equivalences of the form (T). In this connection it is important to notice that the conditions for the material adequacy of the definition determine uniquely the extension of the term *"true."* Therefore, every definition of truth which is materially adequate would necessarily be equivalent to that actually constructed. The semantic conception of truth gives us, so to speak, no possibility of choice between various nonequivalent definitions of this notion.

Moreover, we can deduce from our definition various laws of a general nature. In particular, we can prove with its help the *laws of contradiction and of excluded middle,* which are so characteristic of the Aristotelian conception of truth; i.e., we can show that one and only one of any two contradictory sentences is true. These semantic laws should not be identified with the related logical laws of contradiction and excluded middle; the latter belong to the sentential calculus, i.e., to the most elementary part of logic, and do not involve the term *"true"* at all.

Further important results can be obtained by applying the theory of truth to formalized languages of a certain very comprehensive class of mathematical disciplines; only disciplines of an elementary character and a very elementary logical structure are excluded from this class. It turns out that for a discipline of this class *the notion of truth never coincides with that of provability;* for all provable sentences are true, but there are true sentences which are not provable.[17] Hence it follows further that every such discipline is consistent, but incomplete; that is to say, of any two contradictory sentences at most one is provable, and—what is more—there exists a pair of contradictory sentences neither of which is provable.[18]

13. Extension of the Results to Other Semantic Notions. Most of the results at which we arrived in the preceding sections in discussing the notion of truth can be extended with appropriate changes to other semantic notions, for instance, to the notion of satisfaction (involved in our previous discussion), and to those of *designation* and *definition.*

Each of these notions can be analyzed along the lines followed in the analysis of truth. Thus, criteria for an adequate usage of these notions can be established; it can be shown that each of these notions, when used in a semantically closed language according to those criteria, leads necessarily to a contradiction; [19] a distinction between the object-language and the meta-language becomes again indispensable; and the "essential richness" of the meta-language proves in each case to be a necessary and sufficient condition for a satisfactory definition of the notion involved. Hence the results obtained in discussing one particular semantic notion apply to the general problem of the foundations of theoretical semantics.

Within theoretical semantics we can define and study some further notions, whose intuitive content is more involved and whose semantic origin is less obvious; we have in mind, for instance, the important notions of *consequence, synonymity,* and *meaning.*[20]

We have concerned ourselves here with the theory of semantic notions related to an individual object-language (although no specific properties of this language have been involved in our arguments). However, we could also consider the problem of developing *general semantics* which applies to a comprehensive class of object-languages. A considerable part of our previous remarks can be extended to this general problem; however, certain new difficulties arise in this connection, which will not be discussed here. I shall merely observe that the axiomatic method (mentioned in Section 10) may prove the most appropriate for the treatment of the problem.[21]

POLEMICAL REMARKS

14. Is the Semantic Conception of Truth the "Right" One? I should like to begin the polemical part of the paper with some general remarks.

I hope nothing which is said here will be interpreted as a claim that the semantic conception of truth is the "right" or indeed the "only possible" one. I do not have the slightest intention to contribute in any way to those endless, often violent discussions on the subject. "What is the right conception of truth?" [22] I must confess I do not understand what is at stake in such disputes; for the problem itself is so vague that no definite solution is possible. In fact, it seems to me that the sense in which the phrase "the right conception" is used has never been made clear. In most cases one gets the impression that the phrase is used in an almost mystical sense based upon the belief that every word has only one "real" meaning (a kind of Platonic or Aristotelian idea), and that all the competing conceptions really attempt to catch hold of this one meaning; since, however, they contradict each other, only one attempt can be successful, and hence only one conception is the "right" one.

Disputes of this type are by no means restricted to the notion of truth. They occur in all domains where—instead of an exact, scientific terminology—common language with its vagueness and ambiguity is used; and they are always meaningless, and therefore in vain.

It seems to me obvious that the only rational approach to such problems would be the following: We should reconcile ourselves with the fact that we are confronted, not with one concept, but with several different concepts which are denoted by one word; we should try to make these concepts as clear as possible (by means of definition, or of an axiomatic procedure, or in some other way); to avoid further confusions, we should agree to use different terms for different concepts; and then we may proceed to a quiet and systematic study of all concepts involved, which will exhibit their main properties and mutual relations.

Referring specifically to the notion of truth, it is undoubtedly the case that in philosophical discussions—and perhaps also in everyday usage— some incipient conceptions of this notion can be found that differ essentially from the classical one (of which the semantic conception is but a modernized form). In fact, various conceptions of this sort have been discussed in the literature, for instance, the pragmatic conception, the coherence theory, etc.[6]

It seems to me that none of these conceptions have been put so far in an intelligible and unequivocal form. This may change, however; a time may come when we find ourselves confronted with several incompatible, but equally clear and precise, conceptions of truth. It will then become necessary to abandon the ambiguous usage of the word *"true,"* and to introduce several terms instead, each to denote a different notion. Personally, I should not feel hurt if a future world congress of the "theoreticians of truth" should decide—by a majority of votes—to reserve the word *"true"* for one of the non-classical conceptions, and should suggest another word, say, *"frue,"* for the conception considered here. But I cannot imagine that anybody could present cogent arguments to the effect that the semantic conception is "wrong" and should be entirely abandoned.

15. Formal Correctness of the Suggested Definition of Truth. The specific objections which have been raised to my investigations can be divided into several groups; each of these will be discussed separately.

I think that practically all these objections apply, not to the special definition I have given, but to the semantic conception of truth in general. Even those which were leveled against the definition actually constructed could be related to any other definition which conforms to this conception.

This holds, in particular, for those objections which concern the formal correctness of the definition. I have heard a few objections of this kind; however, I doubt very much whether any one of them can be treated seriously.

As a typical example let me quote in substance such an objection.[23] In formulating the definition we use necessarily sentential connectives, i.e., expressions like *"if . . . , then," "or,"* etc. They occur in the definiens; and one of them, namely, the phrase *"if, and only if"* is usually employed to combine the definiendum with the definiens. However, it is well known that the meaning of sentential connectives is explained in logic with the help of the words *"true"* and *"false";* for instance, we say that an equivalence, i.e., a sentence of the form *"p if, and only if, q,"* is true if either both of its members, i.e., the sentences represented by *"p"* and *"q,"* are true or both are false. Hence the definition of truth involves a vicious circle.

If this objection were valid, no formally correct definition of truth would be possible; for we are unable to formulate any compound sentence without using sentential connectives, or other logical terms defined with their help. Fortunately, the situation is not so bad.

It is undoubtedly the case that a strictly deductive development of logic is often preceded by certain statements explaining the conditions under which sentences of the form *"if p, then q,"* etc., are considered true or false. (Such explanations are often given schematically, by means of the so-called truth-tables.) However, these statements are outside of the system of logic, and should not be regarded as definitions of the terms involved. They are not formulated in the language of the system, but constitute rather special consequences of the definition of truth given in the meta-language. Moreover, these statements do not influence the deductive development of logic in any way. For in such a development we do not discuss the question whether a given sentence is true, we are only interested in the problem whether it is provable.[24]

On the other hand, the moment we find ourselves within the deductive system of logic—or of any discipline based upon logic, e.g., of semantics—we either treat sentential connectives as undefined terms, or else we define them by means of other sentential connectives, but never by means of semantic terms like *"true"* or *"false."* For instance, if we agree to regard the expressions *"not"* and *"if . . . , then"* (and possibly also *"if, and only if"*) as undefined terms, we can define the term *"or"* by stating that a sentence of the form *"p or q"* is equivalent to the corresponding sentence of the form *"if not p, then q."* The definition can be formulated, e.g., in the following way:

$$(p \text{ or } q) \text{ if, and only if, } (if \text{ not } p, \text{ then } q).$$

This definition obviously contains no semantic terms.

However, a vicious circle in definition arises only when the definiens contains either the term to be defined itself, or other terms defined with its help. Thus we clearly see that the use of sentential connectives in defining the semantic term *"true"* does not involve any circle.

I should like to mention a further objection which I have found in the literature and which seems also to concern the formal correctness, if not of the definition of truth itself, then at least of the arguments which lead to this definition.[25]

The author of this objection mistakenly regards scheme (T) (from Section 4) as a definition of truth. He charges this alleged definition with "inadmissible brevity, i.e., incompleteness," which "does not give us the means of deciding whether by 'equivalence' is meant a logical-formal, or a non-logical and also structurally non-describable relation." To remove this "defect" he suggests supplementing (T) in one of the two following ways:

(T′)   *X is true if, and only if, p is true,*

or

(T″) *X is true if, and only if, p is the case (i.e., if what p states is the case).*

Then he discusses these two new "definitions," which are supposedly free from the old, formal "defect," but which turn out to be unsatisfactory for other, non-formal reasons.

This new objection seems to arise from a misunderstanding concerning the nature of sentential connectives (and thus to be somehow related to that previously discussed). The author of the objection does not seem to realize that the phrase *"if, and only if"* (in opposition to such phrases as *"are equivalent"* or *"is equivalent to"*) expresses no relation between sentences at all since it does not combine names of sentences.

In general, the whole argument is based upon an obvious confusion between sentences and their names. It suffices to point out that—in contradistinction to (T)—schemata (T′) and (T″) do not give any meaningful expressions if we replace in them *"p"* by a sentence; for the phrases *"p is true"* and *"p is the case"* (i.e., *"what p states is the case"*) become meaningless if *"p"* is replaced by a sentence, and not by the name of a sentence (cf. Section 4).[26]

While the author of the objection considers schema (T) "inadmissibly brief," I am inclined, on my part, to regard schemata (T′) and (T″) as "inadmissibly long." And I think even that I can rigorously prove this statement on the basis of the following definition: An expression is said to be "inadmissibly long" if (i) it is meaningless, and (ii) it has been obtained from a meaningful expression by inserting superfluous words.

16. Redundancy of Semantic Terms—Their Possible Elimination. The objection I am going to discuss now no longer concerns the formal correctness of the definition, but is still concerned with certain formal features of the semantic conception of truth.

We have seen that this conception essentially consists in regarding the sentence *"X is true"* as equivalent to the sentence denoted by *"X"* (where *"X"* stands for a name of a sentence of the object-language). Consequently, the term *"true"* when occurring in a simple sentence of the form *"X is true"* can easily be eliminated, and the sentence itself, which belongs to the meta-language, can be replaced by an equivalent sentence of the object-language; and the same applies to compound sentences provided the term *"true"* occurs in them exclusively as a part of the expressions of the form *"X is true."*

Some people have therefore urged that the term *"true"* in the semantic sense can always be eliminated, and that for this reason the semantic conception of truth is altogether sterile and useless. And since the same considerations apply to other semantic notions, the conclusion has been drawn that semantics as a whole is a purely verbal game and at best only a harmless hobby.

But the matter is not quite so simple.[27] The sort of elimination here discussed cannot always be made. It cannot be done in the case of universal statements which express the fact that all sentences of a certain type are true, or that all true sentences have a certain property. For instance, we can prove in the theory of truth the following statement:

All consequences of true sentences are true.

However, we cannot get rid here of the word *"true"* in the simple manner contemplated.

Again, even in the case of particular sentences having the form *"X is true"* such a simple elimination cannot always be made. In fact, the elimination is possible only in those cases in which the name of the sentence which is said to be true occurs in a form that enables us to reconstruct the sentence itself. For example, our present historical knowledge does not give us any possibility of eliminating the word *"true"* from the following sentence:

The first sentence written by Plato is true.

Of course, since we have a definition for truth and since every definition enables us to replace the definiendum by its definiens, an elimination of the term *"true"* in its semantic sense is always theoretically possible. But this would not be the kind of simple elimination discussed above, and it would not result in the replacement of a sentence in the meta-language by a sentence in the object-language.

If, however, anyone continues to urge that—because of the theoretical possibility of eliminating the word *"true"* on the basis of its definition—the concept of truth is sterile, he must accept the further conclusion that all defined notions are sterile. But this outcome is so absurd and so unsound historically that any comment on it is unnecessary. In fact, I am rather inclined to agree with those who maintain that the moments of greatest creative advancement in science frequently coincide with the introduction of new notions by means of definition.

17. Conformity of the Semantic Conception of Truth with Philosophical and Common-Sense Usage. The question has been raised whether the semantic conception of truth can indeed be regarded as a precise form of the old, classical conception of this notion.

Various formulations of the classical conception were quoted in the early part of this paper (Section 3). I must repeat that in my judgment none of them is quite precise and clear. Accordingly, the only sure way of settling the question would be to confront the authors of those statements with our new formulation, and to ask them whether it agrees with their intentions. Unfortunately, this method is impractical since they died quite some time ago.

As far as my own opinion is concerned, I do not have any doubts that our formulation does conform to the intuitive content of that of Aristotle. I am less certain regarding the later formulations of the classical conception, for they are very vague indeed.[28]

Furthermore, some doubts have been expressed whether the semantic conception does reflect the notion of truth in its common-sense and everyday usage. I clearly realize (as I already indicated) that the common meaning of the word *"true"*—as that of any other word of everyday language—is to some extent vague, and that its usage more or less fluctuates. Hence the problem of assigning to this word a fixed and exact meaning is relatively unspecified, and every solution of this problem implies necessarily a certain deviation from the practice of everyday language.

In spite of all this, I happen to believe that the semantic conception does conform to a very considerable extent with the common-sense usage—although I readily admit I may be mistaken. What is more to the point, however, I believe that the issue raised can be settled scientifically, though of course not by a deductive procedure, but with the help of the statistical questionnaire method. As a matter of fact, such research has been carried on, and some of the results have been reported at congresses and in part published.[29]

I should like to emphasize that in my opinion such investigations must be conducted with the utmost care. Thus, if we ask a highschool boy, or even an adult intelligent man having no special philosophical training, whether he regards a sentence to be true if it agrees with reality, or if it designates an existing state of affairs, it may simply turn out that he does not understand the question; in consequence his response, whatever it may be, will be of no value for us. But his answer to the question whether he would admit that the sentence *"it is snowing"* could be true although it is not snowing, or could be false although it is snowing, would naturally be very significant for our problem.

Therefore, I was by no means surprised to learn (in a discussion devoted to these problems) that in a group of people who were questioned only 15% agreed that *"true"* means for them *"agreeing with reality,"* while 90% agreed that a sentence such as *"it is snowing"* is true if, and only if, it is snowing. Thus, a great majority of these people seemed to reject the classical conception of truth in its "philosophical" formulation, while accepting the same conception when formulated in plain words (waiving the question whether the use of the phrase "the same conception" is here justified).

18. The Definition in Its Relation to "The Philosophical Problem of Truth" and to Various Epistemological Trends. I have heard it remarked that the formal definition of truth has nothing to do with "the philosophical problem of truth." [30] However, nobody has ever pointed out to me in an intelligible way just what this problem is. I have been informed in this connection that my definition, though it states necessary and sufficient conditions for a sentence to be true, does not really grasp the "essence" of this concept. Since I have never been able to understand what the "essence" of a concept is, I must be excused from discussing this point any longer.

In general, I do not believe that there is such a thing as "the philosophical problem of truth." I do believe that there are various intelligible and interesting (but not necessarily philosophical) problems concerning the notion of truth, but I also believe that they can be exactly formulated and possibly solved only on the basis of a precise conception of this notion.

While on the one hand the definition of truth has been blamed for not being philosophical enough, on the other a series of objections have been raised charging this definition with serious philosophical implications, always of a very undesirable nature. I shall discuss now one special objection of this type; another group of such objections will be dealt with in the next section.

It has been claimed that—due to the fact that a sentence like "snow is white" is taken to be semantically true if snow is *in fact* white (italics by the critic)—logic finds itself involved in a most uncritical realism.[31]

If there were an opportunity to discuss the objection with its author, I should raise two points. First, I should ask him to drop the words *"in fact,"* which do not occur in the original formulation and which are misleading, even if they do not affect the content. For these words convey the impression that the semantic conception of truth is intended to establish the conditions under which we are warranted in asserting any given sentence, and in particular any empirical sentence. However, a moment's reflection shows that this impression is merely an illusion; and I think that the author of the objection falls victim to the illusion which he himself created.

In fact, the semantic definition of truth implies nothing regarding the conditions under which a sentence like (1):

(1)   *snow is white*

can be asserted. It implies only that, whenever we assert or reject this sentence, we must be ready to assert or reject the correlated sentence (2):

(2)   *the sentence "snow is white" is true.*

Thus, we may accept the semantic conception of truth without giving up any epistemological attitude we may have had; we may remain naïve realists, critical realists or idealists, empiricists or metaphysicians—whatever we were before. The semantic conception is completely neutral toward all these issues.

In the second place, I should try to get some information regarding the conception of truth which (in the opinion of the author of the objection) does not involve logic in a most naïve realism. I would gather that this conception must be incompatible with the semantic one. Thus, there must be sentences which are true in one of these conceptions without being true in the other. Assume, e.g., the sentence (1) to be of this kind. The truth of this sentence in the semantic conception is determined by an equivalence of the form (T):

The sentence "snow is white" is true if, and only if, snow is white.

Hence in the new conception we must reject this equivalence, and consequently we must assume its denial:

The sentence "snow is white" is true if, and only if, snow is not white (or perhaps: *snow, in fact, is not white*).

This sounds somewhat paradoxical. I do not regard such a consequence of the new conception as absurd; but I am a little fearful that someone in the future may charge this conception with involving logic in a "most sophisticated kind of irrealism." At any rate, it seems to me important to realize that every conception of truth which is incompatible with the semantic one carries with it consequences of this type.

I have dwelt a little on this whole question, not because the objection discussed seems to me very significant, but because certain points which have arisen in the discussion should be taken into account by all those who for various epistemological reasons are inclined to reject the semantic conception of truth.

19. Alleged Metaphysical Elements in Semantics. The semantic conception of truth has been charged several times with involving certain metaphysical elements. Objections of this sort have been made to apply not only to the theory of truth, but to the whole domain of theoretical semantics.[32]

I do not intend to discuss the general problem whether the introduction of a metaphysical element into a science is at all objectionable. The only point which will interest me here is whether and in what sense metaphysics is involved in the subject of our present discussion.

The whole question obviously depends upon what one understands by "metaphysics." Unfortunately, this notion is extremely vague and equivocal. When listening to discussions in this subject, sometimes one gets the impression that the term "metaphysical" has lost any objective meaning, and is merely used as a kind of professional philosophical invective.

For some people metaphysics is a general theory of objects (ontology) —a discipline which is to be developed in a purely empirical way, and which differs from other empirical sciences only by its generality. I do not know whether such a discipline actually exists (some cynics claim that it is customary in philosophy to baptize unborn children); but I think that in any case metaphysics in this conception is not objectionable to anybody, and has hardly any connections with semantics.

For the most part, however, the term "metaphysical" is used as directly opposed—in one sense or another—to the term "empirical"; at any rate, it is used in this way by those people who are distressed by the thought that any metaphysical elements might have managed to creep into science. This general conception of metaphysics assumes several more specific forms.

Thus, some people take it to be symptomatic of a metaphysical element in a science when methods of inquiry are employed which are neither deductive nor empirical. However, no trace of this symptom can be found in the development of semantics (unless some metaphysical elements are involved in the object-language to which the semantic notions refer). In particular, the semantics of formalized languages is constructed in a purely deductive way.

Others maintain that the metaphysical character of a science depends mainly on its vocabulary and, more specifically, on its primitive terms. Thus, a term is said to be metaphysical if it is neither logical nor mathematical, and if it is not associated with an empirical procedure which enables us to decide whether a thing is denoted by this term or not. With respect to such a view of metaphysics it is sufficient to recall that a meta-language includes only three kinds of undefined terms: (i) terms taken from logic, (ii) terms of the corresponding object-language, and (iii) names of expressions in the object-language. It is thus obvious that no metaphysical undefined terms occur in the meta-language (again, unless such terms appear in the object-language itself).

There are, however, some who believe that, even if no metaphysical terms occur among the primitive terms of a language, they may be introduced by definitions; namely, by those definitions which fail to provide us with general criteria for deciding whether an object falls under the defined concept. It is argued that the term *"true"* is of this kind, since no universal criterion of truth follows immediately from the definition of this term, and since it is generally believed (and in a certain sense can even be proved) that such a criterion will never be found. This comment on the actual character of the notion of truth seems to be perfectly just. However, it should be noticed that the notion of truth does not differ in this respect from many notions in logic, mathematics, and theoretical parts of various empirical sciences, e.g., in theoretical physics.

In general, it must be said that if the term "metaphysical" is employed in so wide a sense as to embrace certain notions (or methods) of logic, mathematics, or empirical sciences, it will apply *a fortiori* to those of semantics. In fact, as we know from Part I of the paper, in developing the semantics of a language we use all the notions of this language, and we apply even a stronger logical apparatus than that which is used in the language itself. On the other hand, however, I can summarize the arguments given above by stating that in no interpretation of the term "metaphysical" which is familiar and more or less intelligible to me does semantics involve any metaphysical elements peculiar to itself.

I should like to make one final remark in connection with this group of objections. The history of science shows many instances of concepts which were judged metaphysical (in a loose, but in any case derogatory sense of this term) before their meaning was made precise; however, once they received a rigorous, formal definition, the distrust in them evaporated. As typical examples we may mention the concepts of negative and imaginary numbers in mathematics. I hope a similar fate awaits the concept of truth and other semantic concepts; and it seems to me, therefore, that those who have distrusted them because of their alleged metaphysical implications should welcome the fact that precise definitions of these concepts are now available. If in consequence semantic concepts lose philosophical interests, they will only share the fate of many other concepts of science, and this need give rise to no regret.

20. *Applicability of Semantics to Special Empirical Sciences.* We come to the last and perhaps the most important group of objections. Some strong doubts have been expressed whether semantic notions find or can find applications in various domains of intellectual activity. For the most part such doubts have concerned the applicability of semantics to the field of empirical science—either to special sciences or to the general methodology of this field; although similar skepticism has been expressed regarding possible applications of semantics to mathematical sciences and their methodology.

I believe that it is possible to allay these doubts to a certain extent, and that some optimism with respect to the potential value of semantics for various domains of thought is not without ground.

To justify this optimism, it suffices I think to stress two rather obvious points. First, the development of a theory which formulates a precise definition of a notion and establishes its general properties provides *eo ipso* a firmer basis for all discussions in which this notion is involved; and, therefore, it cannot be irrelevant for anyone who uses this notion, and desires to do so in a conscious and consistent way. Secondly, semantic notions are actually involved in various branches of science, and in particular of empirical science.

The fact that in empirical research we are concerned only with natural languages and that theoretical semantics applies to these languages only with certain approximation, does not affect the problem essentially. However, it has undoubtedly this effect that progress in semantics will have but a delayed and somewhat limited influence in this field. The situation with which we are confronted here does not differ essentially from that which arises when we apply laws of logic to arguments in everyday life—or, generally, when we attempt to apply a theoretical science to empirical problems.

Semantic notions are undoubtedly involved, to a larger or smaller degree, in psychology, sociology, and in practically all the humanities. Thus, a psychologist defines the so-called intelligence quotient in terms of the numbers of *true* (right) and *false* (wrong) answers given by a person to certain questions; for a historian of culture the range of objects for which a human race in successive stages of its development possesses adequate *designations* may be a topic of great significance; a student of literature may be strongly interested in the problem whether a given author always uses two given words with the same *meaning*. Examples of this kind can be multiplied indefinitely.

The most natural and promising domain for the applications of theoretical semantics is clearly linguistics—the empirical study of natural languages. Certain parts of this science are even referred to as "semantics," sometimes with an additional qualification. Thus, this name is occasionally given to that portion of grammar which attempts to classify all words of a language into parts of speech, according to what the words mean or designate. The study of the evolution of meanings in the historical development of a language is sometimes called "historical semantics." In general, the totality of investigations on semantic relations which occur in a natural language is referred to as "descriptive semantics." The relation between theoretical and descriptive semantics is analogous to that between pure and applied mathematics, or perhaps to that between theoretical and empirical physics; the rôle of formalized languages in semantics can be roughly compared to that of isolated systems in physics.

It is perhaps unnecessary to say that semantics cannot find any direct applications in natural sciences such as physics, biology, etc.; for in none of these sciences are we concerned with linguistic phenomena, and even less with semantic relations between linguistic expressions and objects to which these expressions refer. We shall see, however, in the next section that semantics may have a kind of indirect influence even on those sciences in which semantic notions are not directly involved.

21. Applicability of Semantics to the Methodology of Empirical Science. Besides linguistics, another important domain for possible applications of semantics is the methodology of science; this term is used here in a broad sense so as to embrace the theory of science in general. Independent of whether a science is conceived merely as a system of statements or as a totality of certain statements and human activities, the study of scientific language constitutes an essential part of the methodological discussion of a science. And it seems to me clear that any tendency to eliminate semantic notions (like those of truth and designation) from this discussion would make it fragmentary and inadequate.[33] Moreover, there is no reason for such a tendency today, once the main difficulties in using semantic terms have been overcome. The semantics of scientific language should be simply included as a part in the methodology of science.

I am by no means inclined to charge methodology and, in particular, semantics—whether theoretical or descriptive—with the task of clarifying the meanings of all scientific terms. This task is left to those sciences in which the terms are used, and is actually fulfilled by them (in the same way in which, e.g., the task of clarifying the meaning of the term *"true"* is left to, and fulfilled by, semantics). There may be, however, certain special problems of this sort in which a methodological approach is desirable or indeed necessary (perhaps, the problem of the notion of causality is a good example here); and in a methodological discussion of such problems semantic notions may play an essential rôle. Thus, semantics may have some bearing on any science whatsoever.

The question arises whether semantics can be helpful in solving general and, so to speak, classical problems of methodology. I should like to discuss here with some detail a special, though very important, aspect of this question.

One of the main problems of the methodology of empirical science consists in establishing conditions under which an empirical theory or hypothesis should be regarded as acceptable. This notion of acceptability must be relativized to a given stage of the development of a science (or to a given amount of presupposed knowledge). In other words, we may consider it as provided with a time coefficient; for a theory which is acceptable today may become untenable tomorrow as a result of new scientific discoveries.

It seems *a priori* very plausible that the acceptability of a theory somehow depends on the truth of its sentences, and that consequently a methodologist in his (so far rather unsuccessful) attempts at making the notion of acceptability precise, can expect some help from the semantic theory of truth. Hence we ask the question: Are there any postulates which can be reasonably imposed on acceptable theories and which involve the notion of truth? And, in particular, we ask whether the following postulate is a reasonable one:

An acceptable theory cannot contain (or imply) any false sentences.

The answer to the last question is clearly negative. For, first of all, we are practically sure, on the basis of our historical experience, that every empirical theory which is accepted today will sooner or later be rejected and replaced by another theory. It is also very probable that the new theory will be incompatible with the old one; i.e., will imply a sentence which is contradictory to one of the sentences contained in the old theory. Hence, at least one of the two theories must include false sentences, in spite of the fact that each of them is accepted at a certain time. Secondly, the postulate in question could hardly ever be satisfied in practice; for we do not know, and are very unlikely to find, any criteria of truth which enable us to show that no sentence of an empirical theory is false.

The postulate in question could be at most regarded as the expression of an ideal limit for successively more adequate theories in a given field of research; but this hardly can be given any precise meaning.

Nevertheless, it seems to me that there is an important postulate which can be reasonably imposed on acceptable empirical theories and which involves the notion of truth. It is closely related to the one just discussed, but is essentially weaker. Remembering that the notion of acceptability is provided with a time coefficient, we can give this postulate the following form:

> *As soon as we succeed in showing that an empirical theory contains (or implies) false sentences, it cannot be any longer considered acceptable.*

In support of this postulate, I should like to make the following remarks.

I believe everybody agrees that one of the reasons which may compel us to reject an empirical theory is the proof of its inconsistency: a theory becomes untenable if we succeed in deriving from it two contradictory sentences. Now we can ask what are the usual motives for rejecting a theory on such grounds. Persons who are acquainted with modern logic are inclined to answer this question in the following way: A well-known logical law shows that a theory which enables us to derive two contradictory sentences enables us also to derive every sentence; therefore, such a theory is trivial and deprived of any scientific interest.

I have some doubts whether this answer contains an adequate analysis of the situation. I think that people who do not know modern logic are as little inclined to accept an inconsistent theory as those who are thoroughly familiar with it; and probably this applies even to those who regard (as some still do) the logical law on which the argument is based as a highly controversial issue, and almost as a paradox. I do not think that our attitude toward an inconsistent theory would change even if we decided for some reasons to weaken our system of logic so as to deprive ourselves of the possibility of deriving every sentence from any two contradictory sentences.

It seems to me that the real reason of our attitude is a different one: We know (if only intuitively) that an inconsistent theory must contain false sentences; and we are not inclined to regard as acceptable any theory which has been shown to contain such sentences.

There are various methods of showing that a given theory includes false sentences. Some of them are based upon purely logical properties of the theory involved; the method just discussed (i.e., the proof of inconsistency) is not the sole method of this type, but is the simplest one, and the one which is most frequently applied in practice. With the help of certain assumptions regarding the truth of empirical sentences, we can obtain methods to the same effect which are no longer of a purely logical nature. If we decide to accept the general postulate suggested above, then a successful application of any such method will make the theory untenable.

22. Applications of Semantics to Deductive Science. As regards the applicability of semantics to mathematical sciences and their methodology, i.e., to meta-mathematics, we are in a much more favorable position than in the case of empirical sciences. For, instead of advancing reasons which justify some hopes for the future (and thus making a kind of pro-semantics propaganda), we are able to point out concrete results already achieved.

Doubts continue to be expressed whether the notion of a true sentence —as distinct from that of a provable sentence—can have any significance for mathematical disciplines and play any part in a methodological discussion of mathematics. It seems to me, however, that just this notion of a true sentence constitutes a most valuable contribution to meta-mathematics by semantics. We already possess a series of interesting meta-mathematical results gained with the help of the theory of truth. These results concern the mutual relations between the notion of truth and that of provability; establish new properties of the latter notion (which, as well known, is one of the basic notions of meta-mathematics); and throw some light on the fundamental problems of consistency and completeness. The most significant among these results have been briefly discussed in Section 12.[34]

Furthermore, by applying the method of semantics we can adequately define several important meta-mathematical notions which have been used so far only in an intuitive way—such as, e.g., the notion of definability or that of a model of an axiom system; and thus we can understand a systematic study of these notions. In particular, the investigations on definability have already brought some interesting results, and promise even more in the future.[35]

We have discussed the applications of semantics only to meta-mathematics, and not to mathematics proper. However, this distinction between mathematics and meta-mathematics is rather unimportant. For meta-mathematics is itself a deductive discipline and hence, from a certain point of view, a part of mathematics; and it is well known that—due to the formal character of deductive method—the results obtained in one deductive discipline can be automatically extended to any other discipline in which the given one finds an interpretation. Thus, for example, all meta-mathematical results can be interpreted as results of number theory. Also from a practical point of view there is no clear-cut line between meta-mathematics and mathematics proper; for instance, the investigations on definability could be included in either of these domains.

23. Final Remarks. I should like to conclude this discussion with some general and rather loose remarks concerning the whole question of the evaluation of scientific achievements in terms of their applicability. I must confess I have various doubts in this connection.

Being a mathematician (as well as a logician, and perhaps a philosopher of a sort), I have had the opportunity to attend many discussions between specialists in mathematics, where the problem of applications is especially acute, and I have noticed on several occasions the following phenomenon: If a mathematician wishes to disparage the work of one of his colleagues, say, *A,* the most effective method he finds for doing this is to ask where the results can be applied. The hard-pressed man, with his back against the wall, finally unearths the researches of another mathematician

B as the locus of the application of his own results. If next *B* is plagued with a similar question, he will refer to another mathematician *C*. After a few steps of this kind we find ourselves referred back to the researches of *A*, and in this way the chain closes.

Speaking more seriously, I do not wish to deny that the value of a man's work may be increased by its implications for the research of others and for practice. But I believe, nevertheless, that it is inimical to the progress of science to measure the importance of any research exclusively or chiefly in terms of its usefulness and applicability. We know from the history of science that many important results and discoveries have had to wait centuries before they were applied in any field. And, in my opinion, there are also other important factors which cannot be disregarded in determining the value of a scientific work. It seems to me that there is a special domain of very profound and strong human needs related to scientific research, which are similar in many ways to aesthetic and perhaps religious needs. And it also seems to me that the satisfaction of these needs should be considered an important task of research. Hence, I believe, the question of the value of any research cannot be adequately answered without taking into account the intellectual satisfaction which the results of that research bring to those who understand it and care for it. It may be unpopular and out-of-date to say—but I do not think that a scientific result which gives us a better understanding of the world and makes it more harmonious in our eyes should be held in lower esteem than, say, an invention which reduces the cost of paving roads, or improves household plumbing.

It is clear that the remarks just made become pointless if the word "application" is used in a very wide and liberal sense. It is perhaps not less obvious that nothing follows from these general remarks concerning the specific topics which have been discussed in this paper; and I really do not know whether research in semantics stands to gain or lose by introducing the standard of value I have suggested.

NOTES

[1] Compare Tarski [2] (see bibliography at the end of the paper). This work may be consulted for a more detailed and formal presentation of the subject of the paper, especially of the material included in Sections 6 and 9–13. It contains also references to my earler publications on the problems of semantics (a communication in Polish, 1930; the article Tarski [1] in French, 1931; a communication in German, 1932; and a book in Polish, 1933). The expository part of the present paper is related in its character to Tarski [3]. My investigations on the notion of truth and on theoretical semantics have been reviewed or discussed in Hofstadter [1], Juhos [1], Kokoszyńska [1] and [2], Kotarbiński [2], Scholz [1], Weinberg [1], *et al.*

[2] It may be hoped that the interest in theoretical semantics will now increase, as a result of the present publication of the important work Carnap [2].

[3] This applies, in particular, to public discussions during the I. International Congress for the Unity of Science (Paris, 1935) and the Conference of International Congresses for the Unity of Science (Paris, 1937); cf., e.g., Neurath [1] and Gonseth [1].

[4] The words "notion" and "concept" are used in this paper with all of the vagueness and ambiguity with which they occur in philosophical literature. Thus, sometimes

they refer simply to a term, sometimes to what is meant by a term, and in other cases to what is denoted by a term. Sometimes it is irrelevant which of these interpretations is meant; and in certain cases perhaps none of them applies adequately. While on principle I share the tendency to avoid these words in any exact discussion, I did not consider it necessary to do so in this informal presentation.

⁵ For our present purposes it is somewhat more convenient to understand by "expressions," "sentences," etc., not individual inscriptions, but classes of inscriptions of similar form (thus, not individual physical things, but classes of such things).

⁶ For the Aristotelian formulation see Article [1], T, 7, 27. The other two formulations are very common in the literature, but I do not know with whom they originate. A critical discussion of various conceptions of truth can be found, e.g., in Kotarbiński [1] (so far available only in Polish), pp. 123 ff., and Russell [1], pp. 362 ff.

⁷ For most of the remarks contained in Sections 4 and 8, I am indebted to the late S. Leśniewski who developed them in his unpublished lectures in the University of Warsaw (in 1919 and later). However, Leśniewski did not anticipate the possibility of a rigorous development of the theory of truth, and still less of a definition of this notion; hence, while indicating equivalences of the form (T) as premises in the antinomy of the liar, he did not conceive them as any sufficient conditions for an adequate usage (or definition) of the notion of truth. Also the remarks in Section 8 regarding the occurrence of an empirical premiss in the antinomy of the liar, and the possibility of eliminating this premiss, do not originate with him.

⁸ In connection with various logical and methodological problems involved in this paper the reader may consult Tarski [6].

⁹ The antinomy of the liar (ascribed to Eubulides or Epimenides) is discussed here in Sections 7 and 8. For the antinomy of definability (due to J. Richard) see e.g., Hilbert-Bernays [1], Vol. II, pp. 263 ff.; for the antimony of heterological terms see Grelling-Nelson [1], p. 307.

¹⁰ Due to Professor J. Łukasiewicz (University of Warsaw).

¹¹ This can roughly be done in the following way. Let S be any sentence beginning with the words "Every sentence." We correlate with S a new sentence S* by subjecting S to the following two modifications: we replace in S the first word, "Every," by "The"; and we insert after the second word, "sentence," the whole sentence S enclosed in quotation marks. Let us agree to call the sentence S "(self-)applicable" or "non-(self-)applicable" dependent on whether the correlated sentence S* is true or false. Now consider the following sentence:

Every sentence is non-applicable.

It can easily be shown that the sentence just stated must be both applicable and non-applicable; hence a contradiction. It may not be quite clear in what sense this formulation of the antinomy does not involve an empirical premiss; however, I shall not elaborate on this point.

¹² The terms "logic" and "logical" are used in this paper in a broad sense, which has become almost traditional in the last decades; logic is assumed here to comprehend the whole theory of classes and relations (i.e., the mathematical theory of sets). For many different reasons I am personally inclined to use the term "logic" in a much narrower sense, so as to apply it only to what is sometimes called "elementary logic," i.e., to the sentential calculus and the (restricted) predicate calculus.

¹³ Cf. here, however, Tarski [3], pp. 5 f.

¹⁴ The method of construction we are going to outline can be applied—with appropriate changes—to all formalized languages that are known at the present time; although it does not follow that a language could not be constructed to which this method would not apply.

¹⁵ In carrying through this idea a certain technical difficulty arises. A sentential function may contain an arbitrary number of free variables; and the logical nature of the notion of satisfaction varies with this number. Thus, the notion in question when applied to functions with one variable is a binary relation between these functions and single objects; when applied to functions with two variables it becomes a ternary relation between functions and couples of objects; and so on. Hence, strictly speaking, we are confronted, not with one notion of satisfaction, but with infinitely

many notions; and it turns out that these notions cannot be defined independently of each other, but must all be introduced simultaneously.

To overcome this difficulty, we employ the mathematical notion of an infinite sequence (or, possibly, of a finite sequence with an arbitrary number of terms). We agree to regard satisfaction, not as a many-termed relation between sentential functions and an indefinite number of objects, but as a binary relation between functions and sequences of objects. Under this assumption the formulation of a general and precise definition of satisfaction no longer presents any difficulty; and a true sentence can now be defined as one which is satisfied by every sequence.

[16] To define recursively the notion of satisfaction, we have to apply a certain form of recursive definition which is not admitted in the object-language. Hence the "essential richness" of the meta-language may simply consist in admitting this type of definition. On the other hand, a general method is known which makes it possible to eliminate all recursive definitions and to replace them by normal, explicit ones. If we try to apply this method to the definition of satisfaction, we see that we have either to introduce into the meta-language variables of a higher logical type than those which occur in the object-language; or else to assume axiomatically in the meta-language the existence of classes that are more comprehensive than all those whose existence can be established in the object-language. See here Tarski [2], pp. 393 ff., and Tarski [5], p. 7.

[17] Due to the development of modern logic, the notion of mathematical proof has undergone a far-reaching simplification. A sentence of a given formalized discipline is provable if it can be obtained from the axioms of this discipline by applying certain simple and purely formal rules of inference, such as those of detachment and substitution. Hence to show that all provable sentences are true, it suffices to prove that all the sentences accepted as axioms are true, and that the rules of inference when applied to true sentences yield new true sentences; and this usually presents no difficulty.

On the other hand, in view of the elementary nature of the notion of provability, a precise definition of this notion requires only rather simple logical devices. In most cases, those logical devices which are available in the formalized discipline itself (to which the notion of provability is related) are more than sufficient for this purpose. We know, however, that as regards the definition of truth just the opposite holds. Hence, as a rule, the notions of truth and provability cannot coincide; and since every provable sentence is true, there must be true sentences which are not provable.

[18] Thus the theory of truth provides us with a general method for consistency proofs for formalized mathematical disciplines. It can be easily realized, however, that a consistency proof obtained by this method may possess some intuitive value— i.e., may convince us, or strengthen our belief, that the discipline under consideration is actually consistent—only in case we succeed in defining truth in terms of a meta-language which does not contain the object-language as a part (cf. here a remark in Section 9). For only in this case the deductive assumptions of a meta-language may be intuitively simpler and more obvious than those of the object-language— even though the condition of "essential richness" will be formally satisfied. Cf. here also Tarski [3], p. 7.

The incompleteness of a comprehensive class of formalized disciplines constitutes the essential content of a fundamental theorem of K. Gödel; cf. Gödel [1], pp. 187 ff. The explanation of the fact that the theory of truths leads so directly to Gödel's theorem is rather simple. In deriving Gödel's result from the theory of truth we make an essential use of the fact that the definition of truth cannot be given in a meta-language which is only as "rich" as the object-language (cf. note 17); however, in establishing this fact, a method of reasoning has been applied which is very closely related to that used (for the first time) by Gödel. It may be added that Gödel was clearly guided in his proof by certain intuitive considerations regarding the notion of truth, although this notion does not occur in the proof explicitly; cf. Gödel [1], pp. 174 f.

[19] The notions of designation and definition lead respectively to the antinomies of Grelling-Nelson and Richard (cf. note 9). To obtain an antinomy for the notion of satisfaction, we construct the following expression:

> *The sentential function X does not satisfy X.*

A contradiction arises when we consider the question whether this expression, which is clearly a sentential function, satisfies itself or not.

[20] All notions mentioned in this section can be defined in terms of satisfaction. We can say, e.g., that a given term designates a given object if this object satisfies the sentential function *"x is identical with T"* where *"T"* stands for the given term. Similarly, a sentential function is said to define a given object if the latter is the only object which satisfies this function. For a definition of consequence see Tarski [4], and for that of synonymity—Carnap [2].

[21] General semantics is the subject of Carnap [2]. Cf. here also remarks in Tarski [2], pp. 388 f.

[22] Cf. various quotations in Ness [1], pp. 13 f.

[23] The names of persons who have raised objections will not be quoted here, unless their objections have appeared in print.

[24] It should be emphasized, however, that as regards the question of an alleged vicious circle the situation would not change even if we took a different point of view, represented, e.g., in Carnap [2]; i.e., if we regarded the specification of conditions under which sentences of a language are true as an essential part of the description of this language. On the other hand, it may be noticed that the point of view represented in the text does not exclude the possibility of using truth-tables in a deductive development of logic. However, these tables are to be regarded then merely as a formal instrument for checking the provability of certain sentences; and the symbols *"T"* and *"F"* which occur in them and which are usually considered abbreviations of *"true"* and *"false"* should not be interpreted in any intuitive way.

[25] Cf. Juhos [1]. I must admit that I do not clearly understand von Juhos' objections and do not know how to classify them; therefore, I confine myself here to certain points of a formal character. Von Juhos does not seem to know my definition of truth; he refers only to an informal presentation in Tarski [3] where the definition has not been given at all. If he knew the actual definition, he would have to change his argument. However, I have no doubt that he would discover in this definition some "defects" as well. For he believes he has proved that "on ground of principle it is impossible to give such a definition at all."

[26] The phrases *"p is true"* and *"p is the case"* (or better *"it is true that p"* and *"it is the case that p"*) are sometimes used in informal discussions, mainly for stylistic reasons; but they are considered then as synonymous with the sentence represented by *"p."* On the other hand, as far as I understand the situation, the phrases in question cannot be used by von Juhos synonymously with *"p"*; for otherwise the replacement of (T) by (T′) or (T″) would not constitute any "improvement."

[27] Cf. the discussion of this problem in Kokoszyńska [1], pp. 161 ff.

[28] Most authors who have discussed my work on the notion of truth are of the opinion that my definition does conform with the classical conception of this notion; see, e.g., Kotarbiński [2] and Scholz [1].

[29] Cf. Ness [1]. Unfortunately, the results of that part of Ness' research which is especially relevant for our problem are not discussed in his book; compare p. 148, footnote 1.

[30] Though I have heard this opinion several times, I have seen it in print only once and, curiously enough, in a work which does not have a philosophical character—in fact, in Hilbert-Bernays [1], Vol. II, p. 269 (where, by the way, it is not expressed as any kind of objection). On the other hand, I have not found any remarks to this effect in discussions of my work by professional philosophers (cf. note 1).

[31] Cf. Gonseth [1], pp. 187 f.

[32] See Nagel [1], and Nagel [2], pp. 471 f. A remark which goes, perhaps, in the same direction is also to be found in Weinberg [1], p. 77; cf., however, his earlier remarks, pp. 75 f.

[33] Such a tendency was evident in earlier works of Carnap (see, e.g., Carnap [1], especially Part V) and in writings of other members of The Vienna Circle. Cf. here Kokoszyńska [1] and Weinberg [1].

[34] For other results obtained with the help of the theory of truth see Gödel [2]; Tarski [2], pp. 401 ff.; and Tarski [5], pp. 111 f.

[35] An object—e.g., a number or a set of numbers—is said to be definable (in a given formalism) if there is a sentential function which defines it; cf. note 20. Thus, the term "definable," though of a meta-mathematical (semantic) origin, is purely mathematical as to its extension, for it expresses a property (denotes a class) of mathematical objects. In consequence, the notion of definability can be re-defined in purely mathematical terms, though not within the formalized discipline to which this notion refers; however, the fundamental idea of the definition remains unchanged. Cf. here—also for further bibliographic references—Tarski [1]; various other results concerning definability can also be found in the literature, e.g., in Hilbert-Bernays [1] Vol. I, pp. 354 ff., 369 ff., 456 ff., etc., and in Lindenbaum-Tarski [1]. It may be noticed that the term "definable" is sometimes used in another, meta-mathematical (but not semantic), sense; this occurs, for instance, when we say that a term is definable in other terms (on the basis of a given axiom system). For a definition of a model of an axiom system see Tarski [4].

BIBLIOGRAPHY

Only the books and articles actually referred to in the paper will be listed here.

Aristotle [1]. *Metaphysica* (*Works,* Vol. VIII). English translation by W. D. Ross, Oxford, 1908.
Carnap, R. [1]. *Logical Syntax of Language,* London and New York, 1937.
Carnap, R. [2]. *Introduction to Semantics,* Cambridge, 1942.
Gödel, K. [1]. "Über formal unentscheidbare Sätze der *Principia Mathematica* und verwandter Systeme, I," *Monatshefte für Mathematik und Physik,* Vol. XXXVIII, 1931, pp. 173–198.
Gödel, K. [2]. "Über die Länge von Beweisen," *Ergebnisse eines mathematischen Kolloquiums,* Vol. VII, 1936, pp. 23–24.
Gonseth, F. [1]. "Le Congrès Descartes. Questions de Philosophie scientifique," *Revue thomiste,* Vol. XLIV, 1938, pp. 183–193.
Grelling, K., and Nelson, L. [1]. "Bemerkungen zu den Paradoxien von Russell und Burali-Forti," *Abhandlungen der Fries'schen Schule,* Vol. II (new series), 1908, pp. 301–334.
Hofstadter, A. [1]. "On Semantic Problems," *The Journal of Philosophy,* Vol. XXXV, 1938, pp. 225–232.
Hilbert, D., and Bernays, P. [1]. *Grundlagen der Mathematik,* 2 vols., Berlin, 1934–1939.
Juhos, B. von. [1]. "The Truth of Empirical Statements," *Analysis,* Vol. IV, 1937, pp. 65–70.
Kokoszyńska, M. [1]. "Über den absoluten Wahrheitsbegriff und einige andere semantische Begriffe," *Erkenntnis,* 6, 1936, pp. 143–165.
Kokoszyńska, M. [2]. "Syntax, Semantik und Wissenschaftslogik," *Actes du Congrès International de Philosophie Scientifique,* Vol. III, Paris, 1936, pp. 9–14.
Kotarbiński, T. [1]. *Elementy teorji poznania, logiki formalnej i metodologji nauk* (*Elements of Epistemology, Formal Logic, and the Methodology of Sciences,* in Polish), Lwów, 1929.
Kotarbiński, T. [2]. "W sprawie pojęcia prawdy" (*"Concerning the Concepts of Truth,"* in Polish), *Przeglad filozoficzny,* Vol. XXXVII, pp. 85–91.
Lindenbaum, A., and Tarski, A. [1]. "Über die Beschränktheit der Ausdrucksmittel deduktiver Theorien," *Ergebnisse eines mathematischen Kolloquiums,* Vol. VII, 1936, pp. 15–23.
Nagel, E. [1]. Review of Hofstadter [1], *The Journal of Symbolic Logic,* Vol. III, 1938, p. 90.
Nagel, E. [2]. Review of Carnap [2], *The Journal of Philosophy,* Vol. XXXIX, 1942, pp. 468–473.
Ness, A. [1]. " 'Truth' As Conceived by Those Who are Not Professional Philos-

ophers," *Skrifter utgitt av Det Norske Videnskaps-Akademi i Oslo, II. Hist.-Filos. Klasse,* Vol. IV, Oslo, 1938.

Neurath, O. [1]. "Erster Internationaler Kongress für Einheit der Wissenschaft in Paris 1935," *Erkenntnis,* 5, 1935, pp 377–406.

Russell, B. [1]. *An Inquiry Into Meaning and Truth,* New York, 1940.

Scholz, H. [1]. Review of *Studia philosophica,* Vol. I, *Deutsche Literaturzeitung,* Vol. LVIII, 1937, pp. 1914–1917.

Tarski, A. [1]. "Sur les ensembles définissables de nombres réels. I." *Fundamenta mathematicae,* Vol. XVII, 1931, pp. 210–239.

Tarski, A. [2]. "Der Wahrheitsbegriff in den formalisierten Sprachen" (German translation of a book in Polish, 1933), *Studia philosophica,* Vol. I, 1935, pp. 261–405.

Tarski, A. [3]. "Grundlegung der wissenchaftlichen Semantik," *Actes du Congrès International de Philosophie Scientifique,* Vol. III, Paris, 1936, pp. 1–8.

Tarski, A. [4]. "Über den Begriff der logischen Folgerung," *Actes du Congrès International de Philosophie Scientifique,* Vol. VII, Paris, 1937, pp. 1–11.

Tarski, A. [5]. "On Undecidable Statements in Enlarged Systems of Logic and the Concept of Truth," *The Journal of Symbolic Logic,* Vol. IV, 1939, pp. 105–112.

Tarski, A. [6]. *Introduction to Logic,* New York, 1941.

Weinberg, J. [1]. Review of *Studia philosophica,* Vol. I, *The Philosophical Review,* Vol. XLVII, pp. 70–77.

QUESTIONS FOR STUDY AND DISCUSSION

1. Explain the criterion for the material adequacy of the definition of truth.
2. When is the structure of a language exactly specified?
3. Could a language with a structure exactly specified adequately replace spoken language?
4. Explain the relation between an object-language and a meta-language.
5. Which of these two languages is more formalized and why?

A. J. Ayer

ALFRED JULES AYER (b. 1910) received his B.A. from Oxford University
in 1932 and immediately was appointed a lecturer in philosophy at
Christ Church College, Oxford. In 1946 he joined the faculty of the
University of London and two years later spent an academic year as
visiting professor at New York University. In 1959 he accepted a
professorship at Oxford. The principal exponent of logical empiricism in
Great Britain, Ayer has made accessible doctrines that had been developed
by Russell, Wittgenstein, and the Vienna Circle. Among his important
works are *Language, Truth, and Logic* (1936), *Foundations of Empirical
Knowledge* (1940), *Philosophical Essays* (1954), and *The Problem of
Knowledge* (1956).

Philosophy as the Analysis of Language

THE FUNCTION OF PHILOSOPHY

Among the superstitions from which we are freed by the abandonment of
metaphysics is the view that it is the business of the philosopher to construct a deductive system. In rejecting this view we are not, of course, suggesting that the philosopher can dispense which deductive reasoning. We
are simply contesting his right to posit certain first principles, and then
offer them with their consequences as a complete picture of reality. To dis-
credit this procedure, one has only to show that there can be no first principles of the kind it requires.

As it is the function of these first principles to provide a certain basis
for our knowledge, it is clear that they are not to be found among the so-
called laws of nature. For we shall see that the "laws of nature," if they are
not mere definitions, are simply hypotheses which may be confuted by experience. And, indeed, it has never been the practice of the system-
builders in philosophy to choose inductive generalizations for their premises. Rightly regarding such generalizations as being merely probable, they
subordinate them to principles which they believe to be logically certain.

This is illustrated most clearly in the system of Descartes. It is commonly said that Descartes attempted to derive all human knowledge from

From pp. 46–71 of *Language, Truth, and Logic* by Alfred J. Ayer. Published by Dover
Publications, Inc., and reprinted through permission of the publisher and of Victor
Gollancz Ltd., London.

539

premises whose truth was intuitively certain: but this interpretation puts an undue stress on the element of psychology in his system. I think he realised well enough that a mere appeal to intuition was insufficient for his purpose, since men are not all equally credulous, and that what he was really trying to do was to base all our knowledge on propositions which it would be self-contradictory to deny. He thought he had found such a proposition in *"cogito,"* which must not here be understood in its ordinary sense of "I think," but rather as meaning "there is a thought now." In fact he was wrong, because *"non cogito"* would be self-contradictory only if it negated itself: and this no significant proposition can do. But even if it were true that such a proposition as "there is a thought now" was logically certain, it still would serve Descartes' purpose. For if *"cogito"* is taken in this sense, his initial principle, *"cogito ergo sum,"* is false. "I exist" does not follow from "there is a thought now." The fact that a thought occurs at a given moment does not entail that any other thought has occurred at any other moment, still less that there has occurred a series of thoughts sufficient to constitute a single self. As Hume conclusively showed, no one event intrinsically points to any other. We infer the existence of events which we are not actually observing, with the help of general principles. But these principles must be obtained inductively. By mere deduction from what is immediately given we cannot advance a single step beyond. And, consequently, any attempt to base a deductive system on propositions which describe what is immediately given is bound to be a failure.

The only other course open to one who wished to deduce all our knowledge from "first principles," without indulging in metaphysics, would be to take for his premises a set of *a priori* truths. But, as we have already mentioned, and shall later show, an *a priori* truth is a tautology. And from a set of tautologies, taken by themselves, only further tautologies can be validly deduced. But it would be absurd to put forward a system of tautologies as constituting the whole truth about the universe. And thus we may conclude that it is not possible to deduce all our knowledge from "first principles"; so that those who hold that it is the function of philosophy to carry out such a deduction are denying its claim to be a genuine branch of knowledge.

The belief that it is the business of the philosopher to search for first principles is bound up with the familiar conception of philosophy as the study of reality as a whole. And this conception is one which it is difficult to criticize, because it is so vague. If it is taken to imply, as it sometimes is, that the philosopher somehow projects himself outside the world, and takes a bird's-eye view of it, then it is plainly a metaphysical conception. And it is also metaphysical to assert, as some do, that "reality as a whole" is somehow generically different from the reality which is investigated piecemeal by the special sciences. But if the assertion that philosophy studies reality as a whole is understood to imply merely that the philosopher is equally concerned with the content of every science, then we may accept it, not indeed as an adequate definition of philosophy, but as a truth about it. For we shall find, when we come to discuss the relationship of philosophy to science, that it is not, in principle, related to any one science more closely than to any other.

In saying that philosophy is concerned with each of the sciences, in a manner which we shall indicate,[1] we mean also to rule out the supposition that philosophy can be ranged alongside the existing sciences, as a special department of speculative knowledge. Those who make this supposition cherish the belief that there are some things in the world which are possible objects of speculative knowledge and yet lie beyond the scope of empirical science. But this belief is a delusion. There is no field of experience which cannot, in principle, be brought under some form of scientific law, and no type of speculative knowledge about the world which it is, in principle, beyond the power of science to give. We have already gone some way to substantiate this proposition by demolishing metaphysics; and we shall justify it to the full in the course of this book.

With this we complete the overthrow of speculative philosophy. We are now in a position to see that the function of philosophy is wholly critical. In what exactly does its critical activity consist?

One way of answering this question is to say that it is the philosopher's business to test the validity of our scientific hypotheses and everyday assumptions. But this view, though very widely held, is mistaken. If a man chooses to doubt the truth of all the propositions he ordinarily believes, it is not in the power of philosophy to reassure him. The most that philosophy can do, apart from seeing whether his beliefs are self-consistent, is to show what are the criteria which are used to determine the truth or falsehood of any given proposition: and then, when the sceptic realises that certain observations would verify his propositions, he may also realise that he could make those observations, and so consider his original beliefs to be justified. But in such a case one cannot say that it is philosophy which justifies his beliefs. Philosophy merely shows him that experience can justify them. We may look to the philosopher to show us what we accept as constituting sufficient evidence for the truth of any given empirical proposition. But whether the evidence is forthcoming or not is in every case a purely empirical question.

If anyone thinks that we are here taking too much for granted, let him refer to the chapter on "Truth and Probability," in which we discuss how the validity of synthetic propositions is determined. He will see there that the only sort of justification that is necessary or possible for self-consistent empirical propositions is empirical verification. And this applies just as much to the laws of science as to the maxims of common sense. Indeed there is no difference in kind between them. The superiority of the scientific

---

[1] Discussed in Chapters 3 and 8 of *Language, Truth, and Logic*. [A.J.A.]

hypothesis consists merely in its being more abstract, more precise, and more fruitful. And although scientific objects such as atoms and electrons seem to be fictitious in a way that chairs and tables are not, here, too, the distinction is only a distinction of degree. For both these kinds of objects are known only by their sensible manifestations and are definable in terms of them.

It is time, therefore, to abandon the superstition that natural science cannot be regarded as logically respectable until philosophers have solved the problem of induction. The problem of induction is, roughly speaking, the problem of finding a way to prove that certain empirical generalizations which are derived from past experience will hold good also in the future. There are only two ways of approaching this problem on the assumption that it is a genuine problem, and it is easy to see that neither of them can lead to its solution. One may attempt to deduce the proposition which one is required to prove either from a purely formal principle or from an empirical principle. In the former case one commits the error of supposing that from a tautology it is possible to deduce a proposition about a matter of fact; in the latter case one simply assumes what one is setting out to prove. For example, it is often said that we can justify induction by invoking the uniformity of nature, or by postulating a "principle of limited independent variety." [2] But, in fact, the principle of the uniformity of nature merely states, in a misleading fashion, the assumption that past exerience is a reliable guide to the future; while the principle of limited independent variety presupposes it. And it is plain that any other empirical principle which was put forward as a justification of induction would beg the question in the same way. For the only grounds which one could have for believing such a principle would be inductive grounds.

Thus it appears that there is no possible way of solving the problem of induction, as it is ordinarily conceived. And this means that it is a fictitious problem, since all genuine problems are at least theoretically capable of being solved: and the credit of natural science is not impaired by the fact that some philosophers continue to be puzzled by it. Actually, we shall see that the only test to which a form of scientific procedure which satisfies the necessary condition of self-consistency is subject, is the test of its success in practice. We are entitled to have faith in our procedure just so long as it does the work which it is designed to do—that is, enables us to predict future experience, and so to control our environment. Of course, the fact that a certain form of procedure has always been successful in practice affords no logical guarantee that it will continue to be so. But then it is a mistake to demand a guarantee where it is logically impossible to obtain one. This does not mean that it is irrational to expect future experience to conform to the past. For when we come to define "rationality" we shall

---

[2] Cf. J. M. Keynes, *A Treatise on Probability,* Part III. [A.J.A.]

find that for us "being rational" entails being guided in a particular fashion by past experience.

The task of defining rationality is precisely the sort of task that it is the business of philosophy to undertake. But in achieving this it does not justify scientific procedure. What justifies scientific procedure, to the extent to which it is capable of being justified, is the success of the predictions to which it gives rise: and this can be determined only in actual experience. By itself, the analysis of a synthetic principle tells us nothing whatsoever about its truth.

Unhappily, this fact is generally disregarded by philosophers who concern themselves with the so-called theory of knowledge. Thus it is common for writers on the subject of perception to assume that, unless one can give a satisfactory analysis of perceptual situations, one is not entitled to believe in the existence of material things. But this is a complete mistake. What gives one the right to believe in the existence of a certain material thing is simply the fact that one has certain sensations: for, whether one realises it or not, to say that the thing exists is equivalent to saying that such sensations are obtainable. It is the philosopher's business to give a correct definition of material things in terms of sensations. But his success or failure in this task has no bearing whatsoever on the validity of our perceptual judgements. That depends wholly on actual sense-experience.

It follows that the philosopher has no right to despise the beliefs of common sense. If he does so, he merely displays his ignorance of the true purpose of his enquiries. What he is entitled to despise is the unreflecting analysis of those beliefs, which takes the grammatical structure of the sentence as a trustworthy guide to its meaning. Thus, many of the mistakes made in connection with the problem of perception can be accounted for by the fact, already referred to in connection with the metaphysical notion of "substance," that it happens to be impossible in an ordinary European language to mention a thing without appearing to distinguish it generically from its qualities and states. But from the fact that the common-sense analysis of a proposition is mistaken it by no means follows that the proposition is not true. The philosopher may be able to show us that the propositions we believe are far more complex than we suppose; but it does not follow from this that we have no right to believe them.

It should now be sufficiently clear that if the philosopher is to uphold his claim to make a special contribution to the stock of our knowledge, he must not attempt to formulate speculative truths, or to look for first principles, or to make *a priori* judgements about the validity of our empirical beliefs. He must, in fact, confine himself to works of clarification and analysis of a sort which we shall presently describe.

In saying that the activity of philosophising is essentially analytic, we are not, of course, maintaining that all those who are commonly called philosophers have actually been engaged in carrying out analyses. On the contrary, we have been at pains to show that a great deal of what is commonly called philosophy is metaphysical in character. What we have been in search of, in enquiring into the function of philosophy, is a definition of philosophy which should accord to some extent with the practice of those who are commonly called philosophers, and at the same time be consistent with the common assumption that philosophy is a special branch of knowledge. It is because metaphysics fails to satisfy this second condition that we distinguish it from philosophy, in spite of the fact that it is commonly referred to as philosophy. And our justification for making this distinction is that it is necessitated by our original postulate that philosophy is a special branch of knowledge, and our demonstration that metaphysics is not.

Although this procedure is logically unassailable, it will perhaps be attacked on the ground that it is inexpedient. It will be said that the "history of philosophy" is, almost entirely, a history of metaphysics; and, consequently, that although there is no actual fallacy involved in our using the word "philosophy" in the sense in which philosophy is incompatible with metaphysics, it is dangerously misleading. For all our care in defining the term will not prevent people from confusing the activities which we call philosophical with the metaphysical activities of those whom they have been taught to regard as philosophers. And therefore it would surely be advisable for us to abandon the term "philosophy" altogether, as a name for a distinctive branch of knowledge, and invent some new description for the activity which we were minded to call the activity of philosophizing.

Our answer to this is that it is not the case that the "history of philosophy" is almost entirely a history of metaphysics. That it contains some metaphysics is undeniable. But I think it can be shown that the majority of those who are commonly supposed to have been great philosophers were primarily not metaphysicians but analysts. For example, I do not see how anyone who follows the account which we shall give of the nature of philosophical analysis and then turns to Locke's *Essay Concerning Human Understanding* can fail to conclude that it is essentially an analytic work. Locke is generally regarded as being one who, like G. E. Moore at the present time, puts forward a philosophy of common sense.[3] But he does not, any more than Moore, attempt to give an *a priori* justification of our common-sense beliefs. Rather does he appear to have seen that it was not his business as a philosopher to affirm or deny the validity of any empirical propositions, but only to analyse them. For he is content, in his own words, "to be employed as an under-labourer in clearing the ground a little, and removing some of the rubbish that lies in the way of knowledge"; and so devotes himself to the purely analytic tasks of defining knowledge, and classifying propositions, and displaying the nature of material things. And

---

[3] Vide G. E. Moore, "A Defence of Common Sense," *Contemporary British Philosophy*, vol. II. [A.J.A.]

the small portion of his work which is not philosophical, in our sense, is not given over to metaphysics, but to psychology.

Nor is it fair to regard Berkeley as a metaphysician. For he did not, in fact, deny the reality of material things, as we are still too commonly told. What he denied was the adequacy of Locke's analysis of the notion of a material thing. He maintained that to say of various "ideas of sensation" that they belonged to a single material thing was not, as Locke thought, to say that they were related to a single unobservable underlying "somewhat," but rather that they stood in certain relations to one another. And in this he was right. Admittedly he made the mistake of supposing that what was immediately given in sensation was necessarily mental; and the use, by him and by Locke, of the word "idea" to denote an element in that which is sensibly given is objectionable, because it suggests this false view. Accordingly we replace the word "idea" in this usage by the neutral word "sense-content," which we shall use to refer to the immediate data not merely of "outer" but also of "introspective" sensation, and say that what Berkeley discovered was that material things must be definable in terms of sense-contents. We shall see, when we come finally to settle the conflict between idealism and realism, that his actual conception of the relationship between material things and sense-contents was not altogether accurate. It led him to some notoriously paradoxical conclusions, which a slight emendation will enable us to avoid. But the fact that he failed to give a completely correct account of the way in which material things are constituted out of sense-contents does not invalidate his contention that they are so constituted. On the contrary, we know that it must be possible to define material things in terms of sense-contents, because it is only by the occurrence of certain sense-contents that the existence of any material thing can ever be in the least degree verified. And thus we see that we have not to enquire whether a phenomenalist "theory of perception" or some other sort of theory is correct, but only what form of phenomenalist theory is correct. For the fact that all causal and representative theories of perception treat material things as if they were unobservable entities entitles us, as Berkeley saw, to rule them out *a priori*. The unfortunate thing is that, in spite of this, he found it necessary to postulate God as an unobservable cause of our "ideas"; and he must be criticised also for failing to see that the argument which he uses to dispose of Locke's analysis of a material thing is fatal to his own conception of the nature of the self, a point which was effectively seized upon by Hume.

Of Hume we may say not merely that he was not in practice a metaphysician, but that he explicitly rejected metaphysics. We find the strongest evidence of this in the passage with which he concludes his *Enquiry Concerning Human Understanding*. "If," he says, "we take in our hand any volume; of divinity, or school metaphysics, for instance; let us ask, Does it contain any abstract reasoning concerning quantity or number? No. Does it

contain any experimental reasoning concerning matter of fact and existence? No. Commit it then to the flames. For it can contain nothing but
sophistry and illusion." What is this but a rhetorical version of our own
thesis that a sentence which does not express either a formally true proposition or an empirical hypothesis is devoid of literal significance? It is true
that Hume does not, so far as I know, actually put forward any view concerning the nature of philosopical propositions themselves, but those of
his works which are commonly accounted philosophical are, apart from
certain passages which deal with questions of psychology, works of analysis. If this is not universally conceded, it is because his treatment of causation, which is the main feature of his philosophical work, is often misinter-
preted. He has been accused of denying causation, whereas in fact he was
concerned only with defining it. So far is he from asserting that no causal
propositions are true that he is himself at pains to give rules for judging of
the existence of causes and effects.[4] He realised well enough that the question whether a given causal proposition was true or false was not one that
could be settled *a priori,* and accordingly confined himself to discussing the
analytic question, What is it that we are asserting when we assert that one
event is causally connected with another? And in answering this question
he showed, I think conclusively, first that the relation of cause and effect
was not logical in character, since any proposition asserting a causal connection could be denied without self-contradiction, secondly that causal
laws were not analytically derived from experience, since they were not
deducible from any finite number of experiential propositions, and, thirdly,
that it was a mistake to analyse propositions asserting causal connections
in terms of a relation of necessitation which held between particular events,
since it was impossible to conceive of any observations which would have
the slightest tendency to establish the existence of such a relation. He thus
laid the way open for the view, which we adopt, that every assertion of a
particular causal connection involves the assertion of a causal law, and that
every general proposition of the form "C causes E" is equivalent to a proposition of the form "whenever C, then E," where the symbol "whenever"
must be taken to refer, not to a finite number of actual instances of C, but
to the infinite number of possible instances. He himself defines a cause as
"an object, followed by another, and where all the objects similar to the
first are followed by objects similiar to the second," or, alternatively, as "an
object followed by another, and whose appearance always conveys the
thought to that other";[5] but neither of these definitions is acceptable as it
stands. For, even if it is true that we should not, according to our standards
of rationality, have good reason to believe that an event C was the cause of
an event E unless we had observed a constant conjunction of events like C
with events like E, still there is no self-contradiction involved in asserting

---

[4] Vide *A Treatise of Human Nature,* Book I, Part III, Section 15. [A.J.A.]
[5] *An Enquiry Concerning Human Understanding,* Section 7. [A.J.A.]

the proposition "C is the cause of E" and at the same time denying that any events like C or like E ever have been observed; and this would be self-contradictory if the first of the definitions quoted was correct. Nor is it inconceivable, as the second definition implies, that there should be causal laws which have never yet been thought of. But although we are obliged, for these reasons, to reject Hume's actual definitions of a cause, our view of the nature of causation remains substantially the same as his. And we agree with him that there can be no other justification for inductive reasoning than its success in practice, while insisting more strongly than he did that no better justification is required. For it is his failure to make this second point clear that has given his views the air of paradox which has caused them to be so much undervalued and misunderstood.

When we consider, also, that Hobbes and Bentham [6] were chiefly occupied in giving definitions, and that the best part of John Stuart Mill's work consists in a development of the analyses carried out by Hume, we may fairly claim that in holding that the activity of philosophising is essentially analytic we are adopting a standpoint which has always been implicit in English empiricism. Not that the practice of philosophical analysis has been confined to members of this school. But it is with them that we have the closest historical affinity.

If I refrain from discussing these questions in detail, and make no attempt to furnish a complete list of all the "great philosophers" whose work is predominantly analytic—a list which would certainly include Plato and Aristotle and Kant—it is because the point to which this discussion is relevant is one of minor importance in our enquiry. We have been maintaining that much of "traditional philosophy" is genuinely philosophical, by our standards, in order to defend ourselves against the charge that our retention of the word "philosophy" is misleading. But even if it were the case that none of those who are commonly called philosophers had ever been engaged in what we call the activity of philosophising, it would not follow that our definition of philosophy was erroneous, given our initial postulates. We may admit that our retention of the word "philosophy" is causally dependent on our belief in the historical propositions set forth above. But the validity of these historical propositions has no logical bearing on the validity of our definition of philosophy, nor on the validity of the distinction between philosophy, in our sense, and metaphysics.

It is advisable to stress the point that philosophy, as we understand it, is wholly independent of metaphysics, inasmuch as the analytic method is commonly supposed by its critics to have a metaphysical basis. Being misled by the associations of the word "analysis," they assume that philosophical analysis is an activity of dissection; that it consists in "breaking up" objects into their constituent parts, until the whole universe is ultimately

---

[6] Jeremy Bentham (1748–1832): British jurist and philosopher; a chief expounder of utilitarianism. [J.A.W.]

exhibited as an aggregate of "bare particulars," united by external relations. If this were really so, the most effective way of attacking the method would be to show that its basic presupposition was nonsensical. For to say that the universe was an aggregate of bare particulars would be as senseless as to say that it was Fire or Water or Experience. It is plain that no possible observation would enable one to verify such an assertion. But, so far as I know, this line of criticism is in fact never adopted. The critics content themselves with pointing out that few, if any, of the complex objects in the world are simply the sum of their parts. They have a structure, an organic unity, which distinguishes them, as genuine wholes, from mere aggregates. But the analyst, so it is said, is obliged by his atomistic metaphysics to regard an object consisting of parts a, b, c, and d in a distinctive configuration as being simply $a + b + c + d$, and thus gives an entirely false account of its nature.

If we follow the Gestalt [7] psychologists, who of all men talk most constantly about genuine wholes, in defining such a whole as one in which the properties of every part depend to some extent on its position in the whole, then we may accept it as an empirical fact that there exist genuine, or organic, wholes. And if the analytic method involved a denial of this fact, it would indeed be a faulty method. But, actually, the validity of the analytic method is not dependent on any empirical, much less any metaphysical, presupposition about the nature of things. For the philosopher, as an analyst, is not directly concerned with the physical properties of things. He is concerned only with the way in which we speak about them.

In other words, the propositions of philosophy are not factual, but linguistic in character—that is, they do not describe the behaviour of physical, or even mental, objects; they express definitions, or the formal consequences of definitions. Accordingly, we may say that philosophy is a department of logic. For we shall see that the characteristic mark of a purely logical enquiry is that it is concerned with the formal consequences of our definitions and not with questions of empirical fact.

It follows that philosophy does not in any way compete with science. The difference in type between philsophical and scientific propositions is such that they cannot conceivably contradict one another. And this makes it clear that the possibility of philosophical analysis is independent of any empirical assumptions. That it is independent of any metaphysical assumptions should be even more obvious still. For it is absurd to suppose that the provision of definitions, and the study of their formal consequences, involves the nonsensical assertion that the world is composed of bare particulars, or any other metaphysical dogma.

What has contributed as much as anything to the prevalent misunderstanding of the nature of philosophical analysis is the fact that propositions

---

[7] Gestalt psychology: a school of scientific psychology developed in Germany by Wertheimer, Köhler, and Koffka as a reaction against extreme behaviorism. [J.A.W.]

and questions which are really linguistic are often expressed in such a way that they appear to be factual.[8] A striking instance of this is provided by the proposition that a material thing cannot be in two places at once. This looks like an empirical proposition, and is constantly invoked by those who desire to prove that it is possible for an empirical proposition to be logically certain. But a more critical inspection shows that it is not empirical at all, but linguistic. It simply records the fact that, as a result of certain verbal conventions, the proposition that two sense-contents occur in the same visual or tactual sense-field is incompatible with the proposition that they belong to the same material thing.[9] And this is indeed a necessary fact. But it has not the least tendency to show that we have certain knowledge about the empirical properties of objects. For it is necessary only because we happen to use the relevant words in a particular way. There is no logical reason why we should not so alter our definitions that the sentence "A thing cannot be in two places at once" comes to express a self-contradiction instead of a necessary truth.

Another good example of a linguistically necessary proposition which appears to be a record of empirical fact is the proposition, "Relations are not particulars, but universals." One might suppose that this was a proposition of the same order as, "Armenians are not Mohammedans, but Christians": but one would be mistaken. For, whereas the latter proposition is an empirical hypothesis relating to the religious practices of a certain group of people, the former is not a proposition about "things" at all, but simply about words. It records the fact that relation-symbols belong by definition to the class of symbols for characters, and not to the class of symbols for things.

The assertion that relations are universals provokes the question, "What is a universal?"; and this question is not, as it has traditionally been regarded, a question about the character of certain real objects, but a request for a definition of a certain term. Philosophy, as it is written, is full of questions like this, which seem to be factual but are not. Thus, to ask what is the nature of a material object is to ask for a definition of "material object," and this, as we shall shortly see, is to ask how propositions about material objects are to be translated into propositions about sense-contents. Similarly, to ask what is a number is to ask some such question as whether it is possible to translate propositions about the natural numbers into propositions about classes.[10] And the same thing applies to all the other philosophical questions of the form, "What is an *x?*" or, "What is the nature of

---

[8] Carnap has stressed this point. Where we speak of "linguistic" propositions expressed in "factual" or "pseudo-factual" language he speaks of "Pseudo-Objektsätze" or "quasi-syntaktische Sätze" as being expressed in the "Inhaltliche," as opposed to the "Formale Redeweise." Vide *Logische Syntax der Sprache,* Part V. [A.J.A.]

[9] Cf. my article "On Particulars and Universals," *Proceedings of the Aristotelian Society, 1933–4,* pp. 54, 55. [A.J.A.]

[10] Cf. Rudolf Carnap, *Logische Syntax der Sprache,* Part V, 79B, and 84. [A.J.A.]

x?" They are all requests for definitions, and, as we shall see, for definitions of a peculiar sort.

Although it is misleading to write about linguistic questions in "factual" language, it is often convenient for the sake of brevity. And we shall not always avoid doing it ourselves. But it is important that no one should be deceived by this practice into supposing that the philosopher is engaged on an empirical or a metaphysical enquiry. We may speak loosely of him as analysing facts, or notions, or even things. But we must make it clear that these are simply ways of saying that he is concerned with the definition of the corresponding words.

THE NATURE OF PHILOSOPHICAL ANALYSIS

From our assertion that philosophy provides definitions, it must not be inferred that it is the function of the philosopher to compile a dictionary, in the ordinary sense. For the definitions which philosophy is required to provide are of a different kind from those which we expect to find in dictionaries. In a dictionary we look mainly for what may be called *explicit* definitions; in philosophy, for definitions *in use*. A brief explanation should suffice to make the nature of this distinction clear.

We define a symbol *explicitly* when we put forward another symbol, or symbolic expression which is synonymous with it. And the word "synonymous" is here used in such a way that two symbols belonging to the same language can be said to be synonymous if, and only if, the simple substitution of one symbol for the other, in any sentence in which either can significantly occur, always yields a new sentence which is equivalent to the old. And we say that two sentences of the same language are equivalent if, and only if, every sentence which is entailed by any given group of sentences in conjunction with one of them is entailed by the same group in conjunction with the other. And, in this usage of the word "entail," a sentence *s* is said to entail a sentence *t* when the proposition expressed by *t* is deducible from the proposition expressed by *s;* while a proposition *p* is said to be deducible from, or to follow from, a proposition *q* when the denial of *p* contradicts the assertion of *q*.

The provision of these criteria enables us to see that the vast majority of the definitions which are given in ordinary discourse are *explicit* definitions. In particular, it is worth remarking that the process of defining *per genus et differentiam,* to which Aristotelian logicians devote so much attention, always yields definitions which are explicit in the foregoing sense. Thus, when we define an oculist as an eye-doctor, what we are asserting is that, in the English language, the two symbols "oculist" and "eye-doctor" are synonymous. And, generally speaking, all the questions that are discussed by logicians in connection with this mode of definition are concerned with the possible ways of finding synonyms in a given language for any given term. We shall not enter into these questions ourselves, because they are irrelevant to our present purpose, which is to expound the method of philosophy. For the philosopher, as we have already said, is primarily concerned with the provision, not of *explicit* definitions, but of definitions *in use*.

We define a symbol *in use*, not by saying that it is synonymous with some other symbol, but by showing how the sentences in which it significantly occurs can be translated into equivalent sentences, which contain neither the *definiendum* itself, nor any of its synonyms. A good illustration of this process is provided by Bertrand Russell's so-called theory of definite descriptions, which is not a theory at all in the ordinary sense, but an indication of the way in which all phrases of the form "the so-and-so" are to be defined.[11] It proclaims that every sentence which contains a symbolic expression of this form can be translated into a sentence which does not contain any such expression, but does contain a sub-sentence asserting that one, and only one, object possesses a certain property, or else that no one object possesses a certain property. Thus, the sentence "The round square cannot exist" is equivalent to "No one thing can be both square and round"; and the sentence "The author of *Waverley* was Scotch" is equivalent to "One person, and one person only, wrote *Waverley,* and that person was Scotch." The first of these examples provides us with a typical illustration of the way in which any definite descriptive phrase which occurs as the subject of a negative existential sentence can be eliminated; and the second, with a typical illustration of the way in which any definite descriptive phrase which occurs anywhere in any other type of sentence can be eliminated. Together, therefore, they show us how to express what is expressed by any sentence which contains a definite descriptive phrase without employing any such phrase. And thus they furnish us with a definition of these phrases in use.

The effect of this definition of descriptive phrases, as of all good definitions, is to increase our understanding of certain sentences. And this is a benefit which the author of such a definition confers not only on others, but also on himself. It might be objected that he must already understand the sentences in order to be able to define the symbols which occur in them. But this initial understanding need not amount to anything more than an ability to tell, in practice, what sort of situations verify the propositions they express. Such an understanding of sentences containing definite descriptive phrases may be possessed even by those who believe that there are subsistent entities, such as the round square, or the present King of France. But the fact that they do maintain this shows that their understanding of these sentences is imperfect. For their lapse into metaphysics is the outcome of the naïve assumption that definite descriptive phrases are demonstrative symbols. And in the light of the clearer understanding which is afforded by Russell's definition, we see that this assumption is false. Nor

---

[11] Vide *Principia Mathematica,* Introduction, Chapter 3, and *Introduction to Mathematical Philosophy,* Chapter 16. [A.J.A.]

could this end have been achieved by an explicit definition of any descriptive phrase. What was required was a translation of sentences containing such phrases which would reveal what may be called their logical complexity. In general, we may say that it is the purpose of a philosophical definition to dispel those confusions which arise from our imperfect understanding of certain types of sentence in our language, where the need cannot be met by the provision of a synonym for any symbol, either because there is no synonym, or else because the available synonyms are unclear in the same fashion as the symbol to which the confusion is due.

A complete philosophical elucidation of any language would consist, first, in enumerating the types of sentence that were significant in that language, and then in displaying the relations of equivalence that held between sentences of various types. And here it may be explained that two sentences are said to be of the same type when they can be correlated in such a way that to each symbol in one sentence there corresponds a symbol of the same type in the other; and that two symbols are said to be of the same type when it is always possible to substitute one for the other without changing a significant sentence into a piece of nonsense. Such a system of definitions in use would reveal what may be called the structure of the language in question. And thus we may regard any particular philosophical "theory," such as Russell's "theory of definite descriptions," as a revelation of part of the structure of a given language. In Russell's case, the language is the everyday English language; and any other language, such as French or German, which has the same structure as English.[12] And, in this context, it is not necessary to draw a distinction between the spoken and the written language. As far as the validity of a philosophical definition is concerned, it does not matter whether we regard the symbol defined as being constituted by visible marks or by sounds.

A factor which complicates the structure of a language such as English is the prevalence of ambiguous symbols. A symbol is said to be ambiguous when it is constituted by signs which are identical in their sensible form, not only with one another, but also with signs which are elements of some other symbol. For what makes two signs elements of the same symbol is not merely an identity of form, but also an identity of usage. Thus, if we were guided merely by the form of the sign, we should assume that the "is" which occurs in the sentence "He is the author of that book" was the same symbol as the "is" which occurs in the sentence "A cat is a mammal." But, when we come to translate the sentences, we find that the first is equivalent to "He, and no one else, wrote that book," and the second to "The class of mammals contains the class of cats." And this shows that, in this instance, each "is" is an ambiguous symbol which must not be confused with the other, nor with the ambiguous symbols of existence, and class-membership,

---

[12] This must not be taken to imply that all English-speaking people actually employ a single, precise system of symbols. Vide pp. 70–1. [A.J.A.]

and identity, and entailment, which are also constituted by signs of the form "is."

To say that a symbol is constituted by signs which are identical with one another in their sensible form, and in their significance, and that a sign is a sense-content, or a series of sense-contents, which is used to convey literal meaning, is not to say that a symbol is a collection, or system, of sense-contents. For when we speak of certain objects, *b, c, d* . . . as being elements of an object *e,* and of *e* as being constituted by *b, c, d* . . . we are not saying that they form part of *e,* in the sense in which my arm is a part of my body, or a particular set of books on my shelf is part of my collection of books. What we are saying is that all the sentences in which the symbol *e* occurs can be translated into sentences which do not contain *e* itself, or any symbol which is synonymous with *e,* but do contain symbols *b, c, d* . . . In such a case we say that *e* is a logical construction out of *b, c, d* . . . And, in general, we may explain the nature of logical constructions by saying that the introduction of symbols which denote logical constructions is a device which enables us to state complicated propositions about the elements of these constructions in a relatively simple form.

What one must not say is that logical constructions are fictitious objects. For while it is true that the English State, for example, is a logical construction out of individual people, and that the table at which I am writing is a logical construction out of sense-contents, it is not true that either the English State or this table is fictitious, in the sense in which Hamlet or a mirage is fictitious. Indeed, the assertion that tables are logical constructions out of sense-contents is not a factual assertion at all, in the sense in which the assertion that tables were fictitious objects would be a factual assertion, albeit a false one. It is, as our explanation of the notion of a logical construction should have made clear, a linguistic assertion, to the effect that the symbol "table" is definable in terms of certain symbols which stand for sense-contents, not explicitly, but in use. And this, as we have seen, is tantamount to saying that sentences which contain the symbol "table," or the corresponding symbol in any language which has the same structure as English, can all be translated into sentences of the same language which do not contain that symbol, nor any of its synonyms, but do contain certain symbols which stand for sense-contents; a fact which may be loosely expressed by saying that to say anything about a table is always to say something about sense-contents. This does not, of course, imply that to say something about a table is ever to say the same thing about the relevant sense-contents. For example, the sentence, "I am now sitting in front of a table" can, in principle, be translated into a sentence which does not mention tables, but only sense-contents. But this does not mean that we can simply substitute a sense-content symbol for the symbol "table" in the original sentence. If we do this, our new sentence, so far from being equivalent to the old, will be a mere piece of nonsense. To obtain a sentence which is equivalent to the sentence about the table, but refers to sense-contents instead, the whole of the original sentence has to be altered. And this, indeed, is implied by the fact that to say that tables are logical constructions out of sense-contents is to say, not that the symbol "table" can be explicitly defined in terms of symbols which stand for sense-contents, but only that it can be so defined in use. For, as we have seen, the function of a definition in use is not to provide us with a synonym for any symbol, but to enable us to translate sentences of a certain type.

The problem of giving an actual rule for translating sentences about a material thing into sentences about sense-contents, which may be called the problem of the "reduction" of material things to sense-contents, is the main philosophical part of the traditional problem of perception. It is true that writers on perception who set out to describe "the nature of a material thing" believe themselves to be discussing a factual question. But, as we have already pointed out, this is a mistake. The question, "What is the nature of a material thing?" is, like any other question of that form, a linguistic question, being a demand for a definition. And the propositions which are set forth in answer to it are linguistic propositions, even though they may be expressed in such a way that they seem to be factual. They are propositions about the relationship of symbols, and not about the properties of the things which the symbols denote.

It is necessary to emphasise this point in connection with the "problem of perception," since the fact that we are unable, in our everyday language, to describe the properties of sense-contents with any great precision, for lack of the requisite symbols, makes it convenient to give the solution of this problem in factual terminology. We express the fact that to speak about material things is, for each of us, a way of speaking about sense-contents, by saying that each of us "constructs" material things out of sense-contents: and we reveal the relationship between the two sorts of symbols by showing what are the principles of this "construction." In other words, one answers the question, "What is the nature of a material thing?" by indicating, in general terms, what are the relations that must hold between any two of one's sense-contents for them to be elements of the same material thing. The difficulty, which here seems to arise, of reconciling the subjectivity of sense-contents with the objectivity of material things will be dealt with in a later chapter of this book.[13]

The solution which we shall now give of this "problem of perception" will serve as a further illustration of the method of philosophical analysis. To simplify the question, we introduce the following definitions. We say that two sense-contents directly resemble one another when there is either no difference, or only an infinitesimal difference, of quality between them; and that they resemble one another indirectly when they are linked by a series of direct resemblances, but are not themselves directly resemblant, a rela-

---

[13] Chapter 7. [A.J.A.]

tionship whose possibility depends on the fact that the relative product [14] of infinitesimal differences in quality is an appreciable difference in quality. And we say that two visual, or tactual, sense-contents are directly continuous when they belong to successive members of a series of actual, or possible, sense-fields, and there is no difference, or only an infinitesimal difference, between them, with respect to the position of each in its own sense-field; and that they are indirectly continuous when they are related by an actual, or possible, series of such direct continuities. And here it should be explained that to say of a sense-experience, or a sense-field which is a part of a sense-experience, or a sense-content which is a part of a sense-field, that it is possible, as opposed to actual, is to say, not that it ever has occurred or will occur in fact, but that it would occur if certain specifiable conditions were fulfilled. So when it is said that a material thing is constituted by both actual and possible sense-contents, all that is being asserted is that the sentences referring to sense-contents, which are the translations of the sentences referring to any material thing, are both categorical and hypothetical. And thus the notion of a possible sense-content, or sense-experience, is as unobjectionable as the familiar notion of a hypothetical statement.

Relying on these preliminary definitions, one may assert with regard to any two of one's visual sense-contents, or with regard to any two of one's tactual sense-contents, that they are elements of the same material thing if, and only if, they are related to one another by a relation of direct, or indirect, resemblance in certain respects, and by a relation of direct, or indirect, continuity. And as each of these relations is symmetrical—that is to say, a relation which cannot hold between any terms A and B without also holding between B and A—and also transitive—that is, a relation which cannot hold between a term A and another term B, and between B and another term C, without holding between A and C—it follows that the groups of visual and tactual sense-contents which are constituted by means of these relations cannot have any members in common. And this means that no visual, or tactual, sense-content can be an element of more than one material thing.

The next step in the analysis of the notion of a material thing is to show how these separate groups of visual and tactual sense-contents are correlated. And this may be effected by saying that any two of one's visual and tactual groups belong to the same material thing when every element of the visual group which is of minimal visual depth forms part of the same sense-experience as an element of the tactual group which is of minimal tactual depth. We cannot here define visual or tactual depth otherwise than ostensively. The depth of a visual or tactual sense-content is as much a

---

[14] "The *relative product* of two relations R and S is the relation which holds between x and z when there is an intermediate term y such that x has the relation R to y and y has the relation S to z." (*Principia Mathematica*, Introduction, Chapter 1.) [A.J.A.]

sensible property of it as its length or breadth.[15] But we may describe it by saying that one visual or tactual sense-content has a greater depth than another when it is farther from the observer's body, provided that we make it clear that this is not intended to be a definition. For it would clearly vitiate any "reduction" of material things to sense-contents if the defining sentences contained references to human bodies, which are themselves material things. We, however, are obliged to mention material things when we wish to describe certain sense-contents, because the poverty of our language is such that we have no other verbal means of explaining what their properties are.

As for the sense-contents of taste, or sound, or smell, which are assigned to particular material things, they may be classified by reference to their association with tactual sense-contents. Thus, we assign sense-contents of taste to the same material things as the simultaneously occurring sense-contents of touch which are experienced by the palate, or the tongue. And in assigning an auditory or olfactory sense-content to a material thing, we remark that it is a member of a possible series of temporarily continuous sounds, or smells, of uniform quality but gradually increasing intensity; the series, namely, which one would ordinarily be said to experience in the course of moving towards the place from which the sound, or the smell, came; and we assign it to the same material thing as the tactual sense-content which is experienced at the same time as the sound, or the smell, of maximum intensity in the series.

What is next required of us, who are attempting to analyse the notion of a material thing, is the provision of a rule for translating sentences which refer to the "real" qualities of material things. Our answer is that to say of a certain quality that it is the real quality of a given material thing is to say that it characterises those elements of the thing which are the most conveniently measured of all the elements which possess qualities of the kind in question. Thus, when I look at a coin and assert that it is really round in shape, I am not asserting that the shape of the sense-content, which is the element of the coin that I am actually observing, is round, still less that the shape of all the visual, or tactual, elements of the coin is round; what I am asserting is that roundness of shape characterises those elements of the coin which are experienced from the point of view from which measurements of shape are most conveniently carried out. And similarly I assert that the real colour of the paper on which I am writing is white, even though it may not always appear to be white, because whiteness of colour characterises those visual elements of the paper which are experienced in the conditions in which the greatest discrimination of colours is possible. And, finally, we define relations of quality, or position, between material things in terms of the relations of quality, or position, which obtain between such "privileged" elements.

This definition, or, rather, this outline of a definition, of symbols which

---

[15] See H. H. Price, *Perception*, p. 218. [A.J.A.]

stand for material things is intended to have the same sort of effect as the definition of descriptive phrases which we gave as our original example of the process of philosophical analysis. It serves to increase our understanding of the sentences in which we refer to material things. In this case also, there is, of course, a sense in which we already understand such sentences. Those who use the English language have no difficulty, in practice, in identifying the situations which determine the truth or falsehood of such simple statements as "This is a table," or "Pennies are round." But they may very well be unaware of the hidden logical complexity of such statements which our analysis of the notion of a material thing has just brought to light. And, as a result, they may be led to adopt some metaphysical belief, such as the belief in the existence of material substances or invisible substrata, which is a source of confusion in all their speculative thought. And the utility of the philosophical definition which dispels such confusions is not to be measured by the apparent triviality of the sentences which it translates.

It is sometimes said that the purpose of such philosophical definitions is to reveal the meaning of certain symbols, or combinations of symbols. The objection to this way of speaking is that it does not give an unequivocal description of the philosopher's practice, because it employs, in "meaning," a highly ambiguous symbol. It is for this reason that we defined the relation of equivalence between sentences, without referring to "meaning." And, indeed, I doubt whether all the sentences which are equivalent, according to our definition, would ordinarily be said to have the same meaning. For I think that although a complex sign of the form "the sentences s and t have the same meaning" is sometimes used, or taken, to express what we express by saying "the sentences s and t are equivalent," this is not the way in which such a sign is most commonly used or interpreted. I think that if we are to use the sign "meaning" in the way in which it is most commonly used, we must not say that two sentences have the same meaning for anyone, unless the occurrence of one always has the same effect on his thoughts and actions as the occurrence of the other. And, clearly, it is possible for two sentences to be equivalent, by our criterion, without having the same effect on anyone who employs the language. For instance, "p is a law of nature" is equivalent to "p is a general hypothesis which can always be relied on": but the associations of the symbol "law" are such that the former sentence tends to produce a very different psychological effect from its equivalent. It gives rise to a belief in the orderliness of nature, and even in the existence of a power "behind" that orderliness, which is not evoked by the equivalent sentence, and has, indeed, no rational warrant. Thus there are many people for whom these sentences do, in this common sense of "meaning," have different meanings. And this, I suspect, accounts for the widespread reluctance to admit that the laws of nature are merely hypotheses, just as the failure of some philosophers to recognise that material things are reducible to sense-contents is very largely due to the fact that no sentence which refers to sense-contents ever has the same psychological effect on them as a sentence which refers to a material thing. But, as we have seen, this is not a valid ground for denying that any two such sentences are equivalent.

Accordingly, one should avoid saying that philosophy is concerned with the meaning of symbols, because the ambiguity of "meaning" leads the undiscerning critic to judge the result of a philosophical enquiry by a criterion which is not applicable to it, but only to an empirical enquiry concerning the psychological effect which the occurrence of certain symbols has on a certain group of people. Such empirical enquiries are, indeed, an important element in sociology and in the scientific study of a language; but they are quite distinct from the logical enquiries which constitute philosophy.

It is misleading, also, to say, as some do, that philosophy tells us how certain symbols are actually used. For this suggests that the propositions of philosophy are factual propositions concerning the behaviour of a certain group of people; and this is not the case. The philosopher who asserts that, in the English language, the sentence "The author of *Waverley* was Scotch" is equivalent to "One person, and one person only, wrote *Waverley,* and that person was Scotch" is not asserting that all, or most, English-speaking people use these sentences interchangeably. What he is asserting is that, in virtue of certain rules of entailment, namely those which are characteristic of "correct" English, every sentence which is entailed by "The author of *Waverley* was Scotch," in conjunction with any given group of sentences, is entailed also by that group, in conjunction with "One person, and one person only, wrote *Waverley,* and that person was Scotch." That English-speaking people should employ the verbal conventions that they do is, indeed, an empirical fact. But the deduction of relations of equivalence from the rules of entailment which characterise the English, or any other, language is a purely logical activity; and it is in this logical activity, and not in any empirical study of the linguistic habits of any group of people, that philosophical analysis consists.[16]

Thus, in specifying the language to which he intends his definitions to apply, the philosopher is simply describing the conventions from which his definitions are deduced; and the validity of the definitions depends solely on their compatibility with these conventions. In most cases, indeed, the definitions are obtained from conventions which do, in fact, correspond to the conventions which are actually observed by some group of people. And it is a necessary condition of the utility of the definitions, as a means of clarification, that this should be so. But it is a mistake to suppose that the existence of such a correspondence is ever part of what the definitions actually assert.[17]

---

[16] There is a ground for saying that the philosopher is always concerned with an artificial language. For the conventions which we follow in our actual usage of words are not altogether systematic and precise. [A.J.A.]

[17] Thus if I wish to refute a philosophical opponent I do not argue about people's

It is to be remarked that the process of analysing a language is facilitated if it is possible to use for the classification of its forms an artificial system of symbols whose structure is known. The best-known example of such a symbolism is the so-called system of logistic which was employed by Russell and Whitehead in their *Principia Mathematica.* But it is not necessary that the language in which analysis is carried out should be different from the language analysed. If it were, we should be obliged to suppose, as Russell once suggested, "that every language has a structure concerning which, *in the language,* nothing can be said, but that there may be another language dealing with the structure of the first language, and having itself a new structure, and that to this hierarchy of languages there may be no limit." [18] This was written presumably in the belief that an attempt to refer to the structure of a language in the language itself would lead to the occurrence of logical paradoxes.[19] But Carnap, by actually carrying out such an analysis, has subsequently shown that a language can without self-contradiction be used in the analysis of itself.[20]

QUESTIONS FOR STUDY AND DISCUSSION

1. What does Ayer consider the purpose of philosophy?
2. How does Ayer define a material object?
3. What kind of definitions are provided by philosophy?
4. Explain the method of philosophical analysis.
5. Explain Ayer's theory of meaning.

---

linguistic habits. I try to prove that his definitions involve a contradiction. Suppose, for example, that he is maintaining that "A is a free agent" is equivalent to "A's actions are uncaused." Then I refute him by getting him to admit that "A is a free agent" is entailed by "A is morally responsible for his actions" whereas "A's actions are uncaused" entails "A is not morally responsible for his actions." [A.J.A.]

[18] Introduction to L. Wittgenstein's *Tractatus Logico-Philosophicus,* p. 23. [A.J.A.]

[19] Concerning logical paradoxes, see Russell and Whitehead, *Principia Mathematica,* Introduction, Chapter 2; F. P. Ramsey, *Foundations of Mathematics,* pp. 1–63; and Lewis and Langford. *Symbolic Logic,* Chapter 8. [A.J.A.]

[20] Vide *Logische Syntax der Sprache,* Parts I and II. [A.J.A.]

TOPICS FOR DISCUSSION AND TERM PAPERS

A.

1. Compare Hume's ideas about sense perception with those of Russell.
2. Do logical empiricists and analytic philosophers have the same ideas about the purpose of philosophy?
3. What do these two schools of thought have in common and how do they differ?
4. Explain the preoccupation of these two schools with language.
5. Compare their theories of knowledge with the common-sense idea about knowledge.
6. What new ideas do these schools bring to philosophy?
7. Do these philosophers offer an adequate basis for the discussion of metaphysical problems?
8. To what extent have these schools rejected a priori presuppositions?

B.

1. Compare Hume's theory of knowledge with that of Aristotle.
2. Describe the ideal of knowledge of the logical empiricists. Discuss this ideal taking into account the existentialists' ideas about the nature of being.
3. Compare the aim of philosophy as seen by the analytic school with that professed by Aquinas.
4. Explain what logical empiricists and analytic philosophers understand by metaphysics. How do their views compare with the traditional meaning of this term?
5. Compare the role of the outside world in the process of knowledge as seen by the analytic school and by pragmatism.

RECOMMENDED READINGS

Primary Sources

Ayer, A. J., ed. *Logical Positivism.* Glencoe, Ill.: The Free Press, 1959. Selected papers by major analytic philosophers. See especially the Editor's Introduction; Frank D. Ramsey, "Philosophy"; and Gilbert Ryle, "Philosophical Arguments." Also note the very good, though not complete, bibliography of logical empiricism and analytic philosophy.

Hume, David. *Essential Works of David Hume.* Ed. and with Introd. by Ralph Cohen. New York: Bantam Books, 1965. Contains, with the exception of the *Treatise,* all of Hume's major works and a representative sampling of his essays.

———. *A Treatise of Human Nature.* Garden City, N.Y.: Doubleday & Co. 1961.

———. *Works.* Ed. by T. H. Green and T. H. Grose. London: Longmans, Green & Co., 1875.

Russell, Bertrand. "Logical Positivism," *Revue Internationale de Philosophie, 1950.* Reprinted in *Logic and Knowledge: Essays 1901–1950.* Ed. by R. C.

Marsh. London: Allen & Unwin, 1956. A critical and very interesting discussion.

Ryle, Gilbert, *et al. The Revolution in Philosophy.* London: Macmillan Co., 1960. A collection of BBC Third Programme talks. Excellent introduction to analytic philosophy by the analytic philosophers themselves. Informative and easy to read.

Commentaries

Hempel, C. G. *Fundamentals of Concept Formation in Empirical Sciences.* Chicago: University of Chicago Press, 1952. A clear account of the views of logical positivism on this fundamental problem.

Kraft, V. *The Vienna Circle.* New York: Philosophical Library, 1953.

Mossner, Ernest Campbell. *The Life of David Hume.* New York: Nelson & Sons, 1954. The most authoritative biography of Hume.

Proceedings of the American Catholic Philosophical Association, XXXIV. Washington, D.C., 1960. Among the important papers contained in these *Proceedings* are Ernan McMullin, "The Analytic Approach to Philosophy"; Robert G. Miller, "Linguistic Analysis and Metaphysics"; and W. Norris Clarke, "Linguistic Analysis and Natural Theology."

Runes, Dagobert R., ed. *Twentieth-Century Philosophy.* New York: Philosophical Library, 1943. See Herbert Feigl, "Logical Empiricism."

Smith, Norman Kemp. *The Philosophy of David Hume: A Critical Study of Its Origins and Central Doctrines.* London: Macmillan Co., 1941. The most comprehensive and recent study of Hume's philosophy.

Urmson, J. O. *Philosophical Analysis: Its Development Between the Two World Wars.* Oxford: Oxford University Press, 1956. See Part II, "Logical Positivism and the Downfall of Logical Atomism."

PART FIVE

Introduction

Historical Background

Phenomenology as New Beginning

From Human Finitude to Fundamental Ontology

Freedom as the Absolute Source of Values

Being as Man's Ultimate Concern

Being, Hope, and Fidelity

The World as History—God, Fate, and Human Freedom

I and Thou—The Life of Real Relation

Readings

HEIDEGGER: *The Problem of the Finitude in Man and the Metaphysics of Dasein*

SARTRE: *Existentialism Is a Humanism*

TILLICH: *Being as Man's Ultimate Concern*

MARCEL: *On the Ontological Mystery*

BERDYAEV: *God, Fate, and Human Freedom*

BUBER: *The Life of Real Relation*

EXISTENTIALIST AND PHENOMENOLOGICAL THOUGHT:

Heidegger

Sartre

Tillich

Marcel

Berdyaev

Buber

EDITED BY

Helen James John, S.N.D.

TRINITY COLLEGE, WASHINGTON, D.C.

EXISTENTIALIST AND PHENOMENOLOGICAL THOUGHT:

Heidegger
Sartre
Tillich
Marcel
Berdyaev
Buber

Introduction

Historical Background

The metaphysical revival in twentieth-century Europe has arisen in large measure from the convergence of a profound insight and a powerful method: the insight of existentialism, with its emphasis upon the uniqueness and dignity of the human person, and the method of phenomenology, concerned with the exact description of the whole range of man's concretely given awareness.

The originality of this insight and method is the basis for the judgment held by recent historians that a decisively new period in philosophy has developed: modern philosophy ended in the nineteenth century; contemporary philosophy made its appearance in France and Germany in the work of Henri Bergson (1859–1941) and Edmund Husserl (1859–1938).

The modern period had as its central problem the certitude of human knowledge, especially in the natural sciences. It began when René Descartes (1596–1650), reacting against the widespread scepticism that followed the breakdown of scholasticism, proposed to reconstruct and unify all the sciences through the application of a deductive method modeled on mathematics.

In Germany, the modern tradition was carried forward by Immanuel Kant (1724–1804). In the *Critique of Pure Reason* (1781) Kant explored the possibility of scientific (that is, universal and necessary) knowledge for man. His conclusion established the certitude of the natural sciences, especially Newtonian physics. He held that the mind is endowed with a priori forms of perception and categories of the understanding, which it imposes upon the data of experience. The certitude of science comes, not from things in themselves, for these we can never know, but from the structure of the human mind, which determines the way in which things will appear to us.

This method of salvaging the certitude of science has the effect of destroying the value of speculative metaphysics, as Kant understood that term. Post-Cartesian metaphysics was commonly defined as a knowledge of realities inaccessible to sense experience (God, the world as a total object, the human soul); and Kant's forms of perception and categories of understanding are "empty" and misleading where experiential content is lacking. Thus Kant could assert, in his Preface to the *Critique of Pure Reason*, "I have destroyed reason to make room for faith."

The effect of this destruction was mitigated by the *Critique of Practical Reason* (1788), in which Kant explained man's sense of moral obligation by teaching that the existence of God, the freedom of the will, and the immortality of the soul, while they could never be *proved*, should be held as "postulates of practical reason" required by man's moral life.

In the post-Kantian period, the conclusions of these two *Critiques* inspired two divergent movements of thought. On the one hand, the influence of the *Critique of Pure Reason* worked to turn attention from "metaphysical" to "scientific" problems. Notably, Kant was considered to have shown the futility of proofs for the existence of God. This furthered the scientistic or positivist development of the nineteenth century. On the other hand, the idealist movement, which culminated in the philosophy of G. W. F. Hegel (1770–1831), took over from Kant the view that it is the mind that gives structure to the world of our experience, and not vice versa. The idealists then proceeded to construct through the activity of reason sweeping systematic visions of reality.

Against these two aspects of post-Kantian modern philosophy, the existentialists and phenomenologists vigorously reacted. Søren Kierkegaard (1813–55) and Friedrich Nietzsche (1844–1900), the oddly contrasting pioneers of the existentialist movement, stood in violent revolt against the abstract system-building of the idealists. Although both Bergson and Husserl were very much concerned with the problems of natural science, they worked toward the overthrow of positivism through a "return to the concrete," which extended enormously the range of data recognized as actually and undeniably *given* in man's experience. Man's awareness of the dynamic evolution of his own life, his lived relationships with other men and with God, his recognition of his own power and need to confront Being as such —all these have now emerged as problems offered by experience to philosophy.

Thus a new and vital strength has been given to the philosophy of Being. Since the Kantian "destruction" of "metaphysics" (considered as a science of what lies beyond human experience), many writers today prefer to speak of their work as "ontology" (etymologically, an understanding of Being). Their concern with the problems of Being leads them to give serious attention to the answers these questions have received since the Greek dawn of philosophy; yet the thinkers of our own time, for all their variety, have a recognizable approach—a more concrete and poignant earnestness—that distinguishes their work from the metaphysics of the past.

The phenomenological approach has drawn attention to a wide range of human experience hitherto neglected by philosophers; and at the same time the existential stress on human freedom and responsibility has made metaphysics, the study of being as being, primarily a search for the underlying meaning of man's existence. Thus the problematic of recent existential thinkers seems to converge at two poles: man as the being concerned with his Being, and Absolute Being itself, which can no longer, as Jean-Paul Sartre (b. 1905) points out, be quietly suppressed without causing any disturbance.

The bipolar tension between man and Absolute Being may be found in the metaphysical doctrines of virtually every one of the existentialists. The distinctive perspective and development of this central theme sharply set off their work one from the other; and for this reason, we have chosen our readings, in almost every case, to exemplify the author's view of this relation.[1] The readings from Husserl illustrate the "return to the concrete" —the careful attention to the actual data of experience that characterizes this approach to the understanding of reality. Martin Heidegger (b. 1889) takes up the Kantian question of the possibility of metaphysics; Sartre brings to a grim conclusion what he sees as the implicit atheism of Heidegger.

At the same time, the relation of man to Being has been increasingly seen by other thinkers as an openness to the God who has revealed himself in human history. Protestant theologian Paul Tillich (1886–1965) described God as the object of man's "ultimate concern," while Catholic philosopher Gabriel Marcel (b. 1889) discovers God as the ground of human hope and fidelity. Nicolas Berdyaev (1874–1948), heir of the Rus-

---

[1] A technical terminology for the movement, largely influenced by the vocabulary of modern philosophy, has been worked out by Edmund Husserl and Martin Heidegger, two of the most difficult philosophers. But because of the sharp doctrinal divergences within the movement, even technical terms are rarely used in the same sense by different authors; and there are cases where doctrinal disagreement leads an author consciously to avoid using the terms introduced by his colleagues.

sian Orthodox tradition, sought the meaning of history in the interaction of man, fate, and God; for Jewish thinker Martin Buber (1878–1965), "All the extended lines of relation meet in the eternal *Thou*."

Phenomenology as New Beginning

The desire to establish philosophy as a "strict science," rigorously grounded upon undeniable evidence, was a central motive in the work of Edmund Husserl, leading figure of the phenomenological movement. Having begun his scholarly career with an attempt to derive the basic concepts of mathematics from certain psychological acts, Husserl soon turned to the refutation of "psychologism." In his *Logical Investigations* (2 vols., 1900–01), he vigorously attacked the position that logical and ideal entities can be scientifically treated only from the standpoint of the psychological acts in which they present themselves. Instead, Husserl outlined a theoretical science of "pure logic," embracing both truths or propositions and the states of affairs or things to which such statements refer. To the development of this science Husserl devoted a life of austere dedication and unremitting labor; the papers left behind at his death, now preserved in the Husserl Archives at Louvain, come to some 45,000 shorthand pages. No selections by Husserl are included in this text because reprint rights could not be secured.

Husserl's *Cartesian Meditations* are based on two lectures delivered at the Sorbonne in 1929. In addressing his audience, Husserl underscored the kinship of his own philosophical endeavor with that of the French founder of modern philosophy, René Descartes. Like Descartes, Husserl was keenly aware of the paradoxes and inconsistencies in the root concepts of the science of his day, as well as of the lack of genuine communication among philosophers. And also like Descartes, he hoped, by the painstaking use of a rigorously scientific method, to achieve a radical new beginning in philosophy, so that by starting from undeniable certitudes, he might attain an all-embracing theory of science—a genuinely universal ontology.

Descartes had begun his search for certainty with an attempt to doubt all his previous knowledge. The one proposition that resisted this effort was *Cogito, ergo sum* (I think, therefore I am). This became at once the standard of evidence and the first axiom of Cartesian metaphysics. Husserl likewise began with the insistence on absolute certitude: the phenomenological "reduction" is the act of "suspending" or "putting in brackets" man's spontaneous belief in the factual existence of the objects of his experience. The reduction is found to leave intact all the actual data of experience. (Whatever be the existential status of myself and my office and the world around me, I recognize as given, as appearing phenomena, the sound of my typewriter keys, my effort to think of the next few words, the visualization of an eventual reader for the words I am now writing.) Thus for Husserl, Descartes' *cogito* says at once too little and too much: on the one hand, in the attitude of the reduction, the *ego* of the *ego cogito* is no longer the self factually existing, as a thing among other things in the world. On the other hand, there is given in the *cogito* not only the thinking subject but its *cogitata,* the intentional objects of conscious acts, or *cogitationes.* It is one of the key insights of the phenomenological movement that every conscious act refers to an object distinct from the act itself—perception to the thing perceived, love to the being loved, imagining to the object imagined. These objects are given as immediately as are the subject and its act; transcendental phenomenology explores all those data that survive the reduction's "bracketing" of our natural attitude toward the factually existing world.

Thus, Husserl's endeavor is to begin anew from the self as radical starting point. In *Cartesian Meditations* he set out to clarify fundamental experiences such as the world as "unity comprising all objects" and the ego as the abiding central "pole" of its activities, the givenness of other persons in our experience. Through these explorations he hoped to work out, by an exhaustive and painstaking "self-investigation," the concrete possibility of "philosophy as an all-embracing science grounded in an absolute foundation."

From Human Finitude to Fundamental Ontology

To bring Husserl's new method to bear on the question of Being was the work of Martin Heidegger, who served for a time as Husserl's assistant and later succeeded him as professor of Philosophy at Freiburg.

Where Husserl's concern was directed above all to subjectivity as such, Heidegger, from his earliest philosophical studies as a Jesuit seminarian, had been concerned with the fundamental problem of metaphysics: What is being as being? He approached this question through the phenomenological exploration, not of consciousness for its own sake, but of man as the being who must question Being. *Being and Time,* the massive, difficult work for which Heidegger is best known, appeared in 1927; in the Introduction Heidegger explains that his program will treat, in two parts, the whole question of Being. Part I will offer "the interpretation of *Dasein* [human reality] in terms of temporality, and the explication of time as the transcendental horizon for the question of Being." Part II will provide "the basic features of a phenomenological destruction [or radical rethinking] of the history of ontology, with the problematic of temporality as our clue." [2]

Being and Time includes only a portion of the first of these parts,—"the preparatory fundamental analysis of *Dasein*" and *"Dasein* and temporality." Other portions of the project may be found scattered throughout a

---

[2] Martin Heidegger, *Being and Time,* trans. by John Macquarrie and Edward Robinson (New York: Harper & Row, 1962), pp. 63–64.

long series of shorter studies and lectures, but it is the Heidegger of *Being and Time* who has been most influential. And it is hardly surprising that Heidegger is most often thought of, not as the philosopher of Being, but as the first, and perhaps the gloomiest (certainly the most complicated), of the recent existential prophets of nothingness, anxiety, and abandonment. However, the interpretation of his thought as an atheism was explicitly rejected by him in the famous "Letter on Humanism" written in 1947, where he stated, "Through the ontological interpretation of *Dasein* as Being-in-the-World, there is neither a positive nor a negative resolution of a possible Being-towards-God." And he added that his thought of Being "can no more be theistic than it can be atheistic."

To introduce the reader to Heidegger, we have selected the concluding sections from *Kant and the Problem of Metaphysics* (1929), in which he makes his transition from the problem of human finitude to the grounding of metaphysics. Here, more clearly and more concisely than in *Being and Time* (composed about the same time), Heidegger presents his insight into man's awareness of himself as the being who must be concerned with Being.[3]

The finitude of man is revealed in the very fact that he asks the question concerning Being; in his concern for Being man realizes himself as an essentially limited power-to-be. The fundamental theme of Kant's *Critique of Pure Reason* was precisely the question of the foundation of metaphysics. In its concluding pages, Kant summed up the "whole interest of reason, speculative as well as practical," in three questions: What can I know? What ought I to do? What may I hope? And in the introduction to his lectures on logic, Kant gathered the three questions together in a fourth: What is man? The four questions together reveal man's finitude, because the man who must question concerning his knowledge, his action, and his hope becomes aware of his finitude, in "concern" (*Sorge*). Kant's questions are brought back, in Heidegger's "repetition," from the plane of anthropology to that of metaphysics—to the question of the "essent" (that which is) in its relation to Being.

The whole notion of Being, with its many articulations and relations, finds its origin in philosophy as a fundamental human possibility. When, as men, we ask concerning Being, we ask about "the possibility of comprehending that which, as men, we already understand and have always understood." In every human situation and discourse, our own *Da-sein* (being-there) is manifest to us, as is the Being of other essents. This comprehension is preconceptual, indeterminate, and beyond question. But it constitutes man precisely as man: "Man is an essent in the midst of other essents in such a way that the essent that he is and the essent that he is not are always already manifest to him." For this mode of Being, proper to man,

---

[3] We employ in what follows the translations of Heideggerean terms used by Churchill for *Kant and the Problem of Metaphysics*. As yet no uniformity has been achieved in the English rendering of Heidegger.

Heidegger reserves the term *existence*. As *existing*, as standing forth in the world, man is both dependent upon other essents and answerable to himself as essent. Thus Being is manifest in the finitude of man. "This comprehension of Being itself is the innermost essence of finitude."

The metaphysics of *Dasein* as fundamental ontology joins the Kantian question of the possibility of metaphysics to the revelation of man's finitude. And as the finitude of *Dasein* is discovered in its forgetfulness of Being, the basic act of the metaphysics of *Dasein* must be to wrest from forgetfulness, through remembering, the possibility of the comprehension of Being.

Thus the task of fundamental ontology begins with "everydayness," in order to show how all human activity presupposes the transcendence of *Dasein*, its Being-in-the-World. Here all of man's activity is seen as "thrown," that is, as determined by his dependence upon the essent in totality, and yet as manifesting the need for the comprehension of Being in "concern." This need is concretely recognized in "anxiety" (*Angst*), the "decisive fundamental feeling" that places man before the Nothing.

Freedom as the Absolute Source of Values

Jean-Paul Sartre, most widely known of the existentialists, developed from the method of Husserl and from the perspective opened up by Heidegger a comprehensive view of reality centered upon human freedom. In his massive "essay in phenomenological ontology," *Being and Nothingness* (1943), Sartre presented his philosophy in terms of a dialectic opposition: inert matter as being in itself *(en soi)* and human subjectivity as "negative" being for itself *(pour soi)*. The tension and interrelationships of these two aspects of man's experience are traced through a rich variety of phenomenological analyses, all leading up to the "existential psychoanalysis" in which Sartre describes the fundamental project of man as an effort to become at once, in a fusion of contradictories, being in itself and being for itself. Sartre identified this fusion of contradictories as "the *Ens causa sui* [Being which is its own cause] which religions call God." Man's radical passion is thus to lose himself in becoming God. "But the idea of God is contradictory, and we lose ourselves in vain; man is a futile passion."

In *Being and Nothingness*, Sartre's atheism presents itself as a conclusion arising from description of man's experience of his own being as negation of the inert and absurd being of things. The lecture *Existentialism Is a Humanism* (1946) proceeds in the other direction. Indeed, in its closing lines, Sartre can assert that "Existentialism is nothing else but an attempt to draw the full conclusions from a consistently atheistic position." In drawing these conclusions, he sketches with striking coherence the main lines not only of his atheological position, but also of his ethical principles and his understanding of man. This brief presentation, though obviously a simplification of Sartre's positions, has been regarded as a kind of manifesto of atheistic existentialism. We should note, however, that Sartre's efforts to relate his atheistic conclusions to the teaching of Heidegger have been explicitly repudiated by Heidegger himself.

The principle which Sartre takes as his starting point is that *"existence comes before essence."* In Sartre's usage, this means that man (Heidegger's *Dasein*) *is,* before he can be in any way defined. To begin with, man is nothing; "there is no human nature, because there is no God to have a conception of it." Man exists only as the necessity of choosing himself; he is absolutely free, and as free he bears the complete responsibility for his choices. He must create his own essence, in the sense of his determinate qualities and attributes; and his act of choice is the only source of values. Thus for Sartre, Heidegger's notions of anguish and abandonment, far from expressing man's dependence on the reality that surrounds him, arise from realization of his "complete and profound responsibility." Man is forlorn, "without excuse," for he can depend upon nothing outside himself for justification of his action. (Sartre never faces squarely the question of why, if I am the only source of meaning and value, I should feel any need to justify or excuse myself.)

The position that human freedom is the only ground of value might entail the consequence that human action is pointless and human responsibility meaningless. Sartre evades this consequence by an appeal to the Kantian principle that in choosing for myself I choose also for others; [4] he asserts that a choice that is not based upon freedom *as its motive* is "inauthentic" and grounded in self-deception. Moreover, he contends, no moral code can supply a guide for action, for only the free individual can decide what principle to apply in a given case. All man can do is to act in "despair," relying only upon himself; the eventual meaning of his life is simply the sum of his actions.

This ethical perspective is based upon the "absolute truth" of the Cartesian *cogito,* which Sartre interprets as including the recognition of other subjects with whom I exist. Moreover, while insisting that man has no nature, no essence, Sartre ascribes to the "human condition" the universal situation and limitations of man. In choosing myself and in understanding the purposes of other men, in their diverse historical situations, I recognize each man's free act of self-commitment as the only ground of absolute and universally intelligible being. Freedom becomes at once the only ground of human understanding and the only worthy object of man's moral striving.

---

[4] Sartre's treatment here contrasts strangely with the chapter on "Concrete Relations with Others" in *Being and Nothingness,* in which Sartre sees conflict as the most profound meaning of being for another. The fundamental human relationship in this context is the effort of the subject to maintain his central position in his own world by reducing the other person to the status of an object.

And human finitude, which Heidegger sees as man's openness to Being, becomes the basis of a humanism that sees man as "the heart and center of his transcendence," in the sense that there is no universe other than the universe of human subjectivity.

Being as Man's Ultimate Concern

As we have just seen, Sartre has drawn from Heidegger's analysis of *Dasein* the conceptual framework for what is probably the most radical and consistent atheism of all times. In striking contrast, several contemporary theologians have made use of Heideggerean perspectives to clarify the meaning of Christian revelation for man's life today. The theology of Karl Rahner incorporates into Catholic thought a number of fruitful insights gained from Rahner's study under Heidegger at Freiburg; the "demythologizing" interpretation of Christianity offered by Rudolf Bultmann, a major German Protestant theologian, is even more radically indebted to Heidegger's existentialism;[5] Paul Tillich, perhaps the leading American Protestant theologian of our century, made ample use of Heideggerean concepts and perspectives in the working out of his *Systematic Theology* (3 vols., 1951, 1957, 1963). In fact, the size and scope of Tillich's masterwork, with its persistent and methodical "correlation" of philosophy and theology, cannot but remind the reader of the *Summa Theologica* of Aquinas; Heidegger seems to play in Tillich's thought a role similar to that of Aristotle in Thomism.

Consequently Tillich's views on the relation of philosophy and theology present an interesting and fruitful analogy with those of the medieval theologians. Like Aquinas, Tillich transformed the philosophical concepts that he employed; he was a philosopher in his own right. But his view of philosophy derived rather from the modern than from the classical philosophers. For him, *the* philosophical question par excellence concerns "the character of the general structures that make experience possible." It is, in fact, precisely this question that motivates the Kantian *Critiques*. Philosophy so understood is marked by its disinterested, critical attitude and is defined as *"that cognitive approach to reality in which reality as such is the object."*

In contrast, theology is defined in terms of man's total and personal involvement in it. *"The object of theology is what concerns us ultimately. Only those propositions are theological which deal with their object in so far as it can become a matter of ultimate concern for us."*[6] The attitude of the theologian is an existential one in the sense that he participates in his quest for further knowledge with the whole of his existence. "In all

---

[5] Cf. John Macquarrie, *An Existentialist Theology: A Comparison of Heidegger and Bultmann* (New York: Harper & Row, 1965).
[6] Paul Tillich, *Systematic Theology* (Chicago: University of Chicago Press, 1951), I, 12. The point has been made that this definition of theology would include not only such philosophers as Marcel and Buber, but also Nietzsche, Sartre, and in some moods Bertrand Russell.

existential knowledge both subject and object are transformed by the very act of knowing. Existential knowledge is based on an encounter in which a new meaning is created and recognized." [7] But there is a wide area of co-incidence between the work of the theologian and that of the philosopher. Both must ask the question concerning being. The philosopher, however perfect his detachment, *exists* and cannot fail to be concerned with being. And the theologian cannot make clear the universal validity of that which concerns him ultimately unless he is willing to maintain a critical detachment from every expression of his ultimate concern, even to take the risk of being driven beyond the "theological circle" of his commitment in faith and his concrete situation within the church.

Yet there can be, Tillich insisted, neither a conflict nor a synthesis between philosophy and theology. For any conflict or synthesis must take place *either* on the plane of ontological analysis *or* on the plane of ultimate concern. (One is reminded here of Aquinas' retort to those who charged him with mixing the water of philosophy with the wine of sacred doctrine —that, far from watering the wine, he was changing water into wine!) This meant, for Tillich, that there is one sense in which all modern philosophy is Christian, and another sense in which Christian philosophy is impossible. On the one hand, no philosopher who has lived and worked within Western civilization can escape the fact that Christianity provides the "existential basis" of his thought. "Reality is encountered differently; experience has different dimensions and directions than in the cultural climate of Greece." From this point of view, Marxism has been called a Christian heresy; the early thought of Heidegger was characterized as expressing "the experience of the rejection of Christian existence." [8] On the other hand, if Christian philosophy sets out not to confront reality as such but to support the demands of a church, then the Christianity cancels out the philosophy.[9]

In Tillich's own philosophical thought, as elaborated in the first volume of *Systematic Theology,* man's selfhood, freedom, and finitude are the structures through which he lives, and through which he stands open to being. The special character of man's selfhood, as distinct from that of other beings, is that man has not merely an environment but a *world,* in which all possible perspectives and environments are brought to unity. To confront the world, man must be able to recognize his own distinction from it (Karl Rahner identifies this process with Thomist *abstractio*); apart from the world man's selfhood is empty, unconscious even of itself. For Tillich "the interdependence of ego-self and world is the basic ontological structure and implies all the others."

Tillich draws both on Heidegger and on the history of philosophy in his

---

[7] Tillich, *The Courage to Be* (New Haven: Yale University Press, 1952), p 124.
[8] Alphonse de Waelhens, *La Philosophie de Martin Heidegger,* 3rd ed. (Louvain: E. Nauwelaerts, 1948), pp. 359–60.
[9] Tillich's position here is very similar to that held by the Louvain Thomists in controversy with Etienne Gilson in the 1930s.

treatment of the dialectic of being and nonbeing. He points out the dualism of matter versus idea and of evil versus the good, in which both Plato and Augustine interpreted nonbeing as an actual resistance to being. And along with many other recent observers, Tillich sees at the root of contemporary existentialism a radical encounter with nothingness—a profound experience of man's being as threatened both by death and by the loss of meaning.

In every being short of being itself (God, the power of being), being and nonbeing are in tension, a tension analogous to that of act and potency in classical metaphysics. Man experiences his finitude precisely in looking at himself from the point of view of a potential infinity, in realizing his relation to being itself. In Tillich's thought, as in Kant's, infinity is not an object of human understanding, but a "directing" concept: "Infinity is a demand, not a thing." Yet, while denying that man's awareness of infinity can establish the existence of an infinite being, Tillich asserts that "Being itself manifests itself to finite being in the infinite drive of the finite beyond itself." However, finitude is experienced by man in anxiety, which arises from the ever present threat of nonbeing.

In his discussion of "Finitude and the Categories" Tillich defines the ontological categories as "forms of finitude," related at once to nonbeing and being, and giving rise in man's experience to both anxiety and courage. Awareness of time as an inescapable condition of human experience joins anxiety in the face of death with the courage of self-affirmation in the present. Man's presence in space—his situation in the world and in society—is essential to his being; but no space belongs definitively to any finite being. Man recognizes himself as threatened with the loss of every space, ultimately faced with spacelessness: "Its place knoweth it no more." Courage lies in the acceptance of this ontological insecurity.

The tension of anxiety and courage in all these aspects of man's being leads Tillich to the ontological question in its deepest theological significance. The categories "express the union of being and nonbeing in everything finite. They articulate the courage which accepts the anxiety of nonbeing. The question of God is the question of the possibility of this courage."

Being, Hope, and Fidelity

The eldest of the French existentialists, Gabriel Marcel, has arrived independently of Husserl and Heidegger at a philosophy similarly centered upon man's relation to being and developed by the exploration of concrete human experience. A striking difference between Marcel's thought and that of Husserl, Heidegger, and Sartre may be traced to the experience which Marcel takes as his starting point—the lived communion of man with man, not the Cartesian *cogito*.

Like Sartre, Marcel has expressed his thought in plays as well as in treatises; the essay "On the Ontological Mystery" was first published in 1933 as a postscript to his play, *The Broken World*. This essay is remarkable in that it brings together in a brief form the dominant themes of Marcel's thought. Its design, characteristically, is symphonic rather than logical, for it reflects its author's aversion to systematization. But the sequence of themes—protest against technological society, the distinction of problem and mystery, human relationships in hope and fidelity, availability and openness to God—follows the main lines of a development that led Marcel from his agnostic family background and idealistic philosophical schooling to his conversion to Catholicism in 1929 and to the development of his own Christian existentialism. In "On the Ontological Mystery" he takes as a starting point the tendency of our society to rob man's life of meaning and value by considering only its biological or economic functions; this reaction against technological society seems to have been heightened by his work during World War I as a tracer of lost persons, keenly aware of the grim contrast between the data on file cards and the anguish of a wife or mother.[10]

The distinction of problem and mystery—between questions that can be treated "objectively" and those that involve a man's very being—indicate a series of oppositions running through Marcel's thought. Having and being, reflection and recollection, despair and hope, self-centeredness and availability—each of these distinctions points toward the difference between an objectifying attitude, which reduces the other person to a mere thing, and an openness to the mysterious value of being, which Marcel sees as man's basic ontological need. Like Tillich, Marcel finds the key to the meaning of life in man's participation in being as such; but there is a difference in tone between Tillich's stress on courage and Marcel's appeal to the experience of hope, fidelity, and availability. For Marcel, participation in being lies not in self-affirmation, but in communion with others. And God appears less as the ground of particular beings than as the ground of meaning and value in human love and friendship.

Here also appears the profound contrast between the existentialism of Marcel and that of Sartre. For Sartre, to be is to choose oneself, to establish in one's own liberty the only source of meaning and value; for Marcel, to be *present* to the other, to be available to him, is precisely to find in him, and through him in God, the meaning of one's own life. Thus the famous dictum of Sartre, "Hell is other people," stands in powerful contrast to Marcel's assertion, "To love another is to say to him 'You, you shall never die.' "

---

[10] Cf. Roger Troisfontaines, *De l'existence à l'être* (Louvain: E. Nauwelaerts, 1953), II, 12.

The World as History—God, Fate, and Human Freedom

The importance of time and history in existential metaphysics arises out of the existential concern for the totality of man's life. Purely speculative philosophy tends toward timelessness; pure reason and abstract principles can, in a sense, withdraw themselves from the human world of birth and growth, decay and death. Ever since Plato the philosopher has often considered himself a citizen of the world of eternal ideas, maintaining a dignified superiority with regard to those things that *are* not, because they are not always the same. The existentialists as a group have vigorously rejected this attitude. Heidegger's being toward death, Sartre's vigorous denial of transcendent meanings and values, Marcel's concern with concrete human relationships—all illustrate the turning of philosophy from the heaven of ideas to the world of men. But the turning from merely speculative contemplation on changeless and universal truth to personal engagement in unrepeatable history had been made for the first time long before; it was a distinctive contribution to Western civilization of the Judeo-Christian religious heritage. We have already spoken of Tillich's concern for temporality as a form of human finitude; the more distinctively theological parts of Tillich's work are even more explicit in their concern with man's historical being and God's historical self-revelation.

In the thought of Nicolas Berdyaev the traditions of East and West and the experiences of Marxism and Christianity are brought together in a heightened awareness of the meaning in history. Berdyaev, though distrustful of all formal religious structures, was heir to the rich tradition of Russian Christianity. His language is more explicitly theological than that of Tillich, and his emphasis falls continually upon those aspects of the Christian message that seem most shocking to today's scientific and technical mentality.

Thus, in the "Confession of Faith" with which he concluded his philosophical autobiography, Berdyaev spoke of "objective" things as devoid of reality, as illusions of consciousness; only the subject is real, and can create and know reality. Berdyaev, like the late-medieval German mystics Eckhart and Böhme,[11] set uncreated freedom before Being, which latter concept he viewed as a transcendental illusion. "Original reality is creative act and freedom, and the bearer of original reality is the person, the subject, spirit, rather than Being, nature, or object."[12] Beyond the opposition of God and uncreated freedom (of God and man) lies the divine, transcendent Mystery, where contradictions disappear and logical expression be-

---

[11] Dominican Meister Eckhart (1260–1327) and Protestant layman Jakob Böhme (1575–1624) both taught that God was in some sense above Being. Böhme speaks of God as the *Ungrund,* the ground of all things, "the nothing and the all."

[12] Nicolas Berdyaev, *The Dream and Reality: An Essay in Autobiography,* trans. by Katherine Lampert (New York: Macmillan Co., 1951), p. 286.

comes superfluous. It is hardly surprising that Berdyaev has been described as a "mystical anarchist," [13] nor is it certain that he would have disowned that description.

The Beginning and the End, from which our selection is taken, was originally titled *Essay on Eschatological Metaphysics.* Completed in 1941 but published posthumously in 1952, this book is presented by its author as a view of his total metaphysical vision, "in the light which streams from the End." Driven by his keen sense of the transitoriness and fragility of the world, he sees in the Christian doctrine of the end of time, "not an invitation to escape into a private heaven" but "a call to transfigure this evil and stricken world." Like Dostoevsky, who may have had the most significant influence on his thought, Berdyaev finds himself inescapably confronted with mystery in the sufferings of life. In this perspective, "faith in God arises precisely in virtue of man's longing for deliverance from this evil, suffering, infernal world." [14]

In his discussion of the philosophy of history, Berdyaev begins by contrasting the ancient Greek view of man as part of an unchanging, structured cosmos and the Iranian-Hebrew-Christian expectation that the *Logos,* the meaning of reality, will manifest itself in history. Only from the latter viewpoint is a philosophy of history possible. History now remains incomplete, and we can discover its meaning only by looking into the future. Thus *all* philosophy of history (not only that which is intentionally religious) is eschatological, messianic, prophetic. It looks for the meaning of history in the end toward which it tends, in the hope of a redeeming power, in the promise of what is not yet but shall be. The nineteenth-century myth of progress, Hegel's promise of freedom in the Prussian state, Marx's vision of the reign of the proletariat—all illustrate messianism as the basic theme of history. The messianic hope of the ancient Hebrew was a prototype of the expectation of all men, a hope born of suffering that looks forward to judgment, vindication, and the thousand-years' reign of the saints.

In Christianity, the coming of the Kingdom is not, as the churches would make it, the founding of the churches. Rather it is the transformation of the world by the power of the spirit. Man's life goes forward in cosmic or physical time and in history; it finds its meaning in existential time, where past and future, beginning and end are gathered up as in eternity. Eschatological fulfillment is attained here and now in man's existential decisions; Berdyaev understands the notion of hell as an illusory objectification of an event that takes place only in existential time.

The path of history at once presupposes and denies man's freedom, for in it three distinct and irreducible forces are at work—God, fate, and human freedom. Only in Christ the liberator has fate been conquered; only in Christ's resurrection does history find its meaning beyond history.

---

[13] F. H. Heinemann, *Existentialism and the Modern Predicament* (New York: Harper & Bros., 1958), pp. 154–64.

[14] Berdyaev, pp. 290–92.

Man's life in society manifests the struggle that is fundamental in Berdyaev's thought: the struggle of nature against spirit, of slavery and determinism against freedom and love. Society as nature finds its controlling motives in the desire for predominance and mastery; society as spirit seeks freedom, the recognition of the person, and the realization of love and mercy. (Berdyaev notes that in European thought liberation has been concerned with "natural" reason, morals, and rights.) Spirit at work in history heralds already the coming of the Kingdom of God; in contrast, fate (which Berdyaev sees as demoniacal in its enslaving force) is at work both in the State and in technology, which by its production of unprecedented means of destruction and violence "raises the eschatological question and leads up to the breaking of the seals of history."

The only answer to the threat raised by technology lies in a hierarchic social order, based not upon brute power or even upon an empty notion of equality, but upon charismata, or gifts of the Spirit. Only "a community of emancipated men in the Spirit" can break out of the everyday world of slavery and determinism into the realm of freedom and personal communion. But this eschatological breakthrough is already present in the world today as communion among men and throughout history in *sobornost,* the communion of freedom enlivened by grace that brings men together in the Church, that in its depth is "the mysterious life of Christ within a human communion."

I and Thou—The Life of Real Relation

In the thought of Tillich, Marcel, and Berdyaev we have seen how man's life within the world points beyond itself to its transcendent source and goal. God is manifest as the ground of *Existenz,* as ultimate concern, as source of meaning and value in human love, as longed-for response to human suffering and helplessness. Similar themes animate the thought of Martin Buber, but the Jewish philosopher of dialogue traveled in a different direction than these religious existentialists. Their thought goes from man to God; Buber's begins with an intense and authentic religious commitment that in turn leads to his profound awareness of the significance of man's relation to his fellow men and to other creatures.

Buber's own account of his "conversion" from an individualistic mysticism to the life of real relation is thus crucial for the understanding of his thought:

> What happened was no more than that one forenoon, after a morning of "religious" enthusiasm, I had a visit from an unknown young man, without being there in spirit. I certainly did not fail to let the meeting be friendly, I did not treat him any more remissly than all his contemporaries who were in the habit of seeking me out about

this time of day as an oracle that is ready to listen to reason. I conversed attentively and openly with him—only I omitted to guess the questions which he did not put. Later, not long after, I learned from one of his friends—he himself was no longer alive—the essential content of these questions; I learned that he had come to me not casually, but borne by destiny, not for a chat but for a decision. He had come to me, he had come in this hour. What do we expect when we are in despair and yet go to a man? Surely a presence by means of which we are told that nevertheless there is meaning.

Since then I have given up the "religious" which is nothing but the exception, extraction, exaltation, ecstasy; or it has given me up. I possess nothing but the everyday out of which I am never taken. The mystery is no longer disclosed, it has escaped or it has made its dwelling here where everything happens as it happens. I know no fulness but each mortal hour's fulness of claim and responsibility. Though far from being equal to it, yet I know that in the claim I am claimed and may respond in responsibility, and know who speaks and demands a response.[15]

We have quoted this passage in full both because it presents the central theme of Buber's thought and because it illustrates so beautifully his gift of not merely describing, but of concretely evoking man's lived realization of the presence of God. As a Jewish religious leader under the Nazi persecution or as a worker for Arab-Israeli understanding in Jerusalem, Buber gave charismatic and prophetic expression to his religious convictions. It has been said of him—and it is high praise—that his deeds did not belie his teaching.

The guiding theme of Buber's existentialism is named in the title of *I and Thou,* the seminal work, first published in 1923, of which all his later philosophical writings have been elucidations and developments. From this work we have selected with certain omissions the first part, which introduces the two "primary words," *I-Thou* and *I-It,* and the third and final part, which shows how "the extended lines of relations meet in the eternal *Thou.*" These pages richly exemplify the poetic power of Buber's style, which, like the thought it expresses, is deeply rooted in the revelation of the Old Testament.

The coincidence of Buber's thought with that of Marcel can hardly fail to impress the reader. The two authors reached full development in complete independence of each other, yet the opposition that Marcel traced between problem and mystery, having and being, objective knowledge and availability, corresponds with surprising precision to Buber's contrast of I-It and I-Thou relationships. This correspondence runs through their works on such varied topics as technological society, individual and social relation-

---

[15] Martin Buber, *Between Man and Man,* trans. by Ronald Gregor Smith (Boston: Beacon Press, 1955), pp. 14–15.

ships, and the history of philosophy. An interesting case in point may be seen in their criticism of Sartre. For both Buber and Marcel, Sartre appears as advocate of the self-contained refusal of communion that marks the I-It relation at its most degrading and that reduces the partner in dialogue to the status of a thing for one's use and enjoyment.

Even more than Marcel, Buber was wary of abstract formulations that would reduce the *encounter* with living reality to the level of mere *experience,* possession or exploitation of an object. In *I and Thou* Buber's thought progresses in a kind of meditative spiral, in which the central themes are illuminated from different angles in a series of insights and examples. From this meditation emerges the preeminence of the I-Thou relation and the inevitability of the process whereby every Thou is doomed to become an It. It becomes clear that while the Thou gives meaning to life, the I-Thou encounter remains a grace not to be won by seeking. Moreover, while the I-Thou relation is most profoundly realized in the life of man with man, it is also present whenever man truly encounters reality—in nature, in communion with ideal reality, in the creative impulse of art. I-Thou is the primal relation through which man encounters the world; in the I-It attitude man withdraws from communion in order to master and mold the object of his experience.

God appears to Buber as the eternal Thou, "the *Thou* that by its nature cannot become *It.*" To speak of God in the third person, to enumerate his attributes or demonstrate his existence, would be to claim a blasphemous mastery over God, to make an idol of Him.[16] "God cannot be inferred in anything. . . . Something else is not 'given' and God then elicited from it; but God is the Being that is directly, most nearly, and lastingly, over against us, that may properly only be addressed, not expressed." God may never be regarded as an explanation or a hypothesis; Sartre's critique of God as supernatural artisan making man into an object is a justifiable mockery of an impersonal and depersonalizing theology. But God is present to man as the total meaning of man's life: "Meeting with God does not come to man in order that he may concern himself with God, but in order that he may confirm that there is meaning in the world." And in this meaning are bound up the meaning and value of every encounter in which man enters into real relation. In the encounter with the eternal Thou, man as the being concerned with Being finds the final significance of his concern, the ground of his hope, and the answer to his suffering in the whole of a life lived in openness and communion.

---

[16] A perceptive and sympathetic Catholic criticism of Buber on this point is offered by Gerard Sloyan, "Buber and the Significance of Jesus," in *The Bridge: A Yearbook of Judaeo-Christian Studies,* ed. by John M. Oesterreicher (New York: Pantheon Books, 1958), III, 225.

Glossary

COGITO:
The self considered as subject of its conscious acts (Descartes).

CONSTITUTION:
The act by which an object is made present to consciousness. For example, seeing as "producing" the object as visible (Husserl).

DASEIN:
Human reality as free and open to Being (Heidegger).

EIDETIC:
Relating to universal essences; from εἶδος, Plato's synonym for idea.

EPOCHÉ:
Husserl's synonym for phenomenological reduction.

ESSENCE:
What a thing is, as opposed to the fact that it is.

ESSENT:
Term coined by translator for Heidegger's *Seiende;* that which is, a being.

EXISTENCE:
Nontechnically, *that* things *are,* as opposed to essence, or *what* they are. For Heidegger, man's possibility to be or not be authentically; for Sartre, existence is synonymous with Heidegger's *Dasein.*

FUNDAMENTAL ONTOLOGY:
The ontology of *Dasein* as approach to a general ontology of Being (Heidegger).

HORIZON:
The marginal awareness that accompanies an object explicitly recognized. For example, objects surrounding the one on which seeing is focused; past and future as context for present experience.

INTENTIONALITY:
The property of consciousness by which it is always referred to an object, such as seeing to a thing seen or loving to a person loved.

INTUITION:
For Husserl, the act by which a phenomenon is directly apprehended and rendered explicit; *or,* the object of such an act.

METAPHYSICS:
In its general sense, the understanding of Being, or reality as such; as distinguished from ontology, a knowledge of what lies beyond experience. Heidegger uses *metaphysics* as a knowledge of essents, as opposed to *ontology,* which for him deals with Being.

MONAD:

The concrete self (Husserl).

MYSTERY:

A question whose answer involves the very reality of the one who questions, as opposed to *Problem* (Marcel).

ONTOLOGY:

The study of Being, or reality; the term is generally preferred to *Metaphysics* by the phenomenologists.

PHENOMENOLOGY:

Method consisting in direct contemplation and description of the data of awareness.

PROBLEM:

A question that admits of an impersonal, definitive answer, as opposed to *Mystery* (Marcel).

REDUCTION:

"Transcendental" or "phenomenological" reduction—the act of suspending belief or "putting in brackets" the spontaneous acceptance of things as really existing, so as to consider them as pure phenomena (Husserl). As used by other authors, suspension of philosophical or scientific presuppositions, so as to arrive at a fresh and more complete view of the data of experience.

TRANSCENDENTAL:

Taken from Kant, where it means extending to all possible experience. Used by Husserl to mean pertaining to the data of experience which are left intact by the phenomenological reduction.

Martin Heidegger

MARTIN HEIDEGGER was born in Messkirch (Baden) in 1889. He studied
under Husserl at Freiburg University and his first book, *Duns Scotus'
Doctrine of Categories and Meanings* (1916), shows Husserl's strong
influence. After teaching for several years at Marburg, Heidegger succeeded Husserl as professor of Philosophy at Freiburg in 1928 and served
as rector for a brief period. Since his retirement from teaching, after World
War II, he has lived at his ski hut in the Black Forest. Heidegger's best-
known work is *Being and Time* (1927), a massive and difficult work that
approaches the meaning of Being through the phenomenological analysis
of human reality. *Kant and the Problem of Metaphysics* (1929) offers
in its last section a clearer and more concise presentation of some of
the same questions.

The Problem of the Finitude in Man and the Metaphysics of Dasein

*[Remarks in italics are again inserted by the editor to outline the text.
In the following pages, Heidegger seeks to show how the problem of Being,
the problem of metaphysics, must be traced back to a recognition of man's
finitude, his situation as a fragile and imperfect power-to-be. This project
leads Heidegger to engage in a "repetition," or rethinking of the central
questions of metaphysics as they arise in the work of Aristotle.]*

We have undertaken the present interpretation of the *Critique of Pure
Reason* in order to bring to light the necessity, insofar as a laying of the
foundation of metaphysics is concerned, of posing the fundamental problem of the finitude in man. This is the reason that finitude has been constantly stressed at the beginning of the interpretation as well as in the
course of its development.

.   .   .

From pp. 226–29 of Martin Heidegger, *Kant and the Problem of Metaphysics*, translated by James S. Churchill. © 1962 by Indiana University Press. Reprinted by permission of the publisher.

583

THE PROBLEM OF A POSSIBLE DETERMINATION
OF THE FINITUDE IN MAN

How is the finitude in man to be examined? Is this in general a serious problem? Is not the finitude of man evident always, everywhere, and in a thousand different ways?

In order to uncover the finitude of man is it not enough to adduce at random any one of his many imperfections? But in this way we obtain at best only a proof that man is a finite being. We learn neither in what the essence of man's finitude consists nor yet how this finitude determines man to be the essent that he basically is.

And even if we succeeded in adding together the sum of all human imperfections and "abstracting" what is common to them, we could understand thereby nothing of the essence of finitude. We would not be able to know in advance whether the imperfections of man enable us to obtain a direct insight into his finitude, or whether, on the contrary, these imperfections are merely a simple consequence of this finitude and, hence, are understandable only through it.

And even if we succeeded in doing the impossible, if we succeeded in proving rationally that man is a created being, the characterization of man as an *ens creatum* would only point up the fact of his finitude without clarifying its essence and without showing how this essence constitutes the fundamental nature of the essence of man.

Thus, how the question of the finitude in man—the most common manifestation of his essence—is to be approached is not at all self-evident. The sole result of our inquiry, therefore, is that the question of the finitude in man is no arbitrary exploration of the properties of this being. On the contrary, the question arises as soon as one begins the task of a laying of the foundation of metaphysics. As a fundamental question it is required by this problem itself. Consequently, the problematic of a laying of the foundation of metaphysics must include an indication as to the direction in which the question of the finitude of man must advance.

Finally, if the task of a laying of the foundation of metaphysics admits of an authentic repetition, then the essential connection between the problem of a laying of the foundation and the question inspired by it, namely, that of the finitude in man, must be exhibited more clearly and with greater precision.

The Kantian laying of the foundation of metaphysics begins with a justification of *metaphysica generalis* as that which is at the basis of true metaphysics, i.e., *metaphysica specialis*. But *metaphysica generalis*—under the name "ontology"—is the fixed form of that which in antiquity, and finally with Aristotle, was established as the problem of *prōtē philosophia*, philosophizing in the true sense of the term. However, the question of the *on ē on* (of the essent as such) is mingled in a very confused way here with that of the essent in totality (*theion*). [1]

---

[1] For Kant, general metaphysics or ontology deals with the general conditions of

The term "metaphysics" denotes a conception of the problem in which not only the two fundamental dimensions of the question of the essent but also their possible unity become debatable. This is quite apart from the further question as to whether these two dimensions are sufficient in themselves to exhaust the whole of the problematic of a fundamental knowledge of the essent.

If the question of the finitude in man is to be determined through an authentic repetition of a laying of the foundation of metaphysics, then it is advisable to turn the Kantian question [2] from its orientation on the rigid discipline and fixed system of the metaphysics of the schools and set it on that course which is suitable to its own problematic. This also implies that the Aristotelian formulation of the problem cannot be accepted as definitive.

With the *ti to on* [what is the essent?], the question of the essent is posed, but to pose a question does not necessarily mean that one is capable of mastering and working out the problematic which animates it. The extent to which the problem of metaphysics is still enveloped in the question *ti to on* can be understood if we realize that the formulation of this question does not enable us to determine how it embodies the problem of the finitude in man. Still less can we obtain an indication as to how the finitude in man is to be made the object of our questioning merely by a reiteration of this question. The repetition of the problem of a laying of the foundation of *metaphysica generalis* is not equivalent, therefore, to a simple echoing of the question: What is the essent as such? The repetition must develop as a problem the question which, in brief, we term the question of Being. The purpose of this development is to show in what respect the problem of the finitude in man and the inquiries which it calls for necessarily contribute to our mastery of the question of Being. Basically it is a matter of bringing to light the essential connection between Being as such (not the essent) and the finitude in man.

THE PRIMORDIAL ELABORATION OF THE QUESTION OF BEING AS THE MEANS OF ACCESS TO THE PROBLEM OF THE FINITUDE IN MAN

[*Heidegger proceeds to show that of Aristotle's two questions (What is being as being? What is the totality of beings?) the former must take priority. And the question of the essent as such leads directly to the question of Being—that which makes the essent to be, that is, that which determines the essent as such. But to ask about Being is already to understand Being in some way. We define the essent in terms of what it is, with reference to its*

---

our knowledge; special metaphysics, with its three divisions of cosmology, psychology, and theology, deals with the world, the soul, and God, concerning which we can have no certain speculative knowledge since they lie beyond the limits of our experience. For Aristotle, first philosophy (*prōtē philosophia*) or metaphysics deals both with *on ē on* (being as being) and with the highest being, the divine (*theion*), which Heidegger identifies with the essent in totality. [H.J.J.]

[2] How is metaphysics possible? [H.J.J.]

"whatness," essence, or idea; we ask of the essent whether it is or not, and so determine it as existing. The relation of essence and existence, of what-being and that-being, remains obscure; but neither meaning can be separated from Being as being-true, as expressed in the "is" of every assertion that we make.

In the concluding paragraphs of this section, Heidegger shows that the question of the meaning of Being leads us backward to a more fundamental question: How is it possible for us, as men, to comprehend the concept of Being?]

How is the question, "What is the meaning of Being?" to find an answer if the direction from which the answer can be expected remains obscure? Must we not first ask in what direction it is advisable to look in order from this perspective to be able to determine Being as such and thus obtain a concept of Being with reference to which the possibility and necessity of its essential articulation will become comprehensible? So the question of "first philosophy," namely, "What is the essent as such?" must force us back beyond the question "What is Being as such?" to the still more fundamental question: *Whence are we to comprehend a notion such as that of Being, with the many articulations and relations it includes?*

Therefore, if there exists an internal connection between the laying of the foundation of metaphysics and the question of the finitude in man, the more primordial elaboration of the question of Being now attained will exhibit in a more elemental way the essential relation of this question to the problem of finitude.

But at first sight, this connection remains obscure, above all since one is not generally inclined to attribute such a relation to the question under consideration. This relation is certainly evident in Kant's questions cited above,[3] but how can the question of Being, particularly in the form in which it is now developed, i.e., as a question of the possibility of the comprehension of Being, have an essential relation to the finitude in man? Within the framework of the abstract ontology inspired by the metaphysics of Aristotle, the question of Being may acquire a certain sense and so be presented with some justification as a special problem, a problem that is scholarly but more or less artificial. But there seems to be no evidence of an essential relation between this problem and that of the finitude in man.

If up to this point we have endeavored to clarify the original form of the problem of Being by orienting it on the Aristotelian question, this does not imply that the origin of this problem is to be found in Aristotle. On the contrary, authentic philosophical thinking will be able to come upon the question of Being only if this question belongs to the innermost essence of philosophy, which in turn exists only as a fundamental possibility of human *Dasein*.

---

[3] What can I know? What ought I to do? What may I hope? What is man? [H.J.J.]

When we raise the question as to the possibility of understanding a notion such as that of Being, we do not thereby invent this notion and artificially make a problem of it in order merely to take up again a question characteristic of philosophical tradition. Rather, we are raising the question of the possibility of comprehending that which, as men, we already understand and have always understood. The question of Being as a question of the possibility of the concept of Being arises from the preconceptual comprehension of Being. Thus, the question of the possibility of the concept of Being is once again forced back a step and becomes the question of the possibility of the comprehension of Being in general. The task of the laying of the foundation of metaphysics, grasped in a more original way, becomes, therefore, that of the explication of the intrinsic possibility of the comprehension of Being. The elaboration of the question of Being thus conceived first enables us to decide if, and in what way, the problem of Being in itself bears an intrinsic relation to the finitude in man.

THE COMPREHENSION OF BEING AND THE *Dasein* IN MAN

[Heidegger goes on to explore the relation of Being to the essent that man is. For all its obscurity, Being is revealed to us in our own human reality, our Dasein, *and in the other essents that surround us. This preconceptual awareness or openness to Being gives rise in man to the special mode of Being that Heidegger terms* existence. As existing, *in this sense, man "stands forth into the world," bound up with and dependent upon other essents. Here openness to Being is shown to be the ultimate ground of man's finitude. In consequence, the exploration of* Dasein's *comprehension of Being will be the task of fundamental ontology, the task which Kant termed "the metaphysics of metaphysics."]*

That we, as men, have a comportment [*Verhalten*] to the essent is evident. Faced with the problem of representing the essent, I can always refer to some particular essent or other—whether it be such that I am not and which is not my like, or such that I am myself, or such that I am not but because it is a self is my like. The essent is known to us—but Being? Are we not seized with vertigo when we try to determine it or even to consider it as it is in itself? Does not Being resemble Nothing? In fact, no less a person than Hegel has said it: "Pure Being and pure Nothing are, then, the same."

With the question of Being as such we are poised on the brink of complete obscurity. Yet we should not turn away prematurely but should seek to bring this comprehension of Being in all its singularity closer to us. For despite the seemingly impenetrable obscurity which envelops Being and its signification, it remains incontestable that at all times and wherever the essent appears to us, we have at our disposal a certain comprehension of Being. We concern ourselves with the what-being and thus-being of the essent, acknowledge or dispute its that-being and, at the risk of deceiving ourselves, come to decisions concerning its being-true [*Wahr-sein*]. The assertion of every proposition, e.g., "Today is a holiday," implies an understanding of the "is" and, hence, a certain comprehension of Being.

In the cry "Fire!" we understand that there *is* a fire, that help *is* necessary, that everyone must save himself, i.e., secure his being as best he can. And even when we do not say anything about an essent, even when in silence we assume an attitude toward it, we understand, although implicitly, its mutually compatible what-being, that-being, and being-true.

In every mood wherein "things are this or that way" with us, our own *Da-sein* is manifest to us. We have, therefore, an understanding of Being even though the concept is lacking. This preconceptual comprehension of Being, although constant and far-reaching, is usually completely indeterminate. The specific mode of Being, for example, that of material things, plants, animals, men, numbers, is known to us, but what is thus known is not recognized as such. Furthermore, this preconceptual comprehension of the Being of the essent in all its constancy, amplitude, and indeterminateness is given as something completely beyond question. Being as such is so little in question that apparently it "is" not.

This comprehension of Being, such as we have briefly sketched it, remains on the level of the purest, most assured, and most naïve patency and yet if *this comprehension of Being did not occur,* man could never be the essent that he is, no matter how wonderful his faculties. Man is an essent in the midst of other essents in such a way that the essent that he is and the essent that he is not are always already manifest to him. We call this mode of Being *existence,*[4] and only on the basis of the comprehension of Being is existence possible.

In his comportment to the essent which he himself is not, man finds it to be that by which he is sustained, on which he is dependent, and over which, for all his culture and technique, he never can be master. Furthermore, dependent on the essent that he is not, man is, at bottom, not even master of himself.

With the existence of man there occurs an irruption into the totality of the essent such that, by this event, the essent becomes manifest in itself, i.e., manifest as essent—this manifestation being of varying amplitude and having different degrees of clarity and certitude. However, this prerogative of not being simply an essent among other essents, which last are not manifest to one another, but, in the midst of essents, of *being delivered up to them as such and of being answerable to oneself as essent,* in short, this

---

[4] *Existence* (or *Ex-sistence,* as Heidegger later terms it), like *concern,* is another of Heidegger's "existentials." This term "existence" "is not identical with the traditional concept of *existentia*" which "signifies reality as opposed to *essentia* as the possibility of something." (*Über den Humanismus,* p. 15.) Existence is "The Being to which *Dasein* can and always does dispose itself." (*Sein und Zeit,* p. 12.) It is a "standing forth into the truth of Being"; hence, to assert that "Man ex-sists is not to answer the question as to whether man is real or not but the question as to his essence." (*Über den Humanismus,* p. 16.) [J.S.C.]

prerogative of existing, involves in itself the necessity of a comprehension of Being.

Man would not be able to be, *qua* self, an essent thrown [*geworfene*] into the world if he could not let the essent as such be.[5] However, in order to let the essent be what and how it is, the existent essent [man] must always have already projected that which it encounters as essent. Existence implies being dependent on the essent as such so that man as essent is given over to the essent on which he is thus dependent.

As a mode of Being, existence is in itself finitude and, as such, is only possible on the basis of the comprehension of Being. There is and must be such as Being only where finitude has become existent. The comprehension of Being which dominates human existence, although man is unaware of its breadth, constancy, and indeterminateness, is thus manifest as the innermost ground of human finitude. The comprehension of Being does not have the harmless generality which it would have were it just another human property. Its "generality" is the basic originality of the innermost ground of the finitude of *Dasein*. Only because the comprehension of Being is the most finite in the finite, can it make possible even the so-called "creative" faculties of finite human beings. And only because it takes place in the very bosom of finitude is the comprehension of Being characterized by obscurity as well as by the breadth and constancy which have been noted.

It is on the basis of his comprehension of Being that man is *presence* [*Da*], with the Being of which takes place the revelatory [*eröffnende*] irruption into the essent. It is by virtue of this irruption that the essent as such can become manifest to self. *More primordial than man is the finitude of the* Dasein *in him.*

The elaboration of the basic question of *metaphysica generalis,* i.e., the question *ti to on,* has been thrown back upon the more fundamental question of the intrinsic essence of the comprehension of Being as that which sustains, actuates, and orients the specific question concerning the concept of Being. This more primordial interpretation of the basic problem of metaphysics has been developed with the intention of bringing to light the connection of the problem of the laying of the foundation of metaphysics with the question of the finitude in man. It now appears that we do not

---

[5] The notion of letting-be (*sein-lassen*) adumbrated in *Sein und Zeit* and discussed in this passage in connection with man's situation in the world of essents, later becomes an important factor in Heidegger's conception of what distinguishes the activity of the artist from that of the ordinary man. Although never clearly stated as such, this conception seems to be that the artist differs from the ordinary man who looks upon essents only as objects having value for him as tools, etc., in that the artist lets the essent be what it is in itself. This letting-be, accomplished through restraint (*Verhaltenheit*) and a tarrying by the essent *qua* work of art, is a preservation of it. (See *Der Ursprung des Kunstwerkes, Holzwege,* p. 7ff.) (It is interesting to compare this notion with Keats' "negative capability.")

There is also a suggestion in Heidegger that the activity of the thinker (the true philosopher) is not unlike that of the artist in that the thinker "lets Being be." (*Über den Humanismus,* p. 42.) [J.S.C.]

even have to ask ourselves about the relation of the comprehension of Being to the finitude in man. This comprehension of Being itself is the innermost essence of finitude. We have thus acquired a concept of finitude which is fundamental to the problematic of the laying of the foundation of metaphysics. If this laying of the foundation depends upon the question of knowing what man is, the indefiniteness of this question is in part overcome, since the question as to the nature of man has become more determinate.

If man is only man on the basis of the *Dasein* in him, then the question as to what is more primordial than man can, as a matter of principle, not be an anthropological one. All anthropology, even philosophical anthropology, always proceeds on the assumption that man is man.

The problem of the laying of the foundation of metaphysics is rooted in the question of the *Dasein* in man, i.e., in the question of his ultimate ground, which is the comprehension of Being as essentially existent finitude. This question relative to *Dasein* asks what the essence of the essent so determined is. Insofar as the Being of this essent lies in existence, the question as to the essence of *Dasein* is an existential one. Every question relative to the Being of an essent—and, in particular, the question relative to the Being of that essent to whose constitution finitude as the comprehension of Being belongs—is metaphysics.

Hence, the laying of the foundation of metaphysics is based upon a metaphysics of *Dasein*. But is it at all surprising that a laying of the foundation of metaphysics should itself be a form of metaphysics, and that in a pre-eminent sense?

Kant, who in his philosophizing was more alert to the problem of metaphysics than any other philosopher before or since, would not have understood his own intention had he not perceived this connection. He expressed his opinion concerning it with the clarity and serenity which the completion of the *Critique of Pure Reason* bestowed on him. In the year 1781, he wrote to his friend and disciple, Marcus Herz, concerning this work: "An inquiry of this sort will always remain difficult, for it contains the metaphysics of metaphysics."

This remark once and for all puts an end to all attempts to interpret, even partially, the *Critique of Pure Reason* as theory of knowledge. But these words also constrain every repetition of a laying of the foundation of metaphysics to clarify this "metaphysics of metaphysics" enough to put itself in a position to open up a possible way to the achievement of the laying of the foundation.

·　·　·

THE INCEPTION AND COURSE OF DEVELOPMENT
OF FUNDAMENTAL ONTOLOGY

[*The task of fundamental ontology is to explore* Dasein's *openness to* Being, *in its various modes. Man's being-in-the-world is bound up with the "everydayness" that accounts for his forgetfulness of Being. For all of man's activity is characterized by his relation of dependence on the essent in totality, his "being thrown" into the world, his "lapsing" into forgetfulness. Man's very evasion of Being, thus considered, points up his fundamental need for the comprehension of Being. This need reveals itself in man's "concern," an attitude that gives unity to man's finite openness to Being. Anxiety is the concrete realization of concern, the "decisive fundamental feeling" in which man becomes aware of his finitude as Being confronted with the Nothing, the possibility of his own non-being.]*

The *Dasein* in man characterizes him as that essent who, placed in the midst of essents, comports himself to them as such. This comportment determines man in his Being and makes him essentially different from all other essents which are manifest to him.

An analytic of *Dasein* must, from the beginning, strive to uncover the *Dasein* in man according to that mode of Being which, by nature, maintains *Dasein* and its comprehension of Being, i.e., primordial finitude, in forgetfulness. This mode of Being of *Dasein*—decisive only from the point of view of a fundamental ontology—we call "everydayness" [*Alltäglichkeit*].[6] The analytic of everydayness must take care not to allow the interpretation of the *Dasein* in man to become confused with an anthropo-psychological description of the "experiences" and "faculties" of man. This anthropo-psychological knowledge is not declared thereby to be "false," but it is necessary to show that, despite its exactitude, such knowledge is incapable of coming to grips with the problem of the existence of *Dasein*, i.e., the problem of its finitude. A grasp of this problem, however, is required by the decisive question, namely, that of Being.

The existential analytic of existence does not have as an objective a description of how we manage a knife and fork. It is intended to show how all commerce with essents—even when it seems to concern only the latter—presupposes the transcendence of *Dasein*, namely, being-in-the-world. With this transcendence is achieved the projection, hidden and, for the most part, indeterminate, of the Being of the essent in general. By means of this projection, the Being of the essent becomes manifest and intelligible, although, at first and ordinarily, only in a confused way. In this mode of comprehension the difference between Being and the essent remains concealed, and man himself is presented as an essent among other essents.

Being-in-the-world cannot be reduced to a relation between subject and

---

[6] Everydayness and the associated concepts, "lapsing" (*Verfallen*), "the one" (*das Man*), and "unauthenticity" (*Uneigentlichkeit*), which are the subject of an extended analysis in *Sein und Zeit* are, as Heidegger is at pains to point out here and elsewhere, in no way to be considered as ethical concepts (although that they are often so considered is, in part, Heidegger's own fault—he need not have chosen terms which have such obvious moral and religious overtones). Rather, these concepts refer to a mode of existence which is characterized by that "forgetfulness" of Being discussed above. [J.S.C.]

object. It is, on the contrary, that which makes such a relation possible, insofar as transcendence carries out the projection of the Being of the essent. The existential analytic illuminates this projection (this act of understanding) within the limits imposed imposed by its point of departure. It is not so much a question of pursuing a study of the intrinsic constitution of transcendence as of elucidating its essential unity with feeling and dereliction.[7]

All projection—and, consequently, even man's "creative" activity—is *thrown,* i.e., determined by the dependence of *Dasein* on the essent in totality, a dependence to which *Dasein* always submits. This fact of being thrown [dereliction] is not restricted to the mysterious occurrence of the coming-into-the-world of *Dasein* but governs being-present [*Da-sein*] as such. This is expressed in the movement which has been described as a lapsing. This idea of lapsing does not refer to certain negative events of human life which a critique of culture would be disposed to condemn but to an intrinsic character of the transcendental finitude of man, a character which is bound to the nature of projection as "thrown."

The development of existential ontology, which begins by the analysis of everydayness, has as its sole objective the explication of the primordial transcendental structure of the *Dasein* in man. In transcendence, *Dasein* manifests itself as need of the comprehension of Being. This transcendental need assures the possibility of something on the order of *Dasein.* This need is nothing other than finitude in its most intrinsic form as that which is the source of *Dasein.*

The unity of the transcendental structure of this need, characteristic of the *Dasein* in man, has been termed "concern." The word itself is of little consequence, but it is essential to understand what the analytic of *Dasein* seeks to express by means of it. If one takes the expression "concern"—despite the specific directive that the term has nothing to do with an ontic characteristic of man—in the sense of an ethical and ideological evaluation of "human life" rather than as the designation of the structural unity of the inherently finite transcendence of *Dasein,* then everything falls into confusion and no comprehension of the problematic which guides the analytic of *Dasein* is possible.

In any case, there is reason to believe that the explication of the essence of finitude required for the establishment of metaphysics must itself always be basically finite and never absolute. It follows that this reflection on finitude, which is always to be renewed, cannot succeed by exchanging and adjusting various points of view in order finally and in spite of everything to give us an absolute knowledge of finitude, a knowledge which is

---

[7] Feeling is one of the two ways (the other being understanding [*Verstehen*], which for Heidegger is essentially projection) in which man becomes aware of himself and his world. What is disclosed by feeling in particular is man's dereliction, i.e., that man in the world finds himself cast or thrown into a situation not of his own choosing and among things over which he is not master. [J.S.C.]

surreptitiously posited as being "true in itself." It remains, therefore, only to develop the problematic of finitude as such. Finitude becomes manifest to us in its intrinsic essence if we approach it in the light of the fundamental question of metaphysics as primordially conceived, a method of approach which, to be sure, cannot claim to be the only one possible.

It is clear from the above that the metaphysics of *Dasein* as a laying of the foundation of metaphysics has its own truth, which in its essence is as yet all too obscure. No one dominated by an attitude inspired by a *Weltanschauung,* i.e., an attitude which is popular and ontic, and particularly no one dominated by an attitude—whether approving or disapproving—inspired by theology, can enter the dimension of the problem of a metaphysics of *Dasein.* For, as Kant says, "the critique of reason . . . can never become popular, and indeed there is no need that it should."

Hence, whoever would institute a critique of the transcendental interpretation of "concern" as the transcendental unity of finitude—a critique the possibility and necessity of which no one would deny—must show, first, that the transcendence of *Dasein* and consequently the comprehension of Being, do not constitute the finitude in man, second, that the establishment of metaphysics does not have that essential relation to the finitude of *Dasein* of which we have spoken, and finally, that the basic question of the laying of the foundation of metaphysics is not encompassed by the problem of the intrinsic possibility of the comprehension of Being.

Before presenting an interpretation of transcendence as "concern," the fundamental-ontological analytic of *Dasein* purposely seeks first to provide an explication of "anxiety" [*Angst*] as a "decisive fundamental feeling" in order to show concretely that the existential analytic is constantly guided by the question from which it arises, namely, the question of the possibility of the comprehension of Being. Anxiety is declared to be the decisive fundamental faculty not in order to proclaim, from the point of view of some *Weltanschauung* or other, a concrete existence-ideal but solely with reference to the problem of Being as such.

Anxiety is that fundamental feeling which places us before the Nothing. The Being of the essent is comprehensible—and in this lies the innermost finitude of transcendence—only if *Dasein* on the basis of its essence holds itself into Nothing. Holding oneself into Nothing is no arbitrary and casual attempt to "think" about this Nothing but an event which underlies all feeling oneself [*Sichbefinden*] in the midst of essents already on hand. The intrinsic possibility of this event must be clarified in a fundamental-ontological analytic of *Dasein.*

"Anxiety" thus understood, i.e., according to fundamental ontology, prohibits us from interpreting "concern" as having the harmlessness of a categorical structure. It gives concern the incisiveness necessary to a fundamental existential and thus determines the finitude in *Dasein* not as a given property but as the constant, although generally veiled, precariousness which pervades all existence.

But the explication of concern as the transcendental, fundamental constitution of *Dasein* is only the first stage of fundamental onology. For further progress toward the goal, we must let ourselves be guided and inspired with ever increasing rigor by the question of Being.

QUESTIONS FOR STUDY AND DISCUSSION

1. How is human finitude bound up with the question of Being?
2. How is man aware of Being even before he begins to philosophize?
3. Can you give concrete examples of the kinds of experience that lead Heidegger to speak of everydayness, concern, and anxiety as fundamental modes of man's reality?
4. Why does the treatment of these modes of *Dasein* belong to fundamental ontology rather than to philosophy of man?

Jean-Paul Sartre

JEAN-PAUL SARTRE (b. 1905) studied at the Ecole Normale Supérieure at Paris, and later in Germany (1933–34) under Husserl and Heidegger. During the Second World War he spent nine months in imprisonment; after his release he was active in the resistance movement in Paris from 1941 to 1944. His major metaphysical treatise, *Being and Nothingness,* was published in 1943. He has also expressed his philosophy in novels and plays that have gained widespread attention; among the best known of these are his first novel, *Nausea* (1938), and the plays *No Exit* (1943) and *The Flies* (1943). In 1946 he founded the review *Les Temps Modernes,* which he continues to edit. In 1964, he was offered the Nobel prize for philosophy, but refused it on the grounds that acceptance would place limits on his freedom of self-expression.

Existentialism Is a Humanism

My purpose here is to offer a defence of existentialism against several reproaches that have been laid against it.

First, it has been reproached as an invitation to people to dwell in quietism or despair. For if every way to a solution is barred, one would have to regard any action in this world as entirely ineffective, and one would arrive finally at a contemplative philosophy. Moreover, since contemplation is a luxury, this would be only another bourgeois philosophy. This is, especially, the reproach made by the Communists.

From another quarter we are reproached for having underlined all that is ignominious in the human situation, for depicting what is mean, sordid or base to the neglect of certain things that possess charm and beauty and belong to the brighter side of human nature: for example, according to the Catholic critic, Mlle. Mercier, we forget how an infant smiles. Both from this side and from the other we are also reproached for leaving out of account the solidarity of mankind and considering man in isolation. And this, say the Communists, is because we base our doctrine upon pure subjectivity—upon the Cartesian "I think": which is the moment in which solitary man attains to himself; a position from which it is impossible to regain solidarity with other men who exist outside of the self. The *ego* cannot reach them through the *cogito*.

From the Christian side, we are reproached as people who deny the reality and seriousness of human affairs. For since we ignore the commandments of God and all values prescribed as eternal, nothing remains but what is strictly voluntary. Everyone can do what he likes, and will be incapable, from such a point of view, of condemning either the point of view or the action of anyone else.

It is to these various reproaches that I shall endeavor to reply today; that is why I have entitled this brief exposition "Existentialism Is a Humanism." Many may be surprised at the mention of humanism in this connection, but we shall try to see in what sense we understand it. In any case, we can begin by saying that existentialism, in our sense of the word, is a doctrine that does render human life possible; a doctrine, also, which affirms that every truth and every action imply both an environment and a human subjectivity. The essential charge laid against us is, of course, that of overemphasis upon the evil side of human life. I have lately been told of a lady who, whenever she lets slip a vulgar expression in a moment of nervousness, excuses herself by exclaiming, "I believe I am becoming an existentialist." So it appears that ugliness is being identified with existentialism. That is why some people say we are "naturalistic," and if we are, it is strange to see how much we scandalize and horrify them, for no one seems to be much frightened or humiliated nowadays by what is properly called naturalism. Those who can quite well keep down a novel by Zola such as *La Terre* are sickened as soon as they read an existentialist novel. Those who appeal to the wisdom of the people—which is a sad wisdom—find ours sadder still. And yet, what could be more disillusioned than such sayings as "Charity begins at home" or "Promote a rogue and he'll sue you for damage, knock him down and he'll do you homage"? We all know how many common sayings can be quoted to this effect; and they all mean much the same—that you must not oppose the powers-that-be; that you must not fight against superior force; must not meddle in matters that are above your station. Or that any action not in accordance with some tradition is mere romanticism; or that any undertaking which has not the support of proven experience is foredoomed to frustration; and that since experience has shown men to be invariably inclined to evil, there must be firm rules to restrain them, otherwise we shall have anarchy. It is, however, the people who are forever mouthing these dismal proverbs and, whenever they are told of some more or less repulsive action, say "How like human nature!" —it is these very people, always harping upon realism, who complain that existentialism is too gloomy a view of things. Indeed their excessive protests make me suspect that what is annoying them is not so much our pessimism, but, much more likely, our optimism. For at bottom, what is alarming in the doctrine that I am about to try to explain to you is—is it not?—that it confronts man with a possibility of choice. To verify this, let us review the whole question upon the strictly philosophic level. What, then is this that we call existentialism?

Most of those who are making use of this word would be highly confused if required to explain its meaning. For since it has become fashionable, people cheerfully declare that this musician or that painter is "existentialist." A columnist in *Clartés* signs himself "The Existentialist," and, indeed, the word is now so loosely applied to so many things that it no longer means anything at all. It would appear that, for the lack of any novel doctrine such as that of surrealism, all those who are eager to join in the latest scandal or movement now seize upon this philosophy in which, however, they can find nothing to their purpose. For in truth this is of all teachings the least scandalous and the most austere: it is intended strictly for technicians and philosophers. All the same, it can easily be defined.

The question is only complicated because there are two kinds of existentialists. There are, on the one hand, the Christians, amongst whom I shall name Jaspers and Gabriel Marcel, both professed Catholics; and on the other the existential atheists, amongst whom we must place Heidegger [1] as well as the French existentialists and myself. What they have in common is simply the fact that they believe that *existence* comes before *essence*—or, if you will, that we must begin from the subjective. What exactly do we mean by that?

If one considers an article of manufacture—as, for example, a book or a paper-knife—one sees that it has been made by an artisan who had a conception of it; and he has paid attention, equally, to the conception of a paper-knife and to the pre-existent technique of production which is a part of that conception and is, at bottom, a formula. Thus the paper-knife is at the same time an article producible in a certain manner and one which, on the other hand, serves a definite purpose, for one cannot suppose that a man would produce a paper-knife without knowing what it was for. Let us say, then, of the paper-knife that its essence—that is to say the sum of the formulae and the qualities which made its production and its definition possible—precedes its existence. The presence of such-and-such a paper-knife or book is thus determined before my eyes. Here, then, we are viewing the world from a technical standpoint, and we can say that production precedes existence.

When we think of God as the creator, we are thinking of him, most of the time, as a supernal artisan. Whatever doctrine we may be considering, whether it be a doctrine like that of Descartes, or of Leibnitz himself, we always imply that the will follows, more or less, from the understanding or at least accompanies it, so that when God creates he knows precisely what

---

[1] Both Jaspers and Heidegger have rejected these descriptions of their positions. [H.J.J.]

he is creating. Thus, the conception of man in the mind of God is comparable to that of the paper-knife in the mind of the artisan: God makes man according to a procedure and a conception, exactly as the artisan manufactures a paper-knife, following a definition and a formula. Thus each individual man is the realization of a certain conception which dwells in the divine understanding. In the philosophic atheism of the eighteenth century, the notion of God is suppressed, but not, for all that, the idea that essence is prior to existence; something of that idea we still find everywhere, in Diderot, in Voltaire and even in Kant. Man possess a human nature; that "human nature," which is the conception of human being, is found in every man; which means that each man is a particular example of a universal conception, the conception of Man. In Kant, this universality goes so far that the wild man of the woods, man in the state of nature and the bourgeois are all contained in the same definition and have the same fundamental qualities. Here again, the essence of man precedes that historic existence which we confront in experience.

Atheistic existentialism, of which I am a representative, declares with greater consistency that if God does not exist there is at least one being whose existence comes before its essence, a being which exists before it can be defined by any conception of it. That being is man or, as Heidegger has it, the human reality. What do we mean by saying that existence precedes essence? We mean that man first of all exists, encounters himself, surges up in the world—and defines himself afterwards. If man as the existentialist sees him is not definable, it is because to begin with he is nothing. He will not be anything until later, and then he will be what he makes of himself. Thus, there is no human nature, because there is no God to have a conception of it. Man simply is. Not that he is simply what he conceives himself to be, but he is what he wills, and as he conceives himself after already existing—as he wills to be after that leap towards existence. Man is nothing else but that which he makes of himself. That is the first principle of existentialism. And this is what people call its "subjectivity," using the word as a reproach against us. But what do we mean to say by this, but that man is of a greater dignity than a stone or a table? For we mean to say that man primarily exists—that man is, before all else, something which propels itself towards a future and is aware that it is doing so. Man is, indeed, a project which possesses a subjective life, instead of being a kind of moss, or a fungus or a cauliflower. Before that projection of the self nothing exists; not even in the heaven of intelligence: man will only attain existence when he is what he purposes to be. Not, however, what he may wish to be. For what we usually understand by wishing or willing is a conscious decision taken—much more often than not—after we have made ourselves what we are. I may wish to join a party, to write a book or to marry—but in such a case what is usually called my will is probably a manifestation of a prior and more spontaneous decision. If, however, it is true that existence is prior to essence, man is responsible for what he is. Thus, the first effect of existentialism is that it puts every man in possession of himself as he is, and places the entire responsibility for his existence squarely upon his own shoulders. And, when we say that man is responsible for himself, we do not mean that he is responsible only for his own individuality, but that he is responsible for all men. The word "subjectivism" is to be understood in two senses, and our adversaries play upon only one of them. Subjectivism means, on the one hand, the freedom of the individual subject and, on the other, that man cannot pass beyond human subjectivity. It is the latter which is the deeper meaning of existentialism. When we say that man chooses himself, we do mean that every one of us must choose himself; but by that we also mean that in choosing for himself he chooses for all men. For in effect, of all the actions a man may take in order to create himself as he wills to be, there is not one which is not creative, at the same time, of an image of man such as he believes he ought to be. To choose between this or that is at the same time to affirm the value of that which is chosen; for we are unable ever to choose the worse. What we choose is always the better; and nothing can be better for us unless it is better for all. If, moreover, existence precedes essence and we will to exist at the same time as we fashion our image, that image is valid for all and for the entire epoch in which we find ourselves. Our responsibility is thus much greater than we had supposed, for it concerns mankind as a whole. If I am a worker, for instance, I may choose to join a Christian rather than a Communist trade union. And if, by that membership, I choose to signify that resignation is, after all, the attitude that best becomes a man, that man's kingdom is not upon this earth, I do not commit myself alone to that view. Resignation is my will for everyone, and my action is, in consequence, a commitment on behalf of all mankind. Or if, to take a more personal case, I decide to marry and to have children, even though this decision proceeds simply from my situation, from my passion or my desire, I am thereby committing not only myself, but humanity as a whole, to the practice of monogamy. I am thus responsible for myself and for all men, and I am creating a certain image of man as I would have him to be. In fashioning myself I fashion man.

This may enable us to understand what is meant by such terms—perhaps a little grandiloquent—as anguish, abandonment and despair. As you will soon see, it is very simple. First, what do we mean by anguish? The existentialist frankly states that man is in anguish. His meaning is as follows—When a man commits himself to anything, fully realizing that he is not only choosing what he will be, but is thereby at the same time a legislator deciding for the whole of mankind—in such a moment a man cannot escape from the sense of complete and profound responsibility. There are many, indeed, who show no such anxiety. But we affirm that they are merely disguising their anguish or are in flight from it. Certainly, many people think that in what they are doing they commit no one but themselves to anything: and if you ask them, "What would happen if everyone did so?" they shrug their shoulders and reply, "Everyone does not do so."

But in truth, one ought always to ask oneself what would happen if everyone did as one is doing; nor can one escape from that disturbing thought except by a kind of self-deception. The man who lies in self-excuse, by saying "Everyone will not do it" must be ill at ease in his conscience, for the act of lying implies the universal value which it denies. By its very disguise his anguish reveals itself. This is the anguish that Kierkegaard called "the anguish of Abraham." You know the story: An angel commanded Abraham to sacrifice his son: and obedience was obligatory, if it really was an angel who had appeared and said, "Thou, Abraham, shalt sacrifice thy son." But anyone in such a case would wonder, first, whether it was indeed an angel and secondly, whether I am really Abraham. Where are the proofs? A certain mad woman who suffered from hallucinations said that people were telephoning to her, and giving her orders. The doctor asked, "But who is it that speaks to you?" She replied: "He says it is God." And what, indeed, could prove to her that it was God? If an angel appears to me, what is the proof that it is an angel; or, if I hear voices, who can prove that they proceed from heaven and not from hell, or from my own subconsciousness or some pathological condition? Who can prove that they are really addressed to me?

Who, then, can prove that I am the proper person to impose, by my own choice, my conception of man upon mankind? I shall never find any proof whatever; there will be no sign to convince me of it. If a voice speaks to me, it is still I myself who must decide whether the voice is or is not that of an angel. If I regard a certain course of action as good, it is only I who choose to say that it is good and not bad. There is nothing to show that I am Abraham: nevertheless I also am obliged at every instant to perform actions which are examples. Everything happens to every man as though the whole human race had its eyes fixed upon what he is doing and regulated its conduct accordingly. So every man ought to say, "Am I really a man who has the right to act in such a manner that humanity regulates itself by what I do." If a man does not say that, he is dissembling his anguish. Clearly, the anguish with which we are concerned here is not one that could lead to quietism or inaction. It is anguish pure and simple, of the kind well known to all those who have borne responsibilities. When, for instance, a military leader takes upon himself the responsibility for an attack and sends a number of men to their death, he chooses to do it and at bottom he alone chooses. No doubt he acts under a higher command, but its orders, which are more general, require interpretation by him and upon that interpretation depends the life of ten, fourteen or twenty men. In making the decision, he cannot but feel a certain anguish. All leaders know that anguish. It does not prevent their acting, on the contrary it is the very condition of their action, for the action presupposes that there is a plurality of possibilities, and in choosing one of these, they realize that it has value only because it is chosen. Now it is anguish of that kind which existentialism describes, and moreover, as we shall see, makes explicit through direct responsibility towards other men who are concerned. Far from being a screen which could separate us from action, it is a condition of action itself.

And when we speak of "abandonment"—a favorite word of Heidegger —we only mean to say that God does not exist, and that it is necessary to draw the consequences of his absence right to the end. The existentialist is strongly opposed to a certain type of secular moralism which seeks to suppress God at the least possible expense. Towards 1880, when the French professors endeavored to formulate a secular morality, they said something like this:—God is a useless and costly hypothesis, so we will do without it. However, if we are to have morality, a society and a law-abiding world, it is essential that certain values should be taken seriously; they must have an *à priori* existence ascribed to them. It must be considered obligatory *à priori* to be honest, not to lie, not to beat one's wife, to bring up children and so forth; so we are going to do a little work on this subject, which will enable us to show that these values exist all the same, inscribed in an intelligible heaven although, of course, there is no God. In other words—and this is, I believe, the purport of all that we in France call radicalism— nothing will be changed if God does not exist; we shall rediscover the same norms of honesty, progress and humanity, and we shall have disposed of God as an out-of-date hypothesis which will die away quietly of itself. The existentialist, on the contrary, finds it extremely embarrassing that God does not exist, for there disappears with Him all possibility of finding values in an intelligible heaven. There can no longer be any good *à priori,* since there is no infinite and perfect consciousness to think it. It is nowhere written that "the good" exists, that one must be honest or must not lie, since we are now upon the plane where there are only men. Dostoevsky once wrote "If God did not exist, everything would be permitted"; and that, for existentialism, is the starting point. Everything is indeed permitted if God does not exist, and man is in consequence forlorn, for he cannot find anything to depend upon either within or outside himself. He discovers forthwith, that he is without excuse. For if indeed existence precedes essence, one will never be able to explain one's action by reference to a given and specific human nature; in other words, there is no determinism—man is free, man *is* freedom. Nor, on the other hand, if God does not exist, are we provided with any values or commands that could legitimize our behavior. Thus we have neither behind us, nor before us in a luminous realm of values, any means of justification or excuse. We are left alone, without excuse. That is what I mean when I say that man is condemned to be free. Condemned, because he did not create himself, yet is nevertheless at liberty, and from the moment that he is thrown into this world he is responsible for everything he does. The existentialist does not believe in the power of passion. He will never regard a grand passion as a destructive torrent upon which a man is swept into certain actions as by fate, and which, therefore, is an excuse for them. He thinks that man is responsible for his passion. Neither will an existentialist think that a man can find help through some sign being vouchsafed upon earth for his orientation: for he thinks that the man himself interprets the sign as he chooses. He thinks that every man, without any support or help whatever, is condemned at every instant to invent man. As Ponge has written in a very fine article, "Man is the future of man." That is exactly true. Only, if one took this to mean that the future is laid up in Heaven, that God knows what it is, it would be false, for then it would no longer even be a future. If, however, it means that, whatever man may now appear to be, there is a future to be fashioned, a virgin future that awaits him—then it is a true saying. But in the present one is forsaken.

As an example by which you may the better understand this state of abandonment, I will refer to the case of a pupil of mine, who sought me out in the following circumstances. His father was quarrelling with his mother and was also inclined to be a "collaborator"; his elder brother had been killed in the German offensive of 1940 and this young man, with a sentiment somewhat primitive but generous, burned to avenge him. His mother was living alone with him, deeply afflicted by the semi-treason of his father and by the death of her eldest son, and her one consolation was in this young man. But he, at this moment, had the choice between going to England to join the Free French Forces or of staying near his mother and helping her to live. He ruefully realized that this woman lived only for him and that his disappearance—or perhaps his death—would plunge her into despair. He also realized that, concretely and in fact, every action he performed on his mother's behalf would be sure of effect in the sense of aiding her to live, whereas anything he did in order to go and fight would be an ambiguous action which might vanish like water into sand and serve no purpose. For instance, to set out for England he would have to wait indefinitely in a Spanish camp on the way through Spain; or, on arriving in England or in Algiers he might be put into an office to fill up forms. Consequently, he found himself confronted by two very different modes of action; the one concrete, immediate, but directed towards only one individual; and the other an action addressed to an end infinitely greater, a national collectivity, but for that very reason ambiguous—and it might be frustrated on the way. At the same time, he was hesitating between two kinds of morality; on the one side the morality of sympathy, of personal devotion and, on the other side, a morality of wider scope but of more debatable validity. He had to choose between those two. What could help him to choose? Could the Christian doctrine? No. Christian doctrine says: Act with charity, love your neighbor, deny yourself for others, choose the way which is hardest, and so forth. But which is the harder road? To whom does one owe the more brotherly love, the patriot or the mother? Which is the more useful aim, the general one of fighting in and for the whole community, or the precise aim of helping one particular person to live? Who can give an answer to that à priori? No one. Nor is it given in any ethical scripture. The Kantian ethic says, Never regard another as a means, but always as an end. Very well; if I remain with my mother, I shall be regarding her as the end and not as a means: but by the same token I am in danger of treating as means those who are fighting on my behalf; and the converse is also true, that if I go to the aid of the combatants I shall be treating them as the end at the risk of treating my mother as a means.

If values are uncertain, if they are still too abstract to determine the particular, concrete case under consideration, nothing remains but to trust in our instincts. That is what this young man tried to do; and when I saw him he said, "In the end, it is feeling that counts; the direction in which it is really pushing me is the one I ought to choose. If I feel that I love my mother enough to sacrifice everything else for her—my will to be avenged, all my longings for action and adventure—then I stay with her. If, on the contrary, I feel that my love for her is not enough, I go." But how does one estimate the strength of a feeling? The value of his feeling for his mother was determined precisely by the fact that he was standing by her. I may say that I love a certain friend enough to sacrifice such or such a sum of money for him, but I cannot prove that unless I have done it. I may say, "I love my mother enough to remain with her," if actually I have remained with her. I can only estimate the strength of this affection if I have performed an action by which it is defined and ratified. But if I then appeal to this affection to justify my action, I find myself drawn into a vicious circle.

Moreover, as Gide has very well said, a sentiment which is play-acting and one which is vital are two things that are hardly distinguishable one from another. To decide that I love my mother by staying beside her, and to play a comedy the upshot of which is that I do so—these are nearly the same thing. In other words, feeling is formed by the deeds that one does; therefore I cannot consult it as a guide to action. And that is to say that I can neither seek within myself for an authentic impulse to action, nor can I expect, from some ethic, formulae that will enable me to act. You may say that the youth did, at least, go to a professor to ask for advice. But if you seek counsel—from a priest, for example—you have selected that priest; and at bottom you already knew, more or less, what he would advise. In other words, to choose an adviser is nevertheless to commit oneself by that choice. If you are a Christian, you will say, Consult a priest; but there are collaborationists, priests who are resisters and priests who wait for the tide to turn: which will you choose? Had this young man chosen a priest of the resistance, or one of the collaboration, he would have decided beforehand the kind of advice he was to receive. Similarly, in coming to me, he knew what advice I should give him, and I had but one reply to make. You are free, therefore choose—that is to say, invent. No rule of general morality can show you what you ought to do: no signs are vouchsafed in this world. The Catholics will reply, "Oh, but they are!" Very well; still, it is I myself, in every case, who have to interpret the signs. While I was imprisoned, I made the acquaintance of a somewhat remarkable man, a Jesuit, who had become a member of that order in the following manner. In his life he had suffered a succession of rather severe setbacks. His father had died when he was a child, leaving him in poverty, and he had been awarded a free scholarship in a religious institution, where he had been made continually to feel that he was accepted for charity's sake, and, in consequence, he had been denied several of those distinctions and honours which gratify children. Later, about the age of eighteen, he came to grief in a sentimental affair; and finally, at twenty-two—this was a trifle in itself, but it was the last drop that overflowed his cup—he failed in his military examination. This young man then, could regard himself as a total failure: it was a sign— but a sign of what? He might have taken refuge in bitterness or despair. But he took it—very cleverly for him—as a sign that he was not intended for secular successes, and that only the attainments of religion, those of sanctity and of faith, were accessible to him. He interpreted his record as a message from God, and became a member of the Order. Who can doubt but that this decision as to the meaning of the sign was his, and his alone? One could have drawn quite different conclusions from such a series of reverses—as, for example, that he had better become a carpenter or a revolutionary. For the decipherment of the sign, however, he bears the entire responsibility. That is what "abandonment" implies, that we ourselves decide our being. And with this abandonment goes anguish.

As for "despair," the meaning of this expression is extremely simple. It merely means that we limit ourselves to a reliance upon that which is within our wills, or within the sum of the probabilities which render our action feasible. Whenever one wills anything, there are always these elements of probability. If I am counting upon a visit from a friend, who may be coming by train or by tram, I presuppose that the train will arrive at the appointed time, or that the tram will not be derailed. I remain in the realm of possibilities; but one does not rely upon any possibilities beyond those that are strictly concerned in one's action. Beyond the point at which the possibilities under consideration cease to affect my action, I ought to disinterest myself. For there is no God and no prevenient design, which can adapt the world and all its possibilities to my will. When Descartes said, "Conquer yourself rather than the world," what he meant was, at bottom, the same—that we should act without hope.

Marxists, to whom I have said this, have answered: "Your action is limited, obviously, by your death; but you can rely upon the help of others. That is, you can count both upon what the others are doing to help you elsewhere, as in China and in Russia, and upon what they will do later, after your death, to take up your action and carry it forward to its final accomplishment which will be the revolution. Moreover you must rely upon this; not to do so is immoral." To this I rejoin, first, that I shall always count upon my comrades-in-arms in the struggle, in so far as they are committed, as I am, to a definite, common cause; and in the unity of a party or a group which I can more or less control—that is, in which I am enrolled as a militant and whose movements at every moment are known to me. In that respect, to rely upon the unity and the will of the party is exactly like my reckoning that the train will run to time or that the tram will not be derailed. But I cannot count upon men whom I do not know, I cannot base my confidence upon human goodness or upon man's interest in the good of society, seeing that man is free and that there is no human nature which I can take as foundational. I do not know where the Russian revolution will lead. I can admire it and take it as an example in so far as it is evident, today, that the proletariat plays a part in Russia which it has attained in no other nation. But I cannot affirm that this will necessarily lead to the triumph of the proletariat: I must confine myself to what I can see. Nor can I be sure that comrades-in-arms will take up my work after my death and carry it to the maximum perfection, seeing that those men are free agents and will freely decide, tomorrow, what man is then to be. Tomorrow, after my death, some men may decide to establish Fascism, and the others may be so cowardly or so slack as to let them do so. If so, Fascism will then be the truth of man, and so much the worse for us. In reality, things will be such as men have decided they shall be. Does that mean that I should abandon myself to quietism? No. First I ought to commit myself and then act my commitment, according to the time-honored formula that "one need not hope in order to undertake one's work." Nor does this mean that I should not belong to a party, but only that I should be without illusion and that I should do what I can. For instance, if I ask myself "Will the social ideal as such, ever become a reality?" I cannot tell, I only know that whatever may be in my power to make it so, I shall do; beyond that, I can count upon nothing.

Quietism is the attitude of people who say, "let others do what I cannot do." The doctrine I am presenting before you is precisely ahe opposite of this, since it declares that there is no reality except in action. It goes further, indeed, and adds, "Man is nothing else but what he purposes, he exists only in so far as he realizes himself, he is therefore nothing else but the sum of his actions, nothing else but what his life is." Hence we can well understand why some people are horrified by our teaching. For many have but one resource to sustain them in their misery, and that is to think, "circumstances have been against me, I was worthy to be something much better than I have been. I admit I have never had a great love or a great friendship; but that is because I never met a man or a woman who was worthy of it; if I have not written any very good books, it is because I had not the leisure to do so; or, if I have had no children to whom I could devote myself it is because I did not find the man I could have lived with. So there remains within me a wide range of abilities, inclinations and potentialities, unused but perfectly viable, which endow me with a worthiness that could never be inferred from the mere history of my actions." But in reality and for the existentialist, there is no love apart from the deeds of love; no potentiality of love other than that which is manifested in loving; there is no genius other than that which is expressed in works of art. The genius of Proust is the totality of the works of Proust; the genius of Racine is the series of his tragedies, outside of which there is nothing. Why should we attribute to Racine the capacity to write yet another tragedy when that is precisely what he did not write? In life, a man commits himself, draws his own portrait and there is nothing but that portrait. No doubt this thought may seem comfortless to one who has not made a success of his life. On the other hand, it puts everyone in a position to understand that reality alone is reliable; that dreams, expectations and hopes serve to define a man only as deceptive dreams, abortive hopes, expectations unfulfilled; that is to say, they define him negatively, not positively. Nevertheless, when one says, "You are nothing else but what you live," it does not imply that an artist is to be judged solely by his works of art, for a thousand other things contribute no less to his definition as a man. What we mean to say is that a man is no other than a series of undertakings, that he is the sum, the organization, the set of relations that constitute these undertakings.

In the light of all this, what people reproach us with is not, after all, our pessimism, but the sternness of our optimism. If people condemn our works of fiction, in which we describe characters that are base, weak, cowardly and sometimes even frankly evil, it is not only because those characters are base, weak, cowardly or evil. For suppose that, like Zola, we showed that the behavior of these characters was caused by their heredity, or by the action of their environment upon them, or by determining factors, psychic or organic. People would be reassured, they would say, "You see, that is what we are like, no one can do anything about it." But the existentialist, when he portrays a coward, shows him as responsible for his cowardice. He is not like that on account of a cowardly heart or lungs or cerebrum, he has not become like that through his physiological organism; he is like that because he has made himself into a coward by his actions. There is no such thing as a cowardly temperament. There are nervous temperaments; there is what is called impoverished blood, and there are also rich temperaments. But the man whose blood is poor is not a coward for all that, for what produces cowardice is the act of giving up or giving way; and a temperament is not an action. A coward is defined by the deed that he has done. What people feel obscurely, and with horror, is that the coward as we present him is guilty of being a coward. What people would prefer would be to be born either a coward or a hero. One of the charges most often laid against the *Chemins de la Liberté* is something like this—"But, after all, these people being so base, how can you make them into heroes?" That objection is really rather comic, for it implies that people are born heroes: and that is, at bottom, what such people would like to think. If you are born cowards, you can be quite content. You can do nothing about it and you will be cowards all your lives whatever you do; and if you are born heroes you can again be quite content; you will be heroes all your lives, eating and drinking heroically. Whereas the existentialist says that the coward makes himself cowardly, the hero makes himself heroic; and that there is always a possibility for the coward to give up cowardice and for the hero to stop being a hero. What counts is the total commitment, and it is not by a particular case or particular action that you are committed altogether.

We have now, I think, dealt with a certain number of the reproaches against existentialism. You have seen that it cannot be regarded as a philosophy of quietism since it defines man by his action; nor as a pessimistic description of man, for no doctrine is more optimistic, the destiny of man is placed within himself. Nor is it an attempt to discourage man from action since it tells him that there is no hope except in his action, and that the one thing which permits him to have life is the deed. Upon this level therefore, what we are considering is an ethic of action and self-commitment. However, we are still reproached, upon these few data, for confining man within his individual subjectivity. There again people badly misunderstand us.

Our point of departure is, indeed, the subjectivity of the individual, and that for strictly philosophic reasons. It is not because we are bourgeois, but because we seek to base our teaching upon the truth, and not upon a collection of fine theories, full of hope but lacking real foundations. And at the point of departure there cannot be any other truth than this, *I think, therefore I am,* which is the absolute truth of consciousness as it attains to itself. Every theory which begins with man, outside of this moment of self-attainment, is a theory which thereby suppresses the truth, for outside of the Cartesian *cogito,* all objects are no more than probable, and any doctrine of probabilities which is not attached to a truth will crumble into nothing. In order to define the probable one must possess the true. Before there can be any truth whatever, then, there must be an absolute truth, and there is such a truth which is simple, easily attained and within the reach of everybody; it consists in one's immediate sense of one's self.

In the second place, this theory alone is compatible with the dignity of man, it is the only one which does not make man into an object. All kinds of materialism lead one to treat every man including oneself as an object—that is, as a set of pre-determined reactions, in no way different from the patterns of qualities and phenomena which constitute a table, or a chair or a stone. Our aim is precisely to establish the human kingdom as a pattern of values in distinction from the material world. But the subjectivity which we thus postulate as the standard of truth is no narrowly individual subjectivism, for as we have demonstrated, it is not only one's own self that one discovers in the *cogito,* but those of others too. Contrary to the philosophy of Descartes, contrary to that of Kant, when we say "I think" we are attaining to ourselves in the presence of the other, and we are just as certain of the other as we are of ourselves. Thus the man who discovers himself directly in the *cogito* also discovers all the others, and discovers them as the condition of his own existence. He recognizes that he cannot be anything (in the sense in which one says one is spiritual, or that one is wicked or jealous) unless others recognize him as such. I cannot obtain any truth whatsoever about myself, except through the mediation of another. The other is indispensable to my existence, and equally so to any knowledge I can have of myself. Under these conditions, the intimate discovery of myself is at the same time the revelation of the other as a freedom which confronts mine, and which cannot think or will without doing so either for or against me. Thus, at once, we find ourselves in a world which is, let us say, that of "inter-subjectivity." It is in this world that man has to decide what he is and what others are.

Furthermore, although it is impossible to find in each and every man a universal essence that can be called human nature, there is nevertheless a human universality of *condition*. It is not by chance that the thinkers of today are so much more ready to speak of the condition than of the nature of man. By his condition they understand, with more or less clarity, all the *limitations* which *à priori* define man's fundamental situation in the universe. His historical situations are variable: man may be born a slave in a pagan society, or may be a feudal baron, or a proletarian. But what never vary are the necessities of being in the world, of having to labor and to die there. These limitations are neither subjective nor objective, or rather there is both a subjective and an objective aspect of them. Objective, because we meet with them everywhere and they are everywhere recognizable: and subjective because they are *lived* and are nothing if man does not live them—if, that is to say, he does not freely determine himself and his existence in relation to them. And, diverse though man's purposes may be, at least none of them is wholly foreign to me, since every human purpose presents itself as an attempt either to surpass these limitations, or to widen them, or else to deny or to accommodate oneself to them. Consequently every purpose, however individual it may be, is of universal value. Every purpose, even that of a Chinese, an Indian or a Negro, can be understood by a European. To say it can be understood, means that the European of 1945 may be striving out of a certain situation towards the same limitations in the same way, and that he may reconceive in himself the purpose of the Chinese, of the Indian or the African. In every purpose there is universality, in this sense that every purpose is comprehensible to every man. Not that this or or that purpose defines man for ever, but that it may be entertained again and again. There is always some way of understanding an idiot, a child, a primitive man or a foreigner if one has sufficient information. In this sense we may say that there is a human universality, but it is not something given; it is being properly made. I make this universality in choosing myself; I also make it by understanding the purpose of any other man, of whatever epoch. This absoluteness of the act of choice does not alter the relativity of each epoch.

What is at the very heart and center of existentialism, is the absolute character of the free commitment, by which every man realizes himself in realizing a type of humanity—a commitment always understandable, to no matter whom in no matter what epoch—and its bearing upon the relativity of the cultural pattern which may result from such absolute commitment. One must observe equally the relativity of Cartesianism and the absolute character of the Cartesian commitment. In this sense you may say, if you like, that every one of us makes the absolute by breathing, by eating, by sleeping or by behaving in any fashion whatsoever. There is no difference between free being—being as self-committal, as existence choosing its essence—and absolute being. And there is no difference whatever between being as an absolute, temporarily localized—that is, localized in history—and universally intelligible being.

This does not completely refute the charge of subjectivism. Indeed that objection appears in several other forms, of which the first is as follows. People say to us, "Then it does not matter what you do," and they say this in various ways. First they tax us with anarchy; then they say, "You cannot judge others, for there is no reason for preferring one purpose to another"; finally, they may say, "Everything being merely voluntary in this choice of yours, you give away with one hand what you pretend to gain with the other." These three are not very serious objections. As to the first, to say that it does not matter what you choose is not correct. In one sense choice is possible, but what is not possible is not to choose. I can always choose, but I must know that if I do not choose, that is still a choice. This, although it may appear merely formal, is of great importance as a limit to fantasy and caprice. For, when I confront a real situation—for example, that I am a sexual being, able to have relations with a being of the other sex and able to have children—I am obliged to choose my attitude to it, and in every respect I bear the responsibility of the choice which, in committing myself, also commits the whole of humanity. Even if my choice is determined by no *à priori* value whatever, it can have nothing to do with caprice: and if anyone thinks that this is only Gide's theory of the *acte gratuit* over again, he has failed to see the enormous difference between this theory and that of Gide. Gide does not know what a situation is, his "act" is one of pure caprice. In our view, on the contrary, man finds himself in an organized situation in which he is himself involved: his choice involves mankind in its entirety, and he cannot avoid choosing. Either he must remain single, or he must marry without having children, or he must marry and have children. In any case, and whichever he may choose, it is impossible for him, in respect of this situation, not to take complete responsibility. Doubtless he chooses without reference to any pre-established values, but it is unjust to tax him with caprice. Rather let us say that the moral choice is comparable to the construction of a work of art.

But here I must at once digress to make it quite clear that we are not propounding an aesthetic morality, for our adversaries are disingenuous enough to reproach us even with that. I mention the work of art only by way of comparison. That being understood, does anyone reproach an artist, when he paints a picture, for not following rules established *à priori*?

Does one ever ask what is the picture that he ought to paint? As everyone knows, there is no pre-defined picture for him to make; the artist applies himself to the composition of a picture, and the picture that ought to be made is precisely that which he will have made. As everyone knows, there are no aesthetic values à priori, but there are values which will appear in due course in the coherence of the picture, in the relation between the will to create and the finished work. No one can tell what the painting of tomorrow will be like; one cannot judge a painting until it is done. What has that to do with morality? We are in the same creative situation. We never speak of a work of art as irresponsible; when we are discussing a canvas by Picasso, we understand very well that the composition became what it is at the time when he was painting it, and that his works are part and parcel of his entire life.

It is the same upon the plane of morality. There is this in common between art and morality, that in both we have to do with creation and invention. We cannot decide à priori what it is that should be done. I think it was made sufficiently clear to you in the case of that student who came to see me, that to whatever ethical system he might appeal, the Kantian or any other, he could find no sort of guidance whatever; he was obliged to invent the law for himself. Certainly we cannot say that this man, in choosing to remain with his mother—that is, in taking sentiment, personal devotion and concrete charity as his moral foundations—would be making an irresponsible choice, nor could we do so if he preferred the sacrifice of going away to England. Man makes himself; he is not found ready-made; he makes himself by the choice of his morality, and he cannot but choose a morality, such is the pressure of circumstances upon him. We define man only in relation to his commitments; it is therefore absurd to reproach us for irresponsibility in our choice.

In the second place, people say to us, "You are unable to judge others." This is true in one sense and false in another. It is true in this sense, that whenever a man chooses his purpose and his commitment in all clearness and in all sincerity, whatever that purpose may be, it is impossible for him to prefer another. It is true in the sense that we do not believe in progress. Progress implies amelioration; but man is always the same, facing a situation which is always changing, and choice remains always a choice in the situation. The moral problem has not changed since the time when it was a choice between slavery and anti-slavery—from the time of the war of Secession, for example, until the present moment when one chooses between the M.R.P. [Mouvement Républicain Populaire] and the Communists.

We can judge, nevertheless, for, as I have said, one chooses in view of others, and in view of others one chooses himself. One can judge, first—and perhaps this is not a judgment of value, but it is a logical judgment—that in certain cases choice is founded upon an error, and in others upon the truth. One can judge a man by saying that he deceives himself. Since we have defined the situation of man as one of free choice, without excuse and without help, any man who takes refuge behind the excuse of his passions, or by inventing some deterministic doctrine, is a self-deceiver. One may object: "But why should he not choose to deceive himself?" I reply that it is not for me to judge him morally, but I define his self-deception as an error. Here one cannot avoid pronouncing a judgment of truth. The self-deception is evidently a falsehood, because it is a dissimulation of man's complete liberty of commitment. Upon this same level, I say that it is also a self-deception if I choose to declare that certain values are incumbent upon me; I am in contradiction with myself if I will these values and at the same time say that they impose themselves upon me. If anyone says to me, "And what if I wish to deceive myself?" I answer, "There is no reason why you should not, but I declare that you are doing so, and that the attitude of strict consistency alone is that of good faith." Furthermore, I can pronounce a moral judgment. For I declare that freedom, in respect of concrete circumstances, can have no other end and aim but itself; and when once a man has seen that values depend upon himself, in that state of forsakenness he can will only one thing, and that is freedom as the foundation of all values. That does not mean that he wills it in the abstract: it simply means that the actions of men of good faith have, as their ultimate significance, the quest of freedom itself as such. A man who belongs to some communist or revolutionary society wills certain concrete ends, which imply the will to freedom, but that freedom is willed in community. We will freedom for freedom's sake, in and through particular circumstances. And in thus willing freedom, we discover that it depends entirely upon the freedom of others and that the freedom of others depends upon our own. Obviously, freedom as the definition of a man does not depend upon others, but as soon as there is a commitment, I am obliged to will the liberty of others at the same time as my own. I cannot make liberty my aim unless I make that of others equally my aim. Consequently, when I recognize, as entirely authentic, that man is a being whose existence precedes his essence, and that he is a free being who cannot, in any circumstances, but will his freedom, at the same time I realize that I cannot not will the freedom of others. Thus, in the name of that will to freedom which is implied in freedom itself, I can form judgments upon those who seek to hide from themselves the wholly voluntary nature of their existence and its complete freedom. Those who hide from this total freedom, in a guise of solemnity or with deterministic excuses, I shall call cowards. Others, who try to show that their existence is necessary, when it is merely an accident of the appearance of the human race on earth—I shall call scum. But neither cowards nor scum can be identified except upon the plane of strict authenticity. Thus, although the content of morality is variable, a certain form of this morality is universal. Kant declared that freedom is a will both to itself and to the freedom of others. Agreed: but he thinks that the formal and the universal suffice for the constitution of a morality. We think, on the contrary, that principles that are too abstract break down when we come to defining action. To take once again the case of that student; by what authority, in the name of what golden rule of morality, do you think he could have decided, in perfect peace of mind, either to abandon his mother or to remain with her? There are no means of judging. The content is always concrete, and therefore unpredictable; it has always to be invented. The one thing that counts, is to know whether the invention is made in the name of freedom.

Let us, for example, examine the two following cases, and you will see how far they are similar in spite of their difference. Let us take *The Mill on the Floss.* We find here a certain young woman, Maggie Tulliver, who is an incarnation of the value of passion and is aware of it. She is in love with a young man, Stephen, who is engaged to another, an insignificant young woman. This Maggie Tulliver, instead of heedlessly seeking her own happiness, chooses in the name of human solidarity to sacrifice herself and to give up the man she loves. On the other hand, La Sanseverina in Stendhal's *Chartreuse de Parme,* believing that it is passion which endows man with his real value, would have declared that a grand passion justifies its sacrifices, and must be preferred to the banality of such conjugal love as would unite Stephan to the little goose he was engaged to marry. It is the latter that she would have chosen to sacrifice in realizing her own happiness, and, as Stendhal shows, she would also sacrifice herself upon the plane of passion if life made that demand upon her. Here we are facing two clearly opposed moralities; but I claim that they are equivalent, seeing that in both cases the overruling aim is freedom. You can imagine two attitudes exactly similar in effect, in that one girl might prefer, in resignation, to give up her lover while the other preferred, in fulfillment of sexual desire, to ignore the prior engagement of the man she loved; and, externally, these two cases might appear the same as the two we have just cited, while being in fact entirely different. The attitude of La Sanseverina is much nearer to that of Maggie Tulliver than to one of careless greed. Thus, you see, the second objection is at once true and false. One can choose anything, but only if it is upon the plane of free commitment.

The third objection, stated by saying, "You take with one hand what you give with the other," means, at bottom, "your values are not serious, since you choose them yourselves." To that I can only say that I am very sorry that it should be so; but if I have excluded God the Father, there must be somebody to invent values. We have to take things as they are. And moreover, to say that we invent values means neither more nor less than this; that there is no sense in life *à priori.* Life is nothing until it is lived; but it is yours to make sense of, and the value of it is nothing else but the sense that you choose. Therefore, you can see that there is a possibility of creating a human community. I have been reproached for suggesting that existentialism is a form of humanism: people have said to me, "But you have written in your *Nausée* that the humanists are wrong, you have even ridiculed a certain type of humanism, why do you now go back upon that?" In reality, the word humanism has two very different meanings. One may understand by humanism a theory which upholds man as the end-in-itself and as the supreme value. Humanism in this sense appears, for instance, in Cocteau's story *Round the World in 80 Hours,* in which one of the characters declares, because he is flying over mountains in an airplane, "Man is magnificent!" This signifies that although I, personally, have not built airplanes I have the benefit of those particular inventions and that I personally, being a man, can consider myself responsible for, and honored by, achievements that are peculiar to some men. It is to assume that we can ascribe value to man according to the most distinguished deeds of certain men. That kind of humanism is absurd, for only the dog or the horse would be in a position to pronounce a general judgment upon man and declare that he is magnificent, which they have never been such fools as to do—at least, not as far as I know. But neither is it admissible that a man should pronounce judgment upon Man. Existentialism dispenses with any judgment of this sort; an existentialist will never take man as the end, since man is still determined. And we have no right to believe that humanity is something to which we could set up a cult, after the manner of Auguste Comte. The cult of humanity ends in Comtian humanism, shut-in upon itself, and—this must be said—in Fascism. We do not want a humanism like that.

But there is another sense of the word, of which the fundamental meaning is this: Man is all the time outside of himself: it is in projecting and losing himself beyond himself that he makes man to exist; and, on the other hand, it is by pursuing transcendent aims that he himself is able to exist. Since man is thus self-surpassing, and can grasp objects only in relation to his self-surpassing, he is himself the heart and center of his transcendence. There is no other universe except the human universe, the universe of human subjectivity. This relation of transcendence as constitutive of man (not in the sense that God is transcendent, but in the sense of self-surpassing) with subjectivity (in such a sense that man is not shut up in himself but forever present in a human universe)—it is this that we call existential humanism. This is humanism, because we remind man that there is no legislator but himself; that he himself, thus abandoned, must decide for himself; also because we show that it is not by turning back upon himself, but always by seeking, beyond himself, an aim which is one of liberation or of some particular realization, that man can realize himself as truly human.

You can see from these few reflections that nothing could be more unjust than the objections people raise against us. Existentialism is nothing else but an attempt to draw the full conclusions from a consistently atheistic position. Its intention is not in the least that of plunging men into despair. And if by despair one means—as the Christians do—any attitude of unbelief, the despair of the existentialists is something different. Existentialism is not atheist in the sense that it would exhaust itself in demonstrations of the non-existence of God. It declares, rather, that even if God existed that would make no difference from its point of view. Not that we believe God does exist, but we think that the real problem is not that of His existence; what man needs is to find himself again and to understand that nothing can save him from himself, not even a valid proof of the existence of God. In this sense existentialism is optimistic. It is a doctrine of action, and it is only by self-deception, by confusing their own despair with ours that Christians can describe us as without hope.

QUESTIONS FOR STUDY AND DISCUSSION

1. Trace through this selection Sartre's explication of the principle that existence comes before essence.
2. Summarize and evaluate Sartre's account of the Christian teaching on man and creation.
3. What consequences does Sartre draw from the certitude of the *cogito?*
4. How are Sartre's view of man, his ethics, and his metaphysical position rooted in his doctrine of freedom?
5. What consequences does he draw from his denial of the existence of God?

Paul Tillich

PAUL TILLICH, the son of a clergyman, was born in Germany in 1886 in the province of Brandenburg. He studied theology and philosophy at the Universities of Berlin, Tübingen, Halle, and Breslau, and received his doctorate from Breslau in 1912. That same year he was ordained a minister of the Evangelical Lutheran Church. After World War I he began his academic career at the University of Berlin, where he and fellow intellectuals initiated their idea for the future, which they called "religious socialism." For a decade he wrote and lectured while teaching at various universities throughout Germany. When Hitler came to power, Tillich was dismissed from his position at the University of Frankfurt because he spoke out against the Nazis. He came to the U.S. to take a position at Union Theological Seminary. After his retirement from the seminary in 1955, he was associated with Harvard and the University of Chicago. His most important work, *Systematic Theology* (3 vols., 1951, 1957, 1963), is a comprehensive theological and philosophical synthesis. He died in Chicago in October, 1965.

Being as Man's Ultimate Concern

THEOLOGY AND PHILOSOPHY: A QUESTION

Theology claims that it constitutes a special realm of knowledge, that it deals with a special object and employs a special method. This claim places the theologian under the obligation of giving an account of the way in which he relates theology to other forms of knowledge. He must answer two questions: What is the relationship of theology to the special sciences (*Wissenschaften*) and what is its relationship to philosophy? The first question has been answered implicitly by the preceding statement of the formal criteria of theology. If nothing is an object of theology which does not concern us ultimately, theology is unconcerned about scientific procedures and results and vice versa. Theology has no right and no obligation to prejudice a physical or historical, sociological or psychological, inquiry. And no result of such an inquiry can be directly productive or disastrous for theology. The point of contact between scientific research and theology

Reprinted from pp. 18–28 of *Systematic Theology,* vol. I, by Paul Tillich by permission of The University of Chicago Press. Copyright 1951 by The University of Chicago Press.

lies in the philosophical element of both, the sciences and theology. Therefore, the question of the relation of theology to the special sciences merges into the question of the relation between theology and philosophy.

The difficulty of this question lies partly in the fact that there is no generally accepted definition of philosophy. Every philosophy proposes a definition which agrees with the interest, purpose, and method of the philosopher. Under these circumstances the theologian can only suggest a definition of philosophy which is broad enough to cover most of the important philosophies which have appeared in what usually is called the history of philosophy. The suggestion made here is to call philosophy *that cognitive approach to reality in which reality as such is the object.* Reality as such, or reality as a whole, is not the whole of reality; it is the structure which makes reality a whole and therefore a potential object of knowledge. Inquiring into the nature of reality as such means inquiring into those structures, categories, and concepts which are presupposed in the cognitive encounter with every realm of reality. From this point of view philosophy is by definition critical. It separates the multifarious materials of experience from those structures which make experience possible. There is no difference in this respect between constructive idealism and empirical realism. The question regarding the character of the general structures that make experience possible is always the same. It is *the* philosophical question.

The critical definition of philosophy is more modest than those philosophical enterprises which try to present a complete system of reality, including the results of all the special sciences as well as the general structures of prescientific experience. Such an attempt can be made from "above" or from "below." Hegel worked from "above" when he filled the categorical forms, developed in his *Logic,* with the available material of the scientific knowledge of his time and adjusted the material to the categories. Wundt [1] worked from "below" when he abstracted general and metaphysical principles from the available scientific material of his time, with the help of which the entire sum of empirical knowledge could be organized. Aristotle worked from both "above" and "below" when he carried through metaphysical and scientific studies in interdependence. This also was the ideal of Leibniz when he sketched a universal calculus capable of subjecting all of reality to mathematical analysis and synthesis. But in all these cases the limits of the human mind, the finitude which prevents it from grasping the whole, became visible. No sooner was the system finished than scientific research trespassed its boundaries and disrupted it in all directions. Only the general principles were left, always discussed, questioned, changed, but never destroyed, shining through the centuries, reinterpreted by every generation, inexhaustible, never antiquated or obsolete. These principles are the material of philosophy.

---

[1] Wilhelm Wundt (1832–1920): German pioneer in the development of experimental psychology; his works on logic and ethics grew out of his research in physiology and psychology. [H.J.J.]

This understanding of philosophy is, on the other hand, less modest than the attempt to reduce philosophy to epistemology and ethics, which was the goal of the Neo-Kantian and related schools in the nineteenth century, and less modest also than the attempt to reduce it to logical calculus, which has been the goal of logical positivism and related schools in the twentieth century. Both attempts to avoid the ontological question have been unsuccessful. The later adherents of the Neo-Kantian philosophy recognized that every epistemology contains an implicit ontology. It cannot be otherwise. Since knowing is an act which participates in being or, more precisely, in an "ontic relation," [2] every analysis of the act of knowing must refer to an interpretation of being (cf. Nicolai Hartmann).[3] At the same time the problem of values pointed toward an ontological foundation of the validity of value-judgments. If values have no *fundamentum in re* (cf. Plato's identification of the good with the essential structures, the ideas of being), they float in the air of a transcendent validity, or else they are subjected to pragmatic tests which are arbitrary and accidental unless they introduce an ontology of essences surreptitiously. It is not necessary to discuss the pragmatic-naturalistic line of philosophical thought, for, in spite of the antimetaphysical statements of some of its adherents, it has expressed itself in definite ontological terms such as life, growth, process, experience, being (understood in an all-embracing sense), etc. But it is necessary to compare the ontological definition of philosophy, suggested above, with the radical attempts to reduce philosophy to scientific logic. The question is whether the elimination of almost all traditional philosophical problems by logical positivism is a successful escape from ontology. One's first reaction is the feeling that such an attitude pays too high a price, namely, the price of making philosophy irrelevant. But, beyond this impression, the following argument can be put forward. If the restriction of philosophy to the logic of the sciences is a matter of taste, it need not be taken seriously. If it is based on an analysis of the limits of human knowledge, it is based, like every epistemology, on ontological assumptions. There is always at least one problem about which logical positivism, like all semantic philosophies, must make a decision. What is the relation of signs, symbols, or logical operations to reality? Every answer to this question says something about the structure of being. It is ontological. And a philosophy which is so radically critical of all other philosophies should be sufficiently self-critical to see and to reveal its own ontological assumptions.

Philosophy asks the question of reality as a whole; it asks the question of the structure of being. And it answers in terms of categories, structural

---

[2] *Ontic* means "relative to Being"; *ontological* (as opposed to *ontic*, here) means "relative to the understanding of Being." Tillich has taken over this distinction from Heidegger. [H.J.J.]

[3] Nicolai Hartmann (1882–1950): German philosopher, professor of Philosophy at Göttingen; he combined neo-Kantianism and Husserl's phenomenology in his philosophy. [H.J.J.]

laws, and universal concepts. It must answer in ontological terms. Ontology is not a speculative-fantastic attempt to establish a world behind the world; it is an analysis of those structures of being which we encounter in every meeting with reality. This was also the original meaning of metaphysics; but the preposition *meta* now has the irremediable connotation of pointing to a duplication of this world by a transcendent realm of beings. Therefore, it is perhaps less misleading to speak of ontology instead of metaphysics.

Philosophy necessarily asks the question of reality as a whole, the question of the structure of being. Theology necessarily asks the same question, for that which concerns us ultimately must belong to reality as a whole; it must belong to being. Otherwise we could not encounter it, and it could not concern us. Of course, it cannot be one being among others; then it would not concern us infinitely. It must be the ground of our being, that which determines our being or not-being, the ultimate and unconditional power of being. But the power of being, its infinite ground or "being-itself," expresses itself in and through the structure of being. Therefore, we can encounter it, be grasped by it, know it, and act toward it. Theology, when dealing with our ultimate concern, presupposes in every sentence the structure of being, its categories, laws, and concepts. Theology, therefore, cannot escape the question of being any more easily than can philosophy. The attempt of biblicism to avoid nonbiblical, ontological terms is doomed to failure as surely as are the corresponding philosophical attempts. The Bible itself always uses the categories and concepts which describe the structure of experience. On every page of every religious or theological text these concepts appear: time, space, cause, thing, subject, nature, movement, freedom, necessity, life, value, knowledge, experience, being and not-being. Biblicism may try to preserve their popular meaning, but then it ceases to be theology. It must neglect the fact that a philosophical understanding of these categories has influenced ordinary language for many centuries. It is surprising how casually theological biblicists use a term like "history" when speaking of Christianity as a historical religion or of God as the "Lord of history." They forget that the meaning they connect with the word "history" has been formed by thousand of years of historiography and philosophy of history. They forget that historical being is one kind of being in addition to others and that, in order to distinguish it from the word "nature," for instance, a general vision of the structure of being is presupposed. They forget that the problem of history is tied up with the problems of time, freedom, accident, purpose, etc., and that each of these concepts has had a development similar to the concept of history. The theologian must take seriously the meaning of the terms he uses. They must be known to him in the whole depth and breadth of their meaning. Therefore, the systematic theologian must be a philosopher in critical understanding even if not in creative power.

The structure of being and the categories and concepts describing this structure are an implicit or explicit concern of every philosopher and of every theologian. Neither of them can avoid the ontological question. Attempts from both sides to avoid it have proved abortive. If this is the situation, the question becomes the more urgent: What is the relation between the ontological question asked by the philosopher and the ontological question asked by the theologian?

THEOLOGY AND PHILOSOPHY: AN ANSWER

Philosophy and theology ask the question of being. But they ask it from different perspectives. Philosophy deals with the structure of being in itself; theology deals with the meaning of being for us. From this difference convergent and divergent trends emerge in the relation of theology and philosophy.

The first point of divergence is a difference in the cognitive attitude of the philosopher and the theologian. Although driven by the philosophical *erōs,* the philosopher tries to maintain a detached objectivity toward being and its structures. He tries to exclude the personal, social, and historical conditions which might distort an objective vision of reality. His passion is the passion for a truth which is open to general approach, subject to general criticism, changeable in accordance with every new insight, open and communicable. In all these respects he feels no different from the scientist, historian, psychologist, etc. He collaborates with them. The material for his critical analysis is largely supplied by empirical research. Just as all sciences have their origin in philosophy, so they contribute in turn to philosophy by giving to the philosopher new and exactly defined material far beyond anything he could get from a prescientific approach to reality. Of course, the philosopher, as a philosopher, neither criticizes nor augments the knowledge provided by the sciences. This knowledge forms the basis of his description of the categories, structural laws, and concepts which constitute the structure of being. In this respect the philosopher is as dependent on the scientist as he is dependent on his own prescientific observation of reality—often more dependent. This relation to the sciences (in the broad sense of *Wissenschaften*) strengthens the detached, objective attitude of the philosopher. Even in the intuitive-synthetic side of his procedure he tries to exclude influences which are not purely determined by his object.[4]

The theologian, quite differently, is not detached from his object but is involved in it. He looks at his object (which transcends the character of being an object) with passion, fear, and love. This is not the *erōs* of the philosopher or his passion for objective truth; it is the love which accepts saving, and therefore personal, truth. The basic attitude of the theologian is commitment to the content he expounds. Detachment would be a denial of

---

[4] The concept of a "philosophical faith" appears questionable from this point of view (see Karl Jaspers, *The Perennial Scope of Philosophy* [New York: Philosophical Library, 1949]). [P.T.]

the very nature of this content. The attitude of the theologian is "existential." He is involved—with the whole of his existence, with his finitude and his anxiety, with his self-contradictions and his despair, with the healing forces in him and in his social situation. Every theological statement derives its seriousness from these elements of existence. The theologian, in short, is determined by his faith. Every theology presupposes that the theologian is in the theological circle. This contradicts the open, infinite, and changeable character of philosophical truth. It also differs from the way in which the philosopher is dependent on scientific research. The theologian has no direct relation to the scientist (including the historian, sociologist, psychologist). He deals with him only in so far as philosophical implications are at stake. If he abandons the existential attitude, as some of the "empirical" theologians have done, he is driven to statements the reality of which will not be acknowledged by anybody who does not share the existential presuppositions of the assumedly empirical theologian. Theology is necessarily existential, and no theology can escape the theological circle.

The second point of divergence between the theologian and the philosopher is the difference in their sources. The philosopher looks at the whole of reality to discover within it the structure of reality as a whole. He tries to penetrate into the structures of being by means of the power of his cognitive function and its structures. He assumes—and science continuously confirms this assumption—that there is an identity, or at least an analogy, between objective and subjective reason, between the *logos* of reality as a whole and the *logos* working in him. Therefore, this *logos* is common; every reasonable being participates in it, uses it in asking questions and criticizing the answers received. There is no particular place to discover the structure of being; there is no particular place to stand to discover the categories of experience. The place to look is all places; the place to stand is no place at all; it is pure reason.

The theologian, on the other hand, must look where that which concerns him ultimately is manifest, and he must stand where its manifestation reaches and grasps him. The source of his knowledge is not the universal *logos* but the Logos "who became flesh," that is, the *logos* manifesting itself in a particular historical event. And the medium through which he receives the manifestation of the *logos* is not common rationality but the church, its traditions and its present reality. He speaks in the church about the foundation of the church. And he speaks because he is grasped by the power of this foundation and by the community built upon it. The concrete *logos* which he sees is received through believing commitment and not, like the universal *logos* at which the philosopher looks, through rational detachment.

The third point of divergence between philosophy and theology is the difference in their content. Even when they speak about the same object, they speak about something different. The philosopher deals with the categories of being in relation to the material which is structured by them. He deals with causality as it appears in physics or psychology; he analyzes biological or historical time; he discusses astronomical as well as microcosmic space. He describes the epistemological subject and the relation of person and community. He presents the characteristics of life and spirit in their dependence on, and independence of, each other. He defines nature and history in their mutual limits and tries to penetrate into ontology and logic of being and nonbeing. Innumerable other examples could be given. They all reflect the cosmological structure of the philosophical assertions. The theologian, on the other hand, relates the same categories and concepts to the quest for a "new being." His assertions have a soteriological character. He discusses causality in relation to a *prima causa,* the ground of the whole series of causes and effects; he deals with time in relation to eternity, with space in relation to man's existential homelessness. He speaks of the self-estrangement of the subject, about the spiritual center of personal life, and about community as a possible embodiment of the "New Being." He relates the structures of life to the creative ground of life and the structures of spirit to the divine Spirit. He speaks of the participation of nature in the "history of salvation," about the victory of being over nonbeing. Here also the examples could be increased indefinitely; they show the sharp divergence of theology from philosophy with respect to their content.

The divergence between philosophy and theology is counterbalanced by an equally obvious convergence. From both sides converging trends are at work. The philosopher, like the theologian, "exists," and he cannot jump over the concreteness of his existence and his implicit theology. He is conditioned by his psychological, sociological, and historical situation. And, like every human being, he exists in the power of an ultimate concern, whether or not he is fully conscious of it, whether or not he admits it to himself and to others. There is no reason why even the most scientific philosopher should not admit it, for without an ultimate concern his philosophy would be lacking in passion, seriousness, and creativity. Wherever we look in the history of philosophy, we find ideas and systems which claim to be ultimately relevant for human existence. Occasionally the philosophy of religion openly expresses the ultimate concern behind a system. More often it is the character of the ontological principles, or a special section of a system, such as epistemology, philosophy of nature, politics and ethics, philosophy of history, etc., which is most revealing for the discovery of the ultimate concern and the hidden theology within it. Every creative philosopher is a hidden theologian (sometimes even a declared theologian). He is a theologian in the degree to which his existential situation and his ultimate concern shape his philosophical vision. He is a theologian in the degree to which his intuition of the universal *logos* of the structure of reality as a whole is formed by a particular *logos* which appears to him on his particular place and reveals to him the meaning of the whole. And he is a theologian in the degree to which the particular *logos* is a matter of active commitment within a special community. There is hardly a historically significant philosopher who does not show these marks of a theologian. But the philosopher does not intend to be a theologian. He wants to serve the universal *logos*. He tries to turn away from his existential situation, including his ultimate concern, toward a place above all particular places, toward pure reality. The conflict between the intention of becoming universal and the destiny of remaining particular characterizes every philosophical existence. It is its burden and its greatness.

The theologian carries an analogous burden. Instead of turning away from his existential situation, including his ultimate concern, he turns toward it. He turns toward it, not in order to make a confession of it, but in order to make clear the universal validity, the *logos* structure, of what concerns him ultimately. And he can do this only in an attitude of detachment from his existential situation and in obedience to the universal *logos*. This obligates him to be critical of every special expression of his ultimate concern. He cannot affirm any tradition and any authority except through a "No" and a "Yes." And it is always possible that he may not be able to go all the way from the "No" to the "Yes." He cannot join the chorus of those who live in unbroken assertions. He must take the risk of being driven beyond the boundary line of the theological circle. Therefore, the pious and powerful in the church are suspicious of him, although they live in dependence upon the work of the former theologians who were in the same situation. Theology, since it serves not only the concrete but also the universal *logos,* can become a stumbling block for the church and a demonic temptation for the theologian. The detachment required in honest theological work can destroy the necessary involvement of faith. This tension is the burden and the greatness of every theological work.

The duality of divergence and convergence in the relation between theology and philosophy leads to the double question: Is there a necessary conflict between the two and is there a possible synthesis between them? Both questions must be answered negatively. Neither is a conflict between theology and philosophy necessary, nor is a synthesis between them possible.

A conflict presupposes a common basis on which to fight. But there is no common basis between theology and philosophy. If the theologian and the philosopher fight, they do so either on a philosophical or on a theological basis. The philosophical basis is the ontological analysis of the structure of being. If the theologian needs this analysis, either he must take it from a philosopher or he must himself become a philosopher. Usually he does both. If he enters the philosophical arena, conflicts as well as alliances with other philosophers are unavoidable. But all this happens on the philosophical level. The theologian has no right whatsoever to argue for a philosophical opinion in the name of his ultimate concern or on the basis of the theological circle. He is obliged to argue for a philosophical decision in the name of the universal *logos* and from the place which is no place; pure reason. It is a disgrace for the theologian and intolerable for the philosopher if in a philosophical discussion the theologian suddenly claims an authority other than pure reason. Conflicts on the philosophical level are conflicts between two philosophers, one of whom happens to be a theologian, but they are not conflicts between theology and philosophy.

Often, however, the conflict is fought on the theological level. The hidden theologian in the philosopher fights with the professed theologian. This situation is more frequent than most philosophers realize. Since they have developed their concepts with the honest intention of obeying the universal *logos,* they are reluctant to recognize the existentially conditioned elements in their systems. They feel that such elements, while they give color and direction to their creative work, diminish its truth value. In such a situation the theologian must break the resistance of the philosopher against a theological analysis of his ideas. He can do this by pointing to the history of philosophy, which discloses that in every significant philosopher existential passion (ultimate concern) and rational power (obedience to the universal *logos*) are united and that the truth value of a philosophy is dependent on the amalgamation of these two elements in every concept. The insight into this situation is, at the same time, an insight into the fact that two philosophers, one of whom happens to be a theologian, can fight with each other and that two theologians, one of whom happens to be a philosopher, can fight with each other; but there is no possible conflict between theology and philosophy because there is no common basis for such a conflict. The philosopher may or may not convince the philosopher-theologian. And the theologian may or may not convert the theologian-philosopher. In no case does the theologian as such stand against the philosopher as such and vice versa.

Thus there is no conflict between theology and philosophy, and there is no synthesis either—for exactly the same reason which insures that there will be no conflict. A common basis is lacking. The idea of a synthesis between theology and philosophy has led to the dream of a "Christian philosophy." The term is ambiguous. It can mean a philosophy whose existential basis is historical Christianity. In this sense all modern philosophy is Christian, even if it is humanistic, atheistic, and intentionally anti-Christian. No philosopher living within Western Christian culture can deny his dependence on it, as no Greek philosopher could have hidden his dependence on an Apollonian-Dionysian culture,[5] even if he was a radical critic of the gods of Homer. The modern vision of reality and its philosophical analysis is different from that of pre-Christian times, whether one is or is not existentially determined by the God of Mount Zion and the Christ of

---

[5] Apollo and Dionysius are taken by Nietzsche to symbolize, respectively, the luminous, measured aspect and the dark, passionate aspect of Greek civilization. [H.J.J.]

Mount Golgotha. Reality is encountered differently; experience has different dimensions and directions than in the cultural climate of Greece. No one is able to jump out of this "magic" circle. Nietzsche, who tried to do so, announced the coming of the Anti-Christ. But the Anti-Christ is dependent on the Christ against whom he arises. The early Greeks, for whose culture Nietzsche was longing, did not have to fight the Christ; indeed, they unconsciously prepared his coming by elaborating the questions to which he gave the answer and the categories in which the answer could be expressed. Modern philosophy is not pagan. Atheism and anti-Christianity are not pagan. They are anti-Christian in Christian terms. The scars of the Christian tradition cannot be erased; they are a *character indelebilis*. Even the paganism of naziism was not really a relapse to paganism (just as bestiality is not a relapse to the beast).

But the term "Christian philosophy" is often meant in a different sense. It is used to denote a philosophy which does not look at the universal *logos* but at the assumed or actual demands of a Christian theology. This can be done in two ways: either the church authorities or its theological interpreters nominate one of the past philosophers to be their "philosophical saint" or they demand that contemporary philosophers should develop a philosophy under special conditions and with a special aim. In both cases the philosophical *erōs* is killed. If Thomas Aquinas is officially named *the* philosopher of the Roman Catholic church, he has ceased to be for Catholic philosophers a genuine partner in the philosophical dialogue which goes on through the centuries. And if present-day Protestant philosophers are asked to accept the idea of personality as their highest ontological principle because it is the principle most congenial to the spirit of the Reformation, the work of these philosophers is mutilated. There is nothing in heaven and earth, or beyond them, to which the philosopher must subject himself except the universal *logos* of being as it gives itself to him in experience. Therefore, the idea of a "Christian philosophy" in the narrower sense of a philosophy which is intentionally Christian must be rejected. The fact that every modern philosophy has grown on Christian soil and shows traces of the Christian culture in which it lives has nothing to do with the self-contradicting ideal of a "Christian philosophy."

Christianity does not need a "Christian philosophy" in the narrower sense of the word. The Christian claim that the *logos* who has become concrete in Jesus as the Christ is at the same time the universal *logos* includes the claim that wherever the *logos* is at work it agrees with the Christian message. No philosophy which is obedient to the universal *logos* can contradict the concrete *logos*, the Logos "who became flesh."

QUESTIONS FOR STUDY AND DISCUSSION

1. Compare and contrast philosophy and theology. How does Tillich's own work reflect his view of their relationship?

2. How do the philosophers already studied in this section illustrate Tillich's view that historical Christianity is the existential basis of all Western philosophy?
3. Can you supply historical examples for Tillich's account of philosophical-theological conflicts?

Gabriel Marcel

GABRIEL MARCEL was born in 1889, an only child whose father was at one time French Minister to Stockholm. The opportunity to travel, as well as a sensitivity to tensions in human relationships during his childhood, played a great part in the formation of his philosophy. His work for the Red Cross during World War I gave him a deep realization of the contrast between impersonal, objective knowledge and loving human relationships. Along with philosophical studies, he has written plays and composed musical works. Independently of the German phenomenologists, Marcel reached a very concrete, deliberately unsystematic manner of philosophizing, best exemplified in his *Metaphysical Journal* (1927) and its sequel, *Being and Having* (1935). He converted to Roman Catholicism in 1929. Of Marcel's numerous publications, the closest thing to a systematic view of his thought is found in *The Mystery of Being* (1951), which records the Gifford Lectures he delivered in 1949 and 1950.

On the Ontological Mystery

The title of this essay is likely to annoy the philosopher as much as to startle the layman, since philosophers are inclined to leave mystery either to the theologians or else to the vulgarisers, whether of mysticism or of occultism, such as Maeterlinck. Moreover, the term *ontological,* which has only the vaguest meaning for the layman, has become discredited in the eyes of Idealist philosophers; while the term *mystery* is reserved by those thinkers who are imbued with the ideas of Scholasticism for the revealed mysteries of religion.

Thus my terminology is clearly open to criticism from all sides. But I can find no other which is adequate to the body of ideas which I intend to put forward and on which my whole outlook is based. Readers of my *Journal Métaphysique* will see that they represent the term of the whole spiritual and philosophical evolution which I have described in that book.

Rather than to begin with abstract definitions and dialectical arguments which may be discouraging at the outset, I should like to start with a sort

From pp. 1–30 of Gabriel Marcel, *The Philosophy of Existence,* translated by Manya Harari. Copyright 1948 by The Harvill Press Ltd., London. Reprinted by permission of The Harvill Press Ltd., London, and Philosophical Library, Inc.

of global and intuitive characterisation of the man in whom the sense of the ontological—the sense of being—is lacking, or, to speak more correctly, of the man who has lost the awareness of this sense. Generally speaking, modern man is in this condition; if ontological demands worry him at all, it is only dully, as an obscure impulse. Indeed I wonder if a psychoanalytical method, deeper and more discerning than any that has been evolved until now, would not reveal the morbid effects of the repression of this sense and of the ignoring of this need.

The characteristic feature of our age seems to me to be what might be called the misplacement of the idea of function, taking function in its current sense which includes both the vital and the social functions.

The individual tends to appear both to himself and to others as an agglomeration of functions. As a result of deep historical causes, which can as yet be understood only in part, he has been led to see himself more and more as a mere assemblage of functions, the hierarchical interrelation of which seems to him questionable or at least subject to conflicting interpretations.

To take the vital functions first. It is hardly necessary to point out the role which historical materialism on the one hand, and Freudian doctrines on the other, have played in restricting the concept of man.

Then there are the social functions—those of the consumer, the producer, the citizen, etc.

Between these two there is, in theory, room for the psychological functions as well; but it is easy to see how these will tend to be interpreted in relation either to the social or the vital functions, so that their independence will be threatened and their specific character put in doubt. In this sense, Comte, served by his total incomprehension of psychical reality, displayed an almost prophetic instinct when he excluded psychology from his classification of sciences.

So far we are still dealing only with abstractions, but nothing is easier than to find concrete illustrations in this field.

Travelling on the Underground, I often wonder with a kind of dread what can be the inward reality of the life of this or that man employed on the railway—the man who opens the doors, for instance, or the one who punches the tickets. Surely everything both within him and outside him conspires to identify this man with his functions—meaning not only with his functions as worker, as trade union member or as voter, but with his vital functions as well. The rather horrible expression "time table" perfectly describes his life. So many hours for each function. Sleep too is a function which must be discharged so that the other functions may be exercised in their turn. The same with pleasure, with relaxation; it is logical that the weekly allowance of recreation should be determined by an expert on hygiene; recreation is a psycho-organic function which must not be neglected any more than, for instance, the function of sex. We need go no further; this sketch is sufficient to suggest the emergence of a kind of vital schedule; the details will vary with the country, the climate, the profession, etc., but what matters is that there is a schedule.

It is true that certain disorderly elements—sickness, accidents of every sort—will break in on the smooth working of the system. It is therefore natural that the individual should be overhauled at regular intervals like a watch (this is often done in America). The hospital plays the part of the inspection bench or the repair shop. And it is from this same standpoint of function that such essential problems as birth control will be examined.

As for death, it becomes, objectively and functionally, the scrapping of what has ceased to be of use and must be written off as total loss.

I need hardly insist on the stifling impression of sadness produced by this functionalised world. It is sufficient to recall the dreary image of the retired official, or those urban Sundays when the passers-by look like people who have retired from life. In such a world, there is something mocking and sinister even in the tolerance awarded to the man who has retired from his work.

But besides the sadness felt by the onlooker, there is the dull, intolerable unease of the actor himself who is reduced to living as though he were in fact submerged by his functions. This uneasiness is enough to show that there is in all this some appalling mistake, some ghastly misinterpretation, implanted in defenceless minds by an increasingly inhuman social order and as equally inhuman philosophy (for if the philosophy has prepared the way for the order, the order has also shaped the philosophy).

I have written on another occasion that, provided it is taken in its metaphysical and not its physical sense, the distinction between the *full* and the *empty* seems to me more fundamental than that between the *one* and the *many*. This is particularly applicable to the case in point. Life in a world centred on function is liable to despair because in reality this world is *empty*, it rings hollow; and if it resists this temptation it is only to the extent that there come into play from within it and in its favour certain hidden forces which are beyond its power to conceive or to recognise.

It should be noted that this world is, on the one hand, riddled with problems and, on the other, determined to allow no room for mystery. I shall come back to this distinction between problem and mystery which I believe to be fundamental. For the moment I shall only point out that to eliminate or to try to eliminate mystery is (in this functionalist world) to bring into play in the face of events which break in on the course of existence—such as birth, love and death—that psychological and pseudo-scientific category of the "purely natural" which deserves a study to itself. In reality, this is nothing more than the remains of a degraded rationalism from whose standpoint cause explains effect and accounts for it exhaustively. There exist in such a world, nevertheless, an infinity of problems, since the causes are not known to us in detail and thus leave room for unlimited research. And in addition to these theoretical puzzles there are innumerable technical problems, bound up with the difficulty of knowing how the various functions, once they have been inventoried and labelled, can be made to work together without doing one another harm. These theoretical and technical questions are interdependent, for the theoretical problems arise out of the different techniques while the technical problems can not be solved without a measure of pre-established theoretical knowledge.

In such a world the ontological need, the need of being, is exhausted in exact proportion to the breaking up of personality on the one hand and, on the other, to the triumph of the category of the "purely natural" and the consequent atrophy of the faculty of *wonder*.

But to come at last to the ontological need itself; can we not approach it directly and attempt to define it? In reality this can only be done to a limited extent. For reasons which I shall develop later, I suspect that the characteristic of this need is that it can never be wholly clear to itself.

To try to describe it without distorting it we shall have to say something like this:

Being is—or should be—necessary. It is impossible that everything should be reduced to a play of successive appearances which are inconsistent with each other ("inconsistent" is essential), or, in the words of Shakespeare, to "a tale told by an idiot." I aspire to participate in this being, in this reality—and perhaps this aspiration is already a degree of participation, however rudimentary.

Such a need, it may be noted, is to be found at the heart of the most inveterate pessimism. Pessimism has no meaning unless it signifies: it would surely be well if there were being, but there is no being, and I, who observe this fact, am therefore nothing.

As for defining the word "being," let us admit that it is extremely difficult. I would merely suggest this method of approach: being is what withstands—or what would withstand—an exhaustive analysis bearing on the data of experience and aiming to reduce them step by step to elements increasingly devoid of intrinsic or significant value. (An analysis of this kind is attempted in the theoretical works of Freud.)

When the pessimist Besme says in *La Ville* that *nothing is*, he means precisely this, that there is no experience that withstands this analytical test. And it is always towards death regarded as the manifestation, the proof of this ultimate nothingness that the kind of inverted apologetic which arises out of absolute pessimism will inevitably gravitate.

A philosophy which refuses to endorse the ontological need is, nevertheless, possible; indeed, generally speaking, contemporary thought tends towards this abstention. But at this point a distinction must be made between two different attitudes which are sometimes confused: one which consists in a systematic reserve (it is that of agnosticism in all its forms), and the other, bolder and more coherent, which regards the ontological need as the expression of an outworn body of dogma liquidated once and for all by the Idealist critique.

The former appears to me to be purely negative: it is merely the expression of an intellectual policy of "not raising the question."

The latter, on the contrary, claims to be based on a positive theory of thought. This is not the place for a detailed critical study of this philosophy. I shall only note that it seems to me to tend towards an unconscious relativism, or else towards a monism which ignores the personal in all its forms, ignores the tragic and denies the transcendent, seeking to reduce it to its caricatural expressions which distort its essential character. I shall also point out that, just because this philosophy continually stresses the activity of verification, it ends by ignoring *presence*—that inward realisation of presence through love which infinitely transcends all possible verification because it exists in an immediacy beyond all conceivable mediation. This will be clearer to some extent from what follows.

Thus I believe for my part that the ontological need cannot be silenced by an arbitrary dictatorial act which mutilates the life of the spirit at its roots. It remains true, nevertheless, that such an act is possible, and the conditions of our life are such that we can well believe that we are carrying it out; this must never be forgotten.

These preliminary reflections on the ontological need are sufficient to bring out its indeterminate character and to reveal a fundamental paradox. To formulate this need is to raise a host of questions: Is there such a thing as being? What is it? etc. Yet immediately an abyss opens under my feet: I who ask these questions about being, how can I be sure that I exist?

Yet surely I, who formulate this *problem,* should be able to remain *outside* it—*before* or *beyond* it? Clearly this is not so. The more I consider it the more I find that this problem tends inevitably to invade the proscenium from which it is excluded in theory: it is only by means of a fiction that Idealism in its traditional form seeks to maintain on the margin of being the consciousness which asserts it or denies it.

So I am inevitably forced to ask: Who am I—I who question being? How am I qualified to begin this investigation? If I do not exist, how can I succeed in it? And if I do exist, how can I be sure of this fact?

Contrary to the opinion which suggests itself at this point, I believe that on this plane the *cogito* cannot help us at all. Whatever Descartes may have thought of it himself, the only certainty with which it provides us concerns only the epistemological subject as organ of objective cognition. As I have written elsewhere, the *cogito* merely guards the threshold of objective validity, and that is strictly all; this is proved by the indeterminate character of the *I*. The *I am* is, to my mind, a global statement which it is impossible to break down into its component parts.

There remains a possible objection; it might be said: Either the being designated in the question "What am I?" concerns the subject of cognition, and in this case we are on the plane of the *cogito;* or else that which you call the ontological need is merely the extreme point (or perhaps only the fallacious transposition) of a need which is, in reality, vital and with which the metaphysician is not concerned.

But is it not a mistake arbitrarily to divide the question, *Who am I?* from the ontological "problem" taken as a whole? The truth is that neither of the two can be dealt with separately, but that when they are taken together, they cancel one another out as *problems*.

It should be added that the Cartesian position is inseparable from a form of dualism which I, for my part, would unhesitatingly reject. To raise the ontological problem is to raise the question of being as a whole and of oneself seen as a totality.

But should we not ask ourselves if we must not reject this dissociation between the intellectual and the vital, with its resultant over- or under-estimation of the one or the other? Doubtless it is legitimate to establish certain distinctions within the unity of the being who thinks and who endeavours to *think himself;* but it is only beyond such distinctions that the ontological problem can arise and it must relate to that being seen in his all-comprehensive unity.

To sum up our reflections at this point, we find that we are dealing with an urge towards an affirmation—yet an affirmation which it seems impossible to make, since it is not until it has been made that I can regard myself as qualified to make it.

It should be noted that this difficulty never arises at a time when I am actually faced with a problem to be solved. In such a case I work on the data, but everything leads me to believe that I need not take into account the *I* who is at work—it is a factor which is presupposed and nothing more.

Here, on the contrary, what I would call the ontological status of the investigator assumes a decisive importance. Yet so long as I am concerned with thought itself I seem to follow an endless regression. But by the very fact of recognising it as endless I transcend it in a certain way: I see that this process takes place within an affirmation of being—an affirmation which I *am* rather than an affirmation which I *utter:* by uttering it I break it, I divide it, I am on the point of betraying it.

It might be said, by way of an approximation, that my inquiry into being presupposes an affirmation in regard to which I am, in a sense, passive, *and of which I am the stage rather than the subject.* But this is only at the extreme limit of thought, a limit which I cannot reach without falling into contradiction. I am therefore led to assume or to recognise a form of participation which has the reality of a subject; this participation cannot be, by definition, an *object* of thought; it cannot serve as a solution —it appears beyond the realm of problems: it is meta-problematical.

Conversely, it will be seen that, if the meta-problematical can be asserted at all, it must be conceived as transcending the oppositon between the subject who asserts the existence of being, on the one hand, and being *as asserted by that subject,* on the other, and as underlying it in a given sense. To postulate the meta-problematical is to postulate the primacy of being over knowledge (not of being as *asserted,* but of being as *asserting itself*); it is to recognise that knowledge is, as it were, environed by being, that it is interior to it in a certain sense—a sense perhaps analogous to that which Paul Claudel tried to define in his *Art Poétique.* From this standpoint, contrary to what epistemology seeks vainly to establish, there exists well and truly a mystery of cognition; knowledge is contingent on a participation in being for which no epistemology can account because it continually presupposes it.

At this point we can begin to define the distinction between mystery and problem. A mystery is a problem which encroaches upon its own data, invading them, as it were, and thereby transcending itself as a simple problem. A set of examples will help us to grasp the content of this definition.

It is evident that there exists a mystery of the union of the body and the soul. The indivisible unity always inadequately expressed by such phrases as *I have a body, I make use of my body, I feel my body,* etc., can be neither analysed nor reconstituted out of precedent elements. It is not only data, I would say that it is the basis of data, in the sense of being my own presence to myself, a presence of which the act of self-consciousness is, in the last analysis, only an inadequate symbol.

It will be seen at once that there is no hope of establishing an exact frontier between problem and mystery. For in reflecting on a mystery we tend inevitably to degrade it to the level of a problem. This is particularly clear in the case of the problem of evil.

In reflecting upon evil, I tend, almost inevitably, to regard it as a disorder which I view from outside and of which I seek to discover the causes or the secret aims. Why is it that the "mechanism" functions so defectively? Or is the defect merely apparent and due to a real defect of my vision? In this case the defect is in myself yet it remains objective in relation to my thought, which discovers it and observes it. But evil which is only stated or observed is no longer evil which is suffered: in fact, it ceases to be evil. In reality, I can only grasp it as evil in the measure in which it *touches* me— that is to say, in the measure in which I am *involved,* as one is involved in a law-suit. Being "involved" is the fundamental fact; I cannot leave it out of account except by an unjustifiable fiction, for in doing so, I proceed as though I were God, and a God who is an onlooker at that.

This brings out how the distinction between what is *in me* and what is only *before me* can break down. This distinction falls under the blow of a certain kind of thought: thought at one remove.

But it is, of course, in love that the obliteration of this frontier can best be seen. It might perhaps even be shown that the domain of the meta-problematical coincides with that of love, and that love is the only starting point for the understanding of such mysteries as that of body and soul, which, in some manner, is its expression.

Actually, it is inevitable that, in being brought to bear on love, thought which has not thought itself—unreflected reflection—should tend to dissolve its meta-problematical character and interpret it in terms of abstract concepts, such as the will to live, the will to power, the *libido,* etc. On the other hand, since the domain of the problematical is that of the objectively valid, it will be extremely difficult—if not impossible—to refute these interpretations without changing to a new ground: a ground on which, to tell the truth, they lose their meaning. Yet I have the assurance, the certainty —and it envelops me like a protective cloak—that for as much as I really love I must not be concerned with these attempts at devaluation.

It will be asked: What is the criterion of true love? It must be answered that there is no criteriology except in the order of the objective and the problematical; but we can already see at a distance the eminent ontological value to be assigned to fidelity.

Let us take another illustration, more immediate and more particular, which may shed some light on the distinction between problem and mystery.

Say that I have made an encounter which has left a deep and lasting trace on all my life. It may happen to anyone to experience the deep spiritual significance of such a meeting—yet this is something which philosophers have commonly ignored or disdained, doubtless because it effects only the particular person as person—it cannot be universalised, it does not concern rational being in general.

It is clear that such a meeting raises, if you will, a problem; but it is equally clear that the solution of this problem will always fall short of the only question that matters. Suppose that I am told, for instance: "The reason you have met this person in this place is that you both like the same kind of scenery, or that you both need the same kind of treatment for your health"—the explanation means nothing. Crowds of people who apparently share my tastes were in the Engadine or in Florence at the time I was there; and there are always numbers of patients suffering from the same disease as myself at the health resort I frequent. But neither this supposed identity of tastes nor this common affliction has brought us together in any real sense; it has nothing to do with that intimate and unique affinity with which we are dealing. At the same time, it would be transgression of this valid reasoning to treat this affinity as if it were itself the cause and to say: "It is precisely this which has determined our meeting."

Hence I am in the presence of a mystery. That is to say of a reality rooted in what is beyond the domain of the problematical properly so called. Shall we avoid the difficulty by saying that it was after all nothing but a coincidence, a lucky chance? But the whole of me immediately protests against this empty formula, this vain negation of what I apprehend with the deepest of my being. Once again we are brought back to our first definition of a mystery as a problem which encroaches upon its own data: I who inquire into the meaning and the possibility of this meeting, I cannot place myself outside it or before it; I am engaged in this encounter, I depend upon it, I am inside it in a certain sense, it envelops me and it comprehends me—even if it is not comprehended by me. Thus it is only by a kind of betrayal or denial that I can say: "After all, it might not have happened, I would still have been what I was, and what I am to-day." Nor must it be said: I have been changed by it as by an outward cause. No, it has developed me from within, it has acted in me as an inward principle.

But this is very difficult to grasp without distortion. I shall be inevitably tempted to react against this sense of the inwardness of the encounter, tempted by my probity itself, by what from a certain standpoint I must judge to be the best—or at least the safest—of myself.

There is a danger that these explanations may strengthen in the minds of my readers a preliminary objection which must be stated at once.

It will be said: The meta-problematical of which you speak is after all a content of thought; how then should we not ask ourselves what is its mode of existence? What assures us of its existence at all? Is it not itself problematical in the highest degree?

My answer is categorical: To think, or, rather, to assert, the meta-problematical is to assert it as indubitably real, as a thing of which I cannot doubt without falling into contradiction. We are in a sphere where it is no longer possible to dissociate the idea itself from the certainty or the degree of certainty which pertains to it. Because this idea *is* certainty, it *is* the assurance of itself; it is, in this sense, something other and something more than an idea. As for the term *content of thought* which figured in the objection, it is deceptive in the highest degree. For content is, when all is said and done, derived from experience; whereas it is only by a way of liberation and detachment from experience that we can possibly rise to the level of the meta-problematical and of mystery. This liberation must be *real;* this detachment must be *real;* they must not be an abstraction, that is to say a fiction recognised as such.

And this at last brings us to recollection, for it is in recollection and in this alone that this detachment is accomplished. I am convinced, for my part, that no ontology—that is to say, no apprehension of ontological mystery in whatever degree—is possible except to a being who is capable of recollecting himself, and of thus proving that he is not a living creature pure and simple, a creature, that is to say, which is at the mercy of its life and without a hold upon it.

It should be noted that recollection, which has received little enough attention from pure philosophers, is very difficult to define—if only because it transcends the dualism of being and action or, more correctly, because it reconciles in itself these two aspects of the antinomy. The word means what it says—the act whereby I re-collect myself as a unity; but this hold, this grasp upon myself is also relaxation and abandon. *Abandon to . . . relaxation in the presence of . . .*—yet there is no noun for these prepositions to govern. The way stops at the threshold.

Here, as in every other sphere, problems will be raised, and it is the psychologist who will raise them. All that must be noted is that the psychologist is no more in a position to shed light on the metaphysical bearing of recollection than on the noetic value of knowledge.

It is within recollection that I take up my position—or, rather, I become capable of taking up my position—in regard to my life; I withdraw from it in a certain way, but not as the pure subject of cognition; *in this withdrawal I carry with me that which I am and which perhaps my life is not.* This brings out the gap between my being and my life. I am not my life; and if I can judge my life—a fact I cannot deny without falling into a radical scepticism which is nothing other than despair—it is only on condition that I encounter myself within recollection beyond all possible judgment and, I would add, beyond all representation. Recollection is doubtless what is least spectacular in the soul; it does not consist in looking at something, it is an inward hold, an inward reflection, and it might be asked in passing whether it should not be seen as the ontological basis of memory —that principle of effective and non-representational unity in which the possibility of remembrance rests. The double meaning of "recollection" in English is revealing.

It may be asked: is not recollection identical with that dialectical moment of the turning to oneself (*retour sur soi*) or else with the *fuer sich sein* which is the central theme of German Idealism?

I do not think so. To withdraw into oneself is not to be for oneself nor to mirror oneself in the intelligible unity of subject and object. On the contrary. I would say that here we come up against the paradox of that actual mystery whereby the I into which I withdraw ceases, for as much, to belong to itself. "You are not your own"—this great saying of St. Paul assumes in this connection its full concrete and ontological significance; it is the nearest approach to the reality for which we are groping. It will be asked: is not this reality an object of intuition? Is not that which you term "recollection" the same as what others have termed "intuition"?

But this again seems to me to call for the utmost prudence. If intuition can be mentioned in this context at all, it is not an intuition which is, or can be, given as such.

The more an intuition is central and basic in the being whom it illuminates, the less it is capable of turning back and apprehending itself.

Moreover, if we reflect on what an intuitive knowledge of being could possibly be, we see that it could never figure in a collection, a procession of simple experiences or *Erlebnisse,* which all have this characteristic that they can be at times absorbed and at others isolated and, as it were, uncovered. Hence, any effort to remember such an intuition, to represent it to oneself, is inevitably fruitless. From this point of view, to be told of an intuitive knowledge of being is like being invited to play on a soundless piano. Such an intuition cannot be brought out into the light of day, for the simple reason that we do not possess it.

We are here at the most difficult point of our whole discussion. Rather than to speak of intuition in this context, we should say that we are dealing with an assurance which underlies the entire development of thought, even of discursive thought; it can therefore be approached only by a second reflection—a reflection whereby I ask myself how and from what starting point I was able to proceed in my initial reflection, which itself postulated the ontological, but without knowing it. This second reflection is recollection in the measure in which recollection can be self-conscious.

It is indeed annoying to have to use such abstract language in a matter which is not one of dialects *ad usum philosophorum,* but of what is the most vital and, I would add, the most dramatic moment in the rhythm of consciousness seeking to be conscious of itself.

It is this dramatic aspect which must now be brought out.

Let us recall what we said earlier on: that the ontological need, the need of being, can deny itself. In a different context we said that being and life do not coincide; my life, and by reflection all life, may appear to me as for ever inadequate to something which I carry within me, which in a sense I am, but which reality rejects and excludes. Despair is possible in any form, at any moment and to any degree, and this betrayal may seem to be counselled, if not forced upon us, by the very structure of the world we live in. The deathly aspect of this world may, from a given standpoint, be regarded as a ceaseless incitement to denial and to suicide. It could even be said in this sense that the fact that suicide is always possible is the essential starting point of any genuine metaphysical thought.

It may be surprising to find in the course of this calm and abstract reasoning such verbal star turns—words so emotionally charged—as "suicide" and "betrayal." They are not a concession to sensationalism. I am convinced that it is in drama and through drama that metaphysical thought grasps and defines itself *in concreto.* Two years ago, in a lecture on the "Problem of Christian Philosophy" which he delivered at Louvain, M. Jacques Maritain said: "There is nothing easier for a philosophy than to become tragic, it has only to let itself go to its human weight." The allusion was doubtless to the speculation of a Heidegger. I believe, on the contrary, that the natural trend of philosophy leads it into a sphere where it seems that tragedy has simply vanished—evaporated at the touch of abstract thought. This is borne out by the work of many contemporary Idealists. Because they ignore the person, offering it up to I know not what ideal truth, to what principle of pure inwardness, they are unable to grasp those tragic factors of human existence to which I have alluded above; they banish them, together with illness and everything akin to it, to I know not what disreputable suburb of thought outside the ken of any philosopher worthy of the name. But, as I have stressed earlier on, this attitude is intimately bound up with the rejection of the ontological need; indeed, it is the same thing.

If I have stressed despair, betrayal and suicide, it is because these are the most manifest expressions of the will to negation as applied to being.

Let us take despair. I have in mind the act by which one despairs of reality as a whole, as one might despair of a person. This appears to be the result, or the immediate translation into other terms, of a kind of balance sheet. Inasmuch as I am able to evaluate the world of reality (and, when all is said and done, what I am unable to evaluate is for me as if it were not) I can find nothing in it that withstands that process of dissolution at the heart of things which I have discovered and traced. I believe that at the root of despair there is always this affirmation: "There is nothing in the realm of reality to which I can give credit—no security, no guarantee." It is a statement of complete insolvency.

As against this, hope is what implies credit. Contrary to what was thought by Spinoza, who seems to me to have confused two quite distinct notions, fear is correlated to desire and not to hope, whereas what is negatively correlated to hope is the act which consists in putting things at their worst—an act which is strikingly illustrated by what is known as defeatism, and which is ever in danger of being degraded into the desire of the worst. Hope consists in asserting that there is at the heart of being, beyond all data, beyond all inventories and all calculations, a mysterious principle which is in connivance with me, which cannot but will that which I will, if what I will deserves to be willed and is, in fact, willed by the whole of my being.

We have now come to the centre of what I have called the ontological mystery, and the simplest illustrations will be the best. To hope against all hope that a person whom I love will recover from a disease which is said to be incurable is to say: It is impossible that I should be alone in willing this cure; it is impossible that reality in its inward depth should be hostile or so much as indifferent to what I assert is in itself a good. It is quite useless to tell me of discouraging *cases* or *examples:* beyond all experience, all probability, all statistics, I assert that a given order shall be re-established, that reality *is* on my side in willing it to be so. I do not wish: I assert; such is the prophetic tone of true hope.

No doubt I shall be told: "In the immense majority of cases this is an illusion." But it is of the essence of hope to exclude the consideration of cases; moreover, it can be shown that there exists an ascending dialectic of hope, whereby hope rises to a plane which transcends the level of all possible empirical disproof—the plane of salvation as opposed to that of success in whatever form.

It remains true, nevertheless, that the correlation of hope and despair subsists until the end; they seem to me inseparable. I mean that while the structure of the world we live in permits—and may even seem to counsel —absolute despair, yet it is only such a world that can give rise to an unconquerable hope. If only for this reason, we cannot be sufficiently thankful to the great pessimists in the history of thought; they have carried through an inward experience which needed to be made and of which the radical possibility no apologetics should disguise; they have prepared our minds to understand that despair can be what it was for Nietzsche (though on an infra-ontological level and in a domain fraught with mortal dangers) the springboard to the loftiest affirmation.

At the same time, it remains certain that, for as much as hope is a mystery, its mystery can be ignored or converted into a problem. Hope is then regarded as a desire which wraps itself up in illusory judgments to distort objective reality which it is interested in disguising from itself. What happens in this case is what we have already observed in connection with encounter and with love; it is because mystery can—and, in a sense, logically must—be degraded into a problem that an interpretation such as that of Spinoza, with all the confusion it implies, had to be put forward sooner or later. It is important and must be stressed that this attitude has nothing against it so long as our standpoint is on the hither-side of the realm of the ontological. Just as long as my attitude towards reality is that of someone who is not involved in it, but who judges it his duty to draw up its minutes as exactly as possible (and this is by definition the attitude of the scientist), I am justified in maintaining in regard to it a sort of principle of mistrust, which in theory is unlimited in its application; such is the legitimate standpoint of the workman in the laboratory, who must in no way prejudge the result of his analysis, and who can all the better envisage *the worst,* because at this level the very notion of worst is empty of meaning. But an investigation of this sort, which is just like that of an accountant going through the books, takes place on the hither-side of the order of mystery, an order in which the problem encroaches upon its own data.

It would indeed be a profound illusion to believe that I can still maintain this same attitude, when I undertake an inquiry, say, into the value of life; it would be a paralogism to suppose that I can pursue such an inquiry as though my own life were not at issue.

Hence, between hope—the reality of hope in the heart of the one whom it inhabits—and the judgment brought to bear upon it by a mind chained to objectivity there exists the same barrier as that which separates a pure mystery from a pure problem.

This brings us to a nodal point of our subject, where certain intimate connections can be traced.

The world of the problematical is the world of fear and desire, which are inseparable; at the same time, it is that world of the functional—or of what can be functionalised—which was defined at the beginning of this essay; finally, it is the kingdom of technics of whatever sort. Every technique serves, or can be made to serve, some desire or some fear; conversely, every desire as every fear tends to invent its appropriate technique. From this standpoint, despair consists in the recognition of the ultimate inefficacy of all technics, joined to the inability or the refusal to change over to a new ground—a ground where all technics are seen to be incompatible with the fundamental nature of being, which itself escapes our grasp (in so far as our grasp is limited to the world of objects and to this alone). It is for this reason that we seem nowadays to have entered upon the very era of despair; we have not ceased to believe in technics, that is to envisage reality as a complex of problems; yet at the same time the failure of technics *as a whole* is as discernible to us as its *partial* triumphs. To the question: what can man achieve? we continue to reply: He can achieve as much as his technics; yet we are obliged to admit that these technics are unable *to save man himself,* and even that they are apt to conclude the most sinister alliance with the enemy he bears within him.

I have said that man is *at the mercy of his technics.* This must be understood to mean that he is increasingly incapable of controlling his technics, or rather of *controlling his own control.* This control of his own control, which is nothing else than the expression on the plane of active life of what I have called thought at one remove, cannot find its centre or its support anywhere except in recollection.

It will be objected that even those whose faith in technics is strongest are bound to admit that there exist enormous realms which are outside man's control. But what matters is the spirit in which this admission is made. We have to recognise that we have no control over meteorological conditions, but the question is: do we consider it desirable and just that we should have such control? The more the sense of the ontological tends to disappear, the more unlimited become the claims of the mind which has lost it to a kind of cosmic governance, because it is less and less capable of examining its own credentials to the exercise of such dominion.

It must be added that the more the disproportion grows between the claims of the technical intelligence on the one hand, and the persisting fragility and precariousness of what remains its material substratum on the other, the more acute becomes the constant danger of despair which threatens this intelligence. From this standpoint there is truly an intimate dialectical correlation between the optimism of technical progress and the philosophy of despair which seems inevitably to emerge from it—it is needless to insist on the examples offered by the world of to-day.

It will perhaps be said: This optimism of technical progress is animated by great hope. How is hope in this sense to be reconciled with the ontological interpretation of hope?

I believe it must be answered that, *speaking metaphysically, the only genuine hope is hope in what does not depend on ourselves,* hope springing from humility and not from pride. This brings us to the consideration of another aspect of the mystery—a mystery which, in the last analysis, is one and unique—on which I am endeavouring to throw some light.

The metaphysical problem of pride—*hubris*—which was perceived by the Greeks and which has been one of the essential themes of Christian theology, seems to me to have been almost completely ignored by modern philosophers other than theologians. It has become a domain reserved for the moralist. Yet from my own standpoint it is an essential—if not the vital —question. It is sufficient to recall Spinoza's definition of *superbia* in his *Ethics* (III, def. XXVIII) to see how far he was from grasping the problem: "Pride is an exaggeratedly good opinion of ourselves which arises from self-love." In reality, this is a definition of vanity. As for pride, it consists in drawing one's strength solely from oneself. The proud man is cut off from a certain form of communion with his fellow men, which pride, acting as a principle of destruction, tends to break down. Indeed, this destructiveness can be equally well directed against the self; pride is in no way incompatible with self-hate; this is what Spinoza does not seem to have perceived.

An important objection may be raised at the point we have now reached.

It will perhaps be said: Is not that which you are justifying ontologically in reality a kind of moral quietism which is satisfied by passive acceptance, resignation and inert hope? But what, then, becomes of man as man, as active being? Are we to condemn action itself inasmuch as it implies a self-confidence which is akin to pride? Can it be that action itself is a kind of degradation?

This objection implies a series of misunderstandings.

To begin with, the idea of inert hope seems to me a contradiction in terms. Hope is not a kind of listless waiting; it underpins action or it runs before it, but it becomes degraded and lost once the action is spent. Hope seems to me, as it were, the prolongation into the unknown of an activity which is central—that is to say, rooted in being. Hence it has affinities, not with desire, but with the will. The will implies the same refusal to calculate possibilities, or at any rate it suspends this calculation. Could not hope therefore be defined as the will when it is made to bear on what does not depend on itself?

The experimental proof of this connection is that it is the most active saints who carry hope to its highest degree; this would be inconceivable if hope were simply an inactive state of the soul. The mistake so often made here comes from a stoical representation of the will as a stiffening of the soul, whereas it is on the contrary relaxation and creation.

The term "creation," which occurs here for the first time, is, nevertheless, decisive. Where there is creation there can be no degradation, and to the extent that technics are creative, or imply creativity, they are not degrading in any way. Degradation begins at the point where creativeness falls into self-imitation and self-hypnotism, stiffening and falling back on itself. This may, indeed, bring out the origin of the confusion which I denounced in the context of recollection.

Great is the temptation to confuse two distant movements of the soul, whose opposition is blurred by the use of spatial metaphors. The stiffening, the contraction, the falling back on the self which are inseparable from pride, and which are indeed its symbol, must not be confused with the humble withdrawal which befits recollection and whereby I renew my contact with the ontological basis of my being.

There is every reason to think that such withdrawal in recollection is a presupposition of aesthetic creativity itself. Artistic creation, like scientific research, excludes the act of self-centring and self-hypnotism which is, ontologically speaking, pure negation.

It may perhaps seem that my thesis comes so near to that of Bergson as to coincide with it, but I do not think that this is the case. The terms almost invariably used by Bergson suggest that for him the essential character of creativity lay in its inventiveness, in its spontaneous innovation. But I wonder if by limiting our attention to this aspect of creation we do not lose sight of its ultimate significance, which is its deep-rootedness in being. It is at this point that I would bring in the notion of *creative fidelity;* it is a notion which is the more difficult to grasp and, above all, to define conceptually, because of its underlying and unfathomable paradox, and because it is at the very centre of the realm of the meta-problematical.

It is important to note that the idea of fidelity seems difficult to maintain in the context of Bergsonian metaphysics, because it will tend to be interpreted as a routine, as an observance in the pejorative sense of the word, as an arbitrary safeguard *against* the power of renewal which is the spirit itself.

I am inclined to think that there is something in this neglect of the values of fidelity which deeply vitiates the notion of static religion as it is put forward in *Les Deux Sources de la Morale et de la Religion.* It may perhaps be useful to devote some thought to creative fidelity in order to elucidate this point.

Faithfulness is, in reality, the exact opposite of inert conformism. It is the active recognition of something permanent, not formally, after the manner of a law, but ontologically; in this sense, it refers invariably to a presence, or to something which can be maintained within us and before us as a presence, but which, *ipso facto,* can be just as well ignored, forgotten and obliterated; and this reminds us of that menace of betrayal which, to my mind, overshadows our whole world.

It may perhaps be objected that we commonly speak of fidelity to a principle. But it remains to be seen if this is not an arbitrary transposition of the notion of fidelity. A principle, in so far as it is a mere abstract affirmation, can make no demands upon me because it owes the whole of its reality to the act whereby I sanction it or proclaim it. Fidelity to a principle as a principle is idolatry in the etymological sense of the word; it might be a sacred duty for me to deny a principle from which life has withdrawn and which I know that I no longer accept, for by continuing to conform my actions to it, it is myself—myself as presence—that I betray.

So little is fidelity akin to the inertia of conformism that it implies an active and continuous struggle against the forces of interior dissipation, as also against the sclerosis of habit. I may be told: This is nevertheless no more than a sort of active conservation which is the opposite of creation. We must, I think, go much further into the nature of fidelity and presence before we can reply to this point.

If presence were merely an *idea* in us whose characteristic was that it was nothing more than itself, then indeed the most we could hope would be to maintain this idea in us or before us, as one keeps a photograph on a mantelpiece or in a cupboard. But it is of the nature of presence as presence to be uncircumscribed; and this takes us once again beyond the frontier of the problematical. Presence is mystery in the exact measure in which it is presence. Now fidelity is the active perpetuation of presence, the renewal of its benefits—of its virtue which consists in a mysterious incitement to create. Here again we may be helped by the consideration of aesthetic creativeness; for if artistic creation is conceivable, it can only be on condition that the world is present to the artist in a certain way—present to his heart and to his mind, present to his very being.

Thus if creative fidelity is conceivable, it is because fidelity is ontological in its principle, because it prolongs presence which itself corresponds to a certain kind of hold which being has upon us; because it multiplies and deepens the effect of this presence almost unfathomably in our lives. This seems to me to have almost inexhaustible consequences, if only for the relationships between the living and the dead.

I must insist once again: A presence to which we are faithful is not at all the same thing as the carefully preserved effigy of an object which has vanished; an effigy is, when all is said and done, nothing but a likeness; metaphysically it is *less* than the object, it is a diminution of the object. Whereas presence, on the contrary, is *more* than the object, it exceeds the object on every side. We are here at the opening of a vista at whose term death will appear as the *test of presence*. This is an essential point and we must consider it carefully.

It will no doubt be said: What a strange way of defining death! Death *is* a phenomenon definable in biological terms; it *is not* a test.

It must be answered: It is what it signifies and, moreover, what it signifies to a being who rises to the highest spiritual level to which it is possible for us to attain. It is evident that if I read in the newspaper of the death of Mr. So-and-so, who is for me nothing but a name, this event *is* for me nothing more than the subject of an announcement. But it is quite another thing in the case of a being who has been granted to me as a presence. In this case, everything depends on me, on my inward attitude of maintaining this presence which could be debased into an effigy.

It will be objected: This is nothing more than a description in recondite and unnecessarily metaphysical terms of a common psychological fact. It is evident that it depends upon us in a certain measure to enable the dead to survive in our memory, but this existence is no more than subjective.

I believe that the truth is altogether different and infinitely more mysterious. In saying, "It depends upon us that the dead should live on in our memory," we are still thinking of the idea in terms of a diminution or an effigy. We admit that the object has disappeared, but that there remains a likeness which it is in our power to keep, as a daily woman "keeps" a flat or a set of furniture. It is all too evident that this manner of keeping can have no ontological value whatsoever. But it is altogether different in the case where fidelity is creative in the sense which I have tried to define. A presence is a reality; it is a kind of influx; it depends upon us to be permeable to this influx, but not, to tell the truth, to call it forth. Creative fidelity consists in maintaining ourselves actively in a permeable state; and there is a mysterious interchange between this free act and the gift granted in response to it.

An objection which is the converse of the preceding one may be expected at this point. I will be told: "All right. You have now ceased to decorate a psychological platitude with metaphysical ornaments, but only to make a gratuitous assertion which is unproved and which is beyond all possible experimental proof; this was inevitable as soon as you replaced the ambiguous and neutral term 'presence' by the much more compromising term 'influx.' "

To reply to this objection, we must refer again to what I have already said of mystery and of recollection. Indeed, it is only on the meta-problematical level that the notion of influx can possibly be accepted. If it were taken in its objective sense, as an accretion of strength, we would indeed be faced with a thesis, not of metaphysics, but of physics, which would be open to every possible objection. When I say that a being is granted to me as a presence or as a being (it comes to the same, for he is not a being for me unless he is a presence), this means that I am unable to treat him as if he were merely placed in front of me; between him and me there arises a relationship which, in a sense, surpasses my awareness of him; he is not only before me, he is also within me—or, rather, these categories are transcended, they have no longer any meaning. The word influx conveys, though in a manner which is far too physical and spacial, the kind of interior accretion, of accretion from within, which comes into being as soon as presence is effective. Great and almost invincible is the temptation to think that such effective presence can be only that of an object; but if we believed this we would fall back to the level of the problematical and remain on the hither-side of mystery; and against this belief fidelity raises up its voice: "Even if I cannot see, if I cannot touch you, I feel that you are with me; it would be a denial of you not to be assured of this." *With* me: note the metaphysical value of this word, so rarely recognised by philosophers, which corresponds neither to a relationship of inherence or immanence nor to a relationship of exteriority. It is of the essence of genuine *coesse*—I must use the Latin word—that is to say, of genuine intimacy, to lend itself to the decomposition to which it is subjected by critical thought; but we already know that there exists another kind of thought, a thought which bears upon that thought itself, and is related to a bottled up yet efficacious underlying intuition, of which it suffers the attraction.

It must be added (and this brings us to the verge of another sphere) that the value of such intimacy, particularly in regard to the relation between the living and the dead, will be the higher and the more assured the more this intimacy is grounded in the realm of total spiritual availability (*disponibilité*)—that is to say, of pure charity; and I shall note in passing that an ascending dialectic of creative fidelity corresponds to the dialectic of hope to which I have already referred.

The notion of availability is no less important for our subject than that of presence, with which it is bound up.

It is an undeniable fact, though it is hard to describe in intelligible terms, that there are some people who reveal themselves as "present"— that is to say, at our disposal—when we are in pain or in need to confide in someone, while there are other people who do not give us this feeling, however great is their goodwill. It should be noted at once that the distinction between presence and absence is not at all the same as that between attention and distraction. The most attentive and the most conscientious listener may give me the impression of not being present; he gives me nothing, he cannot make room for me in himself, whatever the material favours which he is prepared to grant me. The truth is that there is a way of listening which is a way of giving, and another way of listening which is a way of refusing, of refusing *oneself;* the material gift, the visible action, do not necessarily witness to presence. We must not speak of proof in this connection; the word would be out of place. Presence is something which reveals itself immediately and unmistakably in a look, a smile, an intonation or a handshake.

It will perhaps make it clearer if I say that the person who is at my disposal is the one who is capable of being with me with the whole of himself when I am in need; while the one who is not at my disposal seems merely to offer me a temporary loan raised on his resources. For the one I am a presence; for the other I am an object. Presence involves a reciprocity which is excluded from any relation of subject to object or of subject to subject-object. A concrete analysis of unavailability (*indisponibilité*) is no less necessary for our purpose than that of betrayal, denial or despair.

Unavailability is invariably rooted in some measure of alienation. Say, for instance, that I am told of some misfortune with which I am asked to sympathise: I understand what I am told; I admit in theory that the sufferers deserve my sympathy; I see that it is a case where it would be logical and just for me to respond with sympathy; I even offer my sympathy, but only with my mind; because, when all is said and done, I am obliged to admit that I feel absolutely nothing. Indeed, I am sorry that this should be so; the contradiction between the indifference which I feel in fact and the sympathy which I know I ought to feel is humiliating and annoying; it diminishes me in my own eyes. But it is no use; what remains in me is the rather embarrassing awareness that, after all, these are people I do not know—if one had to be touched by every human misfortune life would not be possible, it would indeed be too short. The moment I think: After all, this is only a case, No. 75,627, it is no good, I can feel nothing.

But the characteristic of the soul which is present and at the disposal of others is that it cannot think in terms of *cases;* in its eyes there are *no cases at all.*

And yet it is clear that the normal development of a human being implies an increasingly precise and, as it were, automatic division between what concerns him and what does not, between things for which he is responsible and those for which he is not. Each one of us becomes the centre of a sort of mental space arranged in concentric zones of decreasing interest and participation. It is as though each one of us secreted a kind of shell which gradually hardened and imprisoned him; and this sclerosis is bound up with the hardening of the categories in accordance with which we conceive and evaluate the world.

Fortunately, it can happen to anyone to make an encounter which breaks down the framework of this egocentric topography; I know by my own experience how, from a stranger met by chance, there may come an irresistible appeal which overturns the habitual perspectives just as a gust of wind might tumble down the panels of a stage set—what had seemed near becomes infinitely remote and what had seemed distant seems to be close. Such cracks are repaired almost at once. But it is an experience which leaves us with a bitter taste, an impression of sadness and almost of anguish; yet I think it is beneficial, for it shows us as in a flash all that is contingent and—yes—artificial in the crystallised pattern of our personal system.

But it is, above all, the sanctity realised in certain beings which reveals to us that what we call the normal order is, from a higher point of view, from the standpoint of a soul rooted in the ontological mystery, merely the subversion of an order which is its opposite. In this connection, the study of sanctity with all its concrete attributes seems to me to offer an immense speculative value; indeed, I am not far from saying that it is the true introduction to ontology.

Once again a comparison with the soul which is not at the disposal of others will throw light on our subject.

To be incapable of presence is to be in some manner not only occupied but encumbered with one's own self. I have said in some manner; the immediate object of the preoccupation may be one of any number; I may be preoccupied with my health, my fortune, or even with *my inward perfection.* This shows that to be occupied with oneself is not so much to be occupied with *a particular object* as to be occupied in a *particular manner.* It must be noted that the contrary of this state is not a state of emptiness or indifference. The real contrast is rather between the being who is opaque and the being who is transparent. But this inward opacity remains to be analysed. I believe that it consists in a kind of obduracy or fixation; and I wonder if, by generalising and adapting certain psychoanalytical data, we would not find that it is the fixation in a given zone or in a given key of a certain disquiet which, in itself, is something quite different. But what is remarkable is that the disquiet persists within this fixation and gives it that character of constriction which I mentioned in connection with the degradation of the will. There is every reason to believe that this indefinite disquiet should be identified with the anguish of temporality and with that aspiration of man not towards, but *by* death, which is at the heart of pessimism.

Pessimism is rooted in the same soil as the inability to be at the disposal of others. If the latter grows in us as we grow old, it is only too often because, as we draw near to what we regard as the term of our life, anxiety grows in us almost to the point of choking us; to protect itself, it sets up an increasingly heavy, exacting and, I would add, vulnerable, mechanism of self-defence. The capacity to hope diminishes in proportion as the soul becomes increasingly chained to its experience and to the categories which arise from it, and as it is given over more completely and more desperately to the world of the problematical.

Here at last can be brought together the various motifs and thematic elements which I have had to bring out one by one. In contrast to the captive soul we have described, the soul which is at the disposal of others is consecrated and inwardly dedicated; it is protected against suicide and despair, which are interrelated and alike, because it knows that it is not its own, and that the most legitimate use it can make of its freedom is precisely to recognise that it does not belong to itself; this recognition is the starting point of its activity and creativeness.

The difficulties of a philosophy of this sort must not be disguised. It is inevitably faced by a disquietening alternative: Either it will try to solve these difficulties—to give all the answers; in that case it will fall into the excesses of a dogmatism which ignores its vital principles and, I would add, into those of a sacrilegious theodicy, or else it will allow these difficulties to subsist, labelling them as mysteries.

Between these two I believe that there exists a middle way—a narrow, difficult and dangerous path which I have tried to discover. But, like Karl Jaspers in his *Philosophy of Existence,* I can only proceed in this kind of country by calling out to other travellers. If, as it occasionally happened, certain minds respond—not the generality, but this being and that other —then there is a way. But, as I believe Plato perceived with incomparable clarity, it is a way which is undiscoverable except through love, to which alone it is visible, and this brings us to what is perhaps the deepest characteristic of that realm of the meta-problematical of which I have tried to explore certain regions.

A serious objection remains to be mentioned. It will perhaps be said: All that you have said implies an unformulated reference to the data of Christianity and can only be understood in the light of these data. Thus we understand what you mean by presence if we think of the Eucharist and what you mean by creative fidelity if we think of the Church. But what can be the value of such a philosophy for those who are a-Christian—for those who ignore Christianity or who do not accept it? I would answer: it is quite possible that the existence of the fundamental Christian data may be necessary *in fact* to enable the mind to conceive some of the notions which I have attempted to analyse; but these notions cannot be said to depend on the data of Christianity, and *they do not presuppose it.* On the other hand, should I be told that the intellect must leave out of account anything which is not a universal data of thinking as such, I would say that this claim is exaggerated and in the last analysis, illusory. Now, as at any other time, the philosopher is placed in a given historical situation from which he is most unlikely to abstract himself completely; he would deceive himself if he thought that he could create a complete void both within and around himself. Now this historical situation implies as one of its essential data the existence of the Christian fact—quite independently of whether the Christian religion is accepted and its fundamental assertions are regarded as true or false. What appears to me evident is that we cannot reason to-day as though there were not behind us centuries of Christianity, just as, in the domain of the theory of knowledge, we cannot pretend that there have not been centuries of positive science. But neither the existence of Christianity nor that of positive science plays in this connection more than the role of a fertilising principle. It favours the development of certain ideas which we might not have conceived without it. This development may take place in what I would call para-Christian zones; for myself, I have experienced it more than twenty years before I had the remotest thought of becoming a Catholic.

Speaking more particularly to Catholics, I should like to note that from my own standpoint the distinction between the natural and the supernatural must be rigorously maintained. It will perhaps be objected that there is a danger that the word "mystery" might confuse this very issue.

I would reply that there is no question of confusing those mysteries which are enveloped in human experience as such with those mysteries which are revealed, such as the Incarnation or Redemption, and to which no effort of thought bearing on experience can enable us to attain.

It will be asked: why then do you use the same word for two such distinct notions? But I would point out that no revelation is, after all, conceivable unless it is addressed to being who is *involved—committed*—in the sense which I have tried to define—that is to say, to a being who participates in a reality which is non-problematical and which provides him with his foundation as subject. Supernatural life *must*, when all is said and done, find a hold in the natural—which is not to say that it is the flowering of the natural. On the contrary it seems to me that any study of the notion of *created Nature,* which is fundamental for the Christian, leads to the conclusion that there is in the depth of Nature, as of reason which is governed by it, a fundamental principle of inadequacy to itself which is, as it were, a restless anticipation of a different order.

To sum up my position on this difficult and important point, I would say that the recognition of the ontological mystery, in which I perceive as it were the central redoubt of metaphysics, is, no doubt, only possible through a sort of radiation which proceeds from revelation itself and which is perfectly well able to affect souls who are strangers to all positive religion of whatever kind; that this recognition, which takes place through certain higher modes of human experience, in no way involves the adherence to any given religion; but it enables those who have attained to it to perceive the possibility of a revelation in a way which is not open to those who have never ventured beyond the frontiers of the realm of the problematical and who have therefore never reached the point from which the mystery of being can be seen and recognised. Thus, a philosophy of this sort is carried by an irresistible movement towards the light which it perceives from afar and of which it suffers the secret attraction.

QUESTIONS FOR STUDY AND DISCUSSION

1. How does technological society tend to identify man with his vital and social functions?
2. Explain the distinction of problem and mystery. Illustrate the distinction with concrete examples from your own experience.
3. What does it mean to say that hope is situated at the center of the ontological mystery? What does Marcel mean by "creative fidelity"?
4. Trace Marcel's approach to God through "availability." In what sense is Marcel the author of a Christian philosophy?

Nicolas Berdyaev

NICOLAS BERDYAEV, born at Kiev in 1874, was in exile for a time during his youth. After the Revolution he received a chair of philosophy at the University of Moscow, but was expelled by the Bolshevists in 1922 as an upholder of religion. He resided in Paris from 1934 until his death in 1948. Although impatient with the formalism of organized religion, Berdyaev always considered himself a member of the Russian Orthodox Church. His numerous books, written in Russian and widely read in French and English translations, include *Dostoevsky, The Destiny of Man, The Beginning and the End,* and *The Dream and Reality: An Essay in Autobiography.*

God, Fate, and Human Freedom

I

There are two points of view from which the world may be regarded. From one of them the world is above all a cosmos. From the other the world is before all else history. To the ancient Greeks the world was a cosmos, to the ancient Hebrews it was history. The Greeks and the Hebrews lived in different times, not *at* a different time, but in a different kind of time. The view which sees the world as a cosmos is cosmocentric. That which regards the world as history is anthropocentric. The point at issue is this: must man be interpreted in terms of the cosmos or the cosmos in terms of man? Is human history a subordinate part of the cosmic process or is the cosmic process a subordinate part of human history? Is the meaning of human existence revealed in the cyclic movement of cosmic life, or in the fulfilment of history? This is also the issue between a static and a dynamic view of the world, between interpreting the world as primarily in space, and interpreting it as primarily in time. Reality is always historical —it can be nothing else. And what we call "nature" has its history in time, the stars in the heavens have it, so has the crust of the terrestrial globe. But it can be understood as cosmic infinity into which human history breaks, in

From pp. 197–228 of Nicolas Berdyaev, *The Beginning and the End,* translated by R. M. French. Copyright 1952 by YMCA–Press, Paris. Reprinted by permission of Harper & Row, Publishers.

which case there are in it no events which are important in virtue of their own meaning; or it can be understood as entering into human history as a preparatory part of it, and in that case it is given a significant meaning.

No philosophy of history could arise among the Greeks, on account of their cosmocentric way of looking at the world. Their golden age was in the past, and their gift for the creation of myths was due to this. They had no great expectation to turn their minds towards the future. It was only in connection with messianic eschatological thought that a philosophy of history could arise, and that was to be found only in the people of Israel and among the Persians who had influenced them. These people have an intense sense of expectation. They looked for a great manifestation in the future, for the appearance of the Messiah and the messianic kingdom, in other words, for the incarnation of Meaning, of the Logos, in history. It might be said that it is messianism which makes the historical. The philosophy of history is derived from Iranian, Hebrew and Christian sources. The nineteenth century doctrine of progress, which was so non-Christian externally, springs nevertheless from the same source of messianic expectation.

Doubts and objections have been raised about the possibility of a philosophy of history. It is indeed beyond dispute that it is impossible to construct a purely scientific philosophy of history. We live within historical time. History has not yet come to an end, and we do not know what sort of history is yet to come in the future. What element of newness is still possible in the history of mankind and the world? In such circumstances how are we to grasp the meaning of history? Can history reveal itself before it reaches its conclusion?

A philosophy of history has been possible, and it has existed, precisely because it has always included a prophetic element which has passed beyond the bounds of scientific knowledge. There cannot be any other sort of philosophy of history than prophetic. It is not only the philosophy of history contained in the books of the Bible and in St. Augustine which is prophetic and messianic, so also is the philosophy of history of Hegel, Saint Simon, Auguste Comte and Karl Marx.

The philosophy of history is not merely knowledge of the past, it is also knowledge of the future. It always endeavours to bring meaning to light and that can become clear only in the future. When people divide history into three epochs, and from the third synthetic epoch of the future look for consummated fulfilment, for a perfected consciousness of freedom of spirit, and for an embodiment of spirit in a perfect and just state of society, that is prophecy; it is a secularized form of messianism or chiliasm. When Hegel asserts that in the Prussian State there will be a manifestation of that freedom which is the meaning and goal of world history; and when Marx maintains that the proletariat will be the liberator of mankind and will create the perfect social order; or again when Nietzsche affirms that the appearance of the superman as the result of human evolution will make plain the meaning of this earthly life—all alike are sanctioning messianic and prophetic thought, they are all announcing the coming of the thousand years' reign. There is nothing of that sort that can be asserted by science.

In Hegel, history is sacred history. The messianic and prophetic character of the philosophy of history is settled by the fact that the meaning of history depends upon the unknown future. And the difficulty of the philosophy of history is due to the fact that it is knowledge not only of that which has not yet been, but also of that which still is not. It might, therefore, be said that it is prophecy not only about the future but also about the past. Historical reality becomes a thing which cannot be captured, for the present which is with us cannot be retained until the following moment. Everything flows, everything is in a state of movement and change. In actual fact no knowledge contains that concrete reality of the present which we desire to grasp. But the case of the phenomena which the natural sciences study is different from that of the knowledge of history in view of their repeatability and the possibility of experiment. The philosophy of history can be nothing but a religious metaphysic of history. The problem of messianism is of fundamental significance for it.

If we took a deeper view of history we should be able to see that messianism, true or false, open or disguised, is the basic theme of history. The whole tragedy of history is due to the working of the messianic idea, to its constant effect of causing division in the human mind. Messianism is of ancient Hebrew origin, and it is the contribution of the Hebrew people to world history. The intensity of the messianic expectation of the Hebrew people even led to the appearance of Christ, the Messiah, among that people. The messianic idea was foreign to the Greeks, they had a different vocation. The messianic hope is born in suffering and unhappiness and awaits the day of righteous judgment, and, in the end, of messianic triumph and the messianic reign of a thousand years. From the psychological point of view this is compensation. The consciousness of messianic election compensates for the experience of suffering. The sufferings of the Hebrew people, the sufferings of the Polish people, of the Russian people, the sufferings of the German people (and I say of the people, not of the State), and of the labouring classes of society operate favourably to the rise of a messianic frame of mind.

There is also a messianic expectation of mankind as a whole which arises from the enormous suffering of man on this earth. If suffering does not utterly crush a man or a people, it becomes a source of terrible power. Happiness and tranquillity weaken and demoralize and there is nothing more disintegrating than a serene and cheerful scepticism. The appearance of the Messiah is accompanied by constant doubt and questioning whether this is the true Messiah or not. In the Gospels we see this constant questioning about Jesus: is he the Christ? There have indeed been many false Messiahs and many false forms of messianic belief. Anti-Christ will be a false Messiah. Messianic belief may be national or it may be universal, there is an individual messianism and a collective messianism, it is sometimes triumphant and sometimes it suffers, there is a form of messianic hope which belongs to this world and a form which belongs to the other world.

. . .

The one and only true messianic belief is the messianism which looks for a new era of the Spirit, for the transformation of the world and for the Kingdom of God. This messianic belief is eschatological and it stands in direct opposition to all the theocracies of history and to all efforts to turn the State into something sacred. It is only the quest for truth and right in the ordering of society which enters into the true messianic belief.

But those who seek after such an ordering of society may also be seduced by the kingdom of this world and repudiate the Cross. Hebrew messianic belief is still with us in its false form. The deceptions of the messianic consciousness will continue to exist until the end of time, and it is this that makes history a drama. This accounts for the fact that the principal content of history continues to be war. It is the fate of Christianity to find itself, as it were, in an *entr'acte* in history. The spiritual forces of historical Christianity are becoming exhausted, the messianic consciousness in it has been extinguished, and it has ceased to play a guiding rôle in what are known as the great events of history. The creative process goes on, as it were, outside Christianity, and in any case outside the visible Church. Nothing but a transition to eschatological Christianity, and a turning to the light which streams from the future can make Christianity again a creative force. But the transition to eschatological Christianity does not involve the repudiation of the experience of history and culture; on the contrary, recognition of the religious significance of that experience is precisely what it does involve. The messianic theme continues to be the theme of history, and it is a theme which is connected with the problem of time. The philosophy of history is above all a philosophy of time.

History presents itself to us as events in a stream of time—eras, decades, centuries, millenia. But do the events of history take place in that same time in which the phenomena of nature occur? A certain body expanded through the generation of heat, a combination of chemical elements took place, bile was secreted; or, again, the Peloponnesian War broke out, Luther nailed up his theses, the Bastille was stormed. Here is a series of events in which "time" varies in significance and has differing relations to the meaning of the events in question.

I have already written in other books of mine about the fact that there are different sorts of time. At the moment I repeat only the most important points. There is cosmic time, there is historical time and there is existential time. Cosmic time is calculated by mathematics on the basis of movement around the sun, calendars and clocks are dependent on it, and it is symbolized by the circle. Historical time is, so to speak, placed within cosmic time and it also can be reckoned mathematically in decades, centuries and millenia, but every event in it is unrepeatable. Historical time is symbolized by a line which stretches out forward into the future, towards what is new. Existential time is not susceptible of mathematical calculation, its flow depends upon intensity of experience, upon suffering and joy. It is within this time that the uplifting creative impulse takes place and in it ecstasy is known. It is symbolized above all by the point, which tells of movement in depth.

History moves forward in its own historical time, but it cannot either remain in it, or come to an end in it. It moves on either into cosmic time, in which case it makes an affirmation of naturalism and is in tune with the final objectification of human existence, when man takes his place as merely a subordinate part of the whole world of nature. Or it issues into existential time, and this means moving out from the realm of objectification into the spiritual pattern of things.

Existential time, which is known to everyone by experience ("those who are happy do not watch the clock"), is evidence of the fact that time is in man, and not man in time, and that time depends upon changes in man. At a greater depth we know that temporal life is consummated in eternity. The development of the spirit in history is supra-temporal. Hegel is of opinion that in historicity the spirit overcomes history and realizes eternity, but he does not understand the tragedy of history. In existential time, which is akin to eternity, there is no distinction between the future and the past, between the end and the beginning. In it the eternal accomplishment of the mystery of spirit takes place. In consequence of events which occur in existential time there is development and enrichment in history, and a return to the purity of its sources. From time to time limpid springs are brought into view which well up from existential depths and then an illusion is created by which the revelation of the eternal is transferred to the far distant past. Time is not the image of eternity (as in Plato, Plotinus), time is eternity which has collapsed in ruin. Cosmic time and historical time do not resemble eternity. But, nevertheless, Christianity attaches a meaning to time and to history within time.

History in time is the pathway of man towards eternity, within it the enrichment of human experience is accumulated. But it is absolutely impossible to conceive either of the creation of the world within time or of the end of the world within time. In objectified time there is no beginning, nor is there any end, there is only an endless middle. The beginning and the end are in existential time. The nightmare doctrine of predestination became a possibility thanks only to a false and illusory interpretation of objectified time. Upon the same soil springs up the doctrine of the eternal pains of hell. All this is a projection upon the external, upon the realm of objects, of events which take place in existential time. The eternal destiny of man is not a destiny within endless time, the decision upon it is reached through the coming of an end to time. The doctrine of pre-existence is a profound one, for it is based upon the memory of existential time.

The idea of progress has a messianic basis and without that it turns into the idea of natural evolution. Judgments of value are connected with this messianic basis and not with natural evolution, which may lead to what is bad and undesired. Progress must have a final goal and in that respect it is eschatological. But historical progress contains an insurmountable antithesis within it, one which cannot be resolved within history. This antithesis is due to the fact that man is a historical being; it is only in history that he realizes the fullness of his existence, but, at the same time, there is a clash between human personality and history, and it is a clash which cannot be subdued within the confines of history.

Man puts his creative strength into history and does so with enthusiasm. But history, on the other hand, takes no account of man. It uses him as material for the creation of an inhuman structure and it has its own inhuman and anti-human code of morals. History consists moreover in the bitter strife of men, classes, nations and States, of religious faiths and of ideas. Hatred is its controlling power and its most dynamic moments are associated with hatred at its keenest. Men carry on this senseless strife in the name of historical aims, but it inflicts grievous wounds upon human personality and is the cause of measureless suffering among men. In fact, history has become something like a crime.

Yet at the same time we cannot simply cast aside the history of thousands of years nor can we cease to be historical beings. That would be too easy a way out. But it is impossible to see in history a progressive triumph of reason. In Dostoyevsky's *Letters from the Underworld* the hero says: "It's monotonous: they fight and fight, they are fighting now and they fought before; you agree that there is really too much monotony about it all. To put it in a nutshell, you can say anything about world history, things which only the most disordered imagination could put into your head. There is only one thing you cannot say—and that is you cannot call it reasonable." This links up with Dostoyevsky's fundamental theme—the self-will of man and world harmony. Man ranks his self-will higher than his happiness. The will to power and the will to impose unity upon the world by force goad and torment man. Men torment both themselves and others with the illusory aims of historical might and majesty. The foundation and the destruction of kingdoms is one of the chief purposes of history. The first philosophy of history—the Book of Daniel—speaks of this, and there the fate of kingdoms is foreseen. Almighty and majestic kingdoms for the sake of establishing which the sacrifice of numberless men has been made are doomed to perish, and have perished.

All the ancient empires of the East crumbled into ruin; the Empire of Alexander of Macedonia perished and at the time of his death he was aware of the fact that it would do so. The Roman Empire likewise perished, so did the Byzantine Empire. All the theocracies collapsed and we ourselves have witnessed the fall of the Russian Empire. And in the same way all empires which are yet to be founded will perish. The kingdom of Caesar and the glory of it pass swiftly away.

History postulates the freedom of man. The determinism of nature cannot be transferred to history. Dostoyevsky had a profound understanding of this, a deeper sense of it than anyone else. History presupposes human freedom, yet it denies man's freedom and sets it at naught; it scarcely allows him liberty to breathe freely. The tragedy and torment of history are above all else the tragedy and torment of time. History has a meaning solely because it will come to an end. The meaning of history cannot be immanent in history, it lies beyond the confines of history. Progress, which has a habit of offering up every living human generation and every living human person as a sacrifice to a future state of perfection, which thus becomes a sort of vampire, is only to be accepted on the condition that history will come to an end, and that in that end all previous generations and every human person who has lived on earth will be able to enjoy the results of history. Historical pessimism is justified to a remarkable degree, and there are no empirical grounds for historical optimism. But the ultimate truth lies beyond pessimism and optimism. It all goes back to the mystery of the relation between time and eternity. There are such things as moments of communion with eternity. These moments pass, and again I lapse into time. Yet it is not that moment which passes, but I in my fallen temporality: the moment indeed remains in eternity. The task that faces me is that personality as a whole should enter into eternity, not the disintegrated parts of it.

There are three forces which operate in the history of the world—God, fate and human freedom. That accounts for the complexity of history. If it were only God who was active, or only human freedom, that complexity would not exist. It is a mistake to think that Christianity ought to deny fate. What Christianity recognizes about fate is that it can be overcome. Christ was victorious over inevitable fate. But it is only in Christ that fate can be conquered. And those who are outside Christ, or opposed to him, put themselves in subjection to fate.

The terrible power of fate is active in the history of peoples, societies and States. Fate is at work in the formation of great empires, and in the destruction of them, in revolution and counterrevolution, in the insane pursuit of riches and in the ruinous collapse of them, in the seductive lure of the pleasures of life and in its enormous suffering. Fate turns human personality into a plaything of the irrational forces of history. Hegel's "cunning of the reason" is fate. Both irrational forces and rationalizing forces alike are expressions of fate. The power of technical skill, which has been built up by the human reason for the increase of human might, is the work of fate.

At certain times in their history, nations are especially apt to fall into the power of fate, the activity of human freedom is weakened, and a period of Godforsakenness is experienced. This can be felt very strongly in the destiny of the Russian people, and of the Germans as well. Such decrees of destiny are particularly significant in the present era of history. Godforsakenness, accompanied also by enfeeblement of freedom, is an experience both of individual men and women and also of whole peoples. The meaning of history cannot be grasped nor can it be examined in its objectification, for in the view of things taken in objectification, the end of history is concealed from sight.

Given the naturalistic outlook upon history, one can speak only of the youth and old age of a people, one cannot talk about progress. The highest aim that can be acknowledged is only to experience the uplifting impulse which springs from the strength of youth. Decadence, which is both refined and complex, is succeeded by the comparative crudity and primitiveness of the vital forces of peoples. In comparison with the animal world there are endless possibilities of development in the world of human beings, although this does not apply to organic, biological development, in which respect there is rather regress. There is an eternal principle in man which shapes his destiny. But man is not an unchanging quantity in history. In history man does change, he undergoes new experiences, he becomes more complex, he unfolds and develops. There is human development, but it does not take place along a straight ascending line. In the historical destiny of man the part played by freedom varies, and it is impossible to follow Hegel and say that there is in history a progressive development towards freedom.

Freedom such as man has not known may indeed evolve, but so also may human servitude of a kind unknown before. Noumenal realities operate behind the phenomena of history and for that reason only are freedom and development possible. Beyond history meta-history is concealed, and the sphere of the historical is not absolutely isolated from that of the meta-historical. What is happening in existential time lies hidden behind what is taking place in historical time. The appearance of Christ the Liberator is a meta-historical fact and it occurred in existential time. But in that central messianic manifestation meta-history breaks through into history, albeit history receives it in a troubled setting.

It is not that event alone, central and full of meaning as it was, which is meta-historical. A meta-historical element, which is not open to explanation by the determinism of history, is to be found also in every manifestation of creative genius, always a mysterious thing, and in every true liberation from the determining power of the phenomenal world. The meta-historical arrives out of the world of the noumenal into this objective world and revolutionizes it. A real profound revolution in the history of the world is a noumenal revolution, but it gets into a state of tangled confusion owing to the terrible determinism of the phenomenal world. The history of Christianity provides cases in point.

The revolution of the spirit has not been successful in history and, therefore, a transition to eschatological Christianity is inevitable. But in eschatological Christianity there is a retrospective action upon the historical past, an action which resuscitates. The secret of the fascination of the historical past is due to the transfiguring action of memory. Memory does not restore the past as it was, it transforms that past, transforms it into something which is eternal. Beauty is always revealed in creative transformation and is a break-through into the objective world. There was too much that was criminal and ugly in the objective phenomenal reality of the past. That is suppressed by transforming memory. The beauty of the past is the beauty of creative acts in the present. The contradictions of history are amazing: the beauty of the past is seen in association with injustice and cruelty, and, on the other hand, an age which has striven after justice, equality and freedom appears ugly. This is due to the impossibility of attaining completeness within the confines of history and to the illusions of objectifying thought. The end of history means passing through death, yet in order to attain resurrection. Eschatological Christianity is a resuscitating Christianity. The godlessness of Heidegger's philosophy, which is very characteristic of the present day, lies in the fact that from its point of view the present condition of being and the anxiety that belongs to it are unconquerable. Being which inclines towards death is anxiety, and anxiety is being which inclines towards death.

And this is his final word. It is a word which is the very opposite of a religion of resurrection, of an eschatological religion. Hegel's philosophy is godless in another way. There is in it no consciousness of the conflict between the personal and the universal, nor is there any divine pity for suffering man, nor divine compassion for the created thing in its pain. One can become reconciled to the horrors of history and to progress as on its way it deals out death, only if one cherishes the great hope of a resurrection of all who have lived and are living, of every creature who has suffered and rejoiced.

II

. . .

Human societies, and especially those of them which have incorporated Christianity into their experience, undergo in various forms the three temptations which Christ rejected in the wilderness. There is in man a profound need not merely for "bread" which is a symbol of the very possibility of human existence, but also for world-wide unity. And so man follows those who promise to turn stones into bread, and establish the kingdom of this world. People love slavery and authority. The mass of mankind has no love for freedom, and is afraid of it. What is more, freedom has at times been terribly perverted, and even turned into a means of enslavement. Freedom has been wholly interpreted as a right, as a thing which people are entitled to claim, whereas what it really is above all is an obligation and a duty. Freedom is not something which man demands of God, but that which God requires of man.

Freedom, therefore, is not a trifle to be lightly assumed; it is a difficulty and a burden which man ought to take upon himself. And there are but a few who assent to this. Freedom, in the spiritual sense, is aristocratic, not democratic. There is a bourgeois freedom also, but that is a perversion and an insult to spirit. Freedom is a spiritual thing, it is spirit. It issues out of the noumenal world and overthrows the settled order of the world of phenomena.

The ideal of anarchism, if accepted in its ultimate depth, is an ideal which marks the limit of human liberation. It ought not by any means to be taken to denote the rejection of the functional importance of the State in this objectified world. What anarchism ought to oppose is not order and harmony, but the principle of power, that is to say, of force exercised from without. The optimism of most of the theories of anarchism is false. In the conditions of this objectified world we cannot conceive of the ideal society, without evil, strife and war. Absolute pacifism in this world is a false ideal, because it is anti-eschatological. There is a great deal of truth on this subject in Proudhon.

All political forms, democracy and monarchy alike, are relative. What must be supported throughout to the end are those forms, relative as they are, which provide the greatest possibility of real freedom, of the recognition of the value of personality, and which acknowledge the supremacy of truth and right over the State. But the ideal can be nothing but the supersession of all power, on the grounds that it rests upon alienation and exteriorization, and means enslavement. The Kingdom of God can only be thought of apophatically, as achieved absence of power and a kingdom of freedom. Hegel says that "law is the objectivity of spirit," and thus admits that he assigns a realm to objectification. And it is he too who says that the State is a spirtual idea in the *Äusserlichkeit* of the human will to freedom. *Äusserlichkeit* is indeed the fundamental work of the State and of power.

There are two ways of understanding society, and two paths that it follows. Either society is understood as nature or it is interpreted as spirit. Society is either accepted as nature and, therefore, ordered in accordance with the laws of nature, or it is built up as a spiritual reality. In this way the ideals of society, and the character of its conflict are decided. As nature, society is under the power of necessity; its motive power is the struggle for predominance and mastery; natural selection of the strong holds good in it; it is built up on the principles of authority and compulsion, and relations which occur within it are settled as object relations. As spirit, on the other hand, society finds its motive power in the quest for freedom; it rests upon the principle of personality and upon relations which are subject relations. Its controlling motive is the desire that love and mercy should be the basis upon which the fabric of society rests. Society as nature is submissive to the law of the world; as spirit, it desires to be submissive to the law of God. All this has been given a different interpretation by such defenders of the organic idea of society as Schelling, Franz Baader, Möhler, Khomyakov and Soloviëv; but that is just romantic illusion from which one must set oneself free.

As a matter of actual experience society is both nature and spirit, and both principles are at work in it. But the natural predominates; that which is of the world predominates over the spiritual which is of God, necessity predominates over freedom, coercive objectivity over personality, the will to power and mastery over mercy and love. But the great lie has been that the "natural" basis of society, the struggle for existence and predominance, emulation, war, the exploitation of man and scorn of his dignity and worth, coercion of the weak by the strong—that all these have been regarded as eternal and even spiritual foundations of society. And among the ideologists of authority and hierarchical order there has even been an idealization of these vile things, these things that ought not to be. In the eyes of the world society as nature is strength. Society as spirit is truth and right, to which the world may all too often be blind.

Society, as nature, is objectification, self-estrangement of spirit, alienation of human nature into the external, in a word enslavement, which sums it all up. Corresponding to it is naturalism in sociology which endeavours to provide scientific sanction for the selection of a race of the powerful and dominant, and for the crushing of personality by society understood as an organism. Given the organic conception of society some mitigation might have been introduced in the past by the fact of patriarchal relationships. Society as an organism which is constructed upon traditional patriarchal relations, is not rent by the furious and unrestrained strife of men, social groups, classes, tribes and races. It establishes a relative social harmony which is based upon hierarchical inequalities, to which popular religious beliefs give sanction.

In capitalist societies and in those which are known as individualist, which were originally inspired by a set of ideas about the natural state and natural harmony, a conflict of all against all has come to light. And in them the greatest social inequalities have been created, which have the sanction of no popular beliefs at all and of no traditions, and are absolutely shameless. This is a soil which is favourable to the growth of riot and revolt, and they have some right and justice in them, but they assume the character of movements which belong to society as nature, not to society as spirit. Marxism wants to liberate man from the enslaving power of economics, but it looks for the liberating act within economics, to which it assigns a metaphysical significance.

Contrary to the ideas of sociological and economic naturalism, non-objectified spirit does break into the natural life of society with its evil passions and its false ideological sanctions, which are worse than the passions themselves, and with its power of determinism. And in so breaking in, spirit seeks to order society after a different pattern, to introduce freedom, the dignity and value of personality, compassion and the brotherhood of men. This is reflected in distorted form in the philosophically naïve idea of the social contract. In clarifying the conventional and confused state of the terminology it is interesting to note that what ought to be called spiritual right is in fact known as natural right. The "natural" rights of man are precisely those which are opposed to society as nature, to natural determinism in society, and such rights are, therefore, spiritual and not natural.

The doctrine of what is "natural," in the history of European thought, of natural reason, natural morals, and natural right, has very close links with the fight for the liberation of human nature and of nature in general from the stifling suppression they suffered during the middle ages. But the time is at hand when it must be decisively shown that it is precisely the "natural" which is an enslaving power proceeding as it does from the objectified and determinate world. Whereas liberation is spiritual; it proceeds from spirit, which is freedom and lies outside the sway of objective determinism. Some of the greatest misunderstandings are due to this. There is, for instance, no more horrifying misunderstanding than to regard materialism as a philosophy of emancipation and the spiritual view of life as a philosophy which enslaves. Such misunderstanding arises from the fact that men have made use of the spiritual view of life as a means for the enslavement of others, in the interests of sanctions in the realm of ideas, which belong to society precisely as nature, and not to society as spirit. The greatest evil has been not in the primary elements of nature, but in these sanctions in the realm of ideas. And it is all due to a false understanding of spirit.

In actual fact, natural matter is a conservative and reactionary principle, while spirit is a creative and revolutionary principle. Spirit overthrows the naturally servile foundations of society and tries to create society after its own image. It is the non-eternal, transitory character of these servile hierarchical foundations of society which are exposed to condemnation. But the revolution brought about by the spirit, in its own expression in social life, easily falls under the power of objectification, and new and yet newer forms of slavery are continually coming to light. The process of invasion by liberating spirit is interrupted, there is no direct development in a straight line. The real revolution of the spirit is the end of objectification as belonging to this world; it is the revolution of noumena against the wrong line which the world of phenomena has taken. When that time comes the spiritual society, the realm of Spirit, the Kingdom of God will be made plain, decisively and finally.

But the action of fate in history, which dislodges the operation of God and human freedom, gives rise to its own physical embodiments and leads to its own extreme objectifications. The State, that kingdom of this world and pre-eminently of its prince, has had functions to perform which are necessary for this evil world. But there have also been built into it the evil demoniacal will to power and paramountcy, the will to fortify the strength of the iniquitous kingdom of this servile world; there has been a glut of enmity and hatred. And the image of the State will be shown in the final end to be the image of the beast which issues out of the abyss. It is said with much zeal and love that perfection is impossible on earth and so there cannot be a perfect society. And people say this chiefly because they do not want such perfection and because their interest lies in upholding the wrong.

But it is true that there can be no perfect society within this "earthly" scheme of things, and the expectation of such perfection is merely a utopian illusion.

But that is not by any means the question. The question is: is the conquest of this objective world a possibility, not the annihilation of what is "earthly," but its liberation and transformation, its transition to a different scheme of things? And that is an eschatological question. It becomes Christians at any rate to believe that the only kingdom which can achieve success is the Kingdom of God. The Kingdom of God is not merely a matter of expectation: it is being founded, its creation is beginning already here and now upon earth. This requires that we should interpret eschatology in an active and creative way.

III

The most revolutionary and cataclysmic event in the history of the world is the emergence of technological knowledge, that triumphant advance of the machine which is determining the whole structure of civilization. The machine and technical skill have in very truth a cosmological significance. In the machine something new makes its appearance, something which has not hitherto been in the life of the world. The machine is a combination of physical and chemical forces but it is not a natural phenomenon. In addition to inorganic bodies, and organic bodies, organized bodies are making their appearance. This is nature which has been handled by human activity, and subordinated to the purposes of men. By technical skill forces are extracted from the heart of nature which had been asleep and had not come to light in the cycle of natural life. To have achieved the splitting of the atom is paramount to a cosmic revolution which issues from the heart of civilization itself.

At the same time the growing power of technological knowledge in the social life of men means the ever greater and greater objectification of human existence; it inflicts injury upon the souls, and it weighs heavily upon the lives of men. Man is all the while more and more thrown out into the external, always becoming more and more exteriorized, more and more losing his spiritual centre and integral nature. The life of man is ceasing to be organic and is becoming organized; it is being rationalized and mechanized.

Man falls out of the rhythm which corresponds to the life of nature; he gets out of step with nature, he gets further and further away from it (I am not using the word "nature" here to mean the object of mechanical and natural science), and his emotional life, and the life of the soul suffer from deficiency.

The dialectic of technical progress consists in this: that the machine is a creation of man and at the same time it takes a line against man: it is born of the spirit, yet nevertheless it enslaves the spirit. The progress of civilization is a self-contradictory process, one which creates a division in the mind of man. In the life of society, spirit, primitive nature and technology act and react upon each other and are in conflict with one another. Technical knowledge of an elementary kind already exists from the very outset, from the very beginning of civilization. The struggle for life in the teeth of the elemental forces of nature requires it. But at the height of civilization the part played by technical knowledge becomes predominant and takes the whole of life into its scope. This provokes a romantic reaction of the "natural" against technology. Man, suffering from the wounds inflicted by technical civilization would like to return to the organic life of nature which begins to seem to him to be paradise. But this is one of the illusions of the mind. There is no such return to that paradise. A return from the life which is technically organized to the life which is naturally organic is an impossibility.

Both an organic element and a technical element enter into society considered as spirit. Hence arises the problem of the relation between civilization and culture, a question which has arisen with peculiar trenchancy in Russian and German thought. The relation between the two must not be supposed to be a matter of time. The tendency for civilization as a type to predominate over culture always showed itself, already in the ancient world. It is a theme which was known as long ago as the time of the prophets who took up arms against the growth of capitalism.

Culture is still linked with the naturally organic, but civilization breaks that link, for it is possessed by a will for the organization and rationalization of life, by a will for increasing power.

With it goes a dizzying increase of speed, a frenzied acceleration of every kind of process. Man has no time for recollection or for looking inwards into his own depth. An acute process of dehumanization takes place and it is precisely from the growth of human might that it takes its rise. There is paradox in this.

In a bourgeois age of technical civilization an unbounded increase of wealth takes place and these riches are periodically destroyed by fearful wars. There is a sense in which these destructive wars which are brought about by the will to power are the fate of societies which are based upon the dominating influence of technical civilization and steeped in bourgeois contentment. The instruments of destruction are immeasurably more powerful than those of construction. Civilization at its height is extraordinarily inventive in devising means of killing, but it has no resuscitating forces in it. And that is its condemnation.

The part played by technology raises the problem of spirit and the spiritual mastery of life in an acute form. Technology puts into men's hands fearful means of destruction and violence. A group of men who have seized power with the help of technology can hold the whole world under the tyranny of their rule. This means that the question of the spiritual state of men is a matter of life and death. The world may be blown up because of the debased spiritual state of the men who have got possession of the means of destruction. The simpler weapons of time gone by brought no such possibility within the reach of men. The power of technology reaches the limits of the objectification of human existence, it turns man into a thing, an object, a nameless thing. The victory of society considered as spirit would mean that the objectification of human existence would be overcome, it would be the triumph of personalism. The machine raises the eschatological question, and leads up to the breaking of the seals of history.

The major evils and the principal sufferings of life are due not so much to the baseness and wickedness of individual people, but rather to the base and wicked ideas which take possession of their minds, to social prejudices, beliefs which have become vague and cloudy, which have degenerated into a mere inheritance from the environment in which they arose. The evil and suffering which were caused by such people as Torquemada, Philip II, Robespierre and many others and the cruelty they inflicted were not due to the fact that they were themselves vile and evil men, as individual people they were not base and cruel. It was due to the fact that their minds were possessed by evil ideas and beliefs which appeared to them to be good and indeed lofty.

The head of a family, a member of some particular estate, the head of a government department, the director of some enterprise, a prelate of the Church, a general, a minister or a king are liable to be cruel and to spread suffering around them. And the main reason for it is a result of their consciousness of their own position in a hierarchy. By nature and as individual persons it may well be that they are not at all cruel. But the constitution of their minds is by tradition such that it imposes upon them a tendency to be merciless and cruel and to achieve their ends by force. Such people insist with a distorted conscience, upon the honour and might of the family, the estate, the army, the ecclesiastical establishment, the State to which they belong, and in general lay stress upon the principle of authority and the power of rank. What a number of human lives have been crippled and ruined as a result of wrong ideas about the authority of parents and superiors!

The idea of objective rank in a hierarchy based upon the generic and the common is a rejection of the dignity and value of personality; the impress of a fallen state of existence is stamped upon it. It is only the idea of hierarchy in a subjective, spiritual and charismatic sense which maintains the dignity and worth of the man himself, of personality together with all its qualities. Objective hierarchical principles, which are worse than plague and cholera, always sacrifice personality, the living human being who is capable of suffering and joy, for the sake of the family, the race, the class, the State, and all the rest.

The subjective principle of hierarchy on the other hand is a human form of it. It is a hierarchy which depends upon gifts, upon the *charismata* of prophets, apostles, saints; it is the hierarchy of men of genius in human power to create, the hierarchy of personal nobility of character and beauty of soul. There is a metaphysical inequality among human beings in accordance with their individual gifts, and it goes with the preservation and support of personality and the worth of every living creature, of all the children of God. It recognizes an equality of the unequal.

The objective social idea of hierarchy almost never corresponds to the subjective and spiritual idea of it. All too often it includes the selection of the worst, the most debased in personal qualities. The objective principle of hierarchy is a most cunning invention of the objectified fallen world. In that world men who stand at the highest level, judged by their gifts and qualities, are liable to be made victims, they are persecuted and crucified. How tragic is the fate of the prophet and the genius in this world! What a triumph it accords just to the talents of mediocrity, day to day routine and the readiness to adapt oneself! It is only the captains and the men of power who share in that sacrosanct character which is ascribed to tribes and towns, nations and States. But this has been and always is sheer paganism. If only the protagonists of the objective idea of hierarchy would stop talking about the impossibility of equality among men, about the inequality which by nature exists among them and the mastery of some over the others!

The idea of equality as such is in reality hollow and derivative. The primary matter is the idea of freedom, of the value of every man as a person, even if he be a person in only a potential State. And all that equality means is that freedom and worth are secured for every human person, for all men, and that no single man shall be treated as a thing or a mere means to an end. It is precisely in society considered as spirit that a metaphysical charismatic inequality and a qualitative diversity among men should really come to light. In society regarded as objective nature on the other hand a monstous inequality, the lordship of some and the slavery of others is combined with a process of reducing personalities to the same level, with the subjection of personality to the generic mind and the dominance of society over man.

What is needed is to set humanity, pure divine humanity, a human idea of hierarchy and a charismatic sense of it against the fearful slavery of man in objectified society, against the vampire-like tyranny of inhuman and inhumane hierarchical principles and generic ideas. In the last resort this means the substitution of society on a charismatic basis for society established by law, of a society, or to speak more truly, a community of emancipated men in the Spirit. The only thing to set against the servitude of man, which takes the most varied forms, including forms which are liberal and socialist, is personalism which has noumenal foundations. Such personalism, which is social, not individualist, is a personalism of the community.

But a personalist spiritual revolution can only be conceived in terms of eschatology. It means the end of the objectified everyday world, the world of determinism and a transition to the realm of freedom, which is the new era of the Spirit. But this personalism which embraces every living thing is already being established here and now. It is not merely in the future, it is in the present also. It points out the way, although it does not look in an optimistic spirit for victory within the conditions of this world. To the dull and humdrum social world this personalism is miraculous, it meets object-fied nature with resistance, it is a different order of existence.

In order to avoid misunderstanding it must be said that compulsion is inevitable in those parts of the objectified world which are most material in character. It is impossible to endow crude materiality with complete free-dom. But the higher we rise towards spirituality so much the more out of place and intolerable does objectified compulsion become and so much the more ought the freedom of subjectivity, freedom of spirit, to be established. And another thing that must be said is that a true sacred tradition does exist. It is a resuscitating memory through which the link with what is eter-nal in the past is preserved. But the base tradition, tradition which is ge-neric without expressing the "togetherness" of *sobornost,* the tradition of inertia, of objectification instead of spirituality, such evil traditions must needs be overcome.

QUESTIONS FOR STUDY AND DISCUSSION

1. How does philosophy of history depend upon the Judeo-Christian tradition?
2. In what sense are messianism, prophetism, and chiliasm present in Marxism?
3. Explain and illustrate the differences between cosmic, historical, and exis-tential time.
4. Explain and illustrate the tension between spirit and nature.
5. How do Berdyaev's three forces—God, fate, and human freedom—interact in the history of the world?

Martin Buber

MARTIN BUBER was born in Vienna in 1878 and studied philosophy and history of art at the Universities of Vienna and Berlin. Active in the Zionist movement for a Jewish cultural renaissance, he founded in 1916 and edited until 1924 the leading journal of German-speaking Jewry, *Der Jude.* From 1923 to 1933 he taught Jewish philosophy of religion and the history of religions at Frankfurt. In 1938 he left Germany for Palestine, and was professor of Social Philosophy at the Hebrew University, Jerusalem, until his retirement in 1951. From 1949 to 1953 he served as director of the Institute for Adult Education, training teachers to work with the vast numbers of immigrants to Israel. In his last years he was active in working for international understanding, notably in Arab-Israeli relations. He died in Jerusalem in June, 1965. His best-known work is *I and Thou,* first published in 1923; its title presents the central theme, not only of his numerous publications, but of his whole life's work.

The Life of Real Relation

To man the world is twofold, in accordance with his twofold attitude.

The attitude of man is twofold, in accordance with the twofold nature of the primary words which he speaks.

The primary words are not isolated words, but combined words.

The one primary word is the combination *I–Thou.*

The other primary word is the combination *I–It;* wherein, without a change in the primary word, one of the words *He* and *She* can replace *It.*

Hence the *I* of man is also twofold.

For the *I* of the primary word *I–Thou* is a different *I* from that of the primary word *I–It.*

Primary words do not signify things, but they intimate relations.

Primary words do not describe something that might exist independently of them, but being spoken they bring about existence.

Primary words are spoken from the being.

Reprinted with the permission of Charles Scribner's Sons from *I and Thou,* pp. 3–18, 75–81, and 115–20, by Martin Buber (1937, 1958), and by permission of T. and T. Clark, Edinburgh.

If *Thou* is said, the *I* of the combination *I–Thou* is said along with it.
If *It* is said, the *I* of the combination *I–It* is said along with it.
The primary word *I–Thou* can only be spoken with the whole being.
The primary word *I–It* can never be spoken with the whole being.

There is no *I* taken in itself, but only the *I* of the primary word *I–Thou* and the *I* of the primary word *I–It*.
When a man says *I* he refers to one or other of these. The *I* to which he refers is present when he says *I*. Further, when he says *Thou* or *It,* the *I* of one of the two primary words is present.
The existence of *I* and the speaking of *I* are one and the same thing.
When a primary word is spoken the speaker enters the word and takes his stand in it.

The life of human beings is not passed in the sphere of transitive verbs alone. It does not exist in virtue of activities alone which have some *thing* for their object.
I perceive something. I am sensible of something. I imagine something. I will something. I feel something. I think something. The life of human beings does not consist of all this and the like alone.
This and the like together establish the realm of *It*.
But the realm of *Thou* has a different basis.
When *Thou* is spoken, the speaker has no thing for his object. For where there is a thing there is another thing. Every *It* is bounded by others; *It* exists only through being bounded by others. But when *Thou* is spoken, there is no thing. *Thou* has no bounds.
When *Thou* is spoken, the speaker has no *thing;* he has indeed nothing. But he takes his stand in relation.

It is said that man experiences his world. What does that mean?
Man travels over the surface of things and experiences them. He extracts knowledge about their constitution from them: he wins an experience from them. He experiences what belongs to the things.
But the world is not presented to man by experiences alone. These present him only with a world composed of *It* and *He* and *She* and *It* again.
I experience something.—If we add "inner" to "outer" experiences, nothing in the situation is changed. We are merely following the uneternal division that springs from the lust of the human race to whittle away the secret of death. Inner things or outer things, what are they but things and things!
I experience something.—If we add "secret" to "open" experiences, nothing in the situation is changed. How self-confident is that wisdom which perceives a closed compartment in things, reserved for the initiate and manipulated only with the key. O secrecy without a secret! O accumulation of information! It, always It!

The man who experiences has not part in the world. For it is "in him" and not between him and the world that the experience arises.

The world has no part in the experience. It permits itself to be experienced, but has no concern in the matter. For it does nothing to the experience, and the experience does nothing to it.

As experience, the world belongs to the primary word *I–It*.

The primary word *I–Thou* establishes the world of relation.

The spheres in which the world of relation arises are three.

First, our life with nature. There the relation sways in gloom, beneath the level of speech. Creatures live and move over against us, but cannot come to us, and when we address them as *Thou,* our words cling to the threshold of speech.

Second, our life with men. There the relation is open and in the form of speech. We can give and accept the *Thou.*

Third, our life with spiritual beings. There the relation is clouded, yet it discloses itself; it does not use speech, yet begets it. We perceive no *Thou,* but none the less we feel we are addressed and we answer—forming, thinking, acting. We speak the primary word with our being, though we cannot utter *Thou* with our lips.

But with what right do we draw what lies outside speech into relation with the world of the primary word?

In every sphere in its own way, through each process of becoming that is present to us we look out toward the fringe of the eternal *Thou;* in each we are aware of a breath from the eternal *Thou;* in each *Thou* we address the eternal *Thou.*

I consider a tree.

I can look on it as a picture: stiff column in a shock of light, or splash of green shot with the delicate blue and silver of the background.

I can perceive it as movement: flowing veins on clinging, pressing pith, suck of the roots, breathing of the leaves, ceaseless commerce with earth and air—and the obscure growth itself.

I can classify it in a species and study it as a type in its structure and mode of life.

I can subdue its actual presence and form so sternly that I recognise it only as an expression of law—of the laws in accordance with which a constant opposition of forces is continually adjusted, or of those in accordance with which the component substances mingle and separate.

I can dissipate it and perpetuate it in number, in pure numerical relation.

In all this the tree remains my object, occupies space and time, and has its nature and constitution.

It can, however, also come about, if I have both will and grace, that in considering the tree I become bound up in relation to it. The tree is now no longer *It*. I have been seized by the power of exclusiveness.

To effect this it is not necessary for me to give up any of the ways in which I consider the tree. There is nothing from which I would have to turn my eyes away in order to see, and no knowledge that I would have to forget. Rather is everything, picture and movement, species and type, law and number, indivisibly united in this event.

Everything belonging to the tree is in this: its form and structure, its colours and chemical composition, its intercourse with the elements and with the stars, are all present in a single whole.

The tree is no impression, no play of my imagination, no value depending on my mood; but it is bodied over against me and has to do with me, as I with it—only in a different way.

Let no attempt be made to sap the strength from the meaning of the relation: relation is mutual.

The tree will have a consciousness, then, similar to our own? Of that I have no experience. But do you wish, through seeming to succeed in it with yourself, once again to disintegrate that which cannot be disintegrated? I encounter no soul or dryad of the tree, but the tree itself.

If I face a human being as my *Thou,* and say the primary word *I–Thou* to him, he is not a thing among things, and does not consist of things.

Thus human being is not *He* or *She,* bounded from every other *He* and *She,* a specific point in space and time within the net of the world; nor is he a nature able to be experienced and described, a loose bundle of named qualities. But with no neighbour, and whole in himself, he is *Thou* and fills the heavens. This does not mean that nothing exists except himself. But all else lives in *his* light.

Just as the melody is not made up of notes nor the verse of words nor the statue of lines, but they must be tugged and dragged till their unity has been scattered into these many pieces, so with the man to whom I say *Thou.* I can take out from him the colour of his hair, or of his speech, or of his goodness. I must continually do this. But each time I do it he ceases to be *Thou.*

And just as prayer is not in time but time in prayer, sacrifice not in space but space in sacrifice, and to reverse the relation is to abolish the reality, so with the man to whom I say *Thou.* I do not meet with him at some time and place or other. I can set him in a particular time and place; I must continually do it: but I set only a *He* or *She,* that is an *It,* no longer my *Thou.*

So long as the heaven of *Thou* is spread out over me the winds of causality cower at my heels, and the whirlpool of fate stays its course.

I do not experience the man to whom I say *Thou.* But I take my stand in relation to him, in the sanctity of the primary word. Only when I step out of it do I experience him once more. In the act of experience *Thou* is far away.

Even if the man to whom I say *Thou* is not aware of it in the midst of his experience, yet relation may exist. For *Thou* is more than *It* realises. No deception penetrates here; here is the cradle of the Real Life.

This is the eternal source of art: a man is faced by a form which desires to be made through him into a work. This form is no offspring of his soul, but is an appearance which steps up to it and demands of it the effective power. The man is concerned with an act of his being. If he carries it through, if he speaks the primary word out of his being to the form which appears, then the effective power streams out, and the work arises.

The act includes a sacrifice and a risk. This is the sacrifice: the endless possibility that is offered up on the altar of the form. For everything which just this moment in play ran through the perspective must be obliterated; nothing of that may penetrate the work. The exclusiveness of what is facing it demands that it be so. This is the risk: the primary word can only be spoken with the whole being. He who gives himself to it may withhold nothing of himself. The work does not suffer me, as do the tree and the man, to turn aside and relax in the world of *It;* but it commands. If I do not serve it aright it is broken, or it breaks me.

I can neither experience nor describe the form which meets me, but only body it forth. And yet I behold it, splendid in the radiance of what confronts me, clearer than all the clearness of the world which is experienced. I do not behold it as a thing among the "inner" things nor as an image of my "fancy," but as that which exists in the present. If test is made of its objectivity the form is certainly not "there." Yet what is actually so much present as it is? And the relation in which I stand to it is real, for it affects me, as I affect it.

To produce is to draw forth, to invent is to find, to shape is to discover. In bodying forth I disclose. I lead the form across—into the world of *It.* The work produced is a thing among things, able to be experienced and described as a sum of qualities. But from time to time it can face the receptive beholder in its whole embodied form.

—What, then, do we experience of *Thou?*

Just nothing. For we do not experience it.

—What, then, do we know of *Thou?*

—Just everything. For we know nothing isolated about it any more.

The *Thou* meets me through grace—it is not found by seeking. But my speaking of the primary word to it is an act of my being, is indeed *the* act of my being.

The *Thou* meets me. But I step into direct relation with it. Hence the relation means being chosen and choosing, suffering and action in one; just as any action of the whole being, which means the suspension of all partial actions and consequently of all sensations of actions grounded only in their particular limitation, is bound to resemble suffering.

The primary word *I–Thou* can be spoken only with the whole being. Concentration and fusion into the whole being can never take place through my agency, nor can it ever take place without me. I become through my relation to the *Thou;* as I become *I,* I say *Thou.*

All real living is meeting.

The relation to the *Thou* is direct. No system of ideas, no foreknowledge, and no fancy intervene between *I* and *Thou.* The memory itself is transformed, as it plunges out of its isolation into the unity of the whole. No aim, no lust, and no anticipation intervene between *I* and *Thou.* Desire itself is transformed as it plunges out of its dream into the appearance. Every means is an obstacle. Only when every means has collapsed does the meeting come about.

In face of the directness of the relation everything indirect becomes irrelevant. It is also irrelevant if my *Thou* is already the *It* for other *I's* ("an object of general experience"), or can become so through the very accomplishment of this act of my being. For the real, though certainly swaying and swinging, boundary runs neither between experience and non-experience, nor between what is given and what is not given, nor yet between the world of being and the world of value; but cutting indifferently across all these provinces it lies between *Thou* and *It,* between the present and the object.

The present, and by that is meant not the point which indicates from time to time in our thought merely the conclusion of "finished" time, the mere appearance of a termination which is fixed and held, but the real, filled present, exists only in so far as actual presentness, meeting, and relation exist. The present arises only in virtue of the fact that the *Thou* becomes present.

The *I* of the primary word *I–It,* that is, the *I* faced by no *Thou,* but surrounded by a multitude of "contents," has no present, only the past. Put in another way, in so far as man rests satisfied with the things that he experiences and uses, he lives in the past, and his moment has no present content. He has nothing but objects. But objects subsist in time that has been.

The present is not fugitive and transient, but continually present and enduring. The object is not duration, but cessation, suspension, a breaking off and cutting clear and hardening, absence of relation and of present being.

True beings are lived in the present, the life of objects is in the past.

Appeal to a "world of ideas" as a third factor above this opposition will not do away with its essential twofold nature. For I speak of nothing else but the real man, of you and of me, of our life and of our world—not of an *I,* or a state of being, in itself alone. The real boundary for the actual man cuts right across the world of ideas as well.

To be sure, many a man who is satisfied with the experience and use of the world of things has raised over or about himself a structure of ideas, in which he finds refuge and repose from the oncome of nothingness. On the threshold he lays aside his inauspicious everyday dress, wraps himself in pure linen, and regales himself with the spectacle of primal being, or of necessary being; but his life has no part in it. To proclaim his ways may even fill him with well-being.

But the mankind of mere *It* that is imagined, postulated, and propagated by such a man has nothing in common with a living mankind where *Thou* may truly be spoken. The noblest fiction is a fetish, the loftiest fictitious sentiment is depraved. Ideas are no more enthroned above our heads than resident in them; they wander amongst us and accost us. The man who leaves the primary word unspoken is to be pitied; but the man who addresses instead these ideas with an abstraction or a password, as if it were their name, is contemptible.

In one of the three examples it is obvious that the direct relation includes an effect on what confronts me. In art the act of the being determines the situation in which the form becomes the work. Through the meeting that which confronts me is fulfilled, and enters the world of things, there to be endlessly active, endlessly to become *It,* but also endlessly to become *Thou* again, inspiring and blessing. It is "embodied"; its body emerges from the flow of the spaceless, timeless present on the shore of existence.

The significance of the effect is not so obvious in the relation with the *Thou* spoken to men. The act of the being which provides directness in this case is usually understood wrongly as being one of feeling. Feelings accompany the metaphysical and metapsychical fact of love, but they do not constitute it. The accompanying feelings can be of greatly differing kinds. The feeling of Jesus for the demoniac differs from his feeling for the beloved disciple; but the love is the one love. Feelings are "entertained": love comes to pass. Feelings dwell in man; but man dwells in his love. That is no metaphor, but the actual truth. Love does not cling to the *I* in such a way as to have the *Thou* only for its "content," its object; but love is *between I* and *Thou.* The man who does not know this, with his very being know this, does not know love; even though he ascribes to it the feelings he lives through, experiences, enjoys, and expresses. Love ranges in its effect through the whole world. In the eyes of him who takes his stand in love, and gazes out of it, men are cut free from their entanglement in bustling activity. Good people and evil, wise and foolish, beautiful and ugly, become successively real to him; that is, set free they step forth in their singleness, and confront him as *Thou*. In a wonderful way, from time to time, exclusiveness arises—and so he can be effective, helping, healing, educating, raising up, saving. Love is responsibility of an *I* for a *Thou*. In this lies the likeness—impossible in any feeling whatsoever—of all who love, from the smallest to the greatest and from the blessedly protected man, whose life is rounded in that of a loved being, to him who is all his life nailed to the cross of the world, and who ventures to bring himself to the dreadful point—to love *all men*.

Let the significance of the effect in the third example, that of the creature and our contemplation of it, remain sunk in mystery. Believe in the simple magic of life, in service in the universe, and the meaning of that waiting, that alertness, that "craning of the neck" in creatures will dawn upon you. Every word would falsify; but look! round about you beings live their life, and to whatever point you turn you come upon being.

Relation is Mutual. My *Thou* affects me, as I affect it. We are moulded by our pupils and built up by our works. The "bad" man, lightly touched by the holy primary word, becomes one who reveals. How we are educated by children and by animals! We live our lives inscrutably included within the streaming mutual life of the universe.

—You speak of love as though it were the only relation between men. But properly speaking, can you take it even only as an example, since there is such a thing as hate?

—So long as love is "blind," that is, so long as it does not see a *whole* being, it is not truly under the sway of the primary word of relation. Hate is by nature blind. Only a part of a being can be hated. He who sees a whole being and is compelled to reject it is no longer in the kingdom of hate, but is in that of human restriction of the power to say *Thou*. He finds himself unable to say the primary word to the other human being confronting him. This word consistently involves an affirmation of the being addressed. He is therefore compelled to reject either the other or himself. At this barrier the entering on a relation recognises its relativity, and only simultaneously with this will the barrier be raised.

Yet the man who straightforwardly hates is nearer to relation than the man without hate and love.

But this is the exalted melancholy of our fate, that every *Thou* in our world must become an *It*. It does not matter how exclusively present the *Thou* was in the direct relation. As soon as the relation has been worked out or has been permeated with a means, the *Thou* becomes an object among objects—perhaps the chief, but still one of them, fixed in its size and its limits. In the work of art realisation in one sense means loss of reality in another. Genuine contemplation is over in a short time; now the life in nature, that first unlocked itself to me in the mystery of mutual action, can again be described, taken to pieces, and classified—the meeting-point of manifold systems of laws. And love itself cannot persist in direct relation. It endures, but in interchange of actual and potential being. The human being who was even now single and unconditioned, not something lying to hand, only present, not able to be experienced, only able to be fulfilled, has now become again a *He* or a *She,* a sum of qualities, a given quantity with a certain shape. Now I may take out from him again the colour of his hair or of his speech or of his goodness. But so long as I can do this he is no more my *Thou* and cannot yet be my *Thou* again.

Every *Thou* in the world is by nature fated to become a thing, or continually to re-enter into the condition of things. In objective speech it would be said that every thing in the world, either before or after becoming a thing, is able to appear to an *I* as its *Thou*. But objective speech snatches only at a fringe of real life.

The *It* is the eternal chrysalis, the *Thou* the eternal butterfly—except that situations do not always follow one another in clear succession, but often there is a happening profoundly twofold, confusedly entangled.

In the beginning is relation.

Consider the speech of "primitive" peoples, that is, of those that have a meagre stock of objects, and whose life is built up within a narrow circle of acts highly charged with presentness. The nuclei of this speech, words in the form of sentences and original pre-grammatical structures (which later, splitting asunder, give rise to the many various kinds of words), mostly indicate the wholeness of a relation. We say "far away"; the Zulu has for that a word which means, in our sentence form, "There where someone cries out: 'O mother, I am lost.' " The Fuegian soars above our analytic wisdom with a seven-syllabled word whose precise meaning is, "They stare at one another, each waiting for the other to volunteer to do what both wish, but are not able to do." In this total situation the persons, as expressed both in nouns and pronouns, are embedded, still only in relief and without finished independence. The chief concern is not with these products of analysis and reflection but with the true original unity, the lived relation.

We greet the man we meet, wishing him well or assuring him of our devotion or commending him to God. But how indirect these worn-out formulas are! What do we discern even dimly in "Hail!" of the original conferring of power? Compare these with the ever fresh Kaffir greeting, with its direct bodily relation, "I see you!" or with its ridiculous and sublime American variant, "Smell me!"

. . .

The extended lines of relations meet in the eternal *Thou.*

Every particular *Thou* is a glimpse through to the eternal *Thou;* by means of every particular *Thou* the primary word addresses the eternal

Thou. Through this mediation of the *Thou* of all beings fulfilment, and non-fulfilment, of relations comes to them: the inborn *Thou* is realised in each relation and consummated in none. It is consummated only in the direct relation with the *Thou* that by its nature cannot become *It.*

Men have addressed their eternal *Thou* with many names. In singing of Him who was thus named they always had the *Thou* in mind: the first myths were hymns of praise. Then the names took refuge in the language of *It;* men were more and more strongly moved to think of and to address their eternal *Thou* as an *It.* But all God's names are hallowed, for in them He is not merely spoken about, but also spoken to.

Many men wish to reject the word God as a legitimate usage, because it is so misused. It is indeed the most heavily laden of all the words used by men. For that very reason it is the most imperishable and most indispensable. What does all mistaken talk about God's being and works (though there has been, and can be, no other talk about these) matter in comparison with the one truth that all men who have addressed God had God Himself in mind? For he who speaks the word God and really has *Thou* in mind (whatever the illusion by which he is held), addresses the true *Thou* of his life, which cannot be limited by another *Thou,* and to which he stands in a relation that gathers up and includes all others.

But when he, too, who abhors the name, and believes himself to be godless, gives his whole being to addressing the *Thou* of his life, as a *Thou* that cannot be limited by another, he addresses God.

If we go on our way and meet a man who has advanced towards us and has also gone on *his* way, we know only our part of the way, not his—his we experience only in the meeting.

Of the complete relational event we know, with the knowledge of life lived, our going out to the relation, our part of the way. The other part only comes upon us, we do not know it; it comes upon us in the meeting. But we strain ourselves on it if we speak of it as though it were some thing beyond the meeting.

We have to be concerned, to be troubled, not about the other side but about our own side, not about grace but about will. Grace concerns us in so far as we go out to it and persist in its presence; but it is not our object.

The *Thou* confronts me. But I step into direct relation with it. Hence the relation means being chosen and choosing, suffering and action in one; just as any action of the whole being which means the suspension of all partial actions, and consequently of all sensations of actions grounded only in their particular limitation, is bound to resemble suffering.

This is the activity of the man who has become a whole being, an activity that has been termed doing nothing: nothing separate or partial stirs in the man any more, thus he makes no intervention in the world; it is the whole man, enclosed and at rest in his wholeness, that is effective—he has become an effective whole. To have won stability in this state is to be able to go out to the supreme meeting.

To this end the world of sense does not need to be laid aside as though it were illusory. There is no illusory world, there is only the world—which appears to us as twofold in accordance with our twofold attitude. Only the barrier of separation has to be destroyed. Further, no "going beyond sense-experience" is necessary; for every experience, even the most spiritual, could yield us only an *It*. Nor is any recourse necessary to a world of ideas and values; for they cannot become presentness for us. None of these things is necessary. Can it be said what really is necessary?—Not in the sense of a precept. For everything that has ever been devised and contrived in the time of the human spirit as precept, alleged preparation, practice, or meditation, has nothing to do with the primal, simple fact of the meeting. Whatever the advantages in knowledge or the wielding of power for which we have to thank this or that practice, none of this affects the meeting of which we are speaking; it all has its place in the world of *It* and does not lead one step, does not take *the* step, out of it. Going out to the relation cannot be taught in the sense of precepts being given. It can only be indicated by the drawing of a circle which excludes everything that is not this going out. Then the one thing that matters is visible, full acceptance of the present.

To be sure, this acceptance presupposes that the further a man has wandered in separated being the more difficult is the venture and the more elemental the turning. This does not mean a giving up of, say, the *I,* as mystical writings usually suppose: the *I* is as indispensable to this, the supreme, as to every relation, since relation is only possible between *I* and *Thou.* It is not the *I,* then, that is given up, but that false self-asserting instinct that makes a man flee to the possessing of things before the unreliable, perilous world of relation which has neither density nor duration and cannot be surveyed.

Every real relation with a being or life in the world is exclusive. Its *Thou* is freed, steps forth, is single, and confronts you. It fills the heavens. This does not mean that nothing else exists; but all else lives in *its* light. As long as the presence of the relation continues, this its cosmic range is inviolable. But as soon as a *Thou* becomes *It,* the cosmic range of the relation appears as an offence to the world, its exclusiveness as an exclusion of the universe.

In the relation with God unconditional exclusiveness and unconditional inclusiveness are one. He who enters on the absolute relation is concerned with nothing isolated any more, neither things nor beings, neither earth nor heaven; but everything is gathered up in the relation. For to step into pure relation is not to disregard everything but to see everything in the *Thou,* not to renounce the world but to establish it on its true basis. To look away from the world, or to stare at it, does not help a man to reach God; but he who sees the world in Him stands in His presence. "Here world, there God" is the language of *It;* "God in the world" is another language of *It;* but to eliminate or leave behind nothing at all, to include the whole world in the *Thou,* to give the world its due and its truth, to include nothing beside God but everything in him—this is full and complete relation.

Men do not find God if they stay in the world. They do not find Him if they leave the world. He who goes out with his whole being to meet his *Thou* and carries to it all being that is in the world, finds Him who cannot be sought.

Of course God is the "wholly Other"; but He is also the wholly Same, the wholly Present. Of course He is the *Mysterium Tremendum* that appears and overthrows; but He is also the mystery of the self-evident, nearer to me than my *I.*

If you explore the life of things and of conditioned being you come to the unfathomable, if you deny the life of things and of conditioned being you stand before nothingness, if you hallow this life you meet the living God.

Man's sense of *Thou,* which experiences in the relations with every particular *Thou* the disappointment of the change to *It,* strives out but not away from them all to its eternal *Thou;* but not as something is sought: actually there is no such thing as seeking God, for there is nothing in which He could not be found. How foolish and hopeless would be the man who turned aside from the course of his life in order to seek God; even though he won all the wisdom of solitude and all the power of concentrated being he would miss God. Rather is it as when a man goes his way and simply wishes that it might be the way: in the strength of his wish his striving is expressed. Every relational event is a stage that affords him a glimpse into the consummating event. So in each event he does not partake, but also (for he is waiting) does partake, of the one event. Waiting, not seeking, he goes his way; hence he is composed before all things, and makes contact with them which helps them. But when he has *found,* his heart is not turned from them, though everything now meets him in the one event. He blesses every cell that sheltered him, and every cell into which he will yet turn. For this finding is not the end, but only the eternal middle, of the way.

It is a finding without seeking, a discovering of the primal, of origin. His sense of *Thou,* which cannot be satiated till he finds the endless *Thou,* had the *Thou* present to it from the beginning; the presence had only to become wholly real to him in the reality of the hallowed life of the world.

God cannot be inferred in anything—in nature, say, as its author, or in history as its master, or in the subject as the self that is thought in it. Something else is not "given" and God then elicited from it; but God is the Being that is directly, most nearly, and lastingly, over against us, that may properly only be addressed, not expressed.

. . .

Meeting with God does not come to man in order that he may concern himself with God, but in order that he may confirm that there is meaning in the world. All revelation is summons and sending. But again and again man brings about, instead of realisation, a reflexion to Him who reveals: he wishes to concern himself with God instead of with the world. Only, in such a reflexion, he is no longer confronted by a *Thou,* he can do nothing but establish an It-God in the realm of things, believe that he knows of God as of an *It,* and so speak about Him. Just as the "self"-seeking man, instead of directly living something or other, a perception or an affection, reflects about his perspective or reflective *I,* and thereby misses the truth of the event, so the man who seeks God (though for the rest he gets on very well with the self-seeker in the one soul), instead of allowing the gift to work itself out, reflects about the Giver—and misses both.

God remains present to you when you have been sent forth; he who goes on a mission has always God before him: the truer the fulfilment the stronger and more constant His nearness. To be sure, he cannot directly concern himself with God, but he can converse with Him. Reflexion, on the other hand, makes God into an object. Its apparent turning towards the primal source belongs in truth to the universal movement away from it; just as the apparent turning away of the man who is fulfilling his mission belongs in truth to the universal movement towards the primal source.

For the two primary metacosmical movements of the world—expansion into its own being and turning to connexion—find their supreme human form, the real spiritual form of their struggle and adjustment, their mingling and separation, in the history of the human relation to God. In turning the Word is born on earth, in expansion the Word enters the chrysalis form of religion, in fresh turning it is born again with new wings.

Arbitrary self-will does not reign here, even though the movement towards the *It* goes at times so far that it threatens to suppress and to smother the movement out again to the *Thou.*

The mighty revelations to which the religions appeal are like in being with the quiet revelations that are to be found everywhere and at all times. The mighty revelations which stand at the beginning of great communities and at the turning-point of an age are nothing but the eternal revelation. But the revelation does not pour itself into the world through him who receives it as through a funnel; it comes to him and seizes his whole elemental being in all its particular nature, and fuses with it. The man, too, who is the "mouth" of the revelation, is indeed this, not a speaking-tube or any kind of instrument, but an organ, which sounds according to its own laws; and to sound means to *modify.*

The various ages of history, however, show a qualitative difference. There is a time of maturing, when the true element of the human spirit, suppressed and buried, comes to hidden readiness so urgent and so tense that it awaits only a touch from Him who touches in order to burst forth.

The revelation that then makes its appearance seizes in the totality of its constitution the whole elemental stuff that is thus prepared, melts it down, and produces in it a form that is a new form of God in the world.

Thus in the course of history, in the transforming of elemental human stuff, ever new provinces of the world and the spirit are raised to form, summoned to divine form. Ever new spheres become regions of a theophany. It is not man's own power that works here, nor is it God's pure effective passage, but it is a mixture of the divine and the human. He who is sent out in the strength of revelation takes with him, in his eyes, an image of God; however far this exceeds the senses, yet he takes it with him in the eye of the spirit, in that visual power of his spirit which is not metaphorical but wholly real. The spirit responds also through a look, a look that is *formative*. Although we earthly beings never look at God without the world, but only look at the world in God, yet as we look we shape eternally the form of God.

Form is also a mixture of *Thou* and *It*. In belief and in a cult form can harden into an object; but, in virtue of the essential quality of relation that lives on in it, it continually becomes present again. God is near His forms so long as man does not remove them from Him. In true prayer belief and cult are united and purified to enter into the living relation. The fact that true prayer lives in the religions witnesses to their true life: they live so long as it lives in them. Degeneration of the religions means degeneration of prayer in them. Their power to enter into relation is buried under increasing objectification, it becomes increasingly difficult for them to say *Thou* with the whole undivided being, and finally, in order to be able to say it, man must come out of the false security into the venture of the infinite —out of the community, that is now over-arched only by the temple dome and not also by the firmament, into the final solitude. It is a profound misunderstanding of this impulse to ascribe it to "subjectivism"; life face to face with God is life in the one reality, the only true "objective," and the man who goes out to this life desires to save himself, in the objective that truly *is,* from that which is apparent and illusory, before it has disturbed the truth of the real objective for him. Subjectivism empties God of soul, objectivism makes Him into an object—the latter is a false fixing down, the former a false setting free; both are diversions from the way of reality, both are attempts to replace reality.

God is near His forms if man does not remove them from Him. But when the expanding movement of religion suppresses the movement of turning and removes the form from God, the countenance of the form is obliterated, its lips are dead, its hands hang down, God knows it no more, and the universal dwelling-place that is built about its altar, the spiritually apprehended cosmos, tumbles in. And the fact that man, in the disturbance of his truth, no longer sees what is then taking place, is a part of what has then taken place.

Disintegration of the Word has taken place.

The Word has its essence in revelation, its effect in the life of the form, its currency during the domination of the form that has died.

This is the course and the counter-course of the eternal and eternally present Word in history.

The times in which the living Word appears as those in which the solidarity of connexion between *I* and the world is renewed; the times in which the effective Word reigns are those in which the agreement between *I* and the world is maintained; the times in which the Word becomes current are those in which alienation between *I* and the world, loss of reality, growth of fate, is completed—till there comes the great shudder, the holding of the breath in the dark, and the preparing silence.

But this course is not circular. It is the way. In each new æon fate becomes more oppressive, turning more shattering. And the theophany becomes ever *nearer,* increasingly near to the sphere that lies *between beings,* to the Kingdom that is hidden in our midst, there between us. History is a mysterious approach. Every spiral of its way leads us both into profounder perversion and more fundamental turning. But the event that from the side of the world is called turning is called from God's side redemption.

QUESTIONS FOR STUDY AND DISCUSSION

1. Explain and exemplify the contrast between the two primary words, I–Thou and I–It.
2. In what sense is it true that "Through the *Thou* a man becomes *I"*?
3. How does man's relation to God affect his relations with other men?
4. Does Buber tell us anything directly about God? Is "God" as here spoken of to be strictly identified with the God of Abraham and of Isaac?

TOPICS FOR DISCUSSION AND TERM PAPERS

A.

1. Explain what is meant by the phenomenological method. How is it exemplified in the selections in this section?
2. How is existentialist ontology centered upon man? Is such a centering compatible with an authentic theistic position?
3. Why do such purely "human" categories as anxiety, courage, everydayness, and freedom have a role to play in the metaphysical teaching of the authors studied?
4. Can you explain the neglect, in the foregoing selections, of such problems as those of causality, substance, and change?
5. Exemplify, from the selections read, the wider concept of experience that has been claimed as a characteristic of phenomenology.
6. Compare and contrast the very different conclusions drawn from the consideration of human limitation by Heidegger, Sartre, Tillich, and Marcel.
7. Existential philosophy has been described as an exploration of human freedom: is this description relevant to any of the foregoing selections?
8. What place do temporality and history hold in the exploration of man's relation to being?
9. To what extent do the authors just read share Kierkegaard's aversion to system-building? On what grounds?
10. Would you agree with Tillich that Christianity forms the existential basis for all Western philosophy? Can you support your position with examples from the foregoing selections?

B.

1. Husserl claimed that the phenomenologists were "the only true empiricists." How did this new empiricism differ from that of David Hume, Bertrand Russell, or A. J. Ayer?
2. What, if any, relation has the principle "existence precedes essence," as used in this section, to the teaching of Aquinas on the primacy of the act of being?
3. Compare and contrast the approach to God found among theistic existentialists to that employed by the other theistic philosophers whose works you have studied.
4. Would you support or reject the assertion (made in the introduction to this section) that Bergson and Husserl began a radically new, post-modern period in the history of philosophy? If so, how would you characterize this new period?
5. Compare and contrast the attitude toward science and technology found in the authors just read and in the other recent philosophical movements which you have studied. To what extent do historical circumstances (i.e., the disorientation of occupied France, the Marxist revolution in Russia) help to explain these differences? Which attitude do you personally hold?

RECOMMENDED READINGS

Primary Sources

Berdyaev, Nicolas. *The Dream and Reality: An Essay in Autobiography.* Trans. by Katherine Lampert. New York: Macmillan Co., 1951. Chapter 11 gives a concise statement of Berdyaev's "Final Philosophical Outlook."

Buber, Martin. *Between Man and Man.* Trans. by Ronald Gregor Smith. Boston: Beacon Press, 1955. The two essays on education will be of special interest to students.

————. *Eclipse of God: Studies in the Relation Between Religion and Philosophy.* New York: Harper & Bros., 1957. Pages 87–104 give Buber's critique of Sartre and Heidegger.

Heidegger, Martin. *Introduction to Metaphysics.* Trans. by Ralph Manheim. New Haven: Yale University Press, 1959. Chapter 1 takes up the question "Why are there essents rather than nothing?"

————. *Letter on Humanism,* trans. by Edgar Lohner, in *Philosophy in the Twentieth Century.* Ed. by William Barrett and Henry Aiken. New York: Random House, 1962. II, 270–302.

Husserl, Edmund. *Phenomenology and the Crisis of Philosophy.* Trans. and with Introd. by Quentin Lauer. New York: Harper & Row, 1965. Two important essays: "Philosophy as a Rigorous Science" is Husserl's first published justification of phenomenology; "Philosophy and the Crisis of European Man" deals with today's collapse of rationalism.

Marcel, Gabriel. *Being and Having.* With Introd. by James Collins. New York: Harper & Row, 1965. The opening pages of the "metaphysical journal" included in this book contain Marcel's philosophical reflections relative to his baptism, which occurred on March 23, 1929.

————. *The Philosophy of Existentialism.* New York: Citadel Press, 1961. Four essays, the first of which has been reprinted here. "Existence and Human Freedom" is a critique of Sartre; see also "An Essay in Autobiography."

Sartre, Jean-Paul. *Existential Psychoanalysis.* Chicago: Henry Regnery Co., 1962. Selected chapters on human reality from *Being and Nothingness.*

————. *No Exit, and Three Other Plays.* Trans. by Stuart Gilbert. New York: Alfred A. Knopf, 1946. The title play is a good example of Sartre's philosophical drama.

————. "The Wall," in *Existentialism from Dostoevsky to Sartre.* Ed. by Walter Kaufmann. New York: Meridian Books, 1956. Pp. 223–40.

Tillich, Paul. *The Courage to Be.* New Haven: Yale University Press, 1952. Chapter 2, "Being, Non-being and Anxiety," develops in concrete fashion man's encounter with Being and with Nothingness.

Commentaries

Desan, Wilfrid. *The Tragic Finale: An Essay on the Philosophy of Jean-Paul Sartre.* New York: Harper & Row, 1960. The best book on Sartre's ontology available in English. Chapters 9 and 10 offer a penetrating critique of Sartre's "refusal of God."

Friedman, Maurice. *Martin Buber: The Life of Dialogue*. New York: Harper & Row, 1960. Part III, "Dialogue," gives a perceptive and sympathetic account of the nucleus of Buber's philosophy.

Heinemann, F. H. *Existentialism and the Modern Predicament*. New York: Harper & Bros., 1958. A very readable introduction to existentialism, with chapters on Husserl (4), Heidegger (6), Sartre (7), Marcel (8), and Berdyaev (9).

Lauer, Quentin. *Phenomenology: Its Genesis and Prospect*. New York: Harper & Row, 1965. A good general introduction to Husserl. Chapters 7 and 8 summarize the contents of the *Cartesian Meditations*.

Richardson, William J. *Heidegger: Through Phenomenology to Thought*. The Hague: Martinus Nijhoff, 1963. A clear and authoritative account of Heidegger's development. Part I, Chs. 1 and 2, deals with the central problem of *Being and Time* and *Kant and the Problem of Metaphysics*.

Spiegelberg, Herbert. *The Phenomenological Movement: A Historical Introduction*, 2nd ed. rev. 2 vols. The Hague: Martinus Nijhoff, 1965. A basic reference work, including comprehensive bibliographies and a general glossary of phenomenological terms, with detailed studies of Husserl, Heidegger, Sartre, Marcel, and others. The concluding essay on "The Essentials of the Phenomenological Method" is particularly fine.

Thomas, J. Heywood. *Paul Tillich: An Appraisal*. Philadelphia: The Westminster Press, 1963. A general introduction. Chapters 1 and 2 examine and criticize Tillich's view of theology and his teaching on God and revelation.

A 6
B 7
C 8
D 9
E 0
F 1
G 2
H 3
I 4
J 5